# HIS VERY BEST

# HIS VERY BEST

## JIMMY CARTER, A LIFE

## JONATHAN ALTER

**THORNDIKE PRESS**
A part of Gale, a Cengage Company

GALE
A Cengage Company

LIBRARY OF CONGRESS CIP DATA ON FILE.
CATALOGUING IN PUBLICATION FOR THIS BOOK
IS AVAILABLE FROM THE LIBRARY OF CONGRESS.

ISBN-13: 978-1-4328-8452-9 (hardcover alk. paper)

Published in 2020 by arrangement with Simon & Schuster, Inc.

Printed in Mexico
Print Number: 01          Print Year: 2020

To the memory of Alice Mayhew

# CONTENTS

7

## PART THREE: DARK HORSE

## PART FOUR: OUTSIDER PRESIDENT

## PART FIVE: PEACEMAKER

## PART SIX: SWAMPED

## PART SEVEN: GLOBAL CITIZEN

# PREFACE

My previous books — on Franklin D. Roosevelt and Barack Obama — stressed the influence of character on the presidency. I began this one more than five years ago with the same theme in mind. But after the election of 2016, I felt a new urgency. It seemed to me there was no better time to reexamine our superficial assessments of Jimmy Carter. I write out of a fragile hope that the life story of the thirty-ninth president might help light our way back to some sense of decency, account-ability, and seriousness in our politics.

I first met Carter — for a split-second handshake — on the South Lawn of the White House on the Fourth of July 1978, when I was a college intern in his speech-writing office. In early 1980, like so many Americans, I grew disillusioned with him and made the mistake of working for a few weeks as a part-time volunteer on Ted Kennedy's cam-paign against him in the Democratic primaries.

Thirty-five years later, I found myself drawn back to a perplexing leader and to his virtuoso achievement: the 1978 Camp David Accords, which brought peace to Israel and Egypt after four wars and became the most durable major treaty of the postwar era. If he pulled that off, I figured, there must be more to Jimmy Carter than the easy shorthand: inept president who becomes a noble ex-president. When I learned that he would almost certainly have begun to address global warming in the early 1980s had he been reelected, I was hooked. I set out to paint a portrait of perhaps the most misunderstood president in American history.

Carter's prescience on the environment and several other issues was not the only thing that surprised me about him. I knew about his human rights policy but had no clue how much it advanced democracy around the world. I had no idea that ratification of the Panama Canal Treaties, a squeaker in the US Senate, prevented a major war in Central America. Several of Carter's unheralded accomplishments are especially relevant today: normalizing relations with China, which helped set in motion four decades of breathtaking global change; insisting on the first genuine racial and gender diversity in the federal judiciary; curbing redlining, which had so damaged black neighborhoods; providing the first whistle-blower protections and the first inspectors general; and extending the Centers for Disease Control (CDC) for the first time into global health, which presaged the work of his postpresidency. I concluded that he was a surprisingly consequential president — a political and stylistic failure but a substantive and far-sighted success.

From the start of my research, Carter's journey from barefoot farm boy to global icon struck me as an American epic. I wanted to understand how he evolved from a short, timid kid nicknamed Peewee into an ambitious and born-again governor of Georgia; how, straddling two worlds, he advanced miraculously from obscure outsider to president of the United States; how he stumbled as a leader but succeeded in reinventing himself as a warrior for peace.

Carter is warm in public and brisk — sometimes peevish — in private, with a biting wit beneath the patented smile. He is always struggling to do more — for himself and for the world — and to pass what his US Naval Academy rule book called "the final test of a man": honesty. Like all politicians, he exaggerated at times and broke a few campaign pledges. But he fulfilled his famous promise in his 1976 campaign and did not directly lie to the American people, which is no small thing today.

The title *His Very Best* reflects Carter's intensity and his sense of obligation to God, country, humanity, and himself. In his daily, even hourly, prayers, he asks not just "What would Jesus do?" but "Have I done my best?" After cantankerous admiral Hyman Rickover sternly asked the nervous young lieutenant in a job interview for the nuclear navy if he had done his best at Annapolis — and he confessed that he had not — Carter disciplined himself to make the maximum effort in every single thing he did for the rest of his life. (He also entitled his campaign autobiography *Why Not the Best?*) When awarding Carter the Nobel Peace Prize in 2002, the chairman of the Nobel committee said, "Carter himself has taken [from Ecclesiastes 11:4] as his motto: 'The worst thing that you can do is not to try.' Few people, if any, have tried harder."

Whether sprinting as a naval officer through the core of a melted-down nuclear reactor, or laboring to save tens of millions of acres of wilderness, or driving a hundred miles out of his way on rutted roads to talk to a single African farmer, or turkey hunting at age ninety-five, Carter was all in, all the time. Calling him the least lazy American president is not to damn him with faint praise; his long life is a master class in making every minute count.

This is the first full-length independent biography ever written of Jimmy Carter. (His major political contemporaries, Ronald Reagan and Edward Kennedy, have each been the subject of a half dozen.) Fine authors have bitten off chunks on Carter's campaigns, his faith, his presidency, and his postpresidency, and insightful former aides and Cabinet officers have had their say. My more comprehensive book is not in any way "authorized" or "official," but I could not have completed it without the generous cooperation of all the Carters. My beloved longtime editor, the late Alice Mayhew, was also Carter's editor at Simon & Schuster, and she smoothed the way.

Over the last five years, I interviewed the former president more than a dozen times in his home, at his office, over meals, in transit, and by email. I watched him teach Sunday school in Plains, Georgia, and I helped build a Habitat for Humanity house with him in Memphis. I also interviewed Rosalynn Carter — who was kind enough to share for the first time Jimmy's love letters from the navy and portions of her unpublished diaries — as well as their four children, other members of his famously colorful family, and more than 250 people who know him, including former president George H. W. Bush, former vice president Walter Mondale, and several surviving members of the Carter Cabinet. I spent countless hours reviewing thousands of pages of documents at his presidential library in Atlanta and other research facilities and scouring oral histories and unpublished diaries.

My most memorable interviews took place in Plains, the tiny town in southwest Georgia that Jimmy and Rosalynn — married for nearly seventy-five years — have always called home. They met there as infants more than nine decades ago. Jimmy's mother, a nurse, delivered Rosalynn, then brought her nearly three-year-old son over to see the new baby. Plains is a friendly place, but I learned of its harsh past, with a county sheriff described by Dr. Martin Luther King Jr. as "the meanest man in the world." I concluded that the intensity of Carter's commitments in the second half of his life has been at least partial atonement for too often staying silent amid the brutal abuses of civil rights in his own backyard. This stutter-step journey from silence to action on race, rights, and reconciliation has many lessons for citizens of the twenty-first century.

Carter's storied 1976 presidential campaign upended American politics. By beating George Wallace in the Florida primary, he vanquished the racist wing of the Democratic Party, then — with Joe Biden as one of his earliest supporters — took the White House in a brilliant campaign that offered healing, love, and truth. But Carter's presidency bogged down, for reasons often beyond his control. In his last two years, swamped by the Iran hostage crisis and a dismal economy, he was often flailing. One day I asked him to identify the biggest myth about his time in office. He answered: "That I was weak. I made many bold decisions, almost all of which were difficult to imple-

15

ment and not especially popular."*

This is true. Carter was not fundamentally weak. As governor, he was dubbed Jungle Jimmy for his combative nature; "gonzo" journalist Hunter S. Thompson called Carter "a bastard," and he meant it as a great compliment for a man he helped make president. But in Washington, Carter let perceptions of weakness harden and obscure significant — even visionary — achievements. One of my challenges was to separate real weakness from the temporary and often unfair judgment of his contemporaries. In the end, I concluded that his presidency is underrated and that his post-presidency — while pathbreaking and inspiring — offered him fewer levers for change and was marred at times by his ego and is thus a bit over-rated.

Like "weak," the easy depiction of Carter as "incompetent" is not just misrepresentative of his presidency; it's ironic — even ridiculous — to

*A partial list: pardoning Vietnam War–era draft dodgers; imposing nettlesome energy conservation measures; deregulating natural gas prices; canceling dams and other water projects; reducing troop levels in South Korea; canceling the Clinch River Breeder Reactor Project; canceling the B-1 bomber and the neutron bomb; signing the Panama Canal Treaties; returning the Crown of St. Stephen to Communist Hungary; cutting the budget; appointing a Federal Reserve Board chairman to raise interest rates; imposing a grain embargo; boycotting the 1980 Summer Olympics; reinstating draft registration; not attacking Iran; resettling Cuban refugees; preventing development on tens of millions of acres in Alaska.

16

anyone who knows him and his intense dedication to self-improvement, as reflected in the more than two dozen books he wrote on subjects ranging far beyond politics. The man has been frighteningly competent at almost anything he tried to do, professionally or recreationally.

He was the first American president since Thomas Jefferson who could fairly claim to be a Renaissance man, or at least a world-class autodidact. Over the course of his life, he acquired the skills of a farmer, surveyor, naval officer, electrician, sonar technologist, nuclear engineer, businessman, equipment designer, agronomist, master woodworker, Sunday school teacher, bird dog trainer, arrowhead collector, land-use planner, legislator, door-to-door missionary, governor, long-shot presidential candidate, US president, diplomat, fly fisherman, home builder, global health expert, painter, professor, memoirist, poet, novelist, and children's book author — an incomplete list, as he would be happy to point out.

Midway through my research, it struck me that Carter was the only American president who essentially lived in three centuries: His early life on the farm in the 1920s, without electricity or running water, might as well have been in the nineteenth. He was connected — before, during, and after his presidency — to many of the big events and transformative social movements of the twentieth. And the Carter Center, the nongovernmental organization he founded, is focused on conflict resolution, global health, and strengthening democracy — cutting-edge challenges of the twenty-first.

Beyond longevity lies more complexity than applies to most political figures. Carter is a driven

17

engineer laboring to free the humanist within. He once told me that he could express his true feelings only in his poetry, which hints at why he has proved so elusive to journalists and scholars. "Never say you know the last word about any human heart," wrote the novelist Henry James. So this book cannot fully capture the redemptive life of Jimmy Carter. But I've tried my best to get as close as I can.

Jonathan Alter
Montclair, New Jersey
July 2020

# AUTHOR'S NOTE

A note on usage: to accurately convey the vicious racism of Carter's youth and young adulthood, I occasionally quote the N-word but never use it in my own voice. Otherwise I use *black,* the most common usage of the 1970s, when Carter was in government. For older white southerners, like Carter's mother and father, I sometimes use *Miss* or *Mr.* before their first names because that is how they were widely known, though the failure to apply such honorifics to black southerners is yet another racial double standard.

# PROLOGUE
## JUNE 1979

It was just hours before the first day of summer, and the sunny weather in Washington, DC, was perfect for a leisurely drive in the country. But June 20, 1979, was the wrong day for Wednesday golf or a picnic at Bull Run. That week, more than half of the nation's gas stations were running out of gas.

The morning's *Washington Post* reported that local authorities were inundated with requests for carpools from angry motorists who couldn't get to work, yet a small collection of harried reporters and dignitaries managed to find transportation to the White House. There the beleaguered president of the United States was preparing yet another announcement that would lead to eye rolling in the press corps and make little news. The only thing that stood out then about this seemingly minor event was its unusual location: the West Wing roof.

The spring and summer gas shortages marked the worst of a depressing 1979, a year that would later see the seizure of American hostages in Iran and the Soviet invasion of Afghanistan. "Gas stations closed up like someone died," John Updike wrote in his novel *Rabbit Is Rich.* For a generation bonded to cars the way the next would be to smartphones, this was traumatic. Millions of Americans missed work, canceled vacations, and pointed fingers. Public opinion surveys in June 1979 showed Carter's approval ratings in the Gallup poll plummeting to 28 percent, the lowest of his presidency and comparable to Richard Nixon's when he resigned five years earlier. Vice President Walter Mondale later cracked that the Carter White House had gone to the dogs — and become "the nation's fire hydrant."

As usual, the president had few options. A month later, he would offer new, ambitious energy goals as part of his infamous "malaise" speech (though he never used the word), in which Carter delivered a jeremiad against empty materialism. But events all year were largely out of his control, wreaking havoc on the American economy. First came a decision by the Organization of Petroleum Exporting Countries (OPEC) to jack up global oil prices by 14.5 percent virtually overnight — an effort to exploit strikes in Iranian oil fields against the teetering shah of Iran. After the shah fled into exile and was replaced in February by the radical Islamic fundamentalist Ayatollah Khomeini, Iranian oil exports to the United States ceased altogether. Over the next eighteen months, oil prices doubled to nearly $40 a barrel. This represented an astonishing thirteenfold increase in a decade. "Energy is our Vietnam," a White House aide told *Newsweek*.

By the following year, inflation — driven in large part by energy prices — would pass 12 percent, with unemployment over 7 percent for a combined "misery index" of nearly 20 percent. Yet harder to imagine in the twenty-first century was that interest rates in 1980 hit an eye-popping 19 percent.

Even if everything else had gone right for Jimmy Carter in 1979 and 1980 — which it most definitely did not — that was a gale-force economic wind blowing in his face as he sought reelection against former California governor Ronald Reagan.

For two years, a clean-energy pioneer named George Szego had been lobbying the Carter White House to take a look at something he'd cobbled together at his little manufacturing company in Warrenton, Virginia. Szego, an engineer who had fought in the Battle of the Bulge, was hard to ignore. After some hesitation, Carter — himself an engineer — handwrote a reference to this emerging technology into a 1978 speech. Now, a year later, he was making good on his pledge to install it.

At one thirty on June 20, the president climbed an inner staircase to the roof of the West Wing, known as the West Terrace, where he emerged into the bright sunlight for an energy announcement that had nothing directly to do with gas lines. "I've arranged for this ceremony to be illuminated by solar power," Carter joked, as the audience squinted into the sun. He proposed $1 billion in federal funding for solar research, a $100 million "solar bank" offering credits to home owners who installed primitive solar units, and a goal of 20 percent of the nation's energy coming from renewable sources by the year 2000 — just one part of his effort to prepare the United States for a greener future.

The event was meant to publicize an energy source that for years had been of interest mostly to tinkerers and readers of the counterculture

23

*Whole Earth Catalog* but was finally beginning to make its way into the liberal mainstream. To symbolize his commitment to solar, Carter dedicated the rooftop installation of a $28,000 hot water heating system — built by Szego — that would be used for portions of the ground floor of the West Wing.

Like so much else about his presidency, placing a solar unit on the White House roof did Carter no political good at the time. His critics, if they noticed at all, saw it as a stunt to deflect blame from the gas crisis. Carter understood this but didn't care. He meant for the solar panels — visible from Pennsylvania Avenue — to be a symbol of his faith in American ingenuity to tackle the nation's toughest long-term problems.

The president's goal was to develop clean, nonpolluting energy sources and independence from Arab oil. He didn't mention combating climate change, though, the following year, his White House would raise the first official warnings about global warming anywhere in the world.

Carter mentioned how President Benjamin Harrison (he mistakenly called him William Henry Harrison) introduced electric lightbulbs to the White House in 1891, before they were commercially viable or technologically advanced. "A generation from now," Carter said, "this solar heater can either be a curiosity, a museum piece, an example of a road not taken — or it can be a small part of one of the greatest and most exciting adventures ever undertaken by the American people: harnessing the power of the sun."

As it turned out, the thirty-two solar panels became both museum pieces *and* inspirations. President Reagan cut research-and-development spending on alternative energy by two-thirds, wrecking Carter's commitment to clean energy. In 1985 Reagan let Carter's tax credits for solar expire, bankrupting George Szego's company and dozens of others and ceding clean-energy leadership to other countries. With oil prices falling, Reagan's chief of staff, Donald T. Regan, described the roof panels as "just a joke" and ordered them taken down in 1986 as part of a renovation.

After languishing in a government warehouse, the panels were rescued by a professor at Unity College in Maine and used on the roof of the school dining hall. Eventually they were sent to the Smithsonian, the Jimmy Carter Presidential Library and Museum, and a museum in China. It wasn't until 2010 that President Obama put new-generation panels back on the White House roof and dramatically expanded funding for clean-energy development.

Solar power has since become the fastest-growing source of electricity in the United States. It represents just one of many ways a significant American president — buffeted by events — peered over the horizon.

Throughout Jimmy Carter's long life, classmates, colleagues, and friends — even members of his own family — found him hard to read. The enigma deepened in the presidency.

He was a disciplined and incorruptible president equipped with a sharp, omnivorous mind; a calm and adult president, dependable in a crisis; a friendless president who, in the 1976 primaries, had defeated or alienated a good portion of the Democratic Party; a stubborn and acerbic president, never demeaning but sometimes cold; a non-ideological president who worshipped science along with God and saw governing as a series of engineering problem sets; an austere, even spartan president out of sync with American consumer culture; a focused president whose diamond-cutter attention to detail brought ridicule but also historic results; a charming president in small groups and when speaking off the cuff but awkward in front of a teleprompter and often allergic to small talk and to offering a simple "Thank you"; an insular, all-business president who seemed sometimes to prefer humanity to human beings but prayed for the strength to do better.

For some in Carter's orbit, his impatient and occasionally persnickety style — a few dubbed him "the grammarian in chief" for correcting their memos — would mean that their respect would turn to reverence and love only in later years. Only then did many of those who served in his administration fully understand that he had accomplished much more in office than even they knew.

Carter's farsighted domestic and foreign policy achievements would be largely forgotten when he shrank in the job and lost the 1980 election.

He forged the nation's first comprehensive energy policy and historic accomplishments on the environment that included strong new pollution controls, the first toxic waste cleanup, and doubling the size of the national park system. He set the bar on consumer protection; signed two major pieces of ethics legislation; carried out the first civil service reform in a century; established two new Cabinet-level departments (Energy and Education); deregulated airlines, trucking, and utilities in ways that served the public interest;

and took federal judgeships out of the era of tokenism by selecting more women and blacks for the federal bench than all of his predecessors combined, times five. Ruth Bader Ginsburg, whom he appointed to the appellate court, said Carter "literally changed the complexion of the federal judiciary," though he never had a Supreme Court vacancy to fill. Carter did the same for the executive branch, while empowering for the first time the vice president and the first lady, both of whom were given far more responsibilities than any of their predecessors.

So much legislation passed on his watch that major bill-signing ceremonies — a rarity in later administrations — were greeted by the jaded press with yawns. While Carter served only one term, he was, unlike Bill Clinton and Barack Obama, backed by a Democratic Congress for all four years, with a Senate where filibusters were rare. This meant that for all of his problems, he enacted more of his agenda than any postwar American president except Lyndon Johnson, whose legislative program was so big it made the next Democratic president's look underwhelming by comparison. Even little-publicized Carter bills changed parts of American life, from requiring banks to invest in low-income communities to legalizing craft breweries. While Carter suffered several painful defeats — on tax reform, welfare reform, consumer protection, and health care — he won much more than he lost. This scorecard went largely unnoticed, in part because the aggressive post-Watergate press tended to assume the worst about him.

Carter was a Democratic president, but he accomplished many things commonly associated with Ronald Reagan. It was Carter, not Reagan, who ended rampant inflation by appointing Paul Volcker as chairman of the Federal Reserve Board; Carter, not Reagan, who cut the deficit and the growth rate of the federal workforce; Carter, not Reagan, who first broke with the Richard Nixon–Henry Kissinger policy of detente with Moscow by inviting Soviet dissidents to the White House and building the MX missile. Contrary to his reputation, Carter — after some hesitation — showed toughness by placing intermediate-range nuclear missiles in Europe. His Pentagon developed the B-2 stealth bomber and other high-tech weapons that the Soviet Union could not match. He sharply increased the defense budget and approved covert aid to anti-Communist Afghan rebels — the mujahideen — who helped turn Afghanistan into the Soviet Union's Vietnam.

And yet Carter also took risks for peace — and paid a political price for avoiding escalation, most conspicuously in the case of the Panama Canal Treaties. Ratified despite fierce opposition, the treaties prevented the deployment of more than a hundred thousand troops to the Canal Zone and dramatically improved the image of the United States across Latin America.

Carter was the first president with a policy devoted explicitly to promoting individual human rights in other countries. While applied unevenly, the new approach helped hasten the demise of more than a dozen dictatorships, gave hope to dissidents worldwide, and set a new and timeless global standard for how governments should treat their own people. Conservatives who had once thought it naive later admitted that the policy helped win the Cold War. And in the wake of the

28

Vietnam War and CIA abuses that left the United States deeply unpopular in many parts of the world, the humble and respectful approach of the Carter administration offered a model for repairing America's global reputation in the 2020s.

Carter himself made a good argument that his most lasting foreign policy achievement was walking through the door that Richard Nixon had opened to China in 1972. He ended Nixon's and Gerald Ford's unworkable "two-China policy" (which tilted toward Taiwan) and established full diplomatic relations with Peking, a move that launched the world's most important bilateral relationship.

Four decades on, the 1978 Camp David Accords survive as a world-historic achievement — the most successful peace treaty since the end of the Second World War. On at least three occasions, Egyptian president Anwar Sadat or Israeli prime minister Menachem Begin packed their bags to leave Camp David and wreck the summit. Over and over, Carter's inspired tenacity — his wheedling, cajoling, improvising, insisting — saved the day. Franklin Roosevelt's wartime diplomat, Averell Harriman, exulted, "What he has done with the Middle East is one of the most extraordinary things any president in history has ever accomplished." Few remember that the deal nearly collapsed after Camp David. Six months later, at great political risk, Carter traveled to Cairo and Jerusalem and painstakingly put the whole thing back together. After his presidency, Israelis and American Jews grew concerned about Carter's pro-Palestinian sentiments. But deeds are more important than words. The Israelis and

Egyptians have not fired a shot in anger in more than forty years.

Beyond faith, ambition, and grit, there was one constant in the complexity of his story. Today almost every politician wants to be seen as an outsider; Carter was the real thing. As a six-year-old, he was viewed as a country bumpkin when he ventured from his farm in tiny Archery, Georgia, to go to school in the daunting metropolis of Plains, population 406. He was a defiant outsider at the Naval Academy, where he was hazed more viciously than most other plebes, and at sea, where his shipmates thought he spent too much time reading manuals in his bunk. Back in Plains, his tolerant views on race set him outside the circle of his white supremacist neighbors, and in the Georgia State Senate, he never joined the poker games. When, after a period of depression and a born-again experience, he went door-to-door as a Baptist missionary in Pennsylvania and Massachusetts, his accent stuck out. He was elected governor by campaigning against Atlanta's insider "big money boys," then became a pariah to the rednecks who had put him in office. Beginning at 0 percent in the polls, he essentially invented the now-commonplace outsider presidential bid, which was both a campaign strategy and an authentic reflection of his nature. And in office, he avoided clubby relations with Congress and the Washington establishment.

Even Carter's political orientation lay outside the standard categories. He wasn't an angry populist, like his grandfather's patron, Tom Watson, or a devotee of the New Deal, which his father came to loathe. His political roots are easier

30

to discern in the progressive traditions of the turn of the twentieth century, which stressed reform and rejection of special interests. The rest was hard to pigeonhole: he shared Theodore Roosevelt's conservationist ethic and championing of health and safety regulation; Woodrow Wilson's diplomatic courage and global ideals; Calvin Coolidge's personal and budget austerity; Herbert Hoover's engineering background and humanitarian impulses; FDR's longheaded concern for future generations; and John F. Kennedy's "idealism without illusions." His altruistic postpresidency was rivaled only by that of John Quincy Adams — another one-term president — who worked against slavery when he was elected to the House of Representatives after leaving office.

Carter's favorite president was Harry Truman, who was also unpopular in office but grew in stature over time. He placed Truman's famous sign, "The Buck Stops Here," on his desk in the Oval Office and took the idea of accountability so seriously that, when running for reelection, he gave himself poor to middling grades on national television. Like Truman, Carter believed his Baptist faith required a strict separation of church and state. He rarely spoke of his devout beliefs — even to aides — and made a point of not allowing prayer breakfasts or other religious events at the White House. But he occasionally talked to world leaders in private about religious freedom (a conversation with Deng Xiaoping helped spread Christianity to millions in China), and he infused his politics with what one of his speechwriters called a "moral ideology." He thought US control of the Panama Canal a moral injustice to Panamanians; wasteful water projects a moral offense

31

against fiscal responsibility; environmental degradation a moral betrayal of the planet; and war — anywhere — a moral assault on the deepest human values.

Carter's high moral purpose sometimes made him look sanctimonious, especially to skeptics who failed to notice there wasn't enough hypocrisy to bolster the indictment. The critics didn't know yet that there was little to hide. But if his integrity and values were authentic, the gap between the public and private man could be wide.

Zbigniew Brzezinski, his national security adviser, was hardly the only one to notice that Carter had "three smiles": the radiant, toothy, and sometimes contrived grin that delighted crowds and cartoonists; the tight-lipped rictus when he was angry but didn't want to show it; and the relaxed and welcome smile he flashed in private when he found something funny or got off a dry, biting line.

The striking blue eyes told a similar story: loving or contemptuous, soulful or stern. When he was governor and president, the easiest way to get a glare from Carter's icy blues was to move from the merits of a decision to the politics of it. He drew a bright line between campaigning — which he did for governor in 1970 and president in 1976 with a canny grasp of all the angles — and governing, where his high-minded disdain for politics exasperated other politicians and came off as naive.

Carter's 1980 defeat had many causes — the divisive Kennedy challenge in the Democratic primaries; the prolonged captivity of the hostages in Iran; the wretched state of the American economy — but Carter's nature played a role. He

32

seemed as if he were carrying the weight of the world on his shoulders — never a good look. And while he had millions of admirers who liked his Everyman qualities, his modesty stripped him of the aura enjoyed and exploited by other leaders.

Unlike most who reach the summit, Carter did not always possess what soldiers call "command presence." He could bark out orders but lacked an intangible quality that makes people want to charge up the hill behind. This made him an unusual historical specimen: a visionary who was not a natural leader.

Rosalynn, his full partner and closest adviser, thought he was a leader of a different kind. "A leader can lead people where they *want* to go," she said in 2015. "A great leader leads people where they *ought* to go." Her husband was not a great leader — no historians consider him in the first rank of American presidents — but Carter was a surprisingly significant one, a man who lived the advice of the columnist Walter Lippmann to "plant trees we will never get to sit under."

The planting began in a distant America, setting on the horizon, where a real-life Huck Finn launched his own restless adventure.

*Age thirteen, Archery, Georgia, 1937.*

■ ■ ■ ■

# PART ONE:
# SOURCES OF STRENGTH

■ ■ ■ ■

# 1
## DADDY AND HOT

When he was old and allowed himself a reverie, he remembered the soil and the way it felt as it caressed his bare feet. From early March until late October, he almost never wore shoes, even to school. The loam of southwest Georgia was made of dark sand and red clay that spread over his face and his clothes and his house — one day as powder, the next, he said, as pellets the size of grits.

The blue-eyed, freckle-faced boy enjoyed a carefree idyll in the early 1930s that was little different than it would have been in the 1830s or 1730s or even — he liked to say — two thousand years ago, when Jesus Christ walked the earth. Time was measured not by clocks or pocket watches but by the sun and the clanging of the cast-iron farm bell. Until he was eleven, his homestead had no running water, no electricity, no insulation, and no mechanized farm equipment; only slop jars and outhouses, hand-pumped wells, kerosene lamps, ancient mule-driven plows, and black laborers to work the land in a feudal system just one step removed from slavery.

In other ways, he experienced many of the technologies that were coursing through the twentieth century. His boyhood on the farm co-incided almost exactly with the years of the Great Depression, when his family suffered along with the rest of the country. But they were well-to-do by local standards and boasted a telephone (on a shared "party line" with two other families and an operator, Miss Gladys, who knew everyone's business), automobiles (a Plymouth and later a pickup truck), and a large battery-powered radio, shaped like a cathedral, which everyone sat and stared at while the voices of *Little Orphan Annie, Amos 'n' Andy,* Jack Benny, Glenn Miller, and Franklin D. Roosevelt crackled across the small parlor. Atlanta was 160 miles north — as distant as Moscow or Peking, he wrote later, though dreams of the outside world were never far from his mind.

His first universe was Plains, named for the Plains of Dura, the land near Babylon in the Book of Daniel where ancient Israelites refused to bow down to idols. The perfectly flat and circular town, a mere mile in diameter, had been founded only forty years earlier by enterprising merchants anxious to convert the cotton bales that lined the unpaved roads into an outcropping of low-slung buildings that might bring prosperity for them-selves and local farmers.

In summer, Plains lay inside "the gnat belt." Locals learned from childhood the subtle gesture later known as "the Georgia wave": flicking the annoying if harmless insects away from their faces or more often ignoring them altogether. In winter, it was surprisingly cold, and the boy's most unpleasant childhood memories were of shivering all night, even under blankets. Set on the western

38

edge of Sumter County, Plains looked like a movie facade and consisted mostly of a one-sided Main Street — a mere one block in length — that local farmers would visit on weekends by horse and buggy or Model T, eager to get out of the fields to shop and converse. Fewer than half of the town's residents were white.

One of his earliest memories came when he was four years old and first visited the clapboard three-bedroom farmhouse that his family would move to in the country, nearly three miles up the road from Plains. The modest Arts and Crafts "kit house" had been built by the previous owner from materials shipped in a boxcar from Sears, Roebuck, whose catalogue was often a family's only connection to the bounty of the wider world. That day, the front door was locked, but the small boy was able to slip through a window, then come around and open the door from the inside. Daddy's smiling approval of his first useful act remained vivid in his mind. It would not come often.

The house where he was raised lay a few hundred feet down a dirt road — also known as US Route 280 — from a tiny dot on the map called Archery, Georgia, home to fewer than thirty farm families, most of them dependent on his father for work. All but the boy's and one other family were black, a circumstance of his early years that would give him genuine comfort with African Americans and, four decades later, ease his way when he spoke carelessly and needed their forgiveness. West of the family farmhouse, beyond his father's small commissary and the half dozen tenant farmer shacks he owned, was the home of the white foreman of a maintenance section of the Seaboard Air

Line Railroad, plus shacks for the five black railroad workers. The center of the tiny town, if it could be called that, was an African Methodist Episcopal church, which stood across from a small store for black customers, its roof covered by flattened Prince Albert tobacco cans.

That was about it for Archery. Most of the rest was 350 acres of his family's property — not just land but proving ground. The boy took to the soil with an ardor that he would one day apply to every endeavor. He planted himself, early, in futile anticipation of the approval of the person who meant most to him. For the rest of his life, he would pressure himself to measure up to his father's expectations — and his own — and push harder on all fronts when he did not.

Like nearly every white man in the county, Daddy was comfortable upholding a system of rigid segregation and quiet repression that he and most of his family assumed was the natural order of the universe. Within that pernicious system, he prided himself on treating black people with what he, in his blinkered fashion, considered respect. When the boy grew up and became a liberal, he made no secret of his father's racism, but he sometimes sugarcoated the brutal realities of the time.

Daddy always wore a hat — gray felt fedora in winter, straw Panama in summer — and went nowhere without a Home Run or Picayune cigarette dangling from his lips. He was a merchant by background and never one to bend his back much working in the fields. But he refused to pay for skilled labor he could do himself and so became not just a farmer and forester but also a herdsman, blacksmith, carpenter, and shoemaker.

One of the first places the slight, strawberry-blond boy could work alongside his father was in the small machine shop where he turned a hand crank on the forge blower as fast as he could to keep the fire going.

His father called him "son" or Hot Shot — Hot for short — a nickname that, depending on Daddy's mood, recognized his potential or knocked him down a notch. It seemed to fit the boy, one of his sisters said later, because his emotions ran deep, and he was always in a rush to do something significant with his life. Like other southerners addressing their elders, Hot called his father "Sir." He was "my hero" and "best friend." He "worshipped him" even as he waited in vain for outward signs of love and pride.

When he was very young, he fished sometimes with Daddy in Choctawhatchee Creek, a mile north of Archery, where the family fields drained. The Choctawhatchee flowed into other creeks that led near Albany, Georgia, to the Flint River, a great waterway the boy would someday have the power and the passion to protect. Hot spent hours exploring the creek with his playmates and developed there what he called later "an immersion in the natural world that has marked my whole existence."

Daddy introduced the boy to the deep Christian faith that would become a central part of his life. He made church and religion not just instructive but fun by taking Hot and his fellow Sunday school students — the Royal Ambassadors, a kind of Baptist Boy Scout troop — to the local grain mill for sleepovers. After fishing and swimming in a nearby pond and sword fights with corncobs, the boys would gather around as Daddy read Saint

41

Paul's letter to the Corinthians and urged them to be "ambassadors for Christ." Then they lay down to sleep on bags of grain with an aroma so sublime that the boy could still conjure it seven decades later.

Once in a while, Hot was allowed to tag along when Daddy and a buddy went hunting just after sunrise. For quail, he would shout "Point!" as one of the dogs froze — a sign of birds to be flushed. For doves, the responsibilities grew: He ran ahead to retrieve the fallen birds, then arrived at grade school a few minutes late. The feathers still clung to his sweater, a silent boast to classmates that his father had brought him along at a younger age than the other boys could claim. Before long, he was a fine shot himself, a skill he would carry into his midnineties.

Daddy was a stickler for the truth. Hot would say later that his basic integrity and contempt for lying came from him. But there was a harsher side. Much of the time, he was mercilessly competitive with his firstborn son, as Hot would replicate later with his own three sons. Daddy didn't compete at picking cotton or other work in the fields — which he mostly avoided — but he always had to prove he was better on the crude red clay tennis court he built, where his wicked slice beat Hot every time. The same went for fishing and hunting. Constantly losing to his father cut deep. In 1996 the boy, now a former president of the United States, wrote plaintively, "Today I think I could hold my own with him as a marksman and could even outdo him with a fly rod."

South Georgia had a 245-day growing season — an unrelenting pace for the sharecroppers, of course, but also for the family. Hot's complexion

42

was so fair that he sunburned easily, so his parents never let him stay out in the fields at midday. But that hardly offered a reprieve from work. As a child, one of his least-favorite chores was to make several consecutive trips carrying a two-and-a-half-gallon bucket of water in each hand from the spring down a steep incline to faraway fields, where the farmhands often drank one or two dipperfuls before carelessly spilling the rest, a wasting of a precious resource he noticed more than their working conditions.

Mopping cotton was worse. "We despised it," he remembered. An infestation of boll weevils in the 1920s and 1930s ravaged cotton fields across the South, forcing many farmers to turn away from their cash crop. The only way to fend off boll weevils was to mix arsenic, molasses, and water and apply the poisonous concoction to the central buds of every cotton plant. The idea was to attract the insects, then kill them, but mopping often did neither, while leaving a gooey mess — the boy's first evidence of unintended consequences. To protect against the swarms of flies and bees, he wore long pants that became so sticky with hardened molasses that at night they seemed to him to be standing at attention in the corner of his bedroom.

Avoiding chores brought an icy glare from his father that he would later make his own. When Hot was seven, as his family bundled into the car for a picnic, he admitted he had not pruned the watermelons. Daddy stopped the car, opened the door, and told him to get out. "He wasn't going to the picnic," his aunt Sissy remembered. She got out, too, and stayed to help him. "My heart just broke for that little boy," she said. "I'll never

43

forget how he looked out there in the watermelon patch — so little and forlorn." Much later, he attributed his tenacity to his father's insistence that he finish whatever he started. Daddy demanded perfection, and his son would try all his life to provide it.

After school, Hot helped milk eight cows, feed the hogs, and wring the necks of chickens — but these tasks were a small portion of what he eventually did on the farm. Every tool he was allowed to use was a step forward in maturity. Hot started with a hoe, then a hatchet for weeding and chopping stove wood. A big day came when he was allowed to harness a docile mule, Emma, and hitch her to a primitive turning plow. Soon he was less an ordinary boy than a newborn farmer, anxious to learn anything he could about the land. He said later that aspiring to do this work — a man's work — "equaled any other ambition I've ever had in my life."

Finally, after much pleading, Daddy entrusted Hot with the cultivation of his precious crops, a sophisticated task assigned to only a few skilled farmers. He started with corn and sweet potatoes and moved on to cotton — dethroned as agrarian king by depressed prices yet still vital — and peanuts, now the dominant crop in Sumter County. They grew awkwardly in the ground like potatoes but were in great demand everywhere to help feed the new national craze for peanut butter that had begun during the First World War.

Covering as much as twenty-five miles a day, he learned to use turning plows, harrows, and planters. He steered Emma down the rows of the growing plants, commanding her to turn right ("gee")

44

or left ("haw"). Mistakes from an errant blade or poorly handled mule were easy for his father or the black foreman, Jack Clark, to discover. But Hot liked that his skill could be assessed in relation to others'. It was the same habit of mind that would draw him to engineering: "I felt that this was doing all I could possibly do, and that no one on the farm, no matter how strong or experienced, could do it better."

Plowing was a complicated job for a young boy. It required him to acquire broad knowledge of all the elements of successful cultivation: topography; absorption of rain; drainage; crop rotation; clodding (pressing oil from meal); preserving moisture in seedbed preparation; juxtaposition of fertilizer (usually guano, from bird excrement) and seed; insect control; and how to mix, measure, and apply fertilizer — all done in hard, often unforgiving red clay soil under a broiling Georgia sun.

Mules — well known to be smarter than horses — had a way of feigning exhaustion, and Emma was no exception. With temperatures often over one hundred degrees, an aspiring farmer had to learn when his mule was genuinely suffering sunstroke — and when a boy his age might keel over, too. All of this required a prodigious work ethic, a fierce discipline, and an attention to detail that Hot learned when he was barely old enough for school.

On most family farms, little or nothing is discarded, but Daddy took this to extremes. One winter, he cobbled too many high-button ladies' shoes with pointy toes that hadn't been popular since the turn of the century and weren't selling well in the stores. Hot had to wear them to school, where the mocking laughter would echo for him through the years.

There were compensations: a baby alligator, a bulldog named Bozo to help him hunt squirrels, and a pony — a gift that greatly excited him on his seventh Christmas — he called Lady. But his father believed that everyone and everything on the farm — even Lady — must always earn its keep. "There always seemed to be a need for a reckoning in the early days / What came in equaled what went out like oscillating ocean waves," he wrote decades later in the title poem for a collection of his poetry called *Always a Reckoning.* When the colt that Lady bore every year or two didn't fetch a high enough price to pay for Lady's hay and corn, Daddy wanted Hot to make better use of her. "How long since you rode Lady?" he asked, as if even his son's playtime contained a lesson about earning one's way in life.

Daddy didn't like to spend money on veterinarians, so Hot learned to treat problems such as scours, mastitis, and screwworm, and what to do when a calf wouldn't descend to be born. In the slaughterhouse, Daddy and Jack Clark would shoot several two-hundred-pound hogs with a .22-caliber rifle, then slash their throats and let the blood drain into a large pan. When he was small and repelled by this process, his father turned to Jack and said, "The sight of blood is too much for the little boy."

It wasn't. Before long, Hot would eagerly help boil the huge hogs in cast-iron kettles to loosen their hair, then scrape off the follicles with dull knives before washing the liver, heart, kidneys, and other organs and preparing the small intestines to be sausage casings. Chores that others might try to avoid were for him a way to feel closer

46

to his father. As a preteen, he castrated two-week-old piglets, shot edible wild game, and accompanied Daddy to the meetings of the area's eight-family beef club, where the host would slaughter a steer with the help of the group before everyone went home with delectable innards. "We never heard of anything as strange as a vegetarian," he wrote later. The family often gorged on fresh brains, scrambled with eggs.

After school, on weekends, and during blistering summers, Hot joined the black tenant farmers and day laborers his father employed not just in the work of picking cotton and shaking and stacking peanuts, but also in pulling worms and boll weevils out of cotton by hand; planting corn (used for fuel and feed), raising okra, peas, collards, turnips, and cabbage; harvesting timber, then clearing new ground with crosscut saws and dynamite under the stumps; shaking trees until swarms of honeybees dropped into one of the farm's two dozen beehives, then processing the honey (this ended when Daddy was so badly stung that he landed in the hospital); bottling the vanilla and chocolate drinks that his father sold in the surrounding area under the label Plains Maid; shearing sheep for wool and plucking geese for the fine down that filled handmade bedcovers that they transported fourteen miles to Americus, the county seat, for sale in the fancy stores.

As he grew older, the one chore Hot tried to avoid was cutting twenty-five acres of sugarcane and hauling the heavy stalks to the mill in his father's pickup truck, which he was allowed to operate as soon as he could see over the dashboard. He found cutting cane stalks with a machete dangerous and unpleasant, especially

47

with so many rattlesnakes and water moccasins in the sugarcane fields. He preferred working in the mill, where he learned to fire the boiler and burn the stalks.

Above all else, he looked forward to working alongside Daddy in his combination blacksmith and carpentry shop. He learned to use a sledge-hammer, tongs, and anvil to shape and sharpen steel plow points; to shoe mules and horses; to build steel rims for wagons and buggies; and to repair almost any piece of broken equipment. Daddy taught him welding, cobbling, and cabi-netry. His love of woodworking would endure throughout his life.

The multiple skills required for committed work as a farmer and artisan would give him the confidence to set his mind to any task and qualify him for a simple adjective long out of fashion but once high praise: able.

Daddy could be amusing with his friends but had little sense of humor about himself. He once ordered by mail a fancy suit that was so big that it engulfed him like a child when it arrived. Daddy sulked all day about it and skipped church. "And no one in our family blinked or smiled," Hot wrote later. But he likely derived some satisfaction from seeing his father fail to measure up, or he wouldn't have later written a poem about it.

The most memorable rebuke from his father came when Hot was about ten. After a sharp piece of wood penetrated deep into his wrist, causing intense pain, Hot stayed home from the fields. "The rest of us will be here working while Jimmy lies here in the house and reads a book," his father snapped. With Daddy's approval at risk — he

48

called him "Jimmy" instead of "Hot" only when disgusted with him — the boy wrapped a belt tightly around his wrist and pushed it up against a fencepost until the piece of wood was ejected in an eruption of pus. Then he pedaled on his bicycle as fast as he could to join his father in the cotton field. "It's good to have you back with us, Hot," his father said.

Hot remembered all six times his father whipped him, the punishment administered with a long, thin peach tree switch. There might have been many more had his mother not stood between her husband and her children. The first, when he was four or five, was for stealing two pennies from the collection plate at church. "That was the last money I ever stole," he wrote, an assertion that even his worst enemies would never contest. He was whipped for playing with matches in the barn, and for three offenses against one of his sisters, including shooting her in the rear with a BB gun after she'd hit him with a wrench. The final whipping came when Hot retreated to his tree house during a noisy party his parents hosted and didn't respond when his father called for him. By this time, the boy had grown a little sullen and uncooperative; it was the first shadow of his implacable, prickly side.

One day Daddy asked Hot to come with him while he picked up a holiday turkey at a nearby farm owned by an attractive young widow. Hot thought this was strange; they had plenty of turkeys on their own farm. His father, who seemed to know the Webster County property well, directed him to the pen out back and told him to pick out a turkey while he went into the house. Hot followed his instructions and waited a long time. When his father and the dark-haired woman finally exited together, he suspected strongly that they had been doing more than discussing turkeys. His willingness to volunteer this story nearly seventy years later suggests that he never fully extinguished his resentment toward his father.

Hot wondered why — even in the nearly thirteen years before his younger brother was born — Daddy never suggested that he might want to run the farm after he was gone. Why did he treat two of his younger siblings with greater tenderness? Why had he never "showed much emotion or love toward me"? Only much later would his mother tell him that Daddy had wept from missing him when Hot went to stay with his grandparents in Columbus, Georgia, for a week. But this did little to salve the wound. He "despised the discipline he used to shape what I should be." In a poem written decades after his father's death, he confessed:

This is a pain I mostly hide,
but ties of blood, or seed, endure,
and even now I feel inside
the hunger for the outstretched hand,
a man's embrace to take me in,
the need for just a word of praise.

In time Jimmy Carter would understand that the inner steel that took him so far was forged in Earl Carter's foundry and on his farm.

# 2
# THE CARTERS AND THE GORDYS

The tangled history of America is written in Jimmy Carter's genes. One of his ancestors, William Almy, arrived from England in 1630 with John Winthrop, the first governor of the Massachusetts Bay Colony. Winthrop described the new land — in words invoked later by Ronald Reagan — as a shining "city on a hill." Other forebears, Quakers and Baptists, spread to New Jersey, Virginia, and North Carolina. Isaac Carter bequeathed fifty-eight slaves to his children, among them the first James Carter, who commanded a company in the Continental army during the American Revolution before moving to Wilkes County, Georgia, in 1787. This was the year Georgia became the fourth state to ratify the US Constitution — after insisting along with other southern states that the new nation's founding document protect the institution of slavery.

In 1825 the Creek Indians discovered they had been swindled by the state of Georgia. The tribe sold millions of acres to the state for a mere $200,000 in the Treaty of Indian Springs. The traitorous mixed-blood Creek chief who negotiated the fraudulent deal was executed by other chiefs, but it was too late. A lottery was established

51

for white settlers, many of whom were eligible to win Indian land for as little as four cents an acre. The Carters bought land in the late 1820s at those absurdly low prices, and in the 1830s they acquired hundreds more acres, some of it vacated by Indians forced west by President Andrew Jackson on the infamous Trail of Tears.

While Carter pleaded ignorance during his 1976 presidential campaign as to whether his ancestors held slaves, he acknowledged as much after leaving the presidency. By then, he also noted readily that his family's property in Sumter and Webster Counties had originally belonged to the Creeks and other tribes. "To have it taken away from you is terrible," he said in 2006 in reference to the land his ancestors grabbed, comparing the treatment of Native Americans to the plight of the Palestinians in the Middle East.

There was violence in the blood of the peacemaker. Jimmy's great-great-grandfather Wiley Carter shot a neighbor who had publicly accused Carter's wife of adultery. Wiley's son, Littleberry Walker Carter, was stabbed to death in a dispute over receipts from a merry-go-round, and his wife committed suicide on the day of his funeral. Littleberry's son, William Archibald ("Billy") Carter, Jimmy's grandfather, was killed in a dispute over a stolen desk.*

Littleberry and his two brothers fought under Confederate general Jeb Stuart in what Jimmy, when talking to fellow southerners, often called

*"I haven't been very belligerent in my life," Jimmy Carter chuckled when he was in his nineties, just home from yet another peace mission. "Maybe because of that ancestral background."

52

the War Between the States. The Carter boys took part in twenty-one battles, including Gettysburg, where they laid down artillery fire intended to cover Major General George Pickett's fateful assault on the Union lines. Their barrage — and Pickett's Charge — failed, and Gettysburg turned the tide of the Civil War, as President Carter explained to Anwar Sadat and Menachem Begin 115 years later when they came over from nearby Camp David to tour the battlefield.

Wiley Carter left his descendants forty-three slaves and $22,000 each ($300,000 today) — a significant legacy. But after the war, the slaves were freed, and Confederate money was worthless. All they had left was their land. When Reconstruction ended in 1877, the Carters and other white landowners could once again exploit black labor and control state and local politics without fear of interference.

When Billy Carter was killed in 1903, his bereft widow, Nina, couldn't cope with his loss. So control of the family shifted to their sixteen-year-old son, Alton, whom Jimmy later revered as a father figure. Alton sold the sprawling timber farm and moved the family by mule train from Arlington, Georgia, to the newly incorporated and thriving town of Plains. Alton helped raise his four siblings and made sure his younger brother, James Earl Carter, Jimmy's father, got some schooling. Earl made it through the tenth grade at Riverside Military Academy in the Blue Ridge Mountains, which was the most education any Carter had ever received until then.

Earl was already an able detail man — a trait he would pass down to his older son. During the First World War, he joined the Quartermasters

Corps and rose to sergeant, though he never shipped out for Europe. He returned from the army to resume work in Alton's general store — the Plains Mercantile Company — before leaving with his brother's permission to start J. E. Carter's, a grocery and meat market just down Main Street, with a "pressing club" out back where a black worker cleaned and ironed clothes. He owned an icehouse, began brokering peanuts, and borrowed $7,000 — the only debt of his life — to buy seven hundred acres of good farmland in nearby Webster County, where he parceled out some of the land to sharecroppers. Alton marveled that his affable brother Earl was one of those men who "make money every time they lay down their hands."

By the time of his death three decades later, Earl Carter owned a successful seed and fertilizer warehouse, a fire insurance and mortgage company, and nearly four thousand acres of farms across two counties, worked by two hundred men at harvest time. Much of the land was assembled through farm foreclosures, under which Earl would take possession of property when the owners couldn't repay the loans he'd made to them. Jimmy Carter makes no specific mention of the foreclosures in his memoirs. To his wide circle of friends, Earl was known as a warm and gregarious man, an exceptionally hard worker who also knew how to have a good time.

Jimmy's mother was Lillian Gordy Carter, a woman so captivating and irreverent that, during the Carter presidency, she became a frequent guest on the *Tonight* show. The Gordys were descended from slaveholding Scotch-Irish and

54

French colonialists who settled in southwest Georgia in the 1830s, also on land vacated when the Indians were forced westward. Several fought for the Confederacy in the Civil War.

Lillian's grandfather, James Thomas Gordy, a plantation owner and county tax collector, fathered children with his white wife, Harriet, including Jimmy's grandfather. He also fathered a son with his slave Esther Johnson. Their son, Berry Gordy, became the largest black landowner in Washington County, Georgia. His grandson, Berry Gordy Jr., was the celebrated African American founder of Motown Records. Jimmy Carter and Berry Gordy thus shared the same great-grandfather, though neither made note of it.

Lillian's father was James "Jim Jack" Gordy, born in 1863, and named after James Jackson, the young Revolutionary War hero who accepted the British surrender at Savannah and became an early governor of Georgia. Tall, lean, bow-tied Jim Jack was a dandy who skipped town and left his first fiancée at the altar, which led his second fiancée, Ida Nicholson, Jimmy's grandmother, a quiet but strong woman, to insist that he be standing in the church before she dressed for the ceremony and married him. Ida later told Jimmy's sister Ruth that after the wedding, she set aside an hour a day to be alone and scream as loud as she could: "Damn! Damn! Damn!"

Ida grew up hiding her dime-store novel habit by pretending to read the Bible in the parlor. She passed down the reading obsession to her daughter, Bessie Lillian, born in 1898, the fourth of their nine children, including two cousins who moved in when Ida's brother committed suicide. Like her son, Jimmy, and granddaughter, Amy

Carter, Lillian grew up as a bookworm. "I read the almanac, the encyclopedia. I simply had to have something to read," she remembered. When she didn't, she settled for works by Cicero — in Latin. "Some think I'm queer," she said later, though her eccentricities seemed well tolerated by friends and family in both childhood and adulthood.

Jim Jack was a politically engaged former schoolteacher who served for thirty-three years as postmaster of Richland, Georgia, and for a time as a revenue agent charged with destroying bootleg liquor stills. At the post office, he let Lillian, who claimed she was his favorite, sit with him while he worked, and she witnessed him soaking up intelligence from all quarters. He was nimble enough with patronage to hold his postmastership for four decades through both Democratic and Republican administrations in Washington. Jimmy later likened his maternal grandfather to a pollster without polls. He could forecast local election returns with astonishing accuracy and was known as one of the most politically savvy men in Webster and Stewart Counties.

Starting in the 1890s, Jim Jack had political ties to Tom Watson, the fiery agrarian rebel who most personified turn-of-the-century southern populism — the original class-based movement that led to many checks on American capitalism before curdling into racism. Watson ran for vice president and later president on the ticket of the People's Party, an innovative third party implacably opposed to "moneyed interests." Much of the People's Party platform from the 1890s — including the creation of a federal income tax and the direct election of US senators — became law in

56

1913 under President Woodrow Wilson.

When he ran for president, Carter claimed repeatedly that it was his maternal grandfather who gave Congressman Watson the idea for the landmark Rural Free Delivery (RFD) legislation that dramatically expanded American postal service, then the closest connection most Americans had to the federal government. The family long assumed this to be true, but it almost certainly was not. (The idea appears to have originated in Indiana.)

Jim Jack named one of his sons Tom Watson Gordy, hosted Watson overnight in Richland, and helped manage a region in his 1920 US Senate campaign — all in the period after Watson became a virulent racist and anti-Semite who incited the lynch mob that in 1915 hanged Leo Frank, an innocent Jewish businessman wrongly convicted of having murdered a thirteen-year-old girl. Jimmy's mother grew up revering Watson anyway.

Lillian claimed that while "Watson hated blacks," her father was more enlightened. She said he instilled tolerant views on race and religion that she, in turn, conveyed to her children. But there is no record of Jim Jack ever taking issue with the famously vitriolic racism and anti-Semitism of his hero. When his daughter Elizabeth decided in 1933 to marry a Jew, Louis Braunstein, she did so in secret before moving to Chattanooga, Tennessee. Jimmy remembered his Uncle Louie as the strongest man he ever knew — a man who could do twenty-five chin-ups with one arm, though he couldn't change a flat tire.*

*When Carter mentioned that to Jerry Rafshoon, a close adviser who grew up Jewish in the South,

The influenza pandemic of 1918 killed fifty million to a hundred million people worldwide, including one of Lillian's beloved sisters. This inspired her to be a nurse, a career decision that eight decades later would influence her son's passion for curing devastating global diseases. In 1921 she moved eighteen miles down the road from Richland to Plains to work as a nurse in training at the Wise Sanitarium, a sixty-bed hospital that local boosters called "the little Mayo Clinic."

Lillian Gordy met Earl Carter at a dance but was later turned off after watching him do ostentatious half gainers off a diving board into frigid water. "I just didn't like his looks," she remembered. Earl's nickname was changing from Turtle to the more impressive Turk, but he still looked like the former: short, bespectacled, and balding.

Even so, Earl fit Lillian's life plan for herself. After they were caught in a downpour in his Model T, she warmed to him. Earl, then twenty-nine, proposed marriage, Lillian said, mostly because he was upset that his younger sister — newly pregnant — had just announced her engagement. He wanted to be married first. At the time, Lillian was training for several weeks at Grady Hospital in Atlanta. Earl sent the ring to a doctor there, who presented it to her, an approach she didn't appreciate. In an oral history, Lillian sounded as if she agreed to marry Earl so that she

---

Rafshoon replied, "Mr. President, we don't change tires. We hire rednecks for that."

could end her Atlanta training, which she disliked.

But over time she came to love the man who called her "Darlin' " — an endearment Jimmy would later pick up and use with his wife, though it came out as the full "Darling." "He was the kind of Christian who didn't mind if you took a drink," Lillian said. "He was happy all day. He smiled just like Jimmy does." One night shortly after their wedding, they wandered into the yard outside their rooming house at 100 West Church Street and settled under a pecan tree, where they conceived a child.

James Earl Carter Jr. came into the world weighing eight and a half pounds at seven o'clock sharp on the morning of October 1, 1924, in the Wise Sanitarium, making him the first American president to be born in a hospital. Lillian wrote his nickname on his birth record: " 'Jimmy' now — but later of course it will be 'Jim.' " (It never was.) Earl was ecstatic. "He was oohing and aahing so much you'd have thought the baby was Jesus Christ," Lillian deadpanned in 1977. "I knew he wasn't, of course, because I knew I wasn't a virgin."

Gloria would follow in two years. Nicknamed Go-Go, she was taller and more rambunctious than her diminutive older brother and described by Lillian as "more or less the leader of my children," suggesting that birth order (or future positions in life) would not automatically confer leadership qualities on Jimmy. The siblings quarreled often but drew closer as adults living in the same town. Years later, Lillian said that while she had four brilliant children, Gloria was the "most brilliant" and that Jimmy agreed with that assessment.

Ruth, five years younger than Jimmy, was named after one of Earl's former girlfriends, who had died in a car accident. The crash was blamed on a black man who mysteriously disappeared in the aftermath.* While Jimmy and Gloria chafed under their father's discipline, Ruth — whom Earl considered "so much prettier than Shirley Temple" — became his pet. Ruth, nicknamed Boop-a-Doop, enjoyed special stature in the family because as an infant she had nearly died from an undiagnosed illness. When she recovered, Earl held up the baby and said, according to family lore, "She'll have whatever she wants." Ruth later came to believe that her father's doting on her and favoring her so conspicuously over Jimmy and Gloria was "not altogether healthy" and at the root of her depression in the years before she became a well-known evangelist.

Billy came nearly thirteen years after Jimmy, when Lillian was thirty-nine. He was, Lillian said, "a mistake." Earl was the kind of husband who, when informed his wife was pregnant for the fourth time, offered her $1,000 if she had twins. He gave her $500 for Billy, who was born in 1937 and nicknamed Buckshot or Buck. Hot and Buck barely knew each other growing up, which complicated their relationship when the brothers later worked together in the family business. Billy

*Bryan Stevenson of the Equal Justice Initiative determined later that at least three lynchings of black Georgians took place in Sumter County in the late-nineteenth and early-twentieth centuries but could not calculate the number of disappearances.

looked exactly like his father and inherited his good ol' boy nature; he was much closer to Earl than Jimmy was, in part because Earl felt that he had "failed with Jimmy," as Lillian put it, by being too strict. He overcompensated by spoiling Billy, who had a near-photographic memory but little of Jimmy's self-discipline.

After his death, Lillian depicted Earl as a "great man" who backed her in her nursing ambitions, but she admitted that "I always accused him of being kinder to everyone else than he was to me." In later years, the same complaint was sometimes made about Jimmy by certain family members. Jimmy also inherited a fanatical punctuality from his father, who once told a doctor who had kept him waiting, "I'm just as busy as you are."

It was true. Earl loved the adage "idle hands are the devil's workshop." By the 1920s, he was a small-town man on the make; a diversified entre-preneur rather than a tiller of the soil. "He never plowed an acre. He never hoed a row of corn," Lillian remembered. "He had blacks do that." After Jimmy went into politics, he sometimes implied that he grew up poor. When discussing his favorite book, James Agee's *Let Us Now Praise Famous Men,* a depiction of dire poverty in Depression-era Alabama, Carter claimed to an interviewer, "It told accurately what I knew as a child." He might more properly have said, what he *saw* as a child — in the shacks of his family's tenant farmers.

In 1940 those tenant farmers went on strike against Earl Carter and several other landowners in the area. They sought a pay increase from $1.00 a day to $1.25. Earl granted it but no other concessions. He walked to their shacks and told them they had a choice, which he considered a Christian gesture: they could pay what they owed him (mostly from his commissary) and be off his property with their possessions by sunrise, or they could show up as usual at the peanut picker the next morning. Jimmy never doubted that they would remain. "A buck a day wasn't bad pay then," he wrote.

In looking back, Carter liked to recall that his parents treated their black hired help "with great fairness and affection." Perhaps so, relative to other white landlords. Earl did agree at one point to sell 210 acres of his Webster County property to one of his black tenant farmers, an unusual act for the time. But this was hardly enough to distinguish him much from the brutal norm in the Jim Crow South. When Vern Smith, a black reporter for *Newsweek,* went to Archery in 1976 and talked to a few retired field hands with the promise that he wouldn't use their names, they painted a familiar picture. "Mr. Earl, he was sort of a hateful man," said one. "People in those days were *all* kind of mean, and I guess he had to along with the rest of 'em."

Earl Carter was the most prominent figure for miles around, with one exception: Bishop William Decker Johnson of the African Methodist Episcopal Church.

Bishop Johnson — short, reddish-brown face, impeccably dressed, possessing a doctorate in theology — was so brilliant that he was certified to teach public school at age fourteen. The son of an important church elder, he supervised hundreds of AME churches across five midwestern states, but home was Archery, described in 1916

62

by the *Centennial Encyclopaedia of the African Methodist Episcopal Church* as "a little village founded by [Johnson] for the education of the poorest of the poor." He auctioned off twenty-five small plots to black families and built St. Mark's AME Church, which included a chapel, a private industrial school, an insurance company, and a publishing company. Johnson traveled incessantly, but when he came home, it was always a major occasion in the wider community, with the choir from Spelman College often coming down from Atlanta to perform. As a child, Jimmy would marvel over a picture of the bishop standing in front of the Eiffel Tower, and he occasionally accompanied his mother to hear Johnson's sermons at St. Mark's, which featured singing and clapping that was alien to anything Jimmy experienced at Plains Baptist Church. Earl, not surprisingly, did not venture into black churches.

To Jimmy, Bishop Johnson "seemed the epitome of success and power," and he noticed that the bishop defied certain Jim Crow social norms. He would never enter their house from the back, like other black visitors. And yet he would not be so defiant as to approach the front door, an affront to Mr. Earl. Instead, he would pull up to the Carter home in his chauffeured Cadillac or Packard and sound the horn or send his driver round back to let the family know he had arrived. When Earl came out to greet him, the bishop would either sit in the car talking to him out the window, or the two men would stand together under the shade of a large magnolia tree in the Carters' front yard — safe territory for them to converse as relative equals without violating the rigid racial mores of the South.

When he was young, Jimmy mistakenly believed that Bishop Johnson had achieved all of his great success after being born poor in Archery. But he nonetheless absorbed an early life lesson: that it was possible to start out in a tiny rural area and rise to the top without losing ties to home. Carter noted later how remarkable it was that the first eminent person he ever met — the first who could move an audience with words and offer genuine leadership — was black. He wrote that the bishop's good education, along with his social and professional prominence, influenced his attitudes on race and may have kindled his own ambitions. Johnson died when Jimmy was eleven, and his funeral was the most elaborate event anyone in the Plains area could remember, with "Cadillac after Cadillac after Cadillac" bringing senior AME officials from all over the country to Archery.

While Bishop Johnson helped recast Jimmy's ideas of black achievement, it was a black husband and wife down the road who ended up shaping much of his character. On many nights when he was young, Jimmy stayed overnight in the one-bedroom cabin of Jack and Rachel Clark.

Jack Clark, the unofficial foreman of the Carter property, was a gruff, middle-aged black man who always wore clean overalls and carried himself with an air of authority. Earl told his six-year-old son that he should learn about the farm from Jack, so Jimmy followed Jack around with an endless string of questions. Jack rang the big farm bell at around four o'clock every morning to get everyone up "an hour before daylight," which became the title of Jimmy Carter's finest book, published in 2001.

Jimmy would often sleep on lumpy cornstalks

64

on the floor in the main room, where he could peer through the cracks between boards to the earth below. He spent many evenings playing cards and checkers with the Clarks and their relatives, and said that he felt more comfortable there than anywhere in his own house except for his bedroom.

After his mother and siblings died in the 1980s, the former president often suggested that he was raised by Rachel Clark, whom he rarely mentioned when Lillian was alive. "I knew Rachel Clark in many ways better than my mother," he said in 2006, weeping at her grave.

Rachel, born in 1890, was a stately, light-skinned black woman who wore print dresses made from rough-hewn sacks of flour or guano. She signed her name with an *X*. For Jimmy, she had a "gentle touch" and "the aura of an African queen." Later, he would compare her to King Solomon's daughter. He was also impressed by her manual dexterity, which made her the fastest cotton picker for miles around.

When it rained, and the cotton bolls were too damp to pick, Rachel took little Jimmy on excursions. Earl had thrown him into a pond at age three with the words "Swim, son, swim." But it was Rachel, not Daddy or Mama, who taught him the names of flowers and birds and how to fish, using a mixture of crawfish, lizards, crickets, and worms on exactly seven fishing poles to catch perch, catfish, and bass, the latter mistakenly called "trout" by white folks. The stream she favored was a few miles from the homestead, and Jimmy soaked up knowledge and inspiration all the way there and home again. It was "God's holy way" that we be stewards of the earth, she told him, an important early instruction for a boy who would someday fulfill this duty on a historic scale.

It was Rachel, his surrogate mother, who imbued Jimmy with the spirituality that would guide him over time. "Much more than my parents, she talked to me about the religious and moral values that shaped a person's life, and I listened to her with acute attention," Carter wrote. "Without seeming to preach, she taught me how I should behave." In a long poem entitled "Rachel," he wrote that on their fishing expeditions, "She'd tell how praying gave her life a lift, and how it made her act and not just talk — like staying up all night with someone sick. It wasn't empty preaching, like in church. Sometimes I wasn't glad to reach the creek." On the way home, she would put fish she caught in Jimmy's sack so that it would seem as if he'd caught more. "Those might have been the best days I have known," he concluded.

Jack Clark died in the 1960s, but Rachel lived to see Carter as president. In an oral history, she modestly denied doing anything special for him but allowed that the president told her: "You're the cause of me being what I am." Carter would say the same thing publicly on several occasions in his later years.

As a young mother, Lillian was a gaunt, mildly depressed woman with few close friends — a character from a short story by Flannery O'Connor or Eudora Welty. She left all cooking and most child rearing to the black help. If Earl was "Daddy" to the children, Lillian was usually "Mama" but sometimes the more distant "Mother." She admitted that her husband was "a more affectionate father than I was a mother" and

66

did more around the house. When the children were old enough to attend school in Plains, they ate their noontime "dinner" around the corner from school with their aunt Ethel (Earl's sister) and uncle Jack, a veterinarian who was often compensated for his services with opossums. On the campaign trail, Jimmy joked that he'd eaten more opossum — with its "sickly sweet taste" — than any man his age in Georgia.

From the time he first ran for president, Carter's story was always that his father was a tough conservative and his mother a tender-hearted liberal. While this was broadly true, and the tension therein helped forge his character, his mother was a progressive on race mostly in comparison to her neighbors.

Beginning with his 1976 presidential campaign, Carter cast Lillian in the role of integrationist. He liked to say that when he was growing up, his mother was the only person he ever heard praise Abraham Lincoln. In speeches and three of his books, he told the story of how, in 1938, Bishop Johnson's son, Alvan, home from college in New England, was welcomed by Miss Lillian through the front door several times, while Mr. Earl, unable to accept this "breach of southern etiquette," would "leave and pretend it wasn't happening." Carter wrote that his mother also encouraged other black friends to enter that way, especially when her husband was gone, and "as much as their discomfiture would permit, she treated them as equals."

Lillian herself remembered the story differently. While she was proud of receiving Alvan, and said she made sure fourteen-year-old Jimmy listened attentively to stories of his higher education, her flouting of Jim Crow traditions had limits: "I have never had a black person come to my front door to visit me. They respect me too much. They come to my kitchen door." But she added, "If they are in trouble, they know I'm the one who will do it for them." Her help confirmed the impression. "She was about as good a white lady as I've ever seen," one former cook later told a reporter. When any black sharecroppers or tenant farmers who lived on their property died, she would show up at the funeral, frequently with Jimmy in tow, and often delivered a eulogy. Earl "didn't want to go to a black funeral," Lillian remembered. "People just didn't do that." Jimmy later credited his mother with teaching him respect for intelligence and the opportunities of life beyond Archery and Plains. She was a freethinker, embracing Charles Darwin's theory of evolution in the heart of the Bible Belt and devouring accounts in the Atlanta papers of the New York theater. But she disapproved of the plot of Eugene O'Neill's *All God's Chillun Got Wings,* in which a black man, portrayed on Broadway in 1924 by the radical black actor Paul Robeson, marries a white woman. Miscegenation is wrong, she told a *New York Times* reporter in 1977, and she admitted that had she lived in New York in the 1920s, she probably would have joined those picketing the theater.

Lillian claimed in later years that she forbade racial slurs in her house. But that was only after her children had grown up. Willard Slappey, Jimmy's cousin and a frequent presence in the Carter home before World War II, said simply: "We called them niggers then," though he never said specifically that Jimmy did. Where Lillian differed from other whites was in teaching her

68

children not to use the word as an insult. Annie Mae Hollis, the Carters' longtime housekeeper, remembered that when the children got angry with her, they would say, "I don't like you — you go home." And she would reply, "I ain't going nowhere. You goin' to mind me." Then came hugs. "They never did call me anything but my name," she said.

As late as the 1970s, Miss Lillian herself was known to let the word slip out every so often, even in the presence of a reporter, as Eleanor Randolph, on assignment for *Esquire* magazine, learned. But by that time, she was determined that her grandchildren not use it under any circumstances. Billy Carter's son, Buddy, said that she gave him a whipping when he did.

Lillian defined herself as a Christian, but after the children grew older, she ditched services at the Plains Baptist Church, drank whiskey, and loved getting out to play poker or watch professional wrestling in nearby towns. Her friends, indulging her eccentric views, knew better than to tell crude racist jokes in her presence.

At home, she was usually off by herself. When she wasn't tending her pecan trees, which provided her with a little extra income, Lillian could most often be found lying facedown on the edge of her bed with her head bent over a book that was open on the floor. "She loved to laugh," Jimmy remembered in a poem, "and often laughed alone, but didn't seem to care." He added that not many tears fell when she cried: "She had never learned how." Later, he remembered "her crying only as histrionics to emphasize her anger or displeasure. She always liked to be in charge."

All of the Carters read widely, except Earl, who

perused only newspapers and farm journals. Jimmy was partial to Arthur Conan Doyle's Sherlock Holmes stories, the *Tom Swift* boys' adventure series, and Edgar Rice Burroughs's *Tarzan,* and he usually asked Santa Claus for books for Christmas.

The family had a strange habit of reading silently at every meal except Sunday dinner, then arguing about what they read. "A lot of people think it's not polite, but it's just the way we grew up," Jimmy said later. Each of the Carters was in his or her own silent universe, traveling through time and space even as they supped together. Lillian recalled: "When I would say, 'Jimmy, what are you doing?' — I wanted him to do a chore for me — and he would say, 'I'm just reading. What do you want, Mama?' And I'd say, 'Go ahead.' " The children never bothered their mother when she was reading, either.

During the Depression, Archery looked like something out of *Tobacco Road,* the 1932 best seller by Erskine Caldwell that immortalized the poverty of the rural South.

Jimmy glimpsed tramps peering blankly out of boxcars on the trains that passed just seventy-five feet from the house, and he often saw black families with calcium deficiencies eating chunks of chalk from deposits in roadside excavations. Some men preferred prison, where at least they could eat. At his mother's instruction, Jimmy brought lemonade to chain gangs.

Franklin D. Roosevelt's famous First Hundred Days program in 1933 brought hope to much of the country, but it angered many landowners. The Agricultural Adjustment Act, which aimed to raise

70

rock-bottom farm prices by reducing supply, required farmers to plow up their crops and slaughter their piglets in exchange for cash. Earl Carter, who had enthusiastically voted for FDR in 1932, joined other successful farmers in considering these "sacrilegious" acts. "This was my first picture of the difference between political programs as envisioned by Washington and their impact on the human beings I knew," Jimmy wrote later.

Mr. Earl's hero — and Roosevelt's sharpest critic in Georgia — was Governor Eugene Talmadge, a short, bespectacled Democrat known as the Wild Man from Sugar Creek. First elected governor in 1932, Talmadge claimed to be Tom Watson's populist heir, but he resembled more closely later racist demagogues who pretended to side with ordinary people even as they catered to the wealthy.

Arriving at the edge of a small town, Talmadge would strip off his fancy suit in favor of blue bib overalls or old work trousers held up by his trademark red suspenders. Then he ditched his shiny limousine and walked ostentatiously to the rally, where as many as thirty thousand people would watch him mount a tree stump for his fearmongering rant. "The working man in Georgia has got three great friends: Jesus Christ, the Sears, Roebuck catalog, and Old Gene Talmadge!" he yelled. "And the working man of Georgia has got three common enemies." Here he would pause for dramatic effect as his mouth curled into a sneer: "Nigger, nigger, nigger."

Carter wrote later that at age ten, he went with his father to a Talmadge rally and barbecue in Albany. In two books, Carter ignored Talmadge's wildly racist rhetoric and wrote blandly that, while a strict segregationist, Talmadge always made sure a few black farmers had been placed close to the front.

Despite his anger at FDR, Earl went on to serve as a county director of the Rural Electrification Administration, the transformative New Deal program that brought power to much of the American countryside. Even so, he remained so upset about farm policy that he never forgave Roosevelt and — unusual in heavily Democratic Georgia — never again voted for him or for any national Democrat. As for Jimmy, he revered FDR. Like most Democrats of his generation, he grew up knowing no other president. But when he entered politics, the New Deal became something mostly to invoke on ceremonial occasions. It wasn't in his DNA.

Throughout much of Sumter County, Lillian was highly regarded for her nursing. Even her unusual practice of tending to black patients and delivering their babies — in exchange for nothing more than two dozen eggs or a basket of blackberries — was viewed with indulgence and grudging respect by local whites.

For white patients, she received $6 for a twenty-hour nursing shift — good pay during the Depression — though she said she often waived those fees, too. While Earl was proud of her work and paid for all of her medical supplies, he occasionally teased her by calling her "Eleanor" (as in Roosevelt) for the way she was always making sure everything was going well in the black houses. She didn't find it funny.

Carter's later interest in global health issues

owed much to his mother, who treated her family and many others in the area for ground itch, boils, sties, abrasions, and the other common afflictions of rural life. Among the worst was ringworm, which, left untreated, could consume all vital nutrients in the body. Lillian put medicine between her childrens' toes, which prevented the tiny parasites from migrating to the small intestine. Carter noticed that poor families weren't so lucky. This informed his later efforts to combat guinea worm, river blindness, and other diseases in Africa and beyond.

For much of his childhood, Jimmy would barely see his mother for days on end. Lillian was often on duty from two in the morning until ten o'clock at night, with the four hours between the eight-hour shifts just enough time to shower and perhaps wash her uniform before returning to her patients. Jimmy and Gloria dubbed a sturdy black table in the front hall "Mother" because it was where she left them notes when they arrived home from school to find the house empty. As adults, they teased Lillian that the table had been their real mother. But she had no problem with them being what were later known as latchkey kids. "Children who cling to their mothers," she insisted, "grow up to be babies." Any of Jimmy's regrets about being left alone by her were always transcended by his appreciation of her example of social action. He wrote a short poem in the 1980s entitled "Miss Lillian." The opening stanza read:

She would nurse
and when they couldn't pay
she would still be there.

# 3
# MISS JULIA

Lillian always said of her family: "We weren't poor, but we were country." Jimmy saw himself as a country boy from Archery, and his sense of being an outsider — critical to his political success — began in the fall of 1930, when at age six he entered the all-white school in Plains. "I never considered myself part of the Plains society," he wrote of the remote town of about 650. "I always thought of myself as a visitor when I entered that 'metropolitan' community."

In Archery, most — though not all — of his playmates were black. His favorite was Alonzo Davis, known as A.D., who lived on the Carter farm with his aunt and uncle. A.D. was roughly Jimmy's age, but his family didn't know his date of birth. His aunt decided to make it October 1, 1924 — Jimmy's birthday — so that the two boys could celebrate together.

Jimmy fondly recalled how he and A.D. would take the train thirteen miles to Americus to see movies at the Rylander Theatre, though Jim Crow laws forced them to sit in separate railroad compartments and separate sections of the theater. Carter wrote that "we accepted [segregation] like breathing or waking up in Archery every morn-

74

ing." A.D., by contrast, remembered an awkward outing when Miss Lillian brought him along to the Rylander to sit up front with the family and — after enduring stares — he excused himself and fled upstairs to the balcony reserved for black patrons. She asked him, "Why did you go up there, A.D.?" He replied, "I didn't see nobody in there colored but me."

In elementary school, Jimmy was teased for sounding black. Influenced by the inflections of farmhands and playmates, he pronounced "going" as "gwine," "river" as "ribber," "rinse" as "rench." "I rid in the wagon and driv the mules!" he bragged to his parents. Even after he improved his English, Jimmy still felt divided: "From age six until I entered high school, I was two different people: a self-confident young man on the farm with my family and close friends, and a timid and somewhat defensive boy in school with my classmates."

Jimmy was baptized at age eleven in the tank under the pulpit of the Plains Baptist Church. According to the tenets of his faith, which rejected infant baptism, he was thus "born again," though his genuine spiritual rebirth would come three decades later. No pastor at the Baptist church — or at the Methodist church the family also often attended — left any lasting impression on him. The religious activity he remembered most from childhood was collecting nickels to send to Baptist missionaries in China — a devotion he recounted in 1979 to the Chinese leader Deng Xiaoping.

He memorized Bible verses in Sunday school starting at age three but experienced early doubts. Baptist doctrine said that not just Jesus but all believers would be resurrected, even if that meant separating parents from children. By the time he was twelve or thirteen, Jimmy was so anxious on this point that just before "Amen" in his prayers, he would habitually add: "And, God, please help me believe in the resurrection." He had "a nagging degree of skepticism" about the relationship between faith and the science he was learning in school. Jimmy — like both of his parents — often found the services boring. He mostly remembered a game where he and Gloria would amuse themselves evaluating the physical appearances of congregants and guessing how long couples had been married based on how much they looked alike.

When Jimmy and A.D. were fourteen or so, their relationship changed. Jimmy noticed it one day when they approached the pasture gate to the Carter fields. A.D. and the other black teens went ahead to open it for him, then stood back. Jimmy hesitated, thinking it was a prank — maybe they had playfully planted a trip wire for him to fall on his face or hatched a plan to slam the gate on him. It wasn't a joke. They knew intuitively — or their parents had told them — that they now needed to treat Jimmy differently, which they understood to mean letting him pass through the gate first.* In his poem "The Pasture Gate," Jimmy wrote:

We saw it only vaguely then,
  but we were transformed at that place.

*Decades later, when Davis was arrested for murder, Carter privately suggested to the trial judge that it may have been self-defense, and Davis ended up convicted of manslaughter.

> A silent line was drawn between
> friend and friend, race and race.

The Carter children attended Plains High School, which was more than a high school; it educated 250 students from the surrounding area from ages seven to seventeen and was regarded as one of the most progressive public schools in Georgia — though all white, of course, in a town that has always been about half black.*

The main reason for the quality of the school was a brilliant teacher named Miss Julia Coleman, a stout, plain-faced, lame, four-foot-eleven, nearly blind spinster who did as much to shape Jimmy's early development as his parents and Rachel Clark did.† She ended up being the only person other than the biblical prophet Micah quoted in President Carter's 1977 inaugural address, and the only schoolteacher in American history so honored.

"As my high school teacher, Miss Julia Coleman, used to say, 'We must adjust to changing times

---

*Black schoolchildren in Plains and Archery were taught mostly either in churches or private homes, though for a time, the community had a Rosenwald School: one of the scores of black schools across the region built by Julius Rosenwald, president of Sears, Roebuck.

†The absence of a spouse helped Julia Coleman's career; many school districts wouldn't employ married women as teachers and fired those who wed on the theory that they would be supported by their husbands and thus should not take a job from a man. Pregnancy was cause for termination almost everywhere.

and still hold to unchanging principles,' " Carter said less than a minute after being sworn in as president. Beginning in 1930, he had internalized this piece of wisdom that he felt was deeper than a truism. It became the core of his pragmatic but principled approach to public life: a simple idea of committing oneself to the reconciliation of disorienting change and enduring values. In 2003, trying to explain the pressures on children in a rapidly changing world, he told the theologian Martin Marty that Miss Julia's words had been "the most resonating thing in my whole existence."

Miss Julia had first come to Georgia from Texas by covered wagon in the 1890s. She suffered eye hemorrhages so severe that she could read only with the help of thick glasses and a huge magnifying glass; even then, her sister had to read the newspaper to her. She wrote so large that she managed only three or four words a line. Her right leg was shorter than her left, which forced her to stand on her right tiptoes at all times and to walk leaning far forward and with a pronounced limp.

Despite all of this, Julia Coleman began teaching in Plains at age nineteen and rose to be principal and later superintendent of Plains High School, positions rarely held by women. By the time Jimmy was in school, she was already a legend — beloved for her inspiration in the classroom. As an exuberant woman of cultural refinement, she offered a model of how to expand one's interests and contacts. In 1935 Eleanor Roosevelt, whom she met during the 1920s at Chautauqua lectures in upstate New York, invited her to a luncheon at the White House, a great honor not just for her but for all of Sumter County.

Coleman's stories of that visit — when Jimmy was an impressionable eleven — conveyed that big things were possible for people from small towns such as Plains.

For nearly fifty years, Miss Julia taught English from seventh through eleventh (the final) grade — five straight years of instruction for all students. She began each school day with a half-hour mandatory chapel service that included not just Holy Scripture (standard then in most public schools) but also a piece of wisdom about the importance of thinking of the less fortunate, or how the world's evils could not prevent "the ultimate triumph of the Greater Good." She assigned a minimum of thirty to forty pages of reading a night and "ready writing" contests in which students had to complete essays in class in fifteen or thirty minutes — an experience that helped give Carter the speed he needed to crank out so many books after his presidency.

Every Friday, Miss Julia staged debates. Jimmy admitted that his strict life on the farm — away from the other kids — made him feel insecure about speaking in public. His height was also a handicap. For much of high school, he was only a bit over five feet tall. "He wasn't shy, he was little," Gloria remembered. "He was never a leader except in the family." In early presentations, Jimmy was extremely well prepared but had trouble with his halting delivery, a habit he never quite shook. Miss Julia routinely shouted "Projection!" at Jimmy from the back of the room, and over time his confidence grew.

Miss Julia was kind but tough, often asking students, "Where is your brain today?" When students tried to take advantage of her near blindness by illicitly chewing gum, she could hear the snapping or — if they stopped chewing — smell the Beech-Nut or Juicy Fruit on their breath.

Jimmy grew up to be intensely competitive, a product in part of Miss Julia's approach. She awarded gold stars for every ten books read and small bronze medals for every twenty, and Jimmy usually won the most of both in town. The achievement ladder he had begun ascending on the farm now extended to academic life — an ambition less about people pleasing than natural curiosity and a drive to check off whatever boxes of success he could identify.

When Jimmy was in fifth grade, Miss Julia pushed him to read Leo Tolstoy's *War and Peace*. Jimmy assumed beforehand that it was about cowboys and Indians before plowing through all 815 pages. The novel's dissection of Russian feudal society might have been Miss Julia's subtle way of exposing Jimmy to the feudal social structures of the American South. Tolstoy, who corresponded with a young Mahatma Gandhi, combined deep faith with abhorrence of injustice, and Carter read *War and Peace* several more times over the years and mused on its complex themes. Carter came to believe the novel's main messages were that "common, ordinary people" can change history, and that peace is not enough; one must work tirelessly for it.

Miss Julia made all of her students memorize the poem "If —" by Rudyard Kipling, then tested them on it. When explaining the line "If you can make one heap of all your winnings and risk it on one turn of pitch-and-toss," she told the class that she didn't think of a gambler when she read that passage, but perhaps of a man in a political

80

campaign. During Carter's 1970 campaign for governor, a former classmate, Kathryn Bacon Maudlin, wrote him that when Miss Julia analyzed that line, "I thought that her eyes rested on you as she looked around the room."

Jimmy got close to straight As, except in music, one of the only areas of life where he never showed much ability beyond appreciation. Students were also graded every month in "health," "conduct," and "teeth" (where an "OK" sufficed in place of a letter grade). "Good health is good teeth," Jimmy wrote in his eighth-grade workbook, recognizing early the importance of what would become his political trademark. Under the heading "Healthy Mental Habits," he put as number one: "Expecting to accomplish what you intend." He also stressed the importance of making quick decisions and sticking to them, "expecting to like other people and have them like you," and "welcoming fear[lessly] all wholesome ideas and experiences." He ended with a little essay: "A person who wants to build good mental habits should avoid the idle daydream; should give up worry and anger; hatred and envy; should neither fear nor be ashamed of anything that is honest or purposeful."

More playfully, he wrote in Virginia Harris's eighth-grade yearbook:

Now I lay me down to sleep
With a bag of peanuts at my feet,
If I should die before I wake
You know I died with a stomach ache.

Jimmy was in good standing socially in high school in part because of the economic standing of his parents. Starting at age twelve, he could pick up dates for church socials in his father's car. The poor students — whose clothes were made of old sacks and who often smelled or had lice because they couldn't afford to bathe regularly — were often the targets of abuse. While he didn't join in the insults, he didn't come to their defense, either.

Throughout his life, Carter was proud of being a member of Future Farmers of America, where he excelled in everything and especially enjoyed carpentry. He was pleased to be designated a "schoolboy patrolman," a class honor that meant he was the one responsible for keeping order on the school bus, which did not always endear him to his schoolmates. He loved sports but couldn't go out for baseball because, like other farm boys, he was needed in the fields at home after school. Jimmy didn't want his less privileged classmates to know he played a "sissy sport" like tennis, so he took pains to hide his racquet from them. He ran track, and his quickness won him a place on the varsity basketball team despite being five foot four — by far the shortest player, and nicknamed Peewee after a cartoon character.

Dances, mostly church sponsored, included prom cards that matched boys and girls in fifteen-minute intervals for dancing or — more often — taking a walk in the quiet night together, where "heavy petting" was as far as even the fastest girls would go. Jimmy steadily dated a studious brunette, Eloise "Teenie" Ratliff, who came from a less well-off family. Annie Mae Hollis, the Carters' cook, said she was his first true love.

Jimmy misbehaved only once, when, at the end of senior year, he and his male classmates decided to play hooky on April Fools' Day by traveling as a pack to Americus. Of the thirteen boys in the class, all but Thaddeus Jones skipped school. "It's just not right," Thaddeus told them, to taunts of "sissy." When the boys returned to Plains, a male teacher gave them each seven licks, and an angry Earl grounded Jimmy for a month. Carter claimed later that the incident cost him his chance to be valedictorian; others recalled that Teenie Ratliff had slightly better grades, anyway. In the years ahead, he would not always stand up and say, "It's just not right," most conspicuously when it came to the evils of segregation. But he reflected later that the ill-fated escapade reinforced for him the importance of nonconformity and even stubbornness, and it would cure him forever of blindly following the tribe.

Teenie apparently thought Jimmy was already a little too stubborn — and tight with his money. She dumped him for an older, more mature boy with his own car, Lonnie Taylor (the ringleader of the ditching escapade), whom she married. A few other girlfriends followed, though Jimmy took and kept a private oath not to say "I love you" to any girl other than the one he intended to marry.*

The Carter family entered the twentieth century in 1935, when electricity and indoor plumbing came to the farm. Jimmy said later that the day they turned on the lights in his house was one of the most important in his life. The same year, Mr. Earl consulted a mail-order catalogue and bought

*Of the twenty-six members of the class of 1941, Jimmy was the only one who went on to graduate from a four-year college. Thaddeus Jones was the only member of the class killed in the Second World War.

a windmill with an elevated water tank and pipes. This replaced the well pump and provided tap water for the kitchen and a bathroom with a toilet.* Earl even rigged up a makeshift shower by running water through a large tin can with small holes punched in the bottom. Until wind power, Carter recalled, the farm's only energy source came from corn, which fed the animals that worked the land and were eventually consumed. When Carter became president, he intuitively understood alternative energy sources because he had used them growing up.

Another invention that changed their lives was radio. The Carters liked to sit on their front porch and listen to crackling-static renditions of "Yes Sir, That's My Baby" and "Sweet Georgia Brown." Jimmy hungered for sports and news, too. The balloting for president at the 1936 Republican National Convention, which eventually nominated Governor Alf Landon of Kansas, went on so long that the batteries powering the Carters' radio ran out. Jimmy was so entranced that he carried the big radio into the yard and hooked it up to the car battery so he could keep listening.

In 1938 the family gathered to listen to the famous boxing rematch between heavyweight

*Carter wrote of how, when Earl wasn't around, Lillian would occasionally allow A.D. and other blacks to use the new toilet. This was a big change. The outhouses, where Carter said his family wiped themselves with newspapers or pages from the Sears catalogue, had been off-limits to black workers. Even in winter, they were forced to defecate in the woods, using leaves or corncobs.

champion Joe Louis and Max Schmeling, the German boxer who had defeated Louis two years earlier. In Georgia, almost all whites were for the white German (a Nazi) and blacks for the black American. The Carters, as usual, were a little different, with Earl backing Schmeling and Lillian behind Louis. There were no bets in Plains because "no white man would ever bet with a nigger," as "Uncle Buddy" (Alton Carter) explained later. "That just wasn't done." But when a delegation of black tenant farmers came to the Carters' back door and asked if they could listen to the prizefight, broadcast live from Yankee Stadium, Mr. Earl agreed to put the radio by the window and turn up the volume so that they could follow the fight together from under a large mulberry tree in the yard. Louis knocked out Schmeling two minutes and forty-five seconds into the first round.

All that the Carters could hear from outside was a quiet "Thank you, Mr. Earl. Good-bye," as the black farmers walked silently across the railroad tracks and entered a tenant shack. Several of those in the shack were old enough to remember that a black man had been lynched in Americus in 1910 for getting too excited about the victory of Jack Johnson, the first African American heavyweight champion, over Jim Jeffries, hailed as "the Great White Hope." But the jubilation could be contained for only so long. From a distance, "We could hear them screaming for two hours, they were so happy," Lillian remembered. "Daddy was tight lipped," Jimmy wrote later. "But all the mores of our segregated society had been honored."

Earl was in no position to complain about loud

celebrations. The Carters often entertained at home, and the noise kept their young children up well after midnight. When Jimmy was sixteen, his father decided that he wanted a better place to hold parties. With the help of his son and a mule-drawn scoop, he dammed a small stream two miles from home to create a pond and built a cabin on the high bank, which he equipped with a jukebox, billiards, and a Ping-Pong table. Every so often, Jimmy was awakened and told to take a team of mules to the Pond House to pull the car of a drunken reveler out of the water. He would be pulling hard-living family members out of trouble for the rest of his life.

With Earl's encouragement, Jimmy learned to be a tireless entrepreneur when he was six years old. Before long, he earned more than many grown men in the area, who lived on less than $1 a day. Jimmy picked peanuts off the vine (owned by his father) and stacked them in his little wagon, washed them, and soaked them overnight. At four o'clock he rose to boil the peanuts and fill twenty paper bags with a half pound each. Then he pulled the wagon down the railroad bed two miles to Plains to sell his wares — five cents a bag — out of a wicker basket on Main Street. Some of the men at the filling station liked to eat their peanuts with their "dopes," which is what Cokes (Coca-Cola was born in Georgia) were then called. There he began learning about the world beyond his family: the black worker killed for "impudence bordering on assault"; the spinster who stood nude in her window as her suitor drove past. It turned up in his poetry:

Almost ignored, an omnipresent boy,
I learned how merchants cheat, which married
    man
Laid half-a-dollar whores, not always white;
The same ones touting racial purity
And Klansmen's sheeted bravery at night.

When he was nine years old, and it was Gloria's turn to sell peanuts in town, his father helped him use the proceeds from his boiled peanuts to buy five bales of cotton at the depressed price of five cents a pound and store them for a few years. After the local undertaker died, Jimmy sold his cotton at eighteen cents a pound and bought five tenant cabins from the undertaker's estate, which he rented to black families for $2 to $5 a month. Jimmy was now a teenage slumlord and — by his own admission — paid almost nothing for the upkeep of his properties. He rode his bicycle over to the shacks he owned to collect rent, apparently oblivious to the squalor.

When Jimmy went away to college, his father, who had taken over the collections, grew tired of the tenants' demands for repairs and improvements and sold the houses for three times what Jimmy had paid eleven years earlier. In one of his books, Carter depicts his youthful entrepreneurship as nothing more than a prelude to his life as a businessman, as if he were describing his boyhood paper route or lemonade stand. While sensitive in later years to the individual moral dimensions of racism, he seemed unselfconscious then about his participation in an economic system that exploited black people.

During his teenage years, Jimmy and his older cousin Hugh, nicknamed Beedie, collected old newspapers and sold them to markets to wrap fish in; they gathered scrap metal and sold it to a junk dealer at twenty cents per hundred pounds. But their favorite business was using an empty storefront in the summer to sell heavily breaded hamburgers and triple-dip ice cream, which they made themselves in a laborious process. Both were five cents apiece.

At sixteen, Jimmy was hired by the Agricultural Adjustment Administration — the agency his father despised — to measure whether farmers were planting within the often-complex rules on acreage. He and another boy he described as his "assistant" drove all over Sumter County in his mother's 1939 Plymouth. His worst mishap occurred at Uncle Buddy's store on Main Street in Plains, when an irate farmer thought that Jimmy had cheated him out of his government payments. Jimmy didn't back down, and the farmer began pummeling him mercilessly. Uncle Buddy and his clerks finally pulled the farmer off him. In *An Hour Before Daylight,* Carter writes that he was proven correct when federal authorities double-checked his calculations. But he doesn't stop to wonder if there was anything about his teenage attitude that made Farmer Salter want to punch him. It may have been an early example of the stubborn righteousness that would sometimes irritate his contemporaries.

For thirteen generations, not one of Carter's forebears on his father's side had gone to college. By the 1930s, this was about to change. Jimmy's impressive older cousin Don Carter, later a distinguished newspaper editor, graduated from the University of Georgia in 1938. And somewhere

88

around age six, an already willful Jimmy decided he wanted to be not a farmer like his father or one of the other ambitions of kids his age — "railroad engineer," "cowboy," "FBI agent," "John Dillinger" — but to "go to Annapolis" to become a naval officer. The discipline, drive, and exceptionally broad horizons he developed in the navy would make everything in his future possible.

Reverence for the military runs deep in the South, and Earl's army service during World War I was instructive. But these were not the forces propelling Jimmy toward Annapolis. Nor was any glorification of war in his mind. "I didn't join the navy so I could go out and kill people but to get a college education," he remembered. And he wanted to see the world. Miss Lillian's adored younger brother, Tom Watson Gordy, served in the navy when Jimmy was growing up, and the postcards and scrimshaw he sent his favorite nephew from around the world fired the boy's imagination. He would be not just a sailor one day, he said, but a midshipman at Annapolis. "Like a parrot," Carter remembered, he would chirp his ambition.

Tom Gordy, radioman second class, was a champion lightweight boxer in the Pacific Fleet, with a strut like James Cagney. A photograph of him with some of his vanquished rivals hung in the Carters' house in Archery. Jimmy stared endlessly at the boxing picture his uncle gave him, dreaming of adventure far from home. Tom and his wife, Dorothy, whom Jimmy also greatly admired, lived in San Francisco with their three kids, the oldest son named after Jimmy. On leave, they often visited Tom's family in Georgia.

As early as grammar school, Jimmy read books

about the navy, and he wrote to Annapolis, without revealing his age, to inquire about entrance requirements. Worried that he was flat-footed, he rolled his feet over Coke bottles to strengthen his arches. He did push-ups every day and ran long distances to condition himself. "Retention of urine" — bed-wetting — was grounds for rejection. Jimmy didn't understand it. "I was always ashamed to ask whether that last clinging drop would block my entire naval career!" he wrote in his campaign autobiography, *Why Not the Best?,* drawing guffaws from reporters covering his 1976 presidential campaign, their first example of his lifelong habit of offering too much information.

On those rare occasions when Jimmy slacked off from schoolwork, one of his parents was sure to say, "You'll never get to Annapolis this way!" But with excellent grades, his prospects of obtaining a free college education seemed strong. Appointments to service academies are secured through members of Congress, and for years, Earl had contributed money to the campaigns of Democratic congressman Stephen Pace — a champion of peanut farmers in Washington — in anticipation of this moment. Every year Jimmy was in high school, his father brought Jimmy's report card over to Pace's house in Americus when he was home on congressional recess. But Earl was unable at first to secure the favor that he expected. Pace, a graduate of the Georgia Institute of Technology, wasn't impressed by the science and math curriculum at Plains High School, which didn't even offer chemistry. He suggested Jimmy enroll at Georgia Southwestern College, a two-year junior college in Americus, and try again the next year.

Carter later downplayed the year he spent at Georgia Southwestern, omitting it from *Why Not the Best?* He joined a fraternity and ran for freshman class president and for the title Mr. Southwestern, losing both times. Jimmy grew serious about Marguerite Wise, daughter of Dr. Bowman Wise, who, as the town's obstetrician for white babies, had delivered him into the world. He said later that he would have likely stayed with Marguerite had her mother — no admirer of Lillian Carter — not objected. The Wises were a slight cut above the Carters socially, part of local Sumter County society, where the women wore hats and gloves and held teas, all of which Lillian detested. (It didn't help that Lillian was still close to Gussie Abrams, whom the Wise family considered a home wrecker for her long affair with Bowman's brother, Dr. Thad Wise.)

Another date, with Roxy Jo Logan, ended badly when Jimmy — showing off his tumbling skills — fell into a hole and broke his wrist, landing him in the hospital in Atlanta for ten days. Carter was always a good athlete, but this kind of embarrassing recreational mishap would recur periodically for the rest of his life, a sign that he simply didn't know when to quit, even if pressing on wasn't good for him. Sometimes he was just unlucky, like the time he peed on an electric fence and got shocked.

Shortly after the Japanese attack on Pearl Harbor catapulted the United States into World War II, Jimmy left home for the first time and lived in a dorm in Americus during his second semester at Georgia Southwestern. He still worried about his flyweight body preventing his admission to Annapolis. Gloria remembered that at one point he quit a part-time job so that he could lie on his dorm bed and eat bananas. He figured that if he used little energy, he could put on more pounds. Jimmy also tried, without much success, to improve his posture, which would never be good. He felt he wasn't making any progress on his great ambition and, according to his lifelong friend B. T. Wishard, weighed an alternative career path, such as running for governor of Georgia one day — an ambition Carter later insisted he never had at the time.

In early 1942 Congressman Pace refused once again to recommend him for the Naval Academy. This time, though, Mr. Earl stubbornly refused to leave Pace's Americus porch until he had a more definitive answer about his boy's future. Finally, Pace promised an appointment the following spring if Jimmy took math and science classes that weren't available at Georgia Southwestern. That led to a year at Georgia Tech and acceptance into the Naval Reserve Officers Training Corps.

Carter said later that of the four colleges he attended over the years, Georgia Tech was by far the most difficult. The only way he won a degree, he joked on a visit to the Atlanta campus in 1979, was by becoming president of the United States and picking up an honorary doctorate. In truth, he developed strong study habits there and ended up in the top 10 percent of his class, though he received a C in second-quarter Spanish and a D in differential calculus, which he later mastered.

During the 1942–43 school year, the first full year of war, Jimmy listened to war news on the radio and, like other young men his age, was eager to see action. He spent his spare time rooting for the Tech Yellow Jackets football team. Unlike others who ended up in politics, Jimmy wasn't a networker. His roommate in 308 Knowles Hall was a go-getter named Robert Ormsby, who grew up to be president of the Lockheed Corporation. They weren't close.

At noon on June 26, 1943, Earl and Lillian saw Jimmy and his friend Evan Mathis off on the Silver Meteor to Washington, DC, where they would transfer to a bus for Annapolis. Jimmy's anxious parents departed the train station bereft and chose to be apart in their misery. Lillian went fishing alone and wept, while Earl drove with a friend in the opposite direction to fish and drink whiskey until dark. Jimmy was nervous on the long ride north but also excited. He had never been out of the South before.

After registering for school and passing the dreaded physical, he wrote to his parents: "Dear Folks, I have almost finished my second day, and can still say that I'm not ready to come home." It would be more than a decade before he was finally ready to do so — the most important period of growth and change in his life.

# 4
## ANNAPOLIS

When Carter arrived at Annapolis in the summer of 1943, he found an institution shadowed by war. Scores of officers in each of the wartime classes were killed in action not long after being commissioned. The same week Carter was sworn in, President Roosevelt signed an order requiring midshipmen to complete four years of academic work in three. This meant that Carter's class of 1947 would graduate in 1946, with the expectation that all would likely take part in a war they were eager to fight in.

But Annapolis also offered a temporary sanctuary. The makeup of its student body — white, mostly small-town Christians with connections to the navy or to important local politicians — was unchanged since the founding of the Naval Academy nearly a hundred years earlier. So were many of its storied traditions, including "Plebe Summer," the harsh — often vicious — boot camp introduction to navy life. "Look to your right, look to your left," the brutish instructor informed the plebes. "By the end of the summer, one of you won't be here anymore."

That was an exaggeration, but Carter still feared he would wash out, and not just because he was

94

short and skinny for his age. Many of the plebes had gone to prep schools or traveled widely before entering the Naval Academy; Jimmy had neither seen the ocean nor been on a boat bigger than a fishing dinghy. "I was a landlubber in every respect," he remembered.

Like all 2,600 midshipmen, Carter lived for his whole time at Annapolis in mammoth Bancroft Hall, an imposing Beaux Arts pile that in those days was the largest school dormitory in the world. On their first day there, plebes were issued the academy rule book, *The Blue Jacket's Manual,* which Carter so valued that he held on to it long after graduation.

The manual is a time capsule of values that Jimmy took to heart: "Those who serve in ships are expected to exhibit obedience, knowledge, fighting spirit, reliability, initiative, loyalty, self-control, energy, courage, justice, faith in ourselves, cheerfulness and honor, but above all comes absolute truth, the final test of a man." Carter said later that "telling a lie was the worst thing that you could do at Annapolis. You were gone if you told a lie about stepping on the grass. You were out." Several of the other virtues in *The Blue Jacket's Manual* — especially knowledge, energy, self-control, and justice — also became deeply embedded in him.

Among the poems that midshipmen were required to memorize verbatim was "Invictus," by the nineteenth-century English poet William Ernest Henley, which Jimmy had already learned by heart in high school. It would be a few years before Jimmy would develop a strong interest in poetry, but he remembered the poem later as "a miniature sermon on how to live." He connected to the immortal lines "I am the master of my fate. I am the captain of my soul," even if he knew he wasn't yet.

Jimmy and his classmates were also made familiar with the famous speech by President Theodore Roosevelt, a onetime assistant secretary of the navy, about "the man in the arena, whose face is marred by dust, sweat and blood, who strives valiantly, who fails." Throughout his life, Carter would put himself at risk, as Roosevelt recommended, and be a man "who at best in the end knows the triumph of high achievement, and who at worst, if he fails, at least fails while daring greatly."

Even for the many plebes who, like Carter, had already taken college courses, academy classes were rigorous, and no one failed quietly. "Bilging" (flunking) — a common condition in the era before grade inflation — left one "in the bush" or "on the tree." Each week, "bush" and "tree" notices were posted for all to see on company bulletin boards, with offenders restricted to campus and forced to cancel dates with a "hot new drag."

Annapolis alumni often recall that their daily lives as midshipmen seemed to consist largely of lining up in formation and marching somewhere at the sound of bells. Among the punishments Carter said he endured were saluting thousands of times in a row, running a commando obstacle course at dawn, and rowing back and forth across the Severn River. Plebes also had to worry about being "fried" — cited on a whim — for anything that displeased upperclassmen. Unlike instructors, these students were empowered to inflict physical punishment.

96

The hazing was brutal, especially for Carter. "I don't think there was anyone who got more licks with the bread pan, or a broom at night," an exaggerating Carter said at his fiftieth reunion in 1996, while noting with a wan smile that plebe year prepared him well for a later life in politics. Admiral James Stockdale, a Carter classmate and the running mate of Reform Party presidential candidate Ross Perot in 1992, went further: he was sure that surviving the hazing of 1943–44 helped keep him alive during nearly eight years of captivity in North Vietnam.

Hazing likely did little to produce better officers, whose quality did not lessen after the practice slowly ended in the 1960s and 1970s. But it did instill stubbornness — one of Carter's core traits, according to his wife — and weed out weakness. "If one ever showed any weakness, he was assaulted from all sides with punishment and harassment and forced out of the academy," Carter recalled. He was strong and tough minded, but something about Jimmy — his small stature, shy demeanor, refusal to threaten violence — could make him *look* weak, thus subjecting him to more than his fair share of abuse.

The rituals were arbitrary and capricious. Carter was class of 1947, which meant that any upperclassman had the authority to order forty-seven push-ups - - or ninety-four deep knee bends, double the class year. Plebes could be commanded to sleep overnight on top of lockers, march double time in the hot sun, or sing a silly song they had been ordered to memorize. "Square meals" were not nutritious cuisine but a demand that a plebe spend the meal lifting his fork or spoon vertically from the plate and moving it at a 90-degree angle into his mouth. "Pushing out" meant squatting in the mess hall without touching the seat or the back of the chair, a position that plebes could be required to assume for as long as a half hour. They could also be ordered to "submerge," which meant to eat under the table like a dog.

To torture plebes, upperclassmen would stage "cruise box races," in which plebes would be locked inside the wooden trunks used to store belongings for summer cruises, and then race against one another to change into a completely different uniform, with different shoes, socks, tie, trousers, belt, shirt, and jacket, plus a detachable collar, all while scrunched painfully in the dark. Carter's small size helped him in these competitions, and he only lost once, to an even more wiry plebe. More often, when fried, he would be pounded with a hard broom or large serving spoon. "It hurt like heck, particularly with that spoon, because it would make a blister on your butt," Carter remembered.

Jimmy's biggest target was his toothy smile, which thirty years later would be one of his main political assets. "I got beat with a serving spoon twice for [not] wiping a smile off," he reported to his diary. Later, he was beaten four times, "27 licks each time," again for smiling. "Really sore tonight, but was worth it," he wrote. It was hard to predict what would prompt the wrath of the adolescent martinets. Carter was fried for not wearing a neckerchief at a math recitation. And again for a speck of dust on a visor at a captain's inspection. And again for not reporting others as absent. "Over five months til Xmas," he confided to his journal. "Hope I can stand it."

Jimmy learned to repress his anger, which lent

him an intensity in later years. "He would never let it out," a classmate, Arthur Middleton, remembered. "Never kick a chair or throw a book like the rest of us." Carter marched with his icy blue eyes fixed straight ahead.

The indignities mounted: "Johnson told me to get his d—d nose out of his plate, and I did, so he put me under for 7." Raised to avoid profanity, Jimmy wouldn't dare even write out the word *damned* in his diary.

Over time Jimmy grew defiant toward the hazing, especially if a matter of regional pride was at stake. When an upperclassman ordered him several times to learn "Marching Through Georgia," the Union battle hymn celebrating General William Tecumseh Sherman's pillaging march to the sea at the end of the Civil War, he recorded in his diary that instead of obeying, he responded, "Sir? — every time." The upperclassman, a Yankee midshipman named Weidner, "yelled it again and told me not to say 'Sir?' again. He really got mad when I said 'Aye, Aye' with no 'sir.' Told me to come around but I haven't been yet."

After he reported to Weidner's room for his punishment, his tormentors stood him up in front of a wall and beat him for more than an hour. In his poor singing voice, Jimmy belted out a dog food jingle — "I feed my doggy Thrive-O / It makes him so Alive-O" — but refused to sing "Marching Through Georgia." Jimmy, hardly a Confederate diehard, was already trying to soften his southern accent to fit in better, but he was stubbornly proud of his heritage, and singing the most despised song in the South was unthinkable.

By the end of his time at the academy, Jimmy had shed any embarrassment about his family being too "country," and for the rest of his life, he would remain sensitive to antisouthern slights. Once, when Earl and Lillian visited, another parent asked Lillian haughtily if she had acquired her suntan at the beach. A disgusted Lillian replied, "No, I got it in the cotton patch." According to Aunt Sissy, Jimmy told his mother later, "Mama, I've never been prouder of you in my life!"

When Jimmy became a first classman, he didn't do much hazing himself, according to classmates, beyond shouting "Brace up!" or "Square that cap!" at plebes, whom he more often instructed in a good-natured way on how to adapt to the academy.

Carter's near obsession with precision was already in evidence his first year there. On October 1, 1943, he made no mention of his nineteenth birthday, though he did explain that he walked exactly 4.6 miles and 8,642 steps from the boat to the football stadium to watch Navy lose to Cornell 46–7. Carter reported to his diary that he had a 3.478 grade point average in his first term, but the second was looking less auspicious. "I'm practically bilging Bull [English and history] this term. It's partly the teacher but don't guess I've been studying much," he confessed. The slacking off would prove a passing phase. During the winter term, he noted carefully that in his class of 800, he finished 24th in math, 228th in "Dago" (any foreign language; in his case, Spanish), 52nd in Bull, and 178th in "Steam" (fluid mechanics).

Jimmy was already developing a dry, biting take on navy life. In the late spring of plebe year, he complained that the academy hadn't switched yet from blue to white uniforms, which are better in

100

the heat. "We're still in blue service even though the temperature is 90 degrees every day," he wrote in his journal, complaining that "Some Peruvian president gave the admiral a darned medal, & we stood out in the sun for a long time while they made speeches etc." In an early example of the sarcasm that was rarely seen in public when he went into politics, he added: "The navy really uses judgment about everything. Never just blindly follows regulations — Always quick to make a change for the better."

For Jimmy's first two years, the Naval Academy was all white except for cooks, stewards, and groundskeepers. Since its founding in 1841, Annapolis had failed to graduate a single African American midshipman.* After three were driven out of the academy in the 1930s amid appalling racism, Congressman Adam Clayton Powell Jr. of Harlem was so determined to break the color barrier that in 1945 he nominated twelve African Americans. At the end of a rigorous screening process, a Washington, DC, native named Wesley Brown was the only one to enter the academy, class of 1949.

Brown was determined to make it through, and he had help from a group of friendly upperclassmen that included Jimmy Carter.

Two years ahead, Carter was not the most outspoken student in his support for Brown. A Jewish midshipman, Howie Weiss, went so far as to alert his congressman that Brown was being

*West Point did slightly better. In 1936 Benjamin O. Davis became the first black graduate of West Point in the twentieth century.

101

subjected to unwarranted demerits. Carter, too, did the right thing, but more quietly. The price was higher for him because he was a Georgian. "He was treated as if he was a traitor" for lining up with Brown's supporters, a classmate, Walter Moyle, recalled.

Carter and Brown were teammates on the cross-country team, and Carter liked to say that he spent his last year on the team looking at Brown's backside as the plebe led the pack. Even though he was already a star, Brown recalled having to "come around" to rooms of upperclassmen for forty-nine pushups and other hazing. But when he passed Carter's room, Jimmy "told me to hang in there" and later put his arm around him in encouragement. When they parted, Brown — who would become the first African American to graduate from the US Naval Academy — heard another midshipman say of Carter, "Goddamn nigger lover."

Jimmy's second and third years at the Naval Academy were devoted to military training, including learning how to take off and land aging seaplanes on the water. It was a skill — like so many others — that he enjoyed tackling but one that apparently cured him of any desire to be a naval aviator. His first sea duty was on a creaky World War I battleship, the USS *New York,* where he did everything from cleaning the constantly overflowing heads (toilets), to manning a 40-millimeter antiaircraft gun during alerts. Jimmy went far beyond the curriculum in learning to identify the silhouettes of hundreds of friendly and enemy aircraft and ships, which — like his early efforts on the farm in Archery — further fueled his drive to master each new challenge.

With the war nearly over, Carter was fatalistic about his chances of seeing action. He didn't yearn for it like so many of his classmates, focusing instead on classes and sports. Besides varsity cross-country, he played football (the under-140-pound team) and intramural baseball and basketball, with some boxing, wrestling (during which he broke his right shoulder), quail hunting, fishing, and canoeing in rough water when he had the chance. Jimmy also taught Sunday school to the children of faculty at the US Naval Academy Chapel and at the local Baptist church, where his evident piety — a contrast to much of his class — helped keep him grounded in the values of home. He would preach the gospel in one way or another for the rest of his life.

In his second year, Jimmy lived in Bancroft 2259, where one of his roommates, Bob Scott of Phoenix, deepened his interest in classical music. They used their combined $14 monthly pay to buy all four versions of Sergey Rachmaninoff's concertos, with Bob instructing Jimmy on which were superior and why. One of Carter's fondest memories of Annapolis was of Bob turning up the volume on the Victrola during the final movement of Richard Wagner's opera *Tristan and Isolde* — "Liebestod" — and fifteen or twenty midshipmen standing outside the door listening. When they graduated, the two flipped a coin, and Jimmy got the record collection, while Bob took the record player.

Despite Carter's interest in his classes, *Lucky Bag,* the navy yearbook, dispelled any hint that Jimmy was a "slash" — a grind. "Studies never bothered Jimmy," the editors reported. "In fact, the only times he opened his books were when his classmates desired help on their problems." Al Rusher, a future banker from Arkansas who lived down the hall senior year, remembered "an extremely smart" Carter cheerfully helping him with math and other homework, and another friend, Red Herzog, recalled Carter's dorm room as akin to a study hall. For the rest of his life, Carter would usually be smarter than the people around him, but he trained himself early to avoid intellectual arrogance and snobbery.

The help he offered classmates wasn't only academic. Just after Christmas of his senior year, Al Rusher's roommate and closest friend committed suicide by jumping out of an upper-story Bancroft window. Rusher remembered being traumatized afterward, and how Jimmy had invited him to move in with him and three other roommates, despite the crowded quarters. Rusher, who stayed closer to Carter than any other classmate, was grateful for his compassion and sensitivity.

Like so many others of his generation, Jimmy broke down sobbing on April 12, 1945, upon hearing of the sudden death of Franklin Roosevelt, who had been president since he was eight years old. He feared for the future. On August 7, he was on a decrepit destroyer for his summer cruise in the North Atlantic when the loudspeaker blared: "Now hear this! Now hear this!" President Truman came on to announce the dropping of the first atomic bomb, on Hiroshima, Japan. He remembered Truman's flat and nasal voice as the commander in chief explained: "The force from which the sun draws its power has been loosed

104

against those who brought war to the Far East." Nazi Germany had surrendered in early May; now, after the dropping of a second atom bomb, Japan would do the same.

Two months after the war ended, Jimmy turned twenty-one. Earl Carter, a chain-smoker, had promised his son a gold watch if he didn't smoke until he was an adult. That fall, Jimmy went to the store in Bancroft and bought a pack of cigarettes. After one puff, he never smoked another, which he believed was among the most important decisions of his life. Almost all of his immediate family would die prematurely from pancreatic cancer, at least in part from smoking.

As graduation neared, Jimmy effortlessly found his place in the top tenth of the class, officially graduating 60th out of 820, though he was under the misimpression that he was 59th. This was much higher than most modern presidents, including Dwight D. Eisenhower, who finished in the bottom half of his class at West Point. But Ike had been a football star, while Carter admitted that he "did not really excel in any aspect of the academic or military life." Carter left surprisingly few impressions on most classmates and faculty.

Captain Ellery Clark, coach of the Annapolis cross-country team, was an exception. He thought cross-country defined Midshipman Carter's approach to life. "Long-distance runners are a breed of their own," Clark remembered. "They are generally thin, somewhat introverted, friendly as a group, dedicated to self-improvement, [and] intelligent." Clark was especially impressed by Carter's stamina, consistency, and ability to nose out competitors at the finish line.

Red Herzog described his friend as "a loner,"

someone friendly enough but who "did not need other people's close bond of friendship to support his own ego and personality." Like Barack Obama at the same age, Carter was already self-contained and unneedy — rare qualities in politicians. This quiet confidence and security gave him an edge as he moved through life — a sense that he'd earned his self-respect. It would also make him seem aloof and distant in ways that would hinder him politically.

Jimmy missed the war, but his beloved uncle — his inspiration for leaving home and discovering the world beyond Georgia — suffered in ways that would create an awkward drama in his family.

In mid-1941, just as he was graduating high school, Jimmy received a postcard from Tom Gordy saying that he had been transferred to the Pacific island of Guam, where he manned a radio shack. On December 8, 1941 — the day after Pearl Harbor — the Japanese attacked Guam, and Tom was declared missing in action. Soon after, Tom's wife, Dorothy, and their children moved to Archery, where Jimmy's grandparents were then living. In December 1942 a letter from Tom to his mother (Jimmy's grandmother) arrived, relieving his family. "I am well and safe in Japan," Tom wrote. He didn't mention one of his prison duties: burying decapitated American POWs.

That was the last the Gordys and Jimmy heard from Tom for three and a half years. Dorothy, lonely being trapped in rural Georgia with her husband's hostile family, to whom her "city ways were considered strange," as her nephew Jimmy wrote later, returned to San Francisco to live with her parents.

In 1943 the Red Cross declared Tom officially dead. The following year, Dorothy married a fireman.

But Tom Gordy was very much alive, though he was tortured in a slave labor camp and survived on barley soup containing horse hooves — with iron shoes still attached — or bits of cat, dog, and snake. At one point, Gordy injured his hand badly. The only relief he found was to wrap a rag around it and urinate on it, or have a buddy do so.

After the Japanese surrender, Tom returned home weighing less than a hundred pounds. He wrote Jimmy at Annapolis to say that he and Dorothy still loved each other and that Dorothy decided to have her second marriage annulled so that they could be reunited. Jimmy thought this was the beautiful end to his aunt and uncle's wartime love story.

But it wasn't. Jimmy's grandparents and all of Tom's sisters — including Lillian — convinced Tom that Dorothy had committed adultery and that he must divorce her. In his poem "The Ballad of Tom Gordy," Carter wrote:

Tom Gordy soon regained some strength
and craved a normal life,
But mother and sisters told him lies
about his absent wife.

Tom complied reluctantly and soon married someone else, but Jimmy, "furious with Mama," never forgot what happened to his aunt. He made a point of visiting her in 1949 when his submarine docked near San Francisco for repairs. Jimmy was afraid he wouldn't be let in the house, but Dorothy and her family greeted him warmly. In one of his infrequent letters to his parents, he went out of his way to say how wonderful Dorothy seemed and how much he enjoyed the visit, where he "danced and sang" all night. Much later, he described the evening as "one of the most delightful uninterrupted celebrations I have ever known."

Long after Miss Lillian's death, Jimmy still refused to downplay his mother's unforgiving attitude toward her sister-in-law. Carter loved his mother deeply, but he mentioned her mistreatment of Aunt Dorothy in four of his books. At some level, he understood that his recognition of this long-ago injustice was an important part of his journey to remembering his moral duties in a troubled world.

The class of 1947 (though its members graduated after three years in 1946) would eventually become the most accomplished in the history of the US Naval Academy. Besides producing Annapolis's only president of the United States and winner of the Nobel Peace Prize, the class included thirty-four admirals (five of them four-star) and many future government officials. At graduation, the star of the class was Stansfield Turner, later an admiral and Carter's director of the Central Intelligence Agency.

Jimmy's parents came up for their son's graduation and to see him commissioned as an ensign. For the second time that year, they brought someone with them: an eighteen-year-old girl from Plains named Rosalynn Smith.

# 5

# ROSALYNN

Before they moved to the farm in Archery, Earl and Lillian Carter lived on South Bond Street in Plains next door to Edgar and Allie Smith. Mr. Edgar, a tall man with dark, curly hair, had grown up poor and become the head of his household when he was very young after his mother ran off with a traveling salesman. He owned an auto repair shop — the first in Sumter County, his daughter said — and a small farm on the outskirts of town.

Mr. Edgar was beloved in Plains for his friendly checkers games and for driving the school bus, which is where he met and began courting Frances Allethea Murray, whom everyone called "Allie," when she was thirteen. Edgar, nine years older, waited until Allie received her college diploma (her family revered education) before they married at the Plains Methodist Church.

The next year, on August 18, 1927, Allie gave birth to their first child, Eleanor Rosalynn Smith, who was named for her maternal grandmother, Rosa, which is why her name is pronounced "Rose-a-lynn," not "Roz-a-lynn."

The nurse and midwife, naturally, was Lillian Carter, and she would later also help deliver Rosalynn's two younger brothers, Murray and Jerry, and much younger sister, Lillian Allethea, who was named for her. Shortly after Rosalynn's birth, Lillian brought her toddler — just six weeks shy of his third birthday — next door to the Smith house to see the new baby. While Jimmy didn't remember it, the visit later felt almost like kismet.

Edgar lost his $1,000 nest egg after the crash of 1929, but the family got along okay, growing their own food. Miss Allie made their clothes and taught Rosalynn to sew. She described her daughter as the kind of girl who could wear a white dress all day and keep it clean. After Mr. Edgar spanked her for running in the street, he would tell her not to cry, but Rosalynn would go to the outhouse and cry anyway, feeling that her father perhaps didn't love her. "Just having these thoughts troubled me and gave me a guilty conscience for years," she confessed. Reading *Heidi, Hans Brinker,* and *Robinson Crusoe* fired her dreams of escape.

Plains was so small that for a time Rosalynn was one of the only girls her age in town. So it wasn't unusual that in grade school she struck up a friendship with Ruth Carter, who was two years younger.

In 1939, when Rosalynn was thirteen, Edgar fell ill; even eight decades later, she had a hard time talking about it without tearing up. Her father had burned his hand on a blowtorch and when it didn't heal, the Wise brothers, Bowman, Sam, and Thad — small-town doctors determined to be medical pioneers — experimented on him with radium. This likely caused Edgar to develop leukemia, though in a town that revered the Wise family, the connection remained secret for de-

110

cades. Rosalynn blamed herself and her negative thoughts about her father for his illness and compensated by becoming the perfect child, reading detective stories and the Bible to him as he weakened — a caregiver like those she would champion after her husband left the presidency.

One day Edgar called his children to his bedside and told them he would not get better and that he was "depending on you to be strong." He said that he had always wanted to go to college but had not been able to afford it. He instructed that his children go, even if that meant Miss Allie selling the farm. Once again Rosalynn ran to the outhouse to cry. She would later say her childhood ended at that moment.

With Mr. Edgar gravely ill, Miss Lillian brought Rosalynn out to Archery to spend the night with Ruth, where she was relieved to be out of her own sad house. Miss Lillian and another nurse were by Edgar's bed later that night when he died.

Edgar Smith's death at forty-four left his family destitute, living on $18.25 a month in insurance. Allie, only thirty-four, went to work as a seamstress and later a postmistress — a job she held until the year before Carter was elected president. Rosalynn, shaking off feelings that somehow she had been bad and that God didn't love her anymore, helped raise her three younger siblings. She studied hard — rising at five in the morning to do extra homework — and avoided smoking and drinking, as her teetotaler father had requested. Less than a year after Edgar's death, Allie's mother died suddenly, too, leaving the family no money.

Rosalynn thought constantly about how her father would react to everything she said or did.

She made money shampooing hair and set her sights on enrolling in secretarial school at Georgia Southwestern, with ambitions of someday becoming an interior decorator.

Before graduating at the top of her class at Plains High School, Rosalynn — by now a dark-haired, gray-eyed beauty — had fallen in love with the picture of handsome Jimmy Carter in uniform that was pinned to the wall of Ruth's bedroom. Part of his appeal was that he had escaped Plains, as she longed to do. She had spoken to him only once, while eating ice cream in town one day, but plotted with Ruth to cross paths with him during his monthlong home leave in the summer of 1945, when Rosalynn had just finished her first year of college. Finally, three days before he was to return to Annapolis, they chatted at a picnic at the Pond House, where Jimmy teased Rosalynn for making sandwiches with salad dressing instead of mayonnaise. Ruth was going to Americus that night with her boyfriend and suggested that Jimmy ask Rosalynn to come on a double date.

During vacations, Jimmy had been dating Annelle Green, the former Miss Southwestern. But Annelle was at a family reunion in Florida. That Sunday afternoon, Jimmy recalled, he was "cruising" with Ruth's boyfriend in a Ford with a rumble seat and spotted Rosalynn on the steps of the Plains Methodist Church, where she was about to attend a youth meeting. Jimmy jumped out of the car and asked her to a movie, the name of which no one could recall. Rosalynn hopped in, and they took her home to change clothes. He was waiting for her in the front bedroom of her house, where Miss Allie was impressed by "all those amazing teeth, so white, so white." Rosalynn entered, wearing a dress that he would never forget. Jimmy was smitten. Nearly a half century after the double date, he would write of her in a poem entitled "Rosalynn":

I'd pay to sit behind her, blind to what
was on the screen, and watch the image flicker
upon her hair.

I'd glow when her diminished voice would clear
my muddled thoughts, like lightning flashing in
a gloomy sky.

On the ten-mile ride home, they kissed, which stunned her. She had never let a boy kiss her on a first date; her parents hadn't even held hands until they were engaged. "She was remarkably beautiful, almost painfully shy, obviously intelligent, and yet unrestrained in our discussions on the rumble seat of the Ford coupe," Carter later wrote. The next morning, Jimmy told his mother that Rosalynn Smith was the one he was going to marry. Lillian replied, "Jimmy, she's a little girl. She's Ruth's friend." Lillian said later, "What I was really trying to tell him was that I thought he was probably too sophisticated for her."

Jimmy's cousin Hugh Carter claimed in a book that Miss Lillian thought Rosalynn wasn't good enough for her son — that she was "from the wrong side of the tracks" — while Mr. Earl approved. Rosalynn eventually came to believe that the opposite was the case, explaining that it was Mr. Earl who didn't want Jimmy to marry her. "He had all these expectations for Jimmy, and an eighteen-year-old girl from Plains, Georgia, was

113

not in them," she said. In the years ahead, she would occasionally be at odds with Miss Lillian — during Jimmy's early days as governor, they tangled well beyond normal mother-in-law problems — but at the time, she was perplexed by how nice she was to her. The Carters invited Rosalynn to accompany them to see Jimmy off at the station. "I didn't want to go. I didn't think it was right," Rosalynn recalled. But Miss Lillian insisted. Only later, when she learned what Jimmy had said to his mother after their first date, did she understand why she was so solicitous.

As Jimmy returned to Annapolis for his final year, he continued to date other girls, including one he met while on shore leave in New York City during his late-summer cruise. "We were hoping that the war would end while we were here," he wrote Jackie Reid on August 10, 1945, the day after the United States dropped its second atomic bomb, this one on Nagasaki. "Everybody here was listening to the radios and reading the notices in Times Square etc." Had Carter been ordered back to Annapolis even a day later, he would have been among the iconic sailors kissing girls in Times Square on V-J Day when the Japanese surrender was announced.

Jimmy wrote Jackie that "I haven't gotten over the night in New York" and, after inviting her to Annapolis for a football game, insisted, "I'm really looking forward to seeing you, darling." But he was no Lothario. He apologized in his letters for not having the time to write longer ones and apparently didn't get around to sending her a pair of stockings he had promised as a gift.

Jimmy's affections now lay elsewhere. He wrote

114

Rosalynn teasing letters describing her as his "city girl" because she was from Plains. He told her not to wait for him, but when she wrote that she was playing Ping-Pong with boys at college, hinting falsely that she was dating them, he grew furious and told her to stop. At Christmas, he had a final date with Marguerite Wise, to whom he confided that he wanted to marry Rosalynn. She tried and failed to talk him out of it.

Shortly before the holiday ended, Jimmy gave Rosalynn, whom he (and no one else) would later sometimes call Rosie, a silver compact engraved with "ILYTG," for "I Love You the Goodest," a Carter family endearment. Then he proposed. Rosalynn said no. It was too soon. She had promised her father she would finish college. Jimmy understood. They told no one.

On Lincoln's birthday weekend, Rosalynn accompanied Jimmy's parents to Annapolis, her first trip north, for the traditional February Ring Dance. She and Jimmy infuriated Mr. Earl by spending so much time alone together. Jimmy proposed again, and this time she accepted, but they decided to keep it a secret. When she returned home and they announced their plans, neither family was thrilled, though Rosalynn felt that Miss Lillian, always for the underdog, was still in her corner. Rosalynn's only regret was that being a navy wife would likely mean she couldn't fulfill her father's wishes that she complete college. Still, she was in love, and the marriage would bring other benefits. "I had always secretly wanted to get out of Plains, and now I couldn't wait," she wrote later.

After the engagement, Jimmy sent her a copy of *The Navy Wife,* a guidebook for naval officers that categorized possible spouses by type. "The Regal Girl" was "too hard to live up to, talks too much," while "the Athletic Girl" was "too mannish." Then there was "the Clinging Vine," who "goes over fine with the midshipman from Dixie, who like their women to appear helpless, weak, and willing."

The "preferred model," the book said, was "the Natural Girl." She is "easy on the eyes," and "her pretty, soft brown hair has a semblance of a natural wave." She has a "willowy figure," "ready smile," dresses well, and is adaptable to regulations. "She is a good, cheery companion, *an excellent dancer,* never catty, has good manners, and appreciates a midshipman's hospitality." Jimmy underlined this section and wrote in the margin: "You, darling."

The still-callow young man had no idea that the painfully shy girl next door he had fallen in love with would be so much more over the next seven decades: a formidable, shrewd, charming, and fully equal life partner, described by her husband in their old age as "the perfect extension of myself."

They were married at the Plains Methodist Church on July 7, 1946, just two weeks after the Naval Academy graduation and Jimmy's commission as an ensign. Jimmy was twenty-one and Rosalynn, eighteen — the second-to-last girl in her Plains High School class of sixteen to find a husband. They prepared for the wedding in a way that would characterize their long married life: focused on each other with an intensity that didn't always leave room for others. They sent out no invitations and had no attendants or reception — an unusual decision, Miss Allie later said, that was

116

theirs alone.

When the pianist first played "Here Comes the Bride," Jimmy, in his white dress uniform, and Rosalynn, in a white cotton dress and homemade navy-blue top with matching summer hat, hadn't yet arrived. They could hear the wedding march being played a second time as they stepped out of the car. Jimmy grabbed Rosalynn's hand and pulled her up the church steps, and they finally entered together — late to their own wedding. (On the eve of their seventieth wedding anniversary, Jimmy — still proud of his fanatical devotion to being on time — insisted they weren't late and called out the church pianist by name for starting five minutes early.)

Watching them kneel at the altar, Ruth wept. She "felt cheated," she confessed, heartbroken that she was losing her best friend and beloved older brother on the same day — to each other. Ruth was "very jealous," Rosalynn recalled. It would be many years before they could talk comfortably again.

The couple drove in Mr. Earl's Plymouth to the Biltmore Hotel in Atlanta, where Jimmy ran a red light and hit a brand-new car. He had to call his Aunt Sissy to handle the insurance claim before they honeymooned at a mountain resort in Chimney Rock, North Carolina. Both were virgins, which they happily discussed publicly after the presidency.

Jimmy's first assignment, determined by lottery, was one of the worst in the navy. Shortly after the wedding, he reported to Norfolk, Virginia, for duty on the rattrap USS *Wyoming,* a pre–World War I battleship so dilapidated that it was not allowed beyond the Chesapeake Bay. Jimmy was an officer, but he found himself supervising the replacement of toilet paper and mopping a forty-year-old oil-soaked ship. Working on his hands and knees one day, he was shocked by a power line connected to radar equipment but survived without permanent injury.

A year later, Jimmy was transferred to the USS *Mississippi,* another unpleasant experience. His executive officer, L. W. Smythe, appreciated his work as an electronics officer, but the ship's captain, Frederic S. Withington, took a dislike to the self-possessed ensign. Jimmy recalled being summoned one day to the captain's cabin and accused of violating orders. "He didn't even let me in the cabin," Carter remembered. In the corridor, "He berated me about something, punched me in the chest with his finger, and then went back into his quarters and slammed the door [on me]."

Carter chafed at military restrictions on what he could say and do on leave. Early in the 1948 presidential campaign, he grew curious about former vice president Henry Wallace, who was running for president on the Progressive Party ticket. When Wallace — a brilliant former secretary of agriculture who had turned pro-Soviet — made a campaign trip to Norfolk, Jimmy asked permission to see him speak. Commander Smythe was appalled that the young ensign would want to attend a political rally, especially for a radical like Wallace. He told him he would have to choose between seeing Henry Wallace and a prominent naval career, and threatened to place a black mark in his official record if he attended. Jimmy didn't go to the rally but weighed leaving the navy.

Carter confessed later that, like many young officers in the postwar period, he was "fed up with navy life" and might have left had he not felt duty bound to stay. He took the idea that military men served "at the pleasure of the president" — the official commitment — more seriously than many others. But his ambivalence, even cynicism, about his career choice was real. Aboard the *Mississippi,* Jimmy hung a sign over his bunk that read "Who Cares?"

In later years, the story of the sign and his jaded affect would amaze all four of his children, who knew him as a worldly but uncynical man who cared intensely about whatever he happened to be doing at the moment.

Jimmy's absences from home started at twenty-five days a month and grew much longer when his ships left for sea duty. His and Rosalynn's life was what Jimmy called "constant separations interspersed with ecstatic reunions." After nineteen years in Plains, where she felt she was still treated as a child, she appreciated that being a navy wife let her develop "an independence that stayed with me the rest of my life." From that point on, she said, "I felt I could do anything."

After their first son, John William Carter, known as Jack, was born in July 1947, Rosalynn, only nineteen, sometimes cried in exhaustion, but she tried not to let Jimmy know it. She had learned early in their relationship that instead of winning sympathy, tears had the opposite effect. "I became angry and even more withdrawn when I could not see any reason for her tears," he wrote years later. It would not be the last time Jimmy had trouble understanding why others couldn't be as stoic as he was.

The intense ambition that would characterize the rest of his life was by now fully engaged, and the next brass ring was a Rhodes scholarship, which his superstar classmate Stansfield Turner had won the year before. With a sincerity that went beyond platitudes, Carter wrote in his essay that he wanted to use the knowledge of international affairs he would acquire at Oxford to promote world peace. Privately, he figured that the prestigious two-year scholarship would help him achieve his ultimate ambition of rising to the top of the navy to become chief of naval operations.

Carter's main regional rival for the Rhodes in 1948 was a thin, stooped, "real peculiar-looking guy" from Alabama who told Jimmy as they waited for their final interviews that he had no interest in anything that happened after the death of Queen Elizabeth I in 1603. Carter claimed not to be bitter when he lost — his first real setback in life — but his mother said he was devastated. In later accounts, he made a point of noting that the Elizabethan scholar suffered a nervous breakdown at Oxford. Finally, at ninety, perhaps recognizing that this part of the Rhodes rejection story might sound gratuitous, he added that he grieved when he learned that the young man had killed himself.

After two years on surface ships, Carter was now eligible to apply to three elite programs: naval intelligence, naval air force, and submarines. Jimmy chose the latter and set out to be the first member of the Annapolis class of 1947 to join "the silent service." He was admitted to the six-month submarine school in New London, Connecticut, a highly competitive program for sixty junior officers where 15 percent of the class failed to graduate. Carter thrived in that meticulous culture, absorbing the details of all of a submarine's complex systems. While he easily passed the claustrophobia tests, they didn't prepare him for just how cramped conditions were aboard a small submarine, which stank of diesel fuel and sweat. He and his classmates went out on subs in the Atlantic most days to re-create the great submarine battles of World War II — his only real taste of what it felt like to be in combat.

Onshore, the Carters — broadened by travel and reading magazines like the *New Republic* — were becoming more liberal. Jimmy often cited the importance to him of the United Nations' 1948 Universal Declaration of Human Rights, championed by Eleanor Roosevelt, which began his consciousness of the worldwide struggle for human dignity. Jimmy and Rosalynn remembered being the only ones at sub school who supported President Truman over Republican New York governor Tom Dewey, the humorless "little man on the wedding cake" who was expected to win easily. When Truman upset Dewey, no one they knew in New London wanted to talk to them about the election.

A reenergized Carter finished third in a class of fifty-two — a real achievement in the brainiest branch of the navy. With his "dolphins" — submarine insignia — he slid easily into new navy habits that would endure for a lifetime, like wearing his watch with the face on the bottom of his wrist so he could see it while gripping the periscope. (In the Carter White House, more than one ambitious aide adopted the same practice.)

Jimmy's first submarine duty was aboard the diesel-powered USS *Pomfret,* based at Pearl Harbor. But first he obtained shore leave in Plains, where his high school girlfriend — Teenie Ratliff Taylor — had recently been killed along with her husband, Lonnie, and their two young children in a plane crash. There was little time to mourn. Just after Christmas 1948, Jimmy left Rosalynn and eighteen-month-old Jack in Plains, drove all the way to Los Angeles, and flew to Hawaii to report for duty.

On its first patrol, the *Pomfret* was caught in a severe storm that sank seven ships. Carter was violently seasick for five days, with cigarette smoke and diesel fumes in the cramped bunks worsening his agony. His only relief came on the perilously narrow deck, where at least he could vomit over the side.

One night, Carter was standing watch on the conning tower at about two in the morning, when suddenly a huge wave hit the boat. He found himself thrust inside the wave, swimming madly, certain he would be swept into the ocean and drown. He landed, bruised, on top of an artillery gun located about thirty feet behind where he had been standing. He held on to the barrel as tightly as he could. After what felt like an eternity, the wave finally receded, and he scrambled back to the bridge, where he tethered himself in place with a rope. Carter calculated later that if the sub had been traveling at a slightly different angle to the waves, he would have been lost at sea.

Families of the crew were mistakenly informed in Pearl Harbor that the *Pomfret* had sunk seven hundred miles south of Midway Island. Because

Rosalynn was home in Plains at the time, she heard about the storm only after everyone was confirmed to be safe.

A few months later, a senior *Pomfret* officer who had been drinking heavily almost killed everyone aboard when he opened the valves on the starboard side, allowing water to pour into the tanks, while forgetting to open those on the port side. The sub rolled sharply to the right and nearly capsized before high-pressure air was furiously pumped into the tanks. "I realized how fragile was my existence," Carter wrote later. He didn't mention praying to survive, noting only that facing the possibility of death had left him a fatalist who no longer feared it. Carter was a less active Christian than in later years, though he led worship services for his crewmates on Easter and other occasions.

For much of 1949, the *Pomfret* patrolled up the east coast of China from Hong Kong, ostensibly protecting the Nationalist regime of Chiang Kai-shek, which was about to be driven off the mainland by Mao Tsetung's Communist forces. In Qingdao, Carter and his twenty-four crewmates saw the campfires of the Communist insurgents on nearby hillsides. They watched the Nationalists dragoon young boys into their doomed army at bayonet point.

On October 1, 1949, Jimmy's twenty-fifth birthday, Mao proclaimed the establishment of the People's Republic of China, while Chiang's forces retreated to the island of Taiwan. Carter and his shipmates were among the last Americans allowed in China for twenty-two years, until the US Ping-Pong team was invited in prior to President Nixon's historic visit in 1972. Nearly thirty years after that patrol, President Carter

123

normalized relations between the two countries and highlighted his days on the *Pomfret* when hosting Deng Xiaoping at the White House.

The captain of the *Pomfret,* J. B. Williams Jr., left an enduring impression on Jimmy. Captain Williams believed in discipline but was also what Carter described as "a man of gentleness" who never had to chastise subordinates. Williams seemed to share the ideals, hopes, and even fears of his young officers. "We tried never to fail him not because we feared punishment but because we didn't want to let our skipper down," Carter remembered.

Williams, in turn, gave Carter glowing fitness reports that extolled his "remarkably high native intelligence" and "pleasant personality" and went beyond the normal encomiums to suggest big things ahead for the ensign: "It is believed he will be one of the finest of submarine officers." Carter was one of those men, Williams said later, "who no matter what he does ends up being the boss." Because officers don't see their fitness reports when they are filed, Carter didn't know at the time that his hopes of being seen as a leader — not just an achiever — were within sight. In June 1949 he won promotion to lieutenant.

Even so, Jimmy was still having difficulty forming close bonds. His shipmates respected him but didn't often consider him a friend. One described him as a "seaman who never quite got over being seasick" and others as an arrogant southerner.

Unlike the other seven officers serving under Williams, Carter rarely crammed into the commander's tiny stateroom for coffee and an after-dinner poker game. He played cards occasionally in port, reporting to Rosalynn that after winning three pots while drinking, "I'm now ahead one dollar for the whole cruise." But aboard the sub, he mostly saw the poker ritual as three or four hours a night of wasted time. The other young officers remembered his desire to read or work on a technical problem instead. "Jimmy was not one of the guys," recalled Warren Colegrove, whom Carter described as a good friend. "We didn't criticize him or anything, because he was an incredibly determined and responsible officer. But he was always apart with his reading — he never really got close to anybody."

The reading was hardly from a comfortable position. Carter recalled that even in officers' quarters, there was barely enough space for a paperback book to be opened on his chest when he was lying on his back in his bunk. But he said he never felt claustrophobic because of "an embryonic feeling that you were protected in your isolation."

It was in this period that Carter became a true engineer. He recognized that, unlike surface ships, submarines left no margin for error. One wrong move by an officer or even an enlisted man, and everyone dies. Meticulous attention to detail was a way of life, as every precise technical order was confirmed and repeated back to superiors down and back up the chain of command. Carter wasn't the best-educated officer; two of his shipmates had PhDs from Ivy League schools. But he was exceptionally diligent and detail oriented, as a topflight naval engineer and submariner should be. Was this piece of equipment too big, or too small, or wrongly designed, or wrongly operated? He would find out. At the same time, he became fascinated with the complexity of underwater life and read every book about it that he could find.

By this point, the Carters were living in Honolulu, where Jimmy and Rosalynn began what became a lifelong habit of self-improvement — not drearily but in the spirit of adventure. They read art books on the great masters and learned to paint with oils and sketch with charcoal. Rosalynn did a good hula dance while Jimmy, dressed in a Hawaiian shirt (also favored at the time by President Truman), strummed "My Little Grass Shack" on the ukulele, made popular by radio host Arthur Godfrey. Jimmy bought a Studebaker to tool around Oahu and scooped up books on woodworking to improve his formidable DIY skills. The year and a half in Hawaii was such a happy time that they planned to retire there someday. Neither had any idea of the great political adventure ahead.

After the presidency, Carter confessed that in the navy he had too often "compartmentalized" his relationship with Rosalynn. "My almost single-minded commitment to my shipboard duties," he admitted, "rarely included my wife." He lost all of Rosalynn's letters to him, but she kept several of his close at hand through all the moves over the years. These long-hidden, unpublished letters from 1949 and 1950 — when Carter was on the longest cruises of his naval career aboard the *Pomfret* — offer a rare glimpse of a future president's deep love.

On August 18, 1949 — Rosalynn's twenty-second birthday — Jimmy called her collect in Honolulu from the Mare Island Naval Base in Vallejo, California, then wrote:

126

My darling wife,

I just finished talking to you five minutes ago, and I am miserable. I love you so much that it seems my heart will burst, but I can't make you know how I feel on the telephone. I came back to the room as soon as I could to try to tell you in this letter. I kept saying over and over the things I wanted to tell you as I walked back from the waterfront. I have never been so lonely or wanted to see you as much before as I do tonight. You're sick and I can't be with you. I don't know whether or not you were crying. Oh, I hope not, Rosalynn. I don't want you ever to be unhappy.

Rosalynn was newly pregnant with their second son, James Earl Carter III (who would be known as Chip), but it's not clear if she knew it yet or not. In any event, she was upset that Jimmy hadn't been in touch. "You could have written on the way," she said on the phone. Jimmy apologized for that and also for calling her collect on her birthday, explaining that he had only $4 in his pocket when he left Pearl Harbor and wouldn't be paid until the next morning. Then he continued:

Rosalynn, it's probably my imagination, but for about the past month it has seemed to me that you haven't been as affectionate as you used to be. It's not that you haven't been as sweet and kind as always, but you very seldom initiate any show of love. You haven't kissed me more than two or three times a month lately. Did you realize it? It is probably because I haven't been very considerate and because I tease you a lot. I know it must be my fault if

there is anything wrong. Tell me if there is. . . .
I can remember all the times I wanted you to
come over to the couch or table or bed and
put your arms around me like you used to do
without my doing anything.

In the days that followed, Jimmy wrote about
visiting "quite a few nightclubs" while on leave in
San Francisco. Carter was not a teetotaler, then
or later. "The Aloha party was fun and we got
kinda tight," he wrote, though he hastened to add
that he woke up at 0800 the next morning to play
tennis. He looked forward to Rosalynn and two-
year-old Jack coming to San Francisco but worried that his toddler would once again not recognize him. He sent her a money order to pay for
the collect birthday call and told her about the
Quonset hut they would live in on the base, which
cost $35 a month, including cleaning. Jimmy had
received a bank statement from their Pearl Harbor
bank showing they had 93 cents left in their account.

On August 23 Jimmy told Rosalynn that he'd
thought of her all the way through a forgettable
Richard Widmark movie, then again poured his
heart out to his wife:

Oh, Rosalynn, my darling, I love you so very,
very much! I have the least tendency toward a
desire for bachelorhood of anybody in the
world, I reckon. I am miserable away from you
no matter what I am doing. I need you to take
care of me and to love me and to let me love
you. It's funny, but when I first leave you, I
miss more than anything else your mouth and
breasts and body and the way you feel and

128

smell to me when we're making love. But after a day or so those things become less and less important to me, and I want to touch your hair and hold your hand or look at you across the room. When I have been away from you this long, I don't remember particular things about you, but I feel lonely and lost, and it seems that I am not really living but just waiting to live again when you are with me. I hope you have forgotten what I wrote in my first letter about you not being as affectionate as you used to be. I didn't really mean it and know now that it is not so.

When the Korean War broke out in June 1950, Jimmy applied for a better posting. In the fall he received orders to report back to New London, Connecticut, where for the next year he supervised construction of the USS *K-1,* the first new navy ship since the end of World War II and the quietest submarine yet built.

To qualify as one of the four officers aboard once the ship proved seaworthy, Carter needed to write a thesis. After struggling with advanced math at Georgia Tech, he had since mastered differential and integral calculus and now elaborated on a new way of determining the distance of a target ship by the beat of its propellers — essential technology for submarines. While the thesis wasn't quite as original as Carter sometimes claimed, it was well received, and several of his technical findings were later incorporated into naval sonar designs.

After serving on so many rattraps since Annapolis, the *K-1* felt exciting. Carter never seemed to be horrified by the shockingly close quarters

129

onboard; others were. When an electrician's mate suffered a nervous breakdown from claustrophobia, Jimmy helped make sure he was fed intravenously and strapped down before being evacuated.

The K-1's crew walked only when necessary — and in stocking feet — so as not to interfere with the state-of-the-art sonar array mounted forward on the main deck. The ship's official navy mission was to lie in ambush along Soviet submarine lanes, spot its prey, then "nail the enemy with homing torpedoes equipped with electronic ears." Carter's intensity aboard the K-1 was even greater than on the Pomfret. Frank Andrews, the K-1's captain, remembered him as "superb" at finding the bugs in their untested systems. Despite "the big smile and the big laughing," he was "all business, no fooling around; professional; organized; smart as hell." Another officer, Charles E. Woods, shared the stateroom with Carter and said he was as close to him as anyone on the submarine, "but it was not a relationship that I would call a close friendship. He knew his job better and he did it better, with less fuss and bother, than any of the rest of us."

Carter was closer to the enlisted men, including a hospital corpsman with whom he fished for striped bass in port and a quartermaster who helped him improve his celestial navigation. Jimmy, in turn, tutored enlisted men in math. For the rest of his life, he generally avoided prominent people as companions in favor of ordinary folks — often conservative or uninterested in politics — who could teach him a hands-on skill.

Carter was promoted to full lieutenant — his highest rank, equivalent to an army captain — on

June 1, 1952, and that August, his and Rosalynn's third and final son, Donnel Jeffrey Carter, arrived. This meant that Rosalynn was often caring for three boys under five by herself. The couple bought an early-model television set in order to watch New York Yankees games, and Jimmy enjoyed building furniture in the navy hobby shops, which allowed them to save money by renting unfurnished apartments.* "Someday I'd like to have a workshop with my own tools," he wrote his parents.

Other subjects were less pleasant to discuss with Earl and Lillian.

On Christmas leave in 1950, Jimmy — a strong supporter of Truman's desegregation of the armed forces — described how the *K-1* crewmen had voted unanimously to reject an invitation to a fancy party in their honor hosted by the British governor-general of the Bahamas. The reason: their black shipmates were not invited. At home, a sharp argument ensued. Earl snapped, "The governor-general was absolutely right," and left the room. "Jimmy, it's too soon for our folks here to think about black and white people going to a dance together," Lillian told him. This was the last time father and son ever talked about segregation and the last real conversation they would have for the next two and a half years.

*After the Milwaukee Braves moved to Atlanta in 1966, the Carters became Atlanta Braves fans.

# 6

# THE RICKOVER WAY

Rachel Clark, Julia Coleman, Tom Gordy, and J. B. Williams all influenced Jimmy Carter's development, but he often said that Hyman Rickover had a more profound effect on his life than anyone besides his parents. Carter saw Admiral Rickover as resembling his father: "excruciatingly demanding," stingy with praise, and more than a little scary. Later, Carter's subordinates in the statehouse and the White House were struck by how much their Southern Baptist boss from rural Georgia had in common with the Polish Jewish immigrant from Chicago.

Carter liked to say that Rickover was "the finest engineer who has ever lived." This was, of course, an impossible claim to prove, but he was indisputably one of the half dozen most consequential admirals ever produced by the United States. A brilliant innovator and demeaning taskmaster, Rickover was simultaneously revered and despised throughout the military. John Dalton, a future secretary of the navy, said that after he went into government, he ran into Rickover and told him that he had once worked under him. "He was not the least bit gracious — not a pleasant person, no social skills," Dalton remembered.

Most engineering feats going back to the pyramids of Egypt are group efforts. This is also broadly the case with large submarines, which, like all complex modern projects, are designed and built by thousands of people. But one man was most responsible for safely attaching a nuclear power plant to a boat, and he did it two years *before* the construction of the first land-based nuclear power plant for generating electricity. Without Rickover, nuclear submarines would have taken years — possibly decades — longer to design and commission.

Rickover showed how a desk jockey can change the world. After Annapolis and a failed stint as captain of a minesweeper (the crew almost mutinied), he spent most of World War II in Washington, where he received a fine education in bureaucratic maneuvering. By 1948, still a navy captain, Rickover had finagled a joint appointment to the recently established Atomic Energy Commission, which he fully exploited. When the navy needed the permission of the AEC, he provided it. When the AEC needed the cooperation of the navy, he got that, too. The nuclear navy was made possible in part by Hyman Rickover sending permission letters to himself.

The next decade was among the most technologically exciting periods of modern times — comparable to the space program or the development of the Internet. The first nuclear-powered submarine, the USS *Nautilus,* was ordered from the Electric Boat Company in 1951 and commissioned in 1954, with another prototype, the USS *Seawolf,* and a new generation of nuclear-powered aircraft carriers not far behind. This was the most historic shift in naval propulsion since the development of steam-powered ships in the nineteenth century.

According to retired general Colin Powell and others, Rickover's fleet of forty-one nuclear-powered ballistic missile submarines did more than anything else to shift the strategic balance and win the Cold War.* With submarines that could dive silently under the North Pole and roam undetected for months without returning to port, the US Navy controlled all seven seas, a huge advantage. When the Soviets tried to compete, they suffered more than a dozen disastrous accidents before settling for noisier, inferior models.

Even after he became famous, Rickover was so abrasive that he was constantly passed over for promotion by navy brass; congressmen, senators, and presidents routinely saved his job. "Life is a constant fight against stupidity," he liked to say, referring to other admirals and obstructionist bureaucrats. He was interested only in people who shared his fanatic commitment to work. "Most of the work in the world today is done by . . . a 'nucleus of martyrs,' " Rickover said. "The greater part of the remaining workers' energy goes into complaining."

Carter was eager to join the "nucleus of martyrs." But first he had to get past the interview.

Rickover's notorious admissions process would

---

*The winning of the Cold War was multicausal and extended far beyond US military power. But the force projection provided by nuclear-powered aircraft carriers and the deterrence offered by sea-launched ballistic and cruise missiles gave the United States a large advantage on the global chessboard.

today get him fired immediately. He interrogated and insulted applicants, often with obscenities. To measure reaction to stress, he often asked them to open a window that had been nailed shut. He might say, "Either you or a street cleaner will be executed. Who should it be?" Woe to the candidate who said he would save the street cleaner. "No!" Rickover would shout. "Anyone can sweep streets, but the street cleaner cannot do the job of a naval officer!" Other times, Rickover would tell the candidate he was on a sinking boat with five other men, and only one could be saved. He would ask if the applicant was resourceful enough to talk the five others into letting him be the one spared. If the candidate said yes, Rickover brought five of his staffers into the room and said to the candidate: "Start talking."

When one midshipman told him he had a fiancée, Rickover handed him the phone and ordered him to break off the engagement. As the young man began to dial, he ordered him out of his office. He preferred candidates with moxie. After telling another candidate, "Piss me off, if you can," the ballsy applicant swept everything off Rickover's desk and was accepted.

Carter's two-hour interview in early 1952 included a couple of Rickover classics. The admiral would sometimes ask candidates to sit in a chair whose front legs had been shortened by two inches, forcing them to sit at an awkward angle and almost slide out. Carter felt uncomfortable in his seat during the interview but didn't learn until later that this might have been why.

Rickover didn't give Jimmy a hard time about being a "bird hatcher" (an applicant with children) but surprised him by asking what subjects he wished to discuss. Carter replied with the subjects he knew best: current events, naval history, submarine battle tactics, electronics, and gunnery. An unsmiling Rickover peppered him with extremely specific follow-up questions until he couldn't answer them.

When Carter said he liked to read, the interview became a relentless cross-examination on the nuances of Shakespeare, Ibsen, Faulkner, Hemingway, and Herman Wouk's *The Caine Mutiny,* a best-selling novel that year about a mutiny at sea against a tyrannical captain. Rickover asked Carter what kind of music he preferred, and Carter said he liked country and jazz but knew more about classical. Rickover asked for his favorite form of classical, and Jimmy said piano concertos and opera. Rickover leaned in and asked which specific opera he favored. When Carter said Wagner's *Tristan and Isolde,* Rickover asked which movement he preferred, and why. Here, Carter's memory of loving that opera at Annapolis came in handy. " 'Liebestod,' " he said, and explained why, though the satisfaction of giving a good answer did nothing to relieve his cold sweat.

As the interview neared its end, Rickover asked: "How did you stand in your class at the Naval Academy?"

"Sir, I stood fifty-ninth in a class of eight hundred twenty," Carter said, his chest swelling with pride.

After a short pause, the admiral asked: "Did you always do your best?"

Carter started to answer, "Yes, sir," but caught himself as he remembered times at Annapolis when he had put in less than a full effort.

The twenty-seven-year-old gulped and said,

"No, sir, I didn't always do my best."

Rickover, looking him directly in the eyes, said nothing for what felt to Carter like an eternity, then snapped, "Why not?"

Seven decades later, he was still mulling over Rickover's question and its enduring meaning for him: "I've never been able to answer that question — why hadn't I always done my best?"

As Carter sat silently, a cold-eyed Rickover swiveled his chair around to peruse papers on a back table. The interview was over. Jimmy sat silently for several seconds, then left the room. On the way back to his submarine base Carter called Rosalynn and said he had failed. But he had not. Rickover admitted him to the program; Jimmy thought it was because he'd told the truth when questioned about whether he had always done his best.

Rickover's question would change Carter's life. He realized that what he thought of as trying hard fell short of what he was capable of doing. From that day forward — whether he was shelling peanuts, or making peace between Israel and Egypt, or fly-fishing in Siberia — Carter gave it his very best every day, every hour, and — by the accounts of those who knew him well — every minute he was awake.

Carter still often pronounced "nuclear" as "nucular" (a tic that would annoy some Americans when he was president), but he was on the fast track now. With high security clearances, he was detailed for four months in late 1952 to the Naval Reactors Branch of the AEC in Washington, then joined an Annapolis classmate he barely knew, Lieutenant Charles Carlisle, at the Knolls Atomic

Power Laboratory near Schenectady, New York, the sixth place the Carters would live in six years. There the two young officers, still shy of thirty, would run a training program and serve as Rickover's supervisors of the General Electric facility, where work was under way on the nuclear reactor that would power the *Seawolf,* the world's second nuclear-powered submarine.

As senior naval officers on the *Seawolf* prototype, Carter and Carlisle worked with the GE engineers and taught math, physics, and reactor technology (the latter not long after learning it themselves) to noncommissioned officers and to the enlisted men serving under them. Carlisle fell into a rivalry with Carter, who did nothing to defuse the tension. Carter was technically Carlisle's superior because of his slightly higher class standing at Annapolis, and — in his competitive way — he let him know it. The condescension rankled Carlisle.

Still, both were thrilled to be on the cutting edge of the world's most exciting technology. The team constructed the reactor inside a huge steel ball more than two hundred feet in diameter and experimented with a design that used liquid sodium as the cooling system in the *Seawolf*'s power plant. The idea was to make the reactor smaller, quieter, and more efficient than the one that powered the *Nautilus,* which used light water. (Within a few years, Admiral Rickover abandoned liquid sodium, and the *Seawolf* was retrofitted with the *Nautilus*'s light water reactor design.)

As if they weren't busy enough, Carter and Carlisle supplemented their on-the-job training with a semester of nighttime graduate studies in reactor technology and theoretical nuclear physics at nearby Union College. During both the 1970 gubernatorial campaign and the 1976 presidential contest, Carter would be criticized for claiming that he was a "nuclear physicist" — a designation normally requiring a PhD. Jimmy may well have been padding his resume for political purposes, but he was also just following Rickover, who described himself that way, though his only degree was in electrical engineering. "Goddamn it, a PhD isn't worth anything," Rickover told Carter's Annapolis classmate William Crowe when Crowe said he wanted to finish his PhD at Princeton. In truth, the term *physicist,* like *chemist,* does not require a credential. So Jimmy's describing himself as a nuclear physicist wasn't factually inaccurate, even if "nuclear engineer" remained more strictly true — an early example of Carter sometimes inflating his qualifications while not technically lying about them.

Carter was no doubt influenced by Rickover as much as he said, but their personal contact was fleeting, and Jimmy conceded there was no personal bond between them. But Carter was understandably impressed. While he found Rickover "cold and humorless," he thought he was "the smartest man I ever met" and embodied the highest values of a public man. "Rickover has set an example of intelligence, dedication, competence, unselfishness, integrity, and patriotism which are truly inspirational," Carter said in 1973. While invoking Rickover was politically advantageous, his reverence was genuine.

Carter noticed what Rickover had in common with his father. "The absence of a comment was his compliment," he recalled. "Never once did he say, 'Well done, Lieutenant Carter' or 'You did a good job.' " As he grew older, Jimmy had to make a conscious effort to be more supportive of subordinates than Rickover — or his father — had trained him to be. He did not always succeed.

Under Rickover, Carter worked eighty-hour weeks, but his boss put him to shame. Once, on an eleven-hour journey from Washington, DC, to Seattle on a navy plane, Jimmy and other young officers tried to impress the admiral by working all the way. One by one, they eventually fell asleep. When they awoke, Rickover was still up and scribbling his barbed comments on documents. Carter's underlings would later notice the same almost superhuman work ethic in Carter himself — and the same demanding marginalia.

Rickover may have been the last person ever to intimidate Carter; he invariably found something he didn't like in his performance and held him accountable for any problems, even those that were clearly General Electric's fault. But Carter always knew that "he valued me, and he wouldn't have chosen me if he didn't want me."

This was confirmed in his fitness reports: Rickover gave Carter a 3.8 out of 4 overall and reported that he had done an "excellent administrative job" setting up the training program for officers and enlisted men at the Knolls Atomic Lab. Later, he rated him "outstanding" in all categories, with particularly high marks for initiative, force, leadership, loyalty, endurance, industry, and bearing.

"I have a constant drive to do the best I can," Carter told a reporter during his 1976 presidential campaign. "That's what Admiral Rickover and the navy taught me." Like Earl Carter, Hyman Rickover would condition Jimmy to lead his life as if he had something to prove.

In seven decades, Rickover's nuclear navy has experienced no reactor accidents of any kind. The admiral emphasized safety above all, setting a standard for extremely low permissible radiation levels in the entire nuclear power industry.

But in the early years, safety standards were not yet firmly in place. At Rickover's direction, Carter would find himself on the front lines of the first accident of the nuclear age.

On the afternoon of December 12, 1952, something went terribly wrong at the Chalk River Laboratories, a classified research facility 110 miles upstream from Ottawa, Canada. The first experimental nuclear reactor outside of the United States — the National Research Experimental, or NRX — was in trouble.

The sequence of events, hushed up for decades, began with human error: a supervisor confused the numbers on push buttons. Within seconds, under extreme heat, the sheathing around twenty-five fuel rods ruptured and melted. Hydrogen gas explosions blew the four-ton seal of the reactor through the air and straight into the ceiling. More than 10,000 curies of fission products were carried by a million gallons of newly radioactive water all over the floor of the reactor building and into the basement.

Soon the water was more than three feet deep and in danger of leaking into the Ottawa River. While no one had been killed, Canadian officials were gravely concerned. With no prior experience handling accidents, they could only guess the radioactive fallout and what might happen next.

They did know that if the uranium hydride on the fuel rods oxidized, fire could break out. Or the hydrogen that had come into contact with the irradiated water could burn in air, potentially causing a huge conflagration.

Canadian engineers began an elaborate operation to connect a series of hoses and valves to the tops and bottoms of the damaged rods to slow down the water flow. But there was a problem: the radiation levels in the "header room" were much too high to send skilled operators in again and again. So a classified SOS went out to Canadian and US military units involved in nuclear research. Men were needed in Chalk River for dangerous work.

Rickover responded immediately by dispatching crews from AEC facilities. He put Jimmy Carter in charge of a twenty-four-man Knolls Lab team that was sent by train to Chalk River under strict orders of silence. Rosalynn and the other wives were kept in the dark. As one of the few people in the world with the right clearances to enter a nuclear reactor, Jimmy was excited by the secret mission and not unduly concerned about his safety.

At twenty-eight, Carter had essentially been drafted into battle — if only for a minute and a half, the most time anyone on the team would be allowed inside the plant. The radiation experts on-site told team members that their ninety seconds of exposure would subject each man to the maximum amount of radiation considered safe to absorb in a year. Later reports on the accident said that this underestimated the exposure by a factor of 1,000. But the experts had a good excuse for their imprecision: research from the fallout at

142

Hiroshima and Nagasaki was still in its early stages. That meant the risks at Chalk River were largely unknown.

By the time Carter and the other reinforcements from the United States arrived, a mock-up of the affected areas of the plant had been built on a nearby tennis court. There the teams simulated every second of the weeklong operation, racing onto the tennis court to remove as many flanges and turn as many valves as possible in ninety seconds, then practicing again and again to complete more tasks in the allotted time. Bulky television cameras were set up inside the reactor. Each time someone did something to the tubes containing fuel rods or other equipment, the same would be done on the tennis court model. Carter broke his team into eight groups of three, each with a slightly different assignment. When it was time to run down to the deadly basement, everyone wore primitive "anti-C" (contamination) suits and gas masks — an Annapolis cruise box race with much higher stakes. Jimmy and his two partners removed their assigned bolts and pipes and got out of the building in eighty-nine seconds.

Carter had no way of knowing the long-term effects of his radiation exposure. He and the other men, whose urine and feces were examined for six months afterward, joked darkly about whether they would die painful deaths or have to adopt kids. But the salvage operation was a success: despite some environmental damage, the NRX was eventually rebuilt, and the health effects on those who defused the reactor were apparently minimal. A 1982 study by the Canadian government showed no higher incidence of cancer than in the general population.

Carter's knowledge of distressed nuclear reactors would come in handy in 1979, when as president he had to deal with an accident at the Three Mile Island nuclear power plant in Pennsylvania. The absence of severe health effects after Chalk River also made him leery of antinuclear activists who moved past science to scare tactics.

The postwar years were good to Earl Carter. Thanks to shrewd investments during the Depression, he now owned more than four thousand acres in Sumter and Webster Counties, many purchased for less than $15 an acre. In 1949 he sold the farmhouse and moved with Miss Lillian and Billy from Archery to a new house he built back in Plains. His attention shifted from active farming to expanding his thriving supply business, now called Carter's Warehouse. And with Gene Talmadge's son, Herman, ensconced in the governor's mansion after a bloody political fight, Earl found himself drawn more to politics. When a reformer from Americus won a seat in the state legislature and worked with Atlanta moderates to make trouble for Talmadge, the young governor went looking for a conservative Talmadge man with warm relations in the community to unseat him. Earl Carter was the easy choice. He was narrowly elected in 1952.

But he only served a few months. On the Fourth of July 1953, a message reached Schenectady from Plains. Jimmy fell weeping on his bed, then drove home alone on a thirty-day leave granted by Rickover. His father, then fifty-nine, had been released by Grady Hospital in Atlanta after surgery for cancer. The doctors sent him home to die.

It was twelve years since Jimmy had left for college, and he'd visited Plains rarely since. In recent years, he and his parents had corresponded less than they had when he was at Annapolis and rarely spoke by telephone. Now he spent nearly every minute at Daddy's bedside, where Earl kept smoking his Picayune cigarettes. Annie Mae Hollis, who had cared for the Carter children, was in Los Angeles, but she rushed back to Plains to nurse her old boss — and didn't flinch when he vomited on her, a moment Jimmy never forgot. Father and son held the deepest, most searching conversations they'd ever had with each other. Jimmy's youthful resentments eased. He thought he knew his father well but now learned "how diverse and interesting and valuable a man's life could be."

Jimmy confessed later that he was astonished and humbled by his father's accomplishments. He knew Earl was a deacon in the church and active in the Elks Club, but he hadn't fully appreciated the breadth of his civic commitments. Daddy had been a member of the Sumter County School Board since the 1930s, a force on the county hospital board, and such a champion of vocational education that the library at Georgia Southwestern was later named for him.

As Jimmy leaned in for every word, he marveled at his father's equanimity in the face of death. Their long conversations were constantly interrupted by a stream of visitors — more than half of them black, Jimmy said. They came to the door with small gifts or food; often the fresh quail and pecan pie they knew Mr. Earl liked. A surprising number wanted to recount not just his community service but also his quiet acts of generosity that had affected their lives over the years.

Jimmy knew of some of these acts, but now he appreciated them more. Each year, his father had anonymously bought graduation dresses for the many girls at Plains High School who couldn't afford them. When the two-week-old baby of a black tenant farmer died, Earl handcrafted a small wooden casket. A black man who moved to Plains in 1950 said he could not have successfully relocated without a car loan from Earl. And Earl had shown great indulgence to struggling customers of Carter's Warehouse, offering them loans to buy seed and guano fertilizer. Now he went further, asking Jimmy to bring the ledger books to his bedside so that he could cancel the debts of both white and black families that owed him money.

All of this brought Jimmy up short. For all of his success in the navy, he felt "besieged by an unwelcome comparison of the ultimate value of my life with his."

Earl Carter died on July 22, the first of four members of Jimmy Carter's immediate family to die of pancreatic cancer. His children, all present at the end, reacted in different ways. Gloria, who had just been married (for the second time) the week before, handled it fine; Ruth grew depressed; and sixteen-year-old Billy, who had become much closer to his father than Jimmy ever was, fled Plains in tears, returning in a couple of days with a gift for his grieving mother: a green parakeet. The funeral at Plains Baptist Church was jammed, with black mourners allowed to stand at the rear, a rare occurrence in the all-white church. "If I died," Jimmy mused to Gloria, would any friends cry this way? He concluded, "Nobody would care. Not really care."

146

Midcentury America was still a place where a son usually went into his father's business, if he had one. Daddy had long assumed that Jimmy would stay in the navy, and Billy would succeed him someday. But that was now impossible. The teenager was hardly ready to run his father's operations or supervise the harvest. With about $50,000 in the bank and $90,000 in bills, Earl had left his family strapped for cash.

Lillian, bereft, had no interest in being either a merchant or a farmer, despite a tradition in the area of some widows running their late husbands' operations. When local politicians suggested she take Earl's seat in the state legislature, she scoffed; the seat went to Thad Jones, a segregationist friend of the family (and father of Thaddeus Jones, Jimmy's high school classmate killed in World War II) who would later turn nasty toward the Carters. Lillian was disconsolate at the thought of Jimmy returning to Schenectady and urged him to leave the navy and come home, where he was needed. Otherwise Uncle Buddy (Alton Carter) would have to arrange for her to sell Earl's business and some of his land, too.

On the long drive north, Jimmy felt tormented about his future. He had been in the nuclear navy for only eleven months, hardly enough time to make a lasting impression on Rickover, who would be disdainful if he quit. Promotions came slowly in the postwar navy, and the next, to lieutenant commander, was not imminent. But he had one of the most coveted assignments in the entire US military, one he was confident would lead to the very top, CNO, chief of naval operations, or something close to it. If it didn't, he would almost certainly soon command his own submarine (as

Carlisle eventually did) and be eligible to retire just past age forty at half pay for life. He knew that Rosalynn relished her life as a navy wife and wouldn't want to go back to Plains, where even on vacation she felt ordered around by both her mother and her mother-in-law. With no assurance of being a pillar of the community like his father, he might feel stifled, too.

Back in Schenectady, Carter had a beer on the lawn of the navy apartment complex with William Lalor, a fellow officer. "It was agony. His father was the mainstay of that place — the banker and the landowner," Lalor remembered. "He felt that if he didn't go back and take the burden, *the town would die.*"

Since he was six years old, Jimmy had felt like an outsider — first as a hick from Archery venturing to Plains for school, then as a naval officer who would never be one of the boys. For all his confidence, he knew he would face daunting odds against making it to the very top of the navy. Carter's lifelong faith in planning didn't extend to a grand plan for his own life. His ambition was always to reach for the next rung on the ladder. That rung — now coming into view — was to match his father in business and in his standing in the community, and to exceed him where he could, which included understanding that segregation — under assault nationally — was doomed at home, too. Daddy had always beaten him at tennis and anything else where they had competed. Now the grown-up Hot would have a chance not just to even the score but also to rescue Daddy from his poor estate planning.

More than fifty years later, Carter said his reasons for returning home were "still not completely clear to me." In the 1980s, when he had become a warrior for peace, he told his friend Peter Bourne that "God did not intend for me to spend my life working on instruments of destruction to kill people." Decades later, it took poetry to get closer to his tangled feelings. In a poem entitled "I Wanted to Share My Father's World," he wrote that he finally put aside "the past resentment of the boy" and "came to see what he'd become, or always was — the father who will never cease to be alive in me."*

That father was a model of self-reliance. Jimmy would return home not just out of familial obligation — not just because his mother wanted him to — but as part of the same entrepreneurial spirit that led a young George H. W. Bush to light out from Connecticut for Midland, Texas, around the same time. Carter had subordinated himself to his father and then to Rickover. Now Daddy was gone, and quaking in the presence of Daddy Rickover held less appeal. In the navy, no matter how high he rose, he would always be reporting to a commanding officer who would hold his fate in his hands. With Carter's Warehouse, he would be his own boss. It was time to stand up and — in the idiom of the day — be a man.

Jimmy described Rosalynn as "astounded and furious" when he informed her of his decision, which he arrived at without consulting her. Later

*Franklin Roosevelt, Gerald Ford, Bill Clinton, and Barack Obama all likewise lost their fathers before age thirty. "Something's got to be driving you," Obama reflected. "If you have somebody that is absent, maybe you feel like you've got something to prove when you're young, and that pattern sets itself up over time."

he looked back at this male presumptuousness with such regret that it became a staple of his speeches after he left the presidency. Rosalynn cried and screamed at him, claiming she might just stay with their children in the North. Jack was in kindergarten; there was none in Plains, nor access even to a swimming pool. After the freedom to run her own household, she dreaded being trampled on by Allie and Lillian. Her half-hearted threat of divorce — "She almost quit on me," Jimmy remembered — would later stand out as the low point of their marriage, but it had no effect on her husband at the time. "His mind was made up, and he is a very stubborn man," Rosalynn said later.

Now came the scary task of telling his boss. According to Carter, Rickover "thought that if anyone working under him were to resign, that we weren't worth having." A naval aide recalled that the admiral considered Lieutenant Carter's departure after so short a period "a breach of loyalty," but Rickover's chief of staff in Schenectady made the necessary arrangements. Rickover neither personally confronted Carter nor used his final fitness report to malign him.

Even so, Carter's role in one of the US military's most significant and secret projects meant that he was not just another lieutenant; leaving the navy after its investment in him required special dispensation. The congressman who now represented Plains, an ornery segregationist named E. L. "Tick" Forrester, had to write the chief of naval personnel requesting young Carter's honorable release from active duty on the grounds that there was no one else to take Earl Carter's place running an important business in his district. US

150

senator Walter George of Georgia echoed the message. Jimmy won an honorable discharge and enrolled in the naval reserves, where he remained for a decade.

It would be nearly a quarter century before Jimmy Carter saw Hyman Rickover again. The admiral, still on active duty at seventy-seven, arrived in the Oval Office to find the president of the United States standing nervously at attention as if in the navy. Afterward, he wrote his old mentor, "I hope now to repay our nation for the early training you gave me. I'll try never to disappoint you." They later took a ride together on a nuclear submarine and socialized with each other's families. "You worked for me, and now I work for you," Rickover told him, but that could no more be true than if Earl Carter had said the same to his son.

Those eleven years in the navy — especially the final eleven months — would never leave him. Admiral Rickover's example helped render Carter unusually competent and formidable at whatever he undertook. He wasn't dour, rude, and unpleasant like Rickover. But behind his smile lay some of Rickover's intensity and coldness, and it made him a more difficult person than he might have been otherwise.

Rosalynn packed up the boys and the family's meager belongings and met Jimmy in Washington. On the long drive back to Plains, "relations between us remained quite cool," Jimmy remembered. Rosalynn gave her husband the silent treatment for much of the ride, instructing their six-year-old, "Jack, tell your father we need to stop at a restroom." As they drove into Plains, Rosalynn was annoyed by her husband's big smile as he announced, "We're home."

Jimmy, by contrast, felt newly energized about the future. "I had only one life to live, and I wanted to live it as a civilian," he wrote, "with a potentially fuller opportunity for varied public service." In the seven decades to come, he would serve in government for only twelve years. The rest would be spent in the "varied public service" he saw as the duty of a citizen.

*Shoveling peanuts on his farm.*

■ ■ ■ ■

# PART TWO:
# GEORGIA ON HIS MIND

■ ■ ■ ■

# 7
# THE JOINER

Plains, population 650, hadn't changed much since Jimmy was a boy. Downtown consisted of just one block of squat structures on one side of a Main Street barely worthy of the name. There was a gas station and a diner across two-lane US Route 280, the only paved road for many miles. Even in the twenty-first century, Plains never grew big enough for a proper stoplight, just a flashing signal. Visitors from the North tended to find it friendly but desolate.

When they first arrived home, Jimmy, Rosalynn, and the boys moved into Lillian's house, though not for long. Lillian explained later, "There's no house big enough for two women to live together." As a veteran, Jimmy qualified for residence in a new complex that had recently been built a block away. He moved the family in, making him the only American president ever to have lived in a public housing project. It was a difficult period for Rosalynn, who was bored and longed for the independence she'd had as a navy wife. "I pouted for about a year," she confessed, in part because "Jimmy humored me but never sympathized with me."

Her husband spent his time absorbing everything he could about the new businesses he would run. His uncle Buddy, the longtime mayor, became almost a surrogate father to him. Jimmy was shocked to learn that Buddy would not be the executor of his father's estate. Buddy had asked a local judge to designate Jimmy as the executor; he thought that was the best way for his nephew to learn.

For his first year, Carter, not yet thirty, was the sole year-round employee of Carter's Warehouse. The business was a mess. The IRS audited several years of Earl's returns, and the resulting penalties consumed whatever cash was left in the estate. By the end of 1953, Jimmy felt his new responsibilities made building a nuclear reactor in a submarine seem simple by comparison.

An even rougher patch lay ahead. Jimmy received a $10,000 loan to plant crops, but southwest Georgia was struck with one of the worst droughts on record. The Carter lands were parched and the crops worthless, with the exception of one field of peanuts planted with a new variety called Virginia Bunch 67. Jimmy was too proud to ask Lillian or Uncle Buddy to cosign a new loan, which left his farm's total income for 1954 at a mere $280. He was living off war bonds and thanked God that the rent on their public housing unit was only $31 a month.

For two years, Jimmy worried constantly about bankruptcy. He dreaded having to return to a middling navy desk job or take a position with a military contractor. "No matter what happened — if it was a beautiful day or if my older son made all As on his report card . . . underneath it was gnawing away because I owed twelve thousand dollars and didn't know how I was going to pay

158

it," he recalled. Carter later described this as the most stressful period of his life until 1979, when American hostages were seized in Iran.

The Carters were relieved when the harvest for 1955 was better, and they happily paid taxes on $3,600 in income. By the late 1950s, they were clearing more than $8,000 a year, triple Jimmy's navy salary. Rosalynn was now an ace bookkeeper and office manager. Soon the Carters began to invest in expansion, much of it first suggested by Rosalynn, including new spreader trucks to spray liquid fertilizer in customers' fields. "If we were going to live in Plains," she figured, "we might as well be really successful." She said later that their political partnership began in the warehouse business.

Farmers had long stacked peanuts and dried them in the sun before bringing them to market, just as Jimmy did as a six-year-old. But as their businesses grew, both the Carters and their local rival, the Williams family, bought peanut dryers — gas-fired burners that blow hundred-plus-degree air into trailers full of peanuts.

Jimmy was an innovator in the technology of his rapidly changing industry. For the dryers, he personally designed a compressed air system with light sensors that sent out puffs of air at designated intervals. He increased the efficiency of his process by making mechanical improvements to the automated sizers that separated peanuts by size and to his modern shelling system. He also devised a new way to build warehouses with Sheetrock, which was less expensive and more durable. By the mid-1960s, the dryers, sizers, shellers, and other equipment were operated

159

mostly by Billy, though Jimmy and Rosalynn continued to make the major business decisions. Carter's Warehouse now employed about a half dozen workers of both races — and many more during the harvest.

Eventually the Carters decided to process cotton, too, and Jimmy helped design and build an elaborate state-of-the-art cotton gin. His ability to quickly grasp, troubleshoot, and change complex systems would prove central to his later achievements.

After his mother and siblings sold Jimmy much of the land they'd inherited, he invested heavily in real estate, amassing ten working farms on 3,200 acres — close to Earl's total acreage. He made a point of having two tracts that mirrored family holdings acquired by ancestors in 1833 and 1904. With sharecropping on the way out, he hired managers — black and white — and farmhands who rarely lived on his properties.

On their farms, the Carters moved aggressively into planting not just peanuts but also peanut seed: the Virginia Bunch 67 that had proved so hearty during the dismal 1953 harvest. After the new crop was certified as pure seed, they could sell it to farmers across the South to plant. Jimmy soon became an expert on seeds and was later elected president of the powerful Georgia Crop Improvement Association, which supervises the production and distribution of seeds of all varieties — the original source of the state's agricultural economy.

Earl was an accomplished civic "joiner," but Jimmy soon made Daddy look like a slacker by comparison. He assumed his father's roles as a

160

deacon, Sunday school teacher, and member of the Sumter County school, library, and hospital boards. As if that wasn't enough, he was also a Boy Scout master, leader of the Royal Ambassadors, chairman of the Plains Better Hometown Program, state chairman of the Society for the Prevention of Blindness, and, later, state chairman of the March of Dimes. Combined with his leadership in many business groups, it meant many nights out for meetings. "Can't you ever be satisfied?" Rosalynn remembered asking him one night. "Can't we relax and leave well enough alone for a while?" She concluded that it was not in Jimmy's nature to relax.

Above the rest was the Lions Club, where Earl had been an active member. Jimmy spearheaded Lions Club efforts to pave the streets of Plains and build the first public tennis courts and swimming pool — at first for whites only (as mandated by Jim Crow laws) but later integrated. He soon supervised dozens of Lions Clubs across Georgia, a time-consuming responsibility. Carter said later that his motivation for the frenetic networking was to expand his business — "to get people to buy peanuts from me." The Lions connection would also become a critical political network when he ran for governor. Any time Jimmy wanted a toehold in some distant community, he would speak at one of Georgia's 180 Lions Clubs, most in small towns. Hyperactive citizenship was a way to do good and do well at the same time.

As the warehouse expanded, the Carters moved out of public housing and into a house that Jimmy had admired as a child. When he was growing up in Archery, Annie Mae Hollis used to tell Jimmy and his sisters ghost stories about a nearby

161

clapboard house where a "boogie man" once lived. The story went that as you lay in bed inside the haunted house, the covers would mysteriously rise. Others in the area claimed to see ghosts in the window: often a white-gowned woman wandering around the attic holding a lantern. Jimmy loved telling those stories as if they might be true, and he liked the haunted house so much that in 1955 he rented it and moved his family in. Rosalynn and the boys liked it, too.

"Get up! Get up! It's another day in which to excel!" he would exhort his sons when he roused them from bed at sunrise, echoing a line he'd learned at Annapolis. He proved an eager instructor in a thousand areas of life, from farm chores to vocabulary. From an early age, the boys were assigned to argue the side of a point they didn't agree with; Jimmy could argue both sides so well that they weren't always sure where he really stood.

Earl never lost to Jimmy in tennis, and Jimmy would turn out to be intensely competitive with his sons, too. When Jimmy and Jack (the oldest son) played chess, Jack remembered, "eventually I won, and he never played with me again." Much later, when Jeff (the youngest son) got into computers in college, he didn't want his father, an early adopter, to get too interested, lest he try to prove his dominance. Often the competition was healthy: with the Milky Way easy to see in Plains, Jimmy's contests over who could name the most constellations helped stimulate Jeff's lifelong love of astronomy. But it later amused onlookers that he kept such careful score with Rosalynn on fishing trips over who caught more. Even in his nineties, Jimmy almost always shot more birds and

162

caught more fish than his sons. He was better at nearly everything than they were, and he wasn't going to pretend otherwise.

Like Earl, Jimmy made his boys earn their keep. He put Jack to work at age six shoveling peanuts, and all three sons worked in the warehouse as teens for $2.50 a week. On the brighter side, they were allowed to ride motorcycles at age twelve and, when they found rattlesnakes in the peanut bins, were permitted to cut off their heads and cook them like chicken.

Carter was conspicuously thrifty. In 1960 the whole family took a memorable summer camping trip through the southern and mid-Atlantic states. One of the only fights of his parents' marriage that Jack could recall took place when they got to Washington, DC, and Rosalynn insisted that they stop camping. Jimmy was angry about having to pay for a room at the Holiday Inn. It was too extravagant for him.

All three sons remembered their early years as happy and their father as exciting to be around most of the time, but the three would also admit it was harder being the son of Jimmy Carter than being the son of an American president. Carter confessed later to being "extremely strict" with his three sons, "perhaps excessively." For corporal punishment, common in midcentury America, he favored a Kappa Alpha initiation paddle that Lillian brought home from the Auburn University fraternity where she'd served happily for six years as housemother.* Chip (the middle son) remem-

*Jimmy bought her a four-door powder-blue Cadillac so she would have "the prettiest car on campus." The hell-raising fraternity brothers thought "Miz Lillian"

bered that after a paddling, he'd see a reversed "KA" when he looked at his bruises in the mirror.

Carter insisted on high grades. Receiving a B on a report card meant losing a week of TV privileges (though a snowy CBS was the only channel that came through consistently); a C brought two weeks. Once, when Chip was in eighth grade, he received an F on a Latin exam. Jimmy took Chip's Latin textbook to the warehouse every morning for two weeks and taught himself the language. He returned in the evening to tutor his son. When Chip won permission to retake the exam, he passed easily.

Jimmy was often bored by dinner with Rosalynn's family, which he found lacking in substantive conversation. Lillian's table wasn't much better: she sometimes made mean comments about Rosalynn, who could only seethe quietly. Jimmy, too, occasionally spoke sharply to his wife in front of others, including virtual strangers.

Jimmy and Rosalynn adopted Earl and Lillian's eccentric dinnertime tradition: at many meals, everyone in the family read silently at the table. They also sometimes spoke in Spanish if they didn't want the boys (and, later, the Secret Service) to overhear. At other times, Jimmy read aloud to the boys or recited poetry. In 1958, when his sons were eleven, eight, and five, he read a chapter a night of George Orwell's classic *Animal Farm.* Later, he would read to them from the

---

was a "real pistol"; their dates got along with her less well. "I remember you," she told one coed years later. "And I remember I never did like you, either."

works of William Faulkner.

His favorite poet was Dylan Thomas. When asked much later where he was when he first discovered his poems, Carter, open as usual, answered "on the toilet at the back of the warehouse."* One Thomas line in a poem about an official who signs papers — "Hands have no tears to flow" — spoke to his concern with "the insensitivity that's inherent in power," though he confessed he was never entirely sure he understood the poem's meaning. The difficulty of Thomas's poetry only made it more appealing to Carter, whose inner engineer occasionally surfaced to break an opaque poem down to its component parts and diagram every line. He began accumulating all Dylan Thomas collections, biographies, and phonograph records of his readings during the war.

Nearly three decades later, on a state visit to Great Britain, the president of the United States startled his British hosts by inquiring why Dylan Thomas wasn't memorialized in Poets' Corner inside Westminster Abbey. When the bishop giving the tour explained that Thomas was a drunk, Carter pointed out that Edgar Allan Poe and Lord Byron had flaws, too. He followed up with a letter and was eventually credited with initiating the decision to have a stone commemorating Thomas placed at Poets' Corner in 1982. He hung a

*This was also where Martin Luther confessed to first reading the Epistles of Saint Paul. But when he was president, Carter was more discreet, noting that he read Thomas and other poets while sitting on fertilizer sacks.

photograph of Thomas's new Westminster Abbey memorial in his home office in Plains.

Carter's life in politics would not have been possible without the help of his brother.

At the time that Jimmy left home for Annapolis in 1943, Billy was only six years old. Jimmy saw his little brother only rarely for the next dozen years and was jealous that his father had a closer bond with him. Once, when Jimmy was home on leave, Earl complained that Billy was wasting water with a long shower. Billy finally came out and flipped his father a nickel. Jimmy was shocked and envious. He couldn't believe that his father and brother had that kind of relationship.

Only much later did Jimmy realize how much his return to Plains had interrupted Billy's plans to succeed Earl. After high school, Billy married his sixteen-year-old girlfriend, Sybil Spires, and ran off to join the Marines. He flunked out of Emory after running up a $4,000 tab at Manuel's, a legendary Atlanta bar, and bounced around bad jobs. In 1963, after Jimmy was elected to the Georgia State Senate, he invited Billy to come home and help him run the businesses. He gave Sybil a job in Carter's Warehouse, too.

Billy's charm helped the business grow. Unlike Jimmy, he could joke easily with the farmers and salesmen and — despite a wicked temper — didn't take himself too seriously. Jimmy had the respect of their customers and employees; Billy, driving all over Sumter County in his pickup truck with a Pall Mall in his left hand and a Pabst Blue Ribbon between his thighs, had their devotion. Where Jimmy was a joiner, Billy ignored even the Farm Bureau. He avoided church and was contemptu-

166

ous of intellectuals, preferring to consume four or five newspapers a day, then place bets with visitors on the contents of stories.

The brothers quarreled often, especially when the crop didn't come in strong. Jimmy liked to order Billy around, and according to family lore, one night in the 1950s they came to blows under the old Plains water tower. (Jimmy denied it.) Billy would stomp off and drive for hours, swearing not to return as the "hired hand" to his older brother. But Jimmy recalled that his brother would always be back at the warehouse the next day an hour or two before anyone else, ready to work. Jimmy had bought Billy out in the 1950s but in 1971 he gave him one-sixth ownership of the business.

Jimmy's other sibling in Plains was a hell-raiser, too. Gloria routinely hosted Hells Angels and loved showing off her tattoos, which included one of Tweety Bird pushing a lawnmower. Gloria had a son, William (called "Toadie"), from a brief early marriage to a man who beat her. The boy grew up troubled. He stole Billy's car, terrorized his cousins, and punched one of his other uncles. When "Go-Go" and her second husband, Walter Spann, were gone for weeks at a time on long motorcycle trips on their beloved Harley-Davidsons, Toadie often stayed with Uncle Jimmy and Aunt Rosalynn, which caused awkwardness in the family because Jimmy couldn't discipline him the way he did his own children. After the original Pond House burned to the ground, the family was fairly sure Toadie was the arsonist.*

*When he grew up, Toadie served time for burglaries and car theft in Los Angeles and complained about

At home, in Plains, the Carters fell in with a group of prosperous Americus businessmen and their wives. Jimmy and Rosalynn, John and Marjorie Pope, and Billy and Irene Horne called themselves "the Three Musketeers" and socialized often at one another's houses, the Daytona and Sebring auto races in Florida that Jimmy loved in those years, and on weekend jaunts to the Gulf Coast. In pre-Castro Havana, they gambled away the money they set aside for hotel rooms and had to stay up all night before flying home. They took dancing lessons as guests at the Americus Country Club and soon joined the Sumter Squares, a dedicated square dancing group, though Jimmy — an adept dancer — preferred waltzing. By the early sixties, it was on to the Twist.

Even then, the Carters stood slightly apart from the upper crust of Americus society. Jimmy went to the Junior League's black-tie Christmas dances in a blue suit because he didn't yet own a tux. A myth developed inside the family that the Carters were rejected by the all-white Americus Country Club because of their tolerant views on race, which were well known in the area. In truth, they didn't feel entirely comfortable there as guests and decided not to apply for membership.

Instead, they took golf lessons and played avidly

receiving death threats. As governor, Carter intervened with California authorities to have his nephew placed in protective custody. Toadie, a heroin addict, was in and out of state prison before dying young in 1997. He never admitted to burning down the Pond House.

for a time at a public course in nearby Dawson, which Rosalynn said was essential to giving them the contacts they would need to win pivotal Terrell County in Jimmy's first campaign for state senate. No golf, no political career and no presidency. But golf became a memory when other time commitments hurt Jimmy's performance on the links. He wouldn't play any sport in which he couldn't perform up to his own high standards. Carter became the only twentieth-century American president, other than Harry Truman, who didn't golf while in office.

By the early 1960s, small-town social life — the usual gossip and parties — was beginning to bore him; he was worried, one Americus friend said, about "drying up in Plains." The Carters noted later that living where everyone knew everyone's business was surprisingly good preparation for the fishbowl of the White House, but that didn't make it any easier. Events were stirring that would sometimes make Jimmy and Rosalynn feel uncomfortable in the place they called home.

# 8
# "THERE'S NOTHING I CAN DO"

Jimmy Carter's moral stature around the world began with his willingness to speak up on behalf of human rights. But he didn't always do so. While a quiet progressive since his experience in the integrated navy in the late 1940s, he failed to oppose racial discrimination in public until sworn in as governor of Georgia in 1971, nearly three years after the assassination of Martin Luther King Jr., a fellow Georgian he never made a point of meeting. In the eighteen years after he returned home, he would do his best for himself, his family, and his community, but not for his ideals of racial justice. That would come in the second half of his life, which was animated in part by the silences of the first.

"I never claimed to have been courageous during the civil rights movement," Carter said of the momentous events that unfolded before his eyes in the 1950s and 1960s. "I wasn't." Ducking the movement — in what the writer Garry Wills called "a mean and starved back corner of America" — seemed to him to be a practical necessity for his rise in business, civic life, and eventually politics. But it came with a moral cost.

Carter had lots of company among white Americans of every region who also ignored or down-played the repression, racism, and, yes, white ter-rorism of this period. The difference was that Carter considered himself more moral than the average person, which made his years of lying low a more conspicuous part of his life. And yet the consequences of living where he did were of great — and positive — historic import. The emotional stew of sympathy, regret, and faith in redemption would help make him a world-class humanitarian. As he acknowledged, his guilty feelings over not responding earlier and more courageously to the moral imperative of his time — what Carter later called "the secret shame" of all white southerners — helped power the achievements that would one day bring him the Nobel Peace Prize. The intensity of his quest for justice and reconciliation was inseparable from his adult experience in the Jim Crow South.

On May 17, 1954, Rosalynn brought the boys by the warehouse, where Jimmy was listening intently to the radio. By a vote of 9 to 0, the Supreme Court of the United States had ruled in *Brown v. Board of Education of Topeka* that "separate educational facilities are inherently unequal," and that the stigma of segregation harmed Negro children and deprived them of their constitutional rights. The fourteen-page opinion reversed the 1896 *Plessy v. Ferguson* "separate but equal" deci-sion, signaling the most dramatic challenge to the southern way of life since Reconstruction.

Rosalynn remembered Jimmy fearing how their neighbors would react. "I don't know what's go-ing to happen around here," he said. When they looked out on Main Street, they saw little knots of people on the sidewalks and in the stores, talking about a subject that until then was rarely raised but would now condition everything about their lives: racial integration.

Harry Truman had integrated the armed forces, but schools were different. They summoned the white man's deepest fears about his status as the protector of his children, especially his daughters. This was true across the country. In the North, de facto school segregation — and broader racism — endures, its evils often shrouded in hypocrisy. In the South, where they liked their poison straight up, the *Brown* decision brought a furious bolstering of de jure segregation — a Jim Crow revival of legal barriers to equality that Carter witnessed firsthand. "Apartheid reigned," he said later of the land of his birth.

In the immediate postwar period, Georgia had shown a few tentative signs of moving in the right direction. In 1945 Governor Ellis Arnall, a relative moderate, abolished the poll tax. By 1950, the Georgia National Association for the Advancement of Colored People (NAACP) demanded integration — or at least funding equalization — of Atlanta schools, and the subject was taken up for debate. But after *Brown,* a new wave of white supremacy swept the South.

Roy Harris, the segregationist kingmaker of Georgia politics, suggested from his perch on the Board of Regents of the University of Georgia that if the state wouldn't fight to protect segregation, it should "do away with the public school system" altogether. This was not a fringe view at the time. Segregationists embraced a post-*Brown* strategy of "massive resistance," and while the reaction over the next decade to new federal laws and court decisions was less incendiary in Georgia than in much of the Deep South, it was plenty fierce.

It's hard to exaggerate the backlash against *Brown.* Southern states went out of their way to enact some of the nastiest state and local Jim Crow laws since the turn of the century. Hundreds of statues of Confederate war heroes were erected as symbols of defiance. In Atlanta, the state board of education ordered the firing of all black teachers who were members of the NAACP and all white teachers who didn't pledge opposition to school integration. In Sumter County, Jimmy and Rosalynn were derided in whispers as "nigger lovers." And that was for doing next to nothing.

The Carters thought "massive resistance" was futile. They considered themselves realists about the inevitability of integration, which they quietly favored. That realism, of course, also extended to their assessment of how far they could stick their necks out. When he first ran for president in 1976, Carter said that he regretted not being more outspoken about the evils of segregation. "The fact that in 1954 I sat back and required the Warren Court to make this ruling without having crusaded myself — that was obviously a mistake on my part," he said.

Carter's implication is that after 1954, he did better. He did not. Carter would do nothing to support what some historians now call the Second Reconstruction — a period that included the *Brown* decision, the Civil Rights Act of 1957, the Civil Rights Act of 1964, the Voting Rights Act of 1965, and the Fair Housing Act of 1968. As a moderate, Carter believed in the rule of law and objected to outright resistance to federal court decisions, but he was in no hurry to urge compliance.

Several months after the *Brown* decision, Jimmy accepted an appointment to follow in his father's footsteps and sit on the all-white, seven-member Sumter County Board of Education. This was an influential position in the community, complicated by the fact that the area contained two overlapping school systems: one for Sumter County and a smaller one for the city of Americus, the county seat, which, with a population of sixteen thousand, was the biggest town in a forty-mile radius. The county had jurisdiction mostly for rural schools, the vast majority of them black.

The first thing Carter did when he joined the board in late 1955 was to suggest to his fellow board members that they visit every Sumter County school — forty-two in all. The five white schools, including Plains High School, were located in solid brick buildings that the board found to be well supplied for the times. The schools included art, music, sports teams, and up-to-date textbooks.

The same couldn't be said of the district's thirty-seven "colored schools," most of which could not even properly be called schools. Black children were generally taught by one or two teachers in church basements or even private dwellings, many of which were fire hazards. In one schoolroom, Carter saw sixteen-year-old boys assigned to sit in tiny chairs meant for three-year-olds. Later, he was embarrassed to admit that he had been on the school board for several months before it dawned on him that white students took buses to schools, and black students walked to theirs. It was a sign of segregation's power over even a liberal's moral imagination. So-called colored schools offered no art, music, or recreation of any kind, and students were forced to share tattered, outdated textbooks that white schools no longer wanted. Before long, board members cut short their visits to black schools. They had seen enough.

Carter said in later years that he joined the school board to make sure that the public schools in his area didn't close in the face of the threat of integration. In practice, this meant refusing to implement the core of *Brown,* a course of action (or inaction) that was so obvious it required no discussion. Carter and his colleagues knew that if they integrated even a single school, the whole system would have been shut down under a new, explicitly racist state law. The board occupied itself instead with improvements that might come from consolidating one- and two-room schoolhouses for black students into larger, better facilities. They voted to build a few new elementary schools for black children — including one in Plains — and to buy dilapidated school buses to transport black students. But each bus was forced to comply with a new state requirement that its fender be painted black so that everyone knew the color of the young passengers.

Carter never would have been appointed to the school board if, a mere three years after he came home, he had been considered unreliable on school desegregation. Throughout this period, he not only did nothing to carry out *Brown,* he actively catered to the demands of white parents, often as part of his single-minded commitment to fiscal prudence. His very first motion on the board in early 1956 was to use lower-than-expected black enrollment as an opportunity to shift resources from black schools to white ones. He introduced a resolution that called for "leaving off two classrooms from each of the county's three negro elementary school buildings, and then reassigning those six rooms, or the equivalent in equipment, to another project, or building, for the purpose of answering the needs of the white high school pupils of Sumter County, since these rooms are not needed in the negro schools." It may be that his visits to black schools, then just beginning, opened his eyes to the error of that motion. Or perhaps his colleagues found his efficiencies over the top. In any case, the minutes of the next month's board of education meeting record without explanation that two other board members withdrew Carter's resolution.

Later that year, a dozen white parents from the towns of Leslie and De Soto pressured the school board to change the location of its new Negro elementary school because it was too close to a white school and would require white children to pass black children on the same streets. A board member objected that an expensive water line had already been built to the original location. But Carter, wanting to be responsive to the aggrieved white parents, sponsored a resolution that held up construction of the Leslie-DeSoto Elementary Negro School until a new site could be found so as to avoid "friction . . . between colored and white families in these communities." Only when other board members reported that the cost of switching to a new site would be "staggering" did Carter retreat and steer the board back toward the original location, though with a commitment to the white parents that the board would do its best to "minimize simultaneous traffic" between white and black schoolchildren.

A similar issue arose later in Plains. The white businessmen on Main Street — all of whom Carter had known for his whole life — wanted a black school bus stop moved from their line of sight. Black parents, inspired by the early stirrings of the civil rights movement, objected. Lexie Schley, the Carters' black housekeeper, had three teenagers who used the bus stop, and she raised the issue with her boss. "He felt for me," Schley told a reporter later. But Carter answered, "Lexie, there's nothing I can do."

It seemed that nearly every initiative was tinged by race. Carter worked hard to establish the district's first special education classrooms — but only in white schools. After the Soviets launched the *Sputnik* satellite in 1957, and Washington responded with new funding for science and math education, Sumter County received $1,500 in federal funds — for white schools. Carter made a successful motion to transfer four used typewriters to a "colored" high school — but the white high school got new ones.

Carter did vote to allow a pregnant black dropout with an A average and no disciplinary problems to return to class after giving birth, as long as she presented her marriage license and agreed to remain on probation.* And in 1960, in

---

*Young black mothers apparently had equal or, perhaps, better chances of being readmitted to school than white mothers did. Board members often expressed concern that allowing pregnant white students to return to

his first meeting after being elected board chairman, he argued to rehire a black math teacher named William Powell, who was fired from Americus's Colored High School after being falsely accused by the Georgia State Security Office of violating the law by attending NAACP events.

At home with his family, Carter had no problem with the NAACP. But saying so in public was dangerous to his standing in the community and to the continuing success — maybe even the existence — of his business. Instead, he worked on allowing more students, both black and white, who lived outside of Americus to attend the town's schools, which were generally better than those in the countryside.

It was in that context that Carter came into contact with an unusual place called Koinonia Farm, located just seven miles from Plains. The farm would become a flashpoint in the early history of the civil rights movement.

Koinonia (Greek for "fellowship") was a 440-acre multiracial communal farm and Christian community established in 1942 by a white "saint in overalls" named Clarence Jordan. Son of a Georgia banker, Jordan (pronounced "Jerden") became the black sheep of the family — an affable but radical Baptist minister with a PhD in New Testament Greek. Jordan's dream was to live as Jesus did. He and his wife, Florence, and other "Christian brotherhood" families — ranging over the

school would corrupt the morals of other students. This didn't seem to be a concern when black mothers sought readmission.

years from four to about sixty — were committed to racial and economic equality, nonviolence, and stewardship of the land. Pooling their resources, they lived, ate, worked, and worshipped together in spartan conditions and taught skills to the poor of all races.

Martin Luther King Jr., who visited Koinonia in the mid-1950s, called Jordan "my friend, my mentor, and my inspiration," although the two differed on tactics. Jordan chose not to march, favoring interracial pacifist communal living. Segregationists considered this a mortal threat. "I couldn't wait to leave because I was sure the Klan would show up and kill us both," King said. King's close aide, Andrew Young, remembered that "we considered it too radical, too dangerous." When Clarence Jordan once entered the sanctuary of the Plains Baptist Church, about a third of the congregation stood up and walked out. "Koinonia was Communist when we came home," Rosalynn remembered. "That's what everybody said."

In the wake of the *Brown* decision, the Americus chapter of the White Citizens' Council announced an economic boycott of the farm. More than 150 Klansmen and other white terrorists — including members of the Americus police and fire departments — formed a motorcade of seventy cars and drove to Koinonia, where they hissed to Jordan that the sun should never rise on "anyone who ate with niggers." For three years, hooded night riders terrorized Koinonia, spraying bullets onto the property and repeatedly dynamiting the farm's roadside fruit stand. They even fired shotguns at a lighted playground where farm children were playing volleyball.

179

These events generated publicity in the North. On Easter Eve 1957, Dorothy Day, the revered Catholic social activist, took a bus down from New York to serve sentry duty at the entrance gate. One night, the station wagon she was sitting in came under fire. Day felt she had never been anywhere as dangerous as Sumter County. When asked by a Koinonia member why she was shivering, Day said: "That ain't cold, baby. That's scared."

The next month, a huge explosion destroyed a farm supply store in Americus owned by a merchant who had defied the boycott. Instead of bringing the culprits to justice, the mayor and other town elders asked Jordan to close the farm and move away. A defiant Jordan responded by buying supplies from the North and starting a mail-order pecan business with the slogan "Help us ship the nuts out of Georgia."

As the violence escalated, Jordan wrote President Eisenhower, who alerted Georgia governor Marvin Griffin, best known at the time for threatening to cancel Georgia Tech's appearance in the 1957 Sugar Bowl because the other team had a black running back. The governor brought in the Georgia Bureau of Investigation, which resulted in the Sumter County grand jury charging Koinonia Farm with being a "Communist front" that had faked the assaults against it to attract national sympathy. Jordan, who didn't turn away communists or anyone else who dared to visit, was beaten in the streets of Americus — then arrested for disturbing the peace. Black members of the farm were harassed when they ventured into town.

Like nearly every white resident of the area, Carter was unwilling to doubt the findings of the grand jury, which had not bought Jordan's distinction between Jesus Christ and Karl Marx when he appeared before it. Jordan's "Cabbage Patch Gospel," which set the story of Jesus in rural Georgia with the crucifixion as a lynching, would one day become a popular book and off-Broadway musical, but that was far in the future. Even twenty years later, when running for president, Carter waffled on the violence against Koinonia property. "It was done — if it was done — by a fringe element," he said in 1976. "This was a time, I'd say, of very radical elements on both sides."

While the Carters wouldn't dare speak out for Koinonia publicly, they made small private gestures of support. Florence Jordan remembered later that Lillian offered help when someone on the farm got sick. Rosalynn brought pies out to the farm occasionally, and the Carters got involved in the case of Jack Singletary, a white Annapolis graduate and former Koinonia resident who served jail time for being a conscientious objector.

Singletary's farm had no phone, so when his young son fell terminally ill with leukemia, he used a pay phone in a Plains drugstore to call Memorial Sloan-Kettering Hospital in New York to see how his boy was doing. Sumter County sheriff Fred Chappell — viewed later by many veteran civil rights activists as worse than Bull Connor, the infamous Birmingham, Alabama, public safety chief who used dogs and firehoses on black children — demanded that the proprietress of the drugstore deny Singletary further use of the pay phone. Hearing of this, the local merchants' group, which included Carter, intervened. After the boy died, Rosalynn brought the family a ham and shamed the gutless pastor of the Plains

181

Baptist Church into officiating at the burial on Koinonia property.

Jimmy's contact with Koinonia was more fleeting. "I've never met him, and we've been living down the road for thirty-four years," Florence Jordan told journalist Robert Scheer in 1976, seven years after Clarence's death. "People came here from all over the world, but he hasn't come seven miles." Jimmy and Clarence spoke in town only a couple of times, mostly about crop prices. Clarence's nephew Hamilton Jordan (soon to be Carter's closest aide) said his uncle thought Carter was "a nice fella, but just a politician." Eventually Carter's Warehouse and Koinonia did transact some business. Florence recalled that by the late 1960s, Billy Carter regularly broke the boycott to sell to them, the only farm business in the area to do so.

Through the 1950s, Jimmy felt powerless to act. After Klansmen fired at the home of a black couple, Roy and Gussie Jackson, who lived on Koinonia property and had worked for Earl and Lillian, Gussie went to talk to Jimmy at the warehouse. Carter would offer nothing more than his sympathy. "It's a shame and a disgrace on Sumter County that something like this is going on," he told her. "I wish there was some way it could be stopped."

But even when he could have done something, he didn't always do it. Sumter County had a transfer deal with the city of Americus that allowed rural black and white students to go to better schools in town. In 1960, the year Carter became chairman of the county school board, thirty eighth graders applied for transfers, which were usually granted automatically. When only

182

twenty-seven were accepted, it wasn't hard to figure out why: all three of those turned away came from Koinonia, including the Jordans' daughter, Jan. An Americus school official was quoted in the local press as saying that the community feared the three white Koinonia students would "infect" other children with their ideas.

The county board believed — or at least claimed — it had done all it could in the matter. Minutes from the Sumter County School Board meetings indicate that members learned "with regret" that the Americus system would not let the students enroll. But incoming chairman Carter and the other board members "disagreed strongly" with a suggestion from Koinonia residents that the county board write a letter to the city board urging reconsideration. What's more, the county board avoided any connection to the American Civil Liberties Union's lawsuit against the Americus school system, which eventually resulted in the admission of the three students.

For the next two decades, Carter would have little or no contact with Koinonia — until it spawned a program for housing the poor called Habitat for Humanity.

Even as chairman of the county school board, Carter did nothing directly to implement the law of the land: the *Brown* decision. He lamented later that his hands were tied. So he focused instead on school consolidation. Influenced by reports from the Carnegie Corporation and Harvard, he argued in 1961 that consolidating smaller schools into large, higher-quality county schools would lead to major improvements in education and thus the local economy. This was Jimmy's first public campaign, and he authored five columns for the *Americus Times-Recorder* to drum up support. He explained that the plan would save money and address substandard curricula and inadequate library, science, art, and athletic facilities. When opponents argued the plan was a secret path to integration, Jimmy reminded them that the big, new Americus high school he envisioned would be all white.

Carter's cousin Hugh, his brother-in-law Jerry Smith, and his old high school teacher Y. T. Sheffield, now principal of Plains High, led the opposition in Plains, which would lose an elementary school and the upper grades of its high school under the plan. Sheffield grew impassioned and said that the institution he loved would be integrated "over my dead body." (Shortly after integration in the 1970s, he committed suicide.) "Integration then was about like child molestation is today," remembered Warren Fortson, the county attorney. "If you wanted to queer something, you just said it would lead to integration."

That July, Sumter County voted down the plan that Carter and allied boards of education had submitted, with the "No" vote from Plains — the people who knew Carter best — providing the margin of defeat. Jimmy confessed later that his first setback in politics was a "stinging disappointment" and that his family and neighbors had ignored the educational advantages and voted out of racial animus.

On the night after the vote, the Carters went to one of Jack's basketball games, where the results of the school consolidation election were announced for those who hadn't heard. "I sat there at the ball game with my chin up while everyone gloated over our loss, but I was crying inside," Rosalynn wrote. On the way home, they passed their warehouse and found a handwritten sign in capital letters on the door: "COONS AND CARTERS GO TOGETHER."

While admitting he did nothing brave, Carter later sought credit for not being active in enforcing segregation. He did at least try to be decent. One day a black woman drove up to Carter's Warehouse with a wagonload of peanuts and found herself behind some waiting white farmers. "You fellas don't mind if the lady goes first," Carter said casually, waving her ahead. This was the kind of gesture that infuriated white people. For years, Carter feuded with the biggest white supremacist in town, J. W. Sewell, who ran a local sawmill and held Earl's old seat in the state legislature. Jimmy shocked his neighbors by endorsing a moderate woman in her futile campaign against Sewell.

In several books and interviews, Carter told of being visited in 1955 (or sometimes 1958) by the Plains chapter of the White Citizens' Council, which was headed by the town constable and the railroad depot agent. Twice he refused to join, and word got around. One day Carter looked up from sacking wheat seed to find about twenty of his best customers entering his warehouse. His hunting buddy, Paul Toms, explained that they merely wanted to help his business. Jimmy was, after all, the only prominent white man in Plains who hadn't joined. In what he described as a "somewhat shaky voice," Carter politely thanked them for trying to be helpful and for being loyal customers but said he thought the dues to the council just went into the pockets of Atlanta politicians.

185

Another man said that, in that case, he and other members would pay his $5 dues.* After Carter refused the offer, some customers treated him coolly and drifted away, but almost all returned eventually.

Rosalynn said later that she could count the other liberals in Plains and Americus on two hands. By the 1960s, the Carters were finding that their tolerant views, once ignored, were becoming a problem. When Jimmy pulled into the only gas station in Plains one morning, the owner refused to fill up his pickup truck. Carter had to install an underground gasoline tank and pumping station to service his warehouse's vehicles.

In December 1961 Martin Luther King Jr. marched to city hall in Albany, where he and the other activists of the Albany Movement — an important early chapter in their struggle — were arrested. With cells overcrowded, King and his lieutenant, Ralph Abernathy, and two other prisoners, were sent thirty-five miles up the road to jail in Americus.

After a cold wave hit, and one of the imprisoned civil rights workers fell ill, King asked Sheriff Chappell — fresh from persecuting Koinonia — to provide the marchers with more blankets. Instead, Chappell removed the few available blankets, shut off the heat, opened the windows,

*In *Turning Point,* Carter writes, "I finally got desperate, or mad, for I abandoned the polite approach, got a five-dollar bill out of the cash register, and said, 'I'll take this and flush it down the toilet' " — a suspiciously colorful coda attesting to his courage and defiance that he left out of the story in two of his later books.

186

and turned on the fans in the freezing jail. When his prisoners were finally released on bail, he forced them to write a letter thanking him for his decent treatment.

King said later of Sheriff Chappell, "I had the dishonor to meet the meanest man in the world." C. T. Vivian, another important civil rights leader, said that Chappell was the worst of all the sheriffs he confronted in Alabama, Mississippi, and Georgia. One civil rights activist remembered him as a caricature of a vicious, tobacco-spitting southern sheriff: white hair, big jowls, and a face that was red with anger even when he was at rest. Chappell once ran into a white women's restroom to forcibly remove three black women civil rights workers who had dared to use it. He often traveled with a pet chihuahua that snarled on command.

Carter apparently never saw this side of his sheriff, or if he did, he ignored it. When Andrew Young first met Carter in 1970 at Paschal's Restaurant in Atlanta, Young — King's close confidant — told him: "The only man I know in Sumter County is Sheriff Chappell." Carter replied innocently, "Oh, Chappell? He's a good friend of mine." Young was taken aback. Carter insisted later, "He performed well. He was sheriff for a long time. What he actually did in jail with Martin Luther King, we weren't aware of."

Young got to know Miss Lillian and Chip that year, during his first run for Congress, and he decided that both were completely at ease with blacks and "very solid people." But it took Andy Young years to change his impression of Jimmy Carter.

As they prospered, the Carters wanted their own place, and in 1961 they hired an architect and built a three-thousand-square-foot, four-bedroom ranch-style home at 1 Woodland Drive in Plains. The airy brown-brick house was tastefully decorated by Rosalynn. Over time Jimmy built much of the furniture, though he didn't always use it. At social gatherings — even in the governor's mansion, though apparently not in the White House — he often dispensed with chairs and couches in favor of sitting casually on the floor, his bare feet stretched out toward the fireplace.

Contrary to his later image, Carter drank moderately — usually wine or Scotch — and he was among those arguing for the legal sale of alcoholic beverages in Sumter County. This didn't go over well at the Plains Baptist Church, whose deacons would help keep Plains dry into the twenty-first century. For years, his opposition to most blue laws had prevented "Brother Jimmy" from joining their ranks, but in 1962 the congregation relented and elected him a deacon, his first electoral victory.

That year, the US Supreme Court issued another landmark decision that would, like *Brown,* reshape the American South. This one would also affect Carter personally. In *Baker v. Carr,* a Tennessee case, the high court enshrined the principle of "one man, one vote," which meant that courts across the country were empowered to invalidate maps of undemocratic legislative districts. The decision landed especially hard in Georgia, where it led to the demise of the "county unit system,"

188

which for generations gave conservative rural interests a near stranglehold on political power. Under the undemocratic system, a handful of large "urban" counties with hundreds of thousands of voters had been granted six votes each in state elections, while medium-size "town" counties were awarded four votes, and scores of tiny "rural" counties received two votes each. In practice, this meant that Fulton County (Atlanta) got only three times as many votes as a small county even though in population it was more than two hundred times larger.

Carter saw that by curbing the power of old courthouse politicians, *Baker v. Carr* would make a career in politics possible for a moderate like him. Reverend Allen Comish, a renowned Georgia pastor, warned Carter that political life was rough — he would lose friends, suffer personal attacks, and be pressured by special interests. Comish asked him, "If you want to be of service to other people, why don't you go into the ministry or some honorable social service work?" Carter gave him what he called later a "smart-aleck" response: "How would you like to be the pastor of a church with seventy-five thousand members?" It wouldn't be the last time that Carter viewed constituents as akin to congregants.

# 9
## SENATOR CARTER

On October 1, 1962, Jimmy's thirty-eighth birthday, Rosalynn noticed that he had changed from khakis and a work shirt into what he called "Sunday pants." She asked if he was going to a funeral. He said, no, he was driving to town to put an ad in the *Americus Times-Recorder* declaring his candidacy for the Georgia State Senate. The courts had just invalidated the September primary, and a new one — shorn of the county unit system — would be held in sixteen days. Later, Carter said he was amazed and chagrined that he had made such a big decision without consulting Rosalynn.

Business, Lillian remembered, had come to bore Jimmy. But the shyness of his youth had not fully evaporated, and, as he later admitted, he could be "isolated and withdrawn sometimes" — hardly the traits of a natural politician. He wasn't even sure what name to use on the ballot. "For crying out loud, it's *Jimmy*," his friend Warren Fortson, the Sumter County attorney, told him. "James E. Carter is too damn hard to say."

In this race and in all his campaigns over the next eighteen years, Carter ran as a nonpolitician. This was crafty positioning but also an authentic

190

reflection of how he viewed himself. Jimmy was not lacking political assets: he and Rosalynn had friends, relatives, and customers in all seven counties in the district, and Lillian still had stature in rural areas thanks to her years of nursing. The family handed out cards and phoned hundreds of voters, almost none of them black. It would be another four years before enough black voters were registered for them to make up more than a tiny percentage of the electorate. This would be an all-white election, as were almost all elections across the rural South in 1962.

Carter's opponent was Homer Moore, also a young warehouseman. Moore seemed honest enough, but his most powerful backer was a crook. Joe Hurst, a state representative and for twenty-seven years the boss of Quitman County, was a cigar-chomping fixer and moonshiner who wore dark glasses indoors. Through the late 1950s, Hurst had also run the big poker game at the Henry Grady Hotel in Atlanta, where much of the state's business was conducted.

A day or two before the election, Hurst called Sam Singer, a poker buddy and Moore's campaign manager. "Sam, I'm getting ready to stuff the ballot box," Hurst told him. Singer replied that there was no need to do that; Moore would beat Carter without it. "Well, I'm gonna stuff it anyway," Hurst said, according to Singer. "We do it every time, and I don't want my people to get out of practice."

Sure enough, on Election Day, Hurst began to steal votes like a stock villain in a bad movie. Jimmy heard about it and dispatched his friend John Pope to Georgetown, the Quitman County seat. Pope witnessed Hurst ordering scores of vot-

191

ers to cast their ballots for Moore. After an elderly couple was seen voting for Carter, Hurst reached into the pasteboard ballot box, fished out their paper ballots, and made them vote again, this time for Moore.

That night, Carter carried Sumter County easily, and Terrell County as well, which he attributed less to golf than to his and Rosalynn's square-dancing group, good for about 100 votes. ("Had we not square-danced," Jimmy said, "I never would have been elected.") But when the returns came in from Quitman County, they showed Moore winning 360 to 136, deciding the election in his favor.

Before the night was through, it came out that only 333 people — not 496 — had signed in to vote in Quitman County, a clear indication of fraud. Carter heard his mother say to Go-Go, "Jimmy is so naive, so naive." This made him even angrier and more determined to contest the election. Local newspapers — and even some friends — counseled that doing so risked making him look like a crybaby. He pressed forward anyway, and contacted John Pennington, an investigative reporter for the *Atlanta Journal.* Pennington's colorful, well-reported front-page stories soon brought statewide attention to ballot irregularities in Quitman County. He learned that in another election that year, many of the Quitman County votes just happened to have been cast by voters in perfect alphabetical order. Others had been cast by made-up people, prisoners, and the dead, which led to cartoons in the big Atlanta papers of gravestones voting.

As the case moved into court, Carter needed an attorney. Warren Fortson recommended Charlie

Kirbo, a wily native of Bainbridge, Georgia, and an esteemed partner in the top-drawer Atlanta law firm of King and Spaulding. Kirbo wasn't sure at first about the youthful-looking sunburned man who came to see him. He seemed timid. But Kirbo came to be impressed. "He knew more about more subjects than anybody I ever knew," he said of Carter. "And he wouldn't pretend that he knew a subject like most of us do." Kirbo, perfecting the role of country lawyer, spoke with such oracular slowness that his elliptical thoughts seemed especially wise. He was only seven years older than Carter but quickly settled into the role of éminence grise, and would remain so, dispensing advice until Carter left the presidency. Whenever Carter's senior aides in the governor's office or the White House wanted to deliver especially hard truths to him, they always knew to route them through Kirbo.

Within days of the stolen primary, Carter learned the intricacies of election law and grew obsessive about the case; he lost eleven pounds in two weeks and barely slept. Every day, Jimmy and Fortson drove to Georgetown to obtain affidavits from every Quitman County official and voter they could track down, many of whom reported improprieties. With Kirbo's help, they finally got the case before Judge Carl Crow, a respected conservative state jurist known for noisily spitting tobacco into a spittoon while lawyers argued.
Judge Crow ordered the unsealing of a cardboard ballot box that had been located under the bed of Hurst's daughter. Inside were more than a hundred neatly folded ballots bound together with a rubber band. The voter lists and stubs they

should have corresponded to were missing. "When we opened up the ballot box, I nearly fainted," Kirbo recalled. Fortson found it strange that Hurst's people had carefully folded the extra ballots instead of tossing them into the box at random, the normal practice for stuffing ballot boxes. He glimpsed Judge Crow's skeptical expression when he saw the folded ballots just as he was putting a chaw of tobacco in his mouth: "I said to myself, 'We have just won this thing.' " After Judge Crow invalidated all of the Georgetown ballots, Jimmy and his legal team celebrated at the house on Woodland Drive by drinking Old Crow bourbon.

But more twists lay ahead. The general election was only four days away, and Moore's name still appeared as the Democratic candidate, running unopposed because Republicans remained scarce in rural Georgia. Within hours, Fortson's brother, Ben Fortson, the secretary of state, signed a directive ordering local election officials to cross out Moore's name on the ballots and replace it with Carter's. But the harried officials couldn't do all that alone. Thinking ahead, Carter had bought dozens of rubber stamps bearing his name. Jimmy, Rosalynn, Gloria, Lillian, and a few friends worked feverishly on Sunday at all seven county seats stamping "Jimmy Carter" on the paper ballots.

Then, to Carter's dismay, a superior court judge ruled just eleven hours before the polls were to open that the next day's ballot must be blank for state senate — a write-in contest. Election officials, their heads spinning, only had time to cross names off the ballots in about half of the district. In Sumter and Quitman Counties, they intention-

194

ally left Carter's name on and dared the judge to discipline them. He didn't.

Carter ended up winning the new election handily. Moore threatened to appeal the case — Carter's name had been on many more ballots than his — but decided against it. Sam Singer, who was to become Carter's lifelong friend, said Moore told him that after the election, he went to Carter's house in Plains at six in the morning and said, "Jimmy, I quit. You can have it."*

Even so, the incoming senate president, Peter Zack Greer, a friend of Moore's and Hurst's, could have directed that Carter not be sworn in until a legislative committee investigated the matter, thereby jeopardizing his election once again. When the Carters saw Moore and Singer leaving Greer's hotel suite at the Henry Grady Hotel the day of the swearing-in with big smiles on their faces, they grew nervous. Jimmy insisted that he didn't know his fate until the moment Greer asked him to come forward in the senate chamber with the other new senators and take the oath.

The Atlanta that Jimmy Carter encountered upon arriving in the state senate in early 1963 was the most prosperous and tolerant city in the South. But the bar was low. The outgoing mayor, Wil-

---

*To Singer's surprise, Carter didn't include that story about Moore's concession in *Turning Point,* a short book he wrote in 1993 about the disputed election. Carter claimed instead that suspense about the outcome extended all the way to the January swearing-in of new senators — a more dramatic but less accurate rendering of the story.

liam B. Hartsfield, coined the famous slogan "The City Too Busy to Hate," a line that unintentionally implied Atlantans wanted to hate more if they only had the time. These were the years when 160,000 mostly white Atlantans fled to the suburbs. After that, the joke was that Atlanta had become "The City Too Busy Moving to Hate."

The most respected voice in Atlanta belonged to Ralph McGill, the editor and publisher of the *Atlanta Constitution* and an eloquent foe of segregation. Jimmy read McGill's columns and editorials and later credited him with helping Georgia avoid the massive resistance to integration found in Mississippi and Alabama. But he never reached out to McGill, much less to Martin Luther King Jr., who won the Nobel Peace Prize in 1964. If he wanted to continue to represent what he called "the most conservative district in Georgia," he felt he had to be careful about the subject of race.

When he ran for president, Carter bragged that his maiden speech on the Georgia Senate floor was about the "thirty questions" used by registrars in county courthouses across the state to disenfranchise black voters.* But no accounts of Carter's speech have surfaced in senate records or in newspaper stories in either Atlanta or his district. At the time, transcripts of speeches were provided only at the member's request, and Carter — admitting he was "fearful of the news media

*Among the thirty questions: the identity of the incumbent clerk of the superior court, the exact number of Georgia votes in the electoral college, and the US Constitution's description of the application of habeas corpus in Georgia criminal cases. No whites were asked such questions.

196

reporting it back home" — did not ask for one. Even if delivered just as Carter claimed, the speech apparently left no mark on anyone except the rural state senator himself. Like a Catholic sinner in the confessional, he salved his private liberal conscience and protected his public conservative image at the same time.

Carter was more outspoken on the separation of church and state, a central tenet of the Baptist faith dating back to Roger Williams, the founder of the first Baptist church in the colonies. Senator Carter rose to object strongly to a proposed amendment to Georgia's bill of rights reading, "Every man has the natural and inalienable right to worship God according to the dictates of his own conscience." He believed that language was unfair to nonbelievers, and he tried, unsuccessfully, to substitute the text of the First Amendment to the US Constitution. Even as he went on to become arguably the most devout president in American history, he sought — from the start of his political career — to protect the rights of atheists.

Carter devoted most of his efforts in Atlanta to the issue that brought him into politics: education. He served on a special commission that recommended uniform county property tax assessments that would eventually help equalize school funding and make Georgia a national innovator in raising K-12 education standards. As chairman of a new senate committee on higher education, he pushed successfully for the expansion of Georgia Southwestern from a two-year to a four-year college, which made him so popular back home that he was unopposed for reelection in 1964.

When the Georgia General Assembly was in session, Jimmy bunked at a cheap motel and rose at four thirty to begin preparing. He arrived at the capitol before seven — earlier than any colleague — and he worked five days when most of the rest put in four. "He was the hardest-working legislator any of us had ever seen," Sam Singer, his recent adversary, remembered.

Carter took a speed-reading class at Georgia Southwestern to help him fulfill what he ruefully called his "foolish promise" to "read every bill" in its entirety before voting on it — a daunting task when about 1,200 bills reached the floor every year.* "This sometimes made him unpopular because he wouldn't support even a friend's bill if he didn't think it was right," recalled Bobby Rowan, a soon-to-be-powerful state senator from Enigma, Georgia. But assuming the role of class grind also helped Carter wield power without falling prey to what Rowan considered the three afflictions of legislative life: liquor, women, and obesity. While legislators entertained themselves at the Henry Grady Hotel, often in the company of women who were not their wives, Carter was off reading a book or a bill. He amended one

*In their first months in the White House, the Carters, Amy, and many staffers took another speed-reading class from an Evelyn Wood teacher. Carter was clocked at reading and comprehending 1,200 words a minute, the same speed attributed to JFK when he took a speed-reading class as a senator. Carter was unconvinced by the many critics who insisted that the Evelyn Wood approach didn't work. He believed his reading speed had increased fourfold.

legislator's bills so often to delete favors for special interests that the colleague got tired of resisting and wandered over to say, "Go through this and cross out what you don't like."

On the final day of the legislative session (which usually lasted a mere forty days), the senate would vote on a hundred bills — many of them significant. For four years, only Carter and one other senator had any serious idea what was in them. Their recommendations were routinely adopted, giving him outsized power, especially for a freshman. But that power didn't usually extend to Carter's own bills. His refusal to play the game of politics — what he called "grab ass" — meant he never developed the strong personal relationships that could be translated into votes. Carter was routinely described by colleagues as a "loner" and a "straight arrow," and those descriptions, as Hamilton Jordan put it later, "were seldom spoken with affection or even warmth."

It certainly didn't help that Carter made sure to get revenge on the man who ran the lawmakers' poker games: Joe Hurst. For months, he assembled evidence that Hurst ran an illegal distillery, defrauded landowners, and, of course, rigged elections. He turned it all over to the FBI, and Hurst went to federal prison.

By 1963, Georgia was taking its first reluctant steps away from segregation. The new governor was Carl Sanders, at thirty-seven the youngest in the country. Sanders, an urbane lawyer from Augusta, was in many ways Georgia's first "New South governor." He backed JFK and then LBJ and tried to chart a relatively moderate course.

Among Senator Carter's freshman colleagues

was Leroy Johnson, a shrewd Atlanta attorney who, with the demise of the county unit system, became the first African American elected to the Georgia State Senate since Reconstruction. Johnson recalled that most of his white colleagues thought "the ceiling would fall and the seats would crumble" when he showed up. Carter was not among them, but he also didn't go out of his way early on to be friendly. Until the last days of the session, Johnson said, not one senator outside of the more liberal Atlanta delegation spoke to him. "I would walk down the corridors of the senate, and senators would be coming in the opposite direction, and I would say, 'Good morning, Senator.' And the reply would be, 'Mmm.' "

Johnson's ostracism lasted until he arrived late one day to a committee meeting and found that his vote was the tiebreaker. Suddenly all the senators who wouldn't speak to him were acting friendly. But even then, none of his colleagues sought to abolish the rigid traditions of the statehouse. So Johnson didn't announce a desegregation campaign; he just drank out of the "white" water fountain one day and told a guard who tried to stop him that he and his pages would continue to do so. Governor Sanders backed him up, and integration of the capitol began.

Both Johnson and Carter liked to tell the story of how Johnson later taught Jimmy and some colleagues the proper pronunciation of the word *Negro,* which was then the way African Americans preferred to be described. Like LBJ, many white southerners had grown accustomed to using the word *nigra.* Johnson would playfully touch his knee and say, "Knee," then pull his hand upward

200

and add, "Grow." The legislators changed their pronunciation — at least in his presence.*

In 1963, Carter's first year in the state senate, the civil rights movement decided to focus on Sumter County. Organizers from the Student Nonviolent Coordinating Committee (SNCC), a more militant group than King's Southern Christian Leadership Conference (SCLC), moved into Americus, where many of their best recruits were idealistic young teenagers.

In July a dozen black teens lined up at the "whites only" box office of the Martin Theater in Americus. After they were refused entrance, a larger group returned to picket, stage sit-ins, and toss debris over the balcony from the "colored" section, which led to their arrest. On the other side of town, more than thirty black students ranging in age from eleven to sixteen were arrested for demonstrating in a schoolyard. Their punishment included shoveling raw sewage in ninety-degree heat.

*Attitudes died harder. In a special election in 1965, seven black men and one woman were elected to the Georgia House of Representatives, including a twenty-five-year-old activist named Julian Bond. After Bond described the Vietnam War as "murderous aggression," the Georgia House voted 184 to 12 not to seat him for the 1966 session. Carter was in the other chamber and didn't have to vote on the matter, but all of the state representatives from southwest Georgia sided with the majority. The US Supreme Court quickly ruled 9 to 0 that the House had denied Bond's free speech rights and was required under the Constitution to seat him.

On August 8 SNCC organized a rally at the Allen Chapel AME Church, followed by a nighttime march through the black section of Americus, while demonstrators sang "We Shall Overcome." Sheriff Chappell ordered SNCC leaders to make the marchers stop singing. Then he started jabbing a black organizer from the North named Don Harris with his "hot shot" — local lingo for an electric cattle prod usually employed to shock five-hundred-pound cows. By Chappell's own testimony, Harris lay "wriggling and twisting," but he would still not tell the marchers that their singing must stop. Some accounts had Chappell also using the cattle prod on female protesters as young as fourteen.

Americus was wracked by weeks of what were then called "racial disturbances." One demonstrator was killed and twenty-eight wounded, with seven white policemen reporting injuries, mostly from hurled bricks.

Among the scores arrested in Sumter County were twenty young black girls — many of them preteens — who were imprisoned for forty-three days in a filthy, snake-infested jail outside Americus called the Leesburg Stockade. The girls saw themselves as part of Martin Luther King's Children's Crusade, an effort begun in Birmingham, Alabama, in 1963 to enlist youth groups in civil rights protests. After they refused to stop chanting and singing, their jailers took away their bedding and forced them to sleep on the concrete floor, wet from the overflowing toilet. One of the girls, Robertiena Freeman, said later that when the young inmates were let outside, "I remember the guard saying 'Run, nigger, run,' but nobody ran." The girls were told by an older prisoner,

"That's what they want you to do. They'll shoot you [if you do]."*

Civil rights workers from outside the community were treated even more harshly. Stephen Pace Jr., the county prosecutor (and son of the congressman who sent Carter to Annapolis), decided to twist an obscure law and charge Don Harris and three other SNCC workers with sedition — a crime punishable by death. Claude Sitton in the *New York Times* described the sedition charges as "without parallel in the South" for leaders of a desegregation campaign.

Morris Abram, a leading civil rights attorney in Atlanta, filed a motion to stop the sedition case and lost. Not one white member of the Georgia bar, he reported, joined him in condemning the sedition charges. Like those lawyers, Carter was privately concerned about the outrages in his district but publicly silent. Abram would later judge him harshly for having failed that moral test in 1963. "What kind of man would stand aside?" he wondered in the 1970s. Carter "could have said something to the newspapers; at the very least, he could have told a few of his prominent friends that a sedition trial was an absurdity and ought to be viewed as such, but the state senator totally ignored the travesty in his own county and

*Two years later, Freeman, then fourteen, was caught kissing her boyfriend, also black, inside a car. Sheriff Chappell ordered her arrested on the trumped-up charge of "fornication" and carted her off again to jail. Freeman described the ordeal as even worse than her forty-three days in prison in 1963, when at least she could sing and chant with her friends.

concentrated instead on plotting his own future."

Senator Carter could indeed have contacted the press and other influential Georgians; the likely futility of speaking out hardly absolves him of his public silence. He was the kind of moderate Martin Luther King Jr. had in mind that April when he wrote in his classic "Letter from Birmingham Jail" that he had "almost reached the regrettable conclusion that the Negro's great stumbling block in the stride toward freedom is not the White Citizens' Council-er or the Ku Klux Klanner but the white moderate who is more devoted to 'order' than to justice."

Attorney General Robert F. Kennedy didn't intervene in the sedition case, either. In fact, RFK — tacking briefly rightward — chose this moment to announce the indictment of Albany activists on other charges. The civil rights workers jailed for sedition weren't released until the end of 1963, when a federal district court found in their favor.

Throughout this period, President Kennedy remained the closest any politician ever came to being Carter's role model: moderate, energetic, charismatic. On November 22, 1963, Carter was in the warehouse when he learned of Kennedy's assassination. He knelt on the steps and prayed, then cried for the first time in the ten years since his father died. The following weekend, he recalled being sickened at a Georgia Tech football game when some fans booed during a moment of silence for the slain president.

When news of JFK's assassination was announced in Chip's classroom at Plains High School, the teacher said, "Good!" and students applauded. Chip picked up a chair and flung it in the teacher's direction. In the principal's office,

Mr. Sheffield expressed his sympathies over the president's death and sent Chip home, where Jimmy and Rosalynn declined to punish him.

In the fall of 1964, a full decade after the *Brown* decision, Americus High School was finally desegregated. Four black students enrolled without incident, according to the newspapers. In truth, they — like the white Koinonia students — were constantly harassed. White students spit in their food, kicked books out of their arms, flung Coke bottles at their backs. At graduation, the Koinonia students and black students were booed and — as they left school for the last time — pelted with rocks and bricks.

After he signed the Civil Rights Act of 1964, President Johnson told his aide Bill Moyers, "I think we just delivered the South to the Republican Party for a long time to come." His 1964 campaign manager in Sumter County was Lillian Carter, who found her car covered with epithets written in soap and the car antenna bent. At home, she received threatening calls and hateful notes. When Chip's Johnson-Humphrey button was ripped off his shirt pocket, his father told him to "put it back on again, if you want to wear it — and learn to box."

LBJ crushed Arizona senator Barry Goldwater nationally but Goldwater beat Johnson by a 2-to-1 margin in Sumter County, and Howard "Bo" Callaway became the first Republican elected to the US House of Representatives from Georgia since Reconstruction. Callaway was a smart, wealthy army veteran from southwest Georgia — similar enough to Carter to become his main rival in politics.

The summer of 1965 was once again tumultuous in Carter's district. A quietly defiant black college student named Mary Kate Bell decided to run for justice of the peace, the first black candidate in the area in nearly a century. On July 20 she and three fellow activists stood in the "whites only" line as they prepared to help register new voters. They were arrested and jailed, and Bell lost the election. Hosea Williams of the SCLC and John Lewis of SNCC held a press conference announcing that Americus would be the next Selma, where four months earlier — after Lewis and others were beaten on the Edmund Pettus Bridge — Martin Luther King Jr. led a historic march to the Alabama state capitol in Montgomery.

A week after the Americus arrests, two black youths killed a twenty-one-year-old white Marine Corps recruit, Andrew Whatley, in a drive-by shooting, only an hour after a group of about twenty white youths had stood on the same corner, yelling "Nigger! Nigger!" and hurling stones and bottles at passing black motorists and pedestrians. The next day, nearly a dozen black men and boys were beaten and pistol-whipped by a white mob as twenty-five state and local policemen watched and did nothing. Suddenly Americus was a big national story again. More than seven hundred robed Klansmen marched through town in the largest Klan rally in the South in many years. Afterward, black demonstrators carried signs reading, "White sheets don't frighten Negroes no more."

A young reporter for a local Atlanta station, Tom

Brokaw, arrived to find Sumter County full of armed whites in passing cars shouting, "We'll kill any nigger who marches tonight!" When he asked a black teenager if she was scared, the girl replied that she was terrified but would march anyway. "We have no other choice," she said. Brokaw's report from Americus made NBC's *The Huntley-Brinkley Report* and helped launch his storied career; he later remembered the interview as one of the most memorable he ever conducted, though he never learned the girl's name.

Jimmy Carter was scared, too: scared of being connected to the civil rights movement. He felt he had no other choice but to stay silent unless he wanted to see his political career — and quite possibly his business — torched. The one place he did speak out was in his church, now caught up in the racial unrest. The issue was not whether black worshippers could be members of white churches but whether they could enter them at all.

On August 1 newspapers around the world carried a photo of the pastor of the First Baptist Church of Americus with his arms across his chest as he and a group of grim-faced men, including Carter's close friend John Pope, blocked a half dozen peaceful activists of both races, kneeling in prayer, from entering the church. The following week, a larger group led by John Lewis was also rebuffed at the church door in Americus and arrested.

Down the road at the Plains Baptist Church, the deacons looked to Scripture to justify their racism, nodding in agreement as visiting pastors selected verses that "proved" segregation was not just condoned by God but ordered by Him. The governing board, chaired by Jimmy's cousin

Hugh, posted ushers at the door to prevent unknown outsiders and any blacks from entering. Hugh then scheduled a vote on the matter for mid-August.

On the day before the congregation was to vote, the Carters were at the wedding of a relative in Roswell, Georgia, outside Atlanta. As Jimmy gathered his family to return for the climactic meeting, Rosalynn pleaded with him to stay away. She thought speaking out would hurt their business, not to mention the congressional campaign they were planning — a view that later embarrassed her.

The next morning, 250 people crowded the church, far more than usual. Jimmy insisted on a full debate before the vote, though few said much. He found himself standing alone against the other eleven deacons, all of whom recommended approving the resolution barring "Negroes and other agitators" at the door. Lillian remembered the vein in her son's temple throbbing when he rose to speak. Jimmy reminded the congregation that black worshippers had previously been admitted to the church for funerals — including that of his father — and other special occasions. "This is not my house; this is not your house," he said. He and they could keep anyone out of their houses if they wanted. "But I for one will never stand in the doors of this church and keep anyone out."

The vote went 54 to 6 in favor of the resolution, with only Jimmy, Rosalynn, Chip, Jeff, Lillian, and a church member Jimmy described as "an older deaf man who didn't know what was going on" dissenting. But 190 people abstained, which Carter found encouraging. When he called several of the abstainers the next day, some of the younger ones told him that they were with him but afraid to say so in public.

Americus was roiling, with marches, beatings, and arrests (usually of civil rights workers) on a near-daily basis. On the same day that President Johnson signed the Voting Rights Act — August 7, 1965 — comedian and social activist Dick Gregory led a voter registration march to the Sumter County Courthouse. Local officials had tried to slow implementation of the new federal law, but Hugh Carter and other racist white registrars could do nothing as more than 1,700 black citizens crowded into the courthouse to register to vote. There is no record of Senator Jimmy Carter commenting publicly on the landmark bill that, in 1976, while campaigning for president, he would call "the best thing that happened to the South in my lifetime."

Warren Fortson, Sumter County attorney, witnessed the registration drive from his office in the county courthouse. For months, Fortson had tried to organize a biracial committee to talk about the many issues raised by the Sumter Movement. When Americus city officials refused to create such a body, Fortson moved forward on his own, with the quiet backing of Carter and other local moderates, as well as Governor Sanders. But the committee sputtered amid white opposition: while black clergy and civil rights activists were eager to take part, only five white people agreed to serve, and Carter was not among them. Now a petition signed by more than a thousand segregationists called for Fortson's removal as county attorney; his defenders mustered only three hundred names on a petition of support.

On August 3 Carter made his first appearance in the *New York Times,* quoted as saying that Fortson had been the victim of a whisper campaign and was wrongly accused of being a Communist and a member of the NAACP. Fortson said later that Carter "caught a lot of unshirted hell" for his remarks.

When the Carters took a three-week family vacation in Mexico, rumors spread about their whereabouts. Their neighbor Thad Jones Sr. improperly obtained a list of Carter's customers from the US Department of Agriculture (USDA) office in Americus. He and another member of the large local chapter of the John Birch Society, the extreme and fast-growing anti-Communist group, then spread the rumor that the Carter family had left Plains to attend a Communist training camp for civil rights workers in northern Alabama.

After they returned, Carter found that most of his customers were now boycotting his warehouse. He confronted Jones with hotel receipts from Mexico and then spent two weeks crisscrossing southwest Georgia reassuring regular customers that he had simply been on vacation. Years later, several told reporters they were sorry to have been led astray by "Bircher" lies about the Carters.

With his neighbors already "looking at me askance," Jimmy refrained from commenting further on the national story in his backyard. When Gene Roberts, an Atlanta-based reporter for the *New York Times,* approached Carter's Warehouse, hoping to talk to the state senator, "instead of letting me in, he latched the screen door" and mumbled that he had "nothing to say" to anyone from the paper.

Warren Fortson acknowledged later that Carter

was "ducking," but he didn't blame him. As an attorney, Fortson was expected to defend unpopular clients, and his skill-based profession allowed him to move to Atlanta and continue practicing law after he was ostracized in Sumter County. (The president of Georgia Southwestern State University and the manager of a local radio station were also driven out of town for their integrationist views and found work elsewhere.) By contrast, Carter's business was rooted in his community, which meant that the stakes were higher for him. And then there were the political realities. "It wouldn't have done him any good to go around screaming for integration as a state senator," Fortson said later.

"Apartheid reigned," Carter said later of life in the pre–civil rights South. And it did so without much objection from Carter, whose public silence, while common, spoke volumes. His conduct was reminiscent of Abraham Lincoln's response in the 1850s to seeing fugitive slaves forcibly returned to their masters: "I bite my lip and keep quiet."

Jimmy and Rosalynn would compensate for their silence amid entrenched racism with good works in the governor's mansion, the White House, and after his presidency. In doing so, they were models for every white American struggling to make up for past inaction on issues of racial justice. But they also cut their community some slack. "Plains was and is a wonderful place to live," Carter wrote in the 1990s. He had learned there how to find the humanity in people who had done wrong — useful training for the persistent, nonjudgmental diplomacy in which he would excel.

# 10
# THE GREASY POLE

In 1965 Carter was newly reelected to the state senate, which would turn out to be the only reelection of his political career. His "intense ambition," as he described it, brought long days and late nights that he admitted got in the way of family life. But he was restless and eager again to climb the greasy pole. He set his sights on beating Bo Callaway — already making a national reputation in the GOP — when he ran for reelection to the House in 1966.

If Callaway had the seat, the money, and the statewide connections, Carter had something else that would prove a great asset in politics: he was always well prepared. By this time, when asked his profession, he sometimes avoided "farmer" or "businessman" in favor of "planner." Carter had served on several planning boards over the years, and in 1964 he founded the clumsily named West Central Georgia Area Planning and Development Commission. The commission eventually handled grant applications for highways, sewers, emergency services, and other projects in eight counties and twenty-two cities, including plans for the ruins of the notorious Confederate prison at Andersonville, a grim Sumter County tourist site that

Carter helped incorporate into the national park system.

Carter's planning duties — for which he received no pay — brought him occasionally to Washington, DC, where he would seek grants for his state. He helped launch and supervise local Georgia offices of Great Society programs like Head Start and Neighborhood Youth Corps. He was constantly advising towns and counties on the guts of government — land use, consolidating services, disaster preparedness, tax structures — all subjects on which he turned himself into something of an expert. By age forty, Carter had made a name for himself in business and political circles statewide.

Carter's belief in planning, which would shape his entire political career, didn't always account for the old military maxim that plans work only until first contact with the enemy. (Or boxer Mike Tyson's line that "everyone has a plan till they get punched in the mouth.") But overall, his engineering skills and Greatest Generation drive served him and the public well. He understood that the complexities of the modern world demanded disciplined planning for the future, not political improvisations to hold on to power.

In that spirit, Carter prepared methodically for the congressional race. He arranged tutorials on national issues with a University of Georgia professor; he and Rosalynn took lessons on how to improve their memories for names; and he settled on a strategy of distancing himself from national Democrats, especially President Johnson. Instead, he proclaimed, "I'm a Dick Russell Democrat," identifying himself with Georgia's segregationist senior US senator, Richard B. Russell, revered at home and in Washington for his wise counsel (in the 1950s, he had been Lyndon Johnson's mentor) and support for the military. Carter defined himself this way right through Russell's death in 1971; it was a means of signaling that he was a serious man who would make traditional Georgians proud.

Then, in May 1966, came a thunderbolt in Georgia politics. Bo Callaway announced that he was giving up his House seat to run for governor. He was assured of the Republican nomination and viewed the Democratic field as weak. (The popular incumbent, Carl Sanders, was by law not allowed to succeed himself.) With no other prominent Republicans in southwest Georgia, this meant that Carter could likely have won the congressional seat almost without opposition. But Carter's competitive juices got flowing, and he made an abrupt decision. "You'd better get a chair," he advised Rosalynn before telling her he would now run for governor, too. Rosalynn had looked forward to moving to Washington, but Jimmy was adamant. Sensing an opening, and in the grip of his intense rivalry with Callaway, Carter assembled his small crew of volunteers at a Holiday Inn in Albany and persuaded them it was worth the risk.

This was a pivotal moment in Carter's career. As fellow state senator Bobby Rowan said later, "You'd never have heard of Jimmy Carter outside of Georgia if Bo hadn't switched."

The front-runner in the 1966 gubernatorial race was Ellis Arnall, an FDR protege who, as a moderate one-term governor in the mid-1940s, had scaled back prison chain gangs and made Georgia the first state in the country to lower the voting age to eighteen. Now sixty-four and determined to make a comeback, Arnall viewed Carter, who largely shared his politics, as a spoiler. His best bet to win the nomination was to be the only moderate and watch the segregationist Democrats split the redneck vote. Years later, Arnall confessed that he used intermediaries to draw a flashy segregationist, Lester Maddox, into the race. (Maddox denied this.) Maddox, a perennial fringe candidate, ran Atlanta's popular Pickrick restaurant, where he had won national publicity in 1964 for chasing out three black seminary students with a pickaxe handle, which made him a hero to racists across the country.

Carter jumped into the race just twelve weeks before the September Democratic primary. From the start, he ran a disciplined, ideologically hazy campaign focused on integrity and reform — a pattern for the future. But there were signs of his inner progressive struggling to get out. Without drawing attention to it, he campaigned a bit in black churches — one of the first times a white statewide candidate in Georgia did so.

Rosalynn was shy and so nervous that when she arrived at even a small campaign reception, she would lock herself in the bathroom and rehearse her two minutes of lines over and over. Outside a shoe store in Washington, Georgia, she suffered what she later considered to be the worst political experience of her life when a tobacco-chewing Callaway supporter spat on her. Rosalynn usually campaigned alongside her mother-in-law until a couple of weeks before the primary, when Lillian left for what would become a life-changing experience.

Bored with her job managing a small nursing home, Lillian was lying in bed one night watching

Johnny Carson on the *Tonight* show when an ad for the Peace Corps caught her attention: "Age is no barrier," the TV spot said. Lillian was sixty-seven years old and, as she later admitted, suffering from "white guilt." She knew it was safer for her to help dark-skinned people in Africa or India than in Sumter County.

Dispatched to Vikhroli, a village near Bombay, she was assigned to visit families to discuss vasectomies and other forms of birth control. At first, she was desperately homesick. "I couldn't touch the dirt, the blood, the lice, the leprosy," she remembered. "I hadn't the strength to bear the horrible cruelty and indifference." But after praying on a hillside, Lillian found a fortitude she had not thought she possessed. She became a physician's assistant, administering hundreds of inoculations a day, mostly to children. "I have never been so happy," she wrote to her family.

The 1966 election was when Jimmy began assembling the team that would take him to the White House a decade later. All were younger than Carter — often much younger — except for Charlie Kirbo, whose avuncular counsel he came to depend on. Kirbo, who already believed Carter could be president, helped ease his way into the Atlanta establishment, where the increasingly prominent state senator impressed Anne Cox Chambers, owner of Cox newspapers, which published the morning *Atlanta Constitution* and the afternoon *Atlanta Journal.* A bright Kirbo protege, Jack Watson, rode his motorcycle down to Plains and also hit it off with Carter. Touring Berry College, Jimmy met an effusive banker from nearby Calhoun named Bert Lance, who, a few years later, would become his most intimate friend.

One day Jerry Rafshoon, a sharp-witted Jewish adman, heard Carter's radio spots. "Jimmy Carter is his name, Jimmy Carter is his name, Jimmy Carter is his name, number one for governor," a bad country singer twanged. Rafshoon almost drove off the road. "Their ads were beyond horrible," he remembered. He pitched Carter on turning his youth and underdog status into assets with an innovative cinéma vérité commercial highlighting a populist message that began, "*They* say he can't win. *They* say he doesn't have the backing . . ." Rafshoon would handle all of Carter's ads for the rest of his political career.

In a small audience at the Albany Elks Club one weekend, a twenty-one-year-old black-haired University of Georgia student watched the long-shot candidate intently. Carter's voice was so soft and halting that Hamilton Jordan could barely hear. His quick smile struck Jordan as "unnatural and even forced," and his prepared remarks were weak. But he was terrific in the question-and-answer session. When Jordan approached the stage to talk, Carter was immediately impressed by the college student's mind, able to condense complex subjects into clear, simple points. The next week, Carter called him just after sunrise and asked him to organize students at the University of Georgia. At first, Jordan said no. He already had a summer job spraying mosquitoes. But he soon signed on.

For Carter, Jordan fit somewhere between beloved fourth son and respected consigliere. Jordan's charm and humor attracted scores of bright young people to Carter's side; he was a gifted political strategist with an exceptional ability to

217

convince supporters to subordinate their egos to the cause. For most of the next fifteen years, they spoke every day. Carter came to believe that "no other human being" had affected his career more profoundly or beneficially than Hamilton Jordan.

In the summer of 1966 Carter developed into an effective retail campaigner: smart, warm, and looking like a southern-fried Kennedy (at least from a certain angle), a resemblance he traded on then and later. "I can project an image of youth and vigor," he told donors, the latter word a Kennedy favorite. But the Kennedys remained a liability in rural areas. Under the headline "Carter Denies Association with Kennedys," the defensive candidate insisted, "I have never met Bobby Kennedy, talked to him in any way, or talked to him through an intermediary."

By Labor Day, Carter was moving up fast in the polls; he seemed surprisingly well positioned to make the runoff required under Georgia law if no one received more than 50 percent of the vote. He did well in a televised debate and — with the help of Jordan's inspired campus organizing — became the favorite candidate of young Georgians, who saw Arnall as a has-been.

Then, shortly before the September primary, racial strife in a black neighborhood of Atlanta left sixteen people injured. Stokely Carmichael, just emerging nationally as the leader of the Black Power movement, dominated the news for a few days. Carter backed Carmichael's arrest, but the incident helped Lester Maddox.

Even so, as supporters awaited the returns at the Dinkler Plaza in Atlanta, it looked as if Carter would finish a strong second behind Arnall and be in the runoff, which would make him the favorite to be elected. After eleven o'clock, late-reporting rural counties, including Sumter, began going heavily for Maddox. With Callaway already nominated at the Republican state party convention, large numbers of newly minted Republicans had returned to the party of their birth on primary day to vote for Maddox. The final tally showed Carter in third, 2.6 points behind Maddox and far behind Arnall, who would have won a majority and avoided a runoff if Carter hadn't siphoned off liberal votes.

Inside the Carter suite, the mood turned funereal. A gaunt Carter, who had dropped twenty-two pounds in four months running himself ragged, was stunned that he had come in behind "a clown" who was disgracing Georgia. He ran into his driver, John Girardeau, in the hallway, and they hugged in tears.

After midnight, Carter piled his family in the car and drove off without thanking his supporters or even his personal staff. He didn't formally concede for two days.

A couple of weeks later, he called Jordan to apologize for his ungraciousness. But he was bitter. "I'm tired of people saying I ran a good campaign," he said. "It was not good enough because I lost. I never intend to lose another election." In the months that followed, he told anyone in earshot, "You show me a good loser, and I'll show you a loser." When Jordan advised Carter to run for lieutenant governor in 1970, Carter replied, "I'm going to run for governor if I don't get but two votes — mine and Rosalynn's."

"You'll get at least three votes," Jordan told him.

Carter immediately began shifting to the right.

In the runoff between Arnall and Maddox, Carter — leery of alienating Maddox voters he might need four years later — endorsed neither, a decision he later tried to hide.

Arnall grew overconfident and didn't campaign hard in the runoff, which Maddox — consolidating the segregationist vote — won narrowly. Had Carter urged his supporters to vote for Arnall, Maddox might well have been defeated. After the runoff, facing the prospect of either Callaway or Maddox — two ardent segregationists — as governor, Arnall agreed to entreaties to run as a write-in candidate in the general election. But he was now so pessimistic about the outcome that he barely campaigned. Once again, Carter declined to endorse anyone.

In November, Callaway beat Maddox, but Arnall drew just enough write-in votes to keep the Republican from winning a majority. Under the Georgia State Constitution at the time, if no candidate received a majority, the state legislature decided the winner. On January 10, 1967, the Georgia General Assembly, firmly under Democratic control, elected Lester Maddox governor.

Jimmy Carter was devastated.

# 11

# BORN AGAIN

After the 1966 loss, Carter's friend Peter Bourne, a physician, described him as "profoundly depressed." Cousin Hugh remembered seeing Jimmy wandering aimlessly across his peanut fields, shoulders hunched, looking down at the ground or up at the sky.

He was forty-two years old and had given up a sure-thing congressional seat, accrued debts of $66,000, and twice refused to stand up against a racist he detested. Carter knew he was lucky — strong marriage, nice family, wealthy by local standards — but for months, nothing eased his pain. "Everything I did was not gratifying," he recalled. "When I succeeded in something, I got no pleasure out of it. When I failed at something, it was a horrible experience for me." It was, he said, the lowest and most confusing period of his life.

Much later, Carter wrote, "I am embarrassed now to admit that I was so proud and arrogant that I could not believe God would let this person [Maddox] prevail and become the governor of our state." God's mysterious ways confused him. "Heartbroken and discouraged, I felt my life was a failure," he confessed. "And I was disillusioned about my religious faith."

On the surface, Carter had led a devout life. After teaching Sunday school at Annapolis, he often presided at holiday services in the torpedo room of submarines. In port on Sundays, he made a habit of wandering into the first Christian church service he could find, even taking communion at Catholic Mass. Back in Plains, Carter taught the men's Sunday school class in the basement of the Plains Baptist Church, where he avoided explaining that not everything in the Bible was literally true.

In the early 1950s, he began experiencing doubts about God. He viewed his father's death as a "harsh act" of "the God of the Old Testament, a stern, judgmental figure, very different from the loving, forgiving Jesus I knew from the Gospels." Carter later described this period as a "torturous time of searching."

His theological breakthrough came slowly, he said, from an intense period of reading and contemplation. He learned what he considered a simple yet profound truth: God never changed. While he remained a classic New Testament man throughout his life, Carter saw the fusion of the Hebrew Bible and the Gospels as critical. "The turning point for me was the realization that there was no difference between the God of the Old Testament and the God of the New Testament, between the perfect love of Jesus and that of God the Creator," Carter wrote. He knew "the Judeo-Christian tradition" was a modern construct, but he embraced it.

Unlike some Christians, Carter saw no direct

connection between service and salvation. He didn't think people who worked with the poor got into heaven faster. But he believed the example that Christ set centered on love that is self-sacrificing and embraces the despised and dispossessed. Reporters would later joke about Carter's habit of wearing a big belt buckle over his jeans with the letters "JC" instead of his full initials, "JEC." In fairness, he wasn't trying to be Jesus Christ — at least not most of the time — but to follow in his path as much as he could.

Marooned in a town with no library and few people with intellectual interests, Jimmy sent away for volumes of theology by authors of many denominations, including Karl Barth, Martin Buber, Hans Küng, and Emil Brunner. The American theologian Paul Tillich eased his spiritual struggle with his notion that "doubt is not the opposite of faith; it is one element of faith." Dietrich Bonhoeffer, the ecumenical German pastor killed by the Nazis just before the end of the Second World War, was a particular inspiration. His "personal courage has made me feel inadequate in my Christian life," Carter wrote later. Even as he detached service from salvation, he returned again and again to Bonhoeffer's belief that "faith without works is not faith at all but a simple lack of obedience to God." It might be the closest he ever came to a philosophy of life.

Carter was not a scholar of philosophy or theology; Norman Mailer once tested his knowledge of Søren Kierkegaard, whom Carter said he admired, and found it superficial. But his interest in deeper questions was sincere. In early 1965 his friend and state senate colleague Bill Gunter lent him a copy of the recently published *Reinhold Niebuhr on Politics,* and Carter soon described it as "my political bible." Niebuhr was Bonhoeffer's mentor at New York's Union Theological Seminary in 1930 and one of the most influential American theologians of the twentieth century. He wrote that "the sad duty" of politics is "to establish justice in a sinful world." This became Jimmy's handy way of connecting his political ambitions to genuine spiritual commitments. He repeated the line often throughout his political career. On a more personal level, Carter found himself moved by Niebuhr's conviction that "living faith always involves love" and by what Niebuhr called "the creativity of anxiety." Over time, Jimmy interpreted this to mean creatively using sin and setbacks as the engines of self-improvement, prayer, learning, and social justice — the touchstones of his life.

At Thanksgiving 1966, Jimmy welcomed a visit from his sister Ruth Carter Stapleton, who felt she could help her brother overcome his depression and crisis of faith. Ruth herself had faced personal demons in the early 1960s, when she went into a tailspin as a harried wife and mother of four in Fayetteville, North Carolina. Reviewing her life, Ruth decided she "hated" her parents for overprotecting her. She told Lillian that she was taking "an emotional leave of absence from you" for a year — no visits or calls.

Ruth eventually went back to school for a theology degree and tried to get at the root of her pain. Preferring Henry David Thoreau to Baptists, she fashioned an early New Age combination of philosophy, religion, and psychology that she called "inner healing," which she described as "communicating love to the negative repressed aspects in a human being." Ruth bristled when described as a faith healer — she did no laying on of hands — and preferred to focus on personal and spiritual growth.*

Jimmy was one of the first people she tried to help. Separated from her for decades by geography, he had not in recent years been as close to Ruth as he was to Gloria. But now, brother and sister took a walk on their property in Webster County and sat under a tree discussing Jimmy's misfortunes. He felt he had been prideful in the 1966 campaign and had paid for it. Carter wrote later that he told his sister his political life was over — "God has rejected me through the people's vote" — but that he felt making more money was not a worthy aspiration.

When Ruth replied that his defeat would bring a better life and quoted James 1:12 ("Blessed are those who persevere under trial"), "I responded with bitterness," he remembered. "I won't tell you my exact phrase, but I thought it was a bunch of crap."

Ruth told him that her own hurt in North Carolina got so bad that "I had to forget every-

*Over the next decade, Ruth would become a popular lecturer and best-selling author of self-help books for spiritual seekers suffering through broken marriages, crime, alcoholism, and other problems. She advised women to dress well and wear makeup to attract men and feel better about themselves, and she took her own advice. Describing sexuality as "the power of God" helped grow her flock. She even became popular with nuns.

thing I was" and commit completely to Jesus. Jimmy wondered, "What can I do to have this closeness to God?" Ruth recalled asking her brother if Christ came before his family, his business, and his political career. Jimmy said yes to all three but insisted that he had been in politics to serve. When she pressed, he said finally, "I would really rather have the fullness of Christ in my life than be president," an answer Ruth said she didn't fully appreciate at the time — when not even the family realized that his political ambitions extended all the way to the White House.

They then knelt on pine needles and prayed together. Ruth claimed that Jimmy rededicated himself right there to putting Christ first and wept; Jimmy later denied weeping and never confirmed the media narrative in 1976 that this was when he was "born again."

"At the time, I rejected her advice, but I later came to accept it," he wrote. He saw that Ruth's mystical approach didn't match his own religious temperament. While he admitted later to envying the spiritual intensity of "charismatic" Christians like Ruth, who could summon the Holy Spirit and — along with her husband, Robert — speak in tongues, his faith was quieter and more like that of Tillich, who described religion as a "search for truth."

Baptists often divide conversion experiences into two types: those of Paul and Timothy. Paul converted on the road to Damascus; Timothy came to a slower understanding of Christ's importance in his life. Pastor Nelson Price, who became Carter's most important spiritual counselor in the mid-1970s, felt Carter was "a Timothy." Jimmy didn't buy the traditional Baptist view that believers are "born again" when they are baptized as children. "Being born again didn't happen to me when I was 11," Carter wrote. "For me, it has been an evolutionary thing. Rather than a flash of light or a sudden vision of God speaking, it involved a series of steps that have brought me steadily closer to Christ."

The next step after his walk with Ruth came one Sunday in early 1967, when Pastor Robert Harris of the Plains Baptist Church preached a sermon about the Apostle Peter being imprisoned by King Herod. He told his congregation in passing that two Southern Baptist missionaries were in jail in Fidel Castro's Cuba on trumped-up charges. Harris asked, "If you were arrested for being a Christian, would there be enough evidence to convict you?"

The question troubled Carter. "I began to think about the questions the prosecutors might ask me: 'What have you actually done for others in the name of Christ?' 'How many of the very poor families in Plains do you really know?' 'If you're not a Christian, why are you a member of the church?' " The evidence was thin. "I finally decided that if arrested and charged with being a committed follower of God, I could probably talk my way out of it! It was a sobering thought," he wrote.

Jimmy's spiritual anxieties were eased some by circumstances at home. Rosalynn had become pregnant at thirty-nine, thanks to successful surgery to remove a large but benign uterine tumor. Amy Carter was born October 19, 1967. Decades later, Amy said that, around age thirty, she learned "they weren't planning on having me," but everyone was delighted. Her father and much-older brothers doted on her. "She had four fathers," Rosalynn remembered.

Carter later identified 1967 and 1968 as the period when he was gradually born again. In recommitting to Christ and running for governor simultaneously, he seemed to be arguing to himself that he was doing the Lord's work — that, as he told a church publication a few years later, God "wants me to be the best politician I can possibly be." The way to keep this from being a mere rationalization was to connect it to social justice, a la Niebuhr, and to stay grounded by going door-to-door witnessing for Christ. This would be a form of penance for the complacent, self-satisfied approach to his faith that Ruth had helped him identify.

Carter felt he couldn't easily do missionary work in Georgia, where he had become well known, so in May 1968 he joined a lay mission team for two weeks in Lock Haven, Pennsylvania, an industrial town in the mountains. Local volunteers called names out of the Lock Haven phone book and found a hundred people willing to receive visiting Southern Baptists. Dreading the trip, Carter almost backed out, but he made himself fulfill his commitment — a way to extend his spiritual self without putting anything on the line politically in that tumultuous year.

The missionaries went out in teams of two, like Jesus' disciples. Carter's partner was a Texan in his seventies named Milo Pennington, who prayed with him in the car or on the sidewalk before they knocked on the door. If someone was home, Jimmy introduced himself by saying, "I'm a peanut farmer from Georgia." Pennington said that Carter "was never one to talk politics. We were just witnessing for the Lord." At first, Carter thought Pennington was fumbling in his presentation of his own religious experience but then realized that people weren't looking for a smooth appeal. He was amazed at the emotional responses to Pennington's personal stories. Carter, by contrast, was not a natural. "I realized very quickly I didn't have much testimony to give," he remembered. "It was very difficult for me."

Sometimes Milo and Jimmy witnessed beyond the preselected names. As they climbed the stairs of an apartment building one day, they heard cursing from above, ventured farther up, and arrived to find an amused madam of a small brothel and the three prostitutes she supervised. The madam invited them in and spoke with them for two hours, confessing that she had been molested by her father. But when they returned the next day, she would not agree to "sin no more." A visit inside another apartment seemed to be going well until Carter and Pennington employed the standard line that "all of us are sinners," at which point an older woman yelled, "Not me! I don't transgress against God!" — and threw them out.

More often, the pair heard professions of faith that Carter found exhilarating. One woman, Thelma Farwell, invited them for dinner with her family. After he became governor, Carter wrote Farwell that Lock Haven would always have a place in his heart because it was "where I first experienced in a personal and intense way the presence of the Holy Spirit in my life."

The explosive national and world events of 1968 seemed to have little impact on Carter. Over the summer, he spoke to several Georgia church groups about his Lock Haven experience and corresponded with Pennington, signing his letters "Yours in Christ." He traveled a few times to a neighborhood of southwestern Atlanta that was transitioning from all white to all black, and tried unsuccessfully to convince the whites not to abandon their churches.

In the fall, Carter was asked if he would spend a week over Thanksgiving witnessing in an impoverished Spanish neighborhood in Springfield, Massachusetts, this time with a small group from Plains and the surrounding area. During the 1,100-mile drive north, the conversation turned earnest. Jimmy confided that he just wished he could do something to help all the people of the world. Then he went further, expressing a serene confidence that he could do so. "I have no idea of what it is to say, 'It can't be done' or that 'I can't do it,' " Carter said, according to Edwin Timmerman, the music director in the Plains Baptist Church. He told them he had a simple explanation for that confidence: Rosalynn. "She talks to me," he said.

The mission began with doors slammed in their faces. Retreating on Thanksgiving Day to a Springfield suburb, the Plains contingent was detained briefly by police for soliciting without a license. At the station house, they convinced the duty officers that they were legitimate Baptist missionaries and left them a Bible. Carter's roommate at the $3-a-night Springfield YMCA was Jerome Etheridge, an agronomist and fellow Sunday school teacher from Plains who would later devote his life to Baptist missions abroad.*

*Etheridge, who had no abilities as a preacher, moved to Togo, where he dug hundreds of wells and helped

230

At night, they would pray together. "The first time I just bowed my head, but Jimmy got down on his knees, and then I got down on mine," Etheridge recalled.

Jimmy's door-to-door partner was Eloy Cruz, the soft-spoken Cubanborn pastor of a small church in Brooklyn. One day Carter and Cruz met an elderly couple taking care of a sleeping baby. They learned that the young mother of the baby had died suddenly in a freak medical accident, and her grieving young husband — the father of the infant — had gone berserk, threatening to kill their baby and himself. Carter gave the old couple money to buy something in memory of the baby's mother.

On their final day, a landlord in a nearby building mentioned that one of his tenants was a despondent young father who had just lost his wife and relinquished his baby. Carter and Cruz went upstairs and knocked on his door. At first, the father would not open up, and Carter, standing in the hall, quoted Christ from Revelations 3:20:

"Behold, I stand at the door and knock: If any man hear my voice and open the door, I will come to him and sup with him and he with me."

When the father learned that the missionaries in the hall had provided the money for the gift in memory of his wife, he let them in. Years later, Carter remembered the young father's acceptance of Christ that day as "one of the most moving

organize eighty African churches. Carter pointed to him for decades as an example of how one person can make a difference.

religious experiences of my life."

Carter was amazed at how Eloy Cruz reached into human hearts. When he asked him what made his gentleness effective, Cruz said something that he would never forget. "Our Savior has hands which are very gentle," Cruz told him, "and He cannot do much with a man who is hard." Carter used this line often in public and considered Cruz "a great man." But in private he struggled with what he described as his own "impatience" — his hardness. Charles Kirbo, Carter's senior adviser, said early in the 1976 presidential campaign, "It's not often you see someone that gentle who's tough as nails inside." The comment was meant to show that the candidate was tough enough to stand up to the Soviet Union, but it also conveyed a truth about the difference between his public and private selves.

In sermons and speeches in the years ahead, Carter often quoted another line from Eloy Cruz: "A man needs only two loves in his heart: one is a love of God; the other is a love for the person who happens to be in front of you at any particular time." Carter interpreted that to mean that it's easy to love nameless innocent people far away in a foreign country, but "the difficulty comes when you try to love someone right in front of you — on the elevator, across the desk from you, whom you might be inclined to hate."

He would struggle with that "difficulty" for the rest of his life. On one level, he said that the 1968 missions helped make him love the strangers he met every day, rather than just see them transactionally as people who might vote for him, support his policies, or otherwise do his bidding. This warm integrity and soft-spoken friendliness —

conveying a sense that he was truly listening and genuinely cared — helped make Carter an effective diplomat and an unusually appealing politician to meet in person. Andrew Young wasn't alone in describing him as the best one-on-one campaigner he had ever seen.

At the same time, Jimmy's commitment to a Christian life often conflicted with his high standards and prickly temperament. Unlike Eloy Cruz, he often had strong private opinions about the personal qualities of the people right in front of him — especially when he thought they were selfish, incompetent, or lazy. He didn't subscribe to the humorist Will Rogers's maxim "I never met a man I didn't like." And if he wasn't seeking their votes, he didn't much care if they liked him. On her seventieth birthday in 1968, Lillian, about to leave India for home, wrote to her children that they should be "doing as much as you can for everybody, but not worrying if you don't please everyone." Jimmy took the advice to heart.

Not long after his return from Springfield, Jimmy volunteered to chair a weeklong Billy Graham Film Crusade in Americus. Graham, who didn't personally attend this crusade, always insisted that the audience for his events be integrated. This posed a problem for Carter, who was already running hard for governor, just as he had promised Hamilton Jordan the week after his loss in 1966. "Becoming the leader of an integrated religious crusade was not something designed to get me additional votes in a segregated state," he said later. But Carter embraced the challenge, even briefly desegregating the pulpit. During an organizing meeting, he surprised the audience by asking the Reverend Emory Smith, an assistant pastor from a black Baptist church in Americus, to come forward to deliver the closing prayer. More than 3,000 people saw the Graham film *The Restless Ones,* and Carter reported that 515 of them "made decisions for Christ."

Carter felt that his few weeks witnessing for Christ and organizing a Billy Graham crusade were only modest efforts. As he confessed in a speech to a religious group a few years later, "I have been a better businessman, father, politician, and governor than I am a Christian, because in my secular positions I have never been satisfied with mediocrity. I am at best a mediocre Christian." But Carter was never burdened by this knowledge; he knew he had been born again for a purpose beyond renewed faith: to be not a Christian soldier but a Christian citizen.

He would do so as a proud Baptist, but when the Carters worked as a team — as they would for the rest of their lives — they also embodied the ideals of Rosalynn's original creed: Methodism, inspired by founder John Wesley's admonition to "Do all the good you can, in all the ways you can, to all the people you can, as long as ever you can." Prominent Methodists who knew Carter noticed how much he had in common with the founder of their denomination, especially Wesley's righteousness, self-discipline, and indifference to discussion of personal matters.

And yet in 1968, Carter could hardly claim to be living a life of Wesleyan social action. His religious awakening came in the middle of the civil rights movement in the South, but he was conspicuously disconnected from it. As the black churches led the struggle, he hung back, preserving his political options.

In a year of protest and pain, Carter was focused on his inner life. Bill Gunter, his friend from the state senate, said that being born again gave him "a modicum of humility," which Jimmy knew he needed. He believed the "sin of pride" was "the number one sin," and he struggled with what he felt was his own aloofness. In the years ahead, he would often be more humble about his shortcomings as a Christian than he was in discussing his other inadequacies. Whatever the setbacks, his faith would now remain deep and strong. It leavened his intensity with serenity and his impatience with acceptance, at least some of the time.

# 12
# THE CODE WORD CAMPAIGN

The late 1960s saw Jimmy Carter fuse his faith and his ambition. It was almost as if going door-to-door for Christ for three weeks helped motivate him to go door-to-door for himself for three years. For Carter, faith had long been tied to hope. Now those hopes were not gauzy but diamond hard. With the help of Rosalynn and much of his family, he would make them real.

From 1967 through 1970, Carter ran a cunning, tireless, and conspicuously negative campaign for governor. While he didn't say anything explicitly racist, he figured out how to appeal to racist voters, a decision he claimed not to regret. But he knew it was not his finest hour. Nearly a half century later, after answering a few questions about his 1970 campaign, he asked softly, "Are we done talking about this yet?"

On April 4, 1968, Martin Luther King Jr. was assassinated in Memphis. Just outside Plains that night, the owner of the local tavern celebrated the civil rights leader's death by passing out free beer. Carter and his family grieved over King's death; he wished he had known him. But he did not join the 150,000 mourners who marched from the funeral at Ebenezer Baptist Church through the quiet streets of Atlanta. Nor did he respond publicly to the assassination in June of Robert F. Kennedy or attend the infamous 1968 Democratic National Convention, where his party broke apart as Chicago police clubbed antiwar protesters in the streets. It didn't recover until eight years later, when Carter's presidential nomination put a bandage on the still-festering wounds.

In Georgia, the heavy favorite for governor in 1970 was Carl Sanders. At forty-five, Sanders — four years out of the governor's mansion — was by far the most powerful Democrat in the state, thanks in part to his close relationship with J. B. Fuqua, a businessman and former state party chairman who bankrolled the party as it began facing defections to the GOP. Fuqua offered Sanders the use of his corporate jet and made sure that most of the state's other power brokers kicked in for the Sanders campaign. Many were waiting to cash in on his promise to launch the largest road-paving program in Georgia history.

Sanders's ace in the hole was his record. Every reputable Democrat, including Carter, agreed that he had been a good governor and would have been reelected easily in 1966 if the law allowed him to run for a second consecutive term. While his moderation on racial issues was controversial, no one disputed what he had done for Georgia's economy — a $187 million surplus — and for its standing in the nation. Voters especially appreciated that in the early 1960s, he built seventy small airports across the state (mostly with federal money) and — no small matter — helped bring Atlanta big-league baseball (the Braves), football (the Falcons), and basketball (the Hawks) for the first time.

Carter had little maneuvering room. To win the primary, he had to attract the working-class whites who had voted for Lester Maddox for governor in 1966 and George Wallace for president in 1968. (Running as an independent, Wallace had thrashed both Richard Nixon and Hubert Humphrey in Georgia.) But Carter couldn't move so far right that the black and liberal voters he needed against the Republican nominee would stay home in November. Then there was his conscience, which wouldn't allow him to criticize integration directly. His solution was to avoid explicit mention of race in favor of class-based populist appeals to Wallace voters, as well as overtures to moderates on education, the environment, and efficiency in government. It helped that Maddox had been a strident and clownish segregationist governor, best known for riding a bicycle backward for the cameras when he should have been in the capitol during important votes. Carter would spend more than thirty months on the road campaigning nearly full-time — a commitment to retail politics beyond that of any Georgia candidate in modern memory.

The day after he lost in 1966, Carter received a call from a taciturn forty-year-old entrepreneur from Savannah named David Rabhan. Not one for pleasantries — a trait he shared with Carter — Rabhan told Carter that if he ran again for governor, he would ferry him to campaign appearances in the new Cessna 310 twin-engine prop plane he piloted. It was the beginning of an odd and risky but genuine friendship that would extend more than a half century and shape the

238

lives of both men. Carter wouldn't have been elected governor or president without Rabhan — and Rabhan wouldn't have been freed from the Ayatollah Khomeini's prison without Carter.

Straitlaced Jimmy always appreciated eccentrics like his mother, and Rabhan was among them: an artist and gourmand who shaved his head and dressed in a light-blue flight suit and tennis shoes. Rabhan, who inherited or started more than thirty businesses, was part of the Jewish community that funded much of the civil rights movement. He knew the King family so well that he worked out of a small office attached to the Ebenezer Baptist Church when he was building a nursing home for black senior citizens in Atlanta.*

Rabhan became Carter's private pilot, saving him a fortune and allowing him to return again and again to remote Georgia towns that he needed to win. The Cessna often touched down on dirt strips, at night, with no more illumination than the headlights of cars driven by county police who would jump out of their vehicles just before the plane landed for fear of getting hit. Sometimes he and Carter landed so late in Atlanta that they would sleep in a one-bedroom luxury apartment Rabhan kept there. This soon became a classic Rabhan boast. "Jimmy and I are so close we used

*Rabhan recalled pitching Martin Luther King Jr. on starting a string of integrated nursing homes to fund the movement, with Rabhan providing the money and MLK Jr. the status that would bring in business. Rabhan claimed that in April 1968 he was on his way to Memphis to show King blueprints when he heard that he had been shot.

239

to sleep in the same bed," he told the *New York Times* in 1976, a comment that would haunt Rabhan a decade later.

In early 1970, when the campaign was broke and Carter faced a choice between selling his land and dropping out, Rabhan showed up at an airstrip and handed him a signed check with the amount left blank. David Gambrell, the campaign treasurer, was thrilled but feared Carter was doomed anyway. He told Rabhan: "You've bitten into a poison apple." Rabhan didn't care. He became Carter's top donor.

Carter had flown a little at Annapolis in the 1940s and, while unlicensed, was happy to take the Cessna's controls when Rabhan napped. One day when Carter was flying, the engines died, and the plane felt like it was going to go down over the Okefenokee Swamp. Carter was sure they were dead until Rabhan opened his eyes and flipped two fuel switches back on. It was just another of his practical jokes.

As in all of his campaigns, Carter never hired a campaign manager. He preferred that each of his top people report directly to him. Hamilton Jordan, only twenty-five and fresh from doing refugee work in South Vietnam, became the statewide field coordinator.* Jordan was proud that some counties featured two Carter organizations — one headed by conservatives who had supported Maddox four years earlier (and would do so again this

*While in Vietnam, Jordan was exposed to Agent Orange, a carcinogenic defoliant used by American forces to reduce the jungle cover of the enemy. He later developed three different deadly cancers.

240

time when he ran for lieutenant governor) and the other by liberal integrationists — and that they couldn't stand each other.

Carter read a research paper about southern populists sent by an incisive twenty-five-year-old doctoral candidate at Emory University named Joseph L. Powell Jr., better known as Jody. Powell grew up in Vienna, Georgia, where he became the charming but down-to-earth high school quarterback. As a senior at the US Air Force Academy, he was expelled after admitting to an honor code violation on a military history exam. Carter didn't hold it against him. Powell's shame helped make him unusually wise for his age — and always on the lookout for arrogance. Before long, he was hired as Carter's driver and personal assistant.

Traveling with Carter could be a chilly experience. When Powell made the mistake of sleeping until after sunrise on his second morning on the job, he realized that the irritated candidate had stepped into his maroon Chevy and driven off in the dark without him. Two days later, in McRae, Georgia, it happened again, and Powell had to hitchhike to catch up. Stranded in rural counties with few motels, they occasionally had to spend the night in the car, where a sleeping Powell's cigarette ashes once almost set Carter's pants on fire.

More often, they stayed in the homes of ordinary supporters. This would become a tradition in Carter campaigns, simultaneously connecting the candidate to the grassroots and — of critical importance to the tightwad in charge — saving money. Long before GPS, Carter was always certain he knew how to get anywhere in Georgia. "No matter what you thought, he had a better way," Powell remembered. The problem for anyone inclined to resent this trait was that Carter, who seethed and sulked but never screamed, was almost always right.

If Powell came to revere the candidate for his mind and his decency, Carter, in turn, bonded with his amusing young traveling companion. Powell shared his background and love of nature, could keep up with him intellectually, and was fiercely loyal. One day early on, Carter needed a press release and had no one around to prepare it. Powell, the driver, wrote it well and began handling press, too.

As Carter's press secretary in the governor's office and the White House, Powell had a much closer relationship with his boss than most communications aides do. It helped that he was well liked by reporters, who trusted him not to lie. After traveling for months with him during the 1976 presidential campaign, Carter spoke glowingly of a man who was about the age of his sons but had become a close friend. "Jody probably knows me better than anyone except my wife," the candidate said.

Carter's internal polls in late 1969 showed Sanders beating him by more than 30 points. But the polls also revealed that 80 percent of Georgians felt alienated from state government. Their big issues were taxes, school integration, and unfairness in highway construction. The key to winning, Jordan concluded, was to "concentrate heavily on the working man": older, white, male, middle-class voters who watched television instead of reading newspapers, favored George Wallace, and distrusted Atlanta "big shots."

Everything about the 1970 campaign and the ones that followed would be meticulously mapped out months and often years in advance — politics as an engineering project. Carter's TV ads included one featuring Miss Julia Coleman, shortly before her death, praising her former student. The campaign's symbol was the once-lowly peanut, which appeared in ads and spawned peanut necklaces, peanut lapel pins, peanut stationery.

All Carter campaigns from then on would be family affairs. "My wife is my coordinator," Carter liked to say. But this one also took place amid the "generation gap" afflicting so many American families in this period. While Jimmy was running for governor, his sons were sometimes finding ways to run away from him, even if they eventually returned to the fold. In 1968 Jack flunked out of Emory and was on the verge of doing the same at Georgia Southwestern when his father convinced him to join the navy. Two years in, he was asked if he smoked marijuana. Jack said yes and added that he had a couple of LSD tabs, too, just to make sure he would be discharged. His father was disappointed — "a little set in his mouth, the icy stare," Jack remembered — but didn't blow up at him. Jack soon married Judy Langford, who noticed that her father-in-law often barked instructions and his kids never talked back, except to say, "Yes, sir." Years later, after a long career as a family psychologist, Langford understood that Jimmy was simply repeating what had been done to him by his father and Admiral Rickover.

In 1969 Chip and his father hadn't spoken for a year, mostly because of Chip's drug use. They reconnected through Bob Dylan, whose album *The Times They Are A-Changin'* they had enjoyed

243

together. "We talked on the phone in Dylan verses because of the tensions," Chip remembered. Struggling at Georgia Southwestern, Chip drove home to Plains at two in the morning, went to the foot of his parents' bed, and informed them he was addicted to speed. Jimmy's response was to tell his nineteen-year-old son to cut his hair, put away his bell-bottom jeans, and buy a suit. After promoting Powell, he assigned Chip to be his part-time driver in the campaign; that way, he could be with him often enough to make sure he wasn't abusing drugs. Chip's decades of substance abuse had only begun, but he said later that his parents' intervention in 1969 saved his life.

The rest of the family pitched in, too. Jeff, an exceptionally bright teen, stumped often with Rosalynn. When Lillian got home from India, Jimmy felt his mother looked like a skeleton, but she recovered quickly and became an increasingly popular speaker on the campaign trail. Rosalynn's relationship with her mother-in-law improved as they crisscrossed the state together, visiting poultry plants, ladies' teas, and every radio station they could find.

Rosalynn began to notice that many voters mentioned mentally ill or "mentally retarded" relatives who weren't being treated right by the state. Jimmy had two cousins institutionalized at different points for mental illness, but the issue was less personal for her than substantive: Georgia needed community mental health clinics, and it wasn't getting the aid from Washington that it deserved. One day in Swainsboro, Rosalynn learned that Jimmy happened to be in town, too. She waited patiently in the receiving line before shaking hands with her bemused husband and asking with her puckish sweetness what he planned to do about mental health. He promised to do a lot — and did.

After more than two years of campaigning, Carter's formal announcement came on April 3, 1970, in the supreme court room of the state capitol. After promising to reform education and the tax system, he unloaded on Sanders for profiting off his governorship and spending his time "seeking favors with the Washington crowd just to make himself look important." On the trail, Carter offered what would later be called "dog whistles": code words such as "Georgia's heritage," "law and order," "local control," and "respect for Governor Wallace" that sounded innocuous on the surface but signaled to white voters that he was with them on racial issues. He was an early master of the practice.

Carter was also mastering the art of personal voter contact. One day at a factory gate, he told his old state senate colleague Bobby Rowan, "See that man coming here? I'm gonna get him to vote for me." Carter smiled broadly and tried not to ask any question that could be answered with a "No." Afterward, when the voter pledged his support, Carter shared his technique: "Notice how I didn't ask for his vote. I said, 'I want you to *consider* voting for me.'" At small and midsized campaign events, he would arrive early and park himself by the door so that he shook hands with every person entering the room — a simple and effective gesture neglected by many politicians, who convey their self-importance by keeping audiences waiting and often have only enough time to greet a few well-wishers.

For most of his political career, Carter wrote his own speeches, and it showed; the prepared texts were unadorned and usually uninspiring. He paused awkwardly in the wrong places and rarely showed passion or built to an effective oratorical crescendo. He was at his best answering questions, where his direct and enormously well-informed answers often won over skeptics. He would take off his jacket, roll up his sleeves, and respond with great clarity, intelligence, and responsiveness, often double-checking with the questioner that the query had been answered before moving on with a grin. Honing his performance at hundreds of campaign appearances between 1966 and 1970 gave him a huge, unappreciated advantage in the retail politics of early primary and caucus states when he ran for president.

Carter might not have wanted to talk about race on the campaign trail, but events kept intervening. In December 1969 a liberal federal court decision changed the politics of integration across the South. By ordering Atlanta to desegregate its schools by the time classes began in the fall of 1970, the court set up a new battle between the judiciary and school districts, with the once-aggressive Justice Department on the sidelines — where President Nixon wanted it.

This was the beginning of the end of the dream of fully integrated schools in the South. When courts began ordering that children be bused across town to achieve integration, whites quickly pulled their kids out of public schools and placed them in white "Christian academies" rather than have them share classrooms with black students.

Millions of middle-class and affluent white parents have sent their children to these overwhelmingly white private schools ever since.

Carter straddled the issue. He opposed spending public money on private schools and expressed doubts about their standards but made a conspicuous visit to a makeshift white academy in Swainsboro — "some brick chicken house" for fifty kids, according to a Sanders staffer — and praised it.

Although Carter advocated strict compliance with the law, not defiance like Maddox, he strongly opposed busing — a hot-button issue in both the North and the South in the early 1970s. Claiming that he was "deeply resentful" that the South had been singled out for special laws that deprived citizens of "local control," Carter knew just how to thread the needle without sounding like a bigot. "Georgians, like all southerners, have a deep pride," he said on the stump. "They want to manage their own affairs, their own businesses. Some people call this conservatism. But conservatism is not racism [or] hard-heartedness." He knew exactly what the innocuous-sounding words *local control* conveyed: sympathy to conservative resistance to court decisions and the civil rights efforts of the federal government. He accepted being described as a redneck, if it meant that "I'm a working man, close to workers," while disowning the term's racial connotations.

In nearly every speech, Carter attached himself not just to Richard Russell, whom he had embraced in 1966, but also to George Wallace. Fortuitously for Carter, Wallace had been feuding with Sanders since 1962, when both men were first elected governor. After Sanders took office, he refused to let the Alabama governor — famous for his line "Segregation now, segregation tomorrow, segregation forever!" — use the National Guard Armory in Atlanta for a demagogic speech. Coincidentally, Wallace had been invited to speak there by the Georgia Seedsmens Association, a crop improvement trade group that included Carter as a prominent member.

Carter resurrected this slight and turned it into a major campaign issue. Without explicitly endorsing Wallace's racism, he described the snub as discourteous and a sign that Sanders was too close to the national Democratic Party. "I don't think it is right for Governor Sanders to try to please a group of ultraliberals, particularly those in Washington, when it means stifling communications with another state," he said. He said that if elected, he would invite Governor Wallace to speak at the Georgia State Capitol — a promise that Georgia liberals were glad he never kept.

Wallace's own 1970 gubernatorial campaign next door was a rancid racial throwback. It included a print ad with the line "Wake up, Alabama! Blacks Vow to Take Over Alabama" over pictures of seven menacing black boys surrounding a white girl. Much later, long after leaving the presidency, Carter called it "one of the most racist campaigns in modern southern history." But that year, he even stole one of Wallace's slogans: "Our kind of man. Our kind of governor." You didn't have to be a linguistics professor to understand the meaning of "our kind."

Carter liked to think that his populism was merely a variation on the common-man creed of his grandfather's friend Tom Watson — before the bigotry. His billboards featured him looking

248

ordinary — nothing like a Kennedy — under the line "Isn't It Time Someone Spoke Up for *You?*" Other ads said, "Jimmy made it the hard way" and referred to rivals backed by "big money asking for big favors." The populist rhetoric was misleading — Sanders and Carter had comparable net worths — and Carter's class politics lacked economic content; he didn't attack banks — he had, in fact, been quietly trying to start one with some friends in Americus. He nonetheless warmed to the role, quipping that a bank vault he toured in July "looks like Carl Sanders's basement." When Sanders responded that Carter was "the penny-anteist politician I've ever come across," Carter — no doubt noticing that Vice President Spiro Agnew was scoring that year with alliterative jabs — got too cute: "My campaign is based on peanuts, pennies, and people. That's better than one based on bucks, banks, and boondoggles."

Throughout, he was helped by an often-clueless opponent. Sanders's slogan was "Carl Sanders Ought to Be Governor Again" — frequently shortened on literature and bumper stickers to "Sanders. Again" — and it reeked of entitlement. His law firm represented big and unpopular corporate interests, including Georgia Power, and he had personal stakes in several of them. Carter picked up a Republican gibe — "Cufflinks Carl" — and it stuck, though Sanders didn't wear shirts that needed them.

The *Atlanta Constitution* made Carter look bad in many columns and more than a few news stories. Later, he argued, with only slight exaggeration, that the paper thought of him as an "ignorant, racist, backward, ultraconservative, red-necked South Georgia peanut farmer."

Carter's usual response to press taunts was unamused sarcasm — a trait that rarely went over well. For years, he had feuded with the paper's editor and lead columnist, Reg Murphy, who resented what he considered Carter's constant whining about minor errors. Carter's futile effort to get Murphy fired looked petty and faintly ridiculous to Atlantans. But rural voters loved it. "Reg fell right into Hamilton Jordan's game plan, which called for saying the Atlanta papers represented rich liberal interests," remembered Bill Shipp of the *Constitution*. But Carter also managed to alienate Shipp, the top political reporter in Georgia. Late in the campaign, when Shipp was five minutes late to meet the Carter traveling party, Carter ordered the plane to take off without him, leaving him stranded three hundred miles from Atlanta.

Carter aides thought that was a dumb move; they preferred the nastiness to be well orchestrated. The campaign contained a secret dirty tricks unit known internally as the "stink tank." Everyone associated with it insisted that it operated without the candidate's knowledge, which is how such operations usually work.

The stink tank played on both sides of the racial divide. To cut into Sanders's support among black voters, the Carter campaign paid for radio ads boosting a black Democratic rival, C. B. King, an able Albany civil rights activist and lawyer whose gubernatorial bid made him the first black candidate for statewide office since Reconstruction. King was unrelated to Martin Luther King's family, but sharing the same surname didn't hurt in

250

the black community. The stink tank also created a phony "Black Concern Committee" that distributed pamphlets asserting that Sanders didn't care about black people.

More often, the dirty tricks unit sought to exploit the fears of white voters. It printed a "fact sheet" reminding them that Sanders had attended Martin Luther King's funeral and kept George Wallace from speaking in Georgia.

In June a flyer began circulating that contained a photo that had appeared in the *Atlanta Journal* when the Atlanta Hawks clinched an NBA playoff series three months earlier. The caption read: "Former governor Carl Sanders gets champagne shower from Hawks' Lou Hudson." As a part owner of the team, Sanders was hardly out of place at the victory celebration, though he looked wet and — eyes closed — not especially happy about the champagne being poured on his head and nice suit. The reason for the flyer was that Hudson was black. In the context of a racially charged political campaign, a routine sports page photo — soon to be dubbed "the champagne shampoo" — was lethal innuendo.

The man behind the stunt was Carter's Atlanta press secretary, Bill Pope, a Wallace backer with no compunction about using race to win. Without telling Jerry Rafshoon — Carter's friend and media consultant — about it, Pope mailed the flyer to pastors, police stations, country stores, barber shops, and beauticians across the state and personally dropped off stacks for a Ku Klux Klan rally. Bill Shipp wrote that week in the *Constitution* that the leaflet was "a dangerous smear that injected race, alcohol, and high living into the campaign." After the election, Pope admitted he

251

had run "a nigger campaign" for Carter.

By all accounts, Carter didn't see the handbill before it circulated, but he rationalized it afterward. "Carter's attitude was, 'We were trying to show he was a rich guy who owned a basketball team,' " Rafshoon remembered. Even so, the racial undertones couldn't have escaped him. The mud ball had found its target. "I was shocked," remembered Reg Murphy, a strong backer of Sanders in his *Constitution* column. "It changed a whole lot of minds. People said, 'Well, Carl's associating with the wrong crowd.' " Attempting to deflect the story, Sanders immediately sold his shares in the team. But the damage was done.

In late July, after months of trashing Sanders and the press, Carter turned positive and proposed an ambitious reform agenda.

He called himself a "conservative progressive," which sounded oxymoronic but ended up shrewdly melding conservative values with progressive positions on issues. Carter stressed that he had "a businessman's conservative outlook on the economy and efficiency in government." But he remained passionate on the need to fight air and water pollution and upgrade education so that Georgia would no longer have the worst high school dropout rate in the nation.* Rafshoon described his candidate as perfectly in tune with

*With the enactment of the Twenty-Sixth Amendment lowering the voting age to eighteen, in 1971, he also proposed deputizing high school principals and college presidents "so that they can go through the whole student body and register everybody" — an idea far ahead of its time that he ended up enacting.

252

the Georgia electorate: "right of center, but not far right."

After promising a "bombshell" for weeks, Carter went before the press in late August and charged that, while he was governor, Sanders ran a "multi-million-dollar moonlighting business" with J. B. Fuqua, the industrialist who flew him around on his plane. Despite a few incriminating documents, the "bombshell" was mostly a dud, as Carter had fretted privately before detonating it. An indignant Sanders offered detailed denials and relevant context, and the press mostly bought his interpretation, with some newspapers ripping Carter for hyping his charges. But even as Carter risked looking hypocritical by refusing to disclose his own corporate contributions, his attack worked, reinforcing the populist message that "Cufflinks Carl" was too close to the Atlanta establishment.

On the trail in Moultrie, Carter added an antiliberal twist, charging that Sanders "sold out to the ultraliberal wing of the Democratic Party . . . exchanging the favor of Hubert Humphrey for the good will of Georgians." Carter's ads showing Humphrey with Sanders and "the big money boys" and "big city bosses" hammered home just how badly he wanted to win. Two years earlier, Carter — a long shot candidate and private citizen — had alerted Vice President Humphrey that his lonely mother hadn't been visited by any Peace Corps official since she arrived in India; Humphrey not only arranged for the visit, he made sure the official brought Lillian a bottle of Scotch.

One populist Rafshoon ad became a minor classic: "This is the door to an exclusive country club where the big-money boys play cards, drink cocktails, and raise money for their candidate for governor: Carl Sanders," the voiceover said. Then a door with a sign reading "Private Club" — shot secretly, to Rafshoon's delight, at a Jewish country club — swings open on a close-up of a man's hand writing a check. "You and I were not invited. We're too busy working for a living." It didn't matter that Carter, too, had done his fundraising behind closed doors, without disclosure. The ad aligned well with news reports that Sanders had not included black supporters like State Senator Leroy Johnson in his closed-door fund-raisers. And it contrasted sharply with images in the same ad of Carter working twelve hours a day in the peanut fields.

Such was Carter's trust in Rafshoon that he almost never screened his ads or even saw scripts before they were shot. This operating style gave him deniability. When a prominent woman approached him complaining about the country club ad, Carter said truthfully he hadn't viewed it but that as soon as he saw Rafshoon, he'd tell him to take it down. On the phone with Rafshoon from the campaign trail, Carter mentioned the encounter with the woman and said it suggested the ad was working, and Rafshoon should double the buy. They joked that he had promised the supporter that he would tell Jerry to take down the ad the next time he *saw* him, not talked to him. The next time Carter actually saw his media adviser in the flesh was on primary night — too late, of course, to get the anti-Sanders ad off the air.

By the eve of the September 9 primary, the powerful editorial boards of the state's leading newspapers had almost uniformly rejected him. "Jimmy Carter is a classic example of a good man whose high standards have been undermined by political ambition," the *Macon News* wrote. It made no difference. Carter had run an indefatigable, clever, and at least vaguely demagogic campaign, and it had taken him to the verge of a major upset.

After he won the primary by 11 points, nearly enough to avoid a runoff, Carter was up at five thirty the next morning and shaking hands at a factory gate. The *Columbus Enquirer,* the only major Georgia paper backing him in the primary, editorialized, "While a lot of us do not get up at the crack of dawn, many of us must. Jimmy Carter does. He works hard. And he doesn't wait. That's what people like about him."

Sanders knew he was in trouble in the runoff and lashed out, calling Carter a "liar" and "Jimmy the Fabricator." He veered right and charged that Carter was responsible for banning prayer in Georgia's public schools. "How do we reconcile Carter's Sunday school facade today with his efforts to keep God out of Georgia state government six years ago?" Sanders asked, adding, ludicrously, that Carter was "atheistic." Carter's insistence as a state senator in 1964 that the new Georgia constitution mirror the establishment clause in the First Amendment to the US Constitution — one of his proudest moments in office — was now being turned against him. Sanders pledged to spend the last two weeks exposing "this smiling hypocrite."

Nursing a lead, Carter refused to debate. After Sanders appeared onstage with an empty chair,

Carter won the night by noting drily to reporters, "Some folks say the chair was ahead." Sanders, whose origins were more modest than Carter's, printed a flyer announcing that "Carter was born with a silver spoon in his mouth and inherited a 2,000-acre plantation in South Georgia where he makes his profits off the sweat of poor working people." It featured photos of dilapidated tenant shacks on Carter's property with a play on Carter's ads: "Isn't it time someone spoke up for these people?" To distribute the material, Sanders launched what Carter aides called a "smear sheet airlift," which the Carter campaign combated by convincing their volunteers to pose as Sanders workers at rural airports. They intercepted the anti-Carter handbills and burned them.

A pivotal moment in the campaign came shortly before the September runoff. Carter traveled to Augusta and paid a call on Roy V. Harris, a former speaker of the Georgia House and the mastermind of Maddox's 1966 victory. This was not just another visit to a shrewd newspaper editor and political strategist with Richard Russell–style views on race. The man to whom Carter paid homage was a highly influential bigot who had cofounded the White Citizens' Council in Georgia — the same organization whose membership dues Carter took so much pride in having "flushed down the toilet" in the 1950s.

Harris was famous across the South for convincing Arkansas governor Orville Faubus to stand up against Dwight Eisenhower in 1957 when the president sent troops to support the integration of Little Rock schools, a decision that sparked one of the great crises of the civil rights era. His newspaper, the virulently racist *Augusta Courier,* ran screaming, red-lettered headlines viciously attacking blacks, "race mixers," Jews, and Catholics. Harris encouraged harassing phone calls to supporters of integration and depicted the Kennedys, Lyndon Johnson, and Hubert Humphrey as Communist sympathizers. "Niggers are niggers, and no amount of crossbreeding is going to help them any," Harris once said. "The tiniest drop of nigger blood will spoil a man."

Sanders was from Augusta and had been at war with Harris for years in their hometown. Now, overestimating how much things had changed in Georgia, he distributed a cartoon of Carter climbing into bed with the founder of the White Citizens' Council. Harris himself explained how this move backfired on Sanders and elected Carter. "When Sanders denounced me as a segregationist, he drew the line in the sand, and the segregationists lined up from one end of the state to the other against him," Harris wrote in the *Courier.* "The die was cast." Bill Shipp and other savvy political reporters agreed.

Carter also made three visits to hate-mongering former governor Marvin Griffin at his newspaper office in Bainbridge, where, according to Griffin's postelection accounts, Carter "duped" him into thinking he was a conservative segregationist. Griffin fell for the ruse and announced at the Atlanta Press Club that he was endorsing Carter, a move that brought the campaign an important network of segregationist supporters.

Cozying up to Harris and Griffin haunted Carter in later years. He knew that this marred his efforts "to present a picture of my sterling character about racism." This time the enduring struggle within him between his moral vision and his

257

ceaseless ambition would be resolved in favor of the latter. He regretted the tone of the campaign but not his decisions. "If I could rewrite it, I would have made a public statement, 'I don't want any supporters of Richard Russell to support me. I don't want to be associated with Marvin Griffin. I don't want to be associated with Roy Harris — because they're racists and I'm not a racist,'" Carter reflected. "But that would have been the end of my political career."

The September 23 runoff proved anticlimactic, with Carter thrashing Sanders by nearly 20 points. Sanders won about 90 percent of the black vote, and Carter carried about 90 percent of the rural white vote — a polarization that would be replicated countless times and would soon turn the South from solidly Democratic to solidly Republican.

Until the end of his life, Sanders remained bitter toward Carter for "playing the race card." Carter could never admit it, but his hard-edged, dogwhistle 1970 Democratic primary campaign — no racist rhetoric necessary — inadvertently offered a model for Republican candidates taking power throughout the South. And a national candidate, Ronald Reagan, would use code words, too, to defeat him in the presidential election of 1980.*

The general election was not close, either. The

*Lee Atwater, chief strategist for George H. W. Bush and many other GOP candidates, said famously as he was dying of brain cancer in 1991, "You start out in 1954 by saying, 'Nigger, nigger, nigger.' By 1968, you can't say 'nigger' — that hurts you. Backfires. So, you say stuff like forced busing, states' rights. . . . You're

winner of the Republican runoff, Hal Suit, a mild-mannered Ohio native and former WSB-TV anchorman, had no natural base of support. President Nixon declined to campaign for him, sending his daughter Tricia instead. Suit's best bet was to accuse Carter of being a "counterfeit conservative" who betrayed the populist image of the previous summer by becoming part of a "cobweb of power" woven by county bosses he courted.

The message gained traction briefly. Carter's discomfort with being seen as a politician — a major theme of his political career — was obvious during a joint appearance at the University of Georgia. Students cheered Suit and booed Carter, who worried afterward that he had suddenly become the "establishment candidate." Now that the primary was over, he turned on Roy Harris, telling the students that he wouldn't reappoint the white supremacist power broker to the Board of Regents. The next day, he called Harris to apologize and say he had made no decision yet, though he likely had.

With his broad centrist coalition, Carter didn't need the segregationists as much as in the primary. He shifted now to an all-things-to-all-people approach. The *Atlanta Journal* reported that he was wooing "rednecks, whitenecks, and blacknecks."

One night earlier in the campaign, David Rabhan brought Carter over to the Ebenezer Baptist Church to meet Martin Luther King Sr., known

---

getting so abstract now [that] you're talking about cutting taxes, and . . . economic things, and a byproduct of them is [that] blacks get hurt worse than whites."

as Daddy King, who was for Sanders. Rabhan left them alone, and they connected immediately. It was the start of a critical relationship for Carter, who ended the campaign appearing mostly before black audiences.

Carter's senior advisers feared that Rabhan would get them all in trouble, and they didn't like his style: entering fancy fund-raisers in his flight suit and sneakers; making cracks that could blow up the campaign in an instant. Jody Powell began hearing rumblings from reporters about Rabhan's shady business connections. "I told Jimmy to make a deal and get rid of that loon," recalled Charlie Kirbo, who carried more weight than any other adviser.

So, with victory just over the horizon, Carter told Rabhan, "You've done so much for me, but you've never asked me for anything." He wanted to know what he could do for him after the election. Rabhan shrugged at first and couldn't think of something he wanted. Then he made an unusual and — soon enough — historic request: he told Carter that he would like him to say in his inaugural address that it was time to end racial discrimination once and for all. Carter was dismissive; Lester Maddox — certain to be elected lieutenant governor — would be on the inaugural platform in Atlanta in January, and there was no point in showing him up right at the outset.

But once Rabhan locked on to an idea, he rarely let go. There was nothing to write on in the cockpit, so he pulled out a pencil and an old aerial sectional map and scrawled the pledge on race relations in the margin, then handed it to Carter. The soon-to-be governor initialed it and passed the aerial map back to Rabhan, who promptly lost it. But the pledge was firm.*

When Kirbo heard about Carter's promise, he thought it was "political suicide." He would be betraying the people who voted for him. Carter never viewed it that way; he was thinking ahead — far ahead.

Election night was quiet, as Carter exceeded expectations by beating Suit by nearly 19 points. With his yen to quantify, he claimed later that he had made 1,400 speeches in 350 places, mostly off the cuff, and that he and Rosalynn traveled about 1,500 miles a week and shook hands with six hundred thousand Georgians over four and a half years. Carter saw his campaigns as lonely crusades against the odds — and against the same power structure that had held back the civil rights movement. He had largely missed the greatest movement of the twentieth century — playing out in his backyard — but now he would make up for lost time.

When Eloy Cruz sent him a telegram congratulating him, and a secretary prepared the standard response from the governor-elect, Carter wrote on the telegram, "Add: I need your continuing prayers."

*Carter remembered that it was he who wrote out the pledge but otherwise confirmed the story.

# 13
## "HE SAID *WHAAAT?*"

In 1971 the British novelist Anthony Burgess visited the United States and was struck by "the neurosis, the despair, the Kafka feeling that the whole marvelous fabric of American life is coming apart at the seams." In retrospect, the seventies were a painful reckoning for the sixties — a shaggy and confused time that managed to be broad minded and sour at once, a "kidney stone of a decade," as the cartoonist Garry Trudeau put it in his *Doonesbury* comic strip in 1979.

Unfortunately for Jimmy Carter, this was the decade in which he served in high office — four years as governor, then four years as president — and he would inevitably be identified with it.

Shortly before dawn on January 12, 1971, volunteers arrived at the Georgia State Capitol in Atlanta, unpacked 2,500 freshly picked camellias, and stapled them in place. The flower blossoms made up the smiling face and torso of the new governor in an inventive if slightly odd eight-foot-by-four-foot portrait that was soon hung from the colonnade, just above where the swearing-in ceremony was to take place.

As a crowd of five thousand gathered, the scene

reminded reporters of John F. Kennedy's presidential inauguration a decade earlier. Jimmy was young and vigorous, with a full head of Kennedy hair. Rosalynn, looking beautiful in a seafoam-green dress and matching pillbox hat atop her brunette locks, held three-year-old Amy, the same age as Caroline Kennedy when JFK became president. After the US Naval Academy band played "Dixie" and the all-black Morris Brown Concert Choir sang "The Battle Hymn of the Republic," some in the crowd sensed the coming dissonance. Now Carter stepped forward, solemn in an olive suit and brownish-green tie, to take the oath. The sun broke through the clouds and cast its rays on Carter's face, his supporters noticed, at the precise moment that Lester Maddox handed him the state seal.

No one was expecting much from Carter's inaugural address, which he wrote himself while lying in front of his fireplace. Charlie Kirbo advised him to utter the same prideful home-state pabulum he had used in the campaign. "Your goal was to see every Georgian as a law-abiding, well-educated citizen who is proud to stand up in any part of the world and say he is a Georgian," he wrote. The only mention of race Kirbo recommended was a vague promise to do something to help "the ghettos." Jerry Rafshoon came up with "Bigotry is not Georgian," which reminded Carter of the pledge he made to David Rabhan aboard the Cessna.

Without his explicitly planning it, his first words as governor would prove to be more significant than any others he would utter in the next four years. They simultaneously broke his bond with the conservative rural voters who had elected him and put him on a path to the presidency.

After telling the audience that this was "certainly the greatest day of my life," the brand-new governor unexpectedly put daylight between his conservative campaign and what would come next: "The test of a leader is not how well he campaigned but how effectively he meets the challenges and responsibilities of the office." If any onlookers thought this was just a platitude, they were quickly convinced otherwise.

"At the end of a long campaign, I believe I know the people of our state as well as anyone," he said cryptically, another portentous line that only sounded pro forma. He then told the crowd in words that would change his life: "I say to you quite frankly that the time for racial discrimination is over. Our people have already made this major and difficult decision. No poor, rural, weak, or black person should ever have to bear the additional burden of being deprived of the opportunity of an education, a job, or simple justice."

The polite applause masked a moment of disbelief. Carter always claimed that he hadn't changed his message from the campaign, and Hamilton Jordan, trying to discount critical reports about flip-flopping on race, insisted the line was "no big deal." But that's not what eyewitnesses reported. "You could just feel the shock going through the crowd," remembered Judy Woodruff, who was covering Carter for the Atlanta CBS affiliate. Bill Shipp said that he "thought all those [white] guys were gonna fall backward. It looked like a stake had been driven into their hearts." Shipp wrote in the *Constitution* the next day that not long before, Carter's address would have been denounced "as the talk of

264

wild-eyed liberals or Communists or race mixers or worse." He acknowledged that while in many states the line on race would have been like saying "Apple pie is good, and so is motherhood," in Georgia it was unprecedented. "And for George Wallace's old pal, Jimmy Carter, to say such things was unheard of." When the concussion from the cannonade of a nineteen-gun salute shattered windows in the nearby Georgia Department of Justice building, a white worker stuck a long pole with a white flag out the window. The *New York Times* seized on the gesture as a symbol of the surrender of the old era.

This was the first time in memory that the inauguration of a governor outside the New York area appeared on the front page of the *Times.* The story noted that, unlike southern politicians of the previous fifteen years, Carter made no mention of the Supreme Court or school desegregation in his address. In a follow-up four days later, the *Times* reported that "Jimmy Carter, like the South itself, is somewhat of an enigma and a contradiction." Rafshoon said years afterward that, in truth, there was no mystery about what happened: "His liberalism was there all the time, but he couldn't come out of the closet with it until he was governor."

There was a price for that. Senator Herman Talmadge said later that after Carter changed "his stance overnight" on segregation, he lost the support of the state Democratic Party "overnight." Or sooner. Bobby Rowan, Carter's old friend from the state senate, witnessed an impromptu walkout that reporters missed. Before Carter had finished speaking, about a dozen conservative state senators who had supported his campaign headed angrily for the exits. Rowan stayed until the end, but once inside the inaugural reception, he heard one of his colleagues say of Carter: "That nigger-loving bastard."

During the campaign, Carter had run into Vernon Jordan, a black Sanders supporter and civil rights lawyer who would soon head the National Urban League. "Pay no attention to what I say," Carter whispered. "Just watch what I do." After the inaugural, Jordan said to himself, "Okay, *that's* what he meant." The speech would not be the last time Jordan would feel "You know him, but you don't know quite who he is." Rita Jackson Samuels, a veteran of the SCLC and Andrew Young's unsuccessful campaign that year for the House, remembered other black spectators murmuring moments after the speech: "He said *whaaat?*"

Three days after being sworn in, Carter asked Lester Maddox, now the lieutenant governor and president of the state senate, to come to his office. Carter had appeared at a Maddox fund-raiser in Columbus during the campaign and said he was "proud" to support him. But Maddox also had reason to believe that the Carter from the campaign was not the Carter he would be meeting now. He knew that former governor Griffin skipped the inaugural because he felt Carter had camouflaged his liberalism during the campaign. And Maddox himself was angered by Carter's decision to break tradition and exclude him and his wife, Virginia, from joining the Carters in greeting guests in the receiving line at the governor's mansion following the inaugural. Maddox started the conversation by saying he wanted a

266

good working relationship and then explained to Carter the kinds of issues where he could support him.

Carter just glared. With the campaign safely behind him, he chose direct confrontation: He stood very close to Maddox and pointed an intimidating finger in his face. According to Maddox, he said — with a severe tone that reminded the older man of when his father was about to give him a whipping — "I didn't call you to my office to find out when and how you are going to support me. I have just got one purpose: to tell you that if you ever oppose me, even on one issue, I am going to meet you head-on and fight you with the full resources of this office." Looking back, Carter did not recall being "abusive" in the meeting; Maddox was certain that "those are his exact words."

A week later, Senator Richard Russell died. Charlie Kirbo didn't want to move to Washington, so Carter appointed his campaign treasurer, David Gambrell, a moderate lawyer, to serve out Russell's term. Maddox erupted publicly, calling Carter "a bald-faced liar" for posing as a conservative. Maddox claimed that Carter was an "honest, kind, and gentle person before the public," but in private was "angry, mean, and cold." When Carter floated the idea of abolishing the office of lieutenant governor for being "too expensive," Maddox retorted that Carter himself was the big spender and "oughta start being governor and quit trying to be God and king." Carter's effort to eliminate the office went nowhere. Later, Maddox upped the insults, deriding Carter as a "dictator," "traitor," and "Georgia's Hitler."

After he settled in, Carter began making up for

all the years when he sat on the sidelines of the civil rights movement. He hired Rita Jackson Samuels as Georgia's first-ever black woman senior official in state government, assigned to handle consumer complaints. He expanded the number of black Georgians serving on state boards and commissions from three to fifty-five. He appointed Georgia's first-ever black county judge, Horace Ward, and named Jesse Hill Jr., the CEO of an insurance company, as the first African American member of the Georgia Board of Regents, the same body that fifteen years earlier was ready to close the University of Georgia rather than integrate.* When a tense racial standoff nearly turned violent in Hancock County, Carter and his handpicked negotiator defused the incident without scapegoating an unpopular black activist.

Daddy King came for a meeting and broke down in tears; in all his years as a major figure in Atlanta, he had never been in the governor's office before. His daughter-in-law, Coretta Scott King, soon came to meet with Carter, too. The new governor took special pleasure in bringing the black state troopers he hired to country club events, especially Myron Freeman. When the Macon Country Club called the governor's office to say that "another trooper" should accompany Carter, he passed the word back: "I'm coming. I'm bringing Freeman. If he's not allowed in, I'll hold a press conference explaining why." To the

*Ward, an eminent jurist, had been denied entry to the University of Georgia Law School in 1956 because of his race. As president, Carter elevated him to the federal bench.

268

dismay of club members across suburban Georgia, Freeman and other troopers didn't sit in the car outside but ate with the governor in the clubs, thereby integrating them. In the 1930s, the country club set saw FDR as a traitor to his class; now many of the same people saw Jimmy Carter as a traitor to his race.

At the thirty-room Greek Revival–style governor's mansion, the Carters hired "trustys" from the state prison. Among them was a twenty-four-year-old African American cook named Mary Fitzpatrick.

One night in 1970 Mary had gone to a bar in Lumpkin, Georgia, with her cousin, who got into a scuffle with another woman outside. Coming to her cousin's aid, Mary tried to grab the other woman's gun, and it accidentally went off and killed the boyfriend of the other woman, who testified against Mary. An incompetent white court-appointed attorney, hired the day of the trial, instructed her to plead guilty, telling Mary that she would then be tried for manslaughter and freed. Mary took the attorney's advice, only to find herself convicted of first-degree murder and sentenced to life in prison.

"As she explained her case, it was obvious to us that she did not commit the murder," Carter remembered, and he dedicated himself to work on her behalf. When Mary gently encouraged three-year-old Amy to help her cook, Amy fell hard for her, and Mary soon became her indispensable caregiver and, as her case unfolded over the years, virtually a member of the family.

Rosalynn was grateful for Mary's presence but had some trouble adjusting to her new life. She sometimes felt Jimmy was too busy to pay proper attention to her, and tensions developed with her mother-in-law. Lillian, too, wasn't sure of her role. "Sissy, what are we doing here?" she had asked her sister, Emily Dolvin, en route to the inaugural. "We are not limousine people." She insisted at first that she would come to Atlanta just to see professional wrestling. But before long, Lillian convinced herself that she should step into the role of first lady of Georgia. She figured that Rosalynn would be busy tending to Amy, which meant that Lillian would need to be the hostess in the mansion. Rosalynn later acknowledged family strains in this period.

"At some point, Rosalynn had to tell her, 'I am the hostess, and you're not,' " Judy Langford remembered. "That was hard for her to say." Lillian went along, though twenty-five years after the Carters were married, she still sometimes spelled Rosalynn "Rosalyn" when writing her son.

Untroubled by tut-tutting over nepotism, Carter appointed his mother to the Human Resources Board, which oversaw social services in Georgia. Lillian, who had experience as the former manager of a nursing home, wrote to him, "I get gripes everywhere I go." She found the board meetings all talk and no action and complained that "I need something concrete to do." Then came unconvincing protestations of humility that ran in the family: "Please don't think I want to run your business — *I don't* — *I'm too humble.*"

Charlie Kirbo bore the title chief of staff, but he remained more of an informal senior adviser, driving to the state capitol in his pickup truck bearing fresh tomatoes and slow-cooked advice. Kirbo played on Carter's parsimony. One memo for the governor began, "I trust you have taken a look at the consumption of soft drinks at the mansion." He also weighed in often on personnel. At Kirbo's insistence, Carter tried to cut off David Rabhan by refusing to answer his calls for months. One evening, Carter entered the general aviation terminal and, in Rabhan's account, turned beet red when he saw the old friend he had been dodging. "You won't be governor all your life," Rabhan recalled telling him. "But you will be Jimmy Carter all your life." With that, Rabhan left. From then on, his calls were always put through by the switchboard, and Carter adorned the walls of his modern office with four of Rabhan's pen-and-ink drawings of rural shacks. Later, Rabhan hung out in the governor's office, bunked for a time at the governor's mansion, and gave Jeff Carter a job at his fish meal business in California.

Carter enjoyed oddballs but rarely suffered fools. His staff got used to the "tells" of his annoyance or anger. A vein in his temple throbbed, and his jaw moved. Then came an uncomfortable silence and a stare from his "icy blues," enough to make one hide under the desk even though the governor never raised his voice. "He can curl your hair when he wants to chew you out," his close friend Bert Lance wrote. "And he'll flash those eyes at you so brightly you'll need sunglasses."

Favor seekers usually got the icy blues and Carter's tight-lipped fake smile. Georgia, like almost all states, has long suffered under a "pay-to-play" system: campaign contributions and other goodies from lobbyists in exchange for access and favorable legislation. Carter rejected the whole idea, which infuriated old-timers and frustrated his own staff. Barred by the Georgia constitution from seeking reelection, he didn't need to kiss up to donors. But he even stiffed lawmakers he needed to help move bills. When a powerful state legislator asked for a small promotion for his father, a state employee, Carter said no. Later in his term, Carter would horse-trade some, but he saw the job mostly as an engineering challenge — What's the best solution? — and didn't think much of those who did not.

This approach figured in one of the biggest decisions of his governorship: choosing who would control road construction.

In Georgia, all roads led to Jim Gillis Sr. because no roads could be built without his permission. The director of the State Highway Board and his son, Hugh Gillis, a powerful state senator, had a stranglehold on much of Georgia politics. Legislators would line up fifteen deep outside of Jim Gillis's office. If you voted his way, you'd get your highway funding; if you didn't, you got no money for the most important projects in any legislative district: roads.

Carter was advised by his own people to retain the seventy-eight-year-old Gillis, and the *Constitution* published a story saying he would stay. The next day, Carter — who privately called the highway director "a dictator" — announced that he had fired Gillis and replaced him with Bert Lance.

Lance was six feet five inches and 250 pounds, with dark, hooded eyes that darted in fun, not menace — a rumpled, gregarious John Goodman character with a cunning intelligence he applied to everything except himself. The hyperactive son of a struggling Methodist college president, Lance dropped out of college, then married into a banking family, and worked his way up in five years from $90-a-month teller to president of the First National Bank of Calhoun. Lance was impossible to dislike, and his many close relationships in the business world were a big asset for Carter in both Atlanta and Washington. He was the kind of guy who wandered into nearby offices singing Christmas songs but could stiff friends who lent him money.

By all accounts, Lance's performance as highway director was superb. He tripled the number of construction contracts completed by the department while shrinking its staff by more than 25 percent — the model of what Carter wanted from his administration. And he did so without using highway construction to reward friends, punish enemies, and accrue power, as Gillis had.

Shortly after becoming governor, Carter — who confessed to having few intimate relationships — developed an exceptionally close and fateful bond with Lance, arguably closer than with Kirbo or any peer but Rosalynn. Bert's man-crush letters to Jimmy were at once sincere and sycophantic. Lance, never much of a student, made a point of reading and discussing Dietrich Bonhoeffer, whom he knew Carter admired. He wrote the governor that he prayed for him and that his first one hundred days were the best gubernatorial debut ever — "you are just 'Great.' "

Carter replied, "One of the bright spots in my life as governor is having you visit me. Stay close to me. I need your continuing friendship and counsel." In May Lance lent him not just his tennis court but also tennis shoes. Carter vowed to train after a long absence from the courts and

273

beat him: "I'm going to close a twenty-year gap in two weeks. Beware!"

Jimmy and Bert ate lunch together regularly in the governor's office, though Lance, like all visitors, including family, had to reimburse the office for the $2.78 that his "dried out" ham and cheese sandwich cost.

They quarreled occasionally. Lance got up at 4:20 a.m. every weekday to drive seventy-six miles from Calhoun to Atlanta to review the news of the day with Carter before work began. One morning, Lance stood in front of the governor's desk for five minutes and Carter never looked up from his newspaper. Lance stormed out and wrote Carter, "I'm about to quit and go back to Calhoun." To stay, he wrote, he needed to know if Carter wanted to communicate with him through "personal visits, the telephone, or smoke signals." Carter apologized, and Lance accepted. He decided to tutor the governor in introductory political gratitude. "Repeat after me: 'Thank you for your good work,' " he instructed.

But the larger message was adulation. As Carter's first year as governor came to a close, Lance wrote him: "You are the greatest person I have ever known. What else can I say?" More, apparently: "Your accomplishments will go down as being unmatched in the history of our state," he wrote the following year, before adding, "As I heard someone put it the other day: Jimmy Carter is just too good for Georgia." Carter, who saw Lance as "the workhorse and key man" in his major legislative victories, made no effort to convince him otherwise.

If Lance was an example of Carter's success in

cleaning up state government, his relationship with State Senator Leroy Johnson showed him fumbling a chance at reform. Having desegregated the state capitol in 1963, Johnson figured Georgia's new racially enlightened governor might help him become the first black man in Georgia to achieve real power. Carter didn't see it that way, and it cost him.

For generations, Georgia's lieutenant governor — the presiding officer of the senate — decided who would be the chairmen of the various committees. After failing to abolish the office of lieutenant governor, Carter now sought to strip Maddox of his most significant power. He proposed that a special panel of senators — a panel he would control — appoint committee chairmen. And he began promising committee chairmanships to senators who agreed to vote his way on this reform measure and other bills.

Johnson figured this was his chance to make history, so in mid-1972 he asked Carter for the chairmanship of the powerful Senate Judiciary Committee. Carter responded warmly but said he had already promised that position to another senator. Johnson laughed at the memory of what he said happened next: Carter offered him the chairmanship of the Senate Temperance Committee, which had once made decisions important to religious voters but now mostly occupied itself supervising programs to help alcoholics. "I said, 'Governor, I'm a lawyer; I'm not a drinker! I don't want to be chairman of the Temperance Committee,'" Johnson recalled. " 'I want to be chairman of the Judiciary Committee!' And he said, 'No, I can't do that.' "

So Johnson went to see Culver Kidd, the senate

whip, who was known as "the Silver Fox" for his gray mane and political cunning. Kidd, the most powerful lawmaker in Atlanta, was a wheeler-dealer from Central Casting and had a sense of political theater that Carter lacked. He once came to the floor wearing a toga to argue for the Roman prerogatives of the senate. Kidd viewed Carter as a pious hypocrite who wouldn't abide by the time-honored traditions of the capitol. He, more than Maddox, led behind-the-scenes opposition to the governor.

Beyond the racist rhetoric, Kidd and Maddox could be practical if it suited their interests. In 1970, former heavyweight boxing champion Muhammad Ali was having trouble finding a venue for a comeback after boxing authorities stripped him of his crown for dodging the Vietnam War. Johnson helped convince Governor Maddox to let Ali fight in Atlanta, which turned out to be the bout that revived his career. Now Johnson told Kidd he would vote with Maddox against Carter's committee chairmanship reform plan if he got the gavel at Judiciary. Kidd was taken aback. Judiciary was one of the most important power bases in state government. Here was a "nigra" asking one of the nation's most famous segregationists to give him that plum. But when Kidd brought the idea to Maddox, the lieutenant governor said yes.

Johnson took the offer back to Carter, who was incredulous that Johnson would team up with Maddox. "Carter said, 'You can't vote with Maddox — I'm the white hat, he's the black hat.' What Governor Carter failed to realize is that I was not voting with Maddox, I was voting for history as I saw it. And if I did this, then somewhere down the line, other black people could do it. Carter

276

didn't see that. He just saw Maddox was a segregationist, I was black, and I had to vote for anything against him." Given his own background, Carter might have been expected to have a deeper understanding of what Andrew Young — who came to revere Carter but also dealt pragmatically with Maddox — called the "strange, flexible, and complex relationship between black and white southerners."

Johnson would never forget raising his hand to vote in January 1973 to maintain the power of the lieutenant governor to appoint committee chairs. The measure passed 29 to 27, a stunning defeat for Carter, who, as his friend Hal Gulliver wrote in his *Constitution* column, neglected to "crack heads" to win. Maddox was so strengthened by the vote that he was considered the early favorite to be elected governor in 1974, although the momentum ultimately faded. Johnson became the well-regarded chairman of the Judiciary Committee and began hiring black staffers. He was proud that blacks achieving genuine political power was never an issue again in the Georgia State Capitol.

# 14
## JUNGLE JIMMY

Being governor brought out the exacting engineer in Carter — and the righteous warrior. He would prove to be the greatest environmentalist governor in the country, but not before alienating many Georgians with his bold plan to overhaul state government. Both experiences presaged what he would do — and what would be done to him — as president.

The Georgia state bureaucracy hadn't been reorganized since Richard Russell was governor in 1931. In the four decades since, agencies and departments had sprouted like kudzu and become personal fiefdoms or dumping grounds for political hacks. Carter had vowed during the campaign to consolidate and prune them. His stubborn, elbows-out style — an attitude that extended to making fun of a newspaper editor kidnapped and stuffed in the trunk of a car — would lead to a new nickname: Jungle Jimmy.

Shortly after taking office, Carter assembled hundreds of state officials for a meeting in the House chamber. He told them he found the overlap in their duties personally offensive, noting, for instance, that state capitol buildings contained twenty-two government print shops, all underused, when a half dozen would suffice. He quickly won approval of a bill giving him broad power to reorganize as he saw fit — subject to "reverse vetoes" in the 1972 session of the general assembly. Those votes would culminate in an up-or-down vote on the entire reorganization that would essentially determine the success or failure of his governorship.

To staff the "reorg," Carter called up the CEOs of Coca-Cola, Delta Airlines, and other big Atlanta companies and banks and asked to borrow their best young executives for two to nine months, on the corporate nickel. The CEOs were usually silent at first, shocked by the temerity of the governor's request, but most agreed.

Carter expected his team to work eighty- to ninety-hour weeks. He sent back memos with incisive comments but also corrected spelling, punctuation, and grammar, as if he were grading a paper. After Jody Powell wrote an article for local newspapers to go out under the governor's byline, Carter circled every *don't, didn't,* and *aren't,* and scribbled: "Jody, no contractions."*

*Like so much else, Carter's much-maligned insistence as governor and president that his aides spell properly looks better in light of the Trump administration, which issued press releases misspelling the names of Ambassador Jon Huntsman Jr. and British prime minister Theresa May, among countless other typos on everything from official government documents to Twitter posts. "Harmless enough glitches, perhaps," wrote literary critic Michiko Kakutani, "but indicative of the [Trump] administration's larger carelessness and dysfunction — its cavalier disregard for accuracy, details, and preci-

Carter's focus on details often annoyed senior staff, who understood that too much interference from above can make second-level officials more cautious and less inclined to act like leaders within their own departments. In Atlanta and Washington, this trait was widely assumed to be a crippling deficiency that revealed Carter as a small-minded man who failed to look at the big picture. And it is true that instead of playing golf like other governors and presidents, Carter preferred to spend some of his spare time burrowing into policy papers and nitpicking. But as leadership flaws go, this was not serious, and his sometimes obsessive attention to detail often helped him solve knotty problems or peer over the horizon. He underlined articles in the journal *Nature* about carbon dioxide in the atmosphere in 1972, when there was little public interest in the subject, even among scientists. And he read small magazines like the *Washington Monthly* that focused on the mechanics of how government really works, which helped him get under the bureaucratic hood in ways that politicians rarely do.

Not every technocratic idea panned out. Carter famously tried to turn his passion for precision and accountability into a modus operandi called zero-based budgeting, which required government officials to justify every expenditure, not just requests for spending increases. The idea sounded smart, but it generated hundreds of cumbersome forms. And, bureaucrats learned quickly to game the process, placing inessential expenses in the

sion." Carter was at the other, better end of that spectrum.

categories reserved for essential ones — knowing that the essential duties would be funded later by the governor's office or legislators. By the time Carter was endlessly boasting about it nationally on the 1976 presidential campaign trail, zero-based budgeting was already being phased out in Georgia. And after Carter took office, it was dead on arrival on Capitol Hill.

Drafting the reorganization plan consumed most of the first year of Carter's governorship. It reduced the state's sixty-five agencies — containing three hundred separate units — to twenty-two entities, including three umbrella departments of Human Resources, Natural Resources, and Transportation. The idea was to cut bureaucratic overlap and allow Georgians to contact one agency instead of five or six when they had a problem. Now he had to sell the plan to the bureaucracy, the Georgia General Assembly, and the public.

As if restructuring state government wasn't enough, Carter also wanted new policies across the board. This, too, required a planning process, dubbed Goals for Georgia, and he turned to a smart and ambitious thirty-two-year-old state legislator named Sam Nunn to run it. Nunn was disappointed that Carter was so focused on reorganization early in his term that he didn't adopt more of his sweeping policy recommendations. He felt "shuffling boxes [on an organization chart] wasn't going to make much difference."*

*Carter and Nunn had never been close. In 1972 Nunn, in his campaign for the US Senate, ran TV ads saying that Carter had appointed David Gambrell to

281

Carter disagreed, and he grew impatient with subordinates he felt were dragging their feet. "The list is disgusting," he wrote Frank Moore, a top aide, about a tally of unfinished reorg business. When two other aides returned from an unsuccessful mission to force an agency head to speed up his reorganization, as the governor had ordered, Carter snapped, "You sold the farm." But he also encouraged dissent. Anytime Jordan, Powell, or others argued that he was making a wrong decision, he listened attentively. After his attorney general, Arthur Bolton, wrote to apologize for offending Carter over an investigative matter, the governor replied that he wasn't offended and later wrote Bolton thanking him for a compliment, "since I know that you would just as quickly kick my ass if you thought I was doing something wrong."

Carter didn't hesitate to go on the offensive in public. He threatened to campaign against fellow Democrats who opposed his program and accused the State Health Board of being in the pocket of the Georgia Medical Association. Carter had established one of the first state-supported drug treatment programs in the country and didn't

---

fill Richard Russell's seat as a payoff for all the money that Gambrell and his family raised for Carter in 1970. Carter was furious and demanded the ads be withdrawn. "I've never been so surprised and disappointed in anyone before," he wrote Nunn. "I just don't understand you." Nunn said he pulled the ads at the behest of his mother (who disliked attack ads), not the governor, and went on to win the primary and serve twenty-four years in the Senate.

want it pecked to death by commissioners he didn't control.

It was a time of personal face-offs with Jungle Jimmy. Secretary of State Ben Fortson, who used a wheelchair after an auto accident, wheeled into the governor's office to confront Carter over his plans to strip his office of most of its duties. Stomping his foot rail, he snapped, "I've got on an old suit, but it's gonna take some stripping to strip me." As the struggle went public, "Mr. Ben," a popular figure, switched metaphors. "I'm not going to lie down still like a catfish and be gutted," he informed Carter. Warren Fortson saw that his Sumter County friend had been outmatched by his older brother: "Jimmy sailed high without knowing how to play politics." But then, at Warren's suggestion, Carter got smart and found a compromise, turning over securities regulation — a plum — to the secretary of state.

To no one's surprise, this gave Mr. Ben grudging new respect for the governor, whom he described in memorable senate testimony as "made of steel, determination, and stubbornness." Fortson compared Carter to a South Georgia turtle: "He doesn't go around a log. He just sticks his head in the middle and pushes and pushes until the log gives way."

To build public support, Carter stood in the well of the senate for a full day, fielding questions from legislative leaders on the complex details of the plan. This unprecedented closed-door event clinched it for Carter in the House. Speaker George L. Smith told Kirbo he had never seen anybody "do as fine a job as that boy has done," and said that Carter knew more about Georgia than anybody else in the state.

But Hamilton Jordan argued that the sales job and merits of the program had carried them as far as they could in the upper chamber. He knew by then how to motivate his boss: "Governor, they are laughing at *us* and *you* in the senate." It was time, he said, to "punish" those "selfish, petty bastards who use every means of threat and persuasion to get votes."

So Carter got past his diffidence about transactional politics. He blocked the pet projects of those who opposed him and drew on an obscure contingency fund to repair gyms, fix sewage systems, and even fund a high school band to go to the Tournament of Roses parade in California — all in districts of key legislative supporters.

Carter drew the line at indulging Culver Kidd, who was determined to protect the slot machine racket in his hometown of Milledgeville. So great was the Silver Fox's interest in illegal slot machines that he suddenly dangled the idea that he would reverse his position on the reorg, which he had been opposing for months. Kidd passed the word that if Carter gave him a heads-up about state gambling raids in his district, Kidd would do his bidding in the senate. An aide later testified under oath that Carter instructed him, "Tell Senator Kidd to go to the devil." Kidd returned the compliment, calling Carter a bully and a "son of a bitch."*

*Six years later, when Carter was president, Kidd was indicted by a grand jury probing the slot machine scandal. Carter testified by videotape at his trial that he was "appalled by the proposition" but took no action beyond informing the head of the Georgia State Patrol. Kidd was acquitted in a 1978 trial.

As Kidd's power ebbed, the reorg plan advanced — aided in part by the promise of big pay increases for many agency heads, who suddenly started leaning on friends in the senate. Early fears that the entire bill would be reversed by the general assembly evaporated. Given that "we have been criticized all along for not 'playing politics,' " Hamilton Jordan wrote Carter, "it is nothing short of a miracle that you have managed to get as much through the legislature as you have without having to compromise your principles and make a lot of distasteful deals." This "miracle" would be repeated in Washington, though few noticed there, either.

As the general assembly reconvened on February 21, 1972, four-fifths of the bill's 243 provisions had survived the legislative veto, a much higher ratio than predicted by the Atlanta papers, which had opposed government reorganization all along. Tensions ran high in the governor's office until word came through the internal speaker system that a killer substitute went down by one vote — 28 to 27 — on the senate floor. Carter's team rejoiced.

But it was too soon to celebrate. Even after the reorg cleared the senate, it had to be reconciled with the House version. With only a few minutes to go before adjournment at midnight on the last day of the forty-day session, Carter's enemies tried to run out the clock before a vote on final passage. His entire governorship hung by a thread. If not for George Busbee, a future governor of Georgia, who prevented adjournment until the sergeant at arms could round up ducking legislators and enforce the required quorum, the centerpiece of Carter's program as governor would have died.

The reorg didn't lead to immediate savings — staff reductions were by attrition — and most of what Carter wrought was reversed in the 1990s when the Department of Human Resources was broken up. By 2005, there was little left of it, as new species of bureaucratic kudzu sprouted.

But Carter could rightly claim that he had professionalized and changed the culture of state government. His deep knowledge of the gears of government bored the press but yielded big returns for his successors. For instance, when he arrived, the state of Georgia as a whole could not incur debt for construction projects — a major barrier to growth. But after Carter pushed through a 1972 amendment to the Georgia constitution, the state began to issue general obligation bonds, a change that has saved Georgia hundreds of millions of dollars in interest costs in the decades since. Similar farsighted wonkiness would characterize his presidency.

But trouble was encased in his victories. Carter won some legislative battles while standing apart from his fellow Democrats, and lost others in part because of that aloofness. When he became president, he figured he would operate in a similar fashion. But he was drawing a wrong lesson from his experience in Georgia, where he couldn't by law stand for reelection and — by his own admission in 2015 — would have lost had he tried. Only decades later would he recognize that building support in one's own party is essential to governing successfully, not to mention staying in office.

Carter was not just an avid outdoorsman, he was an imaginative one. He had loved rivers since he was a boy, and now he could do something to protect them.

One day Carter and his friend Jimmy Bishop were preparing to go fishing off Little Cumberland Island when a caretaker who doubled as a deputy sheriff put his hand on his gun and threatened to arrest them for trespassing. Bishop identified Carter as the governor to no avail. After Carter's security man reached for his weapon, Carter defused the standoff and reluctantly agreed to leave. Back in Atlanta, he pushed through legislation making all navigable waters in Georgia open to the public and in 1972 ironed out the complex deal that led to the establishment of the Cumberland Island National Seashore, a jewel off the Atlantic coast.

Carter's environmental passions were stimulated in part by his new recreational obsessions. He sometimes snuck away from the capitol in the late afternoon to join new friends like Claude Terry, a whitewater legend, as they canoed or kayaked on the Chattahoochee River, a spectacular waterway surrounded by cliffs that snakes forty miles through the Atlanta area. Barbara Blum, the president of the Sierra Club of Georgia and a major ally in many battles to come, first met the governor when he showed up one day after work in a T-shirt and swim trunks and waited patiently as an instructor gave kayaking lessons. Carter, who had already been practicing nearby at the Georgia State pool, could roll on his second try;

Blum confessed she never got the hang of it.

The Chattahoochee, a bucolic refuge in the heart of the city, became one of his greatest legacies. It would likely have been ruined by urban development in the early 1970s had Carter not intervened. Congressman Phil Burton of California, who controlled environmental legislation in Washington, told the Sierra Club that he couldn't move forward to establish the river as a national park site unless local officials secured undeveloped setbacks of a few hundred feet from the riverbanks to create a natural rustic corridor. Without the setbacks, the cliffs and ledges would be destroyed, and high-rise buildings would go right to the river's edge, which was a deal breaker for Burton.

To protect the river and cliffs, Blum and her fellow environmentalists introduced a limited-land-use planning bill with eminent domain for the setbacks that Maddox and other conservatives predictably denounced. By this time, Maddox had renewed his status as a celebrity segregationist by walking off the set of Dick Cavett's late-night talk show in a huff. And he tried to keep the pot boiling back home, too. When Blum passed the lieutenant governor in the hall one day, Maddox whispered, "Commie."

To build support for the controversial Chattahoochee bill, Carter invited the press down to the river to watch him jump off Diving Rock, a seven-foot ledge. On a river excursion, he nearly banged his head on a rock while rolling in a kayak and wondered aloud what would happen if he died and Maddox became governor. The bill that finally passed in 1973, which established a two-thousand-foot corridor on either side of the river, was the first major land-use legislation in Georgia's history. Further protection of the river from Washington wasn't far behind.

Carter — who had earlier helped found the Georgia Nature Conservancy — also took a brave stand on wetlands, a tough ecological issue because their indispensable role in water quality isn't immediately obvious. Wetlands, critical for preserving delicate but vital ecosystems, are an afterthought for communities hungry for development. With the protections contained in the 1972 Clean Water Act often unenforced, Carter didn't wait for Washington to step in. By his count, 535 projects for draining wetlands in preparation for development were in the pipeline when he took office. Not one was approved while he was governor.

Carter was also among the first politicians anywhere to stand up to the Army Corps of Engineers, which went on an unprecedented dam-building spree in the postwar era. Because the corps was a military unit, he trusted it at first but came to believe it had "abandoned its integrity" by approving hundreds of unnecessary dams and other water projects based on bogus assessments of need. He argued convincingly that the corps was in cahoots with the congressmen who supervised and funded its operations.

It was a scandal in broad daylight. The corps flagrantly underestimated the cost of dams and grossly overestimated the hydroelectric energy generated and the recreation and other ancillary economic benefits for the region. The process, Carter never tired of explaining, worked like this: A junior member of Congress puts a proposed dam in his district on the corps' list. At first, that dam is behind two hundred others. But as the congressman moves up in seniority, his dam moves up, too. "One of a congressman's highest goals in life was to have built in his district a notable dam at federal government expense that would create a lake that could be named for him," he wrote later. Because Washington covered 100 percent of the costs, local objections were few.

Carter was passionate on this issue, and over time he would do more than anyone to disrupt dam development in the United States. He started with a dam on the Flint River backed by the appropriately named Democratic congressman Jack Flynt, a nine-term incumbent best known for personally signing every letter to every constituent (instead of using an autopen like other legislators). Flynt, who would later relinquish his seat to the future Speaker of the House, Republican Newt Gingrich, wanted to dam the upper Flint River at Sprewell Bluffs, near Thomaston, about fifty miles south of Atlanta. This would have dammed what was then the longest free-flowing river in Georgia.

Before making a decision, Carter canoed down the river twice and made a point of learning all about the indigenous shoal bass (which he fished), otter, fox, muskrat, beaver, and bobcat that would be affected by the dam. He devoted more than a hundred hours of his time to meeting with dozens of groups on both sides, from concrete manufacturers to fly fishermen. Flynt was enraged that the governor would dare interfere in a federal project, but Carter later described himself as "impervious to that displeasure." After investigating, he found that the corps was trying to mislead him by arbitrarily tripling existing estimates of economic benefits and falsely claiming the region needed another lake, when a half dozen existed nearby already. Worse, the corps' claim that the dam would control flooding downriver turned out to be bogus. For Carter, the planner and environmentalist, the issue was bigger than the Flint River. He glimpsed a dystopian future where all of America's spectacular rivers were dammed for profit.

On his fiftieth birthday, October 1, 1974, Carter held a press conference to announce that he would use his powers to veto the dam — making him the first governor ever to veto a federally funded water project. Congressman Flynt and the Georgia Chamber of Commerce vehemently objected, but the decision stood. Sprewell Bluffs would be an "important memory" for Carter when he reached the White House and expanded his war on pointless dams.

That year, Carter had one more river to protect: the Chattooga, the backdrop for the 1972 movie *Deliverance,* based on the novel by his friend, the poet James Dickey. Claude Terry, the governor's canoe and kayak instructor, had been a stunt man and technical adviser on the film.

With a TV crew from *NBC Nightly News* filming some of the trip, Carter and Terry decided to try the infamous Section Three of the Chattooga, which contains a class V (the most dangerous) rapid, known as Bull Sluice. The rapid features two six-foot waterfalls in quick succession, among other treacheries, and to Terry's knowledge, no one had ever run it in a tandem canoe. Earlier, they'd hit a rock and been shaken up when, approaching a large ledge, Terry, paddling from the stern, yelled "Right!" above the roar, and Carter wasn't sure if he meant move the boat right or was answering a question in the affirmative. Now he offered to skip Bull Sluice. But Carter, exhilarated that he was "risking my life," was adamant that they try to get into the record books.

Terry was apprehensive. He didn't like the idea of "my bowman facedown" as they went over the falls, a position where he couldn't keep the governor in sight. Sure enough, a photo showed Carter grimly holding the gunwale as if ready to meet his Maker. He emerged thrilled: "It opened my eyes to the relationship between a human being and a wild river," he said. A few days later, Terry overheard Carter calling Washington to talk to Senator Henry "Scoop" Jackson of Washington State, who had not included the Chattooga among rivers to be protected by his federal bill. When Carter was done pushing, all fifty-seven miles of the Chattooga were designated as "wild and scenic," meaning they can never be dammed.

Beyond reorganization and the environment, Carter was an activist — almost hyperactivist — governor with a long list of achievements. On his longtime pet issue, education, he upgraded the higher-ed system with dozens of small but needed reforms and convinced counties to do the same at the elementary and secondary levels. "*Every year,* what money is available is siphoned off into teachers' salaries, retirement benefits, and M & O [management and operations]," he wrote Speaker George L. Smith, urging changes in appropriations. "The Georgia children often don't get any improvements." Carter changed that. He succeeded in obtaining more money for public education, which, in a state where white children were increasingly sent to private academies, meant significantly more money for black schools.

In 1971, white parents began boycotting the Sumter County schools, which sent absenteeism past 50 percent. On a visit home in June, Carter warned that the system was "degenerating rapidly" and that an all-black system would do "an injustice to both black and white citizens."

The following year, the governor joined his family and residents of Koinonia Farm — with whom he now had good relations — in a campaign to disband the Sumter County Board of Education that Carter once chaired. Its members were now shamelessly selling off school property to white academies for next to nothing. Carter knew that endorsing the lawsuit launched by Plains locals — and spearheaded by Billy Carter — to integrate Sumter schools wasn't smart for him politically. He knew it was inevitably a futile effort, "but I just can't stand to see my own county have the worst schools situation in Georgia, which it does," he wrote an old friend from Plains.

Tensions eventually eased. Sumter no longer had the worst situation in Georgia, but it wasn't good, either. Carter's dream of high-quality integrated schools in his county would never come to pass.

During the campaign, Rosalynn had become intensely interested in the problems of the mentally ill and a system for treating them that was unchanged in a century. This was just after the wave of court-ordered deinstitutionalization began, a process that reduced the population of the notorious Milledgeville mental hospital, the state's largest, by three-quarters. But while it was good that medieval mental institutions were shrinking in size or closing, the money didn't follow the patients into the streets, where they often roamed untreated. Rosalynn convinced Jimmy to set up programs that hastened a large expansion in the number of community mental health centers. And he appointed Dr. Peter Bourne, a savvy English-born psychiatrist, to launch methadone clinics for drug addicts as an alternative to jail.

Carter also professionalized the hack-ridden and antediluvian prison system. When he started, almost no Georgia wardens had even college degrees; by the time he left, more than half held advanced degrees. The governor relieved overcrowding by doubling the inmates released on parole, tripling the number of pardons for first-time offenders, and tripling the number of inmates whose civil and political rights were restored. Shortly before leaving office, and outside his official capacity, Carter arranged to bring a "Christian witness" into the prisons to help the chaplains, which he said had worked in federal prisons and should be tried in Georgia.

Carter resisted some federal mandates as meddlesome but enthusiastically enforced any related to energy conservation. After the 1973 Arab oil embargo plunged the nation into an energy crisis, he began phasing out gas-guzzlers from the state motor pool in favor of Chevrolet Novas, a cheap subcompact that burly Bert Lance refused to ride in with him. On occasion, he personally enforced the country's new fifty-five-mile-per-hour speed limit by ordering the troopers who drove him around the state to stop speeders so that the governor himself could give them a lecture.

Ethics was a consistent concern. Well before the

Watergate scandal that would bring down the Nixon White House, Carter issued a new set of standards of conduct for state employees and in 1972 sponsored and signed one of the nation's first "sunshine" laws. The bill lifted secrecy and opened more meetings and records to the public. He overhauled the judicial screening process so that it produced more qualified judges and removed corrupt ones.

Most of the time, he practiced what he preached. As a state senator, Carter had turned down an offer of free eyeglasses from an optometrist, and as governor, he reimbursed a sporting goods store that sent him a single can of tennis balls. Under Highway Department formulas, Plains was eligible to have its last dirt road paved, but because it ran near Billy's house and could raise suspicions of favoritism, Carter stopped it. "What he seemed to be saying was, 'Paved roads all around, except for my town or my brother,' " Lance remembered. However, Lance — while otherwise cleaning up the Highway Department — did accelerate some roadwork in the districts of state legislators Carter needed on key votes. This was done without the governor's knowledge; in a state with plenty of corruption, there was never so much as a whiff of scandal around Carter personally. He entered office with a net worth of about $600,000 and took no action to change that. Even his enemies called him squeaky clean.

All the while, Carter was developing a reputation for being combative and self-righteous. Jerry Rafshoon told him, "You know, *JC* only stands for 'Jimmy Carter.' " Carter laughed but kept swinging. He called the state senate "a cancer" and accused the general assembly of being "the worst in the history of the state." The same tone afflicted his relations with the press. Bill Shipp remembered that Carter was "hard to deal with" compared with other governors. With twice-weekly news conferences, he offered good access but — just as during the campaign — he often went up in reporters' faces if he didn't like what they'd written.

Celestine Sibley, a revered columnist for the *Constitution* who usually wrote about baking apple pies or growing azaleas, found herself accused by the governor of not telling the truth about the legislative maneuvering that surrounded one of his consumer bills. He even wrote a note to state senators saying that Sibley had lied about an interview with him. She played back the tape recording she had made, proving to other reporters that she hadn't. When Carter invited her to his office to discuss the issue, she refused, saying, "You mean you want to insult me publicly and apologize in private?" Carter finally apologized publicly to Sibley but not to the state senators he had misled.

In 1973 Carter, advised by Rafshoon to improve his relations with the *Constitution,* invited Reg Murphy to the mansion for a drink. Murphy remembered it as an unpleasant conversation: "I guess he thought I needed instruction on how to write a column. It was a bit schoolmarmish to me; always 'I really need to tell you what you need to know.' " Murphy felt this made Carter "unlikeable to both supporters and opponents" — more of a seething, disdainful naval commander than a friendly politician.

The next year, Murphy was kidnapped at gunpoint and stuffed in the trunk of a car. This was just two weeks after the highly publicized kidnapping of heiress Patricia Hearst in California, and it jangled nerves across the region. Not Carter's. When Jody Powell informed him of the manhunt under way, the governor put up his hands and quipped, "I've been here all day!" After Carter found out the $700,000 ransom sought from the *Constitution* by the kooky kidnapper included a load of watermelons, he joked to his friend Carlton Hicks, "I didn't do it. I don't like watermelon that much."

Murphy was released unharmed after three days, and the easily apprehended kidnapper, one William A. H. Williams, became a running inside joke for Carter and his team. Powell told friends that Williams "was looking for a small man to put in his trunk, and he couldn't find a smaller man than Reg Murphy." Shortly after Carter was elected president, Chip asked his father what his first act as president would be. "Pardon Williams," he deadpanned.

Carter's friends and senior staff treasured this dark wit, which usually came at the expense of someone else and was thus kept under wraps.

The Carters were enlightened on race but still emotionally connected to their Confederate heritage, a distinction that would be familiar to a later generation of southerners struggling over what to do about Confederate monuments. In April 1972 they traveled to Brazil, and the highlight of the trip was a visit to the town of Americana, where a colony of twenty thousand Confederates had settled after they lost the Civil War because Brazil allowed them to own slaves and establish plantations. (Slavery wasn't abolished in Brazil until 1888.) Their descendants kept southern traditions alive, down to performing Virginia reels and singing "The Yellow Rose of Texas."

"When they spoke, they sounded just like people in South Georgia," Carter marveled. He delivered what amounted to a sermon to several hundred Confederate descendants gathered at the Americana cemetery, which contained the remains of one of Rosalynn's ancestors. The governor told the crowd that it was sad that the Confederates felt they had to leave their own country. To his surprise, he found himself choking back tears as he gave thanks for the Christian spirit of these men. Years later, Jody Powell explained why the Carters and their Georgia entourage were all so genuinely moved: "We discovered part of ourselves that we hardly knew existed."

But Carter was less interested in that old self than a new one struggling to be born. Those southerners had fled rather than reconcile with the government of the United States. He would move in the opposite direction, driving himself relentlessly to transcend his region's tragic past and win a prize that had eluded the Deep South for nearly 130 years. And he would do so with a new consciousness that the entrenched racism of white America must give way to demands for a more just society.

Miss Lillian, with her children Ruth and Jimmy in 1933, nursed both black and white neighbors.

Mr. Earl, an entrepreneur and racist, was extremely strict. His son Jimmy hungered for "just a word of praise."

He knew Rachel Clark, a soulful farmhand, "better than my mother" and told her "You're the cause of me being what I am."

Miss Julia Coleman, the only teacher named in an inaugural address, gave him "the most resonating thing in my whole existence."

5

6

Rosalynn and Jimmy as newlyweds, 1946. "I am miserable away from you," he wrote from sea. Their long partnership changed the role of first lady.

7

8

With a black crewman aboard a submarine, 1952. Carter became an integrationist but hid it upon returning to southwest Georgia.

Admiral Rickover: "Excruciatingly demanding" founder of nuclear navy, sent Carter into the core of a reactor in meltdown.

A county boss literally stuffed the ballot box to beat Carter for state senate. After he fought back and won, he read every single bill introduced.

His failed 1966 campaign for governor led to a bout of depression and born-again missionary work.

Right, Roy Harris, the virulently racist founder of the Georgia White Citizens' Council, gave Carter critical last-minute support before the 1970 primary.

"The champagne shampoo": Carter aides turned this photo of Lou Hudson of the Atlanta Hawks dousing Carl Sanders, his 1970 opponent for governor, into a political attack.

With Coretta Scott King, unveiling a portrait of MLK in the state capitol. When Carter announced in 1971 that "the time for racial discrimination is over," black Georgians rejoiced; whites felt betrayed.

"Risking my life" on the Chattooga River exhilarated him. Tough, stubborn "Jungle Jimmy" had an impressive environmental record in Georgia and later nationally.

15

High-kicking publicity stunt with the Radio City Rockettes to gain name recognition for his long-shot 1976 presidential campaign.

16

Carrying his own bags on the trail. "I'll never lie," he told voters. "I want a government as good and honest as the American people."

17

Jody Powell, Hamilton Jordan: Leaders of the "Georgia mafia" who couldn't stop the aggressive post-Watergate press from ripping their boss.

18

With colorful siblings Billy, Ruth, and Gloria, plus "Remarkable Mother" Lillian, a Peace Corps veteran.

Debating President Gerald Ford after the *Playboy* flap.

19

20

Singles and doubles hitter in Plains, with Ralph Nader as umpire.

21

First Family from upper left: middle son, Chip, and wife, Caron; oldest son, Jack, with infant Jason and wife, Judy; youngest son, Jeff, and wife, Annette; daughter, Amy; president and first lady.

Installing solar panels on the West Wing
roof that President Reagan
later removed.

Cardigan sweater during 1977
fireside chat: despite ridicule,
he was visionary on energy.

"You can go with the rest of
the jackals!" LaBelle Lance
told Carter after the painful
firing of her husband, Bert
(right), which hobbled
the White House.

With Ruth Bader
Ginsburg. Ginsburg
noted that Carter
"literally changed the
complexion of the
federal judiciary."

With Panamanian President Omar Torrijos. The Panama Canal Treaties, which cost several senators their seats, likely prevented a major war in Central America.

Establishing diplomatic relations with Deng Xiaoping's China was central to the development of the twenty-first-century global economy.

Carter empowered women, including Patt Derian (above, left), whose human rights efforts bore fruit. UN Ambassador Andrew Young (right) pioneered a humble, respectful approach to the developing world.

# HELLO!

# My Name Is
# Jimmy Carter
## I'm Running for
# President

*Long-shot campaign for president.*

■ ■ ■ ■

# PART THREE:
# DARK HORSE

■ ■ ■ ■

# 15
## JIMMY WHO?

After twenty years back home in Georgia, where he rarely traveled beyond the state's borders, Carter was shedding his local skin for a new national identity. An intense overachiever most alive when he was evolving into something bigger, he was, as reporter James Wooten put it, "becoming again."

Carter had begun to "go national" within five months of taking office as governor. In the spring of 1971 Jody Powell received inquiries from the Atlanta bureau of *Time* magazine, which was preparing a big story on Carter and the South. The original idea had been to feature all of the young, racially enlightened southern governors who had been elected in 1970, including Carter, John C. West of South Carolina, Reubin Askew of Florida, Dale Bumpers of Arkansas, and Linwood Holton of Virginia, the only Republican of the lot.

Fortunately for Carter, the main story shifted to a detailed look at the way Georgia, with an integrationist governor and a Jewish mayor of its capital city (Sam Massell of Atlanta), was changing. The cover of the May 31, 1971, issue was a drawing of Carter and the headline "Dixie Whistles a Different Tune." The cover story began with Carter's inaugural declaration that "the time for racial discrimination is over" (no credit to Rabhan, of course) and told Carter's colorful peanut-farmer-to-governor tale to a national audience for the first time; it barely mentioned his embrace of George Wallace just nine months earlier. The piece said the governor looked eerily like John Kennedy from certain angles,* and concluded: "Carter is a man as contradictory as Georgia itself, but determined to resolve some of the paradoxes."

The cover story, read by millions, was a critical moment in Jimmy Carter's rise. He would skillfully exploit his new visibility over the next five years.

To build the confidence he needed to thrive on a larger stage, Carter invited several nationally prominent Democrats to stay overnight in the governor's mansion when they passed through Atlanta. Norman Mailer wrote later that he admired Carter's "arrogance" in being unimpressed by them. As he thought about the presidency, he began comparing himself not to George Washington and Thomas Jefferson, but to Senator Edmund Muskie of Maine, Senator George McGovern of South Dakota, and the other 1972 Democratic hopefuls he was checking out. The idea that he could handle the job grew out of these encounters.

Of all the visitors, he most admired the effervescent Hubert Humphrey, especially for his deep knowledge of public policy. And the Carters were charmed by Humphrey's easy laughter when

*After Carter spoke at a fund-raiser in Palm Beach, Florida, three years later, Rose Kennedy, the Kennedy matriarch, said the same thing.

304

four-year-old Amy, tussling with him on the couch, mashed a brownie in his face. Carter noticed that several of the others drank too much, which he thought showed a lack of the discipline it would take to win. They were also all senators, which Carter thought made them ill-informed about how the programs of the federal government actually affected people in the states.

It turned out Carter didn't have much good to say about his fellow governors, either — and the feelings were mutual. At a governors' conference in San Juan, Puerto Rico, in 1971, he argued that the group should go into the poor section of town and perform community service; the other governors preferred to go to the beach. They also snickered at the long string of policy resolutions he wanted them to consider.

Carter hoped to play a prominent role at the 1972 Democratic National Convention in Miami Beach, where McGovern arrived in July just short of the delegates he needed for nomination. At Charlie Kirbo's urging, Carter had joined the doomed "Anybody But McGovern" effort, telling a meeting of Democratic governors that a ticket headed by McGovern would lose every state in the South.

George Wallace, who had won five Democratic primaries before being paralyzed in an assassination attempt in May, expected Carter to place his name in nomination. But Carter — looking for an excuse to distance himself from Wallace — claimed he had already agreed to do so for Scoop Jackson, a hawk on Vietnam and Israel's most fervent supporter in the Senate. Carter was disappointed when his nomination speech for Jackson was barely noticed. Andrew Young suggested that Mc-

Govern select Carter as his running mate to unify the party, but Carter's involvement in the Stop McGovern efforts meant his name was greeted with "vile language" when it was offered in the McGovern suite.

The only good thing Carter's team got out of the 1972 convention was meeting McGovern's prodigy pollster, Pat Caddell, a tempestuous twenty-two-year-old Harvard undergraduate. Caddell, who would go on to coach Gary Hart, Joe Biden, Ross Perot, and eventually Donald Trump on how to appeal to disaffected voters, would, for a time, become one of Carter's closest advisers.*

When McGovern was soon forced to drop his running mate, Missouri senator Tom Eagleton, from the ticket after Eagleton admitted that he had received shock therapy for severe depression years before, Rosalynn quietly called around trying to get Jimmy named as Eagleton's replacement. He wasn't even considered. The party was still so obsessed with the Kennedys that McGovern chose — and the Democratic National Committee ratified — R. Sargent Shriver, a former ambassador and director of the Peace Corps best known as Kennedy's brother-in-law.

A year earlier, Carter's friend Peter Bourne had asked the new governor if he had ever thought about running for president. "No, I haven't," Car-

*In 2012 Caddell, by then a contributor to Fox News and Breitbart News, was the first political figure to suggest that the old Stalinist-Maoist line "enemy of the people" be applied to the American press. President Trump picked it up from him.

ter said. "But if I did, I'd run for four years, the same way I ran for governor." After the convention, Bourne sent Carter an unsolicited memo advising him to start planning for 1976 immediately. He told him that his "charm and discipline" could take him the distance.

Carter began thinking seriously about it. He knew that even had he been constitutionally eligible to run for reelection as governor in 1974, he would have lost. He had antagonized good ol' boys and Atlanta power brokers and a lot of other Georgians in between. He was also a likely loser if he challenged Herman Talmadge for his senate seat that year. So he figured his best career options were to become president of a college — or president of the United States.

The idea of Carter seeking the latter was much more audacious than it would be today, when it's common to run as an outsider with no Washington baggage. In the 1970s the presidency seemed reserved for incumbent senators and governors from big states and other major national figures, not obscure former regional politicians — especially one with his roots in the Jim Crow South.

On October 17, Carter, clad in blue jeans and a T-shirt, met for several hours at the mansion with his advisers. "Governor, we're here to talk about your future," Jordan began with a wry smile. But then the normally voluble twenty-eight-year-old struggled. "It's hard to bring myself to say these words," he said, pausing awkwardly as he and Rafshoon said almost simultaneously, "We think you should run for . . . p-p-p-president." Carter didn't agree right away — not explicitly, anyway — but planning began that evening. With four years until the next election, "We all knew it looked kind of preposterous," Jordan remembered, "but we were serious about it."

From the start, everyone grasped that being a southern farmer with no Washington connections could be converted from a liability into an asset. Carter would be out of office and on the stump for two years before the primaries, while most of his rivals would have to leave the trail and hustle back to Washington to vote in the Senate — a big scheduling advantage. Carter felt his weaknesses included subpar TV skills and a lack of foreign policy experience. Jordan countered that the winding down of the Vietnam War could mean more of a focus on domestic affairs, which played to his strengths.

On November 7, 1972, Richard Nixon and Spiro Agnew won reelection in a historic landslide. The next morning, Carter awakened Rafshoon at six o'clock with the words "I thought I was going to see you after the election." That was the moment Rafshoon understood that Carter definitely wanted to run for president. Later that day, the group of advisers expanded by a half dozen and — out of fear of becoming laughingstocks for their absurdly early planning — pledged secrecy. For months, even in private, the advisers used euphemisms such as "our national effort" and "seeking higher office."

Carter perfected a cryptic tone with other politicians. "Tell Herman I'm not going to run against him for the Senate," he advised a Talmadge aide. "I've got other plans." Even his family couldn't quite grasp the enormity of it. When Jimmy told his mother that he was preparing to run for president, Lillian replied, "President of what?"

Carter began viewing the pursuit of the White

House almost as an engineering project, with Hamilton Jordan as the draftsman. Jordan used his strategic brilliance to turn the early discussions into what became a classic work of political consulting: a sixty-plus-page analysis of how to make Carter president. Without knowing that the Watergate scandal would explode in 1973, Jordan wrote with uncanny foresight about the national mood over the next four years. "Perhaps the strongest feeling in this country today is the general distrust and disillusionment of government and politics at all levels," he wrote. Nixon's election and reelection did nothing to satisfy "the desire and thirst for strong moral leadership." Jordan (and soon Carter himself) believed Ted Kennedy — with his old-fashioned liberalism and sketchy private life — would be a good foil for Carter in 1976. They hoped he would run.

Jordan's strategy centered on a surprise win in New Hampshire. "I believe that your farmer-businessman-military-religious-conservative background would be well received there," Jordan wrote. This seemed a dubious claim. No southerner in either party had proven popular among the flinty Yankees, though Jordan didn't tell his boss that.

The other key state he identified was Florida. Nearly three and a half years ahead of these primaries, Jordan had already mapped out the key elements of Carter's 1976 strategy. The only missing piece — placing an emphasis for the first time on caucuses in Iowa — would come soon.

And yet Carter said later that he didn't make the final decision to run for president until early 1973, when former secretary of state Dean Rusk, then a professor at the University of Georgia, made a special trip to the governor's mansion and urged him on. Rusk's blessing gave him the confidence that he would be taken seriously by the Washington establishment — the same establishment that Carter and Jordan would blast during the campaign.

Everything Carter did during his last two years as governor would be geared toward running for president.

Carter's many trade missions now served a dual purpose: to bring business to Georgia and to burnish his foreign policy credentials. In May 1973 he flew to London, where David Rockefeller, chairman of the Chase Manhattan Bank, was putting together the first members of the Trilateral Commission, a nongovernmental collection of political, business, and academic leaders from North America, Western Europe, and Japan who would meet twice a year to discuss global issues. At the suggestion of the commission's executive director, Zbigniew Brzezinski, a Polish-born Columbia University professor, the organization was looking for a governor from each party. Carter was selected for the Democratic slot.

His membership in the Trilateral Commission was like a golden passport to explore the world. The half dozen meetings he attended over the next three years — for which he prepared assiduously — helped deepen his understanding of the global issues he would face as president. They also introduced him to people who would fill important roles in his administration, including Brzezinski, Cyrus Vance, Harold Brown, W. Michael Blumenthal, Paul Warnke, and Senator Walter F. Mondale. The commission soon became the object of

310

absurd conspiracy theories about a hidden world government, which elevated its worthy but dull closed-door seminars into headlines that redounded to Carter's benefit. He now had instant credibility with the foreign policy establishment — and with voters concerned about his credentials — that might have otherwise taken years to obtain.

The 1973 trade mission climaxed with six days in what Carter always preferred to call the Holy Land, where he met with Israeli prime minister Golda Meir, who shared cigarettes with Jody Powell and arranged for tour guides to drive the visiting Georgia dignitaries around the country in a Mercedes station wagon. Carter wanted to go where Jesus was baptized, so he arranged to bathe in the Jordan River, which he was shocked to see was the size of "a creek." He wrote later that biblical "bonds between Christians and Jews had always been part of my life" and that he "believed very deeply that the Jews who survived the Holocaust deserved their own nation."

Like many first-time visitors, Carter began to appreciate Israel's vulnerabilities. He was struck by how close Israel was to Syrian positions on the Golan Heights, from which Syrian forces could easily shell Israeli villages.

Other things puzzled him. When he visited a synagogue for Friday night Shabbat services, he was surprised by how few worshippers showed up; he wondered why Israelis were so secular. Carter once told Jerry Rafshoon that if he were Jewish, he would be Orthodox.

Much later, he said the plight of the Palestinians moved him on this trip, too, though he met with no Arab leaders and didn't mention Palestinians to the press at the time. Just shy of his fiftieth

311

birthday, this first visit to the Middle East marked the beginning of an interest in the region that over time evolved into something approaching obsession.

In September 1973, nearly a year after he decided to run for president, Carter received an unsolicited letter from one Hayden C. Hewes, director of an outfit called the International UFO Bureau, telling him that "reports have reached our office" that Carter had seen unidentified flying objects. Hewes enclosed one of his questionnaires, which looked like something from the fringe. The governor — genuinely intrigued but also likely knowing there were votes in it — set aside time in his schedule to complete the form by hand and return it within twenty-four hours. The gist of his answer would become one of the most highly publicized incidents of his career.

Carter had reported seeing a UFO outside a Lions Club meeting in Leary, Georgia, in October 1969. (Carter got the date wrong; records show he spoke to the Lions Club in Leary on January 6 of that year.) He noted in his tight script that while he was outdoors waiting with around a dozen men for a seven thirty conclave to begin, the group spotted a silent object in the darkening western sky, about 30 degrees above the horizon. The object — "maybe 300 to 1,000 yards" away — was "about same size as [the] moon maybe," and suddenly "seemed to move toward us from a distance. Stop, move partially away, return, then depart." On the second page of the form, he described the object as "blueish at first, then reddish. Luminous — not solid." Carter declined requests to sketch the object, but he checked the box allowing the organization to use his name.

This was not unique behavior for an ambitious governor in the early 1970s, when UFO sightings captured the public imagination. The following year, California governor Ronald Reagan recounted how he spotted a bright object in the sky as his aircraft approached the Bakersfield Airport and asked his pilot to follow it. He, too, knew this kind of thing had political appeal. Later, when Rafshoon and others tried to warn Carter that he risked looking kooky on the campaign trail, he waved them off. He hadn't reported seeing Martians but simply noticed a flying object that was unidentified; a just-the-facts way to connect himself to certain voters without seeming unhinged.

During the 1976 campaign, Carter would pledge to release all government documents on UFOs, but he found in the White House that this would compromise classified technology projects. Beyond a 1977 request to science adviser Frank Press that NASA review its files, he took no action on UFOs, which disappointed the conspiracy theorists. When asked in later years about the incident, Carter said repeatedly that he thought it was "impossible" to have visitors from outer space.

The story wasn't fully demystified until 2016, when Jere Justus, a former air force scientist, dug through old government reports and figured out that a barium cloud was launched on January 6, 1969, at 7:35 p.m. from Eglin Air Force Base in western Florida, about 234 kilometers from Leary, as part of a scientific project to examine the upper atmosphere with the help of manmade chemical clouds. The reported altitude of the cloud was 152 kilometers, which at that distance from Eglin would have appeared in the sky at an elevation of 33 degrees — almost exactly what Carter speculated.

Carter's evangelical Christianity was another political asset, but he didn't want to be seen as a prude. In 1972 he upset many Georgia Baptists when he successfully pushed through a bill that lowered the state drinking age to eighteen. Like politicians in twenty-four other states, the governor thought it was wrong that a boy could be killed serving his country in Vietnam but couldn't even buy a beer at home. He went even further, opposing blue laws that would outlaw the sale of liquor on Sundays and signing a bill that allowed municipalities in dry counties (Georgia had the most of any state in the United States) to vote on whether to stay dry — which had the effect of turning many Georgia towns wet. His fellow deacons at the Plains Baptist Church thought he had succumbed to sin.

In November 1973 Carter held a tense meeting with representatives of the Georgia Baptist Convention. When a preacher pointed out that the governor had never been a pastor who'd had to deal with the ravages of alcohol in his community, the blue vein throbbed. "Don't tell me I don't know anything about alcohol," Carter snapped, his words caught on a tape recording of the meeting. "I've dealt with alcoholics all my life. Don't tell me what the Bible teaches." This old disagreement with the Baptist hierarchy over alcohol would reemerge when Carter was president and spotted in photographs drinking toasts.

None of the disapproval from bluenoses dampened Carter's faith, but he often questioned his

314

commitment to it. Early in his term as governor, he was asked to speak at the Preston Baptist Church, near Plains, about witnessing for Christ. He counted up 128 people he had reached three years earlier going door-to-door in Lock Haven, Pennsylvania, and Springfield, Massachusetts. Then he thought of the 600,000 people he had met during his campaign. "The scoreboard read, a hundred twenty-eight for Christ, six hundred thousand for me," he recounted ruefully.

Carter said he had never before prayed as much as he did when governor, sometimes twenty-five times a day, either quietly to himself or on his knees in a small private room adjoining his office. He spoke to church groups of the need for "a Christian approach to public service" but canceled the weekly worship service Governor Maddox had held for government employees because it violated the separation of church and state.

One afternoon in late 1973 Carter called in Dr. Nelson Price, pastor of the ten-thousand-member Roswell Street Baptist Church in Marietta, one of the first megachurches in the world. When he told Price he might run for president, Price replied that it was a good time for an evangelical Christian to run because large numbers of previously apolitical evangelicals were now planning to vote for the first time. The men got down on their knees in front of Carter's desk and Price placed his hand on Carter's shoulder and said, "My brother, get your life right because this might be what God has in mind for you."

Not everyone agreed. Around the same time, Vernon Jordan, by now a well-known civil rights leader, and Peter McCullough, the CEO of Xerox Corporation and treasurer of the DNC, stayed overnight at the mansion, where they talked about politics until after one in the morning. When Jordan said he needed to go to sleep, Carter followed him to his room and told him again that he was serious about running. Jordan replied that he wouldn't win, for three reasons: "Number one, no one knows you. Number two, you won't be in office when you're running. Number three, you're a southerner." Carter was undaunted. "I am going to be president," he insisted.

As Carter grew more serious about running for president, black Georgians began to notice that he was sticking his neck out more. He said in interviews that southern whites had been "wrong" on race, had interpreted the Bible incorrectly, and had federal court decisions they despised to thank for allowing them to "save face" during the transition to a more enlightened future.

One day in 1973 Rita Jackson Samuels — who at twenty-nine had become a senior aide — told the governor, "You said segregation was over, but all the portraits in the capitol are of white people." She suggested a portrait of Martin Luther King Jr. Carter agreed but decided the addition would go down easier if King was one of three black Georgians honored. He added Lucy Craft Laney, who founded black schools at the turn of the century, and Bishop Henry McNeal Turner, a pioneer in the AME Church.

When word of the plans leaked, conservative legislators suggested that Carter instead place King's portrait in his outer office, which governors had traditionally decorated as they saw fit. But Samuels remembered Carter insisting, "The picture *will* be placed in the capitol." The painting, by George Mandus, was hung on February 17, 1974, the first anniversary of Martin Luther King Day, a Carter-led precursor to the federal holiday. With Coretta Scott King and other civil rights leaders by his side, the governor and an integrated audience sang "We Shall Overcome," while a sparse collection of protesting Klansmen ringed the capitol outside. The commemoration received national attention. Lester Maddox said that if he were ever returned to the governor's office, he would take the painting down.

Still, the reaction was much more muted than it would have been a decade earlier, which was just what Carter had hoped for. He believed his party had "weathered this aberration toward the Republican Party based on the race issue" and that southern voters would once again make the Democratic Party "their permanent home" — a prediction that proved to be incorrect.

Early one morning in May 1974 Hunter S. Thompson, after a night of heavy drinking, showed up at the gate of the governor's mansion. At first, the famous "gonzo" journalist was denied entry. "I was about two degrees on the safe side of berserk, raving and babbling at Carter and his whole bemused family," Thompson wrote of the origins of a relationship that would help make Jimmy Carter president. He had come to Georgia with Senator Ted Kennedy, who was scheduled to give the keynote address for the Law Day celebration at the University of Georgia Law School in Athens. The ceremony would include the unveiling of a bust of John F. Kennedy's former secretary of state, Dean Rusk, whom Thompson detested for his role in expanding the Vietnam War.

During his overnight stay at the mansion, Kennedy — meeting Carter for the first time — found the governor "puzzlingly changeable in his manner toward me, a trait that would continue." Kennedy felt it was as if he were attending an audition but didn't know why, not realizing that Carter, who had already been secretly running for president for eighteen months, assumed Kennedy would be his main opponent. The Massachusetts senator recognized at once that — unlike his convivial, even fun, relationships with politicians in both parties — he and this governor were just not simpatico. Carter, for his part, thought Ted wasn't as smart as his brothers and believed that his poor response to events at Chappaquiddick — where in 1969 Kennedy had driven his car off a bridge and fled the scene, leaving his young woman passenger to drown — should disqualify him from the presidency. Carter also figured that a diffident Kennedy saw him as a lame-duck southern hick.

Carter offered Kennedy a ride on the governor's plane from Atlanta to Athens the following day, then abruptly revoked the invitation; Kennedy was peeved that he would have to drive seventy-five miles down the highway to Athens and risk being late. After arriving at the law school for the lunchtime reception, Carter learned that Kennedy's prepared remarks overlapped too much with what he planned to say. He decided to throw away his text in favor of a few notes he hastily scrawled in an adjoining room. He wasn't a lawyer, but he would address the conservative Georgia legal establishment about the injustices of its profession.

Thompson had left the boring luncheon several

times to go to his car and refill his "ice tea" glass with Wild Turkey bourbon, which he swigged while raging about the ongoing Watergate affair to anyone nearby. But when Carter stood up, his anger got Thompson's attention. This time he went to his car to retrieve his tape recorder and soon made the only recording of what he called "a king hell bastard of a speech" — one considered by many, including Carter, to be the best he ever delivered.

The governor first impressed Thompson when he said that after theologian Reinhold Niebuhr, "the other source of my understanding about what's right and wrong in this society is from a friend of mine, a poet named Bob Dylan." He explained, "I grew up a landowner's son. But I don't think I ever realized the proper relationship between the landowner and those who worked on the farm until I heard Dylan's record 'I Ain't Gonna Work on Maggie's Farm No More.' " Carter's easy familiarity with Dylan's work would harvest young votes once the 1976 primaries began.

In his speech that afternoon, Carter described himself as a governor "still deeply concerned about the inadequacies of the system of which it is obvious you're so patently proud." He ripped his audience for applying excessive sentences for minor crimes, telling the story of an employee in the governor's mansion who asked him to lend her the $250 she owed the superior court, which had sentenced her to seven years in prison or $750 in fines. This was a side of Carter that he rarely showed as president but presaged the biting attacks on social injustice that he occasionally let loose in interviews after he left office.*

Carter explained that scientists and farmers adapt quickly to change, while lawyers "approach change very, very slowly . . . there's a commitment to the status quo." He said that 50 percent of the state's 9,100 inmates "ought not to be there" and belonged on probation. This was something he could have used his gubernatorial power to commute sentences to alleviate, but — anticipating a presidential campaign where he would need to be tough on crime — he rarely did.†

He had enacted modest ethics reform in Georgia but told his audience that it was lawyers like them who blocked a more ambitious approach. In the same vein, he noted that the Chamber of Commerce represented business but not consumers; the American Medical Association served doctors but not patients; and the Peanut Warehousemen's Association — which he belonged to — represented the peanut warehousemen, but not their customers. All of this anticipated a presidency that would identify more conspicuously with consumers than any before or since.

One anecdote — far ahead of its time in acidly

*One exception was a presidential speech before the Los Angeles County Bar Association in 1978 that included the line, "A child of privilege frequently receives the benefit of the doubt; a child of poverty seldom does."
†Forty years later, the number of Georgia inmates had increased more than fivefold, which means that Carter felt an incarceration rate just 20 percent of today's was still 50 percent too high.

320

capturing rampant violations of civil liberties — left his audience suppressing guilty chuckles:

"I had lunch this week with the members of the judicial selection committee, and they were talking about a 'consent search warrant.' I didn't know what a consent search warrant was. They said, 'Well, that's when two policemen go to a house. One of them goes to the front door and knocks on it, and the other one runs around to the back door and yells 'Come in!' "

Thompson, overreaching for superlatives, wrote that this was "the heaviest and most eloquent thing I have ever heard from the mouth of a politician." He felt the impromptu speech was "the voice of an angry agrarian populist" and, whether one agreed or not, as moving as General Douglas MacArthur's famous "Old soldiers never die" address to Congress in 1951.

Thompson knew little about Carter's record in Georgia, where he'd recently signed a bill offering guidelines for the death penalty that allowed it to pass muster with the US Supreme Court and thus resume again across the United States after a four-year moratorium.* Thompson simply loved the

*In *Gregg v. Georgia,* the high court found Georgia's death penalty statute constitutional. Carter tailored the state's bill in a way that helped make that possible, but he considered himself fortunate that no capital cases came before him either as governor or president; if one had, it's not clear how he would have squared his political ambitions with his evolving moral objections. "In complete honesty, when I was governor, I was not nearly as concerned about the unfairness of the application of the death penalty as I am now," he said in

speech because it ripped the pillars of the establishment.

And yet one of Carter's finest speeches was also a sign of trouble ahead. Speeches are usually meant to rally the audience to your side, not prove the superiority of your argument. While his remarks in the years that followed could be effective, he too often sermonized instead of mobilized, but without the vivid imagery and uplift that make the best sermons sing.

The Law Day speech was nonetheless an instant classic, and for the next two years, Thompson played the forty-five-minute tape dozens of times for "people who would look at me like I was finally over the hump into terminal brain damage." Of course, people listened anyway because a hip, often cynical celebrity journalist was telling them that this obscure governor had something important to say. It's hard to exaggerate the boost Thompson gave Carter with the young reporters he would need to take him seriously as a presidential candidate.

And yet more than two decades later, Carter recalled not Hunter Thompson's reaction but that of his son Jack, who was among the UGA Law School students in attendance. Jack, in a period of estrangement from Jimmy, was apparently unmoved by his father's professed concern for social injustice. This stung Jimmy. "I listened later to your angry claim that you, with your more legal mind, could understand their needs and do much more than I to help the cheerless poor and weak,"

---

2013. "I was looking at it from a much more parochial point of view — I didn't see the injustice of it."

Jimmy wrote in a poem, trying to understand why his son had been so angry and jealous at the time.

A more immediate source of friction was that all three of his sons smoked marijuana, which Carter disliked but also connected to the injustice he was decrying. "I was confident that an arrest would not destroy their lives," he wrote in the poem. "Ours was a prominent family, and I knew the sheriff and judge well. I always felt that they would not want to send 'one of the Carter boys' to the state penitentiary." It gnawed at him that their less privileged neighbors wouldn't fare so well. As president, he would try and fail to decriminalize marijuana.

Jack eventually grew to appreciate what he considered the best speech he ever heard. "Dad really isn't an orator," he observed, "but when he speaks with moral intensity, he makes you believe that what he is talking about is truly important and should be at the core of who you are."

The following year, Jack drove Hunter Thompson to Plains for an interview with his father; Rosalynn had told her son not to let Thompson drive himself for fear he was inebriated. After four hours of conversation, Thompson wrote in *Rolling Stone* that he found Carter "one of the most intelligent politicians I've ever met, and also one of the strangest." Thompson had never felt comfortable around people who talked about Jesus; he thought they were "stupid." But now that strangeness was suddenly cool.

Thompson continued to lay it on thick for the next two years. Carter "could pass for a Fuller Brush man on any street in America," he wrote. "But if Jimmy Carter had decided, 15 years ago, to sign on as a brush and gimcrack salesman for the Fuller people, he would be president of the Fuller Brush Company today, and every medicine chest in the country would be loaded with Carter-Fuller brushes. And if he had gone into the heroin business, every respectable household between Long Island and Los Angeles would have at least one resident junkie."

Thompson had been impressed by Carter's connection to Bob Dylan, which was strengthened after a January 1974 concert in Atlanta, when Dylan and the Band came over to the mansion for late-night scrambled eggs and grits. "First thing he did was quote my songs back to me," Dylan remembered. "He put my mind at ease by not talking down to me." Carter found Dylan "painfully timid" but felt the musician listened intently when they talked about the possibility of Dylan accepting Christ in his life. (Dylan, born Jewish, would convert five years later to Christianity.) Carter's new friend Gregg Allman, whose band was at the peak of its popularity, was at the mansion that night as well, and they all drank J&B Scotch with the governor.

Jimmy and his family always liked meeting interesting new people, and he grasped how associating with celebrities could raise his national profile. He got together with Elvis Presley when the singer passed through town, and he was on hand at Atlanta Stadium in 1974 when Braves superstar Hank Aaron — soon to be a devoted supporter — hit his 715th career home run, breaking Babe Ruth's record.* The governor's splashi-

*The last time Carter and Presley spoke was in the early months of the Carter presidency, shortly before Presley's sudden death, when he called Carter at the

324

est cultural initiative was the Georgia Film Commission, which eventually put Georgia behind only California and New York in movie production. Under Rafshoon's prodding, several well-known films of the 1970s were shot on location in Georgia, including *Deliverance* and *The Longest Yard,* a big hit starring Burt Reynolds as an NFL-player-turned-convict who forms a team to play the prison guards. Carter gave the producers his personal permission to shoot at the Georgia State Prison at Reidsville and to dress four prisoners, playing cheerleaders, in drag.

Richard Nixon, the first president Jimmy ever encountered (at a governors' conference), repeatedly refused to meet with him. The governor couldn't get in to see his domestic policy adviser, John Ehrlichman, or even Ehrlichman's deputy, to discuss the needs of the eighth largest state.

But Carter was slower than many other Democrats to be critical of Nixon on Watergate. At a governors' conference in Ohio in April 1973, he helped circulate a resolution asserting that the presidency remained untouched by "the Watergate affair" — on the very day news broke that Ehrlichman and Nixon's chief of staff, H. R. Haldeman, were being forced to resign over their role in the cover-up.

The October 1973 "Saturday Night Massacre," when Attorney General Elliot Richardson and his deputy resigned rather than carry out Nixon's order to fire Watergate special prosecutor Archibald Cox, changed Carter's assessment. He now

White House; Carter thought he was "stoned."

called Nixon a "paranoiac" and said he had committed impeachable offenses. Rafshoon, believing Carter's rectitude was the perfect antidote to Watergate, phoned Jordan and said flatly: "Jimmy will be the next president."

The same month, Vice President Spiro Agnew — who had received a supportive call from Carter when reports of his own legal troubles first surfaced — resigned after pleading no contest to charges stemming from a kickback scheme when he was governor of Maryland. The new vice president would be House Minority Leader Gerald Ford, an amiable Yale Law School graduate and former University of Michigan football player who had managed to serve for twenty-five years in the House without making enemies.

Carter discussed Watergate often on Atlanta TV, where he perfected his more-in-sadness-than-in-anger analysis of what was happening to the country. His future rival reacted to his own sudden ascension to the presidency much as Carter might have. "I believe that truth is the glue that holds the government together, and not only government but civilization itself," Ford said on the lawn outside his house moments after Nixon told the nation that he planned to resign. "Honesty is always the best policy in the end." The next day, August 9, 1974, Ford took the oath. "My fellow Americans," he said, "our long national nightmare is over."

From the start, Ford set an appealing tone of humility. The new president lived in his suburban home for several more days and was photographed making his own breakfast. But in September he pardoned Nixon, and public opinion turned sharply against him. With the pardon stigmatizing

Ford with many voters all the way through the 1976 election, Carter felt no need to pile on. He rarely mentioned it.

The 1974 midterm elections nonetheless offered Democrats the chance to make the Republican Party pay for Nixon and Watergate. Carter also saw an opportunity to surreptitiously launch his presidential campaign. He offered to travel around the country and advise candidates on speaking, advertising, fund-raising, and thorny issues like abortion and gun control. DNC chairman Bob Strauss — the wisecracking Texas-born Jewish lawyer who was unifying the party after the McGovern debacle — bit on the idea, letting Carter chair a new unit called the Democratic National Campaign Committee, an honorary position he would invest with importance. The assignment offered an easy way to broaden his contacts across the country. As a bonus, Strauss agreed to hire Hamilton Jordan at the DNC, where, under the guise of a staff position, he could work from the inside to advance Carter's interests.

In May 1973 Jordan — thrilled by the chance to infiltrate the national party — left his powerful job as Carter's executive secretary and moved to Washington. It wasn't long before a DNC official accidentally discovered documents Jordan had left on a table that showed Carter was planning a presidential campaign. But Strauss didn't care as long as Carter and Jordan were working sincerely to help the party — and they were. They held six regional workshops with state party leaders exploring how to expand the Democrats' congressional majority the following year.

When word of Carter's presidential ambitions leaked at home, the press had a different reaction.

In July 1974 Reg Murphy of the *Atlanta Constitution* wrote a column headlined "Jimmy Carter Is Running for *What*?" Murphy noted that Carter's own pollster, William Hamilton, had found that Carter's unfavorable ratings in Georgia were 7 points higher than those of Lieutenant Governor Maddox, and that more than a third of voters who backed Carter in 1970 now regretted doing so. "The state needed a good belly laugh," Murphy wrote, "and Carter obliged by announcing he would run for president."

Former governor Ellis Arnall gave Carter's team essential advice on how to tame the Atlanta press: confess that he had little chance, but that Georgians should be proud that one of their own was even running. Carter began saying that he was at the "bottom of the list" of twenty-five possible presidential contenders — behind even Georgia state senator Julian Bond, the only black politician mentioned in the national press. This made Carter seem humble and self-effacing, qualities he hadn't previously been associated with. The gambit worked wonders to improve the tone of home-state coverage, which national reporters looked to for guidance. Their "Jimmy Who?" stories would be more positive.

Among the politicians Carter stumped for in thirty states in the run-up to the 1974 midterms was a bright and assertive twenty-eight-year-old congressional candidate in Arkansas named Bill Clinton. Carter was annoyed that Clinton, who would end up losing that House race, showed up to his hotel an hour late. "Where the devil is William Clinton?" he remembered asking. "I'm William Clinton," replied a strapping, mop-haired former law student — whom the Georgia governor had mistaken for an aide. Afterward, Carter told Jordan, "That kid will go far." So began a long and fraught relationship between two men who came to resent each other.

In the 1974 midterms, the Democrats added to their already sizable congressional majorities, providing buffers that would help Carter when he reached the White House. Unfortunately for him, few if any of the so-called "Watergate Babies" swept into office that year attributed their victories to the governor of Georgia, although he had traveled widely on their behalf and made many useful contacts for 1976. In hindsight, these Democrats felt they owed their election not to a future president but to a disgraced one: Richard Nixon.*

In the fall of 1974 Ted Kennedy announced he wouldn't run for president in 1976, a "firm, final, and unconditional" decision he attributed, as in 1968 and 1972, to family responsibilities, including the cancer diagnosis of his twelve-year-old son, Teddy Jr., whose leg had to be amputated. Kennedy's wayward personal life — he was estranged from his wife, Joan, and both were drinking heavily — was also a factor, as was Chappaquiddick, which was still in the news five years after the accident. Bill vanden Heuvel, the family friend who had handled some of the sensitive conversations with the family of Mary Jo Kopechne (the young passenger who drowned in Kennedy's car), advised that it was still too soon

*Carter made a point of sending a nice letter to every Democrat who lost a congressional primary that year. One of them was to Chris Matthews, who later became a Carter speechwriter and MSNBC anchor.

after the accident to run, and Ted agreed.

Kennedy's decision undid Carter's game plan, which was to have Kennedy on the Left, Wallace on the Right, and roar up the middle. In November Minnesota senator Walter Mondale also decided not to run, saying he wasn't willing to spend another eighteen months "sleeping in Holiday Inns." But new, unexpected candidates emerged, including Arizona congressman Morris "Mo" Udall, a well-liked progressive. (He had jettisoned "liberal" as an unpopular label.) Soon more than a dozen Democrats were exploring possible candidacies, almost all of them better known than Carter.

Wallace, about to be reelected to a third term as governor of Alabama, was definitely in. Carter and his aides had long felt Wallace's appeal had two parts: racism and populism. They began honing theories that Carter could run against the former and embrace the latter, creating the beginnings of a distinctive political identity, even if no one else could see it yet: a southern outsider who wasn't a racist.

Even before being weakened by the 1972 assassination attempt, Wallace was showing signs of vulnerability in parts of the South. Pat Caddell, who'd begun polling in Tallahassee elections as a teenager, made much of Wallace not carrying Florida when he ran as an independent in 1968. The South was no longer monolithic.

To scout the rest of his competition, Carter attended the December 1974 Democratic "mini convention" in Kansas City. There Lloyd Bentsen, a smooth Texas senator getting set to run, asked for his support. Carter replied that he was already backing someone else. Bentsen asked who. Carter smiled and pointed at himself.*

To save money, the Carters bought no liquor for their Holiday Inn hospitality suite at the convention, so Jordan and Rafshoon stole some from Bentsen's suite at the fancier Muehlebach Hotel. They spent their early funds instead on a handsome ten-page brochure with striking photos of Carter shoveling peanuts, working at his desk, consoling hurricane victims, and tossing a Frisbee. This proved important. Over the next two years, tens of thousands of Democrats picked up Carter's green-and-white brochures and liked what they saw. And the slogan that the campaign settled — "Leader, for a change" — contained a wry reference to moving past the failures of LBJ and Nixon.

Heading into 1976, Democrats of all stripes worried about a divided party. That's what had happened in 1972, when Democrats bickered so long at their convention that McGovern didn't deliver his acceptance speech until two in the morning. But momentum seemed to be moving back toward Mayor Richard J. Daley of Chicago (whose Illinois delegation was thrown out of the 1972 convention by party reformers) and other "party regulars." Carter courted Daley, but as the

*Bentsen was the choice of the Atlanta establishment. Senator Herman Talmadge, who despised Carter, organized a secret meeting of Georgia elites to close ranks early behind the Texan. But when Carl Sanders noticed Bentsen was wearing cufflinks, he told Bentsen that Carter had destroyed him with his "Cufflinks Carl" attacks and would do the same to him. The Georgia Stop Carter movement fizzled.

governor of a state with little sympathy for unions, he found himself at odds with much of organized labor — still the most powerful interest group in the Democratic Party. He had better luck with blacks, women, and others on the Left trying to push the old guard out. As the Democratic nominee and president, he would, by turns, bridge such gaps within his party and tumble into them.

Carter postponed his announcement a couple of times. He thought it was "high heeled" — presumptuous — to just stand up and say he was a candidate for president of the United States. He feared people would laugh at him. But on December 12, 1974, the outgoing governor of Georgia became the second candidate — after Mo Udall — to formally announce his candidacy, first at the National Press Club in Washington, then at a rally with two thousand well-wishers (including Apollo 11 astronaut Buzz Aldrin) in the Atlanta Civic Center.

Carter's stilted formal announcements bored the few reporters in attendance, but some noticed there was something different about this campaign. "Being president is not the most important thing in the world to me," he told the Press Club audience. "There are a lot of things I would not do for an office or honor in the world." How much of this was genuine integrity, moral preening, or some combination of the two would take years for the press to sort out. But it was not the kind of thing politicians usually say — nor was the concluding section of the speech, which his aides found "hokey." It came from a question he said Admiral Rickover "asked me and every other young naval officer" under his command: "For our nation — for all of us — that question is: 'Why not the best?' "

In fact, Rickover's question to Carter in 1952 after the young applicant admitted not always fulfilling his potential at Annapolis was a decidedly less egocentric "Why not *your* best?" The change reflected Carter's talent for crafting a compelling personal narrative. "Why Not the Best?" became the title of a cogent and effective campaign autobiography he later dictated and penned alone in spare moments on the campaign trail, then sold to a small religious publisher.*

Jack Carter, still at odds with his father, found the little memoir careerist. "I was put off by the title," he remembered. He'd once asked his father what if striving to do the best you could didn't work. "Well, Jack," his father replied, "that probably means you haven't done your best." Jack, who had worked hard but experienced a checkered career in business, bristled at that.

After experiencing "the worst" government under Nixon, conjuring "the best" was an inspired bet on the triumph of hope over experience. In an end-of-the-year mailing to forty thousand Democrats, Carter wrote: "The person who works hardest usually wins. Nobody will work harder than I will." He would need to. A Gallup poll the month before, just prior to his announcement, had listed thirty-one possible presidential candidates; Carter was not on the list.

Once his campaign was official, Carter flew to Washington for a television interview. Outside the Avalon Theatre, he worked the line of moviegoers,

*The paperback version, published in 1976 by Bantam, became a best seller.

saying, "I'm Jimmy Carter, and I'm running for president." No one had a clue who he was, but he didn't care. He was off and running.

Not long after, he called Jerry Rafshoon and asked to borrow a topcoat for his first trip to New Hampshire as a presidential candidate. He didn't own one. Rafshoon was planning to wear a heavy-weather parka up north, so he took his dark-blue overcoat over to the governor's mansion.

The next time Rafshoon saw his coat was when Carter walked down Pennsylvania Avenue with his family on January 20, 1977, as the newly sworn-in president of the United States.

# 16
## THE LONG MARCH

Jimmy Carter was a famously unlucky president. But as a presidential candidate, he caught many breaks.

The first was that the smiling Sunday school teacher seemed the perfect antidote to the scowling crook who had just left office. In selecting their presidents, Americans have a habit of swinging from one personality extreme to another: dour Hoover to ebullient Roosevelt; grandfatherly Eisenhower to youthful Kennedy. Carter benefited from this pendular effect. After all the bugging and cheating and covering up, here came a candidate who seemed to mean it when he promised not to lie. After the arrogance of an imperial presidency, here was a modest man who listened well. And after four straight presidents who came from Capitol Hill — Kennedy, Johnson, Nixon, Ford — here was the quintessential outsider.

Outsider themes were in the air in the mid-1970s. *Dark Horse,* a 1972 novel by Fletcher Knebel, tells the story of a former New Jersey highway official who comes out of nowhere to win the nomination, pledging "One, that I'll do my best. Two, that I'll be honest with you." Robert Altman's 1975 film *Nashville* opens with a sound truck blaring rural populist messages from an unseen presidential candidate named Hal Phillip Walker — an outsider who is running against lawyers. Carter said he wasn't influenced by either work, but he began sounding nearly identical themes on the stump.

It helped immensely that Carter was unemployed as of January 1975, when his term as governor ended. This allowed him to abandon a long-standing tradition of candidates campaigning only sporadically in the year before a presidential election. With the help of a small charter air company that happened to be established that year in Plains, he traveled an astonishing 260 days before the primaries even began, visiting 250 cities and towns in 46 states. These five-day trips always finished where they began: in Plains, where he would rest, analyze with staff what he was hearing on the trail, go to church with Rosalynn and Amy, and then get up before dawn for another grueling week.

Carter traveled without security, and for more than a year he carried his own bags. After he won some early primaries, and the Secret Service showed up (giving him the code name "Dasher"), agents handled his luggage, but he ostentatiously maintained the practice of carrying at least a garment bag. Artifice without hypocrisy; it worked for him.

Even his name — Jimmy instead of James or Jim — signaled informality and a willingness to buck tradition. What kind of presidential candidate opted for a childhood nickname on the ballot? The answer was: a very different one — an anti-politician who used his relative anonymity to make mistakes when the national press corps wasn't

336

paying attention. And his energy level was astonishing. Eleanor Clift of *Newsweek,* borrowing a description from her children's favorite action hero, called Carter "bionic" — ideal for a presidential campaign.

On the trail, Carter was a fresh face connecting with voters in a fresh way. His quiet confidence conveyed an inner strength that made his long-shot candidacy more plausible. A gentle sense of humor — more in evidence with voters than with the press — took the edge off his grinding ambition.

So did Jimmy's colorful relatives, who offered an appealing contrast to the straitlaced candidate. Billy patented a line for the press, one that he often delivered while swilling alcohol: "My mother went into the Peace Corps when she was sixty-eight, my one sister is a motorcycle freak, my other sister is a Holy Roller evangelist, and my brother is running for president. I'm the only sane one in the family."

White southerners had long borne the nation's collective guilt over race and, not coincidentally, found themselves the butt of demeaning jokes and cultural condescension. Some northern voters could never get past their regional bias; they found Carter's twang and religiosity odd, even foreign. But more exited his events intrigued. At fifty, trim and with ample hair now held in place with hairspray instead of grease, Carter even had some sex appeal, amplified by an air of mystery. "The conventional image of a sexy man is one who is hard on the outside and soft on the inside," Sally Quinn wrote in the *Washington Post* the following year. "Carter is just the opposite."

Hamilton Jordan believed the candidate's secret

weapon was the variety of his life experiences. He could talk commodity prices with Iowa farmers, dam construction with New Hampshire environmentalists, navy traditions with veterans, and the teachings of Jesus with rural Bible Belt Democrats. Women's groups thrilled to the idea of Miss Lillian being "freed" by the early death of her husband to build her own life of adventure, while businessmen were impressed by Carter's hard-nosed management of his company. Miami Cubans cheered when he explained to them (in Spanish, with a southern accent) how his human rights policy could end Castro's domination of Cuba, and blacks loved hearing him use the cadences of a preacher to confess that he had lived his early life in "sinful segregation."

Carter's charm did not depend on backslapping or contrived intimacy. Voters found in him a down-to-earth, surprisingly shy candidate who wasn't always peering over their shoulders looking for someone more important, who believed morality mattered more than power in foreign relations, and who dared talk about boring but important issues (civil service reform!) that other candidates wouldn't touch. When Carter didn't have an answer, he said so, which audiences appreciated.

Jules Witcover, a top political reporter for the *Washington Post,* observed that Carter "combined an easy, warm, personal style with an icy, resolute determination, a kind of soft-sell evangelism that won adherents across the ideological spectrum." Unlike most campaign events — often interrupted by cheers, laughs, and applause — Carter's were strikingly quiet, as if the pastor had left his pensive listeners with important spiritual and temporal matters to ponder.

His message was integrity and decency, wrapped not in cynicism about Washington but in idealism about the country. "If you support me," he told voters, "I'll never make you ashamed. You'll never be disappointed. I have nothing to conceal. I'll never tell a lie." His soon-to-be-famous stump speech always contained the same closing refrain, repeated, Witcover wrote, like his "personal rosary":

"I want a government that is as good, and honest, and decent, and truthful, and fair, and competent, and compassionate, and as filled with love as are the American people."

Love was a new concept in national politics. Hubert Humphrey had spoken of "the politics of joy" in 1968, but the line had clanged in that tumultuous and joyless year.* Eight years later, love was conquering more territory. The idea that *all* Americans were full of love and decency may have been a fatuous contradiction of Reinhold Niebuhr's "sinful world," but it was a brilliant concept for a cynical time. Without being explicitly religious, Carter's love was Christian in spirit. He was asking for the same "leap of faith" for his candidacy that Christians make for the original JC.

Witcover noticed that Carter did especially well with children, who would rush toward him in a way the reporter had never seen while covering

*Lyndon Johnson used love in his infamous "Daisy" ad against Barry Goldwater in the 1964 campaign, but only in an apocalyptic nuclear context: "These are the stakes," LBJ intones after a little girl picks the petals off a daisy with a mushroom cloud in the pupil of her eye. "We must either love each other, or we must die."

339

other politicians. It wasn't that Carter treated children as adults, but that he treated both adults and children as children, "enveloping them with his smile and his message of goodness and love."

In New Hampshire, Hunter Thompson was stunned when he first heard Carter's "mawkish" — almost blissed out — close to his stump speech. He wrote: "It sounded like he had eaten some of the acid I've been saving up to offer him the first time he mentions anything to me about bringing Jesus into my life." But he realized Carter's pitch was just a variation on the old Adlai Stevenson line "In a democracy, people usually get the kind of government they deserve."

"A government as good as its people" was a pander, but in a time of scandal, it also said: We're better than this, and we deserve better, if not the best.

The 1976 election may have been the first since Watergate, but a Democratic victory was by no means assured. Nixon's record forty-nine-state victory in 1972 had not been a fluke. While many liberals insisted on seeing the eight years of Nixon and Ford as a brief interruption in the continuation of FDR's New Deal and LBJ's Great Society, the country — amid a reaction to the excesses of the 1960s and a migration to the more conservative Sun Belt — was, in fact, shifting rightward, especially on social issues.

As that realignment took place, the GOP seemed relatively moderate. The "wing nuts" — racist and anti-Semitic Far Right agitators with a weakness for conspiracy theories — were still confined to the fringes of the conservative movement, thanks to gatekeepers like William F. Buckley Jr.'s *National*

340

*Review* and the organizing limitations of the pre-Internet age. But the racial and cultural resentments that Richard Nixon and Spiro Agnew exploited to mobilize Republicans remained potent. In retrospect, it's hard to see how any Democrat without a base in the South could have won the presidency in 1976.

In the mid-1970s, voters were dispirited but much less partisan than today. Only 25 percent of House seats were in uncompetitive, gerrymandered districts (compared to 60 percent in 2016). The candidates had three-quarters of the country to which they could present their ideas with a legitimate hope of changing minds.

Carter's trek across the country required intense discipline and high standards for himself and his subordinates. Once again, the long, lonely race suited the onetime cross-country runner. He and Rosalynn both felt at home on the road, as they had in the navy and during the 1970 campaign. And they handled rejection well.

When Carter traveled to New York in 1975 to raise money, he was often rebuffed. Gus Levy, the senior partner of Goldman Sachs, asked a subordinate, Robert Rubin (the future Treasury secretary), why he was wasting his time meeting with a former governor who had no chance. The meeting was canceled. Prominent journalists were skeptical, too. Carter would lock on their eyes and say, "I'm running for president, and I don't intend to lose," with a level of confidence that one reporter said "would put Muhammad Ali to shame." The effect could be unnerving, but it was memorable.

That determination to prevail outstripped other values. One day in midtown Manhattan, Carter urged Jerry Rafshoon to move back in with his wife after a months-long estrangement. This wasn't the first time he had tried to be a pastoral marriage counselor. "Did you break your Christian vows?" he had asked Rafshoon earlier. After Rafshoon reminded him he was Jewish, he rephrased it as "Did you break your Judeo-Christian vows?" Now Carter brought up the subject again, urging him to take his wife's hand and tell her how much he loved her. When Rafshoon said that repairing the breach would strip him of the energy he needed to help make Jimmy president, some combination of Carter's dry wit and real priorities kicked in: "In that case, I'll never mention it again."

Throughout 1974 and 1975, Rafshoon's main assignment was to boost Carter's name recognition. The *Washington Post* still identified him, variously, as "Governor Jimmy Collins" and "Jimmie Carter." Game for any stunt, Rafshoon got Carter high-kicking in a chorus line at New York's Radio City Music Hall with the Rockettes, and the photo ran on the wires. Carter also made a soft-spoken and appealing appearance on the TV game show *What's My Line?*, where, even without blindfolds, comedian Soupy Sales and the other panelists had no idea who he was.

"Mr. X has a spiritual quality," said panelist Donna Valeri. "Does he recruit nuns?"

With time nearly expired, movie critic Gene Shalit finally guessed that he was a governor, though he needed help from the moderator to figure out which state.

The Carter campaign's shrewdest move in 1975 was to concentrate on the Iowa caucuses, which in 1972 had been moved up from mid-May to late January, just before the New Hampshire primary. After reviewing the bumper crop of publicity that George McGovern received for finishing second there, Jordan decided to make Iowa the springboard of the Carter campaign — a decision that transformed how almost all future candidates would run for president.

Carter's first trip to Des Moines in February 1975 was a near disaster. The campaign had rented a hotel conference room for a reception, with enough food and Coca-Cola for two hundred people; he attracted only three. Fortunately, no reporters showed up. At Jody Powell's suggestion, Carter began walking down the street and shaking hands en route to the Des Moines City Hall, where he passed out pamphlets to everyone in the building. An idea took hold. Instead of hosting events, they would walk the streets. "Maybe because of that we carried Iowa," Carter said years later.

The campaign acted as if it were 1967 and Jimmy was running for governor again — only smaller. With a mere thirty-five thousand caucusgoers, the Iowa electorate was about the size of his old state senate district. Even so, press coverage was hard to come by. "Anyone with a scratch pad and a tape recorder would send us into ecstasy," Carter remembered. One night in a budget motel, Powell awakened him excitedly to say he had booked him on a widely watched Iowa morning show, though he was vague about the details. On the way to the studio before dawn, Powell casually asked the candidate for his favorite recipe and admitted they were headed for a cooking show. Effortlessly donning a chef's hat and apron on the air, Carter explained how to marinate catfish. The charming segment caught the interest of Iowa reporters.

As usual, he excelled at retail politics. Iowans were impressed — sometimes gobsmacked — by what seemed like his photographic memory for names. Carter remembered not just you but also your children and what town you were from and that your brother-in-law, whom you had mentioned months earlier in passing, worked in insurance over in Waterloo.

He would expend huge effort for a single vote. One day on the road to Marshalltown, Jimmy met an Iowa farmer named Fred McClain. Three weeks later, he drove by again, but McClain was out. Carter left a note on the door: "To Fred McClain. Just stopped by to say hello. Jimmy."* This was followed by a handwritten note, one of thousands the Carters wrote at night or on the drop-down table of Delta flights. Rosalynn often gave Iowans weighing whether to join the cause the family's home phone number in Plains. When they called, she greeted them by their first names and treated them like old friends.

Jimmy and Rosalynn were equally relentless about building an organization. If someone on the campaign trail offered a business card, they would scribble "WH" (Will Help) on it, and the contact information would go on a three-inch-by-five-inch file index card or an organizer's Rolodex, which

*Carter avoided the salutation *Dear* in favor of *To,* followed by the person's first and last names. Jordan felt this was impersonal and asked his boss why he insisted on it. Carter answered that *Mr., Mrs.,* and *Miss* were too formal and just first names too familiar.

was almost always bigger than that of rivals.

And the Carter team hired exceptionally well. Tim Kraft was dispatched to Iowa in August 1975 with a mere $18,125 and built a crack statewide field organization. Chris Brown, the savvy New Hampshire coordinator, brought in gifted organizers who would go on to big careers in politics and government.* They spread the word about Carter's strong environmental record in Georgia, which attracted liberal activists from all over New England. While Carter was usually all business with staffers, they appreciated that he gave them autonomy and support — unless they messed up, in which case no matter was too small for his attention. "Obviously the typing is two or three weeks behind and no one has done anything about it," he wrote his senior staff in July 1975. "The long-distance telephone use is extremely wasteful." After a dozen other such instructions, he concluded curtly: "All of this needs to be done."

In his usual quest for self-improvement, Carter accepted advice on elocution from Carlton Hicks, a Georgia optometrist and loyal friend. Hicks taught him to say "De*troit*" instead of "*Dee*troit." Others reminded him that he didn't have to identify places he had visited as "Paris, France," or "Brussels, Belgium."

On the trail, Carter remained compulsively punctual, a rarity in politics. "Just remember," he reminded Kraft, "I would rather be ten minutes early than one minute late." When pressed for

*One, Jeanne Shaheen, went on to manage Gary Hart's 1984 upset win over Walter Mondale in New Hampshire and later served as the state's governor and US senator.

time, he asked the pilot to fly as low as regulations permitted in order to avoid unnecessary minutes spent ascending and descending. Kraft found Carter's obsession a significant political asset. He noticed that while voters might be accustomed to waiting for tardy candidates, they didn't like it. Time and again, Kraft heard early arrivals comment with pleasant surprise that Carter was there "already." He was rarely hemmed into a corner by a small group of well-wishers because he had, as usual, already greeted them all as they wandered in.

The frugality was unchanged, too. As in the governor's race, Carter usually stayed in the homes of supporters, with no dietary or other requirements except an allergy to Swiss cheese. Originally done to save money, the idea turned out to be inspired. Carter always budgeted time for conversing with the family — the chit-chat he otherwise disliked — and made his bed with navy precision the next morning. After he left and wrote his thank-you note, the families spoke glowingly of him to everyone in town. Their hospitality toward a presidential candidate was often written up in the local paper — and the message of his down-to-earth qualities often spread by word of mouth, the most powerful voter contact tool of all.

When the schedulers couldn't find anyone for him to bunk with, they booked the candidate a moderately priced motel room — sometimes with Rafshoon ("Jerry, do you have to spend so much time in the shower?" Carter would ask) or Kraft, but more often with Powell, whose snoring annoyed him. Before bed, Carter often washed his socks and jockey shorts and hung them on the shower curtain rod to dry overnight. The next morning, after dropping to his knees for prayer, he would begin his ritual sit-ups, which, along with a rigorous diet, kept him at a trim 160 pounds. He would never go above that weight for the rest of his life.

Rosalynn was often hundreds of miles away. She and Edna Langford, Jack's mother-in-law and her close friend, started campaigning in the spring of 1975 in the Florida panhandle, a couple hours' drive from home. As in the 1970 campaign, they looked for the tallest antenna in town, asked the station manager if someone there would like to interview them, then handed out a sheet of questions, which were often used verbatim.

Phil Wise, an ebullient twenty-three-year-old Plains native, showed up that summer to run Carter's state organization out of a storage area in an Orlando Pizza Hut. Wise remembered meeting an important Orlando attorney whose support Rosalynn had sought. After spending a half hour with Rosalynn on one of her seventy-five days in the state, the lawyer told her: "I don't need to meet your husband. Anyone who can snag you as a wife will be a great president."

Rosalynn was proving to be Jimmy's secret weapon: charming, well informed, tireless, and politically shrewd. She spoke well now and was clever: every time she was photographed for a newspaper, she held up a bumper sticker; she figured more people looked at pictures and captions than read stories. In Iowa, she wowed farmers by discussing the prices of corn and fertilizer, and often managed to convert an entire room of undecided voters into Carter supporters. When asked how she and her husband could stand to be in the fishbowl of politics, where everyone knows everything you do, Rosalynn replied routinely, "I live in a town of six hundred and eighty-three, and everyone has always known *everything* I do."

The polls in August 1975, six months before the first primaries, were better for Carter than a year earlier. At least he was on the list — in thirteenth place.

Jordan was unperturbed. He stressed that Carter, by competing in northern states, had the only meaningful campaign strategy to win nationally. If his northern liberal rivals had national strategies, Jordan wrote Carter, they would have been trying to win outside their regions in places like Tennessee and South Carolina. Instead, they all seemed to be playing for an old-fashioned brokered convention, the outcome many pundits were predicting but that Jordan felt was unlikely.

One by one, Carter's Democratic rivals fell away. Lloyd Bentsen was out by January 1976 — too establishment and pro-oil. Former North Carolina governor Terry Sanford and Senator Dale Bumpers of Arkansas exited for personal reasons, and Pennsylvania governor Milton Shapp, the first Jewish presidential candidate in either party, proved hapless on the trail.

R. Sargent Shriver figured it would help that one-third of Iowa caucus-goers were Catholic and his wife, Eunice Kennedy Shriver, was the country's best-known advocate of what was then — three years after the *Roe v. Wade* Supreme Court decision legalizing abortion — first being called the "pro-life" position. But it didn't make up for his late entry. Oklahoma senator Fred Harris was a folksy recent convert to populism who spoke convincingly of "privilege" and other progressive themes years before Bernie Sanders, but he was too quirky and disorganized to get traction. Mo Udall's intelligence and sharp wit helped him win good press, but his organization was sloppy and indecisive, and his glass eye made him look a little strange on television.

Indiana's Birch Bayh, with his strong liberal Senate record and handsome cleft chin, was long seen as the front-runner. He expected great support from women for fighting tirelessly for the Equal Rights Amendment, which had passed the Senate in 1972 and was awaiting ratification by the states. But he erred in attacking the outsider candidates — Carter and Harris — for saying they were nonpoliticians: "Well, I'm Birch Bayh, and *I'm* a politician," he said in a famously unpersuasive ad. "It takes a good politician to make a good president." While Bayh was technically right, voters in 1976 had little use for experience.

"By the time the other candidates woke up," Carter said years later, "I had already won."

There was a serenity to his quest. In the fall of 1975, a year before his election, Carter went to Cambridge, Massachusetts, and hung posters in Harvard Square, hoping to meet the same kind of eager college students who were "Clean for Gene" McCarthy in 1968, when McCarthy attracted idealistic antiwar liberals. Only three freshmen showed up, so he took them out for a leisurely coffee. When he stuck a leaflet through the window of a Boston taxi and the cabbie refused it, Carter told him he would want it for his grandchildren after he became president. In his remarks at Harvard Law School, he described his campaign as a "healing process" that would draw on "the character of the American people." He spent the night in the dorm room of an early volunteer.

In New Hampshire, the candidate wore the same outfit every day: a blue blazer, gray pants, and a "rep" tie (total cost: $42), which he would occasionally leave at a dry cleaner in Concord, the state capital. All eleven members of the Carter family took part in the campaign, which Carter said later gave him a critical edge. Rosalynn appeared in forty-two states over eighteen months. Jack helped in Florida. Chip, the most active, campaigned and fund-raised in every state with a primary except Alaska. Jeff made seventy appearances in New Hampshire. Chip and Jeff and their wives rented part of a house in Manchester so that they could work there full-time before the primary.

In Plains, Gloria took charge of her brother's headquarters in the old railroad depot, which camera crews found picturesque. The story of a peanut farmer from nowheresville perhaps becoming president struck a chord in a country still partial to small-town values and *The Andy Griffith Show.* Carter slid easily into America's most resonant twentieth-century archetype and exploited it skillfully for political gain.

October 1975 was when the campaign began to cohere. Rafshoon filmed Carter in a Florida pulpit and turned the sermon into two ads that began running in Iowa. Because each spot was five minutes long, Iowa voters saw them as news pieces, and they began breaking through. In the ads, Carter says, "I'll never tell a lie. I'll never make a false statement. I'll never betray the confidence you have in me, and I won't avoid a controversial issue. Watch television. Listen to the radio. If I do any of those things, don't support me."

The ads were paid for in part by a series of inspired concerts arranged by the "godfather of rock," Phil Walden, president of Capricorn Records and a friend of Carter from Georgia. The first, by the Marshall Tucker Band, was held at Atlanta's Fox Theatre. Soon Carter would raise money with the help of Charlie Daniels, Willie Nelson, Lynyrd Skynyrd, John Denver, Jerry Jeff Walker, Jimmy Buffett, and the Allman Brothers.* "If it hadn't been for Gregg Allman, I never would have been president," Carter said after Allman died in 2017.

The political risks of being associated with a druggy counterculture never concerned the candidate, even when he saw handmade "Coke Fiends for Carter" signs at his rallies. His admiration of the long-haired musicians was real and reciprocated, with many saying later that they felt a deep, almost mystical connection to him. And the fund-raising advantage offered by the rock concerts was significant. Each ticket stub was used as a receipt to show a contribution that could later be used for matching federal campaign funds. Some rock concerts included voter registration tables at the entrances.

Carter understood just what to do onstage. "I'm gonna say four things," he said at a rock concert in Providence, Rhode Island, in 1975. "First of

*The Allmans, James Brown, and Johnny Cash, as well as many music business managers, also made significant personal donations to the campaign.

all, I'm running for president. Secondly, I'm gonna be elected. Third, this is very important, would you help me? Fourth, I want to introduce to you, my friends and your friends, the great All-man Brothers!" This was followed by thunderous applause. A politician who knew better than to make a speech at a rock concert was guaranteed to win the votes of thousands of grateful fans.*

The candidate was also making inroads in the black community. "Blacks have a kind of radar about white folks," Andrew Young observed. "Somewhere along the line, Jimmy passed the test." It helped immensely that Martin Luther King Sr. came on board. Daddy King had favored former vice president Nelson Rockefeller, who could point to a long history of supporting civil rights and had paid for his son's enormous funeral. When it was clear Rocky wasn't running, King came out for Carter early. He taped a generous endorsement for "this good man" that would be played on black radio for the next year.

Carter's private meeting with the Congressional Black Caucus was also pivotal. Young, who had been elected to the House in 1972, was unsure about how it would go. New York congressman

*Not every concert went smoothly. Before a Jerry Jeff Walker and Jimmy Buffett concert in Portland, Oregon, the soundman was furious that he was owed $500 and approached Carter's suite, threatening to throw a table through a plate glass window if he wasn't paid immediately. Jody Powell introduced him to Carter, who talked him down; the soundman left smiling, and the outdoor concert — attended by thousands more fans than expected — was a big success.

Charlie Rangel hadn't even wanted to meet him. "Why the hell do you want to bring in that Georgia cracker?" he asked Young, who had originally been for Udall. Carter was too conservative for them on busing, affirmative action, and other issues. Asked by caucus members how many black campaign staffers he hired, Carter said he didn't know. The other candidates who preceded him had all said they employed at least one black staffer. Rangel was getting ready to walk out of the meeting in disgust when Young stepped out to call a Carter aide in Atlanta who provided a total number of black staffers that was more than that of all of his rivals combined. Carter began talking about their different functions on the campaign and how he overcame the racist legacy of his family and region. By the time he left, Young remembered, he had the support of virtually the entire Congressional Black Caucus, including Rangel.

That wasn't the only break Carter caught with black voters. In November 1975 President Ford, acting on the advice of Dick Cheney, his conservative chief of staff, made a decision that Carter believed would seal his fate a year later: he dumped Vice President Rockefeller from the 1976 ticket for being too liberal. Tossing Rocky overboard may have been essential to Ford's nomination, but the price was high. The former New York governor's popularity among union households and blacks would have made a Ford-Rockefeller ticket harder for Carter to beat. Ford said later that dropping Rockefeller was the worst decision of his presidency.

The October 25 Jefferson-Jackson Day Dinner in Ames, Iowa — no big deal in advance — turned out to be critical. Kraft worked the Ames straw poll as if it were game seven of the World Series. His volunteers formed carpools to bring supporters to the dinner, where they were given $2 tickets to the balcony. Only those paying $25 for the full "J-J Dinner" were supposed to vote, but the Carter camp had their people infiltrate the dining floor and pick up straw poll ballots to distribute in the cheap seats. Rosalynn handed out oversized Carter buttons in the front row of the balcony to create the impression that the event was heavily pro-Carter. Kraft said later that her presence made the difference. In the straw poll of the 1,094 in attendance, Carter won easily.

After ten months of desperately seeking national press attention, Carter suddenly had the most coveted coverage. That week, R. W. "Johnny" Apple of the *New York Times,* who along with David Broder of the *Washington Post* had great influence inside the press pack, interviewed fifty Iowans and wrote a front-page story — above the fold — saying Carter had a surprisingly "solid lead" in the state. Still, his odds looked steep. When Apple speculated to his boss, Abe Rosenthal, the executive editor of the *Times,* that Carter would be the nominee, Rosenthal told him he was crazy.

In a variation of Kraft's gambit at the Iowa J-J Dinner, Phil Wise learned far in advance that Florida Democrats would hold a presidential straw poll at a special November convention commemorating the US bicentennial. Wise mobilized state party delegates, and Carter won 67 percent. The win was technically meaningless but significant for gaining press attention and building an organization in a state George Wallace was ex-

354

pected to carry.

By Thanksgiving, Carter was finally cracking the guest list for solo interviews on the Sunday political shows. *Newsweek, People,* and the *New York Times Magazine* ran glowing profiles before the end of the year, and in January Carter was the perfectly timed flavor of the month for the rest of the national media, which in those days consisted of only about a dozen powerful news organizations.

Carter still trailed Birch Bayh and several other Democrats in national surveys, but these stories catapulted him beyond the 2 percent to 5 percent range, where he had languished for months, and into serious contention. They also changed the expectations game. Now he would have to win Iowa.

Everyone knew Carter was running a risk with his line about never lying. It resonated after all of Nixon's lies but risked boomeranging. When Rafshoon first showed Charlie Kirbo a television spot that ended with "I'll never lie to you," Kirbo told him, "We're going to lose the liar vote." Rafshoon laughed, but Kirbo said, "I'm serious. If you say, 'I'll never lie to you,' you're just putting a 'Kick Me' sign on your ass. Every son of a bitch who cheated on his wife is gonna vote against you."

Conservative columnists Rowland Evans and Robert Novak were the first to attack Carter as a hypocrite. A January column entitled "Carter Lies" cited nine examples of falsehoods, including whether he'd known Scoop Jackson and Richard Russell (not as well as he claimed) and that he was a "longtime member of the public interest group Common Cause." (Rosalynn was actually the member.) By today's standards, these were exaggerations of little or no consequence, and even Novak admitted the statements were more fibs than lies. But Evans and Novak, who themselves had such a reputation for inaccuracy that they were often dubbed "Errors and No Facts," nonetheless set a pattern of journalists on both the Left and the Right trying to prove that Carter was no different — or actually worse — than other politicians. Just as Kirbo predicted, reporters began working overtime trying to show Carter was lying about not lying.

In late January, about a month before the caucuses, *Harper's* magazine circulated a story by Steven Brill entitled "Jimmy Carter's Pathetic Lies." The headline (not written by Brill) was the worst part for Carter; most of the piece consisted of exaggerations, like the candidate calling himself a nuclear physicist. Most memorably, he told credulous audiences: "Just put 'Jimmy Carter, Plains, Georgia' on the envelope, and I'll get it. I open every letter myself and read them all." Carter did go through the mailbag on weekends, but it strained credulity that he opened and read everything he was sent. Jordan had long warned Carter against exaggeration; he thought it resulted from growing up in rural Georgia, where everything that happened in town was "the biggest" or "the best" or "the greatest." It was a forgivable shortcoming that nonetheless undermined his reputation for honesty.

Beyond causing an annoyed press corps to apply a higher standard to Carter than to other politicians (for the rest of his political career), it wasn't clear whether presenting himself as a truth teller

356

even worked with voters. Rafshoon felt Carter's core integrity came through without showcasing. Pat Caddell disagreed. He believed Carter's line "If I lie, don't vote for me" was critically important. "That's what made our campaign," he insisted. It went straight to the restorative core of his message. Every Carter ad — in text or subtext — was about healing.

The irony of the emphasis on Carter's "little lies" during the 1976 campaign was that it told voters little about how he would govern. While he sometimes spun or shaded the truth in what — a generation later — would have earned him one or two "Pinocchios" from the *Washington Post* fact-checkers, he did not tell "Four Pinocchio" whoppers. Not once during his presidency was he caught in what can fairly be described as a bald-faced lie. In fact, his bigger problems would prove to be what would later be called "TMI" — too much information — about his personal life and a candor about the nation's problems that the public found less satisfying than Reaganesque fantasies.

Part of the problem was stylistic. Carter's rivals — and many reporters and commentators — were irritated by his unironic application of morality to everyday politics. He often played the injured party, accusing opponents whose gibes on issues were completely in bounds of "hurting the country." And he could be elusive when responding to questions. But what looked pious and dodgy to some of the political establishment struck many voters — at least in 1976 — as signs of integrity and an appealing humility in not pretending to have all the answers.

# 17
## FRONT-RUNNER

On January 19, 1976, "Uncommitted" won the Iowa caucuses with 37 percent of the vote. But Jimmy Carter was next at 28 percent, the long-favored Birch Bayh took 13 percent, and the rest of the candidates were in single digits. In the expectations game set up by reporters, Carter had won big.

The results reverberated through American politics. By evening, Carter was in bed in New York, resting up for appearances on all three morning shows, his debut in the national spotlight. After Tim Kraft roused him by phone with the final tallies, he deadpanned: "I guess we won't have to exile you to Alaska now." On TV the next morning, the former Georgia governor came across as the exciting new front-runner, peering forward confidently to New Hampshire and Florida.

In Jordan's 1972 memo, he envisioned New Hampshire as the primary to establish Carter as a serious contender, just as McCarthy in 1968 and McGovern in 1972 had done with impressive second-place finishes there. But now the bar had been raised to actually winning the primary, which was only a little more than a month away. One reason Carter needed to carry New Hampshire, ironically, was to prove to southern whites that he could win away from home.

Fortunately for Carter, Scoop Jackson had a disastrous showing there in 1972 and decided to stay out of the 1976 contest. As in Iowa, the liberals would be split, and Carter would have more conservative Democrats all to himself. This was a huge advantage in a year when Democrats, chastened by McGovern's 1972 wipeout, were open to a moderate.

Just after New Year's, ninety Georgians in the self-styled "Peanut Brigade" landed in Manchester. These older friends and supporters — some of whom had saved for months for the trip — turned out to be a secret weapon. In two weeks of spreading their southern charm to surprisingly receptive Yankees, they contacted about ten thousand voters and often handed out small cellophane packets of peanuts. "Sweetheart, I have not understood a word you've said, but I love the way you said it," a New Hampshire voter with a thick accent of his own told Dot Padgett, a leader of the brigade.

Voters in New Hampshire and in the seventeen other states where Peanut Brigade volunteers would appear were uniformly impressed that so many people would travel so far at their own expense; it must mean Jimmy Carter was a good man. "I'm asking you to vote for someone I personally know" was an extremely persuasive form of canvassing. Hamilton Jordan believed the Peanut Brigade trip to the Granite State gave the campaign a lead there that it never relinquished. It helped that Lester Maddox showed up in New Hampshire to campaign against Carter, which backfired by reminding voters that Carter was a different kind of white southerner.

The months of meticulous planning and careful town-by-town organization were about to pay off. By evening, on February 24, Carter beat Udall in the New Hampshire primary by nearly 6 points, with Bayh, Harris, and Shriver far back. A genial Walter Cronkite interview on CBS News unofficially anointed Carter as the new front-runner, but the Washington establishment remained befuddled. "Jimmy Carter? How can that be?" harrumphed Averell Harriman, wartime ambassador to the Soviet Union and Washington éminence grise. "I don't even know Jimmy Carter, and as far as I know, none of my friends knows him, either."

But younger Democrats took notice. Delaware senator Joe Biden switched his support from Milton Shapp and became the first senator to endorse Carter. As chair of his national campaign steering committee, Biden would appear in dozens of states for Carter in 1976. He joked that at age thirty-three, he was still two years shy of the constitutional age requirement to be president. So, since he couldn't yet run himself, he was backing Jimmy.

In the Carter playbook, the next big challenge was a fortnight later in Florida, which in those pre–Super Tuesday days had a whole primary week all to itself. Carter knew that if he could use Florida to lift the millstone of George Wallace from around the neck of the Democratic Party, he would become a hero for blacks and moderate white southern Democrats — and a giant-killing candidate of destiny.

The intervening week brought the Massachu-

360

setts primary, which had previously been in April and thus had no lore or influence associated with it. So Carter spent most of the week campaigning in Florida. But then he made the mistake of deviating from his game plan and seriously contesting Massachusetts — even letting Powell say he expected to win there. The other candidates ganged up on him, especially after he seemed to say at a candidate forum that his broad tax reform proposal would include eliminating the home mortgage deduction, a third rail in American politics. Even after he retreated and explained the context, the gaffe hurt.

On March 2, Massachusetts voters went to the polls in a blizzard. Jackson was the best organized, and his labor supporters turned out, giving him a surprise victory. Udall came in second, and Wallace, who exploited white resentment toward mandatory school busing in Boston, third. Carter finished a humiliating fourth.

After the returns came in, Bayh and Shriver dropped out, but this was cold comfort to Carter, who called Caddell from Florida and — his telltale temple vein throbbing — said in a slow, furious tone: *"What. Happened?"* When Carter was angry, he routinely turned almost frighteningly quiet. First, Caddell had some good news. He had won Roxbury, the black section of Boston, which meant blacks recognized he was a genuine liberal on race. If he won blacks in the North, Caddell predicted accurately, he would win them in the South. The bad news was that Carter's white support was soft. Voters liked him, but not enough to go vote in a snowstorm. The continued absence of an intense, deeply committed ideological base to draw on when his popularity fell would prove to be the single biggest handicap of his political career.

After Massachusetts, Carter was "off balance," Jordan conceded, and testy with the press. "Do you want to stop talking so I can give you my answer?" he snapped at a reporter. By now, they knew, as Carter's staff did, that the big public smile was rarely sincere and that the candidate was strangely incapable of just shooting the bull like other politicians. Many in the press corps had a soft spot for Harris and especially for Udall, who was funny. (After losing a later primary, he quipped, "The people have spoken — the bastards.")

The "boys on the bus," as the campaign reporters were often called then, asked Carter why he didn't tell jokes on himself, as Udall did. Carter tried a couple of jokes that were on the list of twenty-five not-very-funny ones he kept on a wallet card. A reporter at the back of the room gave Greg Schneiders, Carter's sharp-witted traveling aide, a sideways look. Schneiders cracked, "Carter's idea of a self-deprecating story is to shit on his staff." In later years, Carter displayed a warm, self-effacing sense of humor that amused audiences, but it wasn't much in evidence then.

Schneiders said Carter didn't always understand the niceties of politics: "He was very direct and quite sure he was right, and if people disagreed, they were wrong." Reporters saw that he could be prickly. But he was even-tempered most of the time, and his personal staff had little turnover. That wouldn't have been the case if he was exceptionally hard to work for. On balance, Carter's chilly impatience did not seem to hurt him.

He recalled that in the early primaries, "I got better coverage than I deserved."

Strapped for funds, Udall and Harris decided to skip Florida, another huge break for Carter. Just as he had been the only conservative when Jackson and Wallace avoided Iowa and New Hampshire, now he was the only liberal contesting Florida. Any splitting of the liberal vote would have given Florida to Wallace, a likely death blow to Carter's campaign after the Massachusetts loss.

Reporters expected Florida governor Reubin Askew to endorse Carter, but Askew — along with most other southern Democratic governors — disliked him from their exposure to him at the National Governors Association, where they grew jealous of his rising national profile. It was a sign of political trouble in the years ahead: Carter's "base" in the South wasn't much of a base at all.

Jackson was confident he was moving in the polls after Massachusetts, but he needed to bring Carter to earth. It wasn't easy. After Watergate, dirty tricks were strictly verboten. And Carter was an agile straddler. On abortion, for instance, he criticized the idea of a constitutional amendment banning it but also opposed federally funded Medicaid abortions (which raised hackles within his own administration after the election) and stressed his personal opposition. "I never have thought Jesus Christ would approve abortion," he said. Three years after *Roe v. Wade,* the battle lines on abortion that would condition politics for the next four decades were not yet fully drawn. A nuanced position still worked in the Democratic Party.

The conventional wisdom was that Wallace

would carry rural Florida, while Jackson, with his long and fervent support of the state of Israel, would carry the Jewish condo corridors of Miami-Dade and Broward Counties.

To win, Carter needed a strong share of the black vote. With Caddell's help, he obscured his old opposition to busing, noting that he supported it in certain situations. Anticipating campaigns of the future, he focused his ground game on the barber shops, beauty salons, and funeral parlors that were often the most successful black-owned businesses in the state. A porter and community organizer named Clarence Edwards was exceptionally well connected in that world. Phil Wise was much more confident of success with black voters — and thus of Carter becoming president — after he enlisted him.

For years, Wallace's attacks on "pointy-headed bureaucrats" and other elites were punctuated with his signature line: "Send them a message." In his clever billboards and ads, Carter responded: "This time, don't send them a message. Send them a President." The Carter team sensed that the outsider appeal of southerners could be harnessed to a hunger for respect — a sense that a less fiery candidate than Wallace might actually make it all the way to the White House and do the South proud. For a region that long felt deprived of its rightful place in American society, this was powerful stuff. Before southern audiences, black and white, Carter always got a laugh by saying, "Won't it be great to have a president who doesn't speak with an accent?"

Wallace was not the candidate he had been in 1964, 1968, and 1972. He was fine, he'd tell visitors drily, "except I'm paralyzed." When two state

364

troopers tripped while carrying him aboard a plane in Pensacola, Florida, on February 2, the governor wrenched his knee, requiring a cast. The mishap reinforced the idea that Wallace wasn't up to the challenge physically. His aides tried to make his use of a wheelchair seem in the spirit of FDR, but there was a reason Roosevelt's men threatened the access of any photographer who even tried to take a picture of him in his wheelchair: those images made Wallace look weak, especially because he had become famous for *standing* in the schoolhouse door. But his reactionary message might have been wrong for the times even had Wallace been healthy. Nixon's disgrace lanced the boil of sixties anger, leaving voters ready for healing. Wallace was never the one to bring it.

With his Massachusetts momentum, Scoop Jackson had a good shot in Florida. The transplanted New Yorkers and other snowbirds seemed to gravitate to him, and his strong anti-Communism gave him a claim in the Little Havana section of Miami. He was seen as having an especially strong base in the Jewish community.

Carter had no natural connection to Jewish voters beyond his Jewish uncle Louie Braunstein, who, he informed audiences, had taught the Gordys and the Carters about Passover. At a Florida yeshiva, Jimmy wore a yarmulke that Martin Schram of *Newsday* wrote made him look like " 'Jimmy,' chief of the Mouseketeers on the old Disney TV show." His words supporting Israel were just as strong as Jackson's, but according to Schram, he came across to Florida Jews "like grits at a seder."

Later in the campaign, when weakness with Jewish voters surfaced in other states, Carter mused aloud that Jews feared that Southern Baptists were anti-Semitic. He tried to reassure them that, from their earliest days, Baptists were deeply committed to the separation of church and state. Carter lived this credo as governor and would do so as president, but even then, his church was beginning a sharp shift to the right, and Jews appraising him were slipping from indifferent to suspicious.

These problems were down the road. On March 9 Carter beat Wallace in Florida by 4 points and Jackson by 10. The network news coverage was terrific for Carter, now cast as a man of moderation curing national politics of the scourge of racism. This was an exaggeration, of course, but he had indeed done something no one thought possible: destroyed the 150-year-old racist wing of the Democratic Party.

More immediately, Jackson was in deep trouble. Scoop was a man of integrity and personal modesty — unlike Carter, he carried his own bags and others' without letting anyone know — but he was often dull on the stump. Assessing Jackson's puzzling inability to win votes, political consultants told the story of a dog food company: the CEO complains to his board of directors that their dog food has the best ingredients, best labels, and best marketing, but sales are weak. Why? At the end of the table, a voice pipes up: "Dogs don't like it."

But the big story out of Florida wasn't that the dogs didn't like Scoop; it was that they really didn't like Wallace, who now saw his hopes of being a kingmaker vanish. Carter was charitable after his win, even to the Alabama governor. He told reporters that it was wrong to stigmatize people "because of the times they lived in and when they got their reputation." His instinct for putting himself in the shoes of disreputable — even reprehensible — political leaders first emerged in this period. Carter believed that judging them was complicated and situational, a turn of mind that would help him internationally as a peacemaker.

On the morning after the primary, a problem arose involving Hunter Thompson, whom Jordan had promised a Carter interview without informing the candidate or even Jody Powell. When the flight from Orlando to Chicago was aloft, Thompson plopped down next to Carter. The candidate said stiffly that there was no interview; he was exhausted and needed to sleep. An irate Thompson banged on the cockpit door in a vain effort to get the pilot to turn around. After the plane landed at O'Hare, he immediately caught a flight back to Orlando. He went to a store to buy lighter fluid and proceeded to the motel where Jordan was still asleep. Thompson spread the lighter fluid all around the door, lit it, and smoked Jordan and his girlfriend out of their room. Not long after, he got his Carter interview.

For all his antics, the gonzo legend remained surprisingly invested in a Carter victory. As Carter closed in on the nomination, Thompson wrote him, "I now feel saddled with a personal stake (with regard to my own judgement & credibility) in your candidacy." Even when Carter struggled in the presidency, Thompson stuck by him. In 1977 he described the president as one of the three "meanest men I ever met" — the other two being Muhammad Ali and Hells Angels president Sonny Barger. "But I admire that in him. He'll eat your shoulder right off."

■ ■ ■

Late winter and spring brought a hundred thumb-sucker columns about Carter. *New York Times* columnist James Reston derided outsider candidates for their lack of relevant experience and belittled "Wee Jimmy" for not calling himself "James." Democratic strategist Mark Shields wrote more favorably that "the problem is that no one in Washington owns a piece of Jimmy Carter." *Newsweek,* in a widely quoted line, reported, "It is said around Plains that you love Jimmy Carter in 15 minutes, hate him in six months, and understand him in ten years."

There was anti-southern bias in some of the opposition to him. In March, Charles Morgan Jr. of the ACLU said that a liberal New Yorker confided to him, "I could never vote for anyone with a southern accent." Morgan, a white liberal Alabaman, said he told the man, "That's bigotry, and that makes you a bigot."

For months, Carter had managed to sound liberal to liberals and conservative to conservatives — a purposeful vagueness that only the craftiest politicians can pull off. But now that guile was generating charges that he was "fuzzy" on the issues. The comedian Pat Paulson quipped that there was talk of putting Carter on Mount Rushmore "but they didn't have room for two faces."

Ted Kennedy had said that the front-runner was "intentionally . . . indefinite and imprecise" on issues. When Carter, inside a hotel suite, heard that, his eyes flashed with anger. "I don't have to kiss his ass," he said. The feeling was mutual. Kennedy tended to judge fellow Democrats on a single issue: national health insurance. While Carter favored it in principle, he always added the caveat that any government takeover of the entire system had to be affordable, which he privately thought was not possible.

Carter was a sensible, even logical, mix of conservative and liberal. He was a progressive on racial and international issues, an ardent environmentalist, and a planner with a faith in government — all anathema to the conservative ideology just gaining momentum. But he was also a businessman with no patience for waste and deficit spending and no feel for the labor movement — a political temperament that did not reassure New Deal liberals. His mind was too active to accept liberal ideology as received wisdom. This was attractive to independents and moderate Democrats, but it would prove problematic after he took office.

The best journalists began to see that Carter was connecting on a different wavelength than mere politics. In *New York* magazine, Richard Reeves addressed the elite's question du jour: Is Carter a phony? He concluded that Carter was no phonier than any other politician and that he possessed an insight into the national mood that might take him all the way to the White House. He quoted from Carter's autobiography *Why Not the Best?*:

"Nowhere in the Constitution of the United States or the Declaration of Independence or the Bill of Rights or the Emancipation Proclamation, the Old Testament or the New Testament, do you find the words 'economy' or 'efficiency.' Not that these two words are unimportant. But you discover other words like *honesty, integrity, fairness, liberty, justice, love. . . .* Words which describe what a government of human beings ought to be."

Reeves thought Carter understood that what others perceived as a post-Watergate political crisis was actually a spiritual crisis, and that values were more salient than issues. "Symbolic communication," Reeves wrote. "is the best way to reach Americans drifting in an atmosphere saturated with instant communications." Carter himself believed the Reeves piece had "a great deal of effect" on other journalists.

In Illinois, Carter had been courting Mayor Richard J. Daley of Chicago, last of the big city bosses. While Daley wouldn't endorse him, he did nothing to stop him, either, which sent an important signal to Democrats nationwide. Carter spent only four days campaigning in the state but won big there on March 18.

Just before the next contest, in North Carolina, he first talked publicly about his born-again experience. In the past, Carter had answered questions about his faith only briefly, in part because Jordan — openly worried about what he called "the weirdo factor" — advised him not to raise the subject. But at a closed fund-raiser in Winston-Salem in late March, a donor asked if he would disavow any of his religious convictions to win votes in other regions. Carter answered no and went on to describe his faith in more detail than at any time in the campaign.

When word of the exchange leaked, the Carter team had no choice but to hold a press conference the next day, where the front-runner recounted "a deeply profound religious experience that changed my life dramatically" in 1967. Ever

370

since establishing "a complete commitment to Christ," he said, "I've had an inner peace and inner conviction and assurance that transformed my life for the better." He steered clear of his walk in the fields with Ruth, who had — to her brother's irritation — recently described his supposed born-again moment in dramatic and erroneous detail to the *Washington Post,* even claiming her brother had "cried like a baby," which didn't sound like Jimmy to anyone who knew him.

Carter was candid about the political purpose of speaking out explicitly on religious matters. Referring to the challenges that Al Smith (the Democratic candidate in 1928) and John Kennedy faced over being Catholic, he acknowledged that at first his Baptist faith "created very serious political problems for me" among some Jewish and Catholic voters. He didn't mention the distaste of elites. (Arthur M. Schlesinger Jr., the historian and former Kennedy aide, told a friend, "I can't vote for someone who prays three times a day"). To make himself seem less alien, Carter reminded the press corps that Truman was a Baptist and that Baptists were strong believers in the separation of church and state.

Carter was playing defense on religion, as Smith and Kennedy had, but he also sensed the presence of a huge basket of new voters. Until then, evangelical Christians voted only lightly and not as a bloc; political scientists didn't bother assessing their importance because they had none. Carter saw a chance to inspire them, and he was right: many of the evangelicals who backed him in 1976 had never voted in a national election before. But Carter also inadvertently created a behemoth that would haunt the Democrats. Within four years,

371

the religious voters he brought into politics would not only trend Republican but do so in such numbers that the Christian Right became a major force in American politics.

At the same time, Carter's frank introduction of his personal faith into the campaign changed the way future presidential candidates presented themselves. Even the least religious would all feel obliged to follow Carter's lead and offer professions of faith as part of their campaigns.

George Wallace had forlorn hopes of recovering in North Carolina. By this time, his bitterness toward Carter, whom he viewed as "a warmed-over McGovern," was spilling into print. "He was my friend when I was popular," he told the *New Yorker*'s Elizabeth Drew. "He said he was for me [in 1972] when he thought I might die. . . . He talks about spending all that time on his kneeeeeees. Well, I'm going to church tomorrow, but I don't go around talking about my religion." None of his attacks worked. On March 23 Carter beat him in North Carolina by nearly 20 points, which showed Florida wasn't a fluke. "All they see is the spokes of my wheelchair," Wallace said of the voters.

But Carter was still far from being the presumptive nominee. April 6 brought two potentially pivotal liberal primaries: New York and Wisconsin. Black voters in New York tilted toward Udall, who at the time had the support of black New York politicians. A Udall ad featured tweedy, bow-tied Harvard Law professor Archibald Cox, fired by Nixon as Watergate special prosecutor in the Saturday Night Massacre, ardently endorsing him — a bid for liberal votes.

372

Carter hoped his weakness with Jewish voters, who made up about 40 percent of the New York Democratic primary, would be offset in part by his appeal to Orthodox Jews (who then respected him as a man of faith) and by the support of Mayor Abe Beame. But it wasn't nearly enough. Jackson won New York handily, with Udall second, uncommitted third, and Carter a distant fourth. There were compensations. Jackson's efforts netted him relatively few delegates, and he was nearly broke, having outspent Carter by nearly three to one in the most expensive media market in the country.

Three weeks before the primary, Wisconsin looked like a Carter blowout. Mo Udall's brother, Stu, a former interior secretary under JFK, told him that he was trailing Carter two to one and would lose badly. So Stu canceled a mailing to rural progressive voters and critical last-minute TV ads. But the polls were wrong: Udall was actually surging in the Badger State, where his progressivism was a good fit for liberal Democrats. By the time Mo overruled his brother, it was too late. The Udall campaign called local television stations forty-five minutes after they'd sold their last airtime.

Had he been on the air in the last three days, Udall would likely have won Wisconsin and possibly recovered enough to secure the nomination of a party whose politics more closely resembled his than Carter's. He almost did anyway. On primary night, NBC News and ABC News both projected Udall as the surprise winner. But after midnight, Pat Caddell, analyzing late-reporting rural counties, realized Carter might squeak it out. He passed along a frenzied message to the

Secret Service to contact Carter and make sure he didn't concede.

After two in the morning, it was clear that Carter had edged Udall by fewer than 8,000 votes out of more than 740,000 cast. Jody Powell fastened onto the perfect way to capitalize on Carter's "upset" in a state he had long been expected to win. Borrowing an iconic political image — a smiling Harry Truman holding aloft the 1948 *Chicago Tribune* front page with its premature headline "Dewey Defeats Truman" — he passed Carter an early edition of the *Milwaukee Sentinel* with the headline "Udall Upsets Carter." The photograph of Carter happily displaying the erroneous front page ran across the country and overshadowed the next day's coverage of the devastating New York returns. Despite a poor showing there on April 6, a lucky Carter had wounded Udall and overshadowed Jackson with one deft photograph.

Shortly before New York and Wisconsin, Carter made his biggest gaffe of the primary season, which went unnoticed until after those contests. On April 2 he gave an airborne interview to Sam Roberts of the *New York Daily News* about housing. In the sixteenth paragraph of a story on page 104 of the Sunday edition, he was quoted as saying that while he would not permit any housing discrimination, "I see nothing wrong with ethnic purity being maintained. I would not force a racial integration of a neighborhood by government action."

When Carter used the "ethnic purity" line again in an interview with CBS News, it set off a furor. Besieged by the press at the airport terminal in

South Bend, Indiana, the usually cool candidate was perspiring and dug himself in deeper. He said that what he was actually opposing was "the intrusion of alien groups into a neighborhood simply to establish their intrusion." Then he blamed the press for "trying to make something of it, and there's nothing to be made out of it." In those days, a politician's stubborn refusal to apologize was blood in the water — it just extended the story. "Are such terms as 'ethnic purity' and 'alien group' almost Hitlerian?" ABC News's Sam Donaldson asked him in Pittsburgh.

Now Carter's campaign began to teeter. Julian Bond wrote a piece arguing that his fellow Georgian was slippery and shouldn't be president, while Andrew Young, though still supportive, called the gaffe a "disaster" for the campaign and said Carter would have to "repent" to stay in. After two more days of resisting, the candidate — counseled by Rosalynn — finally apologized with evident sincerity and said he would sooner "withdraw from the race" than use "racist" appeals to win it.

Fleeing home, Carter enlisted the help of Jesse Hill Jr., who proved to be a lifesaver. Hill arranged a large noontime rally in an Atlanta park where Daddy King issued a statement saying "It is wrong to jump on a man for a slip of the tongue" and — in a rousing call-and-response with the black audience — described the beaming candidate at his side as "this man who I love and believe in."

The rally with Daddy King did more than end the worst week of the Carter campaign; it secured the black vote for good. At the lowest depths of his presidency, when other constituencies fled,

African Americans would remain loyal. As Andrew Young said, they knew his heart.

On April 27 Carter thrashed Scoop Jackson in Pennsylvania, effectively ending the Washington senator's campaign. By besting Wallace in conservative Florida, Udall in progressive Wisconsin, and now Jackson in union-dominated Pennsylvania, Carter had vanquished all of his major rivals on their own turf. Michigan, on May 18, was a near repeat of Wisconsin, with Udall finishing just two thousand votes behind Carter. Udall stayed in until the end but never went on the attack. He finished second to Carter in seven major primaries. If nominated, he almost certainly would have failed to carry the southern states that Carter did, likely costing him the election.

Hubert Humphrey might not have done much better. Right after the Pennsylvania primary, Humphrey — about to turn sixty-five — had to decide whether he wanted to run one last time for president. The filing deadline for the June 6 New Jersey primary, which he probably would have won, was the next day. For later generations, this was unimaginably late to jump in, but Humphrey had won the nomination eight years earlier without entering a single primary, and even now hundreds of delegates remained uncommitted or pledged to candidates no longer in the race. A Gallup poll in mid-April showed Humphrey tied with Carter, who was flush with victory but losing altitude nationally.

Amid great suspense about his intentions, Humphrey stood in the Senate Caucus Room and said: "One thing I don't need at this stage of my life is to be ridiculous." He acknowledged later that his bladder cancer, while seemingly treatable (and not known publicly at the time) was a factor in his decision not to run. Humphrey left himself open to a draft, which soon led his many friends in the party to organize an "Anybody but Carter" (ABC) campaign, with Humphrey as the "Anybody" who could be nominated at a brokered convention.

Two later entrants, Idaho senator Frank Church and California governor Jerry Brown, thought the "Anybody" was them. In May, when Church won Oregon and Brown thumped Carter in Maryland, the press jumped on Carter for not closing the sale. Voters still liked him but began experiencing buyer's remorse. With no ecstatic, hard-core supporters to power him through late primaries, he was limping to the nomination.

Just after the Pennsylvania primary, Bob Shrum, a gifted twenty-nine-year-old speechwriter, released a letter he wrote Carter after quitting his campaign. Shrum, who lasted only nine days, didn't like Carter's speaking style; he felt that he talked like an engineer and had an aversion to eloquence. That was true enough, but Shrum jumped to conclusions about Carter's character and convictions based on minimal personal interaction. In a later article, he quoted an unnamed aide calling Carter "a very odd duck," which suggested that the candidate's self-contained contemplative qualities made him some kind of strange loner who shouldn't be in the White House. Shrum's most influential line — one that didn't make news at the time but solidified slowly in the minds of many Democrats — concerned Carter's character: "I am not sure what you truly believe in other

377

than yourself."

This was a damning indictment that helped shape the long-term media narrative about Jimmy Carter. While it may have sounded right at the time, it turned out to be wrong. Carter believed passionately in several ideas larger than himself: peace, human rights, the environment, ethics in government, and tackling knotty problems no one else had the courage to touch. His problem was that these deeply held beliefs and his larger vision of a peaceful world didn't fit into a handy ideological pattern that journalists and voters could identify at a glance. At first, this political agility worked beautifully for him. But he couldn't keep the balancing act going for long. Carter's so-called fuzziness would hamper him for the duration.

So would a belief that politics is for campaigning, not governing. "He's not a politician," Charlie Kirbo reminded other aides in Atlanta. "As president, he will do what he thinks is right, whether it's popular or not, and if elected, he may be a one-term president."

The 1976 election was the first of the post-Watergate era, and it was much cleaner than what had come before. The "bag men" of old who carried around cash from unsavory sources were largely replaced by a transparent process that limited the influence of big money. This new system favored grassroots politicians over establishment candidates with greater access to big donors — an advantage for Carter. That allowed the campaigns to worry much less about fundraising than in later decades, when respect for clean-money reforms waned.*

Even with the nomination in hand, Carter was running himself ragged. In Columbus, Ohio, he was so tired that he mistakenly shook the hand of a department store mannequin. On the last day of the primary season, June 9, Carter won big in Ohio and finished second to Jerry Brown in California and New Jersey. Brown had entered six primaries and won them all, but it was too late to change the outcome.

At two in the morning, Plains was rocking, as townspeople — even the ones who never had any use for their neighbor — mobbed the quaint whitewashed train depot that now represented their town to the world. Carter received a message that George Wallace called. When he phoned back, Wallace said he was releasing his delegates to him, giving him enough to be nominated. But Carter didn't want to win that way. He thought Wallace putting him over the top would taint him. The next morning, he called Mayor Daley, who had said the previous week that he deserved the

---

*Even with the reforms, campaigns still needed money. Joel McLeary, Carter's twenty-six-year-old national finance director, remembered going to Las Vegas, where — without the knowledge of the Carter high command — he raised money from mob lawyer Sidney Korshak. McLeary said one casino owner, seeking favor with Carter, even funneled cash into the Carter campaign by letting McLeary and another man associated with the campaign win $250,000 at a gaming table that featured no cameras, with the understanding that the winnings would "help Carter." McLeary said Carter himself never learned of the gambit.

379

nomination if he won Ohio convincingly. Daley agreed to rally around him, as did Scoop Jackson, who stopped short of releasing his delegates but told Carter he wouldn't stand in his way. It was all over.

Carter took off his business suit and put on blue jeans and a matching jean jacket, his usual wardrobe in Plains. This was intentional, he said later. On the day he was announcing to the world that a big-city boss and a prominent Washington insider were giving him enough delegates to be nominated on the first ballot, he wanted to convey the informality and authenticity that had helped define his insurgent campaign. Every time he had come across as the front-runner instead of the scrappy outsider, he slipped. By contrast, "Whenever we'd project ourselves as the underdog fighting the establishment, fighting a valiant fight, we did all right," he remembered. Those underdog days were over, at least for 1976. Jimmy Carter, the presumptive Democratic nominee for president, was now cloaked in the heavy garments of his party.

# 18
## GRITS AND FRITZ

After clinching the nomination, Carter retreated to Plains to prepare for the Democratic Convention in mid-July and to begin planning for the general election campaign, which didn't begin in earnest until after Labor Day. The plan was to continue to run against Washington from the high road, while having ads and surrogates lash the Nixon pardon and the weak economy around President Ford's neck.

Carter had come further faster than any major party nominee since Republican Wendell Willkie in 1940, and he was now heavily favored to be the next president. But his political standing remained tenuous. He had successfully packaged himself as a man of integrity, accomplishment, and faith — an image that had the added benefit of being largely true. Yet the bond he established with voters was connected to a passing public mood, not deeply shared interests or long-standing political ties. If he owed nobody anything, then nobody owed him much of anything, either.

Carter's southern heritage was a shaky base. Regional pride would prove to be a wide but shallow and temporary phenomenon. And he never developed a hard-core base anywhere else: no fervid farm-belt supporters or special chemistry with a large voting bloc beyond his easy but not deep connection to the black community. While his performance on the stump won him millions of admirers, he never inspired a large following of dedicated "Carterites" who would be for him no matter what.

The bigger challenge was ideological. Carter was the first of what in the Bill Clinton era would be called "neoliberals" (when the label still had positive connotations) or "New Democrats." These weren't corporate Democrats — few had ties to Wall Street — just fiscally conservative moderates still committed to the noble goals of liberalism but open to fresh means of achieving them. Carter didn't go nearly as far as his father in rejecting the New Deal, but he preferred not to see it preserved in amber, either. In this, he was ahead of his time — a leader for socially tolerant, pragmatic, diverse, tech-savvy, green, pro–small business centrists who were still undefined as a political force.

Once the campaign went fully national, Carter risked being seen as too conservative for liberals and too liberal for conservatives — trapped in political purgatory. Democrats had traditionally run left in the primaries, then pivoted to the center in the general election, but Carter was now forced to do the opposite, and it made him uncomfortable. Moving left in 1976 meant moving into the maw of the Democratic Party establishment and its collection of interest groups. He felt that wasn't the right place for a populist outsider who had won the nomination in part by pushing back against those powerful institutional forces.

Carter saw in retrospect that every time a labor boss or Capitol Hill big shot was seen on television headed down to Plains, he lost votes, just as Carl Sanders did in the 1970 gubernatorial campaign when he received all the big endorsements. At the end of the summer, he went to a star-studded party thrown for him by Warren Beatty at the Beverly Wilshire Hotel in Los Angeles. Carroll O'Connor, the actor who played the Queens bigot Archie Bunker on the hit TV show *All in the Family,* mentioned in the Q & A that Carter had won the nomination without the support of all the people in the room. "That's *why* I won the nomination," Carter said with a smile. He was only half joking.

This self-analysis was colored by his memory for personal slights. From Bob Strauss on down, Carter told his team, the Democratic National Committee had been committed to Jackson, Humphrey, or Udall — if not openly, in violation of their supposed impartiality, then privately. He felt he had won the nomination by taking his case directly to the people — and owed little to the DNC, which he had used as a launching pad just two years earlier.

Carter neglected to mention that it was the party rank and file — labor unions, minorities, liberals — who had pulled him over the finish line in Ohio, Pennsylvania, and other critical primary states. With the headiness of nomination, he would discount what the party had done for him and take its support for granted. He downplayed the pain of the 1974–75 recession and other bread-and-butter economic concerns in favor of issues like inflation and budget balancing that were of less interest to most Democrats.

The candidate would later consider his frayed connections to his party the greatest regret of his presidency. "My relationship with the Democratic Party was not particularly good, and I could have done more had I made it a higher priority," he admitted after he left the White House. "It was not a burning commitment or interest of mine, and I think in the long run that was costly."

The more imminent problem was that Carter was sitting on his lead. He neither passionately embraced the old Democratic Party message nor deepened and broadened the one he had crafted for the previous two years. Campaigning on biography and morality had worked brilliantly in the primaries but now brought diminishing returns. Increasingly, Carter gave the impression of running to *be* president, not to *do* big things in office. This wasn't the case; once inaugurated, he would offer a flurry of proposals, many detrimental to his political health. But he didn't put much detail into his plans and policies during the campaign, which made him look less substantive than he actually was.

Arriving in Plains, the press complained about annoying gnats and distant accommodations but mostly considered the Carter home front "a masterful political show," as one reporter put it, full of the cotton-patch characters introduced to the American people over the previous six months. This was when "Miz Lillian" became famous. Lillian liked her nightly bourbon and Fresca and her morning bourbon and coffee, which she would share in the network trailers with Sam Donaldson and other reporters. She could often be found on Sundays complaining about the "hypocrites" at church. The press protected her on the drinking but loved detailing her other indulgences, from the Los Angeles Dodgers to the Thursday afternoon poker games where she and other local women played for dimes. Reporters collected the little shots she took (discussing her children, she said of herself, "Lillian, you should have stayed a virgin") but rarely covered her jealous streak. When a woman sought her autograph on a leaflet signed already by Rosalynn's mother, she snapped, "I sign under no one's name but Jimmy Carter's."

Reporters enjoyed learning that Jimmy's sister, Gloria, and her husband, Walter, devoted much of their time to riding around the country on their Harleys. Walter, wielding a gavel, became the unofficial chief justice of motorcycle racing at Daytona Beach, resolving disputes between the Hells Angels and a rival motorcycle gang, while Gloria kept the bikers' books, so they could figure out who owed each other money. The press never learned that Carter was unhappy when he found out Walter sold bags of Plains dirt to tourists.

For a contrast to Jimmy's enlightened views on race, reporters could always seek out his now elderly uncle and onetime father figure, Alton "Buddy" Carter, who described Archery to a reporter as "not much of a town — it's mostly niggers." Alton's son Hugh ("Cousin Beedie"), the former state senator, ran a store in town where he "made antiques" for unsuspecting tourists and claimed to own the world's largest worm farm, which sold mail-order worms and crickets for fishing bait. Even Amy made a name for herself, raising money for her father's campaign by price gouging the press with her lemonade stand on Main Street.

The summer of 1976 was when the world fell for Billy Carter, who had bought the only gas station in Plains for $10,000 and turned it into a clubhouse for every good ol' boy in the area and the Carter chroniclers in the national press corps.

The Amoco station housed a permanent game of gin rummy under the broken RC Cola clock, where Billy provided rich sidebar material for what he playfully called the "deadbeat" reporters and marooned camera crews. Despite a mild stutter, he was a quip machine ("I got a red neck, white socks, and Blue Ribbon beer") but explained that this didn't qualify him as a Georgia redneck: "A good ol' boy is somebody that rides around in a pickup truck — which I do — and drinks beer and puts 'em in a litter bag. A redneck's one that rides around in a truck and drinks beer and throws 'em out the window."

Ruth, her traveling ministry booming, believed that her younger brother "chose to exaggerate his vices and vitriol," and Billy admitted later that he downplayed his bookishness in order to cash in on his image. But there was intuitive Carter family political calculation here, too. Billy conveniently represented everything his brother couldn't — an almost too-neat balancing of the family ticket. Unlike the candidate, Billy didn't take himself too seriously. "I'm not the Carter who never lies," he liked to say. Jimmy's biggest problem, he told visitors, was that "he's around people that kiss his ass all the time." Jimmy knew that Billy's antics humanized his candidacy. In the years ahead, he might mutter about him in private, but he never distanced himself from his brother in public — no matter what the offense.

Ensconced in Plains, the press corps arranged a

regular softball game that pitted Jimmy and campaign staff versus Billy and reporters. Jimmy was an excellent pitcher, with a deceptive drop-ball pitch that he delivered with maximum spin. At the plate, he was a cagey and consistent singles and doubles hitter. He loaded up his team with young, buff off-duty Secret Service agents, some of them former college and semipro players, and local ringers who hit for power.

The casual dress and ready smiles were deceptive: Jimmy glared at teammates who didn't hustle. When Sam Donaldson razzed him, Carter replied coldly, "Your job is to coach runners at first." Powell said to Donaldson within earshot of Carter, "He can be a real prick, can't he?" — a comment that didn't faze Carter at all. One August afternoon, players and spectators heard a loud explosion from down the street at the gas station, where an electrical fire had started in the soda machine. Until he knew his place would survive, Billy wept uncontrollably, which endeared him further to the press.

The press pack treated Jimmy more skeptically. Reporters liked to joke about "that last clinging drop" — the Carter overshare in *Why Not the Best?* that revealed he was worried that retained urine would keep him out of the Naval Academy. They thought the title was awfully self-regarding for a self-styled "humble" candidate, even if they knew "the best" referred not just to Carter but to the government performance he promised. The short autobiography, by now a best seller, became a handy way of checking his claims against what the folks said at home.

Carter's family tired quickly of the scrutiny. Lillian complained about reporters using flattery to "put the wool in my eye" when they interviewed her. When Kandy Stroud, a reporter for *Women's Wear Daily,* came to interview her in the Pond House, Lillian's first words were: "I don't like women reporters." One unnamed female journalist asked whether her son ever lied. She allowed that the family sometimes told "white lies." The reporter asked how she defined a white lie. Lillian replied, "Remember how when you walked in here, I told you how sweet and pretty you were?"

Jimmy inherited some of that. On an earlier visit to Plains, Stroud felt she had been denied a promised interview. Peter Bourne suggested she just go uninvited to the candidate's house on Woodland Drive. Instead, she called ahead — the home phone was still in the Plains phone book — to make the request. Carter answered, annoyed. He said coldly that if Powell told her to call, "I'll fire his ass." When informed it was Bourne, he said, "I'll fire his ass, too." Then he heard Stroud crying softly. With family and staff, Carter was often unmoved by tears, but this time his mood changed instantly, and he said, "Don't cry. Can you be here by two o'clock?"

One of Carter's appearances at Sunday school with the press corps turned into more than a photo op. After a speaker in church told the biblical story of Jonah and the whale as if it had actually happened, Carter told reporters that he believed in science and that the Bible was allegorical. But when reports of this appeared in the press, Carter, worried he might lose the votes of evangelicals, claimed that he had been misquoted. In trying for both secularists and fundamentalists, he was pleasing neither — and alienating the

388

press. James Perry of the *National Observer* wrote that year, "He is a very tough fellow, he seems to nurse grudges, and he tends to lash out at people who criticize him, even when their intentions are honorable."

Carter didn't care what critics said. Hamilton Jordan worried constantly about his candidate moving either too far left or too far right. He urged him to avoid only two people: Ralph Nader, then at the peak of his fame as a fiery and highly effective liberal consumer advocate, and James Schlesinger, the overbearing Republican hawk who had headed both the CIA and the Pentagon and alienated President Ford. Nader was despised by conservatives; Schlesinger by liberals. Naturally, Carter invited both to Plains.

Nader umpired the softball game, then gave Carter a three-hour guided tour of the pitfalls of Washington.* Carter invited Schlesinger to come talk about China, which he had just visited. The two men fell for each other intellectually and, after the election, would meet to talk about a range of issues on Saturday mornings at six. Schlesinger's strong personality was a big reason why energy — which he considered a matter of national security — became one of the dominant issues of the Car-

*Nader was accompanied by twenty-seven-year-old James Fallows, a former "Nader's Raider" recently hired as a Carter speechwriter, whose searing piece in the *Washington Monthly,* "What Did You Do in the Class War, Daddy?," chronicled his regrets over dodging the draft when he was at Harvard while working-class kids went off to fight — an argument Carter appreciated.

ter administration.

Norman Mailer, then America's most famous novelist, also made the trek, on assignment for the *New York Times Magazine.* He found Rosalynn "immensely alive" and compared her favorably to Jackie Kennedy. Her heart-shaped face reminded him of "a movie star playing a marvelous waitress in a good 1930s film . . . who gives you good cheer about the future of the human condition."

Jimmy, too, impressed Mailer, who felt "Carter's presence had a quintessential American cleanliness, that silvery light of a finely tuned and supple rectitude that produces our best ministers and best generals alike, responsible for both the bogs of Vietnam and the vision of a nobler justice." He didn't find him particularly charismatic, writing "No massing of energy rose like thunder bolts from his brow. You could come near him in a room before you were aware he was there." But he resisted the easy thumbnail assessment: "One would not find the thing that made Carter tick," Mailer concluded, "for it was not a thing but a force that rose from every medium of his experience." He would never be treated so reverentially in the press again.

As he weighed his vice presidential pick, Carter had strong views on the role his number two should play. He wanted to break precedent and have a vice president who, for the first time, was granted some actual power. He knew the long, tortured history of shunned vice presidents and had been horrified to read that his political hero, Harry Truman, had known nothing about the atomic bomb before Franklin Roosevelt died in 1945, just weeks before Truman had to decide whether to use it. He was looking for an "equal partner" who could also connect with the public. "I wanted to see how people reacted when they walked up and down the streets of Plains," Carter remembered. So most of the interviews would be held there.

Charlie Kirbo led the selection process, which he ran quietly out of Herman Talmadge's Senate office. He preferred Scoop Jackson, but Carter wasn't interested. John Glenn, the former Mercury astronaut and Ohio senator, was an early favorite. He piloted his own plane into the airport near Plains, but he didn't stick the landing, and the visit didn't get much better. Glenn brought an aide to the interview, which Carter found off-putting, especially when the senator turned to the aide and said, "Anything else to ask?" Ed Muskie and Frank Church also came down for interviews, but Walter Mondale quickly became the Plains choice, in part because he memorized everyone's name beforehand, including Billy's kids and Cousin Hugh. It helped that Rosalynn and the rest of Plains loved Mondale's wife, Joan, a champion of the arts, and that Mondale's father had been a minister.

"Even though [Carter] was from the South, our backgrounds were similar," Mondale reflected years later. "Fritz" Mondale didn't bring a state into the Democratic column (Minnesota was solidly Democratic) but his strong liberal voting record and deep labor ties helped balance the ticket. More important, Carter trusted him immediately. If not for concern over Mondale's high blood pressure, which delayed a decision, he might have been selected right then. Years later, Carter recalled their instant chemistry and joked,

"And we wanted someone who is handsome."

It was Mondale who was wary at first. He knew that many vice presidents had been "humiliated to death," and that his mentor, Hubert Humphrey, "was ground under Lyndon Johnson's heel." He felt Humphrey was a changed man after he left office — that Johnson's demeaning treatment "had taken something precious out of his being." But he was impressed by how thoroughly Carter had reimagined the vice presidency. And when he told Carter that he wanted to be involved in every dimension of his presidency, not just be given one or two assignments, he liked the fact that Carter quickly agreed.

The closeness between the two would puzzle official Washington, which assumed Mondale was bantering and funny, while Carter was chilly and all business. But this lazy shorthand was belied by their warm and often amusing camaraderie — apparent to all who saw them together. From their first meeting in Plains, they never quarreled and, with one big exception in 1979, would never disagree on anything of great significance.

By the eve of the Democratic Convention, Carter was worried — with good reason — that he might wear out his welcome. Dewey, the 1948 Republican nominee who blew a big lead to Truman, "went around so long acting like he was president that people thought it was time for a change," he told aides. "I don't want that to happen to me."

To maintain at least a little suspense, Carter followed a long-standing tradition in both parties of the presumptive nominee not announcing his running mate before the convention (unless he was the incumbent president sticking with his vice president). When the delegates — more diverse than ever before — gathered at New York's Madison Square Garden on July 12, the guessing game included only white male candidates. After Texas congresswoman Barbara Jordan, famous for her eloquence during the Nixon impeachment case, delivered a stunning keynote address, her name was added to the short list, a first for a woman or an African American.

Beneath the surface of the 1976 convention were signs of tension among Democrats. Ted Kennedy was interviewed on CBS News by Walter Cronkite for a full fifteen minutes and could hardly muster thirty seconds of support for Carter. The wounds from Jerry Brown's last-minute campaign were still so fresh that the California governor could not be trusted to speak in prime time — a harbinger of enduring political trouble for Carter in California. Another omen: the Washington establishment felt slighted by the Carter team. A Washington hostess ran into Hamilton Jordan in an elevator. "By the way, are you called Jordan or Jerden?" she asked him mildly. Hamilton deadpanned, "My friends call me Jerden, but you can call me Jordan." The animus went both ways. Snobby Democratic partygoers were overheard joking about whether the nominee was back at his hotel "watching *Hee Haw,*" a down-home 1970s TV show that featured hicks telling corny jokes.

The debate over the Democratic Party platform was much quieter than in 1968 and 1972. Sam Brown, a left-wing leader of the antiwar movement, and Daniel Patrick Moynihan, a hawkish New York intellectual running for the Senate that year as a Democrat, struck an important deal. Brown wanted a plank criticizing the abuses of

Latin American dictators, and Moynihan wanted language flaying Communist regimes. "I'll denounce your dictators if you denounce mine," Moynihan said. The result was a strong and broad expression of support for human rights, an issue that Carter had mentioned but not stressed during the primaries.

Only the plank on amnesty for Vietnam War protesters generated sustained debate. It called for a pardon of peaceful draft dodgers and for a case-by-case consideration of each Vietnam-era deserter. Left-wingers wanted blanket amnesty and felt that Sam Brown had sold them out — an early sign that parts of the Left would never be satisfied by even Carter's boldest decisions.

Carter had supported the war until 1974 — a full year after the Paris Peace Accords finally ended US military involvement in Vietnam and all troops were withdrawn. That was extremely late for a national Democrat, if standard for a southern politician. Antiwar liberals were also suspicious of Carter for his fuzzy response to the My Lai Massacre, the most notorious of all Vietnam-era war crimes.* He was, however, ahead of many others

*In 1971 Lieutenant William Calley Jr. was convicted by a military court at Fort Benning, Georgia, of the 1968 mass murder of twenty-two South Vietnamese civilians near the village of My Lai. Under intense pressure from the Right, which made Calley into a hero, Governor Carter asked Georgians to turn on their headlights during the day to show support for servicemen on what he called American Fighting Men's Day. In 1976, moving left, Carter said, "I never felt any attitude toward Calley except abhorrence." The press

394

in grasping the class unfairness of the draft —
where poor and middle-class kids who "didn't
have enough money to hide in college" made up a
disproportionately large share of our fighting
forces — and extraordinarily sympathetic to draft
dodgers. Carter welcomed them into his convention (over the objections of liberal Mo Udall) and
allowed Fritz Efaw, a draft cvader who barely
escaped arrest when he returned from Europe for
the occasion, to have his name placed in nomination for vice president. The seconding speech was
delivered by a scraggly Vietnam veteran in a
wheelchair named Ron Kovic, whose life would
be depicted by Tom Cruise in the 1989 film *Born
on the Fourth of July.* In the bicentennial year,
Kovic rocked the hall with a speech that captured
the rawness of the first half of the 1970s:

I am the living death
The Memorial Day on wheels,
Your Yankee Doodle Dandy
Your John Wayne come home,
Your Fourth of July firecracker,
Exploding in the grave.

On Wednesday night, Carter and his family
gathered in suite 2150 of the Americana Hotel
(now the Sheraton New York Times Square) to
watch the balloting. After Ohio put him over the
top, the crowd cheered amid the traditional
Democratic playing of "Happy Days Are Here
Again." Jimmy stood on the Karastan carpet and,

---

found this contradictory, but Carter insisted that one
could simultaneously object to what Calley did and
support the troops.

with what his sister Ruth described as "quiet, brooding emotion," told his guests that he never would have made it this far if he hadn't had someone to run his business in his absence over the previous eight years: "The one person I feel most grateful to, the one I feel did the most to make it possible for me to wage this campaign," he said, turning to the man standing on his right, "is my brother, Billy."

The identity of the vice presidential candidate was the only secret of the convention. On Wednesday the *Children's Express,* a publication put out by preteens, scooped the world by reporting that the choice was Walter Mondale. ("My main advantage is that adults don't think children listen or understand," explained twelve-year-old reporter Gilbert Giles.)

In his rousing acceptance speech on Thursday, Mondale won his biggest applause when he struck the post-Watergate moral themes that had animated the entire campaign season: "The year of our two hundredth birthday, the year of Jimmy Carter's election, will go down as one of the greatest years of public reform in American history." The Garden, festooned with green Carter-Mondale placards printed that afternoon and homemade "Grits and Fritz" signs, erupted. The previous three Democratic conventions — 1964, 1968, and 1972 — had been shadowed by assassination, violence in the streets, and deep party schisms, respectively. Not this time.

When Carter broke precedent and entered the arena dramatically from the back of the convention floor, striding past the delegates, John Chancellor of NBC News called it the best-staged entrance he had ever seen at a convention.* On the podium, the smiling nominee waited for the thunderous applause to die down before beginning his acceptance speech the way he had launched so many of his other appearances in the eighteen months since his improbable journey began in Iowa: "My name is Jimmy Carter, and I'm running for president."

Now came more prolonged cheers, the first of more than two dozen that would interrupt the speech, as Carter beamed wordlessly. Norman Mailer, watching from the press gallery, was hardly the only one smitten by the "astonishingly nice smile." The novelist wrote later, "If the smile was not genuine. then Carter was not just a political genius but an artist of the first Satanic rank."

After another ovation, Carter delivered an impressive if quickly forgotten acceptance speech that lacked a signature line like FDR's "a new deal for America" at the 1932 convention or JFK's promise of "a new frontier" when he accepted the nomination in 1960. This was intentional — an effort, as he told his speechwriters, to strip his rhetoric down to its essentials. The speech was not written, Carter told the *New York Times* the day before, "so that people will be quoting from it in twenty years." They weren't, but more than forty years later, it resonated:

Our country has lived through a time of torment.
   It's now a time for healing.
We want to have faith again!

*He walked right past me, then eighteen years old and working at the convention as an usher.

We want to be proud again!
We just want the truth again!

The theme was how to recover from the "moral decay [that] has weakened our country." The answer, he suggested, was that "love must be aggressively translated into simple justice." Carter softly advocated a revival of spirit — "We have an America that in Bob Dylan's phrase is busy being born, not busy dying" — and used a line that Bill Clinton would borrow sixteen years later: America needs a president "who feels your pain."

It's time for America to move and to speak, not with boasting and belligerence, but with a quiet strength — to depend in world affairs not merely on the size of an arsenal but on the nobility of ideas — and to govern at home not by confusion and crisis but with grace and imagination and common sense.

As the acceptance speech ended, Sam Donaldson somehow got on the podium and stuck his microphone in Carter's face.

"Well, did you think you had a snowball's chance at first?"

"I thought I'd win, yes."

Donaldson asked about the cartoon from the Athens, Georgia, newspaper that Carter kept in his den. The candidate explained how it depicted "me walking in the road carrying a Carter for President sign and the devil walking into hell with a snowball. And this guy is standing there and said, 'I'm betting on the snowball.' "

The happy and surprisingly harmonious Democratic National Convention ended with Daddy King's benediction: "Surely the Lord sent Jimmy

Carter to come on out and bring America back where she belongs." Thirteen years after his son's "I Have a Dream" speech in front of the Lincoln Memorial, the dream that "one day on the red hills of Georgia, the sons of former slaves and the sons of former slave owners will be able to sit down together at the table of brotherhood" seemed to be taking hold, at least in the once-racist Democratic Party. "Strangely enough," wrote essayist Roy Blount Jr., "Jimmy Carter was a surrogate Dr. King." As the stage filled with improbable juxtapositions — George Wallace and Coretta King; Mayor Daley and Gene McCarthy — an exultant Bob Strauss signaled Peter Duchin, whose orchestra began a rousing "We Shall Overcome."

Hubert Humphrey in 1968 and George McGovern in 1972 had both left their conventions trailing the Republican nominees by more than when they entered. Carter came to New York leading by 13 and departed leading by 30 to 35 points. The third week of July 1976 was the high point of his political career.

The Carter campaign seemed suffused by faith, with a candidate who said he prayed silently more than thirty times a day. In a PBS interview in May, Bill Moyers had asked him if he prayed to win. Carter said never — only for guidance and strength. When Moyers asked, "What drives you?" Carter replied that it wasn't "an unpleasant sense of being driven" but a more religious calling:

"I feel like I have only one life to live — I feel God wants me to do the best I can with it. And that's quite often my major prayer: let me live my life so that it will be meaningful. And I enjoy tackling difficult problems, and solving them, and the meticulous organization of a complicated effort."

This was becoming known in theological and socio-philosophical circles as "the servant-leader" model, though a humble, selfless approach to social change was not normally associated with those at the very top. Whatever one called it, finding a path to meaning and goodness resonated powerfully in 1976, even as it invited skepticism. There was something deeply American in Carter's combination of faith in God and faith in himself and his ability to shape the world. It seemed genuine and worked for him politically as long as righteousness didn't become self-righteousness.

In August Tom Wolfe, then celebrated for his nonfiction, devoted a *New York* magazine cover story to the new self-absorption in American life, which he saw as rooted in spiritual pursuits. "The 'Me' Decade and the Third Great Awakening" depicted seekers who dropped acid for divine revelation, sanctified sex as a religion, and committed themselves to cultlike retreats focused on the self. Even mainline churches, Wolfe explained, were going "charismatic" in their religious services. The explanation for Jimmy Carter's appeal, he argued, was the cresting of a "30-year boom" in the wake of World War II that gave Americans the time and money to apply all their talent for excess to themselves.

"Both Carter and [Jerry] Brown had stumbled upon a fabulous terrain for which there are no words in current political language. A couple of politicians had finally wandered into the Me Decade," Wolfe wrote, in the first use of a phrase that would be widely applied to the 1970s:

400

"Ten years ago, if anyone of wealth, power, or renown had publicly 'announced for Christ,' people would have looked at him as if his nose had been eaten away by weevils. Today it happens regularly . . . Harold Hughes resigns from the US Senate to become an evangelist . . . Charles Colson, the former hardballer of the Nixon administration, announces for Jesus . . . and the man who is likely to be the next president of the United States, Jimmy Carter, announces for Jesus. Oh Jesus People."

Wolfe's famous article presaged an irony about the soon-to-be president: Carter may have been the beneficiary of the Me Decade, but beyond his personal relationship with Christ, he never embodied it. He would devote much of his presidency to preaching self-sacrifice and the rest of his life to serving others at least as much as himself.

But first he would have to dislodge the incumbent, who initially seemed to be making it easier for him. For nearly two years, President Ford had been the subject of ridicule. With the 1973 Arab embargo having triggered wild inflation, he launched a lame "Whip Inflation Now" campaign complete with "WIN" buttons that gave comedians good material. After he hit his tennis partner with a serve and slipped on the Air Force One stairs, his clumsiness, while a myth, was immortalized by Chevy Chase's slapstick pratfalls on the first season of NBC's *Saturday Night Live.*

In his 1975 State of the Union address, Ford admitted that "the state of the union is not good." The economy was beset by "stagflation" — a combination of stagnant growth, high unemployment, and inflation that whipsawed business and demoralized the public. And after the fall of Saigon that April, Ford's foreign policy came under attack from Ronald Reagan, who, like Carter, was out of office and had time to launch a vigorous primary campaign.

After Ford won most of the early primaries, Reagan's last shot was North Carolina, where segregation was a fading cause, replaced by a bristling nationalism. The issue that propelled him was Secretary of State Henry Kissinger's negotiation over the future of the Panama Canal. Whenever Reagan said, "We built it, we paid for it, it's ours, and we aren't going to give it away to some tinhorn dictator!" the North Carolina crowds exploded. Reagan won big there and soon had enough delegates to make the Republican National Convention in Kansas City the last multiballot convention of the twentieth century.

To secure the nomination on the fourth ballot, Ford had to agree to a hard-line party platform. Reagan's warm concession speech stole the hearts of even the Ford delegates, but his generous endorsement of the president sewed up the party's wounds. With Reagan, looking to 1980, uninterested in being vice president, Ford offered the second slot on the ticket to Kansas senator Bob Dole, who was then considered a hard-line conservative.

Looking back, Carter saw this as a pivotal moment. Years later, he wrote: "Dole was a disaster at campaigning, alienating African American voters who were loyal to [former New York governor] Nelson Rockefeller, a hero to that community, and costing them New York." And thus the election.

But if Dole was the wrong choice, almost

everything else began clicking for the Republicans. Ford's ability to close a 33-point gap in the ten weeks following the Democratic Convention became political lore. It was partly the result of his skillful campaign and Carter's miscues. But the main reason was a united GOP. All spring and early summer, Reagan and Ford each refused to say he would endorse the other, which meant that conservatives would not tell pollsters they intended to vote for Ford. For all its divisive drama, the Republican convention changed that. Reagan Republicans had nowhere else to go and began slowly but steadily returning to the fold. When they did, Ford cut the gap by two-thirds by Labor Day.

But he still trailed Carter by double digits, and the Ford campaign needed to know why. Dick Cheney, Ford's young chief of staff, had watched the entertaining Carter family show with rising alarm. He knew Ford's personal story couldn't compete. The president was technically from Grand Rapids, Michigan, but had been a creature of Washington for nearly three decades. Born Leslie L. King Jr. — he later took his stepfather's name — Ford had little family besides his wife, Betty, and four fairly ordinary kids. His parents and stepfather were dead, and he had only obscure half siblings. "Everybody knows about Plains, Georgia, and Lillian. Nobody really knows Ford," Cheney wrote in a memo. "He never had a hometown. He never had a mother. He never had a childhood, as far as the American people are concerned."

Ford's challenges were especially acute in the South, which had been slowly trending Republican but now seemed enchanted by a candidate more liberal than the region. "Carter is playing upon two essentially conflicting myths — the 'good ol' boy' rural South and the 'black and white together' new South," Frances K. Pullen, a Tennessee-born woman staffer in Ford's White House, wrote to the campaign's high command. Pullen, whose advice was mostly ignored, argued persuasively that Carter had fused these seemingly contradictory strains of southern culture by highlighting his authenticity and roots.

This "healing southernness," as the scholar Zachary J. Lechner put it, held appeal far beyond the South and was bolstered by popular TV programs like *The Waltons* and the national reach of the Allman Brothers and other southern rock bands. After the 1975 Boston busing crisis showed that racism was flaring in the North, Carter was able to argue that the South had survived such racial strife a decade earlier and was now moving to a warm, hospitable future that was at once tolerant, traditional, and down-home.

And just in case the friendly tone didn't work, the Carter team made sure to have a harder-edged message on the air. In the fall, Rafshoon ran an ad across the South that sold the Georgia candidate as an antidote to "years of coarse anti-southern jokes" and the region's status as "a political whipping boy." The ad concluded, "The South has always been the conscience of America, and maybe they'll start listening to us now." For Latinos in the Southwest, Carter filmed the first-ever political TV ad in Spanish.

All of this worked thematically for Carter through Election Day, but his lead kept eroding anyway. Later, he pointed to the beating he had taken for five days at the Republican Convention, where speakers (in an era of gavel-to-gavel network coverage) had mentioned him unfavorably 113 times from the podium. He also confessed privately that he had become too closely identified with the national Democratic Party — the same insiders he had successfully run away from in both 1970 and the early 1976 primaries. Now, instead of being what he called "a lonely peanut farmer looking for votes," he would go into the industrial Midwest as "the establishment figure" inevitably "saddled" with all the fat and balding down-ballot candidates, many of whom — his children joked — looked like they had answered a casting call for political hacks.*

Carter was determined to run free of these old-fashioned pols. When one of them, Indiana senator Vance Hartke, showed up at an event, Carter was peeved. "If I ever see that son of a bitch again at one of my rallies," he told Jody Powell, "you can be *his* press secretary." But the candidate's days of denying he was a politician were over, and his image grew blurry. Unable to reconcile all of the different Carters they had met over the previous year, voters began to see Ford — their accidental president — as a comfortable old shoe.

As summer wore on, a role reversal was under way. While party leaders trooped to Plains to kiss Carter's ring, Rafshoon said, "Gerald Ford had become a regular guy, getting out and milking cows and going around the country, saying, 'I know what's good for America.' *He* was becoming

*In Ohio one day, Carter referred to politicians variously as "bosses" and "leaders." When Tim Kraft asked him the difference, he quipped, "If they're against me, they're bosses, and if they're for me, they're leaders."

the Jimmy Carter."* And his man-on-the-street ads with Georgians attacking their home-state governor for proving untrustworthy were highly effective.

Rafshoon also felt hampered by the more genteel political culture of the time. For instance, he didn't think he could make an ad featuring the famous 1975 *New York Daily News* headline: "Ford to City: Drop Dead." The president had never actually used those words. Worse, New York Democrats confessed that what the headline reflected — the president's promise to veto an overly generous aid package — had the benefit of galvanizing officials to agree on a more sensible bill bailing out the city that Ford signed two months later. If Rafshoon used the headline, he feared it would resurrect stories about Carter as a liar.

A bigger problem was intensity and commitment. Carter was a world-class retail politician — his warm smile, penetrating gaze, and obvious integrity made him hard to resist in person. But little of that came through on television.

As the race tightened, Pat Caddell grew worried. He could find no area of the country where enthusiastic Carter supporters outnumbered lukewarm ones. And he was stunned to see Carter voters defecting to Ford in the middle of the telephone interviews his poll takers conducted.

*Ford's first campaign manager was Carter's old adversary Bo Callaway, who had to resign the post amid allegations that he had used his position as secretary of the army to win government approval for the expansion of his new ski resort in Crested Butte, Colorado, where Carter would vacation after he lost the presidency.

# 19
## "LUST IN MY HEART"

Carter was a Democrat because everyone he grew up with was a Democrat. It wasn't an important part of his identity. But now, seeking to place himself in a proud tradition, he formally kicked off his fall campaign on September 6 at "the Little White House" in Warm Springs, Georgia, where Franklin Roosevelt recuperated from polio and vacationed. He improbably compared 1976 to 1932, when FDR was first elected amid the Great Depression. Carter liked FDR's last vice president and successor better than Roosevelt, and he worked in a reference to the sign Harry Truman kept on his desk reading "The Buck Stops Here." This intense sense of accountability would be more than a platitude for him.

Jimmy and Rosalynn had campaigned separately since early 1975, spending many weeks apart. But they spoke on the phone as much as possible, and their marriage was strong. The revered political journalist Theodore White wrote later that of all the presidential candidates he covered over four decades, he was "reasonably sure" that only three had not strayed on the trail: Harry Truman, George Romney, and Jimmy Carter. In Virginia, just after Labor Day, Jimmy got a chance to see

Rosalynn's polished stump speech for the first time. It made him weep with pride.

The following week, Carter, channeling Truman, ditched his chartered plane, dubbed Peanut One, in favor of a whistle-stop railroad trip through the East and Midwest. In Pennsylvania, he noticed dozens of reporters in the press car had stopped chatting and were all reading *Playboy* magazine — for the words.

For months, Carter had been talking in the car, on the plane, and in holding rooms to freelance journalist Robert Scheer, a sharp former editor of *Ramparts,* one of the premier left-wing magazines of the 1960s. Scheer was on assignment to conduct what would become the infamous *Playboy* Interview.

Jody Powell had approved the interview out of political calculation. He figured if *Playboy,* with its pass-along readership of twenty million, was good enough for Nobel Peace Prize winners Albert Schweitzer and Martin Luther King Jr. to sit for interviews, Carter should take part. Earlier in the year, Jerry Brown did the *Playboy* interview and the California governor surged in late primaries right after publication. After five hours of conversations, Scheer still felt he didn't have enough about how Carter's faith might conflict with his duties as president, so Powell agreed to schedule a final session for July 21 at the Carters' house in Plains, with a *Playboy* editor, Barry Golson, accompanying Scheer. He figured it might help voters see that the newly anointed nominee wasn't a Southern Baptist prude.

In most matters, he wasn't. He enjoyed what was then known as girl-watching and didn't blanch at dirty language, even if he rarely used it himself and religiously avoided "goddamn." While Jimmy and Rosalynn declined to invite couples who weren't married to stay overnight with them, they tolerated extramarital affairs on their staff, which Scheer described later "as hard-drinking, fornicating, pot smoking, freethinking a group as has ever been seen in higher politics." And Carter's private humor was earthier than reporters realized. One day he saw a woman supporter who had a ribbon signifying her status as a "Carter Ambassador" pinned to her ample bosom. When she moved away, he chuckled to an aide, "Did the other one get a prize, too?"

Powell didn't want Carter to go that far, but he hoped that the long interview would help voters see the man he knew. It turned out to be a disaster. Read in full, Carter came across as an exceptionally thoughtful and intelligent candidate. But few read the entire interview, and comments he made after the three men had stood up in the Carters' living room and moved to the door would prove devastating.

When Scheer asked Carter if his religious views on adultery, homosexuality, and other "victimless crimes" would make him "a rigid, unbending president," Carter said no, explaining that "Jesus teaches us not to judge people." He noted that "the thing that is drummed into us all the time is not to be proud, not to be better than anyone else, not to look down on people, but to make ourselves acceptable in God's eyes through our own actions and recognize the simple truth that we are saved by grace." Then, in response to a question by Golson, came the lines that would stick to him for as long as he was remembered:

"And Christ set some impossible standards for

us. Christ said, 'I tell you that anyone who looks on a woman with lust has already committed adultery.' I have looked on a lot of women with lust; I've committed adultery in my heart many times. This is something God recognizes I will do — and I have done it — and God forgives me for it. But that doesn't mean that I condemn someone who not only looks on a woman with lust but who leaves his wife and shacks up with somebody out of wedlock."

Carter seemed to be mixing standard Baptist teachings with a lame effort to show *Playboy*'s six million mostly male readers that he could relate to them. "Christ says, Don't consider yourself better than someone else because one guy screws a whole bunch of women, while the other guy is loyal to his wife," he said. "The guy who's loyal to his wife ought not to be condescending or proud because of the relative degree of sinfulness." The men in Carter's family knew exactly what he meant because they all remembered that "committing adultery in my heart" is a familiar Baptist sin of pride that every young Baptist boy learns in Sunday school.

Yet even as the interview landed in a 1970s America saturated in sex, it was greeted with prim disapproval. When the magazine appeared on September 22, Walter Cronkite, striving for context on *The CBS Evening News,* said that Carter used "words mild for *Playboy* but perhaps a little racy for Sunday school." Many newspapers printed "shacks up" but not "screws," while the purse-lipped *New York Times* noted that Carter had used "a common but mild vulgarism for sexual intercourse."

Today the *Playboy* interview would likely be a

one-day story; even then, a more "Teflon" candidate like Ronald Reagan might have let it slide right off him. But Carter had a "Velcro" quality to him, the result of his righteousness (which invited charges of hypocrisy) and his inability to develop the casual disarming humor that so often accompanies political success. The *Playboy* imbroglio was the first of a series of episodes that shrank Carter to a smaller-than-life caricature and, as Charlie Kirbo had feared, affixed a semipermanent "Kick Me" sign to his posterior.

Amid the widespread snickering, critics from all corners pounced on Carter for poor judgment for agreeing to the interview in the first place and for his peculiar equation of lusting in one's heart with actual adultery. Campaigns had always been tough, even vicious, and late-night comedians had long poked gentle fun at politicians. But public ridicule night after night on television was new then, and it resonated. Carter was greeted at campaign events with signs saying, "Carter for Playmate of the Year" and "Smile If You're Horny."

Americans were suddenly unsure about their mystery date — and clergymen piled on. "Like many, I am quite disillusioned," said the not-yet-famous Reverend Jerry Falwell Sr. "Four months ago, the majority of people I knew were pro-Carter. Today that has totally reversed." GOP operatives packaged the outraged reactions of clergy into full-page ads in 350 newspapers and mailed similar materials to two million rural households. W. A. Criswell, former president of the Southern Baptist Convention, appeared in a Ford ad preaching to his Dallas congregation with a beaming president nearby. He praised Ford for turning down *Playboy*'s request for an interview.

411

When big-time evangelists Billy Graham and Oral Roberts ignored their own boyhood Sunday school lessons and said piously that they had never lusted in their hearts, Carter's sons turned apoplectic. "People should watch out for people like Billy Graham who go around telling people how to live," Jeff Carter, then twenty-four, said in a radio interview. The next day, Graham appeared publicly with Ford at an event. Rosalynn called the evangelist to apologize on behalf of Jeff, and Graham stopped campaigning with Ford. However, he did nothing to discourage voters from thinking he favored him.

Carter tried to forgive Graham and Roberts, but he had a long memory. Graham was close friends and golfing buddies with nine American presidents between 1945 and 2008; Carter would not be among them. His leadership of Sumter County's Billy Graham Film Crusade in 1968 and their complete theological compatibility (deeper than that of Graham and any other president) meant little now. Carter said later that while he considered Graham "one of my great heroes," he had a new policy as president of not allowing religious sermons in the White House. "I was a stickler for total separation of church and state, a belief which I inherited from my father," he said, noting that this was a central doctrine "followed meticulously" by the Southern Baptist Convention until the late 1970s.

But Carter took the shunning beyond principle. A year after the *Playboy* flap, Graham — accustomed to intimate access — asked to come see him. Carter instructed an aide to tell Reverend Graham that the president could not fit a visit into his busy schedule.*

Oral Roberts also felt the sting. In 1977 Ruth sent her brother an invitation from Roberts to give the baccalaureate address at Oral Roberts University, in Tulsa. "You tell Oral I consider this one of the highest compliments I have ever received," Ruth recalled the president saying. "But tell him I feel so unworthy because I know that there are many other men who — like himself — have never lusted in their hearts, that I have to decline."

Years later, Rosalynn said she never doubted her husband's fidelity. "Everybody thought I ought to be upset, but it didn't bother me because I just trusted him enough not to worry about it," she said. "I did worry about the campaign." So did Hamilton Jordan, who thought that the "goofy" interview and resulting "weirdo factor" might end their hopes for the White House. The polls were inconsistent, but by some estimates, the *Playboy* flap led to a staggering 10-point drop in Carter's support.

Heading into the first of three presidential debates, Ford and Carter were in a statistical dead heat. This left Carter in a subdued, snappish mood. He refused, to the horror of his advisers, to take any practice questions to prepare for the September 23 encounter, preferring to retire to Plains to read

*It wasn't until the last year of his presidency that Carter warmed up to Graham again and invited him and his wife to dinner, in part because Graham had said privately that he didn't think any evangelical group could support Ted Kennedy for president in 1980 because of "the moral issue."

briefing books. Patrick Anderson, Carter's chief campaign speechwriter, described his boss as "close to the edge" in this period.

No presidential nominees had debated on television since Nixon and Kennedy pioneered the forum sixteen years earlier. Nixon believed the 1960 debates had cost him the presidency that year, and he refused to return to the stage for more punishment in 1968 and 1972. The idea seemed dormant, and no debates took place in either party during the 1976 primaries. Newton Minow, an influential former chairman of the Federal Communications Commission, worked tirelessly to revive them. This made Minow a kingmaker. Without the three autumn debates, Carter said just after the election, he would not have had the exposure he needed to be seen on an equal footing with the incumbent president.

But the first debate, at the Walnut Street Theatre in Philadelphia, did not go well for him. Out of the gate, Carter seemed tense, and he bored the audience of ninety million people with a dreary list of statistics. While he recovered some, Carter said later that he lost the debate because of an "overly deferential" attitude toward Ford that stemmed from his respect for the office.

The most memorable moment came with a little less than ten minutes to go, when the audio system at the theater suddenly conked out. Everyone assumed that sound would be restored momentarily, but it inexplicably took twenty-seven minutes before technicians solved the problem. For all that time, both candidates remained standing silently onstage, sipping water, neither daring to chat or move toward the other. If one had smiled and seemed human, he might have won the election right there. Each said later that he feared that the debate would resume and catch him off guard. The moment captured the innate caution of both of the candidates that year.

On the morning after the debate, Carter flew to Texas, where he was confronted yet again with the *Playboy* debacle. Bob Scheer had originally thought the big news from the interview was what Carter had said about Lyndon Johnson: "I don't think I would ever take on the same frame of mind that Nixon or Johnson did — lying, cheating, and distorting the truth," Carter said moments before the session with *Playboy* ended by his Plains front door. "I think that my religious beliefs alone would prevent that from happening to me."

Maligning LBJ posed a big problem in must-win Texas, where Johnson remained a demigod. His widow, Lady Bird, had earlier described herself as "distressed, hurt, and perplexed" by the comment, and Carter phoned her to apologize.* She was a no-show in the greeting party for Carter at the Houston airport, where LBJ's younger daughter, Luci Baines Johnson, introduced the Democratic nominee without mentioning his name. In damage control mode, Carter praised LBJ as the greatest president for human rights "with the possible exception of Abraham Lincoln" and claimed that his line in *Playboy* about LBJ had been taken out of context. After Scheer retrieved the tape and played it for reporters to show Carter was wrong, a shouting match erupted

---

*Carter never met LBJ, but he handwrote a gracious note to him on December 18, 1972, just a month before Johnson's death, to thank him for his "tremendous and unprecedented achievements as president."

415

between reporters fed up with Carter's word games and Jody Powell, who accused them of "nit-shitting" everything the candidate said.*

Peter Bourne, Carter's longtime aide, wrote later that Carter's comments about Johnson "reflected a long-standing tendency on his part to make, often gratuitously, extravagantly negative comments about people in major positions of power and authority." Even when he did so in private, word frequently filtered back to the target of his attacks. It was no wonder he was more respected than liked by other politicians — and that his post-presidency would be marred by such comments.

It wasn't until September 30, nearly three weeks after the *Playboy* story erupted, that the press moved on to a new target. With few substantive issues dividing the candidates, this one was also a "gaffe" story. John Dean, the former White House counsel who had become famous three years earlier for testifying against Nixon before the Senate Watergate Committee, had written an article in the spring of 1976 for *Rolling Stone* recounting how an unidentified "Ford Cabinet member" made racist remarks aboard an airplane about why Republicans didn't do better at the polls with blacks. "I'll tell you why you can't attract coloreds," the Ford administration official told Dean

*Two decades later, Carter still had it in his head that the remarks were off the record. He wrote that Scheer "surreptitiously restarted the tape recorder as we stood at the door." But the transcript shows that well before the "lust in my heart" conversation began, Scheer reminded Carter he was taking notes, and the candidate laughed and said, "Good!"

and singers Sonny Bono and Pat Boone, both of them Republicans. "Because coloreds only want three things: first, a tight pussy; second, loose shoes; third, a warm place to shit." After the *New York Times* identified the Cabinet member as Agriculture Secretary Earl Butz, it took Ford the whole first week of October to fire him — a week that broke his momentum and thus may have helped cost him the election.

The Butz incident also made it harder for Ford to run a racially tinged campaign, as Reagan did four years later. After the Butz story, his campaign advisers felt that employing racial code words (as Carter had in his 1970 gubernatorial campaign) was too risky in the more liberal North. They settled instead on running ads in the South featuring South Carolina senator Strom Thurmond, a onetime segregationist "Dixiecrat" who had become a Republican. "In a presidential election, it doesn't matter who is from the South," Thurmond said in a mild ad that ran across the region. "What matters is who is *for* the South." He argued that on defense, taxes, inflation, gun control, and other issues, Ford sounded more like a southerner than Carter. In another ad, Ronald Reagan asked severely, "Doesn't Mr. Carter owe it to you to explain cutting defense when the Soviet Union is building an aggressive force of staggering size?"

Ford was too decent to attack Carter directly as weak on defense or to pursue a demagogic "southern strategy" like Nixon's in 1968. He refrained from lashing out at Carter by name, calling him only "my opponent." Carter, too, usually observed that now-quaint custom. This toned down the battle for the South and let regional pride gather force on Carter's behalf.

417

It also gave Carter a better chance to win fiscally conservative but socially liberal votes in the suburbs, where this and future presidential elections would be won or lost. "If there's an equal choice between government and private industry, I'll go with private industry," Carter said in one ad. "This is the kind of concept that is generally considered to be conservative." Then he stressed that "I believe in human beings, in equal opportunity," as the announcer intoned, "If you believe government should be sensible but sensitive, vote for Jimmy Carter. A leader, for a change."

It helped that the religious Right remained underdeveloped in 1976. Paul Weyrich, the "Lenin of social conservatism" who had cofounded the Heritage Foundation in 1973, reassured friends on Capitol Hill that Carter's faith was genuine, and, if elected, he might end up appointing more evangelicals than Ford. Right-wingers didn't seem to notice that Carter embraced a new issue: gay rights. With gay voters worried about his evangelical religious beliefs, a group called Gays for Carter took out ads in gay publications pointing out that the Democratic nominee "doesn't believe in legislating morals." Chip appeared later at a gay bar in San Francisco that was sponsoring a tricycle race for charity, the first time in history that an official of a major presidential campaign ever attended a gay rights event.

Cutting the other way, Billy Carter crisscrossed Texas telling enthusiastic audiences that the Carters had always been conservatives, and that he would shoot Cesar Chavez, leader of the United Farm Workers of America union, if he came on his property. Texas voters came to see Carter

418

almost as one of their own. Bert Lance described Billy as the "unsung hero in his brother's election."

But to secure the state, Carter had to nail down the support of "bidness." On October 9, pro-business Democratic governors Dolph Briscoe of Texas and David Boren of Oklahoma sat with Bob Strauss at the Texas-Oklahoma college football game. They agreed that Carter might lose both states if he didn't reaffirm his support for deregulating the price of new natural gas, which they believed was a boon for producers and the larger cause of energy independence. Within days, Carter did so — and Texas, critical to victory, began moving his way. They could worry about the political consequences in the North — where the price of home heating oil would jump — after the election.

Over the summer, Carter had bonded with James Dickey, the celebrated American poet. Carter had been amused in 1972 when Dickey, a Georgia native, showed up drunk to the first screening of *Deliverance.* Now Dickey became virtually the only one whose debate advice he would welcome.

After the first debate, Dickey wrote to Carter that "the slide rule and the calculator" were not enough. He quoted memorable lines from Lincoln and Kennedy and said his friend needed "to catch rhetorical fire, to come out louder and stronger with the greater and more emphatic stress on the key words of the key statements." Dickey, like a lot of Democrats, was afraid that Carter wouldn't get the landslide he needed to govern. The poet couldn't believe he wasn't crushing the "wooden" Ford. "He is a sitting duck for you,"

Dickey wrote at the end of September. With "fire and memorable statements," the race would be over. "You have got the future of all of our lives in your pocket, Jimmy."

The second debate, on October 6, was devoted to foreign policy, an area where Ford was seen to have an advantage.* But here he made the biggest blunder of his political career. In reply to a question from Max Frankel of the *New York Times* about the Helsinki Accords with Moscow, Ford explained that the 1975 treaty required both the United States and the Soviet Union to notify the other of any military maneuvers. Ford finished his answer by saying, "They've done so, so there is no Soviet domination of Eastern Europe, and there never will be under a Ford administration."

Frankel, sensing Ford had misspoken, gave the president a chance to clarify his answer by pointing out in a follow-up question that the Soviet Union was "occupying most of the countries there." But Ford dug himself in deeper:

"I don't believe, Mr. Frankel, that the Yugoslavians consider themselves dominated by the Soviet Union. I don't believe the Romanians consider themselves dominated by the Soviet Union. I

*More than forty years later, the US Senate Intelligence Committee released a report on Russian interference in the 2016 election that included this tantalizing reference to the 1976 election: "In the 1970s the KGB recruited a Democratic Party activist who reported information about then-presidential hopeful Jimmy Carter's campaign and foreign policy plans, according to a former KGB archivist." The "activist" has never been identified.

don't believe the Poles consider themselves dominated by the Soviet Union."

Most viewers didn't seem to notice Ford's gaffe, and an early, unscientific poll showed Ford winning the debate. But pundits feasted on the story, and Carter piled on the next morning. He took note of the Berlin Wall and the three hundred thousand Soviet troops occupying Eastern European countries and charged that Ford had been "brainwashed" on a state visit to Poland, a line (borrowed from attacks on presidential candidate George Romney during the 1968 campaign) he later regretted. He wrote Dickey immediately that "I've tried to follow [your advice] by adding a little 'rhetorical fire,' and I hope I've succeeded," then scrawled at the bottom: "I'll be trying more — J."

The postdebate "rhetorical fire" worked. Ford's momentum stalled once again, and within a week, Carter had regained a 6-point lead in the Gallup poll. Then came the first-ever vice presidential debate, where a snarling and off-kilter Bob Dole blamed "Democrat wars" of the twentieth century for killing or wounding 1.6 million American soldiers — as if a political party was responsible for Pearl Harbor. Mondale replied that Dole was a "hatchet man." After the election, Jordan said that Mondale's performance had given Carter 2 or 3 extra points. "It was a big, big plus for us."

Ford's Poland gaffe and the VP debate were pivotal, but Carter still hadn't closed the deal. Dickey advised him to avoid the kind of "pettiness" that he thought had come to characterize the GOP. He did, and the final debate on October 22 went fine for him, but doubts grew anyway. Was he who he said he was? The racism of Carter's lifelong church in Plains almost doomed him. On Sunday, October 24, Helen Thomas of UPI accompanied Carter to church and asked, "Why are there no blacks here?" A startled Carter replied, "I can't answer that. I guess it's because they don't come."

A week before the election, Clennon King, a black pastor of a storefront church in Albany, Georgia, left a note on the door of Bruce Edwards, the young, liberal minister of the Plains Baptist Church, seeking membership. This was an election eve publicity stunt: Baptists are generally not allowed dual church membership, and local black Democrats believed the Republican mayor of Albany had put King — an erratic ex-con — up to it. But the point of King's provocation was to highlight that the church's 1965 ban on black visitors was still technically in effect eleven years later, the only exceptions being black reporters and Secret Service agents traveling with Carter.

The church's conservative deacons already distrusted Reverend Edwards, in part because he had adopted a biracial child. When Edwards, trying to avoid headlines, said he would let King in, the deacons — happy to embarrass Carter — voted to cancel services on the Sunday before the presidential election rather than integrate. On Sunday, October 31, King showed up with two black children and a pack of reporters to find the church doors locked. At the doorstep, Edwards explained that — over his objections — the deacons had decided to enforce the 1965 decree banning "niggers and other civil rights agitators." Hugh Carter, who as a segregationist a decade earlier had supported the ban, was now afraid his cousin's presidential hopes were slipping away. He

422

shouted to reporters, "No! No! It [the deacons' ban] says negroes — N-E-G-R-O-E-S!" — as if that made it okay. Within minutes, the wire services flashed the story around the world.

The relative civility of the contest now gave way to late hits. Ford's team saw a chance to depress black turnout. James A. Baker — the wily Houston lawyer (and future secretary of state) running Ford's brilliant campaign — sent telegrams to four hundred African American ministers saying that Carter was an "ineffective Christian" who couldn't even manage the integration of his own church and was thus not fit to be president. Appearing in Fort Worth, Texas, Carter tried to walk the line between civil rights and the feelings of neighbors who despised King as an interloping provocateur: "My firm belief, along with the pastor's, is that anyone who wants to join our church, is a member who lives in our community, and who wants to worship with me ought to be accepted, regardless of race."

The same black supporters who had rescued Carter from the "ethnic purity" mess in April now sprang into action again. Daddy King, Coretta Scott King, and Andrew Young organized support for him, and Clennon King's distinguished brother, C. B. King, who had run against Carter for governor in 1970 but backed him since, told a large audience that his brother was "emotionally and mentally disturbed."

After the election, Lillian was still bitter that Clennon King had almost cost her son the presidency. For a moment, she lost sight of the values she had tried to live by. She told reporter James Wooten, "Somebody should have shot that nigger before he came on the lawn." Much later, Andrew

423

Young offered context: "Lillian was good 'til you messed with her children."

The incident eventually led to all the Carters leaving the Plains Baptist Church. Edwards was pushed out, which prompted twenty-five families to announce they were building a new, integrated place of worship in town they would call Maranatha Baptist Church. After the presidency, Maranatha would become the Carters' spiritual home for the rest of their lives.

In the final few days, Ford seemed to gain steam yet again, buoyed by a series of effective ads featuring a patriotic "I'm feeling good about America" jingle. Gallup's final poll put him ahead, 47 percent to 46 percent. The consensus in the political world was that if Americans had voted even a couple of days later, Ford would have won.

On the night before the election, Ford's closing argument featured Joe Garagiola, a retired baseball player and popular NBC sportscaster, tossing him gentle questions that he hit out of the park. The post-Watergate healing that Carter was promising seemed to have already been accomplished by comfortable, experienced Jerry Ford.

As Rafshoon taped Carter's own hourlong election eve appeal at the house on Woodland Drive, he found his candidate tired and snippy. When the camera broke, and Rafshoon tried to fix it, Carter said, "I assume you think you know what you're doing." Then he snapped, "I'll give you ten more minutes," as if he had something more important to do. In a sign of how oblivious Carter was to the importance of television, Rafshoon had to remind him that this appearance would be watched on all three networks and was the last thing that tens of millions of voters would see before they went to the polls.

"Ask Jimmy Carter" turned out to be an effective piece of political persuasion. Dressed in a blue suit and speaking softly, Carter opened by explaining he had begun his campaign as a "lonely candidate" talking with people in the early primary states one-on-one, or with three or four voters at most. Then he surprised experts by winning the nomination. "The reason was, I had a close, personal, direct relationship with the people of this country," he explained, before convincingly answering pretaped questions — some of them pointed — from voters across the nation. Carter knew that Ford's pardon of Nixon remained a major factor, but he never sought to remind voters of it.

At the eleventh hour, Carter received support from a surprising source: George Wallace. For months, Wallace had resisted campaigning for Carter. He even came out to welcome Ford when the president made a campaign stop in Mobile. But Jim Free, the Carter aide assigned to handle him, finally convinced an unenthusiastic Wallace to show up the last week in the Florida panhandle and Jackson, Mississippi, where he told the crowd "It's all right to be a conservative Democrat and vote for Jimmy Carter." The last-minute appeal to regional pride worked. Haley Barbour, who ran Ford's campaign in the southeast and later became chair of the Republican National Committee, said that in 1976 southerners voted with their hearts instead of their brains. He was talking about white voters. Black southerners, many of whom were registered for the first time, also came out in large numbers for Carter. "Hands that picked cotton will pick a president," read one sign. And they did.

On Tuesday, November 3, 1976, after voting in Plains, the Carters flew to Atlanta and arrived at five o'clock at the Omni International Hotel, where they settled into a fifteenth-floor suite to hold hands and await the returns. Little did they know they would be there for nearly eleven hours.

In 1976 the concept of "battleground states" did not exist. The entire country was the battleground. Carter lost Maine, Vermont, and Connecticut but otherwise started strong on the East Coast and in the South, where he would eventually carry every state in the Old Confederacy except Virginia (where government workers outside Washington, DC, feared he would cut their jobs) and every border state except Oklahoma. Mid-evening, New York, Pennsylvania, and Wisconsin went for Carter, but when Ford won New Jersey, Michigan, Illinois (a shocker), and California, completing a sweep on the West Coast, it looked as if the Republican president might pull off the greatest comeback since Harry Truman in 1948. Lester Maddox, running on a fringe right-wing ticket, didn't win enough votes to hurt either candidate, but it seemed for a time that former senator Eugene McCarthy's quixotic third-party bid might tilt the election to Ford. Then Carter began inching back, with Texas his big breakthrough and Ohio finally moving his way.

The election seemed to come down to Hawaii, where Republicans were doing unexpectedly well, and Mississippi. At three thirty in the morning, Governor Cliff Finch of Mississippi called Carter to say he would win there by a whisker. Thanks in

426

part to George Wallace's last-minute appeal, a state that would soon become one of the most Republican in the country put him over the top. Carter didn't exult over the news, but his smile was genuine. His mother, clad in a green jersey with "76" on it, whooped. "I guess it's okay now to tell them you're a Marxist, right?" Powell joked to the president-elect after NBC's John Chancellor finally called the race.

Carter had carried only 45 percent of the white vote, but white southerners and those transplanted to the North grew emotional, much as African Americans did on news of Barack Obama's election in 2008. "Congratulations," a northern friend wrote a weeping Lewis Grizzard, a syndicated southern humorist. "Y'all ain't trash no more." Johnny Cash was exultant, whooping at the TV, "He won! He won! He won!" Carter himself later described the "political redemption" of the South as a critical factor in his election.

By this time, Ford, watching the returns upstairs at the White House, had wandered off to bed. The next morning, his voice a raspy whisper from campaign-induced laryngitis, Ford asked the White House operator to reach Carter. He handed the phone to Dick Cheney, who made the concession by reading what Carter later called a "characteristically gracious" telegram. Republicans were crestfallen. "Contrary to reports that I took the loss badly," Bob Dole deadpanned, "I want to say that I went home last night and slept like a baby — every two hours, I woke up and cried."

Exit polls showed that Carter won on pocketbook issues, with strong majorities among those who felt they were worse off economically than four years earlier — a standard of performance

427

that would come back to haunt him when he sought reelection. Carter carried the popular vote by 50 percent to 48 percent and the electoral college by 297 to 240, but he would have lost with a combined change of just 18,000 votes in Ohio and Hawaii. Twenty states totaling 299 electoral votes were decided by 5 points or less, making for the closest margin in the electoral college since incumbent Woodrow Wilson's razor-thin victory over Charles Evans Hughes in 1916.

At nearly four in the morning, the Carters and their happy entourage left the Omni for the Atlanta airport and the short flight to Albany. One of the press buses was several minutes late, which annoyed Carter, who — in a repeat of what he did to Bill Shipp of the *Atlanta Constitution* in the 1970 campaign — told aides to have Peanut One take off without a large group of reporters who had covered him for more than a year and would now miss the homecoming climax of the whole campaign. He didn't want to make his friends and family gathered to greet him back in Plains wait any longer.

Carter yelled, "Let's go!" but Greg Schneiders ignored the order to clear the aisles in preparation for takeoff and stalled another ten minutes until the second press bus arrived. It was striking how many members of Carter's otherwise loyal inner circle remembered this rigid behavior at the moment of victory. And it got him off on the wrong foot with many of the reporters who would be covering him for four years. "The son of a bitch just got elected, and he's angry that we're late," Curtis Wilkie of the *Boston Globe* said to a chagrined Rafshoon.

The motorcade from Albany arrived in Plains at

428

five thirty, just as dawn was breaking. With his family and thousands of local supporters gathered around him, Carter spoke tearfully from the platform of the tiny old railroad depot that had become the campaign's symbolic headquarters. Peter Bourne, who was there, wrote that the moment was so poignant and meaningful for those in attendance because it represented the American Dream come true — a small-town boy who reaches the heights and returns to share his triumph with those who watched him grow up. The improbability of Carter's victory struck speechwriter Hendrik "Rick" Hertzberg, who said later that electing him was as close "as the American people have ever come to picking someone out of the phone book to be president."

It's easy to forget the historical resonance: more than a century after the Civil War, the son of a staunch segregationist — the loyal citizen of what less than a decade earlier had been one of the meanest counties in the South — had managed for a moment to fulfill Lincoln's admonition in his second inaugural to "bind up the nation's wounds."

Carter was the first president elected from the Deep South since Zachary Taylor in 1848 and the first governor elected president since FDR in 1932. He was the first evangelical Christian president and would be one of the most devout men ever to hold the office. He was also a countercyclical president — the last bulwark, by virtue of his southern heritage, against the political realignment of an entire region. Some reporters were already thinking of him as a fluke; the third accidental president — after Johnson and Ford — in thirteen years.

"In the end, Jimmy Carter won the election but not the mandate," James Naughton of the *New York Times* wrote on election night, already signaling that Carter's ambitious agenda might have trouble. "The voters seemed, in effect, to withhold judgment, as if to say their trust would need to be earned in deeds not declarations." Had a party regular won, that mandate would have been assumed and amplified by his party supporters even without a resounding victory. But many congressional Democrats were privately more comfortable with their old friend and colleague Jerry Ford than with this new stranger in their midst.

Carter's election was a Band-Aid on a ruptured Democratic Party, a party that still dominated Congress but was losing its connection to the voters and to fresh ideas for advancing inclusive capitalism. The existing social contract — the new "deal" FDR struck between the government and the people — was fraying. For ten years, since its big gains in the 1966 midterms, the GOP had been on the march across the country. What the author Kevin Phillips called "the emerging Republican majority" was a powerful coalition of traditional country-club conservatives and middleclass white voters, many of them former Democrats, who were angered by antiwar elites and "welfare," which had become a racial code word. This growing GOP coalition had dominated the election of 1968 (Nixon's and Wallace's combined 57 percent) and 1972 (Nixon's 60 percent), and would give Reagan big victories in 1980 and 1984. Carter managed to hold off the Republican surge in the suburbs and the South. But his election would be the last time a Democratic presidential candidate would win for sixteen years and the last time one would win a majority of the popular vote for thirty-two years — until Barack Obama's election in 2008.

In that sense, Carter was a historical anomaly — an aberration caused by Watergate — and a speed bump in the South's historic transition from solid Democratic to solid Republican. He didn't comprehend these traffic flows of history at the time, but he would struggle with them for the duration of his presidency — along with his own shortcomings as a politician. But Jimmy Carter would do so with a determination and moral vision that would not be properly recognized for decades.

*Symbolic walk down Pennsylvania Avenue on Inauguration Day, 1977.*

■ ■ ■ ■

# PART FOUR:
# OUTSIDER PRESIDENT

■ ■ ■ ■

# 20
# "Let's Go!"

Jimmy Carter was the first president with no Washington experience since Woodrow Wilson. Almost all other presidents, going back to the founders, had been either members of Congress or the Cabinet or army generals or — like the Roosevelts — governors who had previously served a stint in the federal bureaucracy.* Carter had done none of this. He stormed the citadel without the help of any establishment. With the temperament of an outsider and a White House staff as unseasoned as he was, a bumpy ride was almost inevitable.

Even insider presidents were chewed up in this era. Carter's four immediate predecessors served an average of only four years each: Kennedy assassinated. Johnson and Nixon hounded from office. Ford fired by the voters. The movie playing in the heads of many Carter supporters was 1939's *Mr. Smith Goes to Washington.* But before the happy ending, Jimmy Stewart's idealistic and

*Carter launched a new trend: three of the next four presidents — Reagan, Clinton, and George W. Bush — were also governors who had not served in Congress or the Cabinet.

conservationist character is nearly destroyed by corrupt forces in the capital.

Washington wasn't especially corrupt in the late 1970s. And Carter's program made slow but steady progress on Capitol Hill, where he benefited from four years with a Democratic Congress, an advantage Bill Clinton and Barack Obama enjoyed for only two of their eight years. (No Republican president since the 1920s has controlled both houses for four years.)

But Congress was much more independent than it would be in the early twenty-first century. The Democratic majority in 1977 (292 to 143 in the House and 58 to 41 in the Senate) was undermined by an almost total absence of party-line votes. Democrats were divided between old-fashioned northern New Deal–Great Society liberals, southern conservatives who might as well have been Republicans, and rambunctious young Democratic Watergate Babies, elected in 1974, who disliked the stuffy emphasis on seniority and took orders from no one. All factions had enormous pent-up expectations that Carter could not possibly meet.

More broadly, the Democrats had become essentially a collection of interest groups with alliances constantly in flux. The 1970s brought important progressive social movements for the rights of women, homosexuals, and the disabled. But while the ends of liberalism — a more just society, a humane foreign policy — remained intact, how to reach those goals became the subject of fierce debate.

Amid those recriminations, Carter was hampered by seeming to have no distinct political ideology. Reagan, Bush, Clinton, Obama and

436

Trump supporters in Congress might differ from their party's president on a few votes, but they were always playing for the same side. Carter, by contrast, wasn't the quarterback of any particular team; he assembled a new front line on nearly every issue, with no inherited party game plan or ideological playbook to fall back on. Carter thought he had the answers and he saw himself governing on a plane above politics, answerable not to Congress or the Democratic Party or the Washington establishment — the normal bargaining partners of presidents — but to the American people who had placed their faith in him. This assumption of what the political scientist Charles O. Jones called "trusteeship" freed him to peer over the horizon and address critical issues the country would face in the future. He won a lot more than generally assumed and when he lost, he often planted the seeds of future progress. But his policy development was too often missing the axle grease of old-fashioned politics.

The same views that made Carter seem fresh to the country made him a source of suspicion in Washington. "He was confusing to people," his labor secretary, Ray Marshall, remembered. "He was a liberal. He was a conservative. He was a centrist. It depended on the issue." After leaving office, Carter recognized that this had hurt him. "I think the worst mistake I made was not keeping my position as leader of the Democratic Party intact," he said in 2017.

But while his political outlook may have been perplexing at the time, Carter was pioneering center-left "New Democrat" thinking that would be adopted later by Clinton and Obama, though neither would credit him. That was partly because

Carter's achievements and his moral appeal would end up overshadowed by circumstances — stagflation, energy shortages, widespread social angst, and global events largely beyond his control — that would test his resolve and weaken his leadership.

First came the excitement. Not since John F. Kennedy took office sixteen years before had official Washington felt the electric charge of something new in public life. In the days following the election, Carter moved quickly to assemble his team beyond Rosalynn, whom he always described as "my best friend and chief adviser."

As a dedicated planner, Carter had tapped Jack Watson to begin secretly organizing the transition six months before the election — the earliest such effort on record. But Watson had alienated Hamilton Jordan, who now used his close relationship with Carter to assume control over the staffing of the new administration. Jordan blocked Watson from the job he expected: White House chief of staff. When Charlie Kirbo declined to come north (he would fly up twice a month to help out), Carter — noting how Nixon's chief of staff, H. R. Haldeman, had abused his power — decided to leave the critical post empty. Everyone involved except Carter admitted later that this was a mistake.

Jordan was de facto chief of staff but ill-suited even to that. "I do not like to spend a lot of time dealing with politicians" or "going to cocktail parties," he wrote Carter. Nor did he return phone calls from members of Congress, delegating that task to Frank Moore, the Georgian who headed congressional relations. And Moore often stiffed them, too. This would be a problem. Politicians, after all, had good reason to think that they should have direct access to the president's top political advisers.

The president-elect opted to try something that political scientists call "Cabinet government": disempowering the White House staff (which had grown arrogant in recent administrations) in favor of giving Cabinet secretaries more autonomy and freedom to craft policy. Cabinet government was a good idea in theory, but it would saddle Carter with the worst of both worlds: blame without control. Every flap or scandal in one of the agencies would be blamed on the president even if the White House had absolutely nothing to do with it.

Carter loaded his senior White House staff with young Georgians, and he envisioned them as "spokes on a wheel," all with equal direct access to the president at the center.* This would soon prove balky and confusing — and Carter aides couldn't say they weren't warned. During the transition, outgoing chief of staff Dick Cheney rummaged in his closet and found an old bicycle wheel with bent spokes that represented the failed efforts of the Ford White House to do something similar. He presented it to Jordan's team as a gift.

The Georgians would soon be the targets of regional and class biases that had not been a

*Hamilton Jordan, Jody Powell, Bert Lance, Stuart Eizenstat, Frank Moore, Jack Watson, Robert Lipshutz, James McIntyre, and Landon Butler were all Georgians, not to mention Charlie Kirbo and Jerry Rafshoon, who aided Carter from the outside. Only Zbigniew Brzezinski and Midge Costanza were not.

problem for aides to other presidents, a double standard they resented. After FDR and JFK came to office, the press was full of gushing accounts of the smartest minds in the country descending on Washington. In Carter's case, there was no such publicity, despite plenty of talented people working in his administration.*

The best antidote to all the tut-tutting about "the Georgia mafia" was Walter Mondale.

For nearly two hundred years, vice presidents had been little more than "standby equipment" — reminders to presidents of their own mortality. None had any real power beyond the constitutional authority to break ties in the Senate. During the transition, Carter was surprised to learn that the vice president wasn't even briefed on the use of nuclear weapons. With an office in the Senate, the veep had been viewed — in institutional terms — as essentially a member of the legislative branch. That would now change. In Mondale's words, Carter "executivized" and thus revolutionized the American vice presidency.

Why did Carter do this? He had promised Mon-

---

*David Rubenstein, who worked so hard as Eizenstat's deputy that he was known to eat dinner routinely out of the vending machines in the White House basement, went on to become the billionaire cofounder of the Carlyle Group investment firm. James Fallows, Hendrik Hertzberg, and Chris Matthews became renowned journalists. And Ina Garten, an analyst assigned to study nuclear weapons for the Office of Management and Budget (OMB), turned into a TV host and famous cookbook author (*The Barefoot Contessa*).

dale a big role, certainly, and he needed his Washington experience, but there was also a psychological dimension at work: Carter lacked the crippling insecurities of so many other presidents. This allowed him to break with pointless tradition and treat Mondale as what he later called his "assistant president." He explicitly told his staff, "If you get an order from Fritz, it's as if it's an order from me," and passed the word that anyone who undercut the vice president would be gone. When Mondale sent Carter an eleven-page memo on December 9 requesting specific responsibilities (including consultation on every major decision), Carter approved them all.

After taking office, one of his first executive orders placed the VP in the military chain of command. Before that, if the president were incapacitated, the military could make life-or-death decisions for the fate of the planet on its own authority. "Boy, did that change the attitude of the DOD [Department of Defense]," Mondale remembered.

Even the vice president's daily life in the White House would change dramatically. Until Carter, vice presidents weren't granted an office in the West Wing; they were stuck across the driveway in the Old Executive Office Building. "If you're over there, you might as well be in Baltimore," Mondale joked. It was Carter's idea to give Mondale a big suite just down the hall from the Oval Office — something emulated by all of his successors — and he decreed that vice presidential staffers would have the status and perks of his own aides. Where previous presidents could sometimes go weeks without seeing their VPs, Carter made good on his promise and brought Mondale in on almost all significant decisions. They never argued, in part because of good communication. Carter began what would be a tradition for every future vice president: the weekly lunch. Carter and Mondale often had two lunches a week on the schedule: one on domestic issues, the other on national security.

This was a major institutional change for an office once depicted by John Nance Garner, FDR's first vice president, as not "worth a bucket of warm piss." President Eisenhower said he would need a week to think of any big idea that Vice President Richard Nixon had ever contributed and Nixon had even less use for Spiro Agnew. Even such stars as Lyndon Johnson and Nelson Rockefeller were easily marginalized in the vice presidency. The radical shift in the role of the vice president would be one of Carter's enduring legacies — and the most significant strengthening of the American constitutional system in the second half of the twentieth century.

In November the president-elect gathered his transition team at a donor's lush estate on St. Simons Island, off the Georgia coast, but he insisted that his new team experience Plains, too. It didn't always go well. At the Pond House, A. W. Clausen, chairman of Bank of America and an economic adviser to the incoming president, was so thirsty he cupped his hands in a silent plea to staff for water; the attendees, sitting on hard metal chairs, had no snacks and no cups for their Cokes. After several back-to-back sessions, Mondale told Bert Lance — who would be Carter's budget director — that he had learned three things so far about Lance's friend: "First, he has a cast-iron rear end. Second, he has a bladder the size of a football.

And third, his idea of a party is a half a glass of Scotch."

It hardly escaped notice that no fewer than eight members of Carter's Cabinet and national security team were men he met through the Trilateral Commission, a bastion of the establishment. Jordan had famously said during the primaries that "if after the inauguration you find a Cy Vance as secretary of state and Zbigniew Brzezinski as head of national security, then I would say we failed. And I'd quit." He didn't, of course, when both Vance and Brzezinski were named to those very positions.

Both men had redeemed themselves in Carter's eyes by resigning from the Johnson administration over Vietnam. Despite his own tardiness in opposing the war, Carter wasn't going to hire any retreads from the disastrous Kennedy-Johnson "Best and Brightest" foreign policy team.

Vance was a gentleman diplomat from Central Casting. His preference for negotiation over military action in almost any situation — a product of seeing action in the Pacific during World War II and his up-close view of the folly of Vietnam — reinforced Carter's approach. Because Vance's worldview so closely mirrored his own, Carter felt he learned more from Professor Brzezinski, who peppered him every day with ideas, most of which he rejected.

"Zbig," whose Polish family had tangled with both the Nazis and the Soviets, hoped to be Carter's version of Henry Kissinger, his longtime academic rival. Vance and Brzezinski got along fine at first, but soon enough, whole forests of newsprint were consumed covering their enmity, the most hyped story of the administration. Car-

443

ter's growing obsession with foreign affairs made him essentially his own secretary of state and national security adviser, rendering their advice of less importance than journalists realized at the time. While Brzezinski, the more hawkish of the two, eventually won his struggle with Vance, Carter was much too smart and independent minded to fall under his or anyone else's sway.

For Treasury, Carter chose W. Michael Blumenthal, a Jewish refugee from World War II who became the blunt CEO of the Bendix Corporation, and Defense went to Harold Brown, the brilliant president of the California Institute of Technology. CIA was a tougher call.

George H. W. Bush, Ford's CIA director, briefed the president-elect three times on threats he would face around the world. In their final session, on November 19, in Plains, Bush — who was already being credited with having restored the battered agency's morale — offered his resignation but indicated he would prefer to stay on in his post. Carter joked that Bush would be president by 1985 (he was off by four years) but didn't take Bush up on his offer. He wanted his own CIA chief, a decision that would present the incoming administration with its first test.

Instead of Bush, Carter in December selected Theodore Sorensen, who had served as JFK's top policy aide and speechwriter. But CIA director seemed to be the wrong post for him, as Sorensen acknowledged later. (He had hoped to be attorney general.) And he wasn't properly vetted. Sorensen had been a conscientious objector during World War II, and the idea of a onetime pacifist running the CIA raised hackles, as did his alleged use of classified materials in preparing his memoir of the

Kennedy White House, which turned out to be a bogus charge.

As the inauguration approached, Sorensen's nomination was in trouble, with even Senator Joe Biden in opposition. After briefly lobbying for his first choice, Carter began backing away. Sorensen and his wife, Gillian, believed the Georgians treated Sorensen shabbily and that the only person in the Carter camp they could trust was Fritz Mondale — but the vice president–elect was actually among those arguing to cut him loose. Rosalynn Carter wasn't alone in saying later that her husband should have fought harder. Abandoning Sorensen was a sign that the soon-to-be president could be rolled. The CIA job would go to Admiral Stansfield Turner, the star of Carter's class at Annapolis and a Rhodes scholar, who — sacrificing his popularity within his agency — would slash covert operations.

Carter's choice for attorney general was Griffin Bell, a former federal judge forced to resign from his all-white country club before winning Senate confirmation. Bell was an Americus native, but he was not close to Carter, and they would grow more distant over time. They agreed on the importance of an independent Department of Justice, which Carter, in the wake of Watergate, had repeatedly promised on the campaign trail.* To signal their openness, Carter and Bell would join together the first week of the new presidency

*At Bell's suggestion, Carter had even pledged to make the attorney general a non-coterminous office with a five-year term, akin to the head of the FBI or the Federal Reserve. But Carter learned that would be unconstitutional, so he did not pursue it.

to symbolically unlock the heavy front doors of the Justice Department, which had been sealed years earlier after antiwar protesters tried to push their way in.

Carter had often said that the "overriding issue" in his 1976 campaign was "the restoration of faith in our government." Now, as president-elect, he implemented the first rigorous disclosure requirements for all political appointees. Carter announced he would voluntarily release his tax returns every April, setting a standard for transparency respected by all of his successors until Donald Trump. And before taking office, Jimmy and Rosalynn transferred their controlling interest in Carter's Warehouse, Carter's Farms, a lot in Plains, and 3,240 shares of common stock in the American Can Company to a blind trust managed by Charlie Kirbo. "Above all," the trust document said, President Carter "wants the trustee to arrange the assets of the trust so that no one should reasonably assert that [his] actions as President were motivated by a desire to foster his own personal monetary gain or profit."

At first, the Carters seemed headed for a honeymoon with the press. In December ABC's Barbara Walters, hosting her first prime-time special, sat on the wood-frame couch Carter had built in his Plains living room and asked the president-elect if he and Rosalynn slept in a double bed. They said they did. When Walters ended by saying, to the horror of TV critics, "Be wise with us, Governor. Be good to us," Carter replied, "I'll try."

Carter requested a frugal but inclusive "people's inaugural," where no ticket to any event — includ-

ing the customarily expensive inaugural balls —
cost more than $25.* Ordinary people from all
over the country who had volunteered on his
campaign received invitations. This was the last
inaugural for a generation that was not a "donor
event" and the first that offered handicapped access, a still-new concept at the time. (Ramps allowed a morose George Wallace to attend in his
wheelchair.) Determined to be inclusive, Carter
insisted that Richard Nixon, who had been barred
from the Republican Convention the summer
before, also be invited; Democratic senators were
relieved when he declined.

Efforts to make the event eco-friendly brought
mixed results. The reviewing stand for the parade
was made of recycled steel, but the large solar-
power heating unit didn't work well on Inauguration Day, which left eighty-four-year-old general
Omar Bradley, the last living five-star general of
World War II, freezing in his wheelchair, asking
plaintively for more heat.

The preinaugural gala, the first to be televised,
featured Aretha Franklin, Loretta Lynn, Leonard
Bernstein, Warren Beatty, John Wayne, and Linda
Ronstadt, who delighted the Carters by singing
Willie Nelson's ballad "Crazy." Everyone from
Lauren Bacall and Bette Davis to Muhammad Ali
and John Lennon showed up to pay tribute to the
new president. But the festivities were overshadowed by a seating snafu at the gala that became

*In the spirit of frugality, Rosalynn, to the consterna-
tion of fashion designers, wore the same gown to the
inaugural balls that she had to the 1971 gubernatorial
inaugural ball. She had bought the dress from a shop in
Americus.

the first in a series of seemingly minor flaps over the next four years to be blown up by the press and — in a world where perception is reality — take on exaggerated symbolic importance. These incidents usually said next to nothing about the president, but they morphed into colorful stories that lingered (sometimes for decades) and harmed his reputation.

Thomas P. "Tip" O'Neill, the burly Boston Irishman who just two weeks earlier had become Speaker of the House, was seated at the gala with his wife, Millie, in the presidential box. Tip's political experience in Democratic politics went back to 1928, when, as a fifteen-year-old, he worked on Al Smith's presidential campaign. He had long since mastered the art of the favor, the lifeblood of politics, and he thought nothing of requesting a dozen extra tickets for friends and family. When O'Neill found out after the gala was over that some of his clan had been seated in the nosebleed section, his roguish charm turned to fury. That any blame for the mix-up rested at least as much with his top aide as with the Carter transition team did not ease his mood.

O'Neill phoned Hamilton Jordan the next day and said, "Listen, you son of a bitch. When a guy is Speaker of the House and his family gets the worst seats in the room, he figures there's a reason behind it. I have to believe that you did it deliberately." The seating had been an accident, but Jordan's reply wasn't deferential enough for O'Neill, who took to calling the thirty-two-year-old "Hannibal Jerkin." This was unfair to Jordan, who was not a jerk; he was just rumpled, irreverent, and — like the other Georgians — disdainful of the imperial city, which returned the favor.

448

■ ■ ■ ■

Inauguration Day brought temperatures of twenty-eight degrees, frigid for Washington. Carter, dressed in an off-the-rack suit and the overcoat he borrowed from Jerry Rafshoon in New Hampshire, skipped the traditional inaugural morning services at St. John's Episcopal Church on Lafayette Square, "the church of presidents," and went instead to services at the First Baptist Church, which the Carters soon joined (and where Amy was later baptized). He then arrived at the North Portico for coffee with President Ford and the ride down Pennsylvania Avenue.

After taking the oath from Chief Justice Warren Burger, Carter, feeling "strangely calm," opened his inaugural address by thanking "my predecessor for all he has done to heal our land," a gesture of bipartisanship that was remembered long after the rest of the speech was forgotten. He immediately quoted Miss Julia Coleman ("We must adjust to changing times and still hold to unchanging principles") — the first mention of a teacher in an inaugural address. Carter had wanted to use a King Solomon quote from 2 Chronicles 7:14 but was convinced by aides that its references to "sin" and "wicked ways" might be misunderstood by less religious Americans and that it conflicted with his campaign theme that people were fundamentally good. He settled for Micah 6:8 on justice, mercy, and humility.

The address, written by Carter himself, was among the shortest on record, an unadorned and often disjointed blend of his announcement and acceptance speeches, loosely structured as a

449

sermon. "Let our recent mistakes bring a resurgent commitment to the basic principles of our nation," Carter said, conjuring Watergate and the reasons for his election. He pledged to work toward the elimination of all nuclear weapons and stressed the importance he placed on peace and human rights — the twin pillars, he said long after he left office, of his entire public life.

Near the end, the new president explored a farsighted moral theme that would soon become a liability. "We have learned," he said, "that 'more' is not necessarily 'better,' that even our great nation has its recognized limits." Even as he saluted an "undiminished, ever-expanding American Dream," Carter was signaling that he embraced a less materialistic world of reduced expectations — a notion in tune with the 1970s and his personal and prescient ethos of what future generations would call "sustainable growth." Franklin Roosevelt had also skewered material values in his famous 1933 inaugural at the bottom of the Great Depression. But FDR had bolstered his critique with some of the most stirring optimism in American history. While Carter had said in advance that he sought a tone of "sober optimism," he could not convey it — then or later. Instead, he espoused other values — hard work and selflessness — that are also in the American grain. "So together, in a spirit of individual sacrifice for the common good," he concluded, once again channeling Rickover, "we must simply do our best."

The blandly delivered speech was quickly overshadowed by what became the most thrilling part of the day and a new inaugural tradition. Weeks earlier, Senator William Proxmire of

Wisconsin had suggested that after the swearing-in, the new president and his family should get out of the limousine and walk the mile and a half up Pennsylvania Avenue from the Capitol to the White House. Proxmire thought it would be a good symbol of physical fitness. At first, Carter considered it a "rather silly" stunt, and the Secret Service objected. But he decided "the symbolism of our leaving the armored car would be much more far-reaching than simply to promote exercise." It would convey "a reduction in the imperial status of the president and his family."

So, moments after the Carters entered the limo, he leaned forward and told the Secret Service driver to stop, then touched Rosalynn's hand and said, "Let's go!"

When the Carter family got out, the crowd gasped, "They're walking! They're walking!" Onlookers loved the image of smiling Jimmy and demure Rosalynn holding hands and waving, and nine-year-old Amy out front, stepping playfully on the white median strip. Some friends and spectators wept. "When I saw this, a few tears of joy ran down my cold cheeks," Carter wrote later. "It was one of those few perfect moments in life when everything seems absolutely right."

On CBS, White House correspondent Lesley Stahl exclaimed that the gesture "was game changing," while the *New York Times* reported that the forty-minute walk "dramatized in deed the tone of the new president's inaugural address, in which he proposed to help Americans to unite in regenerating a spirit of national comity and openness."

In the decades since, every newly inaugurated president except Reagan has walked at least partway to the White House. But Carter was the only one to walk the entire length and — for post-9/11 security reasons — it will likely never be allowed again.

Before the inaugural balls, Carter assembled his new Cabinet. He asked the members to hold hands and join him in prayer — a request that seemed at odds with his commitment to observe a strict separation of church and state but which Carter considered appropriate because it was nonsectarian and without clergy present. The next day, he surprised Mondale by telling him that he wanted to move aggressively toward a settlement in the Middle East. It hadn't been a campaign issue, but Carter felt it was part of his mission to bring peace to what he routinely called the Holy Land.

From the start, Carter insisted on working on several tracks at once. His first decision, which he mulled while walking down Pennsylvania Avenue, set the gutsy moral tone for his presidency. Instead of embracing something safe and popular, he immediately waded into the most fraught issue of the era: the Vietnam War.

Weeks earlier, the widow of Phil Hart — a newly deceased Michigan senator revered in both parties — had pleaded with President Ford to match his pardon of Nixon with a pardon of Vietnam draft dodgers. It would heal the country, she thought. Like all outgoing presidents, Ford was issuing several pardons, and it would have cost him nothing to include young men who had fled to Canada and elsewhere, often as a matter of conscience. But Ford declined to do so. By contrast, Carter, who had been booed at an American Legion convention in Seattle when he floated the idea during the campaign, had the courage to follow through on something unpopular — and at the very beginning of his term.

Carter would borrow a sign reading "The Buck Stops Here" from the Truman Library and display it in the Oval Office to signal that, like the president he respected most, he would hold himself accountable for what happened on his watch. "He took 'The buck stops here' literally," Jim Schlesinger, Carter's secretary of energy, remembered. That included responsibility for closure on the Vietnam War.

And so, on his first day in office, Carter summoned Max Cleland, a double-amputee Vietnam veteran who was his choice to head the Veterans Administration, and Sam Brown, the antiwar activist slated to be the new director of ACTION, the agency that ran the Peace Corps and domestic national service programs. Cleland and Brown would be the first Carter administration officials sworn in — before even the secretary of state. When Cleland told the president he'd heard that congressional Democrats would support the pardons, Carter replied, "I would do it even if a hundred senators opposed it." Many did. Barry Goldwater called it "the most disgraceful thing that a president has ever done." Cleland thought the decision was rooted in Carter's "sense of Christian forgiveness."

The new president's sweeping unconditional pardon of those who evaded the draft between 1964 and 1973 wiped their criminal records clean and allowed them to return to the United States. The government had no records of how many draft dodgers had fled to Canada and other countries, but estimates put the number at around seventy thousand. Carter's amnesty did not apply to active-duty personnel who went AWOL (absent without leave) or otherwise deserted their units.

If the vicious conservative backlash was predictable, the reaction on the Left set another pattern: no good Carter deed would ever go unpunished. Some former antiwar activists charged that Carter had pardoned the well-educated, middle-class draft dodgers who never served but not the poor and working-class deserters who would have a harder time finding work.

Carter had been president for a day and was already under attack in the press. "Most presidents get a honeymoon," Jody Powell complained to Tim Kraft, the new appointments secretary. "Jimmy didn't even get a one-night stand."

Many veterans who had voted for Carter ten weeks earlier now regretted it, but for the new president, that was a fair price to pay for closing a painful chapter in American history. "This was one of the bravest decisions I've ever seen a president make," remembered Bob Kerrey, who as a Navy SEAL lost part of a leg in combat in Vietnam and went on to serve Nebraska as governor and senator.

Carter knew that he wasn't to everyone's taste — that, as he put it later, "my attitude of piety aggravated some people." But because he had campaigned on integrity, he felt duty bound to stay focused on his campaign promises, which he had assembled in a notebook. Carter described himself as "obsessed, maybe to excess," with the need to carry them out. His record on doing so was mixed, but better than even many of his strongest supporters understood, then or later.

# 21
# THE MORAL EQUIVALENT OF WAR

The cold weather on Inauguration Day continued across the country for a week, with record low temperatures leading to home heating oil shortages, widespread destruction of crops in the South, and scores of people freezing to death. Temperatures plummeted below zero in parts of Georgia, and it snowed for the first time ever in Miami.

The timing of the cold snap had major historical consequences. It helped elevate energy to a top-tier issue — over national health insurance and welfare reform — and set in motion the establishment of the country's first real energy policy. While the details could be mind numbing for reporters, Carter's many bills on energy and the environment had a profound cumulative impact on life in the twenty-first century. His policies sharply reduced dependence on foreign oil, began the transition to green energy, mandated energy efficiency, and moved across a broad front to clean up the environment.

Four years earlier, Arab member-states of OPEC — angry about the United States sending weapons to Israel during the 1973 Yom Kippur War — had launched an oil embargo against the West. The embargo led to many emergency measures, including three-day-a-week driving in Great Britain, fifty-five-mile-per-hour speed limits in the United States, and long lines at gas stations across much of the developed world. The embargo ended in 1974, but "the energy crisis" remained. There were episodic supply disruptions and intermittent debates about how importing large amounts of expensive oil was fueling inflation and clouding the future.

A lull in oil price fluctuations kept energy from being a major issue in the 1976 campaign but now it was front and center again — thanks to a new president who decided to use the cold weather to focus attention on the problem. In his first hours in office, Carter requested that Americans turn down their thermostats to sixty-five during the day and fifty-five at night. The next week, after Tip O'Neill wrote him that "our country and our people are in trouble," he proposed the Emergency Natural Gas Act, which authorized the president to reallocate natural gas supplies as needed between the states.

Carter found a government in disarray on energy. While France, West Germany, and other allies realigned their economies, built nuclear power plants, and otherwise figured out how to cut oil imports after the 1973 embargo, the United States, with its big cars and gluttonous habits, had moved disastrously in the other direction. Oil imports were up nearly 50 percent in four years, and the cost of these imports climbed an astonishing ninefold between 1972 and 1977. Meanwhile, domestic production — hobbled by confused policy making — went into steep decline.

Nixon and Ford took stabs at the problem, but

Carter was the first president to grapple seriously with it. Energy independence was an almost perfect fit for his engineering background and moral imagination. Where right-wingers viewed conservation as largely irrelevant, Carter saw it as a test of discipline, self-sacrifice, and patriotism in the face of a foreign threat. At a deeper level, he viewed wastefulness and lack of stewardship of the natural resources provided by God as fundamentally immoral.

But austerity is a political loser for presidents: all pain for largely invisible gain. And energy conservation is especially unpleasant because it cramps everyone's lifestyle. Carter knew this but remained undaunted. "It's a bitch! I know why no other president was willing to tackle it," he told his family toward the end of his term.

On February 2, two weeks after taking office, Carter signed the emergency bill. That evening, he was scheduled to deliver a televised address from the White House Library to announce that he would develop a comprehensive energy policy within ninety days. In going over the draft, he joked with staff that "Our energy policy will be in the Congress's hands — and [Saudi] Prince Faud's." To add drama, the speech was described as a "fireside chat." When FDR originated fireside chats in 1933, the fireplaces were in the homes of millions of radio listeners; in Carter's revival, the fireplace was on-screen scenery — and a genuine source of heat. With the thermostat in the family quarters already turned down ("It was freezing!" Rosalynn remembered), Jimmy wore a beige cashmere cardigan at dinner, a gift from a friend.

Before the ten o'clock airtime, he was still wearing the sweater. Jerry Rafshoon and Rosalynn thought it might look good on television, though Rosalynn fetched a suit jacket just in case he changed his mind. On the air, the cardigan evoked the children's TV host Mister Rogers; at the time, the look was widely seen as fresh and comforting. "He was folks, and folks is in," a Republican insider told *Time*. "I hate to say it, but from a purely analytical point of view, I loved it." A *New York Times* editorial called Carter's debut performance "masterful."

The president seemed to be squaring with the American people. "I realize that many of you have not believed that we really have an energy problem," he said. Confronting the challenge would "require dedication and even some sacrifice" — the latter a concept that President Nixon had tiptoed up to in 1973 when asking Americans to drive slower and turn down their lights, but that hadn't been heard in so straightforward a way since FDR urged it during wartime rationing.

The difference was that Roosevelt delivered his fireside chats with a buoyant tone, while Carter's approach seemed more eat-your-spinach. During both the Great Depression and the depths of World War II, Roosevelt conveyed that the sacrifices required would be temporary. Carter told Americans that energy prices would go up for years and shortages would be "permanent" — which, it turned out, they were not.

Still, the new president wasn't all doom and gloom. Carter proposed a big government jobs program and committed to full accountability. At biweekly news conferences, he welcomed "the most difficult questions [reporters] can contrive" and answered them with specificity, candor, and enough respect for the audience's intelligence that he spoke at an eleventh-grade reading level.★ This continued throughout his presidency. Judy Woodruff, who covered him in Atlanta and at the White House for NBC News, concluded that "calculating and remote Jimmy Carter presided over one of the most open and accessible administrations since the advent of daily White House press coverage."

The people got a chance to weigh in, too. On a Saturday afternoon in early March, the president sat in a wingback chair in the Oval Office with Walter Cronkite of CBS News to answer questions in an unprecedented two-hour radio program. More than twenty-five million Americans tuned in — including nine million who swamped the phone lines.† On *Saturday Night Live,* Bill Murray impersonated Cronkite, and Dan Ackroyd played Carter as a president so frighteningly competent that he could help callers on everything from fixing a high-speed postal letter sorter to

★The only other modern president who spoke at an eleventh-grade reading level was Herbert Hoover. It may not be entirely a coincidence that Hoover and Carter were defeated for reelection by Presidents Roosevelt and Reagan, who spoke at seventh- and eighth-grade reading levels, respectively. Eisenhower, Kennedy, Nixon, Ford, and Clinton spoke at a ninth-grade level, both Bushes at a seventh-grade level, and Donald Trump at less than a fifth-grade level.

†These were monster ratings by today's standards but not high enough in the days of three networks to let the White House preempt sports or other weekend programming again.

surviving a bad LSD trip: "Okay, you did some orange sunshine, Peter. Relax, stay inside, and listen to some music, okay?" Afterward, Carter's approval ratings reached 75 percent, his all-time high.

Later that month, Carter traveled to Clinton, Massachusetts, for an old-fashioned New England "town meeting," the first of what would soon become a staple of all presidential campaigns. His comments supporting the eventual creation of a Palestinian homeland — a first for an American president — set off alarms in the American Jewish community, but the overall response to his performance was enthusiastic. "I don't know all the answers," the president said.

This public humility was not usually matched in private, where he sometimes tried to show that he knew more than his experts about their subject areas. Bert Lance told Carter that this was counterproductive: subordinates would withhold important information for fear of being embarrassed. "You don't have to prove to anybody that you're the smartest man in the room," he reminded him. "You're the president of the United States."

Other officials found it comforting to see real brains in the presidency. When environmental activists argued that they needed one of their own in the West Wing, Carter agreed and said, "I'm him." It was true. He knew more about, say, the Endangered Species Act and its impact on drilling and dams than almost anyone he could have hired, and he brought that knowledge to bear during the sprint toward a comprehensive energy plan.

All told, Carter spent more than a third of his time during his first hundred days deep in the weeds on energy. His team pulled frequent all-nighters during a hellish three months to come up with the country's first real energy policy: the National Energy Plan.

In a prime-time address on April 18, the still-new president acknowledged that the weather had gotten a lot warmer, but he minced no words on a slow-moving, abstract, and politically uncool issue:

"Tonight I want to have an unpleasant talk with you about a problem unprecedented in our history. With the exception of preventing war, this is the greatest challenge that our country will face during our lifetimes. The energy crisis has not yet overwhelmed us, but it will if we do not act quickly."

An "unpleasant talk"? How contrary to the ethos of optimism that animates most presidencies. Carter struck Churchillian tones and preached sacrifice — including a 10 percent reduction in gasoline consumption. "Those citizens who insist on driving large, unnecessarily powerful cars must expect to pay more for that luxury," he said. Then he borrowed a line from philosopher and psychologist William James that FDR had used in launching the Civilian Conservation Corps during the Depression: "This difficult effort will be the moral equivalent of war — except that we will be uniting our efforts to build and not to destroy."

Columnist William Safire popularized a demeaning acronym for the "moral equivalent of war": MEOW. Even so, early reviews of the speech were again positive. Hedrick Smith of the *New York Times* reported on the front page that Carter was arguing "the time had come for some elemental transformations in the American way of life."

461

Two days later, Carter, still sporting high approval ratings, delivered an address to a joint session of Congress outlining the specifics of his plan. He maintained a somber tone. ("This cannot be an inspirational speech tonight. I don't expect much applause.") But the congressional leadership had already told Carter that his proposed increase in the gas tax was dead-on-arrival on Capitol Hill; his other calls for sacrifice weren't landing, either. The three prime-time energy speeches in three months had lit no fire under Congress.

Even as Carter called Americans to their higher selves, his humble approach ate away at his authority. And unlike war, the energy crisis just wasn't energizing. For millions of people, small wasn't beautiful, as E. F. Schumacher had claimed in a popular book. It was just small.

Just after the election, Hamilton Jordan had predicted that "Jimmy's problem in the White House will be that he's going to try to do everything at once." Sure enough, despite feverish, nearly round-the-clock work early on, energy wasn't the clear priority of his first year, but just one of dozens of initiatives. Carter introduced so many bills that Bert Lance thought "it looked more like a smorgasbord than an agenda."

Carter backed almost anything congressional Democrats favored — with one dramatic exception. On February 21 the president reprised his damn-the-dams policy from Georgia and announced that he would eliminate from his proposed budget nineteen out of more than three hundred water projects in various stages of planning. Carter considered these dams, man-made

462

lakes, and navigational canals to be of "doubtful necessity," and he threatened to veto any public works bill that contained them.

The move would sour his relationship with Congress, setting an acrimonious tone for his presidency. Walter Mondale had strenuously argued that Carter should cancel two or three projects as symbols of his fight against waste but that nineteen was asking for trouble. The president didn't listen. His aim was "front-loaded pain and back-loaded pleasure," as Mondale recalled, but the pleasure never materialized. Veteran senator Russell Long of Louisiana told Carter he had gone to "war with his own best soldiers."

As usual, Carter was right about most of the projects' merits: one violated a treaty with Canada, and another was scheduled to be built on an earthquake fault line. Many of the rest lined the pockets of a small number of wealthy landowners at the expense of taxpayers. The supposed economic benefits to various regions were largely illusory, and the environmental impact was often harmful.

But Carter's so-called hit list was assembled so hastily that it even alienated many environmentalists. Feeling blindsided, Senator Edmund Muskie vowed "to look for anything I can fire back with — anything." Freshman senator Gary Hart of Colorado confided to the White House that there were six water projects in his home state, and three were questionable, but that Carter had killed the wrong three.

Some legislators were notified of the cancellation of a major project in their state or district by the media, without a heads-up from the White House — a cardinal sin in Washington. The old bulls of Capitol Hill, embarrassed that the Georgia rube often knew more about matters under their purview than they did, wanted to "throw a pie in Carter's face," remembered Congressman George Miller, a California liberal.* Jack Brooks, a powerful committee chairman, passed Jerry Rafshoon in the White House one day and snapped, "If that son of a bitch tells me to 'do the right thing' one more time, I'm gonna kick his ass."

After weeks of recriminations, the old bulls attached all nineteen water projects to the president's larger economic package and dared him to veto it. In hindsight, a few Carter aides wished he had. The veto would have been sustained and he could have salvaged some kind of victory from the mess. Instead, he listened to Jordan, who advised against another thumb in the eye of Congress. In the end, his prideful decision had accomplished nothing beyond making powerful new enemies.

Bert Lance believed in retrospect that picking a fight over water projects was the worst political mistake of the Carter administration. Almost everyone else in the White House agreed — except the president himself. He insisted stubbornly that he had been right all along. Carter knew perfectly well that he was expected to offer favors to members of Congress in exchange for support on other issues. He had mostly gotten away with avoiding that game in Georgia and hoped to do so in Washington, too.

*Miller, who was responsible during his forty-year career for spearheading more progressive legislation on health and education than any other member of the House, believed Carter was the best president under whom he served.

This attitude may have been virtuous, but it was unsophisticated about power and what it can accomplish. Patronage and "pork" (federal money pumped into states and districts) can be useful lubricants for a president, as long as they are not exploited in times of crisis. Two years later, when it was time to run for reelection, Carter deputized underlings to dole out favors, often without telling him the specifics. But by then it was too late to reestablish critical relationships with many in his own party.

To Tip O'Neill's credit, he didn't let anger over the water projects slow down the energy bill, which the House approved in August. A few portions of the complicated package of bills also quickly cleared the Senate, including the consolidation of several agencies into a new Department of Energy, which would be headed by Jim Schlesinger. Otherwise, the Senate dawdled on energy for much of the next three years.

The big debate was over the decontrol of natural gas, which had been caught in a regional patchwork of conflicting regulations. Energy-producing southern and western states needed to sell natural gas at higher prices so that oil and gas companies could afford to explore for desperately needed new supplies. Cold-weather northern states believed deregulation was a threat to the environment and an unconscionable concession to corporate America, not to mention a surefire way to jack up home heating bills. Congress was split about fifty-fifty. "We had to force it," Carter recalled. "There was no groundswell."

Energy policy was inherently confusing but Carter didn't do himself any favors in October with the way he chose to sell it. "Suspicion growing that the emperor's top assistants, at least, have no clothes on," speechwriter Jerry Doolittle wrote in his diary as the president embarked on a six-state swing to hawk his plan. "To fight moral equivalent of war, must have moral equivalent of enemy, moral equivalent of order of battle, moral equivalent of victory. (This would not be turning down the thermostat.)"

For Carter's November 8 prime-time speech on energy, Jim Fallows brought in Richard Goodwin, a veteran of both the Kennedy and Johnson White Houses who was widely regarded as one of the best presidential speechwriters ever. But Carter rejected the Fallows-Goodwin draft and penned his own pedestrian version of the address in a single day; he then delivered it poorly. Fallows said later that working as Jimmy Carter's speechwriter was about as rewarding as being FDR's tap dancing instructor.

Carter would give six nationally televised speeches devoted at least in part to energy during his presidency, and none did much to move the upper chamber of Congress. Senate Majority Leader Robert C. Byrd, the fiddle-playing West Virginian sometimes known as "Robert C. Bastard," finally won approval of the National Energy Act of 1978, but it was another two years before he got the Senate to pass watered-down versions of other Carter energy bills — complex legislation on scores of different energy challenges. The president's victories were so fragmented and technical that, even in Washington, few realized he had actually enacted the nation's first comprehensive legislation on the most pressing domestic issue of his time.

The payoff for the country was still over the horizon. Decontrol of natural gas eventually ended twenty-five years of futile efforts to stimulate domestic energy production. Carter's new natural gas regulatory structure encouraging both production and conservation would help make the United States a net energy exporter in the twenty-first century. Liberals disliked the new law because it raised prices temporarily, but long-term the policy actually helped reduce inflation, which was fueled by sky-high global oil prices.

Carter's support from business on natural gas did not extend to other energy issues. After confronting automakers in the Roosevelt Room over their continued love of profitable gas-guzzlers, Carter imposed the first federal fuel economy standards for passenger vehicles: eighteen miles per gallon. The plan, which envisioned hybrids by the early eighties, called for an eventual forty-eight-mile-per-gallon standard by 1995. Twenty-five years after that, fuel economy standards have not yet reached forty miles per gallon, thanks to opposition from the auto industry and Republican presidents.

On the environment, Carter nonetheless presided over the second great public health revolution in American history. The first, at the turn of the twentieth century, was sanitary: it controlled human sewage. Carter's quiet, piecemeal revolution controlled industrial waste. He signed fourteen important environmental bills that for the first time gave the government the muscle to curb pollution of all kinds.

The establishment of the Environmental Protection Agency in 1970 — Richard Nixon's response to twenty million people taking part in the first

Earth Day that April — hadn't by itself done much to end the smog that clung to major American cities and industrial areas. President Ford had begun implementing landmark legislation to build the EPA, but it wasn't until the 1977 Clean Air Act Amendments — pushed hard by Carter and enforced by EPA administrator Doug Costle — that air quality in the United States began to show astonishing improvement. The administration also won a landmark court ruling that forced U.S. Steel to sharply reduce air pollution, leading the entire steel industry to do the same.

Carter's EPA for the first time required companies to list all toxic substances in their products — a huge advance for public health that Americans soon took for granted. The agency moved aggressively to save the planet's ozone layer by banning chlorofluorocarbons in aerosols, and — with the Consumer Product Safety Commission — banned lead paint, which had poisoned thousands of children annually. The EPA's development of market-based emissions trading — so-called cap and trade — eventually eliminated acid rain in the United States and much of Canada and is now used in many countries to fight climate change. The Clean Water Act of 1977 helped end the era where rivers caught fire. Carter was pro-coal — then the largest domestic energy source — but he also signed the first legislation heavily regulating coal mines and the first bill funding the reclamation of strip-mined lands.

Despite the efforts of Reagan (and, later, Donald Trump) to slash budgets and jam environmental efforts into reverse, Carter-era ideas would eventually find their way into laws and regulations

468

with far-reaching implications. New Carter-era regulations required that all appliances disclose their energy efficiency on easy-to-read labels; secured the safe transportation of hazardous waste; and incentivized the use of renewables and privately generated electricity (in the boring-sounding but transformative 1978 Public Utilities Regulatory Policies Act) — huge and positive changes for core American industries and for the environment.

In the forty years since Carter left office, the gross domestic product (GDP) grew six times as fast as energy usage — an impressive achievement. Fuel economy for cars and trucks has improved by more than a quarter, industrial energy savings have doubled, and many everyday appliances are as much as 70 percent more energy efficient. The list goes on. Carter's accomplishments on energy and the environment were not what they might have been had he been reelected in 1980. But they would begin to change how Americans live, and their example offered hope for harder climate change adjustments ahead.

# 22
# THE STEEL MAGNOLIA

First, Carter revolutionized the vice presidency. Then he did the same for the role of the first lady — or, more accurately, Rosalynn and Jimmy revolutionized it together. From the early years of their marriage, they had always been a team, but their relationship in the White House was something new and historic.

Edith Wilson controlled access to her husband, Woodrow, after he suffered a stroke near the end of his presidency. Eleanor Roosevelt carved a new role for first ladies by giving speeches and writing a newspaper column. But even they (not to mention all the other first ladies to that point) were not regarded by their husbands as true partners. Rosalynn was in a category all her own. Carter liked to say that when making important foreign policy personnel decisions, he'd confirm his judgment with "Rosalynn, Cy, Zbig, and Ham." As Hugh Sidey of *Time* wrote, "Note the order."

Jimmy described their "very equal partnership" as "like one person acting in concert," while Rosalynn said, "We developed a mutual understanding about what to do and how to do it." Jimmy saw her as his "antenna" or "lightning rod" to pick up static from the electorate. Bob Strauss, the US trade representative, recalled phoning the president with a particularly touchy personnel problem: "He said, 'I'll get Rosalynn, and you come, and we'll talk about it.' "

The Carters held a working lunch every Tuesday at twelve thirty in the family dining room on the second floor of the White House — a first for a president and his wife. "Well, Rosie," the president would say after the blessing, "what's on your agenda this week?" Then they would nibble salads and discuss personnel, her pet projects, campaign strategy, foreign policy challenges, and other matters of substance. Anything personal that a husband and wife might discuss was left for supper and after hours.

Rosalynn traveled incessantly (eighteen nations and twenty-seven American cities in the first year alone), but at home she went to work every day in the East Wing. She was the first presidential spouse to have her own professional policy staff. When Rosalynn, committed as she was to equal pay for equal work, noticed that East Wing employees were all paid much less than their West Wing counterparts, she complained to Jimmy, who was too cheap to do anything about it until she insisted.

Rosalynn's popularity at least partially compensated for some of Jimmy's shortcomings. She didn't exaggerate, correct grammar, or forget to say thank you. And by Jimmy's own admission, her formidable political instincts were superior to his own. Rosalynn had the full respect of the president's aides, in part because they would ask her to convey political messages to her husband — usually with a bracing dose of realism — that he might otherwise dismiss. Administration of-

471

ficials both feared and respected her, and a nickname took hold: the Steel Magnolia, which Rosalynn didn't mind at all.

After a year in the White House, Jimmy noticed that every time he entered the family quarters, Rosalynn greeted him with a policy question that couldn't wait for their weekly lunch. She needed up-to-date information to communicate properly both within and outside the administration. So the president decided that his wife should attend Cabinet meetings — another first. She was hammered in the press for this, but the Carters didn't care. The first lady sat along the wall with aides and said nothing during the meetings but usually spoke afterward with Jimmy about what had transpired. (The practice did not extend to National Security Council meetings, as she had no formal high-level security clearance.)

One of Rosalynn's most far-reaching projects involved a form of bias identified after the civil rights movement: age discrimination. Working closely with Congressman Claude Pepper of Florida, she helped loosen rules on mandatory retirement in the federal government, a move that quickly extended into the private sector. Soon tens of millions of Americans began working several years longer than permitted in the past.

Rosalynn's most passionate cause remained mental health. As chair of the new Commission on Mental Health, she held hearings across the country and testified before Congress (only the second time a first lady had done so) on the need for community mental health clinics and other reforms. In 1980 her commission's recommendations that mental illness be treated like any other disease were incorporated in landmark legislation.

Within six months of her husband's inauguration, Rosalynn also became a diplomat — a role that even Eleanor Roosevelt never played as first lady. In June 1977 she embarked on a thirteen-day diplomatic mission to seven Latin American and Caribbean nations. She was well prepared, well received, and so effective that an admiring news analysis in the *New York Times* dubbed her "Ambassador Rosalynn Carter." Jimmy privately called her "my number one diplomat" and was hugely proud of the role she played in advancing his human rights agenda.

Rosalynn, as Hamilton Jordan put it, was "one tough lady." In Brazil, she confronted President Ernesto Geisel with the cases of various political prisoners, several of whom were eventually freed. She looked President Alfonso López Michelsen of Colombia in the eye and told him that one of his top Cabinet officers was working with a cocaine cartel. And she returned to Washington with a firm commitment from Francisco Morales-Bermudez, the military leader of Peru, to move toward democracy.

Rosalynn was also essential to Carter's policy of resettling refugees from Southeast Asia. After Saigon fell in 1975, thousands of Vietnamese began fleeing the country by sea. The flotillas of "boat people" in rickety hand-built vessels reached its peak in 1978 and 1979. Rosalynn and Mondale pushed the navy to pick up as many of the refugees as possible, a little-noticed decision that saved thousands of lives at a time when Americans wanted to forget all about Vietnam. Meanwhile, the atrocities of Pol Pot's Khmer Rouge forced hundreds of thousands of Cambodians into refugee camps in Thailand, where they languished for months.

One Friday afternoon in November 1979, Rosalynn and Jimmy sat together in his office, looking at the grim photographs from the Thai camps. By Monday, Rosalynn was on a plane to Thailand, where she plunged into the crowds and cradled an emaciated infant whose mother was too weak from hunger to stand. She kissed another woman on the forehead and said, "Give me a smile." The story was covered all over the world.

After returning to Washington, Rosalynn convinced her husband to accept thousands more refugees than he'd originally planned. Carter doubled the number of refugees from Southeast Asia from seven thousand to fourteen thousand a month, ten times the quota for refugees fleeing wars in the Middle East in the early twenty-first century. All told, nearly a half million immigrants from the region were allowed to resettle in the United States on his watch, 70 percent of the total absorbed worldwide. When Carter learned that Japan had been much stingier than other developed nations — accepting only *four* refugees total — he persuaded Japanese prime minister Masayoshi Ohira to pay for more than half of the UN's resettlement efforts. In 1980, he signed the Refugee Act, which established a permanent public-private international resettlement program within the State Department.

Rosalynn's most historic role came in children's health. At the suggestion of Betty Bumpers, who had spearheaded vaccinations when her husband, Senator Dale Bumpers, was governor of Arkansas, the two women embarked on a state-by-state campaign promoting preschool immunizations. Rosalynn scrounged for seed money in the admin-

474

istration's budget, and the pair eventually convinced thirty-three states to enact bills mandating proof of vaccination before children entered kindergarten or first grade. Before long, early childhood immunization rates had soared past 90 percent, an impressive feat in a country that even then was beset by outlandish conspiracy theories about vaccines. Soon a joke spread: everywhere Rosalynn Carter showed up, kids started to cry — for fear of getting a shot.

The program was a stunning success. Within three years, the US Centers for Disease Control (CDC) reported that the incidence of measles, mumps, rubella, and other communicable diseases among school-age children was "at or near record low levels." A decade later, after a deadly outbreak of measles, Rosalynn and Betty teamed up again to encourage immunizations by age two, and Rosalynn eventually took her crusade abroad. In recent years, anti-vaxxer conspiracy theorists, abetted by the Trump administration, have rolled back some of the progress. But her legacy endures: Rosalynn helped prevent tens of millions of children from getting sick and saved tens of thousands of lives worldwide.

Rosalynn was a feminist and an advocate of affirmative action (now expanded to address gender discrimination), and she pushed hard for Jimmy to hire more women. Carter appointed only two to his original Cabinet — Patricia Roberts Harris as secretary of housing and urban development and Juanita Kreps as secretary of commerce — but he got the diversity message and resolved to act on it. When Joe Califano, secretary of health, education, and welfare, wanted to hire Richard

Beattie, a New York lawyer, for a senior position, Carter wrote Califano, "I've approved Beattie (white male), but this can't go on. It is embarrassing to me." Women and blacks would be represented in Carter's sub-Cabinet in historic numbers.

Carter's respect for women went beyond hiring. For more than thirty years, women who flew in noncombat roles in World War II as part of the Women's Air Corps Service Pilots (WASP) program were denied veterans' benefits; Carter fixed that. And one of the only firm rules he imposed on his speechwriters was to avoid masculine words when also describing women. In a stark departure from precedent, his speeches contained no references to "mankind" or "the common man."

The most permanent effect of the president's interest in diversity was on the federal judiciary. As president-elect, Carter had met at the Georgia governor's mansion with attorney general designate Griffin Bell and Mississippi senator James Eastland, chairman of the Senate Judiciary Committee. Eastland, a virulent racist, was so proud that a southerner had been elected president — he never expected to live to see it — that he pledged to cooperate with Carter. There were limits to Eastland's indulgence — Carter's 1977 proposal to decriminalize marijuana and reexamine sentencing guidelines for cocaine possession was dead on arrival in the Judiciary Committee — but he gave way on judicial nominations. Carter convinced Eastland to move control of nominations for the federal district court out of the hands of senators and give it to newly created semi-independent commissions, which would look for high-quality appointments. Carter's only directive to the commissions was that they undertake affirmative action. He told Coretta Scott King and Daddy King that he would insist that the commissions name at least one black judge from each of the states of the Old Confederacy.

The transformation took a while because the American Bar Association criteria for certifying nominees as "well qualified" was outdated. Adhering to those standards, Bell slow-walked some women and black candidates because they hadn't practiced law long enough or written enough law review articles. Carter sniffed out the hypocrisy in that. "How many law review articles did you write before President Kennedy appointed his Georgia campaign chairman [Bell] to the Fifth Circuit?" he asked. Bell conceded the point.

After the first twelve nominees for the US Court of Appeals were men, women's groups began to pressure the president. So did Rosalynn, who told her husband to pick up the pace, which he did with an executive order urging the commissions to look harder for qualified women and minority candidates. The breakthrough came when the Omnibus Judgeship Act of 1978, designed to ease the intense workload of federal judges, expanded the bench by a third, adding 152 new federal judgeships.

Carter appointed 262 federal judges altogether, by far the most of any president until then and more than any of his successors (including Donald Trump) in a four-year period. He replaced tokenism with thoughtful, systematic affirmative action. All told, he named fifty-five blacks, Hispanics, and other minorities to the federal bench — three times the number serving at the time — including nine to the US Court of Appeals, compared to one by Ronald Reagan, who served twice as long. Among the new judges were forty women, five times as many as appointed by all earlier presidents combined. The best known would be Ruth Bader Ginsburg, a brilliant feminist law professor at Columbia Law School. "People often ask me, 'Well, did you always want to be a judge?' " Ginsburg said years after President Clinton had elevated her to the Supreme Court. "My answer is that it just wasn't in the realm of the possible until Jimmy Carter became president and was determined to draw on the talent of all of the people, not just some of them."

Ginsburg's path to a court appointment wasn't smooth. While known in some legal circles as the "Thurgood Marshall of the women's movement" for arguing a series of landmark cases in the Supreme Court on women's rights, she was passed over for a federal judgeship in New York as a "one-issue" candidate. But after a concerted effort on her behalf, Ginsburg became a finalist to fill a vacancy on the US Court of Appeals for the District of Columbia (the prestigious DC Circuit). Carter's second attorney general, Benjamin Civiletti, was lukewarm on her, in part because her association with the American Civil Liberties Union made her seem "excessively liberal." Assistant Attorney General Barbara Babcock pushed her anyway. As did Sarah Weddington, who as a twenty-six-year-old lawyer argued and won the 1973 *Roe v. Wade* case in the Supreme Court. Weddington was much too liberal for some White House staffers, who thought Carter jeopardized his standing with moderates by hiring her as his top aide on women's issues. But Carter, with Rosalynn's prodding, stuck by her. As the Ginsburg pick hung in the balance, Weddington leaked the selection before a final decision had been made, then rushed downstairs to the Oval Office to confess to the president, who didn't mind. That night, he wrote drolly in his diary that Ginsburg had been "a matter of some controversy."

Carter had the misfortune to be the first president in American history to serve a full four-year term and not fill a single seat on the Supreme Court. If a vacancy had occurred on his watch, he was expected to name Shirley Hufstedler, a widely admired federal judge from California, to fill it. (Hufstedler would become the first secretary of education in 1979.) President Reagan would appoint the first woman to the high court when he nominated Sandra Day O'Connor in 1981, but it was Carter — by expanding the judiciary and committing to diversity — who first changed the face of the federal judiciary. In thousands of cases, his appointees preserved civil rights, protected the environment, and established important precedents that would help shape American law.

Jimmy was proud not only of Rosalynn's work but also of her personal development. He thought she was more relaxed and sure of herself than when they were in the governor's mansion, and he was impressed that, in her early fifties, she was trying things she would never have considered before, including cross-country skiing, swimming, tennis, and jogging. "She's gotten younger, healthier, prettier, more enjoyable to be around," he wrote in his diary after two years in office.

They bickered but loved each other so much that it could be difficult for their children to feel included. "There's a little bit of 'us against the world' that made them so close," Jeff observed. Like the marriage of their successors, Ronald and Nancy Reagan, there was often just no room for anyone else.

Jack, who still had issues with his father, had moved to Calhoun, Georgia, where he worked for his father-in-law's legal practice. Jeff enrolled in George Washington University, where he became a software developer and partner in an early computer mapping business. Chip, the middle son, was the most political of the brood and the one most emotionally invested in being a Carter. He took a job at the Democratic National Committee, but also found himself confronting a messy personal situation.

A month after the inauguration, Chip's wife, Caron, gave birth to a son, James Earl Carter IV. The three of them lived in the White House for a time. But Chip had been cheating repeatedly on Caron since early in the campaign. He confessed later that one of his goals was to sleep with a different woman in all fifty states, and by this time he had made good progress. When Caron finally heard credible rumors and confronted him, he confessed.

In August 1977 Caron made an appointment with the president to discuss her husband's adultery. The wrenching session in Carter's study ended with a tearful embrace. Caron said later that the president had been sensitive and compassionate in discussing the sexual difficulties that often arise in marriage. When Jimmy and Rosalynn learned that Caron and six-month-old James were moving out of the White House, the president suggested that maybe his son should leave instead. Chip and Caron ended up departing together for

Plains, where they tried in vain to save their marriage.

Their divorce shook Jimmy and Rosalynn. When Carter was young, his family didn't know of a single married couple in Plains who split up. Affairs — even living in sin and what were called "bastard" or "illegitimate" children — were common enough, but not divorce. As a child, he'd puzzled over why divorce was worse than adultery but didn't question that both were immoral. As an adult, he tried to discipline himself to be tolerant and nonjudgmental, but his feelings did not change even after three of his four children got divorced. Only Jeff, happily married to Annette, did not.

The Carters were the first family since the Kennedys with a child in the White House, and they tried to make the most of it after so much time on the road. When they weren't traveling, one or both had dinner with Amy every night and often swam with her in the White House swimming pool or bowled in the White House basement. The president designed a tree house for her on the South Lawn, and she roller-skated in the East Room without consequence. Her cat, Misty Malarky Ying Yang, became famous.

Amy recalled being glad that her nanny, Mary Fitzpatrick, could join the family in Washington. After the Carters left the governor's mansion in 1975, Fitzpatrick was sent back to an Atlanta prison, which left Amy, then seven, bereft. When preparing to move to the White House, Jimmy obtained Fitzpatrick's release and arranged to be appointed her parole officer, the first time a president ever performed that function.*

After the Georgia Supreme Court ordered a new examination of Mary's case, she was fully exonerated and pardoned. Carter wrote later that had she shot a white man, she might have been executed for a crime she didn't commit — a personal factor in his growing doubts about the death penalty. Assuming her maiden name, Mary Prince, she moved into the White House and took care of Amy and grandchildren as they came along. She became practically a member of the family and, after the presidency, settled in Plains, where she helped the Carters in all the years that followed.

Amy remained close to her parents. Her dominant impression of her father, then and later, was that he was always focused and in the moment, "able to pay direct attention to the person in front of him and leave other things to the side. He doesn't ever seem distracted." He never complained or said he was having a bad day. When she misbehaved, Jimmy and Rosalynn assigned her to read a book and report back on its contents.

The Carters made a point of sending Amy to the Thaddeus Stevens School, a mostly black public elementary school in Washington, where her best friend was the daughter of the cook at the Chilean embassy. She was the first child of a president to attend public school since Theodore Roosevelt's son Quentin.

This was of a piece with Rosalynn riding the

*Mary's past was used for humor on *Saturday Night Live,* which aired a skit in which actress Sissy Spacek played Amy and cast member Garrett Morris impersonated Mary.

new DC Metro subway around town and visiting patients at DC General Hospital. It helped signal that the administration took a special interest in the fortunes of the District of Columbia. When a magazine depicted Washington as "the crime capital of America," Carter phoned Cher (whom he always called "Cher Allman" because of her brief marriage to Gregg Allman) and asked the now-famous singer to say something nice about the city on television, which she did.

When afforded a respite in Plains a couple of times a year, the Carters happily resumed their old recreational lives: hiking, fishing, and searching the area for Indian arrowheads to add to their collection of more than 1,500.

While they were out of the spotlight, the rest of the family kept America amused. Upon landing in Italy in July 1978, Lillian said she was eager to meet the country's "fine young president," Sandro Pertini, age eighty-two, "since my husband passed away." She added: "I have never met an ugly Italian!" When she playfully called Jordan's King Hussein "a damn foreigner," he didn't seem to mind. The president enjoyed her frequent appearances on talk shows.

Shortly after his brother was elected president, Billy Carter hired a big-time Nashville agent, and by late 1977 he was hauling in $500,000 a year in celebrity endorsements, including peanut-flavored liqueur and, most famously, Billy Beer, which tasted so bad he would often pour the contents into the toilet and fill the can with vodka instead. He hosted an international belly flop contest, played the rube — to his brother's annoyance — on *Hee Haw* and *Hollywood Squares,* boxed with

483

former heavyweight champ Joe Frazier, and vamped with actress Zsa Zsa Gabor.

Even when he was flying high, Billy was beginning his descent. At an Oakland cocktail party, he made reference to "a nigger in a wood pile," just the first of several such indiscretions. When Billy embarrassed himself and the president, the White House routinely declined comment. But Jody Powell occasionally called Chip to ask him to rein in his uncle.

Ruth Carter Stapleton's career flourished. Her audiences increased fivefold, and she made the cover of *Newsweek*. She spent five days counseling pornographer Larry Flynt aboard his pink jet and baptized him in the ocean off the Bahamas. Ruth said Jimmy had "never been good at personal counseling" and that he didn't understand why people got divorced or couldn't just deprive themselves of pleasure when necessary. In Plains, she said, she "tried to help Jimmy understand what most of us are like." He couldn't. "Ruth, there's just no place in my head where I can understand," he told her. "If you're supposed to do a job, you do it."

The president occasionally ran into Rachel Clark in Plains. On a 1977 visit, they recalled their long-ago fishing expeditions. Rachel, living in a nearby housing project, remembered telling him, "Do your best. Don't play. If you do your best, the Lord will take care of you." As they parted, Jimmy asked her to pray for him.

# 23

# HIS INNER ENGINEER

Supreme Court justice Oliver Wendell Holmes famously described Franklin D. Roosevelt as having a "second-class intellect and a first-class temperament." Jimmy Carter was the reverse, with a first-class intellect and a second-class temperament. Meeting FDR was described as "like opening your first bottle of champagne"; Carter, too, could be charming in person, but the champagne had a way of going flat. And yet his decency, sound judgment, and dogged determination to solve problems constituted its own kind of productive temperament in the presidency.

Carter wasn't an arm twister or a backslapper, but he was often persuasive with the logic of his arguments. His inner engineer helped him identify problems, break them down, then try to fix them with the best rational solutions at hand. Like most engineers, he rejected rigid ideology. If ideological consistency was always the right approach, why would the engineer need his tools? This was a utilitarian, data-driven worldview, and it attracted many other smart and moderate people into his orbit.

But engineers are rarely natural motivators and leaders; in corporate America, they often fall just

485

short of becoming CEOs. Having gathered and analyzed the information necessary to reach a rational conclusion, engineers are often bewildered, even aggrieved, when others can't see the obvious empirical truth. According to an old engineering joke, if an optimist sees the glass half-full and a pessimist sees it half-empty, an engineer "sees the glass as twice the size it needs to be." As the writer Malcolm Gladwell put it, "[The engineer] doesn't give free rein to temperament; he assesses the object."

This appearance of bloodlessness might be fine in most circumstances, but not in the glare of the presidency. His charm as a candidate seemed to fade in the White House, which more often brought out his austere and serious side. In private, he sometimes used his intelligence and discipline to intimidate others who hadn't prepared as rigorously for meetings. And in public, his mien was often dour. The historian David McCullough — who would come to know Carter through their advocacy of the Panama Canal Treaties — was hardly alone in noticing that even when the president smiled broadly, he rarely seemed to be having a good time. Carter claimed to be emotionally satisfied in the job; he never regretted seeking it or suffered depression in the White House. But little sense of mischief or joy came through, and this hurt him. "He didn't seem to have the political adrenaline that one responds favorably to," McCullough remembered.

That was ironic because Carter contained vast storehouses of energy. Most mornings, he awoke at six o'clock for some "thinking time," jogged three or four miles on the South Lawn, and often phoned Charlie Kirbo. "He was bad about calling you early in the morning and saying, 'What the heck you doing in bed this time of day?' " Kirbo remembered. "It was usually when he had a problem." Carter frequently rejected Kirbo's basic advice. "He had a policy that I didn't like of being open with everything," Kirbo said. "If he had a problem or scandal of some type, he would just lay it out [publicly]. I spent about half of my time patching up holes that were created by this openness. A lot of times, it served no purpose and was nonproductive. It helped nobody, but that was his policy."

By six thirty, Carter was in the Oval Office, where he often started his workday spinning the huge globe he kept by the Resolute desk. He often rested his fingers on the vast landmass of the Soviet Union and prayed silently for the strength to prevent war. Most days, he held meetings or made calls in the Oval Office in the morning and retreated to his adjoining study in the afternoon, where he would read, think, and pray as Mozart, Bach, Chopin, or some Rachmaninoff played in the background. In the evening, after more work or hosting events, Jimmy and Rosalynn usually read prayers aloud to each other in both English and Spanish (a ritual they followed for twenty years), then retired at around ten o'clock.

Carter later recalled praying more in the White House than at any time in his life. "Even when I was reluctant to share my problems and my unanswered questions with any other human being, including Rosalynn, I was always able to share them with God," he wrote.

Prayers, too, were subject to engineering. The president broke them into "three key questions" for God's guidance, essentially: (1) "Are the goals

I am pursuing appropriate?" (2) "Am I doing the right thing based on my personal moral code, my Christian faith, and the duties of my current position?" (3) "Have I done my best, based on the alternatives open to me?" That focus on his "best" was rarely far from his mind.

Carter struggled sometimes reconciling his faith with his secular obligations. He confessed as much to Pope John Paul II in October 1979 when the pontiff made the first-ever papal visit to the White House. They agreed that if Christ still walked the earth, he would favor the celibacy of priests and the right to live, which meant opposing both abortion and the death penalty. "I told him it was difficult for me as a politician sworn to uphold our laws to live with the concept of permissive abortion," Carter recalled. But he was never one to impose his personal views on anyone else.

The atmosphere in the Carter White House was quiet toil. Carter's personal secretary for six years, Susan Clough, said he never raised his voice, and that his demeanor was genial if businesslike most of the time.* The only chore that he found tiresome was signing photographs. Almost everyone except close staff and celebrities got the simple "Best Wishes, Jimmy Carter." He understood why politicians would need a photo to validate their proximity to power. But like Barack Obama, Carter viewed that neediness as an abstraction — an

*Carter didn't even lose his cool on a state visit to Poland when, during a big speech, an incompetent interpreter translated his promise to learn about the desires of the Polish people into the president desiring them sexually.

488

emotion at one remove — because he had not felt it himself.

Clough viewed her boss as a self-contained, emotionally repressed man who put his feelings "on the shelf" during his presidency. "It's not that he did not have any of the human feelings — it is that he did not *display* or *communicate* feelings," she said, a view Carter agreed with decades later, when he said his emotions were best expressed through his poetry. Clough thought his reserved nature and the inherently transactional nature of his job prevented him from nurturing personal relationships in the presidency. Because he didn't need feedback and back patting and didn't care if people liked him, he mistakenly assumed that others in his orbit felt the same way.

Carter enjoyed warm relations with Mary Prince; Charlie Palmer, who served him throughout as the chief flight steward on Air Force One; and a few African Americans on the household staff. But others found him standoffish. "He didn't want [White House] police officers or agents looking at him or speaking to him," White House usher Nelson Pierce remembered. "He didn't want them paying attention to him by [walking] by. I never could understand why." The Secret Service, which had replaced his campaign code name, "Dasher," with "Deacon" (Rosalynn was "Dancer"), felt the same. There were exceptions over the years among the black agents, with whom he and Rosalynn generally felt more comfortable. After the presidency, Carter loosened up and developed more of a sense of humor, though he still didn't banter as much with his agents as most other presidents did.

Over time, the Carters developed family rituals.

When the weather was good, Jimmy and Rosalynn would go up on the Truman Balcony in the evening and look out on the Washington Monument. They placed Georgia-made rocking chairs there and used the balcony more than any other first family. One night, Rosalynn's brother Jerry Smith muttered, "Anybody that would fight to get a job like this has to have rocks in his head." Jimmy acknowledged the point but told his brother-in-law, "Anytime I get a problem, I can come up here and look at the Washington Monument, just look out, and it boosts me up."

Films had a similar effect. Altogether, the Carters screened 480 movies in four years — a record for a president. Jeff and Chip watched most of them, but Jimmy and Rosalynn tried to see one a week in the White House ground-floor screening room or aboard Air Force One. After watching Sissy Spacek in *Coal Miner's Daughter* in the company of several aides who had no experience in the South, Jimmy told them, "I hope you guys appreciate this movie!"

Books continued to have pride of place in the Carter household. The president especially liked Chinua Achebe's 1958 novel of Africa, *Things Fall Apart,* and Saul Bellow's *Herzog.* Per long-standing family tradition, Amy was allowed to read at the table, which caused a minor flap when she was seen reading during events with foreign heads of state. Jody Powell resented the press focusing on Amy, but it was Jimmy and Rosalynn who included her in everything — even having her play the violin in front of guests.

For all their reserve, the Carters were exuberant entertainers. They especially loved a 1978 jazz festival on the South Lawn, where the president belted out "Salt Peanuts!" with Dizzy Gillespie, who invited him to go on the road. Other visiting artists included cellist Mstislav Rostropovich, opera star Leontyne Price, and pianist Vladimir Horowitz — some of the best classical performers in the world. When Horowitz scouted the East Room and didn't like the acoustics, Carter personally dragged carpets out of nearby halls and — "with our butts in the air" — helped the virtuoso spread them near the piano platform to soften the sound. Horowitz would play a few loud notes, and then they would move or add more carpets — a fun engineering experience for a delighted president. James Schlesinger, who served mostly in Republican administrations, felt the entertainment at the Carter White House was the classiest of the era.

But much of the press remained wedded to its premise that the Georgians were hicks. *Newsweek* depicted Carter as a hayseed leading donkeys into Washington and *Time* published a drawing on its cover of Jody Powell and Hamilton Jordan wearing overalls and no shirts and carrying fishing poles. The press "painted us as country farm people who would bring gingham and square dancing," Rosalynn complained.

Of course, the Carters — eclectic in their tastes — did make room for square dancing, as well as the legends of country music. In 1977 Willie Nelson was invited to the White House fresh from a night in jail in the Bahamas on a drug charge. He found himself talking to the president of the United States about pig farming and the disorienting experience of sleeping in the Lincoln Bedroom. Late in the evening, Chip Carter knocked on the door, offered a tour of the White House,

491

and they ended up on the roof smoking a joint. "How the fuck did I get here?" Nelson asked himself. "Through the front door, by invitation from the man who runs the place." Recalling the Carters singing "Amazing Grace" and "Will the Circle Be Unbroken?" with him in the White House (with the president playing the harmonica for other songs), he wrote, "That was the '70s, when there was a beautiful period of peace in the culture wars, when politicians, rednecks, and hippies were sharing the dance floor and maybe even an occasional joint, all in the name of love."

Artists weren't the only ones asked to stay overnight, often on the spur of the moment. George Forbes, president of the Cleveland City Council, was riding with Carter in the presidential limo in Cleveland and mentioned he had been thinking of going to the National League of Cities meeting the next day in Washington but hadn't made arrangements. Carter flew him back on Air Force One and put him up in the White House. When Forbes joked that the toiletries didn't include an Afro pick, the president made sure the White House staff provided him one.

Even as he enjoyed himself, Carter's frugality and contempt for waste shaped his presidency, from his budget cuts (steep for a Democrat) to his penny-pinching in the Residence.

Carter switched off lights, turned down the thermostat, and insisted that the stairwells be unlocked so he could bound up and down the stairs rather than take the elevator. He figured Thomas Jefferson stood in line for lunch on his Inauguration Day, and Harry Truman washed out his own socks — the least he could do was convince the Secret Service to end its practice of opening the door every time he wanted to go to a different room.

Jimmy replaced Nixon's stretch limousine with a smaller black sedan, while Rosalynn refused to spend the full amount of taxpayer funds set aside to redecorate the White House. And she departed from the normal custom of first ladies by declining to commission an official china pattern. (Friends of the Carters eventually bought them a White House china service, but it arrived after they left office.)

Carter hired his young cousin Hugh Carter Jr., known as "Cousin Cheap," to impose new efficiencies. He told Hugh that having 325 television sets and 220 FM radios in White House offices "makes me sick." To the consternation of staff, many were removed, and Hugh scaled back the $85,000 a year spent in subscriptions to newspapers and magazines.

The president eliminated the nighttime illumination of Washington's many monuments until Bert Lance told him that was dumb, and he reversed himself. The same thing happened the first summer when he ordered the White House air-conditioning turned way down. After members of Congress and other guests showed up sweating, he finally relented.

While Carter had reason to dislike what he called "the ostentatious trappings of power," his ostentatious modesty quickly became unpopular. "We de-pomped the White House, but the American people didn't want that," Jerry Rafshoon remembered. The most conspicuous example was when Carter ordered that "Hail to the Chief" not be played when he entered the room. After a year,

Rafshoon, with Rosalynn's blessing, instructed the Marine Band to strike it up anyway, which Carter reluctantly accepted.

But there was no talking him out of selling the USS *Sequoia,* the 104-foot presidential yacht docked on the Potomac. Every president back to Warren Harding enjoyed the Floating White House, as it was called, for relaxation and the occasional wooing of lawmakers. But Carter didn't see the value in it. Kentucky senator Wendell Ford rebuked Frank Moore, the White House chief of congressional liaison: "Goddamn it, Frank, you're stupid. You take me out on the Potomac with some good Kentucky bourbon that I'll supply, you can get what you want out of me." Instead, Carter decided to set aside for members of Congress five seats on Air Force One, ten seats for state dinners, and three boxes at the Kennedy Center. None of this would leave him feeling trapped with a congressman — his idea of hell, Rafshoon said.

Carter took the downsizing of the presidency so seriously that he planned to sell off Camp David, too. Then he and Rosalynn visited the rustic Maryland retreat and fell in love with it. He told the government officials who ran it that he didn't even want to know how much closing it would have saved.

Upon arriving in Washington, Carter was horrified to learn that, like every president, he was required to pay for all food and drink unconnected to official functions. That was the reason he rarely served hard liquor at small dinner parties. Instead, White House stewards usually offered wine, beer, and aperitifs, with vodka, gin, and Scotch reserved for special requests. Pepsi, long the drink of Republican presidents, was replaced with Coke, with its Atlanta connection.*

Carter didn't like the prices of public, taxpayer-funded events, either, especially the elaborate floral arrangements that could reach $50,000 for a state dinner. The White House florist, Ronn Payne, recalled that a member of his staff was briefly detained by police for picking daffodils in Rock Creek Park that he needed for centerpieces.

The president was also a hawk on travel costs. The elimination of staff cars led to yelps from aides who didn't want to drive themselves to work. And when Cousin Cheap decreed that even the most senior government officials could no longer fly first class on international flights, Bob Strauss — the special trade representative — was asked by a reporter if he would continue to do so. "Until there's a better class, son," he said.†

Even in his personal life, Carter continued to be "tight as bark on a tree," as his old friend Dot Padgett put it. As president, Carter was still wearing suits he bought for less than $100 from a friend and former Georgia state senator who specialized in making clothes for J. C. Penney and other department stores. As the reelection campaign approached, Rafshoon arranged for Carter to receive a couple of nice suits from a fancy

---

*Carter was so cheap that he once tried to make Rafshoon pay for a White House dinner he arranged with a small group of columnists and editors.

†Strauss was careful to pledge his loyalty, but he did so in his own inimitable style: "Mr. President, I'm just a two-bit whore," he told Carter in 1978. "With your inflation, I'm a six-bit whore. But I wanted you to know that when I'm bought, I stay bought."

Washington haberdashery. But he and Bob Strauss had to bury the expense as "props" in the campaign film budget because they knew Carter would explode if he saw the bill. After the presidency, Jimmy often purchased clothes from the Dollar General store in Atlanta. When Rosalynn wanted something nicer for him, she clipped the price tags out so he wouldn't know exactly how much it cost.

Like Mr. Earl, Carter was a stickler for earning what you get. Labor Secretary Ray Marshall noticed that at bill signing ceremonies, Carter, unlike other presidents, wouldn't give you a pen if you hadn't had much to do with passing the bill. He refused to praise people when they didn't deserve it or blame them when he needed a scapegoat. "Politics is about credit taking and blame casting, and Carter didn't have much use for either," Marshall concluded. This would hobble him throughout his presidency.

Carter found politics a distasteful subject. When top aides warned that a certain move wasn't good politics, the president would often peer over his glasses and say, "That's your problem." Landon Butler wrote a note to his staff (and himself): "If you want to get turned down on something, tell the president he needs to do it to get reelected." Butler added that this "willingness to be difficult" — to move forward heedless of the political consequences — was important to his policy success.

Carter believed that good government is ultimately good politics. It often is, but he carried that idealism into the realm of wishful thinking. "I have a good ability to rationalize," he confessed in

2015. "My rationalization was that if I do this, and it's right, even though it's unpopular, in the end I'll be reelected anyway, because people will see that I was right and that it was good for the country." This notion that his job was to worry about the correct policy approach — and assume the politics could be handled later — often exasperated Rosalynn. What if there isn't a "later," she would ask, referring to the possibility of his not being reelected. Stu Eizenstat, Carter's domestic policy chief, wrote that from the start, "the central failure" of the administration was "our inability to combine politics with policy in our decision-making."

The president's disregard for politics fed his appetite for risk — and vice versa. Where Bill Clinton was cautious politically and reckless personally, Carter was the reverse: a man of personal rectitude who often swung for the fences on substance or defied major Washington power centers.

When it came to policy, one of his favorite words was *comprehensive.* He peppered Congress with comprehensive initiatives, usually in the form of a written "Message to Congress" that he worked on personally. With one big exception — health care — he always preferred to start with something ambitious, even if he was fairly sure it wasn't going to survive intact.

As in Atlanta, Carter preferred to be briefed on paper. "I can read faster than people can talk," he told an adviser. He plowed his way through his mountainous in-box every day, writing little comments in the upper-righthand corner of staff memos that were not as snippy as when he was governor. One was repeated over and over:

"Be Bold."

This could be energizing. "In his own scary-smart way, he'd ask, 'What is the right thing to do?' " remembered Tim Smith, a personal aide who was often present. Congressman Abner Mikva, whom Carter later appointed to a federal judgeship, could be scathing about Carter. But he felt his flurry of bold activity on the Hill was the best thing about his presidency: "He thought if you were going to get a second term, it should be for the good things you were doing, not the bad things you were avoiding."

Carter didn't think twice about disappointing supporters. Delaware's Joe Biden, Carter's first backer in the Senate, was strongly opposed to court-ordered school busing in Wilmington. He built bipartisan support for a federal bill limiting the ability of courts to order busing. But Carter rebuffed Biden. He had opposed busing in Georgia but, after a close look, decided Biden's bill was unconstitutional. That soured his relationship with Biden, who in September 1977 said of the president he had bet on: "Nixon had his enemies list, and President Carter has his friends list. I guess I'm on his friends list, and I don't know which is worse."

In the White House, he extended to foreign leaders his annoying habit of calling almost any prominent supporter "my friend," once even referring to Marshal Tito, the Communist dictator of Yugoslavia, as one of his "best friends."* But for all of his ritualized invocation of friends, he had

*This was not in the same league as President Trump saying in 2018 that he "fell in love" with North Korean dictator Kim Jong-un.

498

few in Washington — real or contrived. In letters to members of Congress, Carter rarely scrawled a personal inscription at the bottom. White House logs show his calls to members seeking votes on bills usually lasted only one or two minutes and were — by their accounts — all business. "He liked to tell [them] what he wanted and hang up," Mondale remembered. He often forgot that "Pennsylvania Avenue is a two-way street."

One summer afternoon, Frank Moore convinced the president to invite two powerful and affable moderate southern Democratic senators, Lloyd Bentsen of Texas and Ernest Hollings of South Carolina, over to play tennis. As they walked off the court, the president said good-bye and disappeared into the White House, disappointing his guests, who were hoping he would invite them in for a drink. When Moore asked Carter why he hadn't done so, he replied, "You said to play tennis with them, and I did."

Carter later admitted that he alienated too many members of Congress. In his journal, he described one group of disgruntled House members as "a bunch of disorganized juvenile delinquents" out to "blackmail" him. In one case, Pennsylvania Democrats threatened to vote against his entire domestic program unless he replaced a Republican holdover US attorney, David Marston, who was investigating a Democratic member of their delegation. "I told them in a nice way to go to hell," Carter wrote in his journal, though he later replaced Marston when he thought he had become a showboater. He wrecked any relationship with John Brademas, the astute House majority whip, by not even mentioning him when he gave a major speech in his district — and Brademas was sitting right behind him on the stage. When Chris Matthews was working for Tip O'Neill, he heard an old Washington hand say of Carter: "People don't do their best work when they're being pissed on."

For all that, O'Neill's relationship with Carter was never as bad as legend had it. The speaker had groused at first that the White House should offer more at breakfast meetings than coffee, orange juice, and a roll. A chastened Carter began a proper eggs and bacon (and grits) breakfast, and he happily had dinner or shared a beer with O'Neill on a few occasions. O'Neill preferred Ted Kennedy for president in 1980, and he eventually established a chummier relationship with President Reagan (with whom he could share jokes) than he had with Carter, but he nonetheless came to feel "a genuine affection between us."★ He thought Carter was a good listener — so polite and gracious, in fact, that it could be hard to tell where they disagreed. His major flaw, O'Neill wrote, was that "he never really learned how the system worked." While he found Carter "the smartest politician I've ever known," he had no respect for his political skills.

Carter's showy disdain for playing politics could be its own form of vanity — another moral ticket punched. But it was often just cover for not being very good at it. When his aides did have to work the political angles, he preferred deniability. "You do what you gotta do. Don't tell me," Carter instructed Frank Moore, who usually handled the

★O'Neill denied in his memoirs that he was "closer" to Reagan. He called Reagan the "worst" president he served under.

500

horse trading and perks (a new post office, bridge, or vice presidential visit to the district) that often provided the margin of victory on close legislative votes.

As in Georgia, Carter sometimes held grudges — if the offense seemed grievous enough — but he wasn't the kind of politician who kept score all the time with a little black book in his head. Senior aides attributed this quality in part to his tolerating Rosalynn's often blunt comments made in small meetings, which prepared him to accept milder criticism from others. And if the criticism was valid, Carter would at least try to incorporate it into his job performance.

Carter was prideful but psychologically secure — a huge advantage in the cauldron of the presidency. He avoided saber rattling and military interventions and felt toughest when he was defying the Pentagon. In the summer of 1978 he came under intense pressure to sign a defense bill that authorized a hugely expensive nuclear-powered aircraft carrier. He vetoed it, telling Jerry Rafshoon he "would feel less like a man" if he didn't.

The president was famously stubborn. He once confessed to his sister-in-law, Sybil, "I'm more stubborn than two asses." When asked if her husband was stubborn, Rosalynn just laughed.

While he didn't raise his voice, Carter could be cold and caustic with staff. Reviewing a list of candidates for chairman of the National Endowment for the Humanities, he snapped, "If that's the best you can do, I could have done it myself." He often said the same about speech drafts or messages to Congress he didn't like. Aides grew accustomed to classifying his stares. "Those eyes

501

shone like diamonds when he smiled," remembered Bob Beckel, who worked on the congressional liaison staff. "When he didn't smile, they could cut you in half." But he was never belittling. Jay Beck, who worked for him for more than forty years, described his boss as "emphatic but not mean spirited."

Jack Watson recalled growing passionate one day in his advocacy. "Mr. President," he said, "I urge you to —" Carter turned to him sternly and said, "Don't *urge* me." He meant that he expected his advisers to give him the pros and cons but not press their arguments on him. But with longtime advisers, he didn't always demand the formality that came with the presidency. After taking office, Carter told Rafshoon he should continue to call him "Jimmy," but Rafshoon couldn't bring himself to address the president that way — except once. When Carter gave him a hard time for sending his kids to private school, Rafshoon shot back, "Fuck you, Jimmy!" Bob Strauss didn't miss a beat: "It's fuck you, *Mr. President.*" Carter loved it.

Having been elected by a public fed up with artifice, Carter never seemed to appreciate that the presidency is not just a fishbowl but a theater — a stage from which to project an image. FDR considered himself the second-best actor in America (after Orson Welles), and Reagan, who spent three decades in Hollywood before entering politics, said often that he didn't know how anyone could be president who *hadn't* been an actor. Carter lacked those skills. He sometimes exaggerated stories but disliked occasions that required him to play a role.

One day the communications office designed a

stunt to dramatize the Federal Paperwork Reduction Act. With the cameras rolling, the president was supposed to sweep a tall stack of paper off his desk into a wastepaper basket. Instead of following the script, Carter abruptly told the press that the pile was a "prop" prepared by his staff and that it consisted of blank sheets of paper, not real regulations. That sheepish admission — not paperwork reduction — became the story.

His insistence on transparency sometimes produced undignified headlines. In December 1978 he developed a severe case of hemorrhoids that required him to miss a day's work for minor surgery. Carter feared that the markets would crater if his schedule was canceled without explanation, and he characteristically refused the efforts of aides to concoct a cover story. After he told Jody Powell, "We just have to tell the truth" about it, Bob Strauss reported to friends, "He's weird, but I love the little son of a bitch." Sam Donaldson caught up to Rafshoon outside the West Wing the next day and shouted playfully, "Mr. Rafshoon, how's the president's asshole today?" Rafshoon gave him the finger.

Six weeks later, Carter was in Mexico City toasting Mexican president José López Portillo at a state dinner, and he yet again felt compelled to offer too much information. He extemporaneously recalled his 1965 vacation with his family in Mexico and being "afflicted with Montezuma's revenge." In later presidencies, the awkward diarrhea line would have been lampooned and forgotten within a twenty-four-hour news cycle; in 1979 it overshadowed an important state visit and lingered for years.

■ ■ ■ ■

Carter was usually serious, but he showed occasional signs of a mordant sense of humor. When Terry Adamson of the Justice Department submitted a memo with a typo — "The Attorney Genetal made public a letter he wrote on May 5, 1977" — the president scribbled in the margin, "It's genital."

After the London Summit that year, someone gave the president a membership card that Bob Strauss had used at a strip club during the trip. "Strauss was working very hard on the shoe import negotiations, and I'm told the only thing they were wearing that night at the Reinhold club was just that: shoes," he informed the Cabinet.

Frank Moore once told him, "If it wasn't for you, I'd be running a car wash in Dahlonega, Georgia." Carter deadpanned: "Maybe not running it."

Sometimes his attempts at humor backfired. Visiting HUD headquarters, Carter was asked what should be done for the families of federal employees. The president replied in what he thought was a "humorous" or "half-humorous" vein that everyone "living in sin" should get married, that "those of you who have left your spouses" should "go back home," and that absentee parents should learn their children's names. Reporters took his words at face value; they remembered that a few months earlier, Carter had suggested that Greg Schneiders, who was living with his girlfriend in Americus during the campaign, "do the right thing" and get married. In truth, Carter was indulgent about the private

504

behavior of his aides, not to mention federal employees, but the remarks were nonetheless reported as if he were preaching to them.

Carter never suffered from what the writer H. L. Mencken, defining puritans, called "the haunting fear that someone, somewhere may be happy." But he occasionally made his personal moral values known, especially if flouting them broke the law or reflected on him. After July 1978 press reports of pot smoking by anonymous White House staffers, he told senior staff, "You will obey [the law], or you will seek employment elsewhere."

The Ear, a gossip column in the *Washington Star,* fastened on the fact that ACTION director Sam Brown and his girlfriend, Alison Teal, lived together. Carter invited Brown in for a chat. Brown always felt Carter was "a fabulous boss who backed me to the hilt." But he was a bit taken aback after the president asked, "Do you intend to marry her?" Brown said he wasn't sure. Carter replied pleasantly, "It would be a better thing if you were married." Brown concluded that Carter's belief in marriage came from the same deep and sincere moral place that inspired his amnesty for draft-evaders and his human rights policy. He and Alison soon complied.

In Washington, Carter was often criticized for his focus on detail. While he didn't micromanage the way he had in Georgia, his cast of mind was often more that of a technician than a grand strategist. The veteran CBS News commentator Eric Sevareid recalled going to the White House and stopping first to see Hamilton Jordan, who treated him to a brilliant tour of the global horizon and all of the complex forces at play. Then he went to see Carter, who burrowed into the arcane details of a specific bill that Sevareid quickly forgot. Afterward, he told CBS colleagues, "I get it: Jordan's president, and Carter's chief of staff." What Sevareid didn't get was that Carter was always less interested in geopolitical abstractions than practical applications — and if that didn't impress you, he didn't care.

The public admires presidents with a romantic vision, like JFK, Reagan, and Obama. Carter had one that was grand and cramped at once, as suggested by his view of the space program. Like all scientific questions, the mysteries of space intrigued him. Dr. Robert Frosch, the NASA administrator, recalled that he quickly grasped Frosch's technical explanations of black holes. And he was thrilled when NASA in 1977 launched the *Voyager 2* space probe to study the outer planets of the solar system. It included a gold-plated phonograph record featuring music, greetings in fifty-five languages, the sound of a mother's kiss, and a letter drafted in his name — later dubbed the "Letter to E.T." — telling aliens that his missive was "likely to survive a billion years into our future."

That was the Carter of science, humanity, and wonder. But it competed with the green eyeshade, which fit his brow snugly. He rejected Peter Bourne's advice that he set the nation's sights on reaching Mars, and just the week before the *Voyager* letter, Carter reviewed NASA's budget and wrote tartly in his diary: "It's obvious that the space shuttle is just a contrivance to keep NASA alive." He was right; he saw before almost anyone that the shuttle was a boondoggle. But the miserly part of Carter never understood that, whatever the mission or its cost, Americans needed the spirit of adventure symbolized by the manned space program.

And they needed a tidy frame on their politics. It was often said dismissively that Carter's goals of honest, open government at home and peace abroad were too platitudinous to constitute a vision; he certainly wasn't much good at communicating the big picture. But many of his critics operated on the faulty assumption that only a predictable, ideological domestic policy and a foreign policy based on either McGovernite dovishness or Reaganite hawkishness qualified as a vision.

The most penetrating critique came via former chief speechwriter James Fallows, who in 1979 wrote an incisive piece in the *Atlantic* that Carter never forgave. The article's title, "The Passionless Presidency," missed something essential about Carter personally; his genuine passion for peace, human rights, and the environment would distinguish him and — by extension — his presidency. But Fallows pinpointed how the president's lack of ideology inspired little excitement, even on his own staff: "I came to think that Carter believes fifty things, but no one thing." Fallows wrote that Carter was "perhaps as admirable a human being as has ever held the job" and "probably smarter, in the College Board sense," than any other twentieth-century president. But "the group around him slumbers."

Fallows revealed parenthetically that during his first six months in office, Carter personally supervised the use of the White House tennis court. The anecdote struck a nerve and was still retold decades later as symbolic of Carter's approach to the job. Even though it sounded like the Jimmy Carter everyone thought they knew, the story was mostly false. Susan Clough, who later had a falling-out with Carter and thus no motive to cover for him, said that she forged his initials on these and other routine requests and forged his signature on hundreds of photographs to save him time, a fact that Carter later confirmed.*

Whatever his fussiness, the question of Carter's overemphasis on details has been misunderstood. Few recognized at the time why it would prove essential to most of the historic triumphs of his presidency, from the Panama Canal Treaties, to the Camp David Accords, to the landmark Alaska Lands bill. Once released, his inner engineer knew how to govern.

*Clough was not the only aide Carter authorized to sign his name, a disclosure sure to raise questions in the autograph market.

508

# 24
## "Bert, I'm Proud of You"

Jimmy Carter was both made and unmade by the aftermath of the Vietnam War and the Watergate scandal; he would have been neither elected in 1976 nor defeated in 1980 without the fallout from those events. There was a fearful symmetry to it — the moral bar he raised swung back in his face.

The acrimony came early. Shortly after the inauguration, Bob Woodward of the *Washington Post* asked the White House for comment on a hot story he was preparing: King Hussein of Jordan had been secretly on the CIA payroll for twenty years. The White House reluctantly confirmed the story, a welcome — even amazing — change from the routine denials of the truth from prior administrations. Carter immediately canceled the CIA payments but summoned Woodward and the *Post*'s editor, Ben Bradlee, and asked for a favor. He wanted the newspaper to delay the article a few days because Cyrus Vance was in the Mideast, and he feared it would compromise his efforts there.

The *Post* ran the story anyway, while Vance was still abroad. Carter told Bradlee in a cold fury: "I thought things would be different with the press" than they were under Johnson, Nixon, and Ford. "I was wrong." Jody Powell passed along a message from Carter to the *Post* that Woodward felt amounted to: Fuck you. Woodward wrote later that he had "a sickening sense of foreboding, of here-we-go-again with another president," as if Carter — new and a little testy about an important diplomatic mission — was another Nixon.

He wasn't. But Woodward's attitude reflected a consensus in the Washington press corps that Carter should be seen through a cynical lens that went beyond healthy journalistic skepticism to assumptions of bad faith and worse. Tom Wicker, a longtime columnist for the *New York Times,* later concluded that Carter's press coverage was at least as bad as Nixon's.

Before cable news and the Internet, Carter had no TV networks, blogs, or other partisan forces to watch his back. His contentious relationship with the news media did more than hurt his image. Combined with his own mistakes in handling Congress and his delays in the painful case of Bert Lance, it harmed his ambitious domestic agenda and soured his presidency.

It didn't help that the president rejected the tribal customs of the capital. He could have conquered the Washington establishment with ease had he simply socialized on occasion with Katharine Graham, benevolent publisher of the *Washington Post* and one of the most powerful women in the United States, as Ronald and Nancy Reagan did four years later. The bipartisan collection of formidable insiders who supped at Mrs. Graham's R Street mansion could be snobby, but they had plenty to teach Carter about the folkways and booby traps of Washington.

Instead, the new president thought at first that he could ignore the Georgetown crowd with what he described as "relative impunity." But Carter learned eventually that savvy former Cabinet members, powerful lawyers, and influential columnists were more important in Washington than in Atlanta. "I underestimated that," he admitted. Worse for Carter, the Washington establishment knew it had been too subservient for too long to LBJ and Nixon on the Vietnam War and overcompensated on the gossip circuit at Carter's expense.

This post-Watergate mentality extended to Congress, which — like the Washington press corps — had begun in the midseventies to flex its institutional muscles more than at any time since before World War II. Congress and the press found common ground in sniping at Carter. You didn't have to be a great reporter to find a Democratic senator willing to take a shot at a president from his own party.

As president, Carter was less thin-skinned in public than he had been as governor, but his views of the news media hadn't changed. He despised the annual White House Correspondents' Dinner (where he appeared only twice in four years) — even when he got good reviews for his comic timing and brother Billy jokes. After performing at another press banquet where he was expected to be funny, he complained aboard Air Force One, "They don't want a president; they want Bob Hope."

The first crack in the coalition that elected Carter came when Vernon Jordan, president of the National Urban League, argued publicly that the president was neglecting issues of concern to black

511

voters, particularly expanding welfare and full employment legislation — the unfinished business of the Great Society. "It is not enough for Jimmy Carter to be just a little better than his predecessors," Jordan said.* Even as black voters stayed consistently loyal to the president, Jordan's comments gave permission to white liberals to take him on.

They did so with gusto when Carter abandoned a $50-per-person tax rebate (about $260 in 2020 dollars) that he had promised during the campaign but now felt was inflationary and unnecessary. Carter said later that the decision was the hardest economic call of his presidency. He was making a small but fateful decision that fiscal responsibility trumped political goodies.

The awkward retreat on the rebate obscured that the rest of his 1977–78 economic recovery program — including sharp increases in funding for public sector jobs — was progressive. So were his efforts to save Social Security. In 1977, Carter and congressional Democrats closed their eyes, held hands, and sharply raised payroll taxes, which assured the solvency of the system for the next generation. Three-quarters of Republican House members opposed the bill as a massive tax increase. In 1980, Carter signed a bill to make it easier for the disabled to work and collect Social Security benefits at the same time, which Reagan later tried to repeal.

*In 1980 Jordan was shot and seriously wounded by a racist in Fort Wayne, Indiana. Carter, traveling in Ohio, flew there to visit him in the hospital, the first story covered on the first day of Ted Turner's new Cable News Network.

512

Democrats pocketed such achievements instead of crediting them to Carter's account. And when he compromised on other bills, progressive purists cried foul. Carter didn't like the compromises, either. Some combination of diffidence and annoyance at not getting everything he wanted prevented him from trumpeting his victories. Stu Eizenstat, Carter's top domestic adviser, wasn't alone in lamenting "his politically maladroit way of making a useful compromise look like a defeat."

During the campaign, Carter had hedged on the liberal idea of guaranteeing every able-bodied American a government job, which had been turned into expensive legislation sponsored by Senator Hubert Humphrey and Congressman Augustus Hawkins. But as president, he was forced to choose whether to be a Humphrey-Hawkins full-employment "lunch bucket Democrat" or a liberal but fiscally responsible "New Democrat." He chose the latter, as did Bill Clinton and Barack Obama when they reached office.

In that vein, Carter wasn't about to revive the Depression-era CCC or WPA, but he set out to expand and improve the four-year-old Comprehensive Employment and Training Act (CETA) public sector jobs program, which was plagued by allegations of incompetence and waste. It turned out that the administration itself had leaked many of those negative stories to build public support for reform. This boomeranged, and public support for jobs programs for residents of the inner cities plummeted.

Above all, Carter never developed a good relationship with the labor movement. Raised in a right-to-work state, he was hardly a union man.

He and George Meany, the gruff, cigar-chomping president of the AFL-CIO, didn't get along, in part because Carter refused to pay elaborate tribute to labor. In 1978 Rick Hertzberg, a liberal speechwriter, wrote a speech for delivery to the steelworkers that Carter rejected. "This is the kind of speech that Humphrey would give," the president told Jim Fallows, distinguishing his centrism from the traditional liberalism of the recently deceased senator.

Knowing Carter's stripped-down style, Jerry Rafshoon went through a draft and cut every oratorical courtesy shown the labor audience, as well as most of the applause lines. "Should produce a real winner," Jerry Doolittle noted facetiously in his diary.

Even so, Secretary of Labor Ray Marshall remembered his department working closely in the Senate with Ted Kennedy, the darling of unions, to strengthen collective bargaining and protect the prevailing wage on public projects. But in an era when about 20 percent of American workers belonged to unions — twice the proportion in 2019 — expanding labor rights and union membership didn't have much urgency.

It wasn't until a decade later that economists fully understood that the old industrial economy — the engine powering the mighty American middle class — had begun in the late 1970s to become the "Rust Belt" economy: a dying manufacturing base that would leave millions to settle for lower-paying jobs and reduced incomes. Had Carter somehow seen that Japanese success in the auto industry was the harbinger of a huge economic shift, he might have brought more of the foresight he applied to foreign affairs to the economic future of working Americans.

Instead, Carter believed rampant inflation was a more serious and immediate threat to the economy than comparatively mild unemployment, which was dipping below 5 percent in 1977. This view prevailed. By the time a version of Humphrey-Hawkins finally passed in 1978, it was so watered down as to be mostly symbolic.

Meanwhile, labor law reform — legislation to make it easier to join unions and harder to bust them — was defeated when, after six cloture votes, it fell one vote short of the sixty votes needed to break a Republican filibuster in the Senate. That single-vote loss in 1978 was a watershed event in labor-management relations in the United States, though it wasn't widely recognized as such at the time. The ferocious efforts by a coalition of the GOP and American business to defeat the bill paved the way for new and surprisingly effective corporate union-busting efforts, an outcome Carter never envisioned and, after his presidency, condemned. The seeds of twenty-first-century working-class resentment can be traced in part to these decisions in the late 1970s — and much worse ones for labor to come under Reagan and the Bushes.

Bert Lance and Carter didn't talk every day, as they had in the statehouse, but they remained extremely close until Lance's habits as a banker put a crimp in Carter's presidency.

For years before coming to Washington, Lance ran his Calhoun Bank like a piggy bank. He offered below-market loans and overdraft privileges to friends, relatives, and other favorites — practices that were common in rural America as long

515

as the bank was healthy, which his was. But many of these cozy Georgia relationships looked sketchy under the microscope of federal regulation. After the 1976 election, when Lance was nominated to be director of OMB, the Office of the Comptroller of the Currency opened a brief investigation into his banking history. On the Hill, Lance minimized the irregularities, and no one pursued them. Because of their intimate friendship, Carter was conspicuously incurious about his vetting.

Lance perfected a breezy, casual approach to life in the capital. In a March interview with a business magazine, he coined (or at least popularized) the phrase "If it ain't broke, don't fix it." But his old banking life was catching up with him. In May Lance got word that *Time* magazine was preparing an article detailing how he was facing daunting financial problems because of reversals at a second bank he had recently controlled: the Atlanta-based National Bank of Georgia. Lance told Carter that he couldn't keep his promise to the Senate to sell his stock, because doing so would ruin him financially. He offered to resign. "That's foolishness," the president told him, and Carter — who again declined to look closely at the underlying matter — persuaded the Senate to give Lance an extension on his deadline for divesting himself of the bank stock. This proved to be a fateful decision.

Nothing about Lance's time in government — either in Georgia or Washington — came under suspicion. But by late spring, his personal finances had caught the attention of a Washington press corps gunning for a president who, as Mondale recalled, "seemed so inordinately pure that people were waiting for a way to take the luster off."

*New York Times* columnist William Safire led the charge. Safire was a talented writer and clever analyst who had served Nixon as a publicist and speechwriter for twenty-five years before turning to journalism. In column after column, he set out to dilute the seriousness of Nixon's crimes by inflating one-day Washington flaps into "scandals" that he artfully made smell vaguely of Watergate (often by attaching a "gate" suffix). Unlike many columnists who ranged widely over topics, Safire was like a dog with a bone when he ripped into a story that might damage Democrats.

On the Lance scent, Safire charged the OMB director with receiving a "sweetheart loan" of $3.4 million from the First National Bank of Chicago "on terms so favorable that the main collateral could only be Lance's closeness to the president." The charge didn't bear scrutiny; nor did innuendo that the Securities and Exchange Commission was in the tank for Lance; nor did the suggestion that during the transition, Carter's lack of interest in Lance's dubious banking practices constituted obstruction of justice. Safire's entertaining columns, with headlines like "Broken Lance," "Boiling the Lance," and "The Lance Cover-Up," nonetheless kept the story on the front burner for months and would bring him a Pulitzer Prize.

Media pressure spooked the administration. Treasury Secretary Blumenthal privately believed that "Lance was a corner cutter, not a criminal," but he authorized the comptroller of the currency, John Heimann, to reopen the investigation into his financial history. On August 18 Heimann released a 394-page report that at first glance seemed to exonerate Lance.

It didn't. Robert Lipshutz, the White House

517

counsel, read the exculpatory executive summary that said Lance hadn't broken the law, but he failed to absorb the damning appendix detailing sweet deals offered to friends and family at the Calhoun bank, along with other questionable practices. Lipshutz sent a bland cover letter to Carter at Camp David that led the president to believe there was no problem. Bob Strauss later joked that Carter "hired the only dumb Jewish lawyer in Atlanta." This was a bit unfair to Lipshutz because Carter, who was normally extremely thorough in his preparation, apparently didn't read the appendix, either.

Using the executive summary as his fig leaf, Carter choppered back from Camp David, summoned Lance to his side, and told the press: "My faith in the character and competence of Bert Lance has been reconfirmed." Then, in a line that would haunt him, he smiled broadly, turned to Lance, and said, "Bert, I'm proud of you."

Seven months after setting arguably the highest ethical standard ever established by an American president, Carter managed to come off as clueless and hypocritical at once. Here was a president who that very month had privately returned Muhammad Ali's "Rope-a-Dope" jump rope (valued at a few dollars at most) to the boxer because "Rosalynn and I have set a policy of not accepting personal gifts." And now he was making excuses for a corner-cutting crony.

Jim Schlesinger went to Hamilton Jordan and told him Lance was "dead" politically. But Carter and Lance dug in and privately spread blame on the press, the Washington establishment, and anyone inside the White House who was insufficiently supportive. Stu Eizenstat wasn't alone in later regretting that he didn't brave Carter's ire and recommend cutting Lance loose.★

The only White House aide willing to speak out publicly about Lance was Carter's highest-ranking woman staffer, Midge Costanza, a feminist from Rochester, New York, who handled relations with outside groups as the head of the White House Office of Public Liaison. Costanza, who described herself as "a loud-mouthed, pushy little broad" (and, at the time, was a closeted lesbian), had the guts to say in a television interview that Lance should go. After that, she was frozen out and eventually fired for not being a team player. The contrast between Costanza's treatment and Lance's could not have been starker.

Over Hamilton Jordan's strenuous objections, Lance decided to face his accusers in the Senate. He testified for twenty hours over two days and asked the committee, "Is it part of our American system that a man can be drummed out of government by a series of false charges, half-truths, and misrepresentations, innuendos, and the like?" The testimony went over well, and even some columnists thought the scandal was overblown. But Senator Tom Eagleton spoke for his colleagues when he said the press had mixed rumor and fact to create "guilt by accumulation." Robert Byrd privately advised Lance that more hearings lay ahead, and he should resign. Jordan and Lance's

★The Carter team learned its lesson. A year later, when another longtime loyalist, Dr. Peter Bourne, got in trouble for improperly prescribing Quaaludes to a staffer, he was cut loose in forty-eight hours. But Carter treated Bourne well personally, helping him get a senior position at the United Nations.

own lawyers soon concluded the same.

Carter described September 21, 1977, in his diary as "probably one of the worst days I've ever spent." After tennis the day before, Bert had agreed to resign. But Lance's wife, LaBelle, was still adamantly opposed. Carter invited them back to the White House, where the three old friends from Georgia, heavy with the emotion of the moment, prayed quietly in the study. Jimmy told LaBelle that he could not deal with any of the other important issues facing the country until this was resolved. "I could see that LaBelle was creating a very serious problem for Bert, and, of course, he was trying to accommodate her, as I would Rosalynn," Carter wrote in his diary.

LaBelle had more to say that day to Jimmy. Back home in Georgetown, with an exhausted Bert flopped across their bed, she dialed the White House. As Carter was set to go to a long-scheduled three o'clock news conference, he was told he had an urgent call. LaBelle shouted into the phone that the president had "betrayed" and "destroyed" her husband: "I want to tell you one thing: you can go with the rest of the jackals, and I hope you'll be happy." Then she marched outside and told a throng of reporters that Bert was innocent, and she was "proud to be a servant of God."

As he crossed the driveway to the Old Executive Office Building for the press conference, Carter had his own predatory animals in mind. When reporters yelled from afar, "Are you going to accept his resignation?" the president turned to Jim Schlesinger and said quietly: "Vultures."

But Carter assumed much of the blame for the fiasco, telling reporters he had been the one who had forced Lance to promise to sell his bank stock during the transition so that he could join the administration — a promise Lance couldn't keep — and thus bore responsibility for kicking the whole thing off. "Had he stayed [in Georgia] in a selfish fashion and enriched himself and his own family financially, I'm sure he would have been spared any allegations of impropriety," Carter said. "But he wanted to come to Washington and serve his government."

Afterward, Chief Justice Warren Burger called the president to say, as Carter recorded it, that the Lance case had revealed "the extreme dangers from the press in subverting justice." Henry Kissinger soon phoned to say the same thing. This would be Carter's own takeaway from the episode, but in the meantime, the rift with the Lances wounded him. While Jimmy never seemed to have a best friend, Bert had come as close as any.

The Lance Affair marked a turning point for Carter. Through three months of brutal headlines, he displayed a dithering management style and poor political instincts, and jeopardized his image as a president of impeccable ethical standards. While his approval ratings remained strong, the core of his appeal was eroding. The impression of him as an inept outsider surrounded by Georgia hayseeds solidified in the increasingly hostile press.

Worse, the president lost a trusted adviser who loved the political game and bonded with the business community — a peer who could tell him hard truths. The episode seemed to throw him off balance. According to Jim Schlesinger, who saw him more than any other member of the Cabinet in 1977, Carter began to doubt that he was "this man of destiny" he had imagined himself to be.

The consequences were written across his no-longer-smiling face. "He'd lost his self-confidence," Schlesinger concluded. "You could see it in his public performance." That confidence would return episodically and help power historic achievements. But the mojo of 1976 — already depleted by a closer-than-expected election — was gone now. Everything after Lance would be a slog.

Three weeks after Lance resigned, William Safire conceded in the *New York Times* that "Lancegate is no Watergate." But the allegations he helped spread took on a life of their own. Before long, Lance would face eight federal investigations into his banking practices. In 1980 he went on trial in federal court in Georgia, where jurors learned that members of LaBelle's family had taken advantage of Bert's generosity and used their family bank to feather their own nests. But the evidence of Lance's criminality was weak, and he was acquitted on all charges. The Carters and the Lances eventually repaired their friendship, and Bert went on to chair Walter Mondale's 1984 presidential campaign and become a top adviser to Jesse Jackson in his 1988 bid for the White House. Those who knew him and his forgiving nature were unsurprised to learn that he even became friendly with Safire.

Lance's departure might have doomed Carter's reelection. In his memoirs, Lance recounts that Safire cheerily volunteered to him over lunch in the 1980s that the GOP needed to enmesh him in scandal to prevent him from becoming chairman of the Federal Reserve after the term of Arthur Burns expired in 1978. Republicans, Lance wrote, remembered how Burns, a Republican, had goosed the economy to help Nixon win a landslide reelection in 1972. They feared that Lance, as Fed chair, would make sure that interest rates stayed low to help ensure his friend Carter's reelection in 1980. They were probably right.

In November 1977 *New York* magazine described a "siege mentality" inside the White House. Carter's popularity remained near 60 percent, but the Lance affair brought tougher coverage, especially from the *Washington Post.*

The mid-1970s marked the apex of establishment media power in the capital. At the *Post,* Sally Quinn was riding high, writing deliciously catty profiles for the popular Style section. In December, she described a scene where Hamilton Jordan met the wife of the Egyptian ambassador at a party. Jordan, she wrote, "gazed at her ample front, pulled at her elasticized bodice and was prompted to say, loudly enough for Sam Donaldson and others to hear, 'I've always wanted to see the pyramids.' " The story, reported around the world, threw Jordan into the spotlight.

Two months later, after Jordan and his wife, Nancy, separated, the *Washington Post Magazine* ran what Jody Powell described later as "the trashiest piece of journalism I have ever seen." The story said that after being rebuffed by a woman in a Washington singles bar, Jordan spit his iced drink down the front of her dress. Powell was so angry about the so-called "amaretto and cream" story that he sent the press a thirty-three-page rebuttal that raised legitimate questions about the truth of the story but was much too defensive. "I had underreacted to the pyramids story," Powell wrote later. "I was determined not to make the same mistake again. I did not. I made exactly the opposite mistake, with even more disastrous consequences."

Amaretto and cream was more fun for the press to cover than anything to do with policy, and the story lingered for weeks. "Hamilton had come to be viewed as a politically astute ne'er-do-well," Powell concluded. Two years later, it would make him a sitting duck for Roy Cohn, the scheming New York lawyer, who urged the co-owners of Studio 54, a trendy New York nightclub, to make unsubstantiated claims of cocaine use by Jordan in an unsuccessful attempt at a plea bargain.

As Jordan was distracted by press attacks and handicapped by his own disorderly work habits, the White House he was ostensibly running began to lose focus. Carter's personal discipline was not matched by a disciplined work flow or message. Jordan thought the problem started at the top. In December he wrote Carter a memo arguing that he had spent far too much time on foreign policy in his first year and would suffer serious political consequences if he didn't shift his focus to domestic issues. Carter called the memo "superb" but changed little. And dissatisfaction inside the White House didn't move him. Like Admiral Rickover, he believed officers should feel privileged to be there and were responsible for their own morale.

After leaving office, Carter acknowledged that the consensus view — even on his own staff — was that "we tried to do too much too fast." By not prioritizing, staffers argued in retrospect, the Carter White House had "overloaded the circuits" on Capitol Hill.

Carter himself didn't agree. He felt everyone focused too much on their setbacks. Bob Strauss put it this way: when the team achieved 85 percent of what it wanted, "the public impression was that we had lost fifteen percent."

Frank Moore recalled hard-won victories on foreign policy, the budget, the environment, and civil service reform, as well as deregulation of the airline and trucking industries, and more. "We had thirty pieces [of major legislation] up there, and we passed twenty-six of them," he said. "But the big four didn't pass, so we were 'failures.' " Moore said powerful committee chairmen were also at fault. In the 1970s they — not the White House — determined the sequencing of hearings and votes. By this argument, Carter wasn't entirely to blame for the failure of early bills, which were usually caught up in legislative machinations beyond his control. But he and his staff didn't do themselves any favors, either, alienating Tip O'Neill with their handling of his Boston College buddy, Bob Griffin, who complained of shabby treatment in his job at the General Services Administration.

O'Neill angrily told the president that Moore was now barred from his office permanently and that he had instructed his staff not to talk to him again. Carter would prove to be an ace diplomat in foreign affairs, but this was exactly the kind of situation where his subpar people skills — especially where emotions, not policy, were involved — hurt him. The ban was lifted only when Tip's wife, Millie, intervened.

It was not entirely a coincidence that in the first half of his term, Carter suffered three domestic defeats: on tax reform, welfare reform, and consumer protection. (The fourth, on health care, took place in 1979.)

During the campaign, Carter had famously called the tax system "a disgrace to the human race." Some of his disdain was personal. In Plains, he had eaten at home or at his warehouse. Why, he asked audiences, should big-city businessmen and lawyers get to deduct the cost of their lunches and other entertainment expenses but not the folks who carried a brown bag to work? Why should the average taxpayer subsidize the privileged few? It was a fair populist point — the kind of argument Democratic elites ignored — and he drove it home by ridiculing "the three-martini lunch."

But as he sought to streamline and simplify the system, Carter ran up against what he called "a pack of powerful and ravenous wolves" on the Hill. He didn't fully understand just how hard it would be to beat lobbyists and eliminate the scores of deductions and loopholes that had infested the tax code. Instead of focusing on a savvy strategy to squeeze tax reform through Congress, Carter rose before dawn to study the arcane tax provisions sent to him by Stu Eizenstat, Carter's domestic policy chief. It was the same problem he had had in Georgia: a stubborn wonkiness that placed arriving at the "right" policy solution over the grubby horse trading that might actually produce something.

The high-handed president ignored Senator Russell Long, chairman of the Senate Finance Committee, and Congressman Al Ullman, chairman of the House Ways and Means Committee, the two top tax-writing committees. This was

526

political malpractice. "My advice hadn't been sought. My input's not in it," Long told Eizenstat. "So I figured I could pretty well do whatever I blessed well pleased about it." By the time Carter sought Long's counsel, it was too late. In the end, Congress gutted the president's efforts to close loopholes. After much grumbling, he reluctantly signed the legislation, so as not to hand the Republicans a last-minute issue for the 1978 midterm elections.

Carter didn't know it, but by agreeing to cut the capital gains tax rate from 49 percent to 28 percent, he simultaneously contributed to capital formation and exacerbated income inequality. Economic growth over the next forty years was unevenly distributed, but that was better than no growth at all, which was close to the reality of the 1970s — one of the only decades in history where Americans, on average, ended up with less money (in constant dollars) than when they started.

The tax revolt that would eventually transform American politics began in the Carter years. In June 1978, California voters approved Proposition 13, which slashed property taxes by 57 percent. That ballot initiative ended up wreaking havoc on public services, including the state's fine public school system, where student performance soon plummeted. But Prop 13 offered Republicans across the country a blueprint for how to use tax cuts to achieve political power. What started as Carter's populist promise in 1976 to close loopholes and make "fat cats" pay their fair share became the first of many tax cuts championed by a Republican Party that had found its defining issue for the next generation.

■ ■ ■

Another big 1976 promise was welfare reform, which meant improving federal aid to single mothers and other income support programs that dated back to the New Deal. Carter argued persuasively that the congressional gatekeepers (once again, Russell Long in the Senate and Al Ullman in the House) were "much more conservative" than the administration liberals and that this reality — not anything he did or didn't do — doomed welfare reform. This time, he met with Long and Ullman but considered it "a complete waste of time," though at least Long was "entertaining."

Even as it failed, Carter's early welfare reform bill planted important seeds. For years, Republicans stressed "workfare" — requiring low-income people to work in exchange for welfare or food stamps — while Democrats believed that connecting welfare to work was demeaning. Carter's "work incentives" offered an innovative middle position; a way of using tax credits to "make work pay."

This "third way" proved to be a transformative idea in American social policy. Under Reagan, the landmark 1986 tax bill included a modest earned-income tax credit — a small check from the federal government for the working poor. Clinton and Obama expanded the EITC so dramatically that it boosted the incomes of disadvantaged working families by thousands of dollars a year, giving them a toehold to reach the middle class. This residue of Carter's failed welfare plan — the EITC — is still little known (in part because of its cumbersome name), but it eventually became the most durable and effective antipoverty program since Social Security in 1935.

Carter was less a New Deal Democrat than a Theodore Roosevelt progressive reformer, more concerned about good government and the environment than restructuring capitalism. Like TR, he was a first-rate president when it came to looking after the health and safety of the American public. He hired brilliant and committed progressive experts to run the Environmental Protection Agency, the Federal Trade Commission, the Food and Drug Administration, the National Highway Traffic Safety Administration, the Consumer Product Safety Commission, the National Telecommunications and Information Administration, and more.

Two women sub-Cabinet officials were especially effective. Eula Bingham, a tough Kentucky toxicologist who became Carter's director of the Occupational Safety and Health Administration (OSHA), killed more than 1,000 "nitpicking" regulations on things like toilet seats but saved countless lives with vigorous new regulation of cotton dust, benzene, and lead. When the president's economic advisers argued strenuously that the regulations would hurt business, Carter walked over to Bingham with a smile, put his arm around her, and said, "I'm with Eula on this one." As assistant of agriculture for food and consumer services, Carol Tucker-Foreman implemented the first Dietary Guidelines for Americans (issued since 1980 at five-year intervals) and she helped advance the 1977 Food Stamp Act (enacted through the bipartisan efforts of Senators George McGovern and Bob Dole), which streamlined and expanded the much-maligned food stamp program to the point where it significantly dented hunger in America.

On top of all that, Carter had promised during his campaign to launch a new Consumer Protection Agency devoted to fielding complaints and advocating (often suing) on behalf of ordinary people.. This proposal wasn't as sweeping as tax and welfare reform, but it was central to Carter's political identity as a reformer. In the early 1970s, when liberalism was at its peak, some version of the bill had passed at least one house of Congress five times but was stymied by intransigent Republicans and squabbling Democrats. Now the opposition intensified. Even though the proposed agency was tiny and would have no direct regulatory authority, the idea of a consumer advocate in all federal administrative proceedings angered Republicans. They complained about "Big Government" and launched a campaign against Ralph Nader through the Business Roundtable, an industry group for the Fortune 500. Tip O'Neill said the lobbying over Carter's consumer bill was the most ferocious he had seen in his quarter century in Congress.

By 1977, the tide was turning against the consumer movement and American liberalism in general. Esther Peterson, the revered seventy-one-year-old consumer advocate who had run the Office of Consumer Affairs for Kennedy, Johnson, and now Carter inside the White House, thought that Carter was the greatest consumer champion of the three. But his administration had so many first-rate consumer advocates in its ranks that it became a victim of its own success.

The *Washington Post* editorial page flipped into

opposition, making the strange argument that the Carter administration had appointed enough pro-consumer officials to make the institutionalization of consumer advocacy unnecessary. This was a shortsighted position considering what happened after Reagan was elected in 1980: foxes not just guarding but running all the regulatory chicken coops.

Nader and Peterson were enraged to learn that Frank Moore asked O'Neill to pull the bill from the floor at the end of the 1977 session so as not to alienate the business community, whose support was needed on other legislation. Over the holiday, momentum moved against the bill, as influential Democratic House members Tom Foley, Pat Schroeder, and Leon Panetta (himself an old Nader's Raider) bought the *Washington Post*'s logic and peeled off.

On February 8, 1978, the consumer bill failed in the House, 227 to 189. The vote marked the beginning of a long shift toward increased corporate power in Washington and the country.

Carter did better on unsexy civil service reform and ethics. As in Georgia, he had initially sought to reengineer the entire federal government, promising a sweeping reorganization that would reduce the number of federal agencies from 1,900 to 200. This was a pipe dream. Carter never cared about reorganization in Washington as much as he had in Georgia.

But he cared intensely about good, honest government, and his legislative successes in this area, while generating little publicity at the time, would reverberate in the twenty-first century. The enactment of the 1978 Civil Service Reform Act

— the first substantial reform of the federal workforce since the founding of the civil service nearly a hundred years earlier — was a long struggle that Senate Majority Leader Byrd called the most "tremendous legislative achievement" of his then twenty-seven years in Washington. Carter mobilized his entire Cabinet to lobby for the package and pushed it through with the help of Senate Republicans. The bill overhauled the management of the federal government, making it easier to fire incompetent federal employees but also establishing a 9,200-member Senior Executive Service that protected critical institutional memory and legally shielded experienced career officials (the core of any agency) from political retribution. The Federal Paperwork Reduction Act shortened (though hardly eliminated) the stack of pointless memos on every bureaucrat's desk, and a later bill curbed the seemingly endless forms required for businesses and citizens.

Most significantly, Carter responded to Nixon's corruption of the White House, the FBI, the CIA, the IRS, and other agencies with important ethics reform. He proposed and signed into law the 1978 Ethics in Government Act and the 1978 Inspector General Act, which brought new ethical standards, new transparency requirements, the first whistleblower protections, the first authorized special prosecutors, and — critically — the first formal offices of inspectors general (starting in twelve agencies). The purpose, in Carter's words, was to "root out corruption, fraud, waste, mismanagement in the most effective and enthusiastic fashion."*

*Carter also believed in business ethics, and he signed

532

Carter campaigned after Watergate on ethics and openness, and now he had won significant structural changes that offered new checks and balances in the American constitutional system. The Justice Department set a strong example by winning convictions of senior FBI officials who authorized illegal break-ins against antiwar protesters. (The kinds of warrantless law enforcement abuses Carter had decried in the 1974 Law Day speech Hunter Thompson liked so much). Over the next forty years, what Carter called these "new tools" for accountability grew to seventy-three IGs and fourteen thousand auditors whose work saved taxpayers tens of billions of dollars and led to hundreds of successful prosecutions. Without a process for whistle-blowers and an inspector general, President Trump's infamous phone call with the Ukrainian president would never have come to light in 2019, and he would not have been impeached.* At the same time, Carter's claim at the bill signing that the IGs would

---

the 1977 Foreign Corrupt Practices Act, which prohibits US corporate bribery abroad. As president, Trump complained, "It's just so unfair that American companies aren't allowed to pay bribes to get business overseas."

*The most controversial part of the Ethics in Government Act was the establishment of an Office of Independent Counsel (OIC) — essentially a permanent structure to investigate the executive branch. The independent counsel statute was amended in 1983 and allowed to expire in 1999. Every president in this period, including Carter, resented it.

be protected from political interference (under the 1939 Hatch Act) proved illusory. Upon taking office, Reagan fired all of Carter's inspector generals, while Trump fired any who dared uncover anything unflattering about him.

Even with big bipartisan and farsighted victories on government reform, Carter was learning there were limits to what a president could do in domestic affairs. He would increasingly cast his gaze overseas.

*Sealing peace between Egypt and Israel.*

■ ■ ■ ■

# PART FIVE:
# PEACEMAKER

■ ■ ■ ■

# 25
## HUMAN RIGHTS

After leaving office, Carter often argued that the 1948 Universal Declaration of Human Rights — written by Canadian and French diplomats at the United Nations and popularized by Eleanor Roosevelt — was akin to the Declaration of Independence and US Constitution in its importance. He believed that the values in it were descended from the Sermon on the Mount in the Gospel of Matthew, where Jesus teaches people how they should treat one another.

When the Universal Declaration was issued, Carter was already a well-informed navy lieutenant who supported the United Nations and Harry Truman's 1948 decision to desegregate the armed forces. Truman, he remembered, "was the one who broke the ice" on race relations. But in 1953 Carter returned to Plains and, for the next eighteen years, mostly hid his true feelings about racial discrimination. Now, as president, he would try to make up for lost time, seeking redemption abroad for his years ducking the civil rights movement at home.

A powerful element of the American foreign policy establishment had long claimed that letting Wilsonian idealism interfere with a tough-minded realpolitik approach to foreign relations was soft and naive. They argued that the "national interest" required being critical of Communists who abused human rights but indulgent toward authoritarians who did the same. Carter understood that this double standard drained American foreign policy of its moral authority. Strong, secure presidents representing strong, secure superpowers take on bullies, even if they are allies; weak, insecure presidents from countries in retreat give them a pass in order to pursue poorly defined interests. Carter was strong and secure in his role, even if he didn't always look that way.

The inner strength came from religious and moral conviction. Carter felt that God had created the United States in part "to set an example for the rest of the world" and that America was the "first nation to dedicate itself clearly to basic moral and philosophical principles." In that sense, his new policy was an organic outgrowth of the country's founding ideals and of his own eagerness to consecrate them.

The beauty of the reintroduction of the phrase *human rights* into the foreign policy debate was that it transformed the concept from a Cold War weapon (the United States highlighted repression in Eastern Europe; the USSR highlighted the Jim Crow South) into what Carter called "a beacon of light for all mankind." It injected a growing international movement with energy and purpose, globalized the American civil rights struggle, and set a new moral benchmark for governments and civil society to use in assessing the performance of leaders.*

*The phrase *human rights* was used only sporadically

Carter was a mediocre communicator who often flubbed his applause lines; the columnist Murray Kempton described his television self as "frozen indifference." But there was nothing indifferent in his dogged efforts to put "human rights" into the international vocabulary. The phrase stuck in part because it grew out of the American president's personal history in the South and his authentic religious convictions. Among simple ways of framing public policy, only Franklin Roosevelt's New Deal and Lyndon Johnson's Great Society entered the language with the same permanence, and their policies were limited to the United States.

By the time Carter took office, the human rights debate was already edging into the national spotlight. Liberal Democratic congressmen Don Fraserand Tom Harkin were pushing legislation to stop foreign aid to allies with poor human rights records. And the 1975 Helsinki Accords — the product of detente between the West and the Soviet empire — included provisions (honored mostly in the breach) for human rights in the Soviet Union.

Carter saw a historic opening. He had gingerly raised human rights from time to time on the campaign trail. It was a political winner, uniting liberals critical of Henry Kissinger's support for dictators, ethnic voters upset with Soviet control of nations behind the Iron Curtain, Christians

---

until 1975, when the Helsinki Accords were signed and Carter started running for president. In the two decades that followed, the phrase appeared ten times more often annually in the *New York Times* than it had before.

worried about religious persecution, and Jews concerned about dissidents unable to leave the USSR.

Carter announced his intentions more emphatically in his inaugural address with the line that "our commitment to human rights must be absolute," although most sophisticated listeners knew that the world was much too messy for that. The president's new policy would be selective and inconsistent from the start, especially as applied to strategically important allies. Vital interests would take priority over moral ones, most fatefully in the case of Iran.

But for all the built-in hypocrisy, the message was unmistakable: for the first time, an American president would go beyond promoting American ideals to offering specific critiques of specific countries with specific penalties attached. Carter would aim to condition military and economic aid — and even World Bank and International Monetary Fund loans — on the progress nations made toward ending extralegal killings, detention without trial, censorship, and other abuses. And he would keep the pressure on both Communist and non-Communist regimes.

The first test of Carter's human rights policy came within twenty-four hours. On the day after the inauguration, January 21, 1977, Andrei Sakharov, an esteemed Russian physicist who had won the Nobel Peace Prize two years earlier for his work as a human rights activist, wrote to Carter. Sakharov named political prisoners in the Soviet Union and asked the new president to make good on his promises to improve human rights.

Two weeks later, Carter informed Soviet ambassador Anatoly Dobrynin in a private meeting that he would hold the Soviets to the commitments to human rights made in the Helsinki Accords and that he intended to speak out about Sakharov, whose Moscow apartment had recently been ransacked.* Breaking protocol, he sent Sakharov a forthright letter ("Human rights is the central concern of my administration," the president wrote) that the dissident held aloft for photographers in Moscow so that they could see Carter's signature at the bottom. This enraged the Kremlin but had profound consequences. As Robert Gates, who served as secretary of defense and in other high-level positions of both Republican and Democratic administrations, wrote later, "Whether isolated and little-known Soviet dissident or a world-famous Soviet scientist, Carter's policy encouraged them to press on."

In his letter to Sakharov, Carter exaggerated in calling human rights *the* central concern of his administration; it competed with other priorities. He was already laying the groundwork for a new arms control deal — a major goal of his presidency — and didn't want to antagonize Soviet premier Leonid Brezhnev any more than necessary. He wrote Brezhnev a conciliatory personal letter that included the sentimental line, "As a child, I developed a literary taste by reading your classics."

Brezhnev was having none of it. In a scathing

***

*This was a break from the approach of President Ford, who in 1975 was scheduled to meet with famed novelist Aleksandr Solzhenitsyn, a former Soviet political prisoner, but canceled at the last minute out of fear of jeopardizing detente.

reply, he informed Carter that he would not allow "interference in our internal affairs, whatever pseudo-humanitarian slogans are used to present it." Carter responded covertly by approving expanded CIA support for opposition groups in the Eastern bloc and ordering the region flooded with journals and other printed material favoring dissidents.

Several weeks later, the young Jewish dissident who had helped Sakharov translate Carter's letter, Anatoly (later Natan) Sharansky, was arrested in Moscow on trumped-up charges of treason. Carter protested to Dobrynin and, that fall, to Soviet foreign minister Andrey Gromyko, both of whom responded with stony indifference. Gromyko told Carter during the opening of the UN General Assembly that Sharansky was a "microscopic dot of no importance to anyone."

When Sharansky went on trial in Moscow, Carter — again breaking protocol — called the charges that he was an American spy "patently false" and canceled the sale of certain computers and drilling equipment to the Soviet Union. The case generated huge publicity, with cover stories on Sharansky in *Time* and *Newsweek* that linked Carter's support for him and for the emigration of Soviet Jews (which went up nearly fourfold on his watch) to the seeming collapse of detente with the Soviet Union. In every meeting with a Soviet official for the rest of his time in office, Carter brought up Sharansky.*

*After Soviet premier Mikhail Gorbachev freed Sharansky in 1986, he emigrated to Israel, where he became a conservative politician. While acknowledging that he owed Carter "a debt of gratitude" for speaking out on

On every visit to a closed society, Carter carried the bully pulpit with him, inspiring local populations by giving a speech or holding a live televised news conference that could not be censored, an important tradition followed by his successors.

He worked in private, too. In Warsaw in 1977 he made an unscheduled and highly symbolic visit to the head of Poland's Catholic Church, Cardinal Stefan Wyszynski, and advised Edward Gierek, the first secretary of the Polish Communist Party, to speak more often with the cardinal. "It's never too late" to become a believer, he told Gierek, skillfully exploiting the tension between Gierek's ancestral Catholicism and the atheism of Communist doctrine.

The intersection of faith and human rights provided Carter with some of his most gratifying moments in office. In 1979 Carter and Brezhnev completed what Carter described as a "highly emotional" prisoner swap, trading two Soviet spies being held in the United States for four dissidents in the USSR, including three Jewish refuseniks and Georgi Vins, a Russian Baptist pastor jailed in 1974 for conducting an underground ministry in the Soviet Union. A mere four days after he was transported from prison in a Siberian cattle car, Vins joined the president in Plains for church.

"Up early to prepare my Sunday school lesson, from 1 Kings 21 — about Ahab, Jezebel, and

---

his behalf and for "upgrad[ing] the struggle of dissidents around the world," he argued that Carter "was almost never willing to back his rhetoric on human rights with decisive action." Sharansky didn't specify what that action should have been.

Naboth," Carter wrote in his diary. "Since Georgi Vins is with me, the parallel between this lesson and his persecution in the Soviet Union was remarkable." Vins, sitting next to Rosalynn in the pew, pulled off his shoe, lifted the inner sole, and showed her a small, wrinkled photograph of Jimmy Carter he had kept in prison.

Even as Carter championed dissidents, he was envisioning a post–Cold War world of less hostility toward both the Soviet Union and China. This meant pressing hard but not too hard on human rights. In May 1977, four months into his presidency, he laid out his new foreign policy in a commencement address at the University of Notre Dame. Balancing freedom with better relations with closed societies was only one of the circles he needed to square.

The Notre Dame speech marked a long-overdue course correction for the United States. On one level, Carter defined the pillars of his new foreign policy as stressing human rights, cooperation between democracies, arms control with the Soviet Union, Mideast peace, and nonproliferation. But his bigger point was that the traditional tension between idealism and realism — morality versus power — was a false choice. With the recent resurgence of democracy in India, Spain, Portugal, and Greece, the president was emboldened to strike a theme of confidence that the American system was both morally and economically superior to Communism.

But instead of being triumphal, he used that confidence to champion a different way of thinking about the country's longtime adversaries.* In a soon-to-be-famous line written by speechwriter Jerry Doolittle (and endorsed by Brzezinski, though he didn't see the draft until it was coming off the copier and too late to change), Carter declared the nation "now free of that inordinate fear of Communism" that "led us to embrace any dictator who joined us in that fear."

Carter was venturing where no postwar American president had dared go before: "For too many years, we've been willing to adopt the flawed and erroneous principles and tactics of our adversaries, sometimes abandoning our own values for theirs," he said, citing the decision to fight in Vietnam. "We've fought fire with fire, never thinking that fire is better quenched with water." Freedom would be that potent dousing force. Authoritarians could no longer justify their repression by claiming that they were just fighting Communism.

In a bracing speech that spring, Carter told the United Nations that nations would have to relinquish certain traditional ideas of sovereignty: "No member of the UN can claim the mistreatment of its citizens is solely its own business." His

*A week before the speech, Carter acted on his new approach to Communist regimes by issuing a secret presidential directive that read: "I have concluded that we should attempt to achieve normalization of our relations with Cuba. To this end, we should begin direct and confidential talks in a measured and careful fashion with representatives of the Government of Cuba." For two years, genuine progress was made toward normalization, before it abruptly ended in 1979 when the Cold War revived.

larger argument to the global community was that freedom could actually enhance security by winning governments the sincere support of their people. Under this powerful new worldview, human rights were not just compatible with national interests, they advanced them.

Inside the Us government, Carter institutionalized the concept of human rights by founding a new State Department Bureau of Human Rights and Humanitarian Affairs, which issued "country reports" tracking the behavior of abusive governments. These influential reports helped drive policy decisions.

To run the bureau, Carter and Vance established a new position, assistant secretary for human rights, and gave the job to Patricia "Patt" Derian, an activist of unusual vision and determination who had moved to Mississippi in 1959 to work for civil rights. Vance empowered Derian (even putting her just down the hall from him on the seventh floor), but she clashed with the department's other assistant secretaries, who paid lip service to human rights but gave priority to shopworn strategic objectives and arms sales abroad. They didn't appreciate an outspoken and refreshingly undiplomatic woman mucking around in their pinstriped world.

Derian was so single-minded in her devotion to human rights that US ambassadors winced when they learned she was traveling to their region. Upon arrival in a dictatorship, she never unpacked because she wasn't sure how quickly the regime might force her to leave. Lawrence Eagleburger, a future secretary of state in the Reagan administration, serving as ambassador to Yugoslavia, made a point of leaving Belgrade every time Derian came to town to tongue-lash Josip Tito's Communist government, but he later admitted he was wrong in his assessment of Derian and the policy. "I never thought I'd concede this," Eagleburger said. "A lot of people in a lot of different countries are better off because Jimmy Carter made an issue of it."

Back in Washington, the president sometimes invited Derian to the Oval Office for a firsthand report. Before certain overseas trips, Carter would offer instructions on what to ask for. Derian would also, as Carter remembered, "add her own feelings" in meetings with heads of state. He didn't mind.

Carter's human rights policy was "ambiguous, ambivalent, and ambidextrous," as Hodding Carter (no relation), Derian's husband and the State Department spokesman, described it. His late wife was often frustrated by the lack of support in the State Department and White House. But the policy was historic nonetheless. Roberta Cohen, who worked closely with Derian, credited Carter with "planting the seeds for a change of thinking in the world — seeds that saved not just lives but ideas, and ideas matter."

The new policy was most consistent and effective in the Western Hemisphere, where the United States held more sway than elsewhere. Carter signaled to dictators that the old days of exporting their raw materials to America in exchange for a blind eye to their abuses of power were over. The new policy came as a shock to governments that had fought shoulder to shoulder with the United States against Communism and terrorism.

Each nation now confronted with the new US priorities reacted a little differently.

South America's largest country, Brazil, which had been under military rule since 1964, abruptly canceled its long-standing military treaty with the United States and derided a critical report from Derian's bureau as "unacceptable and tendentious commentaries." While Derian applied pressure over the imprisonment of thousands of leftists, Carter played good cop with Brazilian president Ernesto Geisel, in part because he had another agenda. Brazil was threatening to build a nuclear fuel reprocessing plant, in violation of the 1967 Treaty of Tlatelolco, which aimed to prevent the spread of nuclear weapons to Latin America. With some skillful trade concessions, Carter eventually helped enhance human rights and enforce a treaty that kept Latin America nuclear free — an unheralded victory.

Argentina was also challenging. In 1976 the military government launched a vicious "dirty war" against suspected leftist terrorists, secretly backed by Henry Kissinger. By the time Carter took office, an estimated fifteen thousand people had "disappeared." One publisher, Jacobo Timerman, was imprisoned and tortured in 1977 after publicizing the disappearances. Timerman credited Derian with saving his life, and resourceful American diplomats in Argentina saved hundreds more. "You must have very good contacts," an Argentinian jailer told a prisoner named Alejandro Deutsch as he let him go, "because nobody leaves this place alive." Nearly four decades later, Carter met with grateful members of the Deutsch family in Atlanta.

In Chile, the number of disappearances during

Carter's time in office dropped from hundreds each year to a trickle. The country's infamous strongman, General Augusto Pinochet, felt the heat from the administration over the 1976 car bombing of former Chilean diplomat Orlando Letelier on Washington's Embassy Row. He fired the head of the secret police responsible for the murder and restructured his security services to be somewhat less abusive. Even Alfredo Stroessner, the notoriously brutal president of Paraguay, eventually released eight hundred political prisoners.

In Nicaragua, a Marxist insurgency that called themselves Sandinistas was on the threshold of victory in a long-running civil war. Carter nonetheless cut military and economic aid to Anastasio Somoza, whose family had run the country as its personal fiefdom for more than forty years. As in many countries around the world, Carter sought a "middle way" in Nicaragua between Communism and autocracy. He couldn't find it. In 1979 he proposed to the Organization of American States that the dictator step down and agree to elections. Somoza rejected the deal and tried to flee to Miami with much of the country's treasury in his luggage. Carter ordered him stopped at the border. He resettled in Paraguay, where the following year he was assassinated by Sandinista-backed agents.

While conservatives howled that Carter's actions in Nicaragua proved he was soft on Communism, liberal critics complained that throughout Somoza's rule, his national guard (and those of other dictatorships) was still allowed to train at academies sponsored by the US military. The Carter administration explained the continuation of this tradition by arguing that US generals wined and dined hundreds of Latin American officers at Fort Leavenworth in order to deliver an important message: civilian control of government is ultimately in the interest of the military. Some returned to Latin America with a better understanding of constitutional values and would eventually help democratize their societies; others just picked up pointers from American officers on fighting insurgents and repressing dissidents.

The most conspicuous failures of Carter's human rights policy in Central America came in El Salvador, where the United States backed a right-wing junta against revolutionaries. When Archbishop Óscar Romero — whose left-wing "liberation theology" made him a popular hero — spoke out against the United States for pursuing the Cold War in Central America, the White House secretly tried to convince Pope John Paul II to quiet Romero down. The archbishop would not be deterred. In February 1980 he wrote to Carter "because you are a Christian" and asked the US president to cut off military aid to the Salvadoran army.

Weeks later, a right-wing gunman with ties to the Salvadoran regime burst into a chapel and shot Romero to death while he was saying mass. Nine months after that, just before Carter left office, three nuns and a lay missionary from the United States were killed by what was later determined to be a faction of the Salvadoran military. El Salvador and Guatemala (where Carter's aid cutoff did little to slow the military regime's widespread killing of civilians) showed that insisting on human rights was often not enough to stop officially sanctioned terror.

■ ■ ■ ■

When Carter first talked to Andrew Young in late 1976 about leaving Congress to become his ambassador to the United Nations, Young resisted. He told the president-elect he would better serve Carter's interests by staying in the House of Representatives, where Carter knew almost no one. Young suggested that Congresswoman Barbara Jordan should be his UN ambassador. "But she didn't march with King, and you did," Carter told him. The president-elect felt that the credibility of his human rights campaign abroad depended on its connection to the American civil rights movement.

On the day Young was sworn in, Carter handed him a note that said: "Ask African leaders what we can do together." Young believed the first word, *Ask,* spoke volumes about the transformation under way. In the twenty-five years since decolonization began, African nations had grown accustomed to a patronizing attitude from Washington and implicit demands that Third World countries help the United States in the Cold War in exchange for foreign aid. Carter and Young were determined to listen to these newly independent nonwhite countries with respect — a seemingly obvious but hugely important tonal change in American foreign policy that did much to restore America's standing in the world.

Carter also showed respect by becoming the first American president to visit sub-Saharan Africa while in office: a state visit to Nigeria in 1978. He invited more African heads of state to the White House in his first year than any of his predecessors had in four. Even the dictators were brought into his orbit with the hope of addressing their abuses. "He would negotiate with the devil if he thought he could get a hearing," Young said.

Uganda's dictator, Idi Amin, was an exception. Furious about Carter's denunciation of his human rights abuses, he barred Americans from entering or leaving the country and threatened the lives of a hundred Christian missionaries. Their fates weighed heavily on Carter, who negotiated their release through Saudi Arabia only to find that all of them preferred to remain in remote Ugandan villages to continue their brave work.

In Rhodesia, Carter became convinced that the British, with their financial interests in the region, were "too timid" to make real progress in the endless negotiations under way in London to transition the country from an apartheid state to a democracy. Carter compared the white followers of Prime Minister Ian Smith to the KKK — impactful words from an American president who grew up in the Jim Crow South. Then he followed up with the careful attention to multilateral nuances that he applied to all future diplomatic efforts. In 1980 Rhodesia finally transitioned to majority rule without deepening the country's long-simmering civil war.⋆

The transition in South Africa would take much longer. Carter sent Mondale to Vienna for several meetings with South African president John Vor-

⋆The country held fair elections, which revolutionary leader Robert Mugabe won. Mugabe governed the nation now called Zimbabwe reasonably well for a dozen years before becoming a tyrant.

ster, an implacable racist admirer of Adolf Hitler. When the talks yielded nothing, Carter publicly blasted apartheid and backed a global arms embargo against Pretoria. But he rejected US divestment and boycotts, believing that corporate engagement would encourage liberalization and productive diplomacy. It did, but much too slowly. Reagan reversed most of Carter's majority-rule policy in the region, and Nelson Mandela, imprisoned throughout the Carter and Reagan presidencies, didn't assume the presidency of South Africa until 1994.

Nearby, Carter had to contend with Mobutu Sese Seko, a US ally and the longtime military dictator of the Congo, which he renamed Zaire. When neighboring Angola descended into civil war, Mobutu, with America's backing, intervened against the ruling Marxist regime, which was bolstered by Cuban troops. The messy Angolan proxy war — and another in the Horn of Africa, where the United States sided with Somalia, while the Soviet Union backed Ethiopia — showed that in Africa, the struggle between the superpowers would often take precedence over human rights.

The Cold War also took precedence throughout much of Asia. In Indonesia, the largest Muslim country in the world, the Suharto regime was so anti-Communist and friendly to the United States that Carter was slow to denounce the butchering of left-wing separatists in the province of East Timor, where the death toll from violence and starvation reached 150,000. (He finally joined efforts to free 50,000 political prisoners.)

The Philippines, a critical strategic ally in the Pacific facing a Communist insurgency in its outer islands, offered another example of the clash between "power and principle" (the title of Brzezinski's memoirs). Richard Holbrooke, the talented, egotistical diplomat driving policy in the region, argued that if the Carter administration pushed out longtime president Ferdinand Marcos, and the Philippines fell to a Marxist regime, the fallout would be disastrous not just for human rights but also for the future of the Democratic Party. Carter agreed, though this pragmatism didn't stop him from decrying in his diary the "weak-kneed approach" of those in Washington who would be willing to drop the topic of human rights altogether in order "to appease dictators." And he so disliked dealing with Marcos and his obnoxious, greedy wife, Imelda, that he fobbed them off on Mondale at every opportunity.

Another nettlesome dictator was President Park Chung-hee of South Korea. During his campaign, Carter had alarmed hard-liners by pledging to withdraw American troops from the Korean peninsula, arguing that Park's army was plenty strong to deter North Korean aggression. This stunning proposal challenged Washington's Cold War consensus, and almost no one expected Carter to actually push the policy as president. When he did, not a single member of the US Senate backed the idea. After Major General John K. Singlaub, chief of staff of US forces in South Korea, said publicly that any US troop withdrawals would lead to war with North Korea, Carter relieved him of his command. But the president found it impossible to defy his advisers' nearly united front, and he backed off. In the end, only three thousand out of forty thousand American troops were withdrawn.

During Carter's visit to Seoul in 1979, President Park angered him by delivering what Carter called in his journal "an abusive harangue" about how even that tiny reduction in forces — just 0.5 percent of the six hundred thousand South Korean troops already defending the country — would jeopardize his national security.

Carter ignored Park's rudeness because he had what he considered a higher purpose: saving his soul. On the last day of his visit, after official business was completed, he talked to the South Korean president about becoming a Christian. Like Gierek in Poland, Park never fully embraced Christianity, but Carter's unusual decision to raise the matter strengthened religious freedom in South Korea.

Four months after Carter's visit, Park was assassinated. Carter never met his successor, General Chun Doo-hwan, but he threatened to pull all US troops if Chun executed Kim Dae-jung, a human rights activist and future Nobel Peace Prize winner wrongly accused of being a Communist. The South Korean regime didn't want to give Carter the satisfaction of releasing Kim Dae-jung on his watch, so it wasn't until the Reagan administration that he was freed. But Kim Dae-jung knew who had saved him. When he was elected president of South Korea in 1998, he invited Patt Derian to his swearing-in and told her that he wouldn't be alive without the efforts of the Carter administration.

The worst human rights violation to occur in Asia during Carter's term was the genocide in Cambodia. From 1975 to 1979, Pol Pot's Khmer Rouge killed an estimated 1.7 million people, more than one-fifth of the population. In 1978

Carter declared Cambodia the worst violator of human rights in the world, and he joined international condemnation of the regime, though he later admitted, "I should have denounced them more forcefully." While direct military intervention was out of the question, what Carter did next was out of character.*

In late 1978 Communist Vietnam (backed by the Soviet Union) invaded Communist Cambodia (backed by China) and removed the murderous Khmer Rouge. This should have been welcome news for the president, even if he didn't yet know the full extent of the Cambodian genocide. But Carter faced a political and moral dilemma. He knew that accepting Vietnam's attack on its genocidal neighbor would validate aggression and complicate efforts to normalize relations with China. To bond with Beijing, he would have to criticize Hanoi.† This left Carter once again favoring geostrategic considerations over moral ones.

Only years later did it become clear just how entangled the United States had been in the continuation of the Khmer Rouge. "I encouraged the Chinese to support Pol Pot," Brzezinski told the *New York Times* in 1998. While he said he considered the Khmer Rouge "an abomination,"

*After Nixon destabilized Cambodia with a secret bombing campaign, Ford evacuated Phnom Penh in 1975 and left millions of civilians to a bloody fate. The United States wanted nothing more to do with the region. That disengagement left Carter little room to force change in Cambodia.
†It would be seventeen years before US diplomatic relations with Vietnam were established.

the national security adviser remained wedded to the old Nixon-Kissinger formula of "playing the China card" against the Soviet Union.

It got worse. With US-Soviet tensions growing sharply in 1980, the United States voted in the United Nations to seat the remnants of Pol Pot's government in exile instead of the new Cambodian leaders, who may have been the puppets of Vietnam (and thus the Soviet Union) but at least weren't genocidal maniacs. Carter's explanation — that he was siding in the United Nations with China, Australia, and Western Europe against the Soviet Union, Vietnam, and Cuba — was practical but unpersuasive even in parts of his own State Department. Would China have really reversed course and broken its new diplomatic relations with the United States if America voted against seating the Khmer Rouge in the United Nations? Not likely. That US vote — described by Cyrus Vance in his memoirs as "extremely distasteful" but necessary to maintain alliances and show respect for the exiled Cambodian prince Norodom Sihanouk — was a measure of Cold War thinking in that era. Too often, Carter, despite his best intentions, allowed a narrow and often mistaken definition of "the national interest" to prevail.

Even at its best, Carter's emphasis on human rights never fully moved from episodic initiatives into a structured and systematic policy. And after the Soviets invaded Afghanistan in late 1979, the idea faded. The revival of the Cold War took the heat off authoritarian regimes that were successful in portraying themselves as ardently anti-Communist. Carter deleted references to "disappearances" in his 1980 Human Rights Day proclamation and scaled back his invocations of human rights in his speeches.

Patt Derian was unhappy. Arguing that Argentina and other human rights abusers were now getting off lightly, she threatened to resign. And while friends in the State Department talked her out of it, she believed with good reason that human rights policy had not been implemented aggressively enough, especially in the second half of Carter's term. A few months after leaving office, a briefly demoralized Carter agreed that "the results of our commitment were often disappointing."

Reagan's ascension to the presidency seemed at first to signal an end to human rights as an animating principle of American foreign policy. Right-wing Argentine diplomats literally broke out the champagne; they knew that the United States would now prevent the United Nations from looking too closely into their human rights abuses. Jean-Claude Duvalier, Haiti's dictator, rearrested all of the political prisoners he had freed when Carter took office.★

But even after Reagan's first secretary of state, Alexander Haig, said human rights would take a "backseat" to fighting terrorism, neither he nor other Reagan-era policymakers fully abandoned the Carter policy. In fact, a new generation of conservative thinkers committed to the promotion

★Neoconservatives took their cues from a 1979 essay by Reagan's UN Ambassador Jeane Kirkpatrick, "Dictatorships and Double Standards," that argued — wrongly, it turned out — that authoritarian regimes could peacefully evolve into democracies, but Communist regimes could not.

of global democracy began echoing it. Many of these policymakers (including Elliott Abrams, Reagan's hawkish assistant secretary of state for human rights) reappeared in important positions in the administration of George W. Bush, who made the expansion of democratic values central to his foreign policy.

The seeds that Carter planted slowly bore fruit. In 1981 Brazil, Bolivia, Peru, and Uruguay were already moving away from dictatorships. Argentina returned to democracy in 1983; the new president, Raúl Alfonsín, described himself as a "Carterite" and said America's human rights policy had saved thousands of lives. Carter's legacy contributed to democracy building in Chile, Ecuador, Colombia, Costa Rica, and even Paraguay. In the 1970s, only one or two Latin American nations were democracies; by the early 2000s, only one or two were not.*

In Western Europe, Carter's policy helped save NATO. In 1977 the Italian Communist Party came close to winning parliamentary elections; for months afterward, it was poised to enter the government, weakening or even cracking the Western alliance. Richard N. Gardner, Carter's ambassador to Italy, crisscrossed the country delivering an understated but effective speech: that the kinds of people who would persecute Andrei Sakharov simply couldn't be trusted to protect basic freedom in Europe and maintain NATO. The human rights speeches embarrassed the once-fashionable Italian Communists, and —

*Only Venezuela, which had long enjoyed the strongest democracy on the continent, moved toward dictatorship in the 2000s.

even before the 1978 left-wing kidnapping of a former prime minister — their power in Italy receded.

Many historians of the Cold War stress the importance of "soft power": nonmilitary cultural factors that cause catalytic change inside closed societies. Placing an emphasis on human rights was one example. But Carter was also an early believer that Western music could help hollow out the Soviet system. In 1977 the White House helped the Nitty Gritty Dirt Band become the first rock-and-roll band to play on Russian soil, part of an infusion of Western values that Soviet premier Mikhail Gorbachev later said "taught the young there was another life." Anatoly Dobrynin, who served as the Soviet ambassador in Washington through five presidencies, conceded in his memoirs that Carter's human rights policies "played a significant role" in the Soviet Union loosening its grip at home and in Eastern Europe. Once liberalization was under way, Dobrynin concluded, it couldn't be controlled.

Václav Havel, the dissident playwright who in 1993 became prime minister of the Czech Republic, put it in psychological terms. He argued that Carter's policy not only inspired him in prison, it also undermined "the self-confidence" of the Soviet bloc, which imperiled the strength and legitimacy of the state. Meanwhile, the self-confidence of Eastern Europe's human rights organizations grew.

A new global movement was taking shape, as authoritarian regimes on both the Right and the Left bent to the democratic revolution sweeping the globe in the 1980s and 1990s. The concept of human rights became permanently encoded in the global conversation — and dissidents no longer felt so alone when the prison door clanged shut at night. For all the legitimate worries about resurgent authoritarianism in the twenty-first century, around half of the nations of the world now live under some form of democracy — more than twice as many as in 1980. This is a tribute, in part, to the work of Jimmy Carter.

# 26
# PANAMA CANAL SQUEAKER

If there is a gene for duty, responsibility, and the will to tackle messy problems with little or no potential for political gain, Jimmy Carter was born with it. Nothing showed this better than his determination to give the Panama Canal back to Panama. His success in doing so almost certainly prevented a long and bloody guerilla war against the United States in Central America.

When it opened in 1914, the Panama Canal transformed global commerce. By linking the Atlantic Ocean to the Pacific in Central America, the canal cut more than eight thousand miles off the old voyage around Cape Horn. This helped make the United States a dominant global power. But the canal was born in struggle and misery. After French efforts failed amid tens of thousands of deaths from malaria and yellow fever, President Theodore Roosevelt ensured that the fifty-mile canal would be dug by the United States. Roosevelt backed Panamanian independence from Colombia in exchange for a long-term lease to build and manage it. The lopsided 1903 treaty granted the United States control of the canal "in perpetuity."

For seventy-five years, most Americans assumed

the Canal Zone was American territory ("as much a part of the United States as Omaha, Nebraska," according to one midcentury journalist). In truth, it wasn't; Panama never formally relinquished sovereignty. But under the treaty, the Panamanian government had no say in what happened inside the Canal Zone. Stationed there in the 1920s, a young major named Dwight D. Eisenhower came to believe the treaty was unfair to the Panamanians. He and other thoughtful military officers and diplomats knew the colonial wound it represented was buried deep in the psyche of Latin America, poisoning relations with aggrieved nations that saw it as a symbol of disrespect, even contempt.

In 1964 Panama broke diplomatic relations with Washington after President Johnson sent US troops to quell three days of unrest that left twenty Panamanians and four American soldiers dead. To restore diplomatic ties, LBJ agreed to begin renegotiating the treaty, but the outlines of the deal he proposed were met with fierce opposition in both countries. While Presidents Nixon and Ford launched fresh talks with the charismatic if combative new Panamanian leader, General Omar Torrijos, neither had the political will to push them to completion. During the transition, Ford told Carter that he considered the canal more pressing than the Middle East or arms control talks with the Soviet Union — but he had made no progress on it.

It wasn't hard to understand why. Ronald Reagan had come within a whisker of winning the Republican nomination by accusing Ford of being "blackmailed" by Torrijos. If Ford hadn't been so weakened by the Reagan challenge and the right-wing onslaught over the Panama Canal, he likely would have beaten Carter. In the fall of 1976, forty-eight senators sponsored a resolution saying they would never "give away the canal" — fifteen more than were needed to block any treaty.

After the election, Rosalynn, Kirbo, Lance, and Jordan all advised Carter that renegotiating the treaty was a classic second-term issue: a political suicide mission to be undertaken only when he would no longer face the voters. The president predictably rejected their counsel. "Suppose there is no second term?" he told Rosalynn. Even so, Carter said later that if he had known beforehand how brutal the opposition would be, he might have taken a pass, as every president since William Howard Taft had done.

With no progress toward renegotiating the treaty for a dozen years, Panama in the 1970s had become a tinderbox. Nearly every day, angry activists chanted that the United States was an "imperialistic colonial power." Most analysts agreed that some form of combat was nearly inevitable. Once Panamanians attacked the canal, the Americans could never relinquish control without being seen as giving in to terrorists. Then the Canal Zone would become a perpetual war zone.

The Joint Chiefs of Staff testified before Congress that at least a hundred thousand troops would be necessary to defend the canal if it were sabotaged, which they considered likely. The result would have been an "utter disaster" for the United States, wrote Adam Clymer, who covered the story for the *New York Times*. With endless guerrilla war in Panama and ruined relations throughout Latin America, "We would have had Vietnam all over again."

In his usual methodical way, Carter closely read the entire 1903 treaty and scores of other reports and documents. During his August 1977 vacation, he devoured *The Path Between the Seas,* David McCullough's magisterial account of the building of the canal, which dealt at length with three of Carter's lifelong interests: engineering, disease control, and peacemaking.* For the president, the Panama Canal was not just a matter of national security. Jim Schlesinger noticed that after reading McCullough's book, Carter began seeing US control of the canal as immoral — what he later called "a diplomatic cancer" and "a symbol of subjugation." The president believed his human rights policy would ring hollow as long as a condescending United States insisted that Panamanians remained incapable of operating the canal. The issue, he wrote later, was a "litmus test throughout the world" of whether the United States would bully "a small and relatively defenseless nation that had always been a close partner and supporter."

To jump-start the talks, Carter tapped Sol Linowitz, an experienced diplomat and former CEO of Xerox Corporation, and former ambassador Ellsworth Bunker (Ford's Panama negotiator). Linowitz soon became so identified

*The president recommended the book to everyone involved in the treaty debate, and it would soon be cited by both sides on the Senate floor. McCullough dropped everything for three months to help lobby for the new treaties.

with the issue that he was hanged in effigy on Constitution Avenue. Overwhelmed by Carter's "insatiable curiosity," he found himself lying to the president by claiming that he did not know certain facts that he actually knew, such as how many tons were shipped through the canal a year. Linowitz figured that if he answered the question, Carter would ask him to break down the amount of traffic in each direction, then pose another hard, factual question, and another. But Linowitz felt that Carter, having curbed some of his Georgia habits, stopped short of micromanagement. His basic instructions were just to "use your best judgment."

The talks were going nowhere until Linowitz had a burst of inspiration: negotiate two treaties instead of one. That way, overall approval of the handover would not be threatened by the thorny question of what would happen in a crisis. By mid-May, the United States and Panama had the outlines of a deal. One treaty specified joint operation of the canal until the turn of the century, at which point the United States would give Panama total control. The second document was a vaguely worded "neutrality treaty" that tried to assure Panama that, while the canal would always remain open and neutral, the United States had no explicit right to intervene militarily.

Over the summer, opposition began to swell in the United States, where polls consistently showed that only about a third of Americans believed the canal should be turned over. Given that, the Senate's initial response would be unimaginable in twenty-first-century Washington. And yet on August 7, with the treaty details (and Panamanian approval) still pending, Carter sent telegrams to all one hundred members of the Senate with a request that they not comment publicly on the treaties until they had seen the full text of the agreements. All Republicans agreed except for senators Strom Thurmond of South Carolina and Jesse Helms of North Carolina — the two reigning right-wing "nuts" (Carter's description, in his diary). Without talk radio or cable news to egg them on, even hard-core opponents kept their mouths shut for a month.*

To build momentum and a sense of inevitability, Carter hosted Torrijos and seventeen other Latin American heads of state at the White House on September 7 for a televised signing ceremony and state dinner. The president seemed in his element — as exhilarated as anyone in Washington had ever seen him. "Carter clearly enjoyed his role as the political emancipator of a downtrodden people," Brzezinski wrote tartly. The president used the event to meet individually with several of the visiting right-wing dictators and press them — often successfully — to show their appreciation of the historic treaty by improving their records on human rights. Over the objections of the State Department, Andrew Young arranged for Carter to also meet briefly with a few left-wing Latin American leaders in exchange for their successful efforts to keep Cuban leader Fidel Castro from loudly championing the handover of the canal — an important element in winning approval.

President Ford showed up, which lent a biparti-

---

*By contrast, when President Obama signed a deal with Iran in 2015 to limit its development of nuclear weapons, dozens of Republican senators denounced the agreement before reading the text.

san feel to an event and was the beginning of thirty years of friendship and cooperation between the old rivals.* Backstage at the ceremony, Torrijos broke down in tears as he thanked Carter for ending generations of frustration and despair. Throughout the festivities, Carter treated the still-dicey ratification of the deal as a fait accompli. Some senators felt pressured, but they held their tongues.

Even Ronald Reagan promised Carter in an August phone call that he would not comment on the treaties until briefed by Linowitz and Bunker, though he quickly reneged by telling the press that he didn't believe the Joint Chiefs truly favored the "giveaway." The former California governor renewed his 1976 attacks and began misinforming conservative audiences that once the United States relinquished sovereignty, Panama could nationalize the canal overnight. Beyond asserting that the canal was "ours," Reagan's argument was essentially that Panamanians were too immature to run it. Other right-wingers went further, calling Panamanians "subhuman" and Torrijos a "drunken dictator."

The Panama Canal united what was then called the New Right (later known as the Republican base) at least as powerfully as abortion, school prayer, and other social issues. It harkened back to more than two dozen pre–World War II military interventions in Latin America undertaken in the spirit of the 1823 Monroe Doctrine, which gave the United States wide latitude in the Western

*Ford's former chief of staff, Dick Cheney, who was running for Congress from Wyoming, became a strong opponent of the treaties.

570

Hemisphere. What became a bristling, go-it-alone nationalism inside the GOP seemed to flare about every twenty years: in the 1950s with Robert A. Taft, in the 1970s with Ronald Reagan, in the 1990s with Pat Buchanan, and in the 2010s with Donald Trump. But in each of those periods (until the last), the Republican Party still contained a powerful establishment wing that often supported intervention yet also believed in the importance of diplomacy and multilateralism.

After the treaty texts were submitted to the Senate, Carter began to assess the order of battle. On his desk, he kept a large private notebook and entered every relevant bit of intelligence about undecided senators. Initially, he had fewer than thirty commitments — well under half of what he needed for ratification. Most Democrats would eventually be in support and most Republicans in opposition, but a majority took their time making up their minds. Ten would remain on the fence until the debate on the Senate floor.

Carter knew he had no chance without Majority Leader Byrd, who told reporters that the treaties faced "an uphill battle." The Carters hosted him and his wife, Erma, for a three-hour dinner at which Byrd told the president that he would have to contact all hundred senators individually, or the treaties had no hope for success. Carter did so, with a three-page handwritten letter that looked personal but was actually a well-printed copy.★ Rosalynn, who would soon be calling the

---

★Susan Clough carefully matched the ink in the form letter to Carter's personalized salutations; several senators believed the letter had been written just for them. In many cases, Carter followed up with a call.

spouses of fence-sitting senators, arranged a White House playdate with Amy for the Byrds' grandchildren, which seemed to charm them. After visiting Panama, Byrd would become an essential ally.

Carter had less luck with Barry Goldwater, the best-known Republican in the Senate, who told the president privately that turning over the canal was the right thing to do because of the threat of guerrilla warfare but wrote his constituents that he would oppose the treaties. Several other senators did the same.

The key GOP senator was Tennessee's Howard Baker, the affable and effective Senate minority leader who went on every short list for president after his famous Watergate question "What did the president know and when did he know it?" At first, Baker, known as "the Great Conciliator," seemed like a no. He was disturbed that the chief Panamanian negotiator, Rómulo Escobar Bethancourt, went public with his interpretation that the cloudy language in the neutrality treaty meant that the United States had no right to intervene militarily to keep the canal open. Baker said that was a deal breaker.

Carter jumped on the problem. He warned Torrijos that he could currently count on only fifty-five of the sixty-seven votes needed for ratification and urged him to come to Washington. Torrijos flew in and overruled his own negotiator, hammering out language that authorized the United States to "act against aggression" but — mindful of the plebiscite at home — toughened the part about America having no "right of intervention" in his country's internal affairs. On October 23, Panamanian voters went to the polls and approved the treaties overwhelmingly. Their fate now rested in Washington, where much of the first half of 1978 would be devoted to debating them.

Carter worked on Baker from all angles. He invited William Weaver, a major Nashville business leader and owner of the "Grand Ole Opry," to the White House, where he stood up in the East Room and dramatically announced his support. A critical moment came on January 3, when Baker visited Panama with a congressional delegation (about half the Senate would make the trip in a six-month period) and concluded that sabotage of the canal was a genuine national security threat. After winning a personal commitment from Torrijos to abide by any Senate amendments to the treaty, he moved toward support. More than sixty thousand letters poured into Baker's office, the vast majority opposed to the treaties, but Jim Cannon, Baker's top aide, knew that his boss was "more responsible than he is ambitious." When Cannon advised Baker that voting yes would prevent him from becoming the Republican nominee for president in 1980, the senator snapped, "So be it."

After Baker had sided with Carter on several other votes, the president thanked him for doing "the right thing." Baker replied that with any more "right things," he'd lose his seat in the Senate.

In early 1978 Carter returned to the prime-time fireside chat format that had worked so well a year earlier. He had one good line, arguing that Panama would no more likely close the canal than the United States would close the interstate highway system. But otherwise the speech flopped. Jim Fallows noticed that nearly every time Carter had a clear choice between good and bad writing in the drafting process, he chose the latter. "A leaden, heavy, shapeless, and disorganized piece of work . . . per JC instructions," Jerry Doolittle noted in his diary. "Apparently public expectations so low that nobody particularly noticed [it] sucked."[*]

Hamilton Jordan said he had a "shaky feeling" about the outcome: "A third of the people for it, and we need two-thirds of the Senate." To get it, the White House devised a strategy of courting state and local elites in order to build a "fire wall" to protect senators from political harm. The "Establishment" — both in the states and nationally — would try to come to the rescue.

While the State Department sponsored more than five hundred information sessions around the country, the most effective lobbying came from Carter himself. He hosted more than a dozen intimate personal briefings for wavering senators' home-state newspaper editors, bankers, lawyers, and other powerful community leaders. The briefings were factual and persuasive, and they gave attendees a thrill when the president, Secretary of Defense Harold Brown, or members of the Joint Chiefs of Staff patiently explained how easy it would be to blow up the canal and harm the United States if the treaties were not ratified. After returning home, these influential citizens usually delivered a message to their senators: we've got your back.

But when the Senate debate opened on February 8, Carter was still nineteen votes short of

[*]Fallows and Doolittle departed at the end of the year, and as Carter developed a better working relationship with his speechwriters, the speeches improved.

ratification. The death of Hubert Humphrey in January had been a blow; Carter had been hoping that Humphrey — emaciated from cancer — still had enough of his old clout to round up errant Democrats.* The White House hatched a rescue plan: an amendment to the treaty backed by both Byrd and Baker that guaranteed the canal would stay open under any circumstances (including if it was losing money) and that the United States could intervene to keep it open. The idea was to let senators tell their constituents that they had voted to *strengthen* the treaties. This helped with the polling and was enough to immediately bring aboard Democrats Lloyd Bentsen, John Glenn, and Richard Stone, and moderate Republican Charles Percy of Illinois. But even with them, ratification remained unlikely.

The most surprising supporter of the treaties outside the Senate was the Oscar-winning actor John Wayne, a conservative Republican and icon of cowboy integrity. Wayne's first wife was Panamanian, and his next two were also Latinas, and he and Torrijos had become fishing buddies. He let Bob Pastor — Carter's top aide on the issue — ghostwrite dozens of letters and articles in support of the treaties, many of which pointed out that "General Torrijos has never followed the Marxist line." Wayne contacted every senator and, as he told the president, "all the people who write

---

*Humphrey was touched that Carter invited him to Camp David, which he had never visited before, not even when he was vice president. Carter also sent him a photograph of Humphrey sitting in the president's chair behind the Resolute desk in the Oval Office with the inscription "This desk should have been yours."

me hysterical letters." When Wayne saw Reagan's fund-raising letter attacking the treaties, he privately scolded his old friend: "Dear Ronnie," he wrote. "I'll show you point by God damn point in the treaty where you are misinforming people. This is not my point of view against your point of view. These are facts."*

Some attempts at arm-twisting failed. Walter Mondale, Russell Long (finally on board), and Bob Strauss paid a visit to Wendell Ford, a Kentucky Democrat, who told his staff afterward that the trio called him "a traitor and the skunk at the garden party" and threatened him with a primary challenge. Ford voted no anyway. Georgia Democrats Herman Talmadge and Sam Nunn delayed committing for many months and voted yes only to avoid embarrassing the first-ever president from their state.

Supporters were heartened when hawkish Democrat Tom McIntyre of New Hampshire decided to deliver an impassioned speech attacking "the bully boys of the radical Right." He told his wife as he left for the floor, "Come and watch me lose my seat."

By mid-February, the White House feared the treaties were doomed when a bizarre tale surfaced of a secret diplomatic cable that was recovered in a factory lunchroom in North Carolina. The cable disclosed the existence of a sealed indictment of Moises Torrijos, brother of the Panamanian

*Carter expressed his gratitude, and in 1979 a cancer-stricken Wayne welcomed him to his Los Angeles home, one of his final visitors other than family. "He wished he could share his lunch with me but only had one straw!" Carter wrote in his diary.

general, for shipping cocaine into the United States. As rumors circulated, the Senate convened an extremely rare closed-door session, during which Robert Byrd pointed to Jesse Helms and all but accused him of concocting a scare story to block the treaties. When the Senate Intelligence Committee produced no evidence directly connecting the Panamanian leader to drugs, the matter ended inconclusively.*

By now, the White House lobbying had grown fierce. Bob Beckel, a deputy assigned to push the treaties, cut deals with senators that would have horrified the president if he knew the details. Sugar subsidies, Amtrak routes, weather stations — everything below major legislation was on the table. Beckel revealed later that, without the knowledge of higher-ups, he received $50,000 in cash from a businessman who favored the Panama deal to conduct opposition research aimed at finding senators' points of vulnerability in their private lives. Edward Brooke of Massachusetts, a moderate Republican and the first black senator since Reconstruction, said the pressure from unnamed Democratic operatives was so heavy-handed — so dependent on threats he refused to specify — that he almost switched from support to opposition.

Carter was lampooned in the *Wall Street Journal* for acting like Monty Hall, host of the TV game show *Let's Make a Deal,* but in private, he often

*In 1989, eight years after Omar Torrijos was killed in a 1981 airplane crash and succeeded by Manuel Noriega, newer stories of Panamanian drug dealing were substantiated, and President George H. W. Bush ordered an invasion that led to Noriega's removal from power.

confessed that he despised playing that game. "His heart wasn't in it. He felt himself unclean when he lobbied a senator," Jim Schlesinger remembered.

Every leverage point was nonetheless exploited. Senator Howard Cannon, a wavering Nevada Democrat, was a Mormon. The president called contacts in Salt Lake City, urging them to remind Cannon that the Mormon church had no official position on this issue. When Carter tracked down the editor of the locally influential *Las Vegas Review-Journal* and convinced him to back the treaties, Cannon finally had the cover he needed.

The historic vote on giving up the canal — the so-called resolution of ratification — was expected to come first, with the neutrality treaty submitted later. Sensing tactical advantage, Byrd and the White House reversed the order, scheduling the neutrality treaty — ostensibly an easier vote — for mid-March. But with two days to go, Carter told his diary, "This has been one of the worst days of my political life, knowing that we were lost, regaining a little hope." He sent Vance and the rest of his senior team to the Hill full-time and failed at lunch to convince Mississippi's John Stennis to vote yes. This only intensified his will to win. As tension mounted, he "worked over a problem like a piece of broken machinery he was mending in his hand, taking the time to do the job right," as Norman Mailer had described Carter's nature in 1976.

There was new trouble in Panama, where General Torrijos, furious about the proposed amendments and facing dissension at home, was now threatening to reject the treaties. Carter dispatched Hamilton Jordan and Deputy Secretary of State Warren Christopher to Panama to calm him down. Torrijos was a hothead who caused angina in Washington, but he and Jordan developed a bond, partly over their mutual regard for attractive women. In the end, the general did nothing to stop ratification.

Arizona's Dennis DeConcini almost did. DeConcini, a freshman Democrat out of his depth, saw the treaties as a roundabout way to help Arizona. He wanted Washington to prop up his state's major industry by buying $250 million worth of copper for the Defense Department's strategic minerals reserve. Carter and the Pentagon weren't about to pay off DeConcini this way, and for several days it looked as if Carter would lose the whole thing. To try to look substantive, DeConcini introduced a hard-line amendment giving the United States a blank check to invade Panama at will. It won broad support among Republicans but caused rioting in Panama and horrified Senate liberals.

After much haggling, the senators finally struck a compromise and rewrote the treaty to say the US military could step in only to keep the canal open, not as a broad colonialist "right to intervention" in Panama to quell labor strikes and restore order in the streets. Just off the floor, Byrd, who had the power to make the freshman's life miserable, told DeConcini, "It has to be like this, Dennis. I will not accept any changes." DeConcini had little to do with "the DeConcini Amendment" but was allowed to announce it as if it were his own.

On March 16, 1978, the neutrality treaty was approved with one vote to spare, 68 to 32. Inside the White House, staffers went charging down the hall carrying half-empty wine bottles. "It was the first display of emotion I've seen around the joint," Jerry Doolittle noted that day. But the celebration was tempered by the knowledge that a handful of senators said they were still not committed to giving back the canal. Carter felt the second vote would be tougher, in part because, for the first time, a Senate debate had been broadcast on the radio, which had the effect of hardening positions on both sides.

S. I. "Sam" Hayakawa had voted for the neutrality treaty — with the help of promised economic assistance to California logging towns — but the eccentric Republican decided to hold out on the handover treaty. Hayakawa was a seventy-one-year-old retired professor who had become popular among conservatives in 1968, when, as acting president of San Francisco State College, he pulled the cables out of a loudspeaker while black student protesters were addressing a rally. Elected in an upset in 1976, he was best known in the Senate for wearing colorful tam-o'-shanters (berets) and for falling asleep in hearings. Hayakawa's widely quoted position on the Panama Canal was: "We stole it fair and square."

Carter, Mondale, and Baker hatched a plan to play on the senator's vanity. One day in early April, Baker called the president, with Hayakawa listening in from the Senate minority leader's office. "Mr. President, do you need to meet with Sam Hayakawa from time to time on foreign affairs?" Baker asked. Carter knew Hayakawa could hear the conference call, and he replied effusively that he would greatly benefit from the senator's

580

wise counsel.

Hayakawa came by the White House, where he lectured the president on foreign policy and gave him a copy of his book *Language in Thought and Action.* That night, Carter forced himself to read the dense academic tome, first published in 1949, and the next day, he called him to discuss it. A suspicious Hayakawa asked Carter questions about his book and the nuances of semantics, his specialty. Could any other American president have stayed awake to read the book, much less answer the questions to the senator's satisfaction? Carter did.

Hayakawa then said he would like a regular meeting every two weeks with the president to discuss foreign affairs. Carter replied brilliantly, "Sam, I couldn't possibly limit our visits to every two weeks. I might want to hear your advice more often!" Hayakawa agreed. He voted yes, and that was the last time S. I. Hayakawa ever spoke to Jimmy Carter.

Shortly before the second vote, Senator James Abourezk, a Lebanese American Democrat from South Dakota, called Dan Tate of the White House congressional relations staff. "Danny," he said, "I was taking a piss and looked into the toilet and saw Jimmy Carter's face."

The firebrand liberal told Tate that because he hadn't been placed on the House-Senate conference committee on the deregulation of natural gas — a perch that would have allowed him to try to gut a bill he despised — he was going to make a 180-degree turn and come out against the hand-over treaty. This was a potential disaster for the White House. Abourezk had been one of the first

581

to endorse it, and Carter had assumed he was a solid yes.

As Senators Ted Kennedy and John Culver tried to reason with him, Abourezk suddenly bolted out of the Dirksen Senate Office Building toward the Senate floor, with Culver and Kennedy — Harvard football teammates in the early 1950s — in portly pursuit. Abourezk barricaded himself in a telephone booth in the Senate cloakroom and began calling reporters to tell them that he was switching positions on the Panama Canal. Culver lit pieces of paper on fire and slid them under the door to smoke his colleague out. It was partly fun and games for the senators, but the fate of the treaties genuinely hung in the balance.

Carter was angry. He found Abourezk "flighty" and "trying to blackmail me," but "there's no possibility of that succeeding," he wrote in his diary. The president asked Prince Sultan, the Saudi defense minister, to work on Abourezk, the most pro-Arab member of Congress. Just in time, Carter got word directly from Riyadh that Abourezk would vote yes. The Saudis were happy to put the American president in their debt.

On April 18, 1978, the Senate engaged in a long and historic debate, with the outcome in doubt until just before the six o'clock roll call. All day, Carter wrote in his diary, "We were planning for massive violence in Panama if the treaties were defeated." But by the same 68-to-32 margin as on the neutrality treaty, with no senators switching either way, the Senate voted to turn over the Panama Canal on December 31, 1999. The bipartisanship was striking, with sixteen Republicans backing a Democratic president and ten

Democrats defying him. As Carter told Robert Byrd, "You're a great man; it was a beautiful vote." But Byrd warned his colleagues of the political damage ahead: "Your badges of courage may be the dents in your armor."

Getting sixty-eight votes, Carter said, was even harder than getting elected president, and he wanted to celebrate the accomplishment by visiting Panama in June. But Rafshoon didn't want him to go. He thought Carter would be seen as going down there to give away the canal. And he was even more unhappy when Carter announced to his staff that he intended to give his speech in Spanish. But the address, delivered in passable Spanish with David McCullough and a few senators at his side, was wildly popular in Panama. It was the first time in American history that a full presidential address was delivered in a foreign language, much less given in another language overseas.

Unfortunately for Carter, the ordeal was not over. After the treaties passed, Torrijos announced that if they had failed, he had given orders to his armed forces to blow up the canal. This set off alarms in the House, which, along with the Senate, would have to approve legislation by October 1, 1979, to fund the joint operation of the canal for the next twenty years. Otherwise the treaties wouldn't go into effect.

Then Torrijos began shipping arms to the leftist Sandinista rebels in Nicaragua, a move that inflamed Congress. The critical votes for the funding legislation were nearly as hard to get as the Senate ratification because they involved all 535 members of Congress, not 100.

Carter considered this unanticipated chore

"extremely unpleasant." He thought he was past Panama only to find himself mired in it again. "We had them [House members] over in groups of thirty or forty ad nauseam," he recalled. "It was horrible. Night after night after night after night, going through the same basic questions. It was politically damaging for them to do it, and they were tortured." Later, Carter argued that this kind of "tedious work" constituted political leadership as much as being "a great communicator." He had a point.

For a time, it looked as if the House would unravel the treaties. Strong majorities voted to prevent troop transfers out of the Canal Zone, and — with members in a punitive mood — canceled most economic aid to Panama. They even met in secret for the first time in 150 years to weigh bogus allegations related to Panama's relationship with the Sandinistas. While the Senate moved to protect the treaties, the overwhelmingly Democratic House ended up approving a first bill to implement the treaties by a mere two votes. By the time the final measures passed in September 1979, Carter was done with the issue. "Has been a bitch ever since more than two years ago," he wrote in his diary.

Giving the Panama Canal to Panama would prove over time to be one of the wisest decisions ever made for democracy in the Western Hemisphere — and not just because the Panamanians have, by all accounts, managed the canal well since 1999. The handover engendered significant goodwill. For generations, tinhorn dictators had used resentment of arrogant gringos to gain and hold power. *Yanqui go home!* was one of the most politically potent epithets in the region. Now it had been replaced, at least for a time, with mutual respect.

That respect did not extend to domestic American politics. In the 1978 midterm elections, five Senate Democrats who backed the Panama Canal treaties lost their seats. (Republicans netted three seats but were still in the distinct minority.) In retrospect, it's clear that the Panama Canal debate helped create the modern conservative base. Direct-mail wizard Richard Viguerie and Terry Dolan of the recently founded National Conservative Political Action Committee (NCPAC) had obtained millions of "pledges" from Republicans to oppose relinquishing sovereign territory — a device used later by conservative activist Grover Norquist to lock in support for tax cuts. And the canal debate helped pioneer a form of paid advertising the Right would effectively deploy for years: the infomercial.

In 1980 eight Democratic senators who supported the treaties were defeated, with the canal votes especially harmful to Frank Church, John Culver, George McGovern, and Herman Talmadge, whose half-century family dynasty in Georgia politics, so beloved by Mr. Earl, came to an end. Senator Robert Morgan said he lost to John P. East in North Carolina almost entirely because of his Panama vote. And that's not even counting the unquantifiable political damage to Carter himself.

After Reagan was elected, William F. Buckley wrote that Reagan won by losing on Panama. If he had supported the treaties, he would never have been nominated in 1980. But if he had successfully defeated them, there would have been an insurrection in Panama, and, proven wrong about the deadly consequences of rejecting the treaties, he would not have beaten Carter. Upon taking office in 1981, Reagan didn't touch the treaties he had railed against. He privately considered them a "success story" that required no modification, much less abrogation. But he refused to admit he had been wrong in his career-making opposition.*

Reagan's timing was, as usual, impeccable. His use of the issue in his campaign for president tapped into post-Vietnam bitterness about the declining role of America in the world. By 1978, Carter was a major target of that bitterness — the personification of American retreat.

In betting so heavily on the canal treaties, Carter risked his other priorities. After the vote, Howard Baker told him that he and other Republicans would not be able to support the Strategic Arms Limitation Talks treaty — SALT II — no matter what was in it. "They said that they had gone as far as they could as a Republican party in supporting my basic positions," Carter remembered.

The Panama Canal victory nonetheless testified to the power and occasional virtue of elites, who — as the founders understood — can sometimes offer a cooling saucer for the heat of public opinion. Ratification of the treaties was clearly in the national interest of the United States, as even most opponents admitted later. And for all of

*In 1989 President George H.W. Bush, fed up with the erratic leadership of Manuel Noriega, who was accused of drug dealing, invaded Panama and removed Noriega from power. His stated reason was in part "to protect the integrity of the Panama Canal Treaties."

Jimmy Carter's grousing about how "horrible" it was to entertain members of Congress night after night, he was perfectly cast for the thankless but historic task of securing ratification. His speechwriter Rick Hertzberg saw it as the quintessential Carter achievement, one that rewarded his hard work, offered no political dividends, and drew on an alleged personal liability that was actually more often an asset. Carter's excessive attention to detail — mentioned in nearly every critique of the man — helped lead to two of the greatest triumphs of American foreign policy in the last quarter of the twentieth century. The first was in Panama. The second — an even longer shot — was in the Middle East.

# 27
## CAMP DAVID

Carter was more critical of Israel and supportive of Arabs than any other president, especially after he left office. And yet he also did more for the security of the State of Israel than any American president other than Harry Truman, who first extended diplomatic recognition to the newborn nation in 1948.

Consider the reality on the ground when Carter assumed office, and what he did to change it. Four times between 1948 and 1973, neighboring Arab states launched wars aimed at destroying Israel. In each of those conflicts, the strongest Arab military force by far — the only one capable of "driving Israel into the sea" in the common formulation of the day — was the Egyptian army. In 1979 Carter secured peace between Israel and Egypt, and neither country has made war on the other in all the decades since.

The Camp David Accords and the treaty that resulted did more than save tens of thousands of Egyptian and Israeli lives; they dramatically reduced the odds of general war — even superpower confrontation — in the Middle East. While Carter fell short of his dream of brokering a comprehensive regional settlement that produced a homeland for the Palestinians, his handiwork has remained remarkably intact, making it the most important and durable peace treaty anywhere in the world since the end of World War II.

It's an improbable tale: a south Georgia peanut farmer with no foreign policy experience who educates himself in the nuances of the most complex conflict in the world, and then — when history offers him the chance — defies his advisers and dives in headfirst. His religious faith and long interest in the Holy Land fueled a risky but ultimately magnificent obsession, one that tested not just his prodigious diplomatic skills but every ounce of his patience.

For a decade, the Middle East had been engulfed in war and its messy aftermath. In the 1967 "Six Day War," Israel shocked the world by using lightning-fast military strikes to seize the gargantuan Sinai peninsula, along with the tiny Gaza Strip, from Egypt; the strategic Golan Heights from Syria; and the West Bank, home to hundreds of thousands of Palestinians, from Jordan. After the war, the UN Security Council voted unanimously in its famous Resolution 242 that "territories occupied in the recent conflict" must be returned. Since the resolution lacked the definite article (*the* territories occupied), Israel long argued that it didn't have to return *all* the land. It would offer "land for peace" only if the Arabs recognized its right to exist and pledged not use these "occupied territories" as access corridors to attack it.

Six years later, Arab states did just that. Led by Egyptian president Anwar Sadat, they launched a surprise attack on the holiest day of the year for

589

Jews. The 1973 Yom Kippur War, which nearly escalated into a broader conflagration, ended with an emergency US airlift of arms to Israel and a superpower standoff; President Nixon actually ordered the Pentagon to go on a higher state of nuclear alert. In the wake of another setback at the hands of Israel, the bitter Arab states banded together to create the OPEC cartel, which led to energy shortages and rampant inflation in the United States.

After that, events took a slight turn for the better. At the 1973 Geneva Conference, the United States and the Soviet Union used their newly warming relations to build on the UN-sponsored cease-fire that ended the Yom Kippur War. Secretary of State Henry Kissinger launched what came to be known as "shuttle diplomacy": a series of trips to Jerusalem and Arab capitals to negotiate military disengagement from the Golan Heights and the Sinai. Sadat, a relative moderate, acknowledged that the State of Israel was not going away.

But by 1976, tensions were rising again. Egypt expelled its 19,000 Russian advisers — a relief to the United States — but was still legally at war with Israel, still participating in a total boycott of Israel that extended to any direct communications, and still preventing Israeli ships from passing through the Suez Canal.

The plight of the Palestinians continued to be a sticking point. By 1978, hundreds of thousands were living as refugees in the West Bank and Gaza Strip — many in teeming refugee camps — under the thumb of the Israeli army. Arab nations backed Yāssir 'Arafāt's Palestine Liberation Organization to the hilt, even — and sometimes especially — when it committed terrorist acts against Israelis.

Carter respected the deal Kissinger struck, which called for no US contact with the PLO until it recognized Israel's right to exist. But he sympathized with Palestinian refugees and felt his human rights policy made it impossible for him to avoid discussing them. When he went to the United Nations in March 1977 and shook hands with everyone in the room, including the Palestinian representative, it caused a stink.

Carter's original idea was to reconvene the Geneva Conference. But Israel feared that Moscow — which agreed to let the PLO be part of the Arab delegation — would tilt any Geneva agreement toward the Arabs. It was hardly surprising that in March 1977 Israeli prime minister Yitzhak Rabin arrived in Washington looking grim. Carter found Rabin "very stubborn and somewhat ill at ease." He was also distracted. Rabin was soon forced to resign as prime minister over financial irregularities connected to a New York bank.

A month later, Carter had a very different reaction to his first meeting with Anwar Sadat. "A shining light burst on the Middle East scene for me," he wrote in his memoirs. From the start, Carter and Sadat would become, according to both men, genuinely close friends — sharing hometown stories and personal ambitions "as though we were tying ourselves together for a lifetime." Carter described Sadat as a man "I would come to admire more than any other world leader."

In May Carter flew to Geneva to meet with Syrian president Hafiz al-Assad, the first of many times Assad's good humor would prove deceptive.

The Syrian leader soon found several ways to — in Carter's words — "sabotage" the Geneva Conference. This proved to be a blessing in disguise for Carter. At Camp David, he wouldn't have to deal with the Soviet Union or with Arab countries other than Egypt.

The following month, Israeli voters elected their country's first conservative prime minister, Menachem Begin of the right-wing Likud Party, a man who often referred to the West Bank by its biblical name, Judea and Samaria, and believed the Jews had an ancient claim to it. This view raised a new issue in Israeli politics: settlements. A few hardy Israeli settlers had begun building encampments on Palestinian land in the West Bank — a major provocation.

There were scattered Israeli settlements in the Sinai desert, too, but the land there had no biblical significance. Besides some army garrisons, the Sinai settlement plans were mostly for resort cities by the Red Sea. The people in the area were Bedouin nomads, not Palestinians.

When Begin arrived in Washington, Carter found him at first glance "quite congenial, dedicated, sincere, deeply religious." He thought he would be a stronger leader than Rabin. But any hopes evaporated when Begin returned home and recognized a few early and temporary West Bank settlements as permanent.

Looking to shake things up, Sadat told the Egyptian parliament that he would be willing to travel to Jerusalem to explain his support for the PLO. Six days later, an excited Begin — thrilled by this recognition of Israel — used American channels to invite Sadat to Israel, and he quickly accepted. Sadat's three-day trip to Jerusalem,

November 19 to 21, 1977, capped by an emotional speech to the Knesset, made Camp David possible. It was described by Carter in his memoirs as "among the most dramatic events of modern history."

The euphoria did not last.* The governments of Syria, Iraq, and Libya all called for Sadat's assassination, and even Arab Americans were critical of him. Palestinians made it clear that they rejected any contact with Israel. After back-channel feelers between Israel and Egypt went poorly, the odds for Mideast peace in 1978 receded.

Carter was at a crossroads. He told Brzezinski that he faced a simple choice between abandoning peace efforts and getting much more involved personally. They tossed around the idea of inviting both Sadat and Begin to Camp David for talks, and a split developed. "We had quite an argument at breakfast, with me on one side, and Fritz, Cy, Zbig, and Ham on the other," Carter recorded in his diary. "I think we ought to move much more aggressively on the Middle East question than any of them seem to."

In February he invited Sadat to Camp David, where their friendship deepened, and in March he forged a good connection with Israeli defense minister Ezer Weizman — a highly decorated war hero — that would prove important in the fall.

In May Begin returned to the White House to commemorate the thirtieth anniversary of the

---

*An enduring anti-Carter neoconservative talking point is that Sadat's visit to Jerusalem — not Camp David — brought peace between Egypt and Israel. This is at odds with Sadat's own view and with the actual sequence of events.

establishment of the State of Israel and witness Carter's announcement of plans for a Holocaust memorial.★ Their meetings went badly. Carter now viewed Begin as "a small man with limited vision, and my guess is he will not take the necessary steps to bring peace to Israel."

Vance and Mondale took separate trips to Israel and Egypt in this period, and both returned pessimistic. But instead of backing off, the president decided to take a momentous risk: use Camp David as the site for a high-stakes summit. "Are you willing to be the scapegoat?" Rosalynn asked him. "What else is new?" he said with a shrug. Mondale tried to dissuade him: "They get over here, and this blows up in your face, it could destroy your presidency." The vice president suggested diplomats work out something first. Carter said peace would never happen that way. Brzezinski argued that any conference would have to include the other Arab states. A deal won't happen that

★The word *holocaust* was only then coming into wide usage. Carter originally wanted the museum to define holocaust broadly to include other genocides and emphasize universalism and human rights. However, his choice for chairman of the commission that would build the memorial, Elie Wiesel, a Holocaust survivor, viewed the Holocaust as a uniquely Jewish experience. Wiesel prevailed and came to appreciate the president's interest in the project. When it was completed fifteen years later, few knew that the idea for the US Holocaust Memorial Museum originated in the Carter White House. In recent years, the Simon-Skjodt Center for the Prevention of Genocide has helped broaden the museum's mission to encompass Carter's original goal.

way, either, Carter replied.

Carter dispatched Vance to the region with secret invitations for Begin and Sadat to come meet with him at Camp David in the fall. Neither wanted to be seen sabotaging peace prospects, so both men quickly accepted, though each had sharply different expectations. Begin saw a chance to neutralize the Egyptian army, which remained an existential threat to Israel; Sadat hoped to vindicate his bold trip to Jerusalem and make the United States a permanent ally. Neither truly needed a deal, which made the odds of success long.

After the August 8 announcement of September talks at Camp David, Carter was deluged with warnings from advisers, friends, and outsiders. None could see a clear route to success, and the president himself had only the vaguest sense of how to proceed. Many cautioned that the summit was all downside — a fatal distraction that would further deplete his political capital. Kissinger, who would later admit he was jealous of Carter's achievement, called him to warn that presidents should never negotiate personally, because they expose themselves unnecessarily to failure.★

"I slowly became hardened against them," Carter wrote later. "And as stubborn as at any other time I can remember."

In 1942 Franklin Roosevelt, worn down by the

★The only precedent for an American president brokering a peace deal between warring parties was Theodore Roosevelt's settlement of the Russo-Japanese War in 1905. But Roosevelt never ventured to the site of the talks in Portsmouth, New Hampshire.

burdens of war, needed a peaceful place of refuge that was closer to the White House than his other homes in Hyde Park, New York, and Warm Springs, Georgia. He found it in Catoctin Mountain Park, a rocky, forested area of Maryland sixty miles north of Washington. Roosevelt called his then-secret retreat Shangri-La, and one of his first guests was Winston Churchill. Later, Dwight Eisenhower, who brought Soviet premier Nikita Khrushchev there in 1959, renamed the rustic cottages and cabins nestled in 140 wooded acres for his grandson, David, who would end up marrying Richard Nixon's daughter Julie.

The Carters loved Camp David so much that they spent almost every other weekend there. With the longer stays, that added up to nearly one-quarter of his entire presidency — far more than any other president.

As the summit approached, Carter insisted that the only chance for success at Camp David was leak-proof secrecy, a requirement that would almost certainly be unworkable in today's wired world. Over the objections of Rafshoon and Powell, he barred reporters and photographers from the area and instructed that no one invited should be in contact with the media for the duration of the summit. Carter felt that if the parties had to explain their positions every day in the press, they wouldn't have the flexibility to change them without losing face. His more immediate motivation for the blackout was to keep Begin from talking to William Safire, an implacable foe of his Mideast policy. This proved to be an unfounded concern because the New York Times wasn't publishing during the conference, thanks to an eighty-eight-day New York newspaper strike.

The original plan called for three days at Camp David, six at most. No one dreamed they would be there so much longer. Carter knew that the atmosphere would be tense. For a quarter century, the four wars between the two countries, in 1948, 1956, 1967, and 1973, had touched almost every family in the two delegations. Several attendees, including Sadat and Weizman, had ordered attacks that killed the loved ones of those who would soon be sleeping in cabins only a few yards away.

And then there were the dynamics between the principals. Going into the summit, Carter fretted that "Sadat seemed to trust me too much, and Begin not enough." Sadat trusted Carter as a personal friend and as a cudgel to convince America's strongest ally in the region — Israel — to go along with him. This was unrealistic on Sadat's part, but the assumption in the Egyptian delegation that Carter could "deliver" Israel would be hard to shake. Begin worried that Carter was pulling the United States away from Israel after three decades of being wary but dependable allies and that the American president's hunger for a historic deal would overshadow his good sense. He didn't trust Carter to protect his country.

Carter knew that Sadat and Begin had more in common than either cared to admit. Both were devout but militant men who had spent years on the lam or in prison. Both were willing to bloody their hands to achieve political aims. Their common target — the British, who had occupied Egypt and Palestine for decades — considered them terrorists.

The CIA profiles assembled for the summit focused more on their differences, which went far beyond tribal enmity between Muslims and Jews. Sadat was a larger-than-life charmer who saw himself as a major actor on the world stage. The CIA called that thirst for publicity his "Barbara Walters syndrome" but suggested he had loftier aims: a "Nobel Prize Complex." Begin was a passionate and intransigent right-wing lawyer with the weight of tragic Jewish history on his shoulders. Where Sadat floated above the trees with airy convictions, Begin was in the weeds, inspecting every word.

Born on a farm at the end of the First World War, Sadat — descended from slaves — grew up with a burning desire for Egyptian independence from Great Britain. The enemy of his enemy was his inspiration, whether Mahatma Gandhi or Adolf Hitler. In 1942 Sadat was arrested in Cairo for conspiring with Nazi spies. After escaping from jail, he joined Mohamed Kamel (his friend, future foreign minister, and disenchanted subordinate at Camp David) to plan the assassinations of pro-British government officials and British soldiers. In 1951, six years after Hitler committed suicide in his Berlin bunker, Sadat was still praising him for fighting Winston Churchill. By then, Sadat had developed into a religious but not fundamentalist Muslim who recalled learning from a *Reader's Digest* article he read in prison that God is merciful and loving.

In 1952 Sadat, then a dashing young army officer, joined the pan-Arabist strongman Gamal Abdel Nasser in his revolution against the Egyptian king. When Nasser died in 1970, Sadat cut a deal with the clandestine militants of the Muslim Brotherhood that eased his way to power. He threw out the Soviets and raised Egypt's profile internationally with his charismatic leadership. The 1973 Yom Kippur War — when Egyptian troops pierced Israeli lines and crossed the Suez Canal — made him popular at home, and even a collapsing economy hadn't weakened his authority.

By contrast, Menachem Begin operated in the Middle East's only democracy and governed in a fragile parliamentary coalition with ministers from the opposing Labor Party, which had dominated Israeli politics since its founding. His grip on power was much more tenuous than Sadat's. But Begin was an exceptionally tough politician. Growing up short and pale in Poland, he watched his father proudly bloodied when he fought back against anti-Semites who were tormenting a rabbi. He explained to Carter: "Mr. President, from that day forth, I have forever remembered those two things about my youth: the persecution of helpless Jews, and the courage of my father in defending their honor." Begin was radicalized by contact with Vladimir Jabotinsky, a militant Zionist leader, and, after earning a law degree, he became a Zionist activist with a scholarly bent and fluency in nine languages.

When the Nazis invaded Poland in 1939, Begin went to the Soviet Union, where he was imprisoned and sent to Siberia. In 1941 he and other Jewish prisoners were freed by the Soviets to go fight the Nazis in Palestine. His parents and most of the rest of his family died in the Holocaust.

At thirty, Begin — disguised as a bearded Hasidic Jew — was named commander of the Irgun, the underground paramilitary force inspired by Jabotinsky and committed to driving the British out of Palestine. With a British bounty on his head that made him a legend, Begin ordered Irgun attacks on British troops, Arab villages, and, most infamously, Jerusalem's King David Hotel, where, in 1946, a warning to clear civilians from the building wasn't heeded, and a powerful bomb killed ninety-one people, mostly civilians.

The Haganah, the official Jewish army, tried and failed to crush Begin's more radical Irgun, with the help of a talented officer named Moshe Dayan, who wore a black eyepatch after losing an eye in battle. Following Israel's 1948 War of Independence, Begin insisted he hadn't been a terrorist, a claim that even prominent Jews like Albert Einstein and Hannah Arendt refused to accept. In the decades that followed, Begin wasn't a war hero like Dayan and Weizman but a Likud Party backbencher whose implacable will and talent as an orator eventually took him to the pinnacle of Israeli politics.

On Monday, September 4, 1978, Carter taped a speech at the White House in garbled Spanish in the morning, then departed for Camp David, anxious about what lay ahead. He had left Walter Mondale nominally in charge back in Washington, where key votes needed high-level attention. The vice president would travel back and forth to Camp David; Carter would stay there for the duration of a conference that extended across thirteen exhausting days.

Jimmy was joined by Rosalynn and Amy, and Begin by his wife, Aliza. Sadat arrived without family; his wife, Jehan, had to attend to an ill granddaughter. The three official delegations totaled forty-four people, with another eighty in support staff and base personnel. Cabins usually

600

occupied by one or two people would now house several, with most sleeping on cots. No interpreters were needed because all negotiations were to be conducted in English. The guests all assumed the telephones in their cabins were tapped. They weren't, but the presumption of surveillance kept them from breaking the rules against contacting outsiders (except their own governments).

Carter hoped to use the bucolic camp to encourage informal, free-flowing dialogue. His efforts to tamp down the pressure by appearing in casual attire were less successful. More than once, the president wore a chocolate-brown sport shirt, tan slacks, and desert boots — a fashion crime in historical photographs. Begin, rejecting the ahead-of-its-time informality of Israeli political culture, usually appeared in a dark suit, white shirt, and tie. Sadat, with his jolly smile, ever-present pipe, and bespoke white leisure suits, cut the most dashing figure.

For any chance of success, Carter would have to stay neutral. It wouldn't be easy, for by this time, Sadat was practically a member of his family. Even Amy had a special relationship with the Egyptian president, who — when he visited the White House — always made a point of saying good night to her before she went to bed. One day at Camp David, Amy was playing a board game with a friend and eating crackers. Sadat snuck up behind her, bent down, and ate the cracker right out of her hand before it could reach her mouth. After the conference, Miss Lillian was so entranced that she asked her son, "Jimmy, is Anwar Sadat married?"

To set the table for the summit, Carter decided to begin with separate conversations with each leader shortly after arrival. On the terrace behind Aspen Lodge (Carter's cabin), Sadat told the president that he had a comprehensive proposal "here in my pocket" that would include full diplomatic relations and the end of the Arab boycott of Israel. "We can do it, Mr. President! We can do it!" he said.

But Sadat was demanding complete Israeli surrender on questions Carter had thought were yet to be negotiated. "Jimmy was shocked by Sadat's plan," Rosalynn reported in an unpublished diary that offers a fresh angle on the summit.

As for Begin, all he wanted to do at Camp David was agree on some very small things and a few broad principles, then announce that at least talks between Israel and Egypt had started again. For Carter, this would represent failure.

The next day, a nervous Carter asked Begin to come to the porch of Aspen Lodge a little before three in the afternoon, the scheduled time for the first three-way meeting. He wanted to warn him about Sadat's plan. The Egyptian leader arrived and slowly read aloud his entire proposal, which took an hour and a half. When he finished, Carter broke the tension by joking that Begin could just sign the document right there, which cracked everyone up. Begin complimented Sadat on the thoroughness of the proposal, and they slapped each other on the back, but the good cheer was a put-on.

When Jimmy and Rosalynn were alone, he silently mouthed his frustration to her, concerned that someone might be eavesdropping. The two leaders needed to "stop assing around."

Back at his cabin in the evening, Begin told Dayan, Weizman, and the rest of his delegation that Sadat's outrageous plan had even called for Israel to pay war reparations to Egypt, as if Israel had lost four wars rather than won them all. "What chutzpah! What impertinence!" Begin scoffed.

On day three, Carter stepped on a land mine. In their three-way meeting, he asked mildly if Begin might respond favorably to Sadat's courageous trip to Jerusalem with a concession. Begin grew indignant and said that no concession was necessary; it also took courage, he said, for Israel to welcome with open arms the Egyptian commander of a surprise attack on Yom Kippur, when all of his people were in synagogue.

Sadat downplayed Egypt's surprise attack of five years earlier as merely "a strategic deception." Now it was as if the bloodiest battles of the 1973 war were being fought again inside Aspen Lodge. A shouting match broke out, with Sadat the louder of the two. Sadat said all the good feelings from his Jerusalem trip were gone. He was offering Israel full diplomatic recognition, an end to the boycott of Israeli products, and security. But a continuing Israeli presence in the Sinai — garrisons, settlements, and the like — was non-negotiable. He shouted his bottom line: "Security, yes! Land, no!"

Rosalynn was working in an adjacent bedroom and could hear raised voices. "They were brutal with each other, personal, and Jimmy had to break into arguments at certain points," she recalled. He told her later that the two leaders had been "mean" to each other.

The three-way meeting was a disaster — three hours of bitter argument over both fundamental differences and peripheral issues. Sadat eventually calmed down long enough for an eloquent reverie that ended with his dream of all three leaders, representing three nations and three religious traditions, coming together again on Mount Sinai: "This is still my prayer!" It was a reminder that the deep faith of all three men was often the only thing holding the summit together.

The meeting had its moments of humor, especially when they laughed over how their wives must have reacted to pictures of each of them kissing Barbara Walters of ABC News at various points earlier in the year. But on substance, Begin and Sadat just kept butting heads. Begin pointed out that only 2,000 to 2,500 Israelis were living in a mere thirteen small settlements in the vast Sinai desert. Why couldn't they stay in their homes? At this point, Sadat said angrily that a "stalemate" had been reached, and everyone should depart Camp David. He rose and headed for the door, with Begin not far behind. Carter physically blocked their path.

That was when the president began to earn his rightful place in the long history of the Middle East. He was now, by his own admission, "desperate." But he knew intuitively that he could fall back on character traits — stubbornness, resourcefulness, attention to detail — that might help him play for time. He quickly retrofitted the role of neutral mediator and seized control of the process. Raising the already-high stakes, he announced that the United States was not a bystander; it had a strong security interest in the Middle East, and failure here could mean a global war.

Instead of mediating, Carter from now on would be initiating. He would do so with the Single Text technique pioneered by Roger Fisher, a Harvard Law School professor and expert on negotiations, who had explained it to Cyrus Vance that summer on Martha's Vineyard.* Following Fisher's approach, the arbiter drafts a document that he assumes agreement on unless one of the parties objects to something in it. After that section is amended, another draft is submitted, further narrowing the dispute.

Carter informed Begin and Sadat that he would prepare a summary of all the outstanding issues they now identified in the talks: about a dozen major areas of disagreement. Then he would come back with a "strong proposal" about what should be done.

When the three men reconvened in the afternoon, tempers flared again. Carter realized now that he would have to separate the two leaders like a parent or teacher with squabbling children. From then on, he would negotiate with each individually. It would be a long ten days before Sadat and Begin were in the same room at the same time again. In the meantime, Carter would meet for many hours alone with each one, a level of personal diplomacy unmatched by any other American president.

By coincidence, the near breakdown of the talks occurred on the same day that the news media was allowed its only visit. Reporters had been kept

*The Single Text technique, explored in the book *Getting to Yes: Negotiating Agreement Without Giving In,* by Roger Fisher and William Ury, would soon influence a whole generation of negotiators in diplomacy, law, and business.

several miles away from Camp David and fed largely useless scraps of information by spokesmen. Now they were bused in for a mere forty-five minutes and seated in bleachers to witness an evening ceremony featuring the US Marine Band. Even from a distance, the press corps could tell that all three leaders looked glum and the talks were not going well.

Beyond that, reporters got nothing. After the press buses were loaded to leave, Jerry Rafshoon noticed that Barbara Walters was not aboard. He found her hiding in a stall in the ladies' room. She'd hoped in vain to stay behind and find out what was happening.

At a reception that night, Rosalynn sat on a ledge on the Laurel Lodge patio and talked with her friend Anwar. She was sorry to see him so sad and noticed his unwillingness even to use Begin's name. "I've given so much, and 'that man' acts as though I have done nothing," he said. Later that evening, Carter, Mondale, Vance, Brown, and Brzezinski implored the Egyptians to give them more time.

"My good friend Jimmy, we have already had three long sessions," Sadat replied. "I cannot leave conquered land to Israel." Carter spoke up for Begin — "an honorable man, tenacious" — and past midnight won a commitment from Sadat to stay a little longer and keep an open mind.

After a rough day, Jimmy offered Rosalynn his take before bed: Begin might be happy that Sadat's proposal was so harsh because it gave him an escape route. He could tell the Israeli public that he had tried for peace, but Sadat didn't want it. And Sadat was being so "tough and mean" because he calculated that "Begin didn't want to

606

negotiate in the first place, so why give in on anything?"

He told Rosalynn that he and Sadat could have reached a peace agreement in ten minutes, and that Sadat claimed he and Weizman could have done the same. As she wrote in her diary: "When Sadat trusts someone — and he trusts Jimmy and Weizman — he will work with them and go all out with them. When he doesn't — and he doesn't trust Begin at all — he can be abusive and feels like all is in vain, so why waste the time." By contrast, she felt Begin harbored "no such hard feelings" but was simply "locked into positions by his past and is absolutely rigid about them."

It all added up to a toxic environment when the Israeli and Egyptian leaders were in each other's presence. Friday was supposed to be the day the three leaders went fly-fishing together, but the tension in the talks led to the trip being scrapped. Carter played tennis and didn't enjoy it. A bike ride turned into an occasion to vent to Brzezinski about how Begin thought failure would play better than success for him at home. The Carters and Cy Vance did something rare: they drank at lunch.

To save the summit, the president knew he had to find a way to tamp down arguments about the West Bank. He decided to tell the Egyptians that it was not right for Sadat to negotiate on behalf of Syria's Assad and Jordan's King Hussein; they weren't present and couldn't speak for themselves. This meant that any agreement on the Israeli occupation of the West Bank would have to be a vague, nonbinding framework for self-rule and more talks, not a peace treaty resolving the fate of the Palestinians.

That night, the Begins hosted Shabbat dinner for the Israeli and American delegations at Laurel Lodge. The Carters enjoyed the singing and rejoicing and connected with the Begins, at least for now. Begin told Jimmy, "She's a remarkable woman, Mrs. Carter." The president naturally agreed. "She's not Jewish?" Begin joked. Rosalynn laughed but reflected years later that she wasn't sure if Begin really liked them: "Jimmy and I come across as exotic to Jewish people."

As he worked all the next day with his advisers formulating the American peace plan, Carter made what would turn out to be a historic decision. He realized that for any chance of success, the parties would have to strike two separate agreements: a highly specific bolted-down treaty on Israel pulling entirely out of the Sinai, and a second, much more ambiguous "accord" on the West Bank. The president, always straining to be comprehensive, would have to do what King Solomon abhorred: split his baby in two — as he had done in the case of the Panama Canal Treaties.

If ancient enmities and the bitterness of four wars weren't enough, cabin fever set in. Begin joked that Camp David was "a concentration camp deluxe," and his delegation chuckled about digging escape tunnels. Despite all the meetings, both sides had plenty of time to watch a nonstop loop of movies in Laurel Lodge. Four chess matches between Begin and Brzezinski were seen as major entertainment. (Each won two, with Begin claiming falsely that he hadn't played in many years.*) "It all reminded me of the World

*The two men had met in the 1950s, when Brzezinski traveled to Israel to study the Irgun, which was mod-

608

War II films about submarines," Weizman recalled. "Here we were, in the enclosed, claustrophobic atmosphere of Camp David, with Jimmy Carter at the periscope."

Carter was always looking for a route ahead to avoid icebergs. First, he would need to restore trust, which had been damaged badly in the first four days of the summit. Then he would have to convince Begin that the security situation in the Sinai desert was different for Israel than in the populous West Bank — that Israel could safely withdraw all forces from the Sinai, and the United States would help him refortify those forces along the new border with Egypt. The good news was that it seemed Dayan and Weizman were prepared to help him make this case. Or were they?

After church on Sunday, Carter agreed to a request by Begin and took the group to the battlefield at Gettysburg, a half-hour drive over the border in Pennsylvania. Begin left part of his team behind at Camp David to draft a statement he had dictated that essentially rejected all peace proposals and ended the conference. He even instructed members of his delegation privately to make plans to pack their bags. But he told Weizman he would show Carter the courtesy of reading his new proposal before leaving Camp David.

The president squeezed into his limo between Begin and Sadat, who both kept the conversation pleasant with anecdotes about their time in jail. (Begin called prison "my university.") Carter had instructed that there be no negotiations during

eled on the Polish underground.

the Gettysburg outing, though he hoped it would remind them of the consequences of failed diplomacy. The geography of the battlefield was completely familiar to the former military leaders in both delegations, all of whom had studied it in their own countries and were excited to visit.

As a National Parks tour guide escorted them around, Carter, who had earlier walked the battlefield with the southern historian Shelby Foote, interjected knowledgeable insights. Begin stayed quiet during most of the tour, but at the cemetery, he began speaking softly. "Four score and seven years ago, our fathers brought forth on this continent a new nation." Suddenly all eyes were on Begin, who recited Lincoln's entire Gettysburg Address from memory and with great emotion.

Back at Camp David, Carter and his team presented the American plan to the Israelis. Begin disliked it immediately. But he worried about Carter cutting a separate deal with Sadat, so he canceled plans to depart. Instead, he invoked a 1975 agreement that President Ford had made between Israel and the United States that gave Israel the chance to see any American diplomatic proposals regarding the Middle East before they were submitted to other parties. He asked that Carter not show his plan to Sadat until the Israelis had amended it.

Carter, proud of his handiwork, replied sharply that he hadn't drafted the document expecting it to be changed much — an expectation about to be dashed again and again. The major stumbling block was the Carter draft's reliance on United Nations Resolution 242, from 1967, which decreed the "inadmissibility of acquisition of territory by war." Resolution 242, perhaps the best-known UN document ever, put forward the "land for peace" swap at the heart of this and every other negotiation with Israel: give land seized in 1967, get full diplomatic recognition and peace. Begin wasn't only not pulling out of the occupied territories, as required by Resolution 242; with the new settlements, he was moving farther in.

Carter grew furious with the Israeli leader. "Do you reject United Nations Resolution 242?" he asked, his voice rising. "To delete this phrase would mean that we have no basis for negotiation now or in the future. What you say convinces me that Sadat was right: what you want is land!"

Begin now put on his lawyer hat. He said placidly that because the United Nations had decided that Israel was not the aggressor in the 1967 war, he saw 242 as merely a starting point for talks.

Afterward, as the Carter team watched the US Open tennis tournament on television, Brzezinski said he had noticed that when Carter got mad, Begin got polite. Vance thought Weizman was embarrassed by his prime minister's conduct.

As they resumed discussions that evening, Carter was still angry. He told Begin he "won't beat around the bush": he would not have invited him to Camp David in the first place if he had known he wanted to stay in the occupied territories forever.

"What you want to do is make the West Bank part of Israel," Carter said coldly. "It looks like subterfuge."

He wondered what had happened to the "full autonomy" Begin had pledged earlier to the Palestinians on the West Bank. Begin's view was that "autonomy is not sovereignty," and, given the West Bank's very close proximity to Israel, his country needed to maintain ultimate control over all security questions. This would be the essential Israeli position for decades to come.

Carter found himself giving his dictionary and thesaurus a workout, as he would for the rest of the summit. The Americans and Israelis argued over almost every sentence in the long US proposal, engaging in Talmudic debates over the meaning of *autonomy, self-rule, authority, withdrawal, refugees, devolution,* and *minor modifications.*

Begin's combination of intransigence and legalistic hairsplitting exasperated Carter beyond anything his aides had ever seen. When, after a long discussion of the status of East Jerusalem, Begin said again that he could not accept the language of Resolution 242, the president crumpled up the papers in front of him and threw down his pencil. "You will have to accept it!" he shouted. Begin told him to stop threatening him, and Carter stewed.

Carter wrote in his diary that he admired Weizman and Dayan but doubted Begin's "rationality." Rosalynn told Brzezinski later that her husband thought Begin was a "psycho" that night.

At three thirty in the morning, after six hours of haggling and recriminations, the parties staggered off. Despite the late hour, Carter asked Dayan to speak with him on the Aspen Lodge terrace. He liked Dayan — considered him a friend — and believed that if the general were Israel's prime minister, a peace deal would have been signed already. Dayan told him he was wrong about Begin. He did want peace, but he had promised at home to protect the Sinai settlements. If the settlers were allowed to wait a while before leaving, maybe something could be worked out.

As the one-eyed war hero strolled out to meet the driver of his golf cart at four o'clock, he walked right into a tree. Blood streamed from Dayan's nose, a symbol of more confrontations to come.

Carter napped for two hours, then got up early and incorporated the Israeli objections into the American draft. He met alone with Sadat and asked him an intriguing question: Would he allow Jews from any nation, including Israel, to live in Cairo? Sadat replied, "Of course." Carter then pointed out that it was not logical to prevent them from living for a time in sandy Sinai settlements where they were not displacing anyone.

"Some things in the Middle East are not logical," Sadat replied.

After tennis and lemonade, Carter paid an unscheduled visit to Weizman, who had stripped off his clothes for a nap. "Mr. Weizman!" Carter said on entering the cabin, which was strewn with dirty clothes and empty liquor bottles. A startled Weizman quickly dressed and took a walk with the president. Carter learned that Weizman and Egypt's minister of war, General Mohammed Abdel Ghany el-Gamasy, had made important progress on the delineation of military zones in the Sinai and the arms that would be allowed in them — critical elements of any deal.

But Carter remained pessimistic. "Jimmy said he thought the whole thing was breaking down," Rosalynn wrote in her diary. "We didn't eat much dinner! He said he didn't want to see a movie."

After thirty-six hours with almost no sleep, the president went to bed more tired than he had ever been in his life.

On day eight, a still-exhausted Carter again arose early for his usual "thinking time." He had to face reality: a summit planned for three or four days had lasted a full week with no real signs of progress. His original idea to help Begin and Sadat talk through their differences had proved to be a pipe dream. As the author Lawrence Wright put it, "Their hatred and distrust for each other really did seem to be three thousand years old."

Carter felt even worse when he went on a long bike ride and pedaled past Sadat's cabin, where he saw the Egyptian president and his advisers on the porch shouting at one another. Carter's worries intensified when Sadat, arriving late to their meeting, "seemed very troubled and was somewhat evasive in his greetings." He held a piece of paper in his hand that Carter feared was an announcement that would end the Camp David negotiations.

Meanwhile, the Israelis were preparing to do just that. Begin ordered his advisers to draft a statement saying he welcomed future negotiations, but the conference was over. Dayan told the US ambassador to Israel, Samuel Lewis, that he was departing for Israel right away and went to his cabin to pack. When Vance heard that, he rushed to the cabin and talked Dayan out of it.

Knowing that failure was imminent, the president now moved quickly. He sat down with a yellow legal pad and a large map of the Sinai peninsula and, in three hours, handwrote a new proposed agreement on the Sinai. It was a rough draft, but Carter figured that if Sadat agreed in principle, at least he would have something specific to show the Israelis.

Carter walked the six-page document over to Sadat's cabin. The document essentially said UN Resolution 242 applied and that Israel and Egypt would explicitly commit to "a peace treaty between them" after three months of negotiating over the Sinai. Sadat casually made a couple of changes and said, "It's all right." Carter promised to bring back a typed, much more detailed version.

Things didn't go as well with the Israelis. After Carter went to Laurel Lodge for a friendly dinner with the delegation, Begin asked to see him alone. "This is the most serious talk I have ever had, except once when I discussed the future of Israel with Jabotinsky," Begin informed him. He acknowledged that Israel had repeatedly endorsed Resolution 242 in the past but insisted it could not be included in any peace treaty.

Carter felt the meeting was "unpleasant and repetitive." He pointed out to Begin that opinion polls in Israel had long shown support for a Sinai deal along the lines he was proposing. Finally, the president stood up, signaling that he had heard enough. He accused Begin of throwing away everything: peace for his war-weary people, the cheers of the world, long-sought diplomatic recognition from Arab nations, long-needed access to the Suez Canal, and permanent security for Israel. For what? Just to keep a few illegal settlers on Egyptian land in the Sinai?

Rosalynn had spent the day in Washington, where she helped Amy get her ears pierced. When she returned, she went for a late-night walk with her husband. He was angry and discouraged.

■ ■ ■ ■

At this point, almost any other president would have cut his losses and returned to the White House to attend to the dozens of other problems piling up on his desk. Key votes on civil service, natural gas deregulation, and the veto override of a defense bill all awaited Carter's attention.

Instead, he dug in and got creative. He decided to violate a centuries-old diplomatic tradition requiring that leaders negotiate only with leaders of comparable official status. He handpicked one member of each delegation to help him and Cyrus Vance draft the final "Framework for Peace" agreement for the West Bank and Gaza.

Carter and Vance chose the two most brilliant legal minds on the premises: Aharon Barak — soon to become a justice of the Supreme Court of Israel — and Osama el-Baz, a Harvard-trained lawyer. Barak (no relation to Ehud Barak, a later Israeli prime minister) had Begin's trust, and el-Baz was the most militant of the Egyptians, which meant that if he agreed to something, the rest of the delegation would be more likely to go along.

The four men worked together for nearly eleven hours, deep in the weeds. They settled on vague language regarding Jerusalem and finessed the Resolution 242 problem in part by placing the entire text of the historic resolution in the appendix, where it would be present but not highlighted. It felt to Carter like they were getting very close.

Carter was impressed by Barak but suspicious of el-Baz, who made it seem as if Sadat had reversed his position on a subsidiary question involving the West Bank. When el-Baz admitted he had never discussed it with Sadat, Carter turned icy — such anger was now almost his default mode at the summit — and said el-Baz was being disloyal to his leader. When he heard afterward that el-Baz had once helped organize PLO terrorists, his irritation turned to dread.*

At four o'clock Rosalynn awoke, and soon Jimmy did, too, thinking about Sadat. He told Rosalynn, "I'm worried about his safety." Carter remembered that when he had gone to Sadat's cabin at nine thirty that evening, the lights were out, and el-Baz told him Sadat had retired and wasn't to be disturbed. This was odd, Carter thought. Sadat was a night owl. He summoned Brzezinski, who arrived still in his pajamas. Together they instructed the Secret Service to place extra security near Sadat's cabin.

The next morning, Carter was relieved to see Sadat strolling past Aspen Lodge. He joined him on a long walk, where they envisioned constructing a major highway from Jordan to the Sinai — a tangible symbol of peace and mutual economic development that would remain an unfulfilled dream. They discussed how Carter's southern heritage gave him a sensitivity to the problems of the Middle East. His region had, Sadat said, "lived under an occupying power and been torn apart by racial prejudice [but] was resurgent."

Carter then returned to his study to work on new drafts of the Framework agreement for the West Bank and Gaza, which he planned to show

*El-Baz was not being disloyal to Sadat, and he was not sympathetic to terrorists. In the years that followed, he cooperated closely with the Israelis.

to Begin and Sadat that day. As Rosalynn prepared to chopper to Washington for a luncheon, he happily beckoned her to sit on his lap. "I think it's all coming together now," he said.

In fact, it was all coming apart. For days, Weizman had believed that a Moshe Dayan and Sadat one-on-one — a meeting between two old warriors — might be the breakthrough that was needed. He wanted Dayan to meet with Sadat to talk through old grievances. Carter agreed with Weizman that Dayan and Sadat — both pragmatists — might agree on innovative solutions for the West Bank. Bad idea.

When the two former battlefield combatants sat down together, they began not by discussing the West Bank but by arguing about the other deal: the one involving the Israeli withdrawal from the Sinai. The poisonous feelings from the 1973 war were still so present that the meeting collapsed in acrimony. Dayan was backing construction from scratch of a large new Israeli resort city to be located in the northern Sinai. Sadat's hard line on making all Israelis leave the area angered him, and he suddenly echoed Begin's old rejection of any treaty. Sadat, still frosted from his meeting with Dayan, told Carter he would negotiate only on *when* the Israeli garrisons and settlements would be withdrawn from the Sinai, not *if*.

Having blown his matchmaking, Weizman — the most eager for peace of any of the Israelis — grew depressed and spent the next twenty-four hours watching movies in Laurel Lodge. For the third or fourth time (everyone had lost count), the Israelis were ready to settle for a meaningless fig leaf agreement or just leave without anything.

When Rosalynn returned in the afternoon, she

618

found Jimmy, Ham, and Zbig in the swimming pool. What happened today? she asked. The response was: "All bad. We've failed." Brzezinski pulled her aside to say that Jimmy was really discouraged and ready to give up. Talk turned to how Jerry Rafshoon might "present the failure."

Everyone was worn out and ready to go home. Carter directed Mondale to handle the political fallout. Vance came by Aspen Lodge, and he and Carter had a couple of martinis. The secretary of state said that they had accomplished all that could be expected: a lot of small, substantive agreements and a sense that Egypt was now a full partner in the search for peace.

Vance could see that Carter's natural impatience was in conflict with the patience required for diplomacy. Not for the first time, Vance said his long experience in diplomacy had taught him "it always seems to be darkest before it's light." This was cold comfort for the president. "Jimmy told me he was just sick of the whole situation and ready to quit and go home," Rosalynn noted. The blame for the summit's failure, they believed, rested squarely with Begin and his obsession with settlements in the Sinai.

On their second Friday in the woods, Carter made plans to salvage something. He would ask for the final proposals from both sides that day, draft something vague on Saturday, have the parties issue some kind of joint communique on Sunday, and somehow rationalize spending two weeks at Camp David in an address to the nation on Monday. It was better than nothing.

Carter was meeting with Secretary of Defense Harold Brown on unrelated matters when Vance walked in, his face white. Sadat had asked him for a helicopter to take him immediately to the Washington airport. The Egyptians were all packed and ready to go.

Carter wrote later, "This was one of the worst moments of my life. I went to my bedroom, knelt down, and prayed, and — for some reason — decided to change from my sport shirt and jeans to a suit and tie."

He rushed to Sadat's porch and brushed past the Egyptian advisers to meet with him alone. Carter had to pull the emergency cord. He told the Egyptian president that if he unilaterally broke off negotiations, it would severely harm relations between Egypt and the United States, and Egypt would have to ally with the Soviet Union again. He said Sadat was "violating his personal promise to me" and damaging one of his most precious possessions: "his friendship and our mutual trust."

As on day three, Sadat was adamant about leaving, but "I was dead serious, and he knew it," Carter wrote in his memoirs. "I had never been more serious in my life." He argued that departing would damage Sadat's reputation as the world's foremost peacemaker and prove his Arab critics right when they charged that going to Jerusalem was foolish.

Sadat looked shaken. He explained that he was leaving because Dayan told him the Israelis wouldn't sign a substantive agreement, and he didn't want to sign something that was just peace platitudes. Sadat was worried that Israel would brag about peace without giving up anything.

Carter, thinking quickly, committed to him that if either nation rejected any part of the agreements, none of the proposals would stay in effect.

This formulation would later become standard in many government and private negotiations: the parties agree to everything — or they agree to nothing.

The president wanted to make sure the Israelis couldn't brag about having achieved peace unless they agreed to give something up. It was an imaginative way of letting Sadat out of his box. Sadat stood silently for what seemed to Carter like a long time, then agreed that with this commitment: "I will stick with you to the end." These were sweet words for Carter. They pledged themselves to secrecy — Jimmy told Rosalynn she couldn't even record it in her diary — and went back to their cabins.

Carter was still proceeding with "failure plans," but he didn't want to give up on either the broad Framework agreement on the Palestinians or the separate, more specific deal on Israeli withdrawal from the Sinai.

To keep things light and social, Carter and Mondale went to Sadat's cottage to watch the Muhammad Ali–Leon Spinks heavyweight title fight, live from the Superdome in New Orleans. Sadat, a huge Ali fan, served them tea made from boiled mint and honey. He seemed calmer. After Sadat retired, Carter finally reached Ali at one thirty in the morning to congratulate him on his win and invite his young daughter to come visit Amy. Ali was thrilled that they had watched his fight from Camp David.

Before bed, Jimmy told Rosalynn that while parts of their time here had been "among the most unpleasant he had ever experienced in his life," he knew there was no way either Begin or Sadat would have stayed were it not for him.

Day twelve would determine whether the agreements reached at Camp David would be window dressing or historic.

Negotiators worked all day on the language of both the broad Framework agreement and the specific Israel-Egypt peace treaty on the Sinai. Some Framework disputes were too difficult to resolve. On Jerusalem, the most sensitive of all issues, the parties resorted to side letters. Sadat wrote one endorsing permanent Jewish control of the Western Wall, the holiest site in Judaism, and the United States wrote one reconfirming its long-standing view that Arab East Jerusalem was part of the West Bank. The latter would soon almost dynamite the whole summit.

Rosalynn had planned a bike ride with Jimmy, Amy, and Amy's friend Mika Brzezinski, Zbig's eleven-year-old daughter, but Jimmy begged off. They were down to the short strokes. Carter and Dayan discussed how much time Israeli settlers — some of whom had been there for more than a decade — would have to leave the Sinai. (The answer: it varied.) A newly invigorated Weizman told Carter that if Begin went home and tried to kill the treaty, he would resign as defense minister and try to form a new government.

Carter, sensing victory, asked Sadat if there was anything extra he could do for him. The Egyptian president said that his ailing economy needed wheat and maize. Carter told him he would get it from Congress. Sadat agreed to let UN forces stay in parts of the Sinai and, critically, agreed not to have the Egyptians do the dismantling of the Sinai settlements; that would be handled by the Israelis.

"We're going to get it!" Jimmy told Rosalynn. "Up until now," Rosalynn wrote in her diary, "he felt Sadat had been planning, more or less, to embarrass Begin."

At eight thirty in the evening, Begin, Dayan, and Barak from the Israeli delegation came to Aspen Lodge for the final negotiating session at Camp David. Many differences had been resolved. "You've restored my faith in lawyers!" an exuberant Carter told Barak. On the surface, Begin continued to resist on the Sinai settlements, charging the Americans with issuing "ultimatums" and asking him to commit "political suicide." In truth, Begin's political situation was in flux. Earlier in the day, Dayan and Weizman arranged a call to Israel's powerful minister of agriculture, Ariel Sharon, who was at home on his farm. When Sharon signed off on the Sinai deal, provided that it be submitted to the Knesset, Begin's opposition to it weakened.

After nearly three hours of arguing, Begin finally agreed that he would present what he viewed as the central question to the Knesset within two weeks: "If agreement is reached on all other Sinai issues, will the settlers be withdrawn?"

Carter asked Begin if — back in the scrum of Israeli politics — he would take a position on the question. Begin replied that he wasn't sure, but he would sign an agreement and let all members of his Likud Party vote their consciences. That was all Carter needed to hear. The deal on the Sinai was done.

The larger Framework accord on the West Bank and Gaza was dicier. Israel committed to withdrawing many of its military forces from the West

Bank and, for the first time, formally recognized that the Palestinians were entitled to "autonomy," even if Begin haggled over nearly every word relating to it. After a five-year transition period, the Palestinians would get statehood, though no one at Camp David yet used that term. In the meantime, the parties agreed to new, separate negotiations between both Israel and Jordan and Israel and the Palestinians — important mileposts in the peace process.

Carter cared intensely about this part of the deal — the part that he believed (mistakenly, it turned out) could eventually bring lasting peace to the Mideast — and he insisted on a clause saying there would be no new Israeli settlements on the West Bank constructed "during the negotiations." He and Vance believed "during the negotiations" clearly meant during the five-year transition period to full autonomy. But Begin interpreted "during the negotiations" to mean no new settlements for just three months — the length of time set aside to finish negotiating the Israel-Egypt Sinai deal. That imprecise language, likely the result of fatigue and the lateness of the hour, would cause continued bad feelings between Carter and Begin.

It was Sunday, September 17, 1978, the thirteenth and final day of what had been expected to be a three-day conference. Begin and Sadat hadn't seen each other since the trip to Gettysburg a week earlier, and Carter hoped they would sit down together and sign a historic agreement that afternoon in Washington.

On a morning stroll, the president told Sadat about the late-night breakthrough on the Sinai.

When Sadat was convinced that the dismantling of the settlements could pass the Knesset, he said he would sign the deal.

His advisers were despondent over his decision. But because Sadat was effectively the dictator of Egypt, with near-total control of the parliament, they had little room to resist. (Had Egypt been a democracy, the Camp David Accords would never have been completed.) Mohamed Kamel, the Egyptian foreign minister who had served time in jail with Sadat and considered him almost like an older brother, thought Sadat was desperate for a deal to cement his place in history. A day earlier, Kamel had resigned in protest, though he agreed to Sadat's request that he not announce it until they returned to Egypt. This was the last chance Kamel and others in the sullen Egyptian delegation had to sink the agreement.

They argued that Begin had not committed to withdrawing fully from the West Bank and insisted that Carter had sold out the Palestinians to please American Jews and get reelected. The latter was untrue and entirely unconvincing: everyone knew perfectly well that an immediate Palestinian state was a nonstarter in both Israel and the United States in 1978. That these were the Egyptians' best final arguments for rejecting the deal showed how little they had actually given up at Camp David in exchange for winning back twenty-three thousand square miles of Egyptian territory in the Sinai.

When Kamel and the other Egyptian advisers raised their concerns with Sadat, he turned on them. "All of you are plumbers! You don't do anything with anything," he said. "I am a statesman. I know my objective." He told them that if he didn't sign, "Your grandchildren will be fighting in the Sinai, and there will be war after war." This was Sadat at his most courageous — risking everything, including his own life, for peace.

At noon, Vance gave the Israelis the side letter from the United States on the status of Jerusalem, and it landed like an artillery shell. The letter had no legal significance and was merely a restatement of long-standing US policy initiated by President Johnson's UN ambassador Arthur Goldberg and repeated by his successors: it said that Arab East Jerusalem, taken in the 1967 war, was occupied territory. It was attached to the Framework agreement at the last minute because Sadat asked for it.

The Israelis were irate over the side letter, which they considered a grave insult. It was one thing to address the issue years earlier in obscure letters from obscure ambassadors; this was much more explosive — including a retreat from Jerusalem in the most momentous document since the founding of Israel. For nearly two thousand years, Jews at the Passover seder have universally exclaimed, "Next year in Jerusalem!" Now the United States seemed to be saying that the ancient Jewish capital — the spiritual center of their faith — was not truly theirs.

Dayan informed Vance that the Israelis would sign no agreement that contained any such letter, and Barak reinforced the point to Carter. Begin told his delegation to pack up and get ready to leave immediately.

Carter seemed out of options. If he withdrew the letter, Sadat couldn't sign without betraying the Palestinians, who had already received much less than Sadat and the Egyptians had hoped for.

The president was already preparing the signing ceremony for that evening in Washington. Rafshoon had alerted the networks to a major announcement. But now the summit would end in humiliation.

Then came one of those human moments that so often determine the course of events. Ken Hays, the deputy chief of protocol, had earlier received a request from the Israeli delegation for signed presidential photographs for Begin's grandchildren. Susan Clough had the good sense to ask Hays to find out their names. Carter disliked autographing pictures, and, according to Clough, he wasn't in the mood for it. But he quickly agreed to his secretary's suggestion that he personally walk the pictures over to Begin — and he signed them with "Love and Best Wishes" instead of his standard "Best Wishes."

Begin received Carter coolly, but when he looked down and saw the kind inscription Carter had written for his granddaughter on the top photograph, he somberly spoke her name aloud and that of a couple of his other grandchildren, telling the president a bit about each. His lips trembled, and his eyes filled with tears. So did Carter's. He had hoped to write, "This is where your grandfather and I brought peace to the Middle East." They exchanged a few words about grandchildren and war. Begin was suddenly friendlier but repeated that the Jerusalem letter was fatal. As he was leaving, Carter told Begin that he and Barak had redrafted the letter on Jerusalem. He asked Begin to please take a look, then walked back to his cabin, still dejected.

About fifteen minutes later, Begin called Carter and said that the new, more anodyne letter — with the American ambassadors mentioned only in passing — was acceptable. Was the deal back on? Maybe not, because Begin, at the eleventh hour, had decided to submit new language on a couple of clauses. With things hanging by a thread, it seemed like these final caveats would be deal breakers with the Egyptians.

When the president learned that Begin had — for the first time — gone to Sadat's cabin, he broke into a sprint to get there, concerned they might quarrel again. Upon arriving, he ran into a happy Begin in a golf cart returning from what he described as a "love feast" with Sadat, who had moved past clauses and caveats to the bigger picture.

After twenty-three drafts, Menachem Begin was finally on board, overcoming — at least for now — his fear of opposition from old friends at home and showing what Carter called "a surprising flexibility that made it possible for us to achieve success." Begin wrote no memoirs and never said publicly that the individually inscribed photographs for his grandchildren influenced him, but Carter came to believe they were critical to the outcome.

The Sinai deal was done, but Begin had one more gambit: a move that Carter later considered a betrayal. He sent the president a letter in late afternoon of the final day clarifying that the moratorium on West Bank settlements would be for only three months. Carter told Barak that this was not what they had agreed to the night before, which was no new settlements until full autonomy was achieved — in five years. Three months and five years were awfully far apart, but it was too late to revisit.

More than two years later, as he prepared to leave office, Carter got some clarity on what Begin had wanted at Camp David: "Begin showed courage in giving up the Sinai," he wrote in his diary. "He did it to keep the West Bank."

In the flush of triumph, Carter was much too optimistic about the chances of true regional peace by the early 1980s. "If the Palestinian authority is well run and controls terrorism, it will be extremely difficult for Israel to slice away any significant territory after five years of Palestinian consolidation," he wrote on the final day of the summit in a portion of his diary that he — not surprisingly — chose not to publish. "The process, if well conducted, becomes virtually irreversible."

As it turned out, the Palestinians did not "control terrorism," the Israelis continued to "slice away" territory for their settlements, the peace process was not "well conducted," and there was nothing "irreversible" about it. In fact, Carter recognized later that Camp David may have inadvertently hurt the cause of a Palestinian state — a cause to which he would dedicate himself in the years ahead.

What he didn't grasp then was that taking the Egyptian army off the table as a threat to Israel did more than bring peace between warring countries and ensure the security of Israel from its most formidable foe. It also removed Egypt's powerful military as a deterrent to Israel's launching preemptive strikes against Palestinian fighters in Lebanon and other countries and to building many more settlements on the West Bank.

These were questions for another day. First came completion of what would be known as the Camp

David Accords. Rosalynn phoned Jimmy to recommend that he have the documents signed at Camp David in case the parties changed their minds. Jimmy told her he would have the stack of papers initialed before they boarded the helicopters to ride back to the White House through a thunderstorm. Cyrus Vance made sure all the i's were dotted and t's crossed. At five thirty he told Carter, "That's it." Carter called Rosalynn first and said, "We're coming home!" She burst into tears. Then all three leaders embraced and prepared for a triumphant return.

In a sign of just how oblivious he was to the theater of the presidency, Carter had earlier in the day directed that an afternoon ceremony be scheduled at the State Department. There the three foreign ministers (he didn't know Kamel had quietly resigned) would sign the agreements. An agitated Rafshoon immediately overruled the president and scheduled a prime-time live signing ceremony and remarks by the three leaders in the East Room.

Upon everyone's arrival at the White House at around ten thirty, the mood finally turned celebratory. When Begin saw his wife, he cried, "Mama, we'll go down in history books!" Dayan told Ambassador Samuel Lewis that Carter was one of the smartest, shrewdest, and ablest people he had ever met, and he couldn't understand why Americans had doubts about him. Not since John F. Kennedy spent thirteen days on the Cuban Missile Crisis in October 1962 had an American president devoted so much time to a single issue. But it seemed worth it now.

Flanked by Begin and Sadat, Carter explained to the world that they were signing two agreements, one between Israel and Egypt and one that spelled out how Israeli forces would withdraw from most (though not all) of the West Bank and Gaza and negotiate directly with the Palestinians and Jordan as part of a five-year path to "full autonomy" for the Palestinians.

Staring down at his prepared statement, Sadat gestured toward Begin, but mostly he focused on Carter and his courage. So did Begin. "The Camp David conference should be renamed," Begin said, as Carter beamed beside him. "It was the Jimmy Carter conference. The president took a great risk for himself and did it with great civil courage." Begin was impressed by Carter's diligence: "I think he worked harder than our forefathers did in Egypt building the pyramids."*

Carter would believe for the rest of his life that his grit and the courage of Begin and Sadat were secondary: "We finally got an agreement because we all shared faith in the same God — we all considered ourselves the sons of Abraham."

En route to the Capitol the next night for an address to a joint session of Congress, Jimmy asked Rosalynn if she knew how the verse from the Sermon on the Mount that begins "Blessed are the peacemakers . . ." ended. Rosalynn remembered the line concluding with "for they shall inherit the earth." Jimmy was fairly sure it was "Blessed are the peacemakers, for they shall be called the children of God." With Begin and Sadat already in the balcony and no time to check a Bible (Google was twenty years in the future),

*Like many Jews, Begin believed that Jewish slaves in Egypt built the pyramids. The archeological record shows the laborers were Egyptian.

631

he went with his gut, turned out to be right, and the words brought a thunderous ovation.

Afterward, the House chaplain told Cyrus Vance that in all his years there, he had never seen such an outpouring of emotion. But there was dread, too. "When we left Camp David, I was certain Sadat would be killed, and I was certain he knew it," Mondale said later.

In late September Carter surged 11 points in the Gallup poll to a 56 percent approval rating, but it didn't last, in part because of growing skepticism that Israel and Egypt would actually sign the treaty as planned. Within hours of the agreement, Begin began telling supporters in the United States and Israel that he had given up too much. The Knesset nonetheless quickly approved the dismantlement of the Sinai settlements, which should have paved the way for the final treaty. But it did not.

Six months after his historic achievement, Jimmy Carter — amid enormous political risk — would have to travel to the Middle East and put the whole thing back together again.

# 28
## RECOGNIZING CHINA

As a boy, Jimmy sent a nickel every week to Baptist missionaries building hospitals and schools in China. As an officer aboard a submarine and celebrating his twenty-fifth birthday, he glimpsed the campfires of the Chinese Communists on the brink of victory in their 1949 revolution. And now, as president, he saw a chance to build on Richard Nixon's historic opening to the People's Republic of China by normalizing relations with the most populous nation on earth. This, he said later, turned out to be the most historically significant decision of his presidency. It allowed China's entrance into the global economy and helped ignite the most rapid and extensive modernization in the history of the world.

With China now poised to be the world's largest economy, it's hard to imagine the wrenching poverty of the mainland in the 1970s. During the Cultural Revolution, which lasted from 1966 to Mao Tse-tung's death ten years later, the Chinese leader had killed or exiled to the countryside a whole generation of "counterrevolutionaries" — educated elites and middle-class strivers — sending China's per capita income below that of sub-Saharan Africa. Save for the sound of bicycle bells, the broad prewar boulevards of Beijing and Shanghai were eerily quiet in 1979 because they carried few cars.* Cheap black-and-white television sets with snowy images remained luxuries shared by several families or an entire village. Private enterprise was strictly forbidden, which meant that shops and restaurants were run by the government and located mostly in ramshackle tourist hotels off-limits to ordinary Chinese. Hardly any new office or apartment buildings had been built anywhere in the country in the forty years since the outbreak of World War II. Few Chinese had ever glimpsed a Westerner in person. Almost all still wore rough-hewn Mao suits and were barred from leaving the country.

For twenty-two years after the Chinese Revolution, there was little contact between the United States and China — no travel, trade, or cultural exchanges of any kind. In 1971 Mao allowed the US Ping-Pong team to visit, followed by National Security Adviser Henry Kissinger and, the next year, President Nixon himself. For the seven years after this historic breakthrough, the United States pursued a peculiar "two China policy": tentative contacts with Communist China (George H. W. Bush headed the US liaison office in Peking in 1974 and 1975) and continued full diplomatic relations with Taiwan. Chiang Kaishek, the wartime ruler of Nationalist China who had fled to Taiwan after losing to the Communists, ran his small, increasingly prosperous authoritarian state under the protection of the United States. When Chiang died in 1975, his sons took over, but

*The official translation of *Peking* changed to *Beijing* that year.

without his authority or deep support among American anti-Communists.

During the second 1976 presidential debate, Carter had accused President Ford of "frittering away" an opportunity to improve ties with mainland China. Ford's 1975 trip there had yielded little, in part because the United States was pursuing detente with the Soviet Union, which now had hostile relations with Peking and resented American presidents playing "the China card." China, in turn, was angry that Washington wouldn't, in the words of Chinese state media, "make up its mind" about which China it recognized. Ford's hands were tied by domestic politics. Ronald Reagan and the right-wing China lobby badgered him throughout his presidency to protect the interests of Taiwan. Had Ford won the 1976 election, full diplomatic relations and economic and cultural ties with the mainland would likely have taken much longer to establish.

Carter didn't feel that kind of heat from Democrats, though Walter Mondale cautioned that it might be a second-term issue and Cyrus Vance argued, accurately, that improving relations with China would complicate SALT II talks with the Soviet Union. The president brushed them off and began to rethink US policy. He stepped up low-level contacts and made sure that his son Chip represented him as part of an April 1977 congressional delegation to China — a symbolic imprimatur of family that the Chinese appreciated.

The momentous policy shift came almost exactly six months after Carter took office. At a July 30, 1977, meeting of his foreign policy team, the president abruptly announced that he wanted

Vance — scheduled to depart for Peking in August — to introduce the idea of full normalization into discussions with the Chinese. Brzezinski remembered Carter saying that his entire political experience told him that it doesn't pay to prolong or postpone difficult decisions — a governing philosophy that, contrary to his undeserved reputation for fuzzy indecisiveness, Carter usually applied. At a pivotal historic moment for the two countries and the world, he didn't temporize.

To kick things off, Vance and the head of the US liaison office in Peking, Leonard Woodcock, had an encouraging meeting with an emerging new Chinese leader, seventy-three-year-old vice premier Deng Xiaoping, who had been rehabilitated only ten months earlier, not long after Mao's death.* But throughout 1977, normalization remained on the back burner. The United States was busy with the Panama Canal Treaties and Mideast peace. Woodcock, a former president of the United Auto Workers (UAW), and his deputy, Stapleton Roy, a career diplomat, nonetheless began secret negotiations to move the relationship forward, with Carter monitoring their work closely. In February 1978 the president met secretly with Huang Zhen, the Chinese liaison in Washington, to feel out the Chinese position.

All of the preliminary talks were run out of the White House because of loyalty to Taiwan in the State Department. This setup strengthened

*During the Cultural Revolution, Deng was forced to work for four years at a tractor factory in rural Jiangxi Province, and his son, Deng Pufang, became a paraplegic after being thrown out of a window by the Red Guards, the Maoist shock troops.

636

Brzezinski's hand against Vance. Carter decided that the Taiwan lobby was so powerful and meddlesome that the early planning for normalization had to be kept out of public view. He said later that establishing diplomatic relations with China and the development of the B-2 Stealth bomber were the two biggest secrets of his administration.

In May 1978 Carter dispatched Brzezinski to Peking — over Vance's objections — with the historic message that "the United States has made up its mind" to recognize the People's Republic as the true China. The grand strategic goal was to put the Soviets on the defensive by exploiting China's hostility toward them. (At the Great Wall, Brzezinski joked to his Chinese hosts, "First one to the top gets to fight the Russians!") The initiation of cultural and scientific exchanges would be important, too. As a goodwill gesture, Brzezinski presented Chairman Hua Guofeng with a moon rock, encased in Plexiglas, that dazzled a group of gawking Chinese scientists. The highlight of the trip was a two-hour dinner with Deng, the wily and unusually pragmatic leader, barely five feet tall, who was consolidating his power in the Politburo and was on the threshold of becoming one of the most consequential figures in the three-thousand-year history of China.

Deng was a harsh authoritarian. That year he crushed the "Democracy Wall Movement" — a burst of free expression — and he did the same a decade later when Chinese tanks attacked young protesters in Tiananmen Square. But the old hard line was evolving. Once he took firmer control, Deng usually favored sidelining political rivals instead of imprisoning them, exiling them to the countryside, or killing them.

And he completely reversed Mao's shunning of Western education. In July, Frank Press, the White House science adviser, arrived in Peking with a delegation of academics. Press awakened Carter at three o'clock in the morning Washington time to say that he was sitting there with Deng, who had a question for the president. Under Mao, not a single Chinese student had studied in the United States since World War II. Deng asked Press if he could send five thousand Chinese students to American colleges and universities. Carter was annoyed to have been awakened by that question. He enjoyed telling the story of how he snapped, "Tell him to send a hundred thousand," and hung up the phone.

The educational exchanges would exceed the wildest expectations of both Carter and Deng. By 2015, more than 350,000 Chinese students — mostly the full-paying children of the Chinese elite — studied in the United States every year, a development that aided Chinese modernization and kept several floundering American colleges afloat.

Back in Washington, Press learned just how committed Carter was to normalization. He told the president that the Soviets weren't happy to learn that the United States was giving a few computers to China (though none with highly advanced technology). "I don't give a shit what the Soviets think," Carter replied. When Vance went to Moscow for the short strokes on the SALT II deal, the Soviets suddenly told him that they wanted to go slow. The deal wasn't dead, only delayed several months, which Carter felt was an acceptable price to pay for warming relations with China. Only two and a half years later would the consequences of the delay for US-Soviet relations come into view.

Carter personally handled the final China negotiations in mid-December by sending detailed instructions to Woodcock and Roy in Peking. Not surprisingly, the sticking points involved Taiwan. China's priority was to end the American military presence there altogether. The United States was willing to yield on the deployment of American forces on the island but refused Deng's demand that it close the US embassy in Taipei and stop selling arms to Taiwan. Carter, directing the talks remotely, promised that only defensive weapons would be sold to Taiwan. He added that he would announce as part of the agreement that all disagreements between China and Taiwan would be resolved peacefully — a critical provision that might be tested in the twenty-first century. Deng, with classic diplomatic finesse, didn't agree to these demands, but he didn't object, either. The deal was done.

With word beginning to leak, Carter stunned the world on December 15, 1978, by walking into the Oval Office at nine in the evening and announcing the agreement, which was timed to a similar proclamation in Peking.

Reagan and other conservative Republicans, including George H. W. Bush, criticized the new policy, but not in strident Cold War terms, and Richard Nixon supported it without reservation. The press reaction was highly positive, with Deng becoming *Time* magazine's Man of the Year. Because presidents have broad authority to extend diplomatic recognition, anti-Communists on the Hill had few options to scuttle the deal, especially after Carter threatened to veto any effort to do so. The president later expressed pleasant surprise at how well normalization went. China proved less intransigent — and the Taiwan lobby less effective — than he had expected.

If Nixon and Mao cracked the door, Carter and Deng swung it wide open, and the result was a radically different future for the world. Two days after the announcement, the Central Committee of the Communist Party of China launched a new series of fundamental economic reforms. The rigid Communist regime was moving to embrace capitalism. "It doesn't matter if a cat is black or white, so long as it catches mice," Deng liked to say. His notion of "socialism with Chinese characteristics" was a discreet way of saying that after thirty years of Marxist-Leninist dogma on the economy, China would return to its older traditions of education, industriousness, and trade with the West.

It was no coincidence that US diplomatic recognition of China and new permissions for entrepreneurship occurred in the same week. Deng now rapidly decollectivized agriculture, eased the way for most forms of private enterprise, and created special economic zones for foreign investment. (Banking reforms, lifting rigid price controls, and other reforms would come a few years later.) The new leader was signaling that he felt that diplomatic, cultural, and economic relations with the United States were central to developing China. When Carter invited him to visit the United States at some point in the future, Deng responded immediately, "I'll be there next month."

But first the State Department had to deal with

a furious Taiwan. Over the Christmas holiday, Warren Christopher traveled to Taipei to assure the government that despite ditching its two-China policy, the United States would maintain good relations with Taiwan. Enroute from the airport to his hotel, the secretary of state's motorcade was trapped for an hour by a mob that pelted his limousine with eggs, mud, and paint and shattered car windows. The demonstrators waved identical printed placards reading "Carter Is a Bastard" — more evidence that the angry protesters (usually banned in Taiwan in that period) were encouraged by the government. Christopher and his rattled entourage were unhurt but infuriated that the Taiwanese regime had allowed the riot.

January 1, 1979, was the official date for the start of formal diplomatic relations. At a special ceremony that day at the US Liaison Office in Beijing, Deng and Woodcock, soon to become the first US ambassador to China in thirty years, drank toasts of champagne and Coca-Cola. The two men each wore hastily assembled lapel buttons depicting, for the first time, intertwining Chinese and American flags. "Three decades of acrimony over the Korean War, the Taiwan issue, the Vietnam War, our UN status — all that bitterness seemed to melt away, forgotten like the snows of winter on a warm spring day," Ji Chaozhu, Deng's Harvard-educated interpreter and later the Chinese ambassador to Great Britain, wrote of the event.

On January 29 Deng Xiaoping arrived in Washington on a state visit, and the two leaders signed dozens of agreements approving the first significant cultural, educational, and scientific exchanges and settling lawsuits left over from the long period of estrangement. Carter found Deng "small, tough, intelligent, frank, courageous, personable, self-assured, friendly." The most dramatic point came when Deng asked to meet alone with Carter (and an interpreter) in the Oval Office, where he confided to the president that he planned to invade Vietnam shortly. Carter was surprised. "The first thing you will do after normalization is war?" he asked. "They insulted us," Deng explained. "We need to teach them a lesson."

Then Deng went further, warning that if the Soviets came to the defense of their ally, Vietnam, there would be a major Sino-Soviet war with millions of casualties. "They will drown in many people's wars," he said in a remark so chilling that both Carter and Brzezinski intentionally left it out of their memoirs. Deng's plan to attack Soviet-backed Vietnam brought his trip to Washington into sharper focus: if Carter was playing the China card against the Soviet Union, then Deng was playing the America card against the same country — but in a more hard-edged fashion.

Carter was in a bind. Brzezinski warned him that "any such hostilities will generate major international turmoil." But if he decried China's invasion of Vietnam, he would derail the historic US-Chinese rapprochement. So he tilted toward China. "Do me a favor and make it brief," Carter told Deng. It was. Three weeks later, when Deng was safely back in Beijing, two hundred thousand Chinese troops crossed the border, but Vietnam's battle-tested army put up stiffer than expected resistance, and China quickly withdrew — a small taste of what the Americans had gone through.

Deng later told the Italian journalist Oriana Fallaci that he saw Vietnam as "the Cuba of the East" — a Soviet military outpost in China's backyard — and he described the invasion as a "defensive counterattack." He wasn't especially proud of "the lesson." When the US sponsored a UN resolution denouncing the invasion, China did not use its power to veto it.

While the secret of the impending war preoccupied Carter's advisers, Deng's visit proceeded as if nothing was amiss. Carter invited Richard Nixon to the state dinner, his first trip back to the White House since his tearful farewell four and a half years earlier. The invitation stimulated more press coverage than all of the transformative normalization initiatives combined, which annoyed Carter.

At public events that week, Deng asked for Amy to come forward. When she did, he put his outstretched hand at the level of his head to show they were exactly the same height, which always got a big laugh. At a Kennedy Center gala, Deng was entertained by the Harlem Globetrotters basketball team, John Denver, and the Joffrey Ballet. Everyone sang "Getting to Know You" from *The King and I,* and Carter felt "a genuine sense of emotion" as Deng put his arms around American children singing a Chinese song. When Republican senator Paul Laxalt saw that, he knew he wouldn't be able to block normalization. There was no way to beat little children singing Chinese songs, he said.

Deng gave no interviews to American journalists, but he set off on a tour across America that would display his human side.

At a rodeo near Houston, Deng donned a ten-

643

gallon cowboy hat, which led to whistling and cheering from the crowd and became an iconic image. "In one simple gesture," wrote Orville Schell, a China expert, "Deng seems to not only end thirty years of acrimony between China and America, but to give his own people permission to join him in imbibing American life and culture."

During the White House banquet on the final night, Deng leaned over to thank Carter for his direct involvement in reconciling the two countries and asked if there was anything China could do for him. Carter recalled his childhood practice of giving five cents a week to Baptist missionaries. He mentioned a revered woman missionary from the late nineteenth and early twentieth centuries named Lottie Moon, and noted that Mao had expelled all missionaries and banned Bibles and churches in China. "I finally responded, 'Yes, there are three things that I would like: for your government to let people worship freely, to own Bibles, and for our missionaries to return.'"

Carter described Deng as "kind of taken aback" by the requests. But the next day, as they bid good-bye, the Chinese leader brought up the subject of Christianity in China unprompted. He said he must reject Carter's request for the admission of missionaries into China. "Missionaries were arrogant and lived like kings when our people were poor," Carter later quoted Deng as saying. But Deng added that, upon reflection, he thought Chinese should be allowed to practice the religion of their choice, and he said he would lift restrictions on Bibles.

Two years later, when the Carters visited China as private citizens, they were pleased to learn that the government was now providing paper for the printing of Bibles. They were sold in churches, which were packed with new worshippers. During Mao's reign, the country contained only about five million Christians, almost all of them driven underground. By 2015, there were an estimated seventy million Christians inside China, which, to the chagrin of authorities, was on its way to becoming one of the largest Christian nations on earth, even if thousands who shunned state-sanctioned churches were forced to remain in the shadows. If the president's appeal to Deng was even partly responsible for this historic change, it would still make Jimmy Carter among the most successful Christian missionaries of all time.*

While Deng lived another eighteen years, he never set foot outside China again. But it was not because he disliked his trip to the United States. When Carter turned ninety in 2014, one of Deng's daughters, Deng Rong, gave him a scrapbook of the historic visit.

Jimmy Carter didn't cause the rise of modern China; nor did Deng Xiaoping. That was the work of hundreds of millions of ambitious Chinese. But the underappreciated partnership of the two leaders helped birth the global economy. To show rivals in the Chinese Communist Party that his move toward capitalism could bear fruit, Deng needed the cooperation of the United States. This made Carter's 1979 normalization more than a

*This account comes from Carter. Because the conversation was impromptu and not part of the formal talks, no State Department or National Security Council note taker was present, and the interpreter, Ji Chaozhu, wrote nothing of it in his memoirs.

mere addendum to Nixon's opening to China seven years earlier. Without Carter's bold determination, Nixon's two-China policy might well have extended for many years, delaying or even preventing China's emergence on the world stage. Deng also normalized relations with Japan in 1978, and ties to Western Europe were blossoming. But by engineering a dramatic upgrade in what became the most critical bilateral relationship of the twenty-first century, Carter accelerated the pace of change and shaped it for the better.

At Carter's direction, the Pentagon established a strong relationship with China's military, the People's Liberation Army, which would soon be an important ingredient in the Chinese economic miracle. Harold Brown visited Beijing in 1980, and senior Chinese military officers — several of them frail octogenarian veterans of Mao's Long March in the early years of the Chinese Revolution — traveled to Washington. Deng had instructed the military to carry out retirement in its ranks. The concept was at that time entirely foreign in China, where, for centuries, most Chinese simply worked until they died. The Chinese military and political leaders asked their American counterparts a basic question: How do you retire? The Pentagon officials explained generational turnover, and the Chinese brought the ideas home, where they helped inject dynamism into the Chinese bureaucracy and, soon, into business.

Advice from the Carter administration on energy was much less helpful for the world. When Jim Schlesinger went to China, he was told the Chinese had a chance to buy nuclear reactors from France, which relies heavily on nuclear power plants. While a strong supporter of nuclear power, Schlesinger advised the Chinese that they should seek cheaper forms of energy. They took his advice and embarked on a huge development of coal, a decision with disastrous effects on climate change.

In the four decades after normalization, China's economy soared, even as its harsh authoritarian system remained. The stunning rise of China has been a great boon to the American economy, especially the tech and agriculture sectors. But it has also worsened global warming, indebted the United States to Chinese banks, and led to cheating and other threats to intellectual property, fair trade, and American strategic interests. The hope of American presidents that closer cultural and economic ties would produce an increasingly democratic country adhering to Western values has not been fulfilled. In recent years, the Chinese government has trampled even harder on human rights (most conspicuously in Hong Kong) and reversed much of the religious tolerance that Carter pushed on Deng, with Christians spied on in church and millions of Muslim Uighurs sent to detention camps. By the 2020s, the relationship between the US and China was shifting from cooperation to competition and possible confrontation.

But only the most narrow-minded American nationalist could argue that China's ending its bristling isolation and hostility toward the West and moving toward capitalism and global economic integration did not represent historic progress. Imagine the level of alienation and confrontation in a world where the United States and China have no diplomatic relations; today's tensions might be producing talk of war. And consider the economic transformation. Before Carter, American farmers, tech companies, and other producers had no access to the vast Chinese market, and American consumers paid higher relative prices. By 2020, the two countries — despite their disputes — were headed toward $1 trillion in annual trade.

In the last four decades, more than a billion Chinese peasants have joined the middle class, where they contribute — through trade and technology — to global development and human knowledge. Today that extends to confronting pollution and global warming, a struggle China has now joined. Without Carter and later American presidents who favored engagement, an aggressive and repressive China would have risen anyway — this was its destiny based on its immense size and entrepreneurial culture. But the world is safer because China's rise came with a web of commercial and educational connections to the West that began under Jimmy Carter.

None of this was discernible in 1979. In the short run, normalizing relations between the United States and China proved of little consequence to either the world or the political fortunes of the American president. Other wheels of history were turning even faster.

*American hostages seized at the US embassy in Tehran, November 4, 1979.*

■ ■ ■ ■

# PART SIX:
# SWAMPED

■ ■ ■ ■

# 29
## THE FALL OF THE SHAH

Jimmy Carter had a decent enough first two years as president — with historic foreign policy triumphs, reduced unemployment (down from 8 percent to 6 percent), and the fulfillment of campaign promises on a great many issues. Despite inflation and various headline-making White House miscues, the 1978 midterm elections had gone relatively well for Democrats. The country as a whole remained behind the president, if in a lukewarm fashion. His reelection, while hardly assured, seemed like a reasonable bet.

By contrast, the second half of Carter's tenure — 1979 and 1980 — would prove to be one of the worst two-year periods in recent history. Carter's luck had run out. At one point, his approval ratings cratered into the mid-20s, lower than Richard Nixon's during the worst of Watergate. Like all presidents, he was judged by how he responded to the problems that now pressed in on him. In this, he was found wanting, even if many of the circumstances he confronted were beyond his control.

One global event stood above the others: the Iranian Revolution, which rivals the Russian and Chinese Revolutions in its twentieth-century importance and shapes the landscape of the Middle East to this day. The Iranian Revolution led to the Iran-Iraq War, which left 1.5 million dead; severe repression inside Iran, which exported Shiite fundamentalism in ways that harmed human rights globally; Iranian-backed terrorist organizations (e.g., Hezbollah) that destabilized Lebanon and killed hundreds in bombings; a nuclear weapons program that threatened world peace; and dangerous twenty-first-century tensions with Israel, Saudi Arabia, and the United States.

The revolution was a fiasco for American interests. Its aftereffects would help boost inflation and interest rates in the United States to unthinkable heights, wound America's pride, and contribute mightily to sending Jimmy Carter into early retirement.

It is ironic that the single most destructive event of Carter's presidency largely escaped his habitually intense focus until it was too late. Carter admitted later that he didn't consider the Iranian Revolution to be "that big a deal," especially compared to other challenges. "I didn't see [it] as the major burning issue on which I needed to focus all of my attention."

The timing of the tumultuous events in Iran could not have been worse for the president. Carter was so busy with other matters in late 1978 and early 1979 that he began waking up at five o'clock — an hour earlier than usual — and still could not clear his in-box by the time he went to bed. The imminent collapse of the Camp David Accords, the complex summit with Deng Xiaoping, and a revolt of feminists all competed for his attention.

And so the Carter administration's reaction to events in Iran was everything Carter himself was not: undisciplined, disorganized, and poorly informed. But even if the president had given the revolution more of his attention it's unlikely he could have done more than buy a little time. Carter was in no position to stem the tide of history. Having just spent twenty-five years failing to prop up the government of South Vietnam, the United States was understandably reluctant to take ownership of what happened in Iran.

The origins of the Iranian Revolution can be traced back to the ancient Persian Empire, which prided itself on its distinctive culture. European powers long threatened that pride and used the country as a pawn. During the Second World War, British and Soviet forces advancing through the Middle East needed oil for the Allied war effort and so jointly deposed the Nazi-sympathizing shah of Iran, then installed his more pliable twenty-one-year-old son, Mohammad Reza Pahlavi, on the Peacock Throne.

Young and bright, the shah did well for several years before appointing a reformer, Mohammad Mosaddegh, as prime minister. Mosaddegh alarmed the West, and not just because he hosted meetings with foreign heads of state while wearing his pajamas. He began nationalizing the Anglo-Iranian Oil Company and amassing political power. In 1953, fearing for his safety, the shah went on "vacation" outside Iran, while the CIA's Kermit Roosevelt Jr. (Theodore's grandson) helped engineer a coup against Mosaddegh that led to the shah's full restoration. "I owe my throne to God, my people, and to you," the shah told

Roosevelt.

The 1953 coup foreshadowed everything that happened in Iran in the 1970s: American cold warriors felt they could manipulate Iranian politics from the outside; Iranian dissidents saw their ruler as an irredeemable American puppet.

Through five US presidencies, the diffident, urbane shah of Iran made great strides in modernizing his country, which built good universities and gave rights to women. Iran became America's staunchest ally in the region, a major oil exporter and key strategic bulwark against the neighboring Soviet Union. But at the same time, the shah authorized his secret police (SAVAK) to hold more than two thousand political prisoners, infiltrate dissident groups, and torture critics of his corrupt regime in the name of fighting suspected Communists.

In 1963 the shah faced a challenge from a then-obscure but fiery cleric named Seyyed Ruhollah Khomeini, a onetime student of Greek philosophy whose brilliant command of the Koran and mesmerizing black eyes left his audiences transfixed. Khomeini, who often made his most important decisions while sitting in a trancelike state, gave the shah's embrace of blasphemous ideas like coeducation, high fashion, and Hollywood a name: "Westoxication." Oblivious to income disparities, the shah in 1971 commemorated the 2,500th anniversary of the founding of the Persian Empire by Cyrus the Great with a $200 million private celebration — arguably the most expensive party in history — in a country where the average per capita income was $250 a year.

The shah exiled Khomeini to Turkey and later Iraq, where he was largely ignored by Western

intelligence analysts for the next thirteen years —
a costly mistake. During his exile, the ayatollah's
son died mysteriously at the hands of the Iranian
government. His hatred of the shah grew more
personal.

Carter later described November 15, 1977, as "an
augury." That morning, he held a welcoming
ceremony for the fifty-eight-year-old shah on the
South Lawn of the White House. The Iranian
embassy paid nearly three thousand well-dressed
supporters to come to Washington to cheer on
their leader. They gathered on the nearby Ellipse
next to noisy anti-shah protesters whose ranks
had been infiltrated by SAVAK agents.* As the
twenty-one-gun salute rang out, Iranians broke
through a small fence and began attacking one
another with placard handles and nail-studded
two-by-fours. The melee left ninety-two people
injured before park police broke it up with tear
gas.

With the wind blowing north, the dignitaries
and press on the South Lawn were all left cough-
ing and dabbing their eyes with handkerchiefs.

*SAVAK's torture techniques were no secret. When
Jerry Doolittle, who wrote Carter's talking points for
the event, learned that the shah was presenting Carter
with a handmade tapestry in honor of the US bicentennial that depicted George Washington and the Iranian
ambassador and "contains 120 to 160 knots per square
centimeter," he included a never-delivered fake talking
point for the amusement of the White House staff that
said "and it is extremely difficult to tie knots that small
with no fingernails."

Many walked out early, but Carter had to power through his speech, which impressed even skeptical reporters. "It was *really* rough," Carter wrote in his diary. "I took it perhaps better than anyone else, because I didn't want to admit that it was hurting me so bad."

After the tear gassing, Carter pulled the shah into his private study and told him gently that he thought SAVAK was mostly to blame for the riot and that Iran needed to improve its human rights record. The shah bristled. At a state dinner that night, the president deadpanned in his toast, "There is one thing I can say about the shah: he knows how to draw a crowd."

Six weeks later, Carter flew to the Middle East, his first trip to the region as president. After Saudi Arabia, he and Rosalynn stopped off in Iran to talk with the shah about energy and Soviet meddling in the Horn of Africa. While there, on New Year's Eve, Carter toasted the shah at a reception in Tehran with a line that would haunt him until the end of his days: "Iran, because of the great leadership of the shah, is an island of stability in one of the more troubled areas of the world."

Within months, Iran had fallen into a cycle of street demonstrations and crackdowns. After weeks of unrest, twenty thousand demonstrators gathered in Tehran's Jaleh Square on September 8, 1978, to protest the imposition of martial law. Government troops opened fire, killing as many as two thousand people. Secular Iranians who had remained on the sidelines now joined the struggle against the shah.

The day after the Jaleh Square massacre, the president took time away from what would be his greatest triumph — Camp David — to tend briefly to what would be his greatest failure: Iran. But when Carter called the shah, he barely got a word in. In a flat, strange monotone, the shah said he would continue to pursue both order and democratization. Carter agreed this was a good idea, and the White House released a statement from Camp David regretting the loss of life but asserting continued full support for the shah. That was the last time the two men spoke until the shah was in exile.

If the US government wanted to prop up the shah, this would have been the time to try. But the Carter administration was constantly distracted and badly divided. Cyrus Vance, busy with SALT II and Camp David, wanted to turn the shah into a powerless constitutional monarch as in Great Britain or Sweden. Zbig Brzezinski, busy with the details of normalizing relations with China, pushed what came to be known as option C: a military coup in which senior officers would declare martial law to bolster the shah and restore order in the streets. Given the bad feelings generated by American involvement in the 1953 coup in Iran, Carter was always against option C.

For most of the autumn of 1978, the odds of regime change in Tehran appeared small. American officials reasoned that authoritarian leaders in almost every Muslim nation in the region had at some point put down protests that threatened their rule. The shah seemed likely to do the same. No one in Washington could yet imagine that a seventy-six-year-old cleric dressed in black could turn one of the most prosperous and cosmopolitan nations in the Middle East into a theocracy.

Visitors to the palace were soon describing the

shah as "shattered" and possibly on the brink of a nervous breakdown. Secretary of the Treasury Michael Blumenthal, whom Carter asked to make a side trip to Iran while in the region, remembered a pale and vacant-looking near zombie. (It would later come to light that the shah was suffering from Waldenstrom's disease, a rare blood cancer in the process of transforming into a more dangerous form of non-Hodgkin's lymphoma.) When Senator Robert Byrd visited Tehran, on a detour at the president's request, he reported that the shah viewed his problems as unrelated to the level of support he was receiving from the Carter administration.

It quickly became clear that the shah was making bad decisions — when he made decisions at all. He allowed Khomeini to leave exile in Iraq and decamp to France, where the ayatollah settled in Neauphle-le-Château, a small village outside Paris that provided the perfect base for him to appeal to the global media. Khomeini struck Canadian American television journalist Robert Mac-Neil as "the calmest, stillest man I ever met," eerily convinced that "he could turn the clock back."

In the meantime, the United States remained in the dark about the shah's intentions. Would he crack down further? No one knew. Carter blamed his ambassador in Tehran, William Sullivan, a career diplomat, who was smart and brave but also erratic and — by Carter's lights — insubordinate. Sullivan took off most of the tumultuous summer of 1978, leaving it to dissenting deputies to inform Washington that fundamentalist opposition to the shah was rising dangerously in Iran. As late as October 27, Sullivan — who was personally focused on combating the Iranian Communist Party — told Washington, "Our destiny is to work with the shah."

The shah told Sullivan that autumn that while he appreciated America's support, he didn't see what the Carter administration could do for him concretely. This wasn't 1953, the shah said; public statements by US officials asserting that they were backing him were just fueling more unrest.

After his fall, the shah claimed that advice from Washington had been "confusing and contradictory," and he blamed Carter for undermining his "self-confidence." Henry Kissinger insisted later that the refusal of the United States to send the shah more antiriot weapons (though he had plenty) demoralized him because he "relied on the US as a safety net."

But the shah was making his own decisions and bore responsibility for them. On November 6 he shocked his team by empowering a mild-mannered general who foreswore the use of force against the protesters. The tone of the shah's announcement was apologetic, a feeble promise of long-delayed democratization after order was restored. As the fatalistic shah himself anticipated, this tardy effort to appease the resistance did nothing to stabilize the country.

SAVAK officers presented the shah with the names of revolutionary ringleaders to be arrested and new plans to flood Tehran's squares with police to crush the protests. Over the objections of his family and advisers, the shah turned them down, arguing that while dictators can shoot at will, a true monarch doesn't fire on his own subjects. "I will not pass on the throne to my son on a foundation of blood," he told them. And there were practical considerations. If he crushed a rebellion on one Tehran street, he explained to several visitors in late 1978, it would quickly pop up on another.

Carter knew none of this. He continued to believe the regime would do what it took to stay in power. The shah had SAVAK, a large and loyal army, and a huge treasury to draw on. What did he have to fear from a handful of scraggly slogan-eers from the campuses and mosques with no weapons or money to buy them? Of course, this view had the added benefit of not requiring the president to do anything.

But by late fall of 1978, Ambassador Sullivan felt that everything he had thought about Iran since his arrival nearly two years earlier was mistaken. He reversed his assessment 180 degrees from sharply pro-shah to what Carter called "obsessive" support for abdication. In a soon-to-be-infamous November 9 cable entitled "Thinking the Unthinkable," Sullivan, for the first time, envisioned Iran without the shah. His analysis was surprisingly upbeat, with rosy predictions about the pro-Western orientation of young army offi-cers. The ambassador even ventured that the shah's military and Khomeini might unite over their mutual anti-Communism to form a viable government. The result would be an Islamic republic tilted toward the West with an empowered parliamentary system and Khomeini as spiritual leader in a "Gandhi-like" role.

That "Gandhi-like" description of Khomeini would trail Carter for the next forty years, even though he rejected the idea of the Iranian military coordinating with Khomeini, and he never came close to comparing the ayatollah to the revered

662

Indian leader. Not surprisingly, Sullivan's cable soured his relationship with the president.

As the revolution gained steam, Carter was upset that no one had told him just how much Khomeini — 2,500 miles away in France — was controlling events in Iran. His supporters secretly spread his sermons on thousands of small cassette tapes, leading to strikes and a revolutionary fervor that brought millions of ordinary Iranians into the streets.

While no one could have predicted the final outcome — theocracy without a fight — the intelligence failure was colossal.* For years, any effort to understand the Iranian opposition had been discouraged for fear of angering the shah, whom Presidents Nixon and Ford had somehow allowed to become the chief source of information about dissenters. As late as August 1978, a breathtakingly incompetent CIA assessment found that Iran "is not in a revolutionary or even prerevolutionary situation." And now there was apparently no surveillance of the ayatollah in France to offer advance word on his proclamations or his larger goals for Iran. The president's relationship with his old Annapolis classmate Stansfield Turner deteriorated. The CIA director admitted later that his agency had "let Carter down badly on Iran."

The bureaucratic recriminations distracted from the deeper problem: the US government knew virtually nothing about the repercussions of imposing rapid modernization on a traditional

*Sullivan's predecessor as ambassador was Richard Helms, a former CIA director who proved especially invested in the shah. It was understandable why Iranian militants feared the CIA.

Muslim society. Senior officials couldn't even pronounce *Shiite* properly, much less explain the difference between Shia and Sunni Islam. Gary Sick, the top NSC aide on Iran, recalled hearing Turner in the hall one day explaining to Walter Mondale what an "ayatollah" was.

Carter was a quick study, but even he had little time to steep himself in the complexities of Iran. In early 1979 he had his hands full rescuing his greatest achievement.

Because Camp David was a set of accords, not a formal peace treaty, there was work to be done after the conference. Per the agreement, the Israeli Knesset took a vote on the Accords and, on September 28, 1978, approved them by a four-to-one margin. Carter hoped that would pave the way for the final treaty and allow him to worry about the other problems on his plate, but it did not.

Before the ink on the Camp David Accords was dry, the deal was already falling apart. Every Arab head of state (except Egypt's) met in Baghdad to denounce the agreement, and it quickly became apparent that the three-month deadline for completing final negotiations on the West Bank (December 17) would not be met.

Carter fretted in his diary on November 29 that even Sadat had grown "very, very negative in his attitude" toward the accords. But it was Begin who emerged as the major impediment. The day after leaving Camp David for Washington, the Israeli prime minister was already backing away from the deal, privately informing American Jewish leaders that Carter favored Sadat over him and that nothing had been finalized.

664

When Begin came by the Oval Office before returning to Jerusalem, Carter gave him a little plaque that said "Shalom, Y'all." but he was angry that the prime minister was now publicly backing new settlements on the West Bank. He is "acting in a completely irresponsible way," Carter wrote in his diary that evening. "He's trying to welsh on the deal."

Preoccupied with salvaging Camp David and normalizing relations with China, Carter now looked to the wrong sources on Iran. On November 21, at Brzezinski's urging, he invited Iran's silky ambassador in Washington, Ardeshir Zahedi, in for what turned out to be an unsatisfying chat. Zahedi, famous for buying influence in Washington with lavish parties, told the president that the shah was growing stronger politically, militarily, and psychologically — all untrue. He insisted that no political structure was in place to allow for national elections in Iran — refusing to consider what should have been a good option for channeling public anger. And he nominated himself as the next prime minister — an idea that went nowhere when he returned home a few weeks later.★

Other efforts to get a handle on Iran fared no

★Zahedi had some credibility with Carter because in 1977 he was among the ambassadors from Muslim countries who handled the negotiations that ended the violent takeover of three buildings in Washington, DC, by radical Hanafi Muslims. The terrorists took 150 hostages and killed one before the standoff ended after three days.

better. Carter asked a seasoned diplomat, George Ball, who had been his first choice for secretary of state, to take a fresh look at Iran policy. After two weeks of intense study in early December, Ball issued unworkable recommendations and told Carter privately that the shah was through; the professional and middle classes supported the protesters.

But Brzezinski still had not given up on option C. If the shah was too mired in his funk to make a decision to put down the resistance, he argued, the United States "should make it for him." For Brzezinski, Schlesinger, and other Cold War hawks, the specter of a Soviet Union with client states in Afghanistan (where a pro-Soviet regime took power in 1978), possibly Pakistan, and now perhaps even Iran was a strategic fiasco. Both asked to be dispatched to Tehran to work on the man Schlesinger called "a wobbler." But Carter was at heart a peacemaker and moralist, not a geopolitical thinker or gung-ho interventionist. He barred any trip aimed at egging on the shah.

On November 30 Vance told the president that the British were abandoning the shah. Carter started edging in the same direction. "We personally prefer that the shah maintain a major role in the government," Carter told reporters at a breakfast on December 7. "But that is a decision for the Iranian people to make." With the press full of stories that US support for the shah was all about oil, Carter knew he had room to distance himself from him. Mondale urged Carter not to assume responsibility for a military solution. That could mean blood on *his* hands, he told the president, not just the shah's.

For weeks, the shah had been vacillating. "On Monday, Wednesday, and Friday, he would authorize the rough handling or the shooting of demonstrators; on Tuesday, Thursday, and Saturday, he would have bouts of conscience and apologize about it," Jim Schlesinger remembered.

The passive days grew more frequent. Once the resistance was confident the shah's army wouldn't shoot, street protests surged. Just before Christmas, the shah told Sullivan that he might take "a vacation" abroad. He hoped that after he departed, the military might crack down harshly, then bring him back. When Sullivan warned the shah against such a gambit, Brzezinski instructed the ambassador that he must neither approve nor disapprove of such an action.

On December 26 the indecisive shah asked Sullivan point-blank what the United States wanted him to do. Sullivan told him, "The United States could not make such a decision for the shah." America supported his efforts to restore law and order, but whether to use military force was his call. Generations of US hard-liners and Iranian exiles would point to this meeting as proof that the shah fell because the United States failed to back him at a pivotal moment — a claim unsupported by the record. Refusing to offer advice does not constitute abandonment.

But even after Sullivan's meeting with the shah, the Carter administration remained badly split on what US policy should be. Vance wanted an unequivocal rejection of force; shooting protesters wouldn't work, he said, and would harm US efforts to stay on good terms with the successor government. Brzezinski pressed again for the shah to call on Iran's heavily armed military to end the protests once and for all. At Camp David on December 28, Carter decided to support empowering the generals, but only to prevent further bloodshed, not save the shah's throne. He and Vance agreed on language in a cable urging the shah to stop the uncertainty and "choose without delay" some form of interim military government to end the chaos.

The cable either came too late or went ignored. At the end, the shah was in an accommodating mood. Instead of an iron fist, he offered an olive branch, asking a moderate, elegant, Western-educated opposition leader, Shahpur Bakhtiar, to form a civilian government. Bakhtiar, destined to be the Kerensky of the Iranian Revolution, was described by Sullivan as a "determined, even quixotic man" uninterested in advice from Americans.* To win the support he needed from his coalition, Bakhtiar declared that the shah would have to leave the country.

As 1979 began, every major Carter adviser except Brzezinski agreed it was time for the shah to leave Iran, at least temporarily. Sullivan's assessment was that if the shah departed, Bakhtiar had a chance; if the shah stayed, Bakhtiar had none.

But if he did decide to flee, where would he go? After all those years of friendship, the US government felt duty-bound to be the shah's travel agent. During a White House meeting on January 3, Vance left the room to arrange a safe haven for the shah at the Palm Springs, California, estate of Walter Annenberg, publisher of *TV Guide* and a

---

*Amid the Russian Revolution that overthrew Czar Nicholas II, Aleksandr Kerensky held power for four months during 1917 before being removed by the Bolsheviks.

668

friend of Ambassador Zahedi's.

Carter rejected the pessimism about Iran he saw in all of his senior advisers except Vance. Their predictions of civil war and the Soviet Union exploiting the chaos seemed overblown to him. Still, he agreed to dispatch Air Force general Robert "Dutch" Huyser, the blunt, red-faced deputy commander of Allied forces in Europe, to Tehran to make sure the Iranian military (some of whose commanders he knew from an earlier posting) didn't splinter when the shah left.

The shah later charged that Carter sent Huyser to "neutralize the army" so it would not block the forces overthrowing him. If this was Carter's intention — and there is no evidence for it — Huyser himself said he did just the opposite: he told Iranian army officers that if firing warning shots over the heads of demonstrators did not quell the protests, "move to focusing on the chests." Huyser recounted that "I got stern and noisy with the military," but to no effect. The top generals, he said, were "gutless."

None of this stopped a collection of armchair coup plotters in New York City who would spend most of the next year pressuring Carter on matters related to Iran. The Chase Manhattan Bank, headed by David Rockefeller, became the headquarters of Project Eagle, an effort by the shah's well-heeled American friends to save his throne. This group, run by a Chase banker named Joseph Verner Reed Jr., favored what Kissinger called a "Bonapartist" solution: installing a military strongman who would handle security while the shah continued his nation building. Carter, by contrast, believed that Iran could return to the quasi-democratic principles of its 1906 constitution. Jim Schlesinger thought the president's hope for democracy was preposterous and naive. But Carter stuck with it anyway, assuring Schlesinger and Brzezinski that the Iranian parliament could become a source of stability and that a genuinely nonaligned Iran need not be viewed as a setback for the United States. On both counts, he was tragically mistaken.

On January 4, 1979, Jimmy, Rosalynn, and Amy traveled to the island of Guadeloupe for a combination Caribbean vacation and four-power summit. Carter noted later that with the advent of the less personal G-7, G-8, and G-20 summits, this may have been the last time the leaders of the West relaxed together in an informal setting without their allies and legions of staff. He spent hours with French president Valéry Giscard d'Estaing (who struck him as the most fiercely anti-Israel leader he had ever met), amiable British prime minister James Callaghan (the foreign leader Carter got along with best after Sadat), and foul-tempered West German chancellor Helmut Schmidt (who treated Carter with arrogant disdain).

At a private lunch on a balcony overlooking the ocean, the heads of state eyed topless women bathers passing below. "Jim [Callaghan] complained strenuously that his back was turned to the beach," Carter wrote in his diary. He later went scuba diving (to a depth of fifty feet) and spent a whole day helming a trimaran (a multihull boat) — "one of the most enjoyable times I've ever had."

The oblivious leaders of the West had no idea that the impending Iranian Revolution would upend world history. They expected that the Arab states would use the turmoil in Iran — the second largest oil exporter in the world — as an excuse to jack up global oil prices even further. But as they enjoyed the sunshine, they couldn't see that skyrocketing oil prices and supply disruptions would help wreck all of their careers. Within a few years, each would be pushed out of office by conservatives. In that sense, Carter's replacement by Ronald Reagan in 1981 was just part of a powerful global shift to the right.*

Away from the other leaders, Carter — clad only in his bathing suit — sat on a small refrigerator in an alcove of his cottage and took a call from Vance, who reported from Washington that the Iranian military was finally preparing for a bloody crackdown. Vance and Mondale, recalling American support for ill-advised coups against Mohammad Mosaddegh in Iran in 1953, Ngo Dinh Diem in South Vietnam in 1963, and Salvador Allende in Chile in 1973, wanted Carter to make it clear the United States wouldn't back it. Brzezinski, who had accompanied Carter to Guadeloupe, argued strenuously that if the United States prevented the shah or his military from finally acting decisively, Carter would "shoulder a massive historical responsibility." World politics, he told the president, is "not a kindergarten." The half-naked Carter sided with Brzezinski. He was

*Callaghan was the first to go, beaten that spring by Margaret Thatcher. Giscard d'Estaing was succeeded by the more liberal François Mitterrand but only after being fatally weakened from the Right by an ascendant Jacques Chirac, a future prime minister. Schmidt was succeeded by conservative Helmut Kohl.

disturbed by the impending bloodshed but agreed not to change the instructions to Huyser.

Then nothing happened. The shah said his talk of a bloody crackdown was meant only to pressure Bakhtiar, in whom he had already lost confidence. He resumed his procrastination and vacillation, as did the Carter administration.

As the revolution gathered strength, Carter's team squabbled. Vance and Sullivan pressed their case for using a diplomat to launch a dialogue with Khomeini in Paris. Brzezinski thought it ridiculous that an elderly religious fanatic would be swayed by this. Carter wanted to enlist the French, which prompted an intemperate Sullivan cable calling French involvement a "gross and perhaps irretrievable mistake." Carter felt Sullivan's cable "bordered on insolence." He told Vance to fire him but was talked into leaving him in place until the immediate crisis passed.

For all the bickering, the big picture in early 1979 didn't look so bad. At best, the Carter White House figured, Iran would end up like Iraq, where the dictator Saddam Hussein ruled cruelly but — in that period — remained on relatively good terms with the United States. At worst, Iran would be another Libya, where the mentally unstable despot Mu'ammar Gadhafi had a poor relationship with Washington. With little understanding of the Ayatollah Khomeini, no one could envision an outcome more negative than that. Brzezinski cautioned that "nothing could be worse than a half-assed coup," but he remained sorely tempted to sponsor one anyway.

On January 11 a perplexed General Huyser met with the shah to ask the critical question: You have

672

four hundred thousand troops. How did you lose control? The shah turned around the question, asking Huyser, "Could you, as commander in chief, give the orders to kill your own people?" Huyser replied, "Your Majesty, we are not talking about me, we are talking about you." The shah sat silently; Huyser had his answer.

On January 12 Khomeini announced his intentions of returning to Iran. Fearing (rightly) that this would mean the end of the Bakhtiar government, Carter called President Giscard d'Estaing to ask him to do anything he could to postpone the ayatollah's departure from France. Giscard d'Estaing reported back later in the day that Khomeini, afraid of being killed upon returning to Iran, was delaying his trip.

Carter grew concerned about the shah's safety and sent word that he should leave "promptly." When the shah finally departed for Egypt on January 16, Carter found the end of his thirty-eight-year reign strangely anticlimactic — in part because his leaving was long expected and draped in the ludicrous cover story that he was going "on vacation." To the president's relief, the shah decided to skip Palm Springs and settle with his family in Morocco, the second of seven countries he would live in during the frenzied last eighteen months of his life.

While the Iranian Revolution was going full force, President Carter was preoccupied with a domestic issue that felt a million miles away from the Middle East: the case of Bella Abzug, the crusading former New York congresswoman. A January 15 Cabinet meeting involved more discussion of Abzug than of the shah, who would leave Iran the next day. By the end of that tumultuous week, Carter joked that it reminded him of the naval academy, where on Monday morning, cadets would be prompted by upperclassmen to shout, "Oh, boy, another week to excel!" Then on Friday, they would shout, "Oh, boy, another week shot to hell!"

The Abzug case typified how Carter's good intentions often went awry. Over the objections of Rosalynn, who recognized Abzug's divisiveness, Carter had followed the advice of several female aides and appointed the prominent feminist as chair of the newly established National Advisory Committee for Women. The high-profile committee grew out of the historic 1977 Women's Conference in Houston, where Rosalynn spoke. The part-time position was unpaid, but Abzug had a White House office and staff, and the notoriously penny-pinching president was infuriated to learn that she had racked up the highest long-distance phone charges of anyone in the Executive Office Building.

With a voice that could "boil the fat off a taxi driver's neck," as Norman Mailer put it, "Battling Bella" was irresistible to the press. She had a habit of standing before cameras on the White House driveway and attacking the budget cuts of the president who appointed her — the kind of dissent (and disloyalty) that Carter had tolerated in his first two years but now felt was undermining his administration. On January 12 Abzug's advisory committee issued a press release criticizing Carter for prioritizing the defense budget over welfare programs. While Abzug refrained from attacking Carter publicly that day, inside the White House she lit into him with her usual abrasive

674

tone in front of the entire advisory group.

He did not take kindly to the tongue-lashing. By this time, the feminists and the White House were fed up with each other. Anne Wexler, a savvy Washington operative who was now a senior adviser to the president, recommended Abzug be fired that afternoon, and Rosalynn agreed — although, in another ham-handed move, women were never publicly associated with Carter's decision. When Hamilton Jordan told her she was fired, Abzug said she had been "scapegoated," and soon twenty-two of the remaining thirty-nine members of the committee quit in protest. (Abzug was replaced by Lynda Johnson Robb, LBJ's older daughter.) Gloria Steinem, channeling the outrage of feminists, called Abzug's firing "the Friday Afternoon Massacre" and told Rafshoon that it would doom Carter's 1980 reelection campaign.

"We are pushing hard to keep Khomeini out of Iran," Carter wrote in his diary on January 17. Except they weren't. Two days earlier, Warren Zimmermann of the US embassy in Paris had been dispatched to a cozy French inn near the Khomeini compound to meet with Ibrahim Yazdi, a smooth Iranian American physician from Houston who was perfectly cast for the role of appeasing the Americans. At the inn, Zimmermann and Yazdi worked together to make sure that the ayatollah's return didn't cause violence — a distinctly different mission than keeping him out of the country.

Washington had privately warned Khomeini that if he tried to seize power, the Iranian army would intervene "to protect the constitution." Yazdi, smooth as ever, wanted to know what that meant.

Zimmermann told him that it meant essentially that the army would protect the parliamentary system but the United States had no plans to push for the continuation of the monarchy, as it had in 1953.

This was just what Khomeini wanted to hear; now he didn't have to worry as much about a military coup. With a cunning that surprised secularists, he began a shrewd charm offensive, announcing that "nonintervention in other people's affairs" would be the foreign policy of the revolutionary government.*

At this point, Carter and Bakhtiar, both of whom should have known better, still trusted the ayatollah's empty promises. Bakhtiar told the United States he would "close the airports and permit Khomeini to enter only if he promises to do so as a religious leader, not as a political heir," Carter wrote in his diary on January 23.

What if, in hindsight, Washington had told Bakhtiar that Khomeini's "promises" were worthless and that he should do everything he could to keep the ayatollah from coming home like a conquering hero? Might that have helped Bakhtiar to consolidate power and survive? Maybe. More likely, news of Bakhtiar's consorting with the enemy — with America — would have made the street protests even bigger and accelerated the revolution.

Still, a more adept — and less distracted — American president might have at least played for time, using every overt and covert tool at his and

*By the 1980s, Khomeini's government was subsidizing Hezbollah and other terrorist groups operating inside foreign countries.

the CIA's disposal to make sure the ayatollah didn't leave France until Bakhtiar had better odds of solidifying his position. Even granting how few options he had at this pivotal moment, Carter's lack of diplomatic and clandestine imagination is striking.

In the meantime, Khomeini was smart enough to at least sound reasonable. On January 27 he issued a friendly first-person statement directed to the US government. "You will see we are not in any particular animosity with the Americans," the ayatollah wrote mildly. He pledged that the coming Islamic republic would be "a humanitarian one."

Bakhtiar by now thought Khomeini's return was inevitable, but he believed naively that the ayatollah could be dispatched to the holy city of Qom to be "drowned in mullahs" — persuaded by other clerics to abide by their standard separation from politics. Sullivan cabled that the Iranian army had also "come around to accepting Khomeini's arrival." Infantilized over the years by the shah — who had taken away their autonomy — and now facing small-scale mutinies, the senior Iranian officers had decided to stay on the sidelines. Brzezinski admitted later to "a misperception on my part": he had thought the army would rally behind the shah, as it had in 1953, but it was more divided, undisciplined, and feckless than he knew.

For a day or two, it seemed as if Bakhtiar might be the tough, decisive leader Iran's allies were looking for. He told Washington he planned to arrest the ayatollah when he landed in Tehran. After a bitter debate that pitted Brzezinski and Harold Brown (both in favor of the arrest) against Vance and his department, Carter backed the idea on

January 24. But when Khomeini again delayed his departure, Bakhtiar changed his mind. With revolutionary violence surging, he saw that seizing the ayatollah would cause untold bloodshed in the streets.

More dramatic ideas were scotched, too. Iranian Air Force general Amir Hossein Rabii told his American counterpart in Tehran, Brigadier General Richard Secord, that he intended to shoot down the ayatollah's plane, with Bakhtiar's support.* Secord warned him against it, and Rabii backed off. Brzezinski heard separate reports of a plan to sabotage Khomeini's plane and told his staff it wasn't a good idea.

For years, neoconservatives have claimed a more Reaganesque American president would have stiffened the royal spine and somehow transformed an ailing and passive man into a dynamic defender of dynasty. In his nineties, Henry Kissinger still insisted that if Carter had sent the right signal, the shah — "psychologically dependent" on the United States — might have taken the steps necessary to secure his regime.

A close reading of the shah in this period suggests otherwise. In his final weeks in power, he proved he was an autocratic sovereign but not a blood-thirsty tyrant. Had he succumbed to American pressure, the shah fully understood that he would have ended his days as a Persian King Canute: flailing against the revolutionary tides of history and killing thousands of people in the

*In 1989 Secord pleaded guilty to lying to Congress about his role in arms sales to Iran, an outgrowth of his role in the Reagan-era Iran-Contra scandal.

process. Then the United States might have felt obliged to intervene in a bloody and endless civil war. The world would later see how that turned out in Iraq, a country much smaller than Iran.

It is nonetheless hard to exaggerate the blow the Iranian Revolution dealt to US geopolitical interests. Four decades on, Washington still confronts the dangers posed by Iran nearly every day. Gary Sick, who served on Carter's National Security Council, wrote later that for years, foreign policy decisions had resembled a chessboard, with two opponents (usually the United States and the Soviet Union) competing but playing by roughly the same rules. The Islamic Revolution, by contrast, was "the player who smashes his fist into the board and showers the pieces about the room in an emotional demand for a fresh board, new players, and a radically restructured rule book."

In the short term, Khomeini's hurricane blew away much of the political and historical credit Carter had won for Camp David and for normalizing relations with China. He interrupted oil supplies, further emboldening OPEC to cripple the US economy. By conservative accounts (denied by the Russians and absent from their archives), Carter's passivity encouraged the Soviet Union to move openly into Afghanistan and made his tough rhetoric toward Moscow after the invasion sound tinny. And, of course, the revolution set in motion events that led to the seizure of the US embassy in Tehran.

None of this was clear in early 1979, when Carter had to prepare for the Deng trip, contend with a feminist rebellion, and — most critically — try to revive Camp David, which was in shambles. This was exasperating, not just for Carter and his team but also for the public, which thought the whole thing had been settled the previous September. After Begin returned to Washington in early March for talks that ended badly, Carter was, he wrote later, "convinced the peace effort was at an end." That night, after Rosalynn went to bed, the president put on a heavy coat and sat on the Truman Balcony alone, wondering what he could possibly do to save his handiwork.

Out of "desperation," Carter decided to travel to the Middle East for one more try at peace. This was madness, he was told by several senior advisers; a wild and unnecessary risk. Nothing would dramatize failure like a futile and embarrassing state visit. Presidents were supposed to go to summits and sign agreements *after* messy negotiations had been completed, not venture abroad in search of a signature when they were deadlocked. Carter's dogged insistence on getting his hands dirty had been dangerous enough at Camp David, but with so much else going on in the world, indulging his Middle East obsession was now almost radical. To make matters worse, Saudi Arabia threatened to cut off aid to Egypt and even reduce oil supplies to the United States if Carter made the trip. "It got kinda ugly," Carter recalled. "I was way out on a limb." With the president's poll numbers already low, Jody Powell advised him that he would likely face a public relations disaster if he left the country.

In a replay of the run-up to Camp David, Carter grew stubborn. He was going to the Middle East whether anyone liked it or not. Sadat had been thrilled by the idea of "my friend Jimmy" visiting Egypt, and that was good enough for him.

On March 8 Air Force One landed in Cairo, and Jimmy and Rosalynn "felt a glow of welcome, warmth, and friendship." Within an hour, Carter and Sadat resolved their outstanding issues, and Sadat gave Carter "my full authority" to negotiate on his behalf with the Israelis. As the Sadats and Carters traveled from Cairo to Alexandria in a vintage open-air train, millions of Egyptians cheered — the most enthusiastic crowds of Carter's lifetime. Many held placards with a picture of Sadat and Carter and the line "Men of Peace."

In Israel, Carter was met by demonstrators — a reminder that he was now in a democracy. And he was shadowed by a busload of prominent if short-sighted American Jewish leaders — skeptical of Camp David — who had flown over to "keep Carter honest," as one told Jerry Rafshoon. Carter recorded later that an emotional visit to Yad Vashem, the Holocaust memorial in Jerusalem, gave him a better feel for Begin's extreme caution on anything related to the security of the state. But their meeting went as poorly as the one in Washington.

Begin said, essentially, that Carter's trip was a waste of time; he couldn't sign or even initial any treaty until every section of it had been submitted to the cabinet and the Knesset for extensive debate — an interpretation of Israeli law that other of the country's leaders told Carter was bogus. The president informed the prime minister that he was obstructing everything they had accomplished at Camp David, and they quarreled until after midnight. Carter returned to his room depressed. "He was so completely disgusted," Rosalynn wrote.

At Hamilton Jordan's suggestion, Carter decided to go over Begin's head, which proved to be brilliant advice. Carter asked to address a closed-door meeting of the Israeli cabinet — an unprecedented event for an American president or any other outsider. He found the ministers, including right-winger Ariel Sharon, more receptive to peace than Begin, who kept interrupting his colleagues. The ministers worried that Egypt's treaties with other Arab nations would legally supersede its peace treaty with Israel and that the return to Egypt of Israeli-dug oil wells in the Sinai would interrupt Israeli oil supplies. Carter, deeply knowledgeable about obscure energy policy options, reassured them on these and other points.

But progress proved elusive. Rosalynn noticed that Jimmy "had a stricken look on his face" after he met alone with Begin. She asked what happened. "All negative," he said, more déjà vu from Camp David. Carter went almost directly from that meeting with Begin to the Knesset, where he delivered a heartfelt speech carried live on Israeli television. Columnists in Israel and the United States agreed that Carter's Knesset speech was so persuasive that it would bring the Israeli government around. Midway through, the president infuriated Begin by saying that the Israeli people were ready for peace but their leaders had not yet shown the courage for it. Polls of Israeli voters showed this argument helped highlight Begin's obstructionist position.

Carter watched silently as Far Right members of the Knesset who despised the Camp David Accords heckled the prime minister mercilessly, a parliamentary tradition. This made the president feel friendlier toward him. "You see, I'm only one member!" Begin whispered to him with a smile that suggested he took perverse pleasure in the scorching attacks. "Being charitable to Begin," Rosalynn wrote later. "He has had to completely change his positions. To accept the Camp David agreement went against all he had fought for all his life."

But Carter's time in Israel was running out. When Begin insisted on resubmitting the American proposals for yet more Cabinet debate, Jimmy told Rosalynn, "I believe he just enjoys making others uncomfortable and being rude." Carter's senior advisers reported more fruitless meetings, and the Americans prepared for a humiliating departure. "Everyone was so pessimistic and 'down,'" Rosalynn reported to her diary. But she urged her husband to extend the trip. "We have come so far, and one more night might give time for something to break."*

Carter summoned Moshe Dayan, and the Israeli foreign minister urged him to remove any mention of allowing an Egyptian presence in the Gaza Strip — a proposal that the president correctly predicted he could sell to Sadat, who never considered Gaza part of Egypt. With the United States reiterating its long-standing guarantee of Israeli oil supplies, the parties were now only inches apart.

But the president still had to persuade Begin, a mission almost sure to prove futile. He called and asked him for breakfast the next morning before

---

*CBS News reported at the time that the parties were on track for an agreement all along, making the whole trip look contrived. But the memoirs of American and Israeli officials indicate otherwise.

the presidential party departed the King David Hotel for the airport. Before the meeting, a smiling Begin asked Jordan and Rafshoon, "You boys like the King David? You know, I blew it up once. Don't worry, I won't do it today!" — a reminder of Begin's most infamous deed.

After yet more circular discussions, Carter rose to depart in failure when a lifetime of persistence and creative impatience kicked in. "With obvious frustration, I made one final effort," he recalled. He went over the relatively minor details of new American oil supply guarantees and an exchange of ambassadors and — more soulfully — read Begin the generous statement to be issued by Sadat in Egypt if a deal was completed.* It may have been the last of these that did the trick — no one quite knew for sure. Begin, who always seemed to hold out until the last possible moment, finally committed to signing the entire agreement if Sadat did. Carter insisted that press reports saying he did so only because of a vague new promise of more US aid to Israel were not accurate.

On the way down from Carter's suite in the King David, the Carters and Begins got stuck in a broken elevator for twenty minutes, six feet above the lobby. Security forces finally found a crowbar and tore off the door. Carter remembered the two couples awkwardly descending "with our butts coming down backward off the ladder" — the "breech birth" of a historic treaty.

Carter then flew to Egypt, where he blurted upon arrival: "I feel like I'm coming home." In a

*The exchange of ambassadors did not happen, thanks to continued chilliness in the Israeli-Egyptian relationship.

lounge at the Cairo airport, Sadat kept his promise and readily signed off on the new language Carter had negotiated without him.

"It's a miracle! It's a miracle!" the Egyptian leader exulted.

As they strolled across the tarmac, Sadat's wife, Jehan, told Rosalynn tearfully that none of this would have been possible without their husbands' deep faith in God. Rosalynn agreed. Then the presidential party flew to Andrews Air Force Base, triumphant but still a little nervous about final approval from the Israeli cabinet. When it came the next day, by a vote of 15 to 0, a fatigued president could finally bask in his historic triumph.

On March 26, 1979, Carter, Begin, and Sadat sat on the South Lawn and signed the most significant peace treaty since the Japanese surrendered to the United States at the end of World War II. The three men linked hands in a pose that captured the moment for all time: joyous, almost sacred, and full of hope. At the luncheon afterward, Ezer Weizman brought his severely disabled son, Shaul, who had been shot in the head by an Egyptian sniper near the Suez Canal in 1970. The president, his eyes welling with tears, watched as Anwar Sadat rose to embrace him.

"We pray that the season of weeping is past, that now will come a time to heal, a time to build up, a time to laugh, a time to dance," Carter said in his toast at the state dinner that evening. "We pray that at last the children of Abraham have come to the time of peace."

They had not. Begin and Sadat were jointly awarded the 1978 Nobel Peace Prize (Carter was not included, in part because he forgot to arrange to be nominated) but little progress was made on a wider regional peace. For the rest of his presidency, Carter would try and fail to persuade Begin to move forward on autonomy for the Palestinians — and, through back channels, to convince the Palestinians to accept a formula that would lead to statehood.* Neither budged. After he left office, Carter's dreams of completing the work of Camp David foundered on the harsh realities of the Middle East. In October 1981 Sadat was assassinated while reviewing a military parade in Cairo. Begin, for his part, treated Carter coolly when he stopped in Israel in 1983 and stiffed him entirely on a visit in 1987.

As president, Carter, almost inadvertently, achieved critical longtime American strategic goals: removing the Soviet Union from relevance in the Mideast, strengthening US relations with Egypt, and splintering the Arab League, whose unity as a regional alliance was rarely in the inter-

*Seth Anziska, an American Orthodox Jew, wrote an intriguing revisionist history of Camp David in 2018 entitled *Preventing Palestine: A Political History from Camp David to Oslo.* He argues that all three parties set up a framework for Palestinian autonomy that delayed justice. Dennis Ross, a longtime American negotiator in the region, writes that Anziska "too often seems to absolve the Palestinians of any responsibility for their predicament. They were excluded from talks but essentially because they chose to be — from 1977 until 1988. The idea of autonomy that originated at Camp David did not ensure that Palestinian statehood would be denied later on."

est of the United States. But the failure to forge a comprehensive regional peace would prove to be the greatest regret of his life.

And yet for Egypt and Israel, Carter's prayers were answered. In all the years since, not a single shot has been fired in anger between them, a chilly but surprisingly permanent peace.

On February 1, 1979, the Ayatollah Khomeini, after fourteen years in exile, boarded an Air France charter flight bound for Tehran with more than a hundred international journalists aboard, a guarantee that the plane would not be shot down. He was greeted by huge and rapturous crowds. Like Vladimir Lenin arriving at Saint Petersburg's Finland Station in 1917, back from exile in Switzerland, this was a momentous revolutionary event.

Within days of his arrival, Khomeini named Mehdi Bazargan, a scholar and former deputy to Mohammad Mosaddegh in the early 1950s, as his provisional revolutionary prime minister. Bakhtiar was out after just five weeks in the job. Bazargan assured the United States that the thousands of Americans still in Iran would be safe during the revolution. Sullivan took this as a sign that Khomeini would prove to be more reasonable than expected. Huyser, by contrast, feared the worst. He'd seen a spike in anti-American sloganeering in the streets.

On Sunday, February 11, 1979, commemorated later as the founding day of the Islamic Republic, a mob trapped Iranian officers and twenty-six senior American military personnel in a bunker beneath the American military compound. In a gesture of goodwill that he would not repeat,

Khomeini arranged for the hostages to be released unharmed after a few hours. Washington remained largely clueless about events on the ground in Tehran. As he negotiated the freedom of the Americans with a Khomeini aide, Sullivan's other phone rang. It was Undersecretary of State David Newsom calling from Washington to say Brzezinski wanted to know if a coup was still possible. Sullivan was enraged. "Tell Brzezinski to fuck off," he said. When Newsom noted that this was not a particularly helpful comment, Sullivan replied, "You want it translated into Polish?" and hung up.

Three days later, February 14, rampaging pro-Khomeini militants assaulted the US embassy itself in the so-called Valentine's Day attack, which presaged the more momentous takeover nine months later. Under orders from Sullivan, marine guards repelled this first attack without exchanging fire; the ambassador worried that if American soldiers killed any Iranians, a bloodbath would ensue. Diplomats inside dove under their desks and tried to shred documents. Mohammad Yazdi, still close to Khomeini, intervened to free the Americans. He declared that foreign embassies should be protected, and they were — at least for a time.

The following day, four Iranian generals were executed on the roof of a high school — more proof that US intelligence remained blind when it came to Khomeini's intentions.

On February 21 Sullivan, acting on instructions, met with Bazargan and told him the United States looked forward to good relations and would keep its embassy open. The reason for this decision required no explanation: Tehran was a critical post from which to monitor the neighboring Soviet Union and, not incidentally, make sure the new revolutionary regime did not shift orbit.

Once again, Carter could not devote his full attention to the issue. As the Iranian Revolution — one of the most pivotal events of the second half of the twentieth century — came to an end, the president was focused more on Afghanistan, Mexico, and Nicaragua. In Kabul, US ambassador Adolph "Spike" Dubs had been kidnapped from the embassy the previous week and killed during a shoot-out with three terrorists. In Mexico, Carter's February 14 state visit had been marred by a tiff over trade with President José López Portillo, who was bad-mouthing the United States. And in Nicaragua, Carter's decision to withdraw US support for the corrupt regime of Anastasio Somoza had boosted the fortunes of the Sandinistas, who threatened to turn the Central American country into another Cuba.

In 1949, conservatives had asked bitterly, "Who lost China?" Now Henry Kissinger and others asked, "Who lost Iran?" Their answer was Jimmy Carter.

From exile, the shah gave interviews holding the US president personally responsible for his fate. He claimed he had failed to act decisively because he couldn't count on Washington's support. Leaks out of the State Department suggested the opposite — that Carter had sided for too long with the shah, the army, and Bakhtiar.

Brzezinski got Carter so worked up about the leaks that the president summoned a group of State Department officials to the White House for a humiliating dressing-down, made worse because the officials knew that Brzezinski leaked even more than they did. With a red-faced Cyrus Vance at his side, Carter told the diplomats they had been disloyal. If the false stories didn't end, he said, "I'm firing all of you." Then he rose and left. Walking back to his office, Assistant Secretary of State Leslie Gelb decided to quit. He wasn't alone.

Word of the president's touchiness spread throughout Washington. His policy of holding back and hedging his bets had been a mess. Instead of mobilizing the American and Iranian governments to back Bakhtiar to the hilt and resist a dangerous revolution, he had reached out to Khomeini and retreated to post-Vietnam platitudes about nonintervention. And it had bought him nothing.

Carter and his team cannot be held responsible for the Iranian revolution and its aftermath. The tectonic plates of history were shifting beneath their feet. But they were blindsided by the depth of Iranian hatred of the United States for imposing a "puppet" on their proud country for thirty-five years. And so, with the support of all of his advisers, Carter decided to pursue full diplomatic relations with the ayatollah's regime, "whom we thought would be friendly to us and work with us."

# 30
## THE "MALAISE" SPEECH

In a classic episode of *The Simpsons,* the citizens of Springfield wait in excitement for the unveiling of a statue. When they see that it depicts Jimmy Carter with the inscription "Malaise Forever," they heckle the assembled dignitaries: "Aw, come on!" "He's history's greatest monster!" Then they pull down the statue and start a riot.

Everything connected to Carter's famous "malaise speech" was a little odd, starting with the fact that he never actually used the word *malaise* in that address or any other. And yet the timing was perfect. The most curious, confessional, and intensely moral television address ever delivered by an American president took place in the most frazzled and dispirited peacetime year of the late twentieth century.

The year 1979 stood out for being one of the most conspicuously unpleasant of recent decades. It opened on the Iranian revolution and closed on the Soviet invasion of Afghanistan, with sky-high inflation, long lines at the gas pump, open warfare in the Democratic Party, and the seizure of American hostages in Tehran in between.

Although the word *malaise* wasn't in the speech, it accurately described the national mood. The

691

Me Decade zest for spiritual enlightenment and "self-actualization" that Tom Wolfe had depicted in 1976 had descended into self-parody. Jerry Rubin, the onetime Yippie protester and member of the Chicago Seven, had catalogued his seventies journey through "est, gestalt therapy, bioenergetics, rolfing, massage, jogging, health foods, tai chi, Esalen, hypnotism, modern dance, meditation, Silva Mind Control, Arica, acupuncture, sex therapy, Reichian therapy."

Now the country was entering what one historian called the "Great Funk." The previous November, more than nine hundred Californians under the spell of cult leader Jim Jones had died in a mass murder-suicide near Jonestown, Guyana, just the latest omen of a decline that was seen to include everything from New York City's bankruptcy to platform shoes for men. America in 1979 struck more than a few critics as reminiscent of the last decadent days of the Roman Empire, with fiddling politicians and orgies at nightclubs.

American institutions felt soiled. The once-great Ford Motor Company produced the Pinto — a butt-ugly car with an exploding gas tank. Ten years after the United States thrilled the world with the first moon landing, Carter had to call the prime minister of Australia to apologize after pieces of the disintegrating NASA Skylab space station landed on the country. The following evening, three days before the malaise speech, Commissioner of Baseball Bowie Kuhn was forced to cancel the second game of a Chicago White Sox doubleheader after Disco Demolition Night — a radio promotion climaxing in a bonfire of despised disco albums on the pitcher's mound — turned into a riot with racist and homophobic undertones that tarnished the national pastime.

Carter was not the first Democrat to identify what he called "a crisis of confidence" in the nation. Robert F. Kennedy had said in a speech at Kansas State University in 1968 that the country was "deep in a malaise of spirit" and suffering from "a deep crisis of confidence." Mo Udall, no one's idea of a scold, told the 1976 Democratic Convention, "We have lost our confidence and lost our way. The fact is that our country hasn't been working very well."

Three years later, it was working worse, and the sense of national decline was now laced with fear.

At four in the morning on March 28, 1979, more than one hundred alarms went off in reactor number 2 at the Three Mile Island Nuclear Power Plant near Harrisburg, Pennsylvania. Instruments in the control room indicated that radioactivity had been released into the surrounding area.

By morning, panic was spreading fast across the country. A hit film released twelve days earlier, *The China Syndrome,* starring Jane Fonda, Michael Douglas, and Jack Lemmon, included a character saying that if a nuclear core melted, it would "render an area the size of Pennsylvania uninhabitable." The president, rusty but still conversant in nuclear engineering, dropped everything to study the details of the large gas bubble forming in the containment facility.

Carter's experience as a planner in southwest Georgia also came in handy. He smoothly coordinated with northeastern governors and activated thousands of emergency personnel under plans that — with characteristic foresight — he had ordered upgraded in 1977. Stockpiles of medicine, cots, and communications equipment were ready for immediate use if necessary.

On Sunday, April 1, the Carters choppered to the reactor site to learn firsthand about the incident and — by having their pictures taken there — to calm the public. The visit took some political guts because it would also associate the president with the embattled and unpopular nuclear industry.* By this time, it was clear the nuclear core had not melted down, and the radiation risks were minimal. Carter made a reassuring statement afterward, but the resulting photographs of the president and first lady wearing goofy yellow booties — standard footwear inside any plant — overshadowed his expert handling of the crisis.

No deaths, injuries, or potential health hazards were ever connected to Three Mile Island, but it would be more than three decades before another nuclear power plant was commissioned in the United States.

Carter had been off balance all year long. At Rick Hertzberg's suggestion, he agreed reluctantly to structure his 1979 State of the Union address

*Carter drew an important if little-understood distinction between uranium reactors like Three Mile Island, which he generally considered safe, and certain models of plutonium reactors, which he viewed as too risky to build. In a classic sign of his choosing science and safety over politics, the president had essentially written off winning Tennessee — which he had handily carried in 1976 — by withdrawing support for the Clinch River Breeder Reactor, a hugely popular plutonium project in that state.

around the idea of his administration building a "New Foundation," a phrase he used thirteen times in the speech. Afterward, even William Safire liked the idea of Carter finally crafting his own New Frontier or Great Society, both of which came into common usage only through repetition. But three days after the speech, when a reporter asked if the New Foundation would stick, Carter said it was just something his speechwriters came up with and thus abandoned his best chance to have a theme for his presidency.*

At Rosalynn's urging, Jerry Rafshoon had moved inside the White House the year before to supervise speechwriting and communications, which everyone agreed needed help. Soon the newspapers were full of stories about "Rafshoonery": PR gimmicks to control Carter's image. One idea, recommended by Rosalynn, was to sideline the long-serving White House barber and bring in a stylist, who changed the president's part from right to left, a decision that the press and much of the public found disconcerting. Rafshoon and the rest of the senior staff were under no illusions that even smart cosmetic changes could do much to help. Jody Powell said that any president looks good in blue jeans when he's popular and bad in them when he's not.

Even so, Rafshoon tried to keep the president focused on what would much later be called "optics." He reassured Carter in a memo that he had not failed to provide leadership; he had merely failed "to *look* like you're providing leadership. . . . You're going to have to start looking,

*Barack Obama tried briefly to resurrect the "New Foundation" before abandoning the effort.

talking and acting like more of a leader if you're to be successful — even if it's artificial," he wrote him.

That started with his speeches, which weren't working. The fault lay not with his speechwriters (who had little access to the president, which made their jobs much harder) but with Carter's preference for laundry lists of facts over reasoned arguments and his poor delivery: underpowered voice, misplaced emphasis, inexplicable smiling, and bulging eyes. His insistence on deleting rhetorical flourishes gave him the worst of both worlds on the podium: words with no music, delivered in a singsong rhythm.

Rosalynn worried constantly that Jimmy was in political peril. On April 9 she invited Pat Caddell — who worked on contract to the DNC — for a two-hour breakfast. Caddell, still under thirty but with a beard that bore a distinctive white stripe, had not until then had as much influence on the president as the press believed. Carter drew a rigid line between campaigning and governing and had little time for polls.* But the first lady found Cad-

*Caddell's memo during the transition advising the president-elect to run "a continuing political campaign" after he assumed the presidency was later seen as the founding document of what consultants called "the permanent campaign" — the efforts of all presidents from Carter forward to act as candidates for reelection almost from the moment they took office. But Carter, while appreciating Caddell's sophisticated analysis of his polls, rarely met with him and ignored that memo and others Caddell sent him in 1977 and 1978. It wasn't until 1979, when the president's thoughts turned

696

dell fascinating. The scowling pollster — fully inhabiting the role of Old Testament prophet — laid out the "crisis of confidence" he felt was afflicting the country. When Rosalynn looked stricken, he bucked her up by quoting Napoleon: "Glory comes only in great danger." Rosalynn and Jody Powell suggested he put his dark thoughts on paper.

Two weeks later, Caddell delivered a seventy-five-page memo entitled "Of Crisis and Opportunity." Inside the White House, the tome was quickly dubbed "Apocalypse Now," and not just because Caddell was working on the marketing of Francis Ford Coppola's epic film by that title. Caddell painted a gloomy picture of a crisis that "threatens the political and social fabric of the nation." America, he feared, might rot from inside as France had in 1940 before the Nazis took Paris in a matter of days. Caddell quoted John Maynard Keynes and Alexis de Tocqueville, among many others, and cited passages from *The Culture of Narcissism: American Life in an Age of Diminishing Expectations,* a popular sociological analysis by Christopher Lasch, and *Leadership* by James Mac-Gregor Burns, an FDR biographer.

In his memo, Caddell hastened to add that the malaise he was describing was not Carter's fault but the product of long-festering mass psychological problems that went back to Vietnam and Watergate and had led to the historically high levels of pessimism he found in his polls. The good news was that Caddell thought Carter could seize

---

to reelection, that Caddell was invited into the inner circle.

the moment to become a great president "on the order of a Lincoln, a Roosevelt, a Wilson, and a Franklin Roosevelt" and "reshape the structure, nature, and purpose of the United States in fundamental ways." How to ground this grandiosity in reality? The pollster didn't say.

Carter didn't react immediately to Caddell's ideas, but he did speed-read *Leadership,* hoping to reverse engineer his relationship with the public. Burns argued that "transformational leadership" (as opposed to the everyday "transactional" kind) "seeks to satisfy higher needs." Good leadership didn't seem to be something a driven president could learn with just a little more practice, like how to dry peanuts, or draw a map of the West Bank, or fly fish.

But it was a sign of Carter's commitment to self-improvement that he was willing to try. On May 30, at Caddell's suggestion, he hosted a White House dinner to explore the distemper of the American people and what he could do about it. Carter was disappointed with the evening, though he thought Jesse Jackson had some insights into how to move to higher ground. "Everyone was concerned with getting him out of chicken-shit," remembered Charles Peters, the editor of the *Washington Monthly,* referring to the minor announcements he made nearly every day. "We were trying to get him to think in bigger terms and to be truthful — to bring out the better part of himself."

Walter Mondale didn't attend the dinner, but he read Caddell's memo and thought it was "crap." Carter didn't know it, but Mondale was at that moment contemplating an act undertaken by only two vice presidents in American history: resigning his office.★ "I became really depressed when the economy was going to hell, and we couldn't seem to get anything done," Mondale recalled. He still felt friendly toward Carter and grateful that his job responsibilities had been upgraded. But looking to his own career, he saw the vice presidency as more of a graveyard than a stepping-stone for his presidential ambitions.

Mondale decided to have an aide, Mike Berman, research the legalities of resigning. He weighed three options: resign immediately; announce that he would not be on the 1980 ticket; or stay with Carter in the primaries the following year before announcing at the Democratic National Convention that he was withdrawing from the ticket for personal reasons. He leaned toward the third option and went fishing in northern Minnesota on May 29 to weigh his future. He brought communication gear to allow him to consult with confidants and his wife, Joan, who wrote him as he departed: "I'll be better if you quit."

But he didn't. Mondale's caution, loyalty, and faith that he could still exert influence proved decisive. He returned from vacation the first week of June refreshed and determined to fight internally for his views. A month later, this decision would be tested, then tested again.

By spring, energy inflation had driven overall inflation into double digits, resurrecting grainy images of frantic Germans taking wheelbarrows of cash to the grocery store during the hyperinfla-

★The only two were John C. Calhoun in 1832 and Spiro Agnew in 1973.

tion of the Weimar Republic a half century earlier. But gas prices at the pump weren't high enough to curb consumption. An unwieldy — even absurd — lightly regulated gasoline allocation process meant that rural service stations had plenty, while cities often experienced shortages. Much of the public thought the whole crisis was a hoax perpetrated by greedy oil companies that Carter refused to slap down. One popular sign read: No Gas My Ass.

The first long gas lines appeared in May in California, where motorists hoping to fill up their tanks were told by service stations that they could purchase only a few gallons at a time. By early summer, the shortages had spread across the country. Truckers, idled by crippling shortages of diesel fuel, staged demonstrations in thirty states before launching a strike. They shot out the tires of truckers they viewed as scabs, vandalized fueling stations, and in Levittown, Pennsylvania — a planned community for the middle of the middle class — set off a melee after blocking an intersection where angry suburbanites cheered them on.

After tense meetings, the White House overhauled the gas allocation system and helped settle the truckers' strike but won almost no credit for its role. Carter appeared in a prime-time NBC News special on the gas lines, offering little beyond hope that decontrolling oil prices would stimulate more production. It was cold comfort.

In June, a month when Carter was mostly out of the country, his poll numbers plummeted into the low 30s. Unlike most other presidents, he had few die-hard supporters outside of the black community to break his fall. After four days in Europe, he returned briefly to Washington before leaving June 23 for a G-7 summit in Tokyo. The highlight of the trip was a meeting with Emperor Hirohito, now an amiable old man who talked easily with the American president about their mutual interest in marine biology and poetry.

Otherwise the summit was most noteworthy for what Carter and his entourage were missing in Washington. "Back home, everything is going down the drain," Rick Hertzberg, who was traveling with the presidential party, wrote in his journal on June 27. "We are out of touch with the country to a frightening degree. How is it possible that we left on this trip without doing something, anything, any appearance of anything, about the gas lines?"

Congress was asking the same question. When Mondale briefed a bipartisan group on the Tokyo summit, they told him they were afraid to go home over the Fourth of July recess. That's how angry their constituents were about the gas lines. "Nothing [has] added so much water to our ship," Stu Eizenstat, whose portfolio as chief domestic policy adviser included energy, wrote Carter in an impassioned memo delivered to Japan. "Nothing else has so frustrated, confused, angered the American people — or so targeted their distress at you personally." Eizenstat urged the president to shift the blame to "a clear enemy": namely, the OPEC cartel.

The Carters were scheduled to stop in Hawaii for a short vacation after the G-7 summit, a chance to revisit their happy navy days there. Over Rafshoon's objections, the president heeded Eizenstat's advice and canceled the sojourn. He arrived home on July 2 and went immediately into

701

meetings, barely able to stay awake. Carter was expected to address the nation on July 5 after a day of rest at Camp David. Rafshoon made the mistake of alerting the heads of the three networks, who cleared their prime-time schedules for what they assumed would be a major address about the gas crisis.

The speechwriters realized immediately that for all of Eizenstat's exhortations, they had nothing fresh to say. Carter had delivered four energy speeches to the nation, each proving less effective than the one before. Rosalynn felt another would be disastrous.

The president got up early on the Fourth of July and read an updated and much better memo from Caddell with growing excitement. He considered it "one of the most brilliant analyses of sociological and political interrelationships I have ever seen."

Caddell's influence over the Carters had been slowly growing, and by now, he had become "almost a Rasputin," Jordan recalled. "He was kind of in Carter's head and in Rosalynn's head." At Caddell's urging, the president decided to cancel his energy speech and let Caddell spend a few days turning his thoughts into the draft of an address. Caddell's speechwriting technique consisted of ranting aloud and letting a fellow data geek, Wayne Granquist, a talented Office of Management and Budget official, put it in written form.

On a conference call from Camp David, Carter told his senior staff that he did not want to "bullshit the American people." When Deputy Press Secretary Rex Granum asked what reason he should offer for the change of plans, Carter, sounding petulant, said, "Don't give an explanation. Just cancel the damn speech."

The lead story in the July 5 *New York Times* — "President Cancels Address on Energy; No Reason Offered" — kicked off a feverish guessing game. "What the Heck Are You Up To, Mr. President?" the *New York Post* asked in a banner headline. When Carter mysteriously stayed at Camp David after the cancellation, rumors spread that he had suffered a nervous breakdown. "President Carter has reached the low point not only of his administration but perhaps of the postwar presidency," *Times* columnist Tom Wicker wrote that week. "Mr. Carter's celebrated cancellation of his energy speech may well have been the worst public relations blunder since Richard Nixon's 'Saturday Night Massacre.' " Polls showed the president's popularity plummeting even lower than in June, with the *New York Times*/CBS News poll putting his approval rating at 26 percent — as low as Nixon at the bottom of Watergate.

Carter summoned a half dozen senior aides — plus Pat Caddell — to a July 5 meeting at Camp David to discuss Caddell's draft. The session turned into a conversation about national narcissism, not policy or plans for what Carter would tell the nation. Eizenstat wrote later that he "almost felt I was at a seance, not a serious meeting with the leader of the free world." He argued that Caddell's ideas raised expectations of changing the culture the president could not possibly meet, given how resistant energy and inflation were to easy solutions. Rosalynn reiterated that giving the same old speech on energy would be pointless. The others mostly agreed. "You've become part of the Washington system," Rafshoon

703

told the president. "You were elected to kick ass and haven't."

Mondale was having none of this. He was apoplectic, so angry that others worried he might have a heart attack. Behind Carter's back, the vice president had earlier told Eizenstat that Jimmy and Rosalynn must have drunk Pat Caddell's Kool-Aid, a reference to the poison-laced beverage Jim Jones had made his followers swallow seven months earlier. As a student, Mondale had read some of the same sociology Caddell referenced. It wasn't relevant, he told Carter. "We got elected on the grounds that we wanted a government as good as its people," Mondale reminded the group through gritted teeth. "Now, as I hear it, we want to tell them we need a people as good as the government; I don't think that's going to sell." The idea that endless gas lines and horrendously inflated prices for essential household items were only "psychological" problems appalled him. If we question Americans' "mental stability," he said, "I think we're goners."

The vice president was astonishingly blunt with Carter, considering that others were in the room. He argued that his boss was fatigued and not thinking straight. Then he hit harder. "You have a style problem," he told the president. "You can't uplift people." He wheeled on Caddell to tell him his speech draft was "the craziest goddamn thing I've ever read" and his half-baked proposal for a new constitutional convention "the worst idea I've ever heard." The first lady patted the pollster on the knee to comfort him; Caddell — not yet thirty years old — remembered he was "shaking like a leaf" because the vice president of the United States had just said he was insane.

704

Carter decided to move forward with a speech that addressed Caddell's themes. Then he rose to take Mondale for a walk around the compound to cool him down. He found his vice president still "quite distraught." Carter asked for Mondale's support but did not get it. To appease him, he threw Caddell out of Camp David for a couple of days.

Carter had entered a period of reflection and self-criticism unlike any in the history of the presidency. Years before ritualistic "listening tours" became standard for politicians, he decided he wanted to "reach out and to listen to the voices of America," as he explained later. The difference was, later politicians asked voters about *their* problems; Carter already knew what those were. These meetings would be more about *his* problems — a largely sincere effort to learn how and why he was messing up. It never seemed to occur to the president that the peculiar process he had set in motion might worsen the very problem it was designed to address.

All told, more than 130 leaders from different sectors would chopper to Camp David over the next ten days. The president knew that for political reasons, he would need to make every constituency — labor and business, teachers and preachers — feel heard. The first group, on July 6, consisted of eight governors, followed by "wise men" John Gardner of the watchdog group Common Cause; Panama negotiator Sol Linowitz; and Clark Clifford, a smarmy fixture of the Washington establishment who appealed to Carter mostly because he had first come to Washington with Truman. Carter sat on the floor of Aspen Lodge, taking notes. "Their criticisms of me were much more severe" than the governors', he wrote, "including the basic question: Can I govern the country?"

Carter found the meeting with members of Congress unhelpful, and the one with economists "the worst of the week." In one of the later meetings, he listened attentively to the thirty-two-year-old governor of Arkansas, Bill Clinton, who struck a characteristically upbeat tone, telling the president, "Don't just preach sacrifice." Clinton thought Carter should also remind the American people "that it is an exciting time to be alive." It was good advice that Carter did not take.

On the evening of July 10, the president — in transition from government engineer to national pastor — finally heard some of the Reinhold Niebuhr–style moral reasoning and spiritual insight that he craved. He gathered clergy from all major denominations to be part of what White House staffers dubbed "the God Squad." Rabbi Marc Tanenbaum saw Carter as a Moses-like figure returning from the wilderness with a new vision for his people that rejected "unrestrained consumerism" and "mindless self-indulgence." Robert Bellah, a brilliant sociologist of religion, offered "the covenant model" for creating a sense of mutual obligation on the part of the government and the American people. Others made reference to the long religious tradition of the "jeremiad," named for the Hebrew prophet Jeremiah, who lambasted his people for worshipping false idols.

They were pushing on an open door. Carter considered this the best meeting of the week. He had grown up with a father who made use of every

706

part of the pig in his stew and punished his children if they didn't clean their plates. The president loathed shopping and extravagance; he was not a fan of the celebrity worship he felt was typified by *People* magazine and, in private, he often derided the commercialism and greed he saw throughout corporate America. (This, in an era when CEOs made around fifteen times as much as their average employees; in 2018 they made four hundred times as much.) Carter genuinely believed that Americans should not be let off the hook for the corruption of their values. He told the God Squad that just blaming OPEC for the country's mood would be "self-righteous," hypocritical, and ahistorical. In a private preview of the dovish views on foreign policy that would characterize his postpresidency, he informed the group, "We've been interfering in OPEC countries' lives and most other countries' lives rather heavily for a long time."

But the president didn't want to be what Mondale called a "scold" or a "grouch," either. "How much can the American people take?" he asked Bellah. Now the conversation turned in a direction that Carter found especially helpful. Bellah said the president should forget about politics and tell the American people what he'd promised in his first campaign: The truth. The real truth. The group agreed with Bellah's advice that Carter become "a teaching president." Tanenbaum, at Carter's request, offered a blessing, and the meeting ended with everyone holding hands.

To meet some of the regular Americans he would ask to make sacrifices, the Carters — with Caddell in tow — ditched the press pool and flew to the Pittsburgh suburb of Carnegie, where they

707

chatted on the porch of William Fisher, a twenty-nine-year-old machinist who had gathered a few friends. Fisher screwed up his courage and told the president the country was on a "downhill spiral." Carter shocked him by nodding his head in agreement. Back at Camp David, Carter hosted sixteen prominent journalists. Their conflicting reports of his mood — some claimed he seemed emotional, others said he was calm — further heightened the national drama around what was going on with the president.

For ten days, Carter's team agonized over what should be in the speech. Rafshoon told the president he thought giving Caddell's version would be "counterproductive, even a disaster." But Eizenstat's draft, which stuck mostly to energy policy, was boring. It was up to Rick Hertzberg to take the best of both drafts — plus what he had heard Carter say in the Camp David sessions — and weave them together.

The address the president delivered was actually three speeches in one: he would hold himself accountable for his shortcomings (a section he wrote alone); wrestle with the questions of confidence, community, sacrifice, materialism, and moral obligation first raised by Caddell and turned into moving prose by Hertzberg; and offer a more aggressive plan for confronting the energy crisis, written by speechwriter Gordon Stewart, based on Eizenstat's policy recommendations.

In the past, Carter often sniped that he would only rehearse speeches as a personal favor to Rafshoon. This one was different. He agreed to be coached by Stewart, a playwright and theater director. The practice sessions took place inside

708

the small Camp David movie theater, which was decked out to resemble the Oval Office, with lights and a teleprompter. Stewart believed Carter's delivery wasn't nearly forceful enough to hold an audience. He used an old director's trick by saying, in essence, "I'm bored. I'm going to get up and start walking toward the door, and I would like to see if you can stop me." Carter was annoyed at first, but he made his delivery more urgent, adding strong and effective hand gestures.

The president was internalizing the speech, making it his own. FDR had described the presidency as "preeminently a place of moral leadership," and this, Carter felt, was the moment for it, the right occasion to "witness" and maybe even redeem.

On July 15 the president of the United States addressed an expectant audience of a hundred million Americans in front of a curtain in the Oval Office. The title of the thirty-three-minute speech was "A Crisis of Confidence." He began by noting that it was exactly three years since he had accepted his party's nomination and "promised you a president who is not isolated from the people." But he realized his speeches and press conferences had become "increasingly narrow" and focused on Washington. The country's problems, he asserted, "are much deeper than gasoline lines or energy shortages, deeper even than inflation or recession." By this point in the speech, his staff and many viewers noticed his voice modulation and hand movements were much improved. And his lacerating self-criticism — unprecedented from an American president — made for historic television.

"I got a lot of personal advice" at Camp David, he said. "Let me quote a few of the typical comments that I wrote down. This from a southern governor [Richard Riley of South Carolina]: 'Mr. President, you are not leading this nation — you're just managing the government.'

" 'You don't see the people enough anymore.'

" 'Some of your Cabinet members don't seem loyal. There is not enough discipline among your disciples.'

" 'Don't talk to us about politics or the mechanics of government, but about an understanding of our common good.'

" 'Mr. President, we're in trouble. Talk to us about blood and sweat and tears.'

" 'If you lead, Mr. President, we will follow.' "

Carter then read several of the energy-related comments he heard at Camp David and in his visits to the homes of everyday Americans. He ended this unflinchingly honest section with one: " 'When we enter the moral equivalent of war, Mr. President, don't issue us BB guns.' "

Here Carter moved to the Caddell-inspired part of the speech, which had been revised enough from its original version that Mondale — while still not considering it good — could live with it. After citing the collective American pain of the Kennedy and King assassinations and Watergate, Carter argued that an "invisible" threat — "a crisis of confidence" — "strikes at the very heart and soul and spirit of our national will." The crisis was reflected "in the growing doubt about the meaning of our own lives and in the loss of a unity of purpose for our nation."

It was when the president got to *why* Americans had lost confidence that he slipped into a sermon

710

from the bully pulpit that was bracing and true but also risky, considering that he was addressing a country full of people who love to shop:

"In a nation that was proud of hard work, strong families, close-knit communities, and our faith in God, too many of us now tend to worship self-indulgence and consumption. Human identity is no longer defined by what one does, but by what one owns. But we've discovered that owning things and consuming things does not satisfy our longing for meaning. We've learned that piling up material goods cannot fill the emptiness of lives which have no confidence or purpose."

Here was the president of the United States confronting the American people over their materialism. It was a moment of breathtaking honesty that had no precedent and will almost certainly never be repeated. Even in tough times, future presidents would stop well short of truly challenging their audiences.

The politics of true candor (as opposed to the mere claim of it) were terrible. Richard Wirthlin, the pollster for Ronald Reagan's 1980 presidential campaign, wrote later that when he heard these lines about "self-indulgence" and "consumption," he knew instantly that Carter had stepped on a "strategic land mine" and that Reagan could beat him. At the moment Carter said, "In a nation that *was* [Wirthlin's emphasis] proud of hard work, strong families . . ." the Republican pollster almost fell out of his chair. Even if Carter hadn't intended to insult Americans, Wirthlin noted, he had succeeded: "How else were voters to feel about a president who spoke about American greatness in the past tense?"

That was a partisan shot that Reagan was

already preparing to take, and his sunny optimism would make him the perfect messenger for it. Carter, by contrast, was working in a different vernacular. His form of inspiration sounded more like the civil rights movement than the familiar patriotic patter of presidents. As he said in one memorable passage of the speech:

"One of the visitors to Camp David last week put it this way: 'We've got to stop crying and start sweating, stop talking and start walking, stop cursing and start praying. The strength we need will not come from the White House, but from every house in America.' "

After explaining that there were "two paths" for America — "fragmentation and self-interest" or "common purpose and the restoration of American values" — Carter came to the "pivot," to policy the speechwriters had worked on for so long. The seams showed, but it was serviceable: "On the battlefield of energy, we can win for our nation a new confidence, and we can seize control again of our common destiny."

Carter went on to a vivid description of the energy crisis and what to do about it. His action plan sounded strong at the time but has produced mixed results in the years since.* Carter did not

*Carter stressed alternative energy sources such as oil shale, gasohol, and solar. But the primary goal — cutting oil imports in half by 1990 — proved unrealistic. The supposedly powerful energy ideas in the speech, including oil import quotas, a windfall profits tax, and an energy security corporation, petered out over time, and Carter's plan for massive investment in public transportation was blocked by the highway lobby.

712

shrink from the implications of his plan — "There is simply no way to avoid sacrifice," he said — but he tried to end on an upbeat note: "Whenever you have a chance, say something good about our country. Let us commit ourselves together to a rebirth of the American spirit. Working together with our common faith, we cannot fail."

When the speech ended, Carter's top aides, watching on TV down the hall in the Roosevelt Room, erupted in cheers. The commentary on the networks was glowing, but Rafshoon noticed that more than one analyst said the president had addressed the "malaise" in the country. He soon learned that Caddell had gone behind his back to brief the networks and reporters beforehand, employing the word, which Rafshoon and the speechwriters had intentionally avoided. By the next day, it was everywhere, even though Carter himself never used it. Within hours, Carter's eloquent appeal to traditional American values of self-reliance and patriotic self-sacrifice was being interpreted in some quarters as a humorless downer message that blamed the American people for their own problems.

Public reaction was nonetheless enthusiastic. The president had held an adult conversation with voters, and most responded as adults. The White House mail room reported the most letters and telegrams ever received in peacetime. The vast majority of them were positive. Overnight polls showed strong majorities believed the speech inspired confidence and would generate widespread acts of sacrifice. Carter's job approval ratings surged 11 points, a huge jump, even if his old numbers were so low that this took him up only to the high 30s.

The journalist Theodore White later summarized the reaction: "No president since Abraham Lincoln has spoken with such sincerity to the American people about matters of spirit." The next day, Carter spoke to thousands of county officials in Kansas City and union members in Detroit, where he won the most rousing ovations of his presidency.

Even habitually skeptical senators like Daniel Patrick Moynihan were impressed. Business and labor leaders across the spectrum backed both Carter's sense of urgency and his various proposals for energy independence. He even got credit for being positive. "The president's comments on the mood of America were indeed welcome," wrote Reginald H. Jones, chairman of General Electric. "As a nation, we've had too much negativism."

The heads of the National Conference of Catholic Bishops, the Southern Baptist Convention, and dozens of other churches signed a letter applauding the president's "call to action" and his willingness to advocate "a return in part to the simplicity that distinguished earlier generations."

The *New York Daily News,* the largest-circulation newspaper in the country, called the speech "by far the best formal address [Carter] has delivered as president," and the *Baltimore Sun* editorialized, "Suddenly last night, the nation saw an old friend, the man who had won the presidency by appealing to the decency, the faith, and the selfless patriotism of his fellow citizens." The "sermon" could be historic, the paper said, "if the president uses this moment to bring to the country the sustained leadership that so far has been beyond

714

his grasp."

Rick Hertzberg was proud to have been part of a "truthful and prescient diagnosis" of what was wrong with the country. "But a president who sets out to diagnose a problem had better be able to offer a plausible solution to it," Hertzberg wrote years later. Carter couldn't. Nor could the other populist politicians — on both the Left and the Right — that Pat Caddell would advise over the next forty years. By offering few real answers to the underlying economic problems afflicting voters, they risked worsening the very alienation they had sought to address.

Still, Carter's malaise speech was a success, at least at first, and might have marked a turning point for his popularity. But then he wrecked it with the worst decision of his presidency.

At Camp David the previous week, Jordan and Powell and a few of the "wise men" began talking about a possible reshuffling of the Cabinet. Carter resisted at first but soon decided some kind of shake-up would show "vigor" and leadership. "You should fire people who are disloyal or no good," Rosalynn advised him.

And so, on July 17, two days after his historic speech, Carter appeared unannounced at the early-morning senior staff meeting in the Roosevelt Room and spoke in what Eizenstat called a "shocking" and "brutal" tone — the harshest in the dozen years that Eizenstat had known him. He announced that Jordan would be his new chief of staff, and a powerful one.

At ten thirty, a severe president convened a special Cabinet meeting with no note taker and no staff except Jordan, who had swapped his casual wardrobe for a blue suit and tie. Several of those present would describe this as one of the strangest and most unsettling meetings they ever attended. Carter said bluntly that some of them had been "disloyal."

After confused discussion, the president accepted a suggestion by Attorney General Griffin Bell that as a pro forma step, his Cabinet resign en masse, allowing him to accept whichever resignations he chose. Nobody seemed to remember that six years earlier, Nixon had done the same after his 1972 reelection, and it had generated a lot of criticism at the beginning of his second term. Defense Secretary Harold Brown recalled being among the few raising objections to Carter's request. "He was acting like Moses — breaking stone tablets — when he should have been aspiring to be Jesus," Brown recalled. Carter left the Cabinet Room, and Jordan passed out questionnaires for Cabinet members to assess how well their subordinates were coordinating with the White House, an exercise that amounted to a final burial of the ill-fated idea of Cabinet government.

The next few days proved disastrous for Carter. Instead of accepting the resignations of a couple of Cabinet members, which would likely have been viewed as an uncontroversial shake-up, he accepted five — half his original Cabinet. Jordan and Rafshoon told him it would make him look tougher if he dispatched several people at once, which Rafshoon admitted privately was "awful advice."

Each departure had its own dynamic. At Camp David, several days before the speech, Carter had accepted Jim Schlesinger's resignation, which he had offered twice before. (Members of Congress and Washington wise men felt he had been arrogant and unhelpful as secretary of energy.) The Georgians thought Treasury Secretary Mike Blumenthal was a leaker and too self-serving. They complained that when the economic news was good, he announced it; when it was bad, he let the White House handle the fall-out. (Staff acrimony had grown so bad that Carter sent Blumenthal a note upbraiding him for freelancing his views in the press and ended with a simple "Stop it.") And yet years later, Carter said, "If I had to do it all again, I wouldn't have let him go."

Carter had written in his diary in early 1979 that hard-charging Joe Califano was "one of the best and strongest" Cabinet members. But Califano had lobbied on the Hill against Carter's plan to carve a new Department of Education out of the Department of Health, Education, and Welfare he headed. The Carter team considered this unforgivably disloyal. Rosalynn also blamed Califano for her mental health legislation having stalled in Congress and suspected, correctly, that he was leaking to his friends at the *Washington Post.* And she disliked his antismoking campaign, which made Carter enormously unpopular in North Carolina and other tobacco-producing states. (Rosalynn figured smoking was an issue for the second term, when Carter planned to introduce a $2-a-pack cigarette tax.)* Mondale thought Califano's unquestioned competence should allow him to get off with a reprimand, but his advice did not prevail.

The Cabinet reshuffling also included Attorney

---

*"On smoking, you were right, and I was wrong," Carter told Califano in 2015.

General Bell — who had long intended to return to Atlanta but resented the appearance that he had been canned. After a phone call in which Transportation Secretary Brock Adams told the president his remaining would depend on how much Carter backed his programs (hardly the best approach to keeping one's job), the president accepted his resignation, too.

The global reaction to the resignations was alarming. Countries with parliamentary systems assumed that the American government had fallen. The consensus on the Hill was that the Cabinet "purge" negated anything the president had done to repair his image in his recent speech. "He's like a football player who was behind in the game, then catches the ball and is breaking through to daylight, when he suddenly runs out-of-bounds," House Majority Whip John Brademas said. In his memoirs, Carter acknowledged, "I handled the Cabinet changes very poorly."

Mondale, on the road pushing SALT II, was blindsided by the extent and timing of the purge. People he met kept asking him, "Are we falling apart? Has the government stopped operating?" On returning to Washington, he took Eizenstat to lunch at a Chinese restaurant on Wisconsin Avenue and poured out his heart, despondent over the clumsiness of Carter's recent decisions and his loss of influence on "a ship that seemed rudderless." How could the Carters prefer crazy Pat Caddell's advice to his? Revisiting his June decision not to quit, the vice president told Eizenstat that he just might do so after all, or at least withdraw from the ticket. Mondale claimed later that he was merely blowing off steam and had not been serious about quitting in either June or July.

718

By this time, Ted Kennedy was making noises about entering the race, which Mondale thought was outrageous and potentially suicidal for Democrats. This ended any talk of his resigning.

Even without a vice presidential resignation, the summer was a fiasco for the White House. Carter had just told the nation that he was going to be a leader and not a manager — and then flunked his first test of leadership after the speech. "That day, he was a gone duck," Jim Schlesinger said of the purge. All over the country, others were coming to the same conclusion. He had squandered his last, best chance to reestablish his connection to the American people.

By August 1, the fan mail to the White House had dried up, and Carter's poll numbers cratered. Cynics wondered whether his approval ratings might go below the inflation rate. Mario Cuomo, the lieutenant governor of New York and an admirer of the president, joked privately, "Jimmy Carter must be the sexiest man in the country. Everywhere I go, people say, 'Fuck Carter.' "

And that was all before interest rates neared 20 percent and American hostages were seized in Iran.

# 31
# TOUCHING BOTTOM

When Jimmy was young, his father thought he would make money planting ten acres of tomatoes on his property. The tomatoes didn't sell well, so Earl Carter boiled a huge batch of them and told his son to bottle two hundred gallons of catsup. But Mr. Earl miscalculated. In the Georgia heat, the catsup fermented, and scores of bottles began exploding in his commissary and neighboring stores. Jimmy had to clean up the mess.

So it was in the summer and fall of 1979, only this time, it was Jimmy's catsup that began exploding, as a series of events — large and small, personal and political — stained his presidency tomato red.

Carter's single biggest domestic setback was his failure to tame inflation, which had been surging since the 1960s for reasons that even Nobel Prize–winning economists didn't fully understand. Their classic definition of the causes of inflation — too much money chasing too few goods — was a partial explanation. Presidents Johnson and Nixon had pliant Federal Reserve chairmen "print money" to pay for the Vietnam War and expensive domestic programs and to boost economic growth just before elections. Then Nixon abandoned the gold standard, devalued the dollar, and, in 1971, slapped on rigid federal wage and price controls, which so distorted markets that they worsened inflation when they were lifted. Finally, the 1973 Arab oil embargo sent oil prices — the foundation of many other prices — through the roof.

By the seventies, prices at the grocery store (and everywhere else) were gyrating wildly. The inflation rate went from 4 percent in 1971, to 12 percent in 1974, to 6 percent in 1977, to 13 percent in 1979. This was hugely disorienting and eroded not just purchasing power but also the value of money in the bank. Economists had long believed that when inflation went up, unemployment went down. But the seventies saw frequent combinations of sluggish growth amid high inflation — a phenomenon dubbed stagflation.

Carter's battle against inflation had been an awful slog from the start. In early 1978, with inflation over 7 percent, he hired Bob Strauss to fly around the country jawboning CEOs to slow their price increases. That failed, as did efforts to hold down inflation with renewed antitrust actions against semi-monopolized industries. Carter then decided to hire a colorful know-it-all economics professor named Alfred Kahn to serve as "inflation czar." Kahn, who had done a good job implementing airline deregulation, tilted right. "Congress and Labor were our natural enemies," he said later, blaming government spending and generous labor contracts for continued inflation.

In 1979 Kahn drafted a series of complicated "voluntary guidelines" for business and labor. The guidelines — the product of an elaborate accord among CEOs, unions, and the White House to restrain wages and prices — ended up "guiding" almost no one.

The final straw for Carter came in mid-1979, when his economic advisers told him that the best-case scenario was reducing inflation by 1.25 points. That was pathetic, Carter thought. After two and a half years, he was out of patience. As the bond market continued to react badly, the president decided the best way forward was to soothe anxious investors.

Carter had started with a strong populist distrust of the Establishment, which, even as late as July 1979, he was calling "snobbish, arrogant, distrustful, especially of people like us." But after being told at Camp David that he was a ham-handed bush leaguer with an arrogant staff, the president decided he had to hire some pillars of the Establishment.

To replace Blumenthal as secretary of the treasury, Carter offered the job to David Rockefeller and brought on Lloyd Cutler (an impeccably credentialed Washington lawyer) and Hedley Donovan (the silver-haired former editor in chief of Time Inc.) as senior advisers. When Rockefeller turned down Treasury, Carter tapped Federal Reserve chairman G. William Miller, who, unlike many administration officials, had a good relationship with the White House. That left a critical vacancy at the Fed. Carter's fate, and that of the American economy, would turn in no small part on his choice to fill it.

Paul Volcker, a rumpled, cigar-chomping six-foot-seven-inch veteran of Nixon's Treasury department, was the chairman of the powerful Federal Reserve Bank of New York. Volcker was a Wall

Street guy, but he wasn't a banker; he was a bank economist. In 1979, economists were roughly divided into Keynesians and free marketeers. Volcker, having been burned by some of Nixon's failed Keynesian remedies, was increasingly in the latter category, though with a pragmatic and non-ideological turn of mind. He had a reputation as a canny and unpretentious public servant, and on July 15 he had listened approvingly to Carter's "malaise" speech. Volcker often voted Democratic and thought Carter was right to address the sour and divisive mood in the country.

A few days after the Cabinet shake-up, Bill Miller invited Volcker to come talk to Carter about replacing him at the Fed when he became Treasury secretary. Sprawled on the couch in the Oval Office, cigar in hand, Volcker gestured at Miller, sitting nearby. "You have to understand," he told Carter. "If you appoint me, I favor a tighter policy than him [Miller]." Carter assured him that he believed in the Fed's independence, but Volcker knew that Carter's political advisers — worried he might hurt Carter in 1980 — opposed him. The meeting was short, and Volcker felt he had talked too much. He was certain he would not get the job. If he hadn't — if Bill Miller had been replaced by someone similarly loyal to Jimmy Carter — the history of the next forty years might have unfolded in a dramatically different way.

This counter-factual almost happened. As he weighed his options, Carter was warned that Volcker might not be a "team player." His thoughts turned to A. W. "Tom" Clausen, the CEO of the San Francisco–based Bank of America, which he had built into the largest commercial bank in the United States. Clausen had served on Carter's transition team, and the president admired him for his interest in the developing world. He sensed Clausen would be more cooperative at the Fed — more like Miller — than Volcker would.

Carter phoned Clausen in California to see if he wanted to come east to talk about the job. While the president spoke, Clausen's wife, Peggy, sat next to her husband on the porch of their country home. When it became clear what the call was about, Peggy shook her head vigorously from side to side and mouthed an elongated "No." So Clausen told Carter that he and his wife didn't want to move to Washington just then. Once Clausen had declined, Volcker was the only candidate left.

Former Carter aides like to argue that Peggy Clausen changed American history: had she let her husband become chairman of the Fed, he would have been far more cognizant of the sensitive politics at play. Interest rates would not have skyrocketed, and Carter would not have faced voters in November 1980 with such a dismal economy.

With Volcker's appointment apparently still pending, Jerry Rafshoon took a call from Bert Lance, who had been advised by counsel not to be in direct touch with the president until his legal case was resolved. "You gotta tell Jimmy that if he appoints Volcker to the Fed, he'll be mortgaging his reelection to him," Lance said, urgency in his voice. Rafshoon rushed to the Oval Office, but the president was behind closed doors. He went by Powell's office, where the press secretary was writing a press release. "We're about to announce that Paul Volcker is the new Fed chairman," Powell said casually, not recognizing the consequences of

724

the decision.

Carter didn't need Lance to tell him he was rolling the dice with Volcker's appointment. He might have ended up preferring Clausen had he been interested, but he understood that Volcker would do what it took — namely, raising interest rates — to bring down inflation, whatever the political consequences. Rosalynn, for one, seemed to have little idea of the excruciating path ahead and told friends how excited she and Jimmy were that he had appointed Volcker and that they could now finally solve the inflation problem.

It helped that Carter was tightfisted by nature. Like his passion for energy conservation, his long-standing fiscal conservatism allowed him to elevate prosaic economic questions into matters of moral principle. Moving right felt right. Loose money was like gluttonous energy consumption, a luxury the nation could no longer afford. If that meant administering the harsh medicine prescribed by the bond market, he could live with it. Besides, this was not as nonpolitical a decision as he and his aides would later claim. Continued double-digit inflation, he felt, would wreck his chances at reelection. He had to try something, even if it made things worse before they got better.

Carter did more than just appoint Volcker; he resolved to challenge liberal Democrats who didn't seem to care all that much about inflation and the way it ate away at savings. "The budget commitment will be to control inflation," Carter told the press, explaining his domestic priorities for the year ahead. "It will be very austere, stringent, tough fiscal policy."

This was true only relative to the proposals of

725

very liberal Democrats. For all of the moaning in Congress and the press over his austerity, Carter rarely vetoed domestic spending bills. And he remained committed to investments in education and health. By the end of his presidency, Carter had doubled funding for Head Start and boosted spending 50 percent for poor schools and child nutrition — hardly a Scrooge-like budget.

Carter's successors nonetheless benefited from his political guts. By swallowing his doubts and appointing Volcker, he set in motion powerful economic forces that would eventually put the United States on a path of stable if inequitable low-inflation growth for the better part of forty years. They would also help cost him reelection.

When shambling Paul Volcker got the job, he traveled to Washington without his wife, who was in ill health, and rented a cheap one-bedroom apartment. He had "practically nothing in savings," he remembered, because he had spent most of his career in public service.

Once in place, Volcker moved fast. On August 16, ten days after he took over, the Fed raised the discount rate — the rate it charges for loans to banks — to 10.5 percent, a modern record. But two more rate increases in the next month did nothing to slow what had become 15 percent inflation, unprecedented in peacetime, and the markets lost faith in the Fed.

So Volcker decided to pull the fire alarm. On Saturday, October 6, 1979, he broke Fed chairmen's long tradition of silence and assembled the news media for a historic announcement. The country's central bank had long controlled the *price* of money (interest rates). Now, however, he

726

was going to let the market influence the *amount* of money (the money supply) pumped into the banking system through a series of complicated Fed "targets." This attempt to stabilize the economy by controlling the supply of money was known as monetarism and had been championed by Milton Friedman, the hugely influential University of Chicago economist who won a Nobel Prize for his free market theories. Volcker was revolutionizing the way central bankers had acted since the founding of the Federal Reserve System in 1913.

Like all Fed chairs, Volcker pretended he knew exactly what he was doing; he had to, in order not to spook markets. In truth, as he would later admit, he was experimenting. Volcker was like an oncologist trying various harsh treatments to save the life of the patient without killing him.

At the White House, Charles Schultze, the chairman of the Council of Economic Advisers, called Volcker with a final plea: raise interest rates again if you must but don't lock the Fed into a rigid monetarist system. That would likely lead to even higher interest rates and guarantee a recession. Volcker was unresponsive, though he had by then edged away from a pure Milton Friedman approach. He dodged questions from reporters about whether the Fed's new strategy for fighting inflation would slow growth and raise unemployment. In private, he did not dispute that an election-year recession would be the inevitable result. He was not hostile to Carter, merely "indifferent" to his political fate, as the journalist William Greider put it.

Amid worries about foreign policy and the

economy, Carter had to contend with another exploding catsup bottle closer to home: a seven-month federal investigation into Carter's Warehouse over vague allegations that money had been diverted from the warehouse into the 1976 campaign. Paul Curran, the special counsel in the case, deposed the president for four hours at the White House on September 5, in what was the first deposition ever taken from a sitting American president. Before the deposition started, Carter told Curran he thought the probe was a "travesty." He wrote in his diary that the fault was not with Curran "but with a weak attorney general [Griffin Bell, who had appointed Curran] and [with] our system of justice."

Carter was also angry with Bell's replacement, Benjamin Civiletti, who gave the president what Carter described privately as a "ridiculous reason" for appointing a special prosecutor in the case: because there was not enough evidence to prosecute Carter, "the special prosecutor was needed to determine whether the accusers were guilty of perjury!" Exclamation points were rare in Carter's diaries, and a sign of extreme annoyance.

Unlike Presidents Clinton and Trump, Carter never went public with his unhappiness over the inquiry. And he did not gloat when the 180-page report concluded with a full exoneration. The special counsel reported on October 16 that no money had been diverted from the warehouse and that while Billy Carter had overdrafts in one account, Billy's loans from Bert Lance's National Bank of Georgia were not illegal, as a former Carter's Warehouse employee had alleged.

Unfortunately for Carter, this would not be the end of Billy's legal troubles. His brother had become an alcoholic and had done things after Jimmy became president that would soon embarrass him.

Back in April, the president had gone fishing alone one day on a pond near Plains. A vicious-looking, oversized swamp rabbit approached his flat-bottomed boat, hissing and baring its teeth. Carter slapped the water with his paddle, to no effect, before the rabbit noticed something else and swam away. After returning to Washington, Carter recounted what he thought of as a humorous yarn to Jody Powell on the Lincoln Balcony. Powell laughed and said it couldn't be true: rabbits don't swim. As they joshed about the story, Carter asked if White House photographers had any pictures. They did, and the enlarged grainy photos proved the president right.*

In mid-August, the Carters boarded the *Delta Queen* for a leisurely riverboat trip down the Mississippi River, where a relaxed president had a gin and tonic with a group of passengers. Chatting with Brooks Jackson of the Associated Press, Susan Clough made the mistake of telling him the rabbit story. Jackson's lighthearted article ran on page one of the August 30 edition of the *Washington Post* ("Bunny Goes Bugs: Rabbit Attacks President") with an accompanying cartoon of a rabbit emerging from the deep under the word *Paws* — a spoof of the movie poster for the 1975 blockbuster killer-shark film *Jaws*.

The "Killer Rabbit" story exploded, running in

*The photo of Carter in the boat and the rabbit swimming off wasn't released by the Carter White House. After Reagan became president in 1981, it was leaked.

almost every newspaper in the country and many abroad. The anecdote became shorthand for a hapless president, as if even swamp rabbits thought Jimmy Carter was an easy mark. Good-natured laughter turned into ridicule, with Carter's ordinary flaws stretched into character defects and an innocuous fishing anecdote transformed into a symbol of incompetence. The story kept percolating right into 1980, when folk singer Tom Paxton released a song about the incident called "I Don't Want a Bunny Wunny in My Widdle Wow Boat."

Carter was obviously annoyed by the over-the-top coverage, but he had to be a good sport about it in town meetings and sessions with reporters. Even years later, he was forced to pretend the whole thing was funny. The rest of the world thought so. Dave Barry wrote in his humor column that "the enormous swimming rabbit" was the single most memorable event of the entire Carter presidency, and Carter's 1976 chief speechwriter, Patrick Anderson, speculated later that the story resonated because even when the president tried to make light of it, he seemed incapable of laughing at himself. Jody Powell had a different take on why such stories stuck to Carter: the hostile media. He told a reporter, only half facetiously, that having been in the White House for a while, he was "beginning to think Richard Nixon got a raw deal."

Unable to fend off inflation or a swamp rabbit, the last thing Carter needed was a flap that alienated an important constituency. But he got one.

Andrew Young, the first African American ever to serve in a senior foreign policy post, was a top-notch UN ambassador when it came to fulfilling his main duty: repairing US standing in the world after the deeply unpopular Vietnam War and revelations of rampant CIA abuses abroad. Carter's and Young's success in reviving American ideals anticipated Barack Obama's improving America's image in the world after the disastrous Iraq War — and gave encouragement to those hoping to do the same in the post-Trump era.

But Young's basic modus operandi — "I'd rather ask forgiveness than permission" — made him a target. In 1977 he had been forced to apologize twice for off-the-cuff comments that were accurate but inconvenient, first for charging that "Britain invented racism," and then after attacking Presidents Nixon and Ford for neglecting Africa. He took heat again in 1978 for suggesting that there are "hundreds, perhaps thousands of political prisoners" in the United States, by which he meant people jailed "much more because they are poor than because they are bad." Once again, he was penalized for uttering the truth.

The story that ensnared Young in the fall of 1979 and alienated many Jewish voters was not a gaffe. It was the ironic result of a well-intentioned effort to protect Israel from criticism. In pursuing that goal, Young met with a representative of the PLO, a violation of US policy that alarmed American Jews — even though both the United States and Israel were at that very moment trying to establish secret contact with the Palestinians.

As usual, the backstory was more complicated than the public understood. In August Young was serving a brief stint as the president of the UN Security Council, a rotating position with a set of responsibilities different from those of an ambassador. He worried that a pending UN report (rumored to have been authored by Yāssir 'Arafāt himself) that pushed Palestinian statehood and bashed Israel would necessitate a high-profile American veto, which would set off demonstrations around the Arab world and hamper efforts to convince the PLO to recognize Israel's right to exist.

Young figured it was best to block or delay the report. Arab diplomats told him that Zehdi Terzi, a well-regarded Christian lawyer who was the PLO's nonvoting representative to the United Nations, was the only one who could convince 'Arafāt to back off. The ambassador of Kuwait suggested that Young and Terzi meet at his house over the weekend. To keep it looking casual, Young wore jeans and brought along his six-year-old son.

Of course, the soon-to-be famous meeting on August 11 wasn't casual, and when a State Department official asked Young about it, he told the truth. But Young made the mistake of also telling Yehuda Blum, the Israeli ambassador to the United Nations, that the meeting was, in fact, substantive. The Israelis, worried about much more serious American overtures to the PLO, leaked the story, and the press went wild trying to figure out if Young had strayed from US policy.

Deputy Secretary of State Warren Christopher hoped to replace the ailing Cyrus Vance as secretary of state and feared Carter would name Young instead. Christopher's ambitious aides convinced Vance that Young had misled him about the purpose of the meeting. This was rich because it was almost certainly State Department officials — not Young — who had been deceptive by hatching a phony cover story for the press that the visit

732

was merely "social." In any event, Vance went to the White House on August 14 and informed Carter that Young lied and had to go. It's me or Andy, Vance said. Carter admired and appreciated Young but felt obliged to side with his secretary of state.

Young remembered telling Carter that his conscience was clear and he felt he had done nothing wrong, but that if he stayed, demonstrations by Jews outside the UN would be followed by counterdemonstrations by blacks, and the whole mess would jeopardize Carter's reelection. The president accepted Young's resignation, and they parted on good terms. If he had to do it over again, Carter said after Vance's death, he would have kept Young and cut Vance loose.

The one thing blacks and Jews agreed on was that Carter was to blame for the debacle. Black leaders thought Carter had succumbed to Jewish pressure to fire a civil rights hero; Jewish leaders were angry that they were blamed for Young's downfall instead of "the long knives at the State Department."

Carter used an August 30 speech at Emory University to say that both the black and Jewish communities had experienced "too much pain, too much suffering" to be at odds with each other.* He knew he would need both communities to get reelected. Benjamin Hooks, executive

---

*Another flashpoint was affirmative action, which many Jews, among other whites, felt was coming at their expense. In the landmark 1978 *Regents of the University of California, Petitioner, v. Allan Bakke* case, which focused on admission to medical school, the Carter administration filed a brief supporting affirmative action but opposing quotas — anticipating where the

733

director of the NAACP, threatened that unless black leaders received greater cooperation from Carter, "I'm going to find somewhere else to take my vote." He and other blacks decided not to bolt, but many Jews — located in critical swing states — did.

Carter's fund-raising took a hit. Jewish donors accounted for a significant chunk of the contributions to the Democratic National Committee, and Evan Dobelle, treasurer of the DNC, informed the president that his support among Jews was also being hurt by the sale of F-15 fighter jets to Saudi Arabia. Carter refused to pander. "You want me to change my policy to make your job easier," he told Dobelle coldly. "You do your job, and I'll do mine."

Carter's political problems with American Jews were rooted in cultural differences. Stuart Eizenstat, the president's most senior Jewish adviser, noted that while Carter's Baptist beliefs led him to honor Israel, his rural roots meant that growing up he never had much contact with Jews. Eizenstat felt that while Carter obviously knew about the two millennia during which persecuted Jews were expelled from country after country, culminating in the Nazi Holocaust, "I do not think he fully internalized the collective impact on Israeli attitudes." But Eizenstat and Jerry Rafshoon were adamant that Carter bore no trace of anti-Semitism and had no tolerance for it. And his other Jewish advisers and officials, including Bob Lipshutz, Bob Strauss, and four Jewish Cabinet secretaries — Treasury Secretary Michael Blu-

Supreme Court came down.

734

menthal, Defense Secretary Harold Brown, Commerce Secretary Philip Klutznick, and Transportation Secretary Neil Goldschmidt — reported nothing to suggest any bias.

This didn't break through to some Jewish voters. In 1980, despite Camp David, Carter would receive a mere 45 percent of the Jewish vote, making him the only Democratic candidate in modern times to lose a majority of it.

In December 1978 Carter had decided to take up running, which he had not done consistently since his cross-country days at Annapolis. He went from jogging a mere mile and a half his first day to as many as eight miles along paths near Camp David. If he and Rosalynn were in town at the same time, they tried to sneak away at four o'clock in the afternoon for an under-the-radar run in Rock Creek Park. Soon running became an obsession for the president, who was hypercompetitive even with himself. In June 1979 he ran with the troops at five fifteen in the morning in South Korea, and in August he jogged around the deck of the *Delta Queen* until passengers not associated with the presidential party complained — at which point he ran onshore. Running six-and-a-half-minute miles, Carter reduced his weight from 157 pounds to 149 and his resting pulse rate from 60 to 40.

Carter preferred shorter uphill runs to marathons. So he and Dr. William Lukash, his personal physician and running buddy, helped design a brutal 6.2-mile course in the Catoctin Mountains near Camp David. Carter could complete the steep course in around fifty minutes but resolved to shave time off his personal best.

On September 15, No. 39 (fitting for the thirty-ninth president) donned a yellow headband, the short shorts of the day, and black socks, and joined 750 other runners, including Olympic marathoners and weekend enthusiasts, in the Catoctin Park 10K Race. *Sports Illustrated* would report that it took guts for Carter to make his debut as a road runner at this shaky moment in his presidency, but Carter expressed no doubts about how he would do. He never did.

On a scale of 1 to 10, experts rated the difficulty of the Catoctin course an 8. Around the halfway mark, Carter passed a water station, reached for a cup, missed it, and kept climbing a long, steep hill. Suddenly "his face was ashen. His mouth hung open, and his eyes had an unfocused look," according to *Washington Post* columnist Colman McCarthy, who was running nearby. Dr. Lukash and a Secret Service agent rushed up to grab the president under the arms to keep him on his feet. Carter tried to continue; he never had — and never would — know when to quit. But his legs didn't work, and he crumpled. As an ambulance approached, he staggered instead into a waiting car that took him back to Camp David. Two hours later, the smiling president, looking well, presided over the awards ceremony. "They had to drag me off," he said. "I didn't want to stop."

The stories afterward practically wrote themselves, as the press succumbed to the temptation to add the indelible image of Carter collapsing during the race to the malaise speech, the killer rabbit, and Andrew Young's final flap, all of which occurred within a span of two months — irresistible symbols of the president's haplessness. Little wonder Carter was in danger of being the first incumbent president since Rutherford B. Hayes denied renomination by his party.

In September 1979 he trailed Ted Kennedy in the polls by a margin of 2 to 1.

# 32
## READY FOR TEDDY?

The press and political world had believed Ted Kennedy was running for president as far back as December 1978, when Carter wasn't yet halfway through his term. At the Democratic Party's midterm "mini-convention" in Memphis, Kennedy overshadowed Carter and gave a barn-burning speech that included the classic line "Sometimes a party must sail against the wind. We cannot afford to drift or lie at anchor. We cannot heed the call of those who say it is time to furl the sail."

The sea metaphor contained everything a misty-eyed progressive could want: the defiance of prevailing conservative winds in politics; the glamour of sailing with the Kennedys at Hyannis Port; the romance of guiding the ship of state back to the magical kingdom of Camelot. And by saying explicitly that the Democratic Party should not be the party of McKinley, Harding, Coolidge, and Hoover — all Republicans — Kennedy was cementing the charge that Carter was not just a centrist Democrat but a crypto-Republican.

By early 1979, Kennedy was holding planning sessions for a 1980 campaign, though he claimed in his memoirs that he didn't make a final decision to run until he felt outraged by the pessimism of the July malaise speech. He told friends that the president of the United States should not wring his hands and act as if the job is too big for him. His sister-in-law Jackie Onassis thought the malaise speech lessened the grandeur of the office, and Washington power broker and éminence grise Averell Harriman — who ten months earlier had called Camp David one of the greatest presidential triumphs ever — told friends, "I would never imagine a president talking that way about our country."

That didn't mean Ted had the full support of his team. William vanden Heuvel, a close family friend, was serving in Geneva as US ambassador to the European office of the United Nations. He relayed word to Kennedy that if he ran, he would "divide the country, lose the election, and bring to power the forces we've been fighting our whole lives."

Carter signaled he would play rough. At a June 11 dinner for sixty Democratic House members at the White House, Connecticut congressman Toby Moffett asked about Kennedy. "If Kennedy runs, I'll whip his ass," the president said, before repeating the line for other House Democrats who might not have heard it the first time. Carter thought his feisty answer was the best thing for morale in the White House since Willie Nelson performed months earlier.

When Americans for Democratic Action, the most influential of the old-line liberal groups, met that month in Washington, Arthur M. Schlesinger Jr. invoked his flawed "cycles of history" theory to suggest that a revival of 1930s-style full-blown governing liberalism was just about to commence.

He was at least forty years early, but the ADA didn't care. The group's members endorsed Kennedy and helped spread the new progressive line: that the president of their own party lacked "leadership." Repeated often enough, it stuck.

Why the intraparty venom? Many of the same northern liberal Democrats who would revere Carter in the twenty-first century disliked him in those years for what they saw as his hypocritical combination of piety and pettiness, his indifference to expensive social programs, his opposition to federally funded abortions, and — most important — his anemic approval ratings, which they worried would drag down the entire Democratic ticket in 1980. Vanden Heuvel, for one, figured that — as in 1968, 1972, and 1976 — Kennedy never really wanted to run but was doing so only because he thought Carter was a certain loser to Reagan.

A collection of congressional Democrats who supported Kennedy thought the president so politically weak that in September they plotted to go to the White House and tell him he should not seek reelection. They chickened out, but the Kennedy rebellion grew so fierce through September and October that John White, the Carter-appointed chairman of the DNC, felt obliged to say he was neutral.

It's hard to understand in retrospect why so many Democrats wanted to throw a smart and decent man overboard. Beyond embarrassment over an uninspiring president who seemed in over his head — and fears of a crushing defeat — lay a century-old regional schism that was reopening in the party. Pat Caddell's shorthand was oversimplified but not wrong: "Southerners took over; now

740

Yankees unhappy." The big issue in the South had been integration — not Social Security, Medicare, and other "entitlements" (a bloodless pejorative first applied in the Carter administration) that were seen as birthrights in the North. The fact that Carter had helped save Social Security and wasn't challenging other entitlements didn't count for much with liberals.

Carter didn't absorb that the old orthodoxies still held sway among a majority of Democrats. He saw austerity as morally superior to profligate spending and shared the conservative critique that stagflation was the product not only of external forces like OPEC but also of ever-expanding social programs. This turned out to be faulty economics; the next four decades proved that increased government spending under both parties did not ignite inflation. And it was lousy politics. Fiscal hawks don't win many votes.

Mondale aides grasped this and were freaked out by Labor Day polls showing Kennedy with a 35-point lead over Carter. But Caddell and the Georgians felt sure the survey findings weren't real. Caddell liked to point out that the public's view of presidents had changed since Watergate and that voters now distinguished between personal approval — where Carter continued to rate highly on integrity and honesty — and job approval, where the unpopularity of the dreary energy crisis and the Panama Canal treaties pulled down his ratings. "Why is he perceived as a weak leader?" Caddell asked. "I think it's because he has taken on unpopular causes."

When he was a Harvard undergraduate, Caddell occupied the same room in Wigglesworth Hall that Kennedy had lived in two decades earlier. He asked Bob Shrum — a top aide to Kennedy — to hand deliver a letter to his boss reminding them of this connection and adding: "I'm the King's man, and you have moved to kill the King. We will beat you." The senator did not reply.

So much about politics is personal: Kennedy and Carter just never liked each other. During the 1976 campaign, Kennedy was understandably offended by Carter's refusal to reach out to him. He was, after all, the most prominent Democrat in the Senate and a man known to have useful allies across the aisle. After the election, he thought the president lectured him and his colleagues and only gave "the *appearance* of listening." Kennedy grew restless when he attended Carter's earnest White House seminars on obscure issues, which he considered nothing more than occasions for Carter to show off his knowledge. And the hard-drinking senator resented not being offered liquor at these colloquies, which the White House did not view as social events. Carter, meanwhile, seemed aggrieved by what he saw as patrician condescension. He believed that Kennedy, still a few years away from achieving greatness as a senator, felt entitled to the presidency. Kennedy wrote later that as cold as Carter could be to other politicians, "he reserved a special place in his animus toward me."

The irony was that the two men — or at least their underlings — worked together on some of the most impactful legislation of the 1970s. To a later generation of progressives, "deregulation" sounds threatening. But economic (not health and safety) deregulation was essential to the future of transportation and other industries that had been protected from competition and become bloated and inefficient. Most deregulation was backed strongly by both Carter and Kennedy, and even by Ralph Nader and other reformers. They all recognized that certain long-in-the-tooth regulatory agencies had been taken over by the industries they were supposed to monitor — so-called "regulatory capture."

The most conspicuous example was the Civil Aeronautics Board (CAB), which, since the New Deal, had developed baroque bureaucratic systems for strictly controlling airline routes, fares, service, and entrance to the market. For decades, passengers dressed up for trips to the airport as if they were going to a fancy restaurant; air travel was, by definition, luxury travel. In the mid-1970s, it was hard to fly from New York to Los Angeles for less than $1,400 (in 2019 dollars). After Alfred Kahn, a Carter favorite as chairman of the CAB, dissolved his own agency, sartorial standards plummeted with the fares; Kahn received letters from passengers complaining about sitting next to disheveled hippies.

Kahn worked closely with a brilliant young lawyer on Kennedy's Judiciary Committee staff named Stephen Breyer, who had developed the academic arguments for reform and was impressed there was "a reader in the White House" — Carter — who absorbed them.* The 1978 deregula-

---

*Just after losing the 1980 election, Carter swallowed his hard feelings toward Kennedy and appointed Breyer to the US Court of Appeals for the First Circuit. Republicans could have easily blocked the nomination and waited a couple of months until Reagan took office and appointed a Republican. But that's not how the

tion of the airline industry they fashioned led over time to a quadrupling of air travel, which meant tens of millions of Americans could see their families more often and vacation far from home. The new law brought much lower fares on major routes, higher fares on others (especially to small cities), and endless disruption and consolidation in a now-cutthroat industry. The bill's free market reforms allowed the emergence of companies like Federal Express, whose conservative founder, Fred Smith, could never bring himself to admit that he wouldn't be in business if it weren't for Carter.

While the CAB had become a silly agency, abolishing it altogether hurt the battered flying public, which has little recourse for bad service. Within a few years, an experience that Americans once looked forward to became — thanks to Carter and Kennedy — an affordable but often uncomfortable part of life.

Another joint project, trucking deregulation, also had a major impact on the American economy. On July 1, 1980, when, ironically, his tensions with Kennedy were at their peak, Carter signed the Motor Carrier Act — "a miracle achievement, since nobody thought it would ever pass," he wrote. The landmark bill created a new, more flexible regulatory structure that cut red tape and

---

game was played then. GOP senator Strom Thurmond, the incoming chairman of the Senate Judiciary Committee, knew Breyer and respected Kennedy, and he made sure the nomination was approved. In 1994 President Bill Clinton elevated Breyer to the Supreme Court.

eventually helped tamp down inflation by sharply reducing shipping costs — a payoff that came under Reagan.

Deregulation generated a half million new truck-driving jobs in the 1980s and eventually slashed all logistical costs by nearly a third — a huge productivity boost. Under the old rules, trucks were often required to make return trips empty and use pointless circuitous routes. Carter's reform allowed American companies to adopt "just-in-time" delivery systems that helped Walmart, Amazon, and thousands of other businesses thrive, though neither Carter nor Kennedy got any credit for it.

Carter saw airline, trucking, and railroad deregulation as part of his comprehensive plan to change the relationship between the government and the free enterprise system. With the consumer in mind, he also began gingerly deregulating communications (accelerating the suit to break up AT&T and enabling more cable TV) and financial services (though in a way favorable to consumers seeking loans, not Wall Street). He even signed a bill exempting home brewers from harsh regulations imposed during the Depression to prevent anyone from competing with large breweries. Within a few years, craft breweries went from a small handful to more than four thousand, though nobody other than a few grizzled former White House staffers have thought to hoist one in tribute to Jimmy Carter.

Beyond their personality clash, the big substantive conflict between Carter and Kennedy was over Kennedy's signature issue: health care. Focused on his energy bill and other priorities, Carter slow-walked plans for national health insurance, refusing in the first half of his term to make good on his well-publicized campaign promise to Doug Fraser of the United Auto Workers (UAW) that he would push for "universal" and "mandatory" coverage.

Instead, Carter and Califano, who also didn't work well with Kennedy, were busy improving the slipshod administration of the gargantuan Medicare and Medicaid programs and launching a dizzying array of innovative prevention programs that would save lives. Legislatively, the president was much more interested in his own bill to control hospital costs, which he viewed as critical to fighting inflation. It also happened to be a useful excuse to procrastinate on a broader health care bill. He informed Kennedy in mid-1978 that because of inflation, which was running as high as 30 percent in the health care sector, it would be years before a comprehensive national health insurance program would be affordable. He suggested coverage be expanded in phases.

Kennedy loathed the idea of phased-in coverage. Ironically, in the decades ahead, he would be the driving force on Capitol Hill behind exactly that, providing critical leadership in the enactment of the Children's Health Insurance Program (CHIP) under Bill Clinton, the 2006 Medicare prescription drug benefit under George W. Bush, and other phased-in health care expansion. But at the time, Kennedy thought Carter's incremental approach was woefully inadequate. And he was oblivious, if not hostile, to arguments about the dangers of rising budget deficits.

Brushing aside doubters, Kennedy thought Carter was "squandering a real opportunity to get something done." He told the president in a phone conversation in June 1978: "I don't think you can go to an elderly group and say, 'You're in . . . the second phase [of coverage], but if we pass the first [phase] and hospitals keep their costs down and the economy doesn't go so much into a deficit, then you might be phased in.' "

At the same time, Kennedy was wary of aiming too high. He wanted to supplement employer-based insurance and pay for it with some kind of progressive tax increase (though the top marginal rate was already 70 percent). To the dismay of some on the Left, Kennedy did not propose a single-payer system (later called Medicare for All), which he favored personally but thought was "politically impossible" to pass, even with heavy Democratic majorities in Congress. The main thing, he argued, was to join with the White House on a big bill that covered everyone.

This proved elusive. First, Carter and Kennedy clashed over whether to propose legislation before the 1978 midterms. With some justification, Carter argued no — any bill would be gutted because Congress couldn't stand up to the American Medical Association, the American Hospital Association, the US Chamber of Commerce, and other powerful interests in an election year. Kennedy was frustrated by Carter's lack of interest; his aides remember the boss entering the Oval Office for what they expected to be a three-hour meeting and leaving, deflated, after twenty minutes. Carter, who described Kennedy as "emotional about this issue and also knowledgeable," might have been right about the political odds of passage at that juncture, but he would have helped himself and his party had he more loudly and sincerely embraced the goal of universal coverage.

Not feeling the love, Kennedy grew adamant about moving forward without the president. Matters came to a head on July 28, 1978. In the Oval Office, Kennedy asked Carter to have Joe Califano delay a press conference in which the administration was scheduled to announce the broad outlines of its modest plan. He wanted time to study it. Carter agreed and was shocked when, at three o'clock that afternoon, Kennedy held his own press conference to denounce Carter's plan as insufficient. Kennedy "betrayed our trust," Carter wrote in his diary, by "blasting us." But he took bitter satisfaction in the now-public split: "In the long run, though, it helped because we've been dreading the liberal image of putting forth an expensive health care system, and Kennedy made us look [fiscally] responsible and conservative with our plan."

The hard feelings worsened in 1979. In February Carter instructed Califano to tell liberal members of Congress the harsh truth: that Kennedy's proposal "would be excessively expensive and impossible to pass." Califano, who had run domestic policy in LBJ's White House and had strong liberal credentials, agreed wholeheartedly. His priority, too, was hospital cost containment, which would have saved the public about $30 billion in hospitalization costs — real money in 1979.

"This is *the* vote to fight inflation," Carter wrote Tip O'Neill. He was right that with health care inflation running at a shocking 20 to 30 percent a year, urgent action was required. The problem, as Stu Eizenstat noted, was that by failing to link hospital cost containment to expansion of coverage in the same bill, the Carter plan was "all pain

748

and no gain, a serious strategic mistake."

There was no reason an ambitious president couldn't both contain hospital costs and move toward universal coverage. To Kennedy's credit, his passionate advocacy essentially forced Carter to craft a new bill that did so. After more than two years of delay, the president in mid-1979 finally coughed up his own moderate but impressive and achievable health insurance plan. It was along the lines of what he had promised the United Auto Workers in 1976 but came too late for him to win praise for finally fulfilling a campaign pledge.

Carter's bill was better than anything that would be produced by Congress for decades. Under it, no American would have to pay more than $1,250 a year in out-of-pocket costs, with anything above that handled by national catastrophic coverage. The bill federalized and expanded Medicaid (fully insuring an additional sixteen million people); funded generous prevention programs; paid all prenatal, delivery, and infant care; and created a framework to transition to full universal coverage over four years.

Carter knew Kennedy wouldn't like the bill and might attack it. But he once again refused to embrace the standard courtesies of politics — the ones he had also ignored two years earlier on the water projects. Instead of at least trying to reach out to Kennedy to bring him aboard beforehand, he let Califano blindside the Massachusetts senator by unveiling the proposal publicly without giving Kennedy a private heads-up.

That left Kennedy steaming. As with other clashes between the White House and liberals on the Hill, Walter Mondale mediated. He held two tense meetings with Kennedy. The vice president remembered being shocked that Kennedy — for all his noise about his own health bill — had not even managed to convince the relevant Senate committee chairmen to hold any hearings on it. This told Mondale all he needed to know about Kennedy's motives. "I think he had decided to run for president, and he wanted to hit us with this national health insurance thing," Mondale recalled.

The differences between Kennedy and Carter on health care, nuclear power, and other issues struck Mondale — whose Senate record was nearly as progressive as Kennedy's — as relatively minor. "Why, at this point in American history, decide to act in a way that would elect Reagan?" Mondale asked later. "The answer is that he thought that Carter was unworthy of being president. That was just plain irresponsible."

The Kennedy people ascribed the exact same political motives to Carter. They convinced themselves that Carter was some kind of Machiavellian president who actually wanted Kennedy to run against him so he could use the senator as a foil to stage a comeback. They claimed that if Carter really didn't want him in the race, he would have simply supported Kennedy's doomed health insurance bill. "What would the downside have been?" Carl Wagner, a senior Kennedy aide, wondered. The downside was that Carter genuinely didn't support the Kennedy bill, and it was against his principles to back major legislation he didn't like just for political reasons, especially when it had no chance of passage and his alternative did.

On June 12, 1979, Carter announced that his

plan was now backed by almost all of the important Democrats in Congress, including Senator Russell Long (chairman of the key Senate committee), Congressman Harley Staggers of West Virginia (chairman of the key House committee), and even California congressman James Corman, the ardent liberal who had been Kennedy's longtime cosponsor in the House.

Despite Carter's political weakness at the time, he likely had the votes to pass the bill had Kennedy merely maintained a sullen silence. But the senator did not have it in him to do so. "Kennedy, continuing his irresponsible and abusive attitude, immediately condemned our health care plan," Carter wrote bitterly in his diary. "He couldn't get five votes for his." This was an accurate head count. As Califano put it, Kennedy's all-or-nothing approach "had less chance of passing than putting an elephant through a keyhole." It never even came up for a vote in the Committee on Labor and Human Resources, where Kennedy served as a member but not yet as chairman. If it had, the liberal lion — famous in later decades for rounding up votes — did not have the Democratic support necessary to send it to the Senate floor, much less secure final passage.

But Kennedy's fervent opposition was enough to kill Carter's belated effort at major health care reform. Long, Staggers, Corman, and the other influential backers wouldn't move forward in the face of it. A year later, after Carter beat Kennedy for the 1980 nomination, the White House made a final effort to move legislation, and, again, Kennedy declined to take part. To make matters worse, the president couldn't even get a watered-down version of his hospital cost containment bill through the House, where it lost 234 to 166. Carter had blown an earlier opportunity to do so in 1979 by refusing to cut what he considered to be a crass deal (in truth, a minor federal appointment in Chicago) with influential Illinois congressman Dan Rostenkowski. Now he called dozens of Democratic members only to find that many were, in his words, "bribed" by the hospital industry. "This is the worst example of a powerful special interest that I've seen since I've been in office," Carter wrote that evening.*

Decades later, Kennedy and Carter each tried to blame the other for the disappointments of 1979. Kennedy wrote in his 2009 memoirs that had the president joined him in passing comprehensive national health insurance, "it would have been a huge victory for Carter. And it would have been much more difficult for me to challenge him for the nomination." Carter, like Mondale, felt Kennedy had already decided to run against him and was just looking for a platform. But in retrospect, he wished he had handled the Kennedy challenge better and confessed that the failure to achieve universal coverage was his greatest regret on domestic policy.

As in most failures to communicate, both men were at fault. It was Carter's responsibility to look past their rivalry and better manage his relationship with Kennedy — even when the senator shivved him. That was an important part of his

*Frank Moore said hospital cost containment lost because board members of hospitals lobbied congressmen while home in their districts by saying: "If you vote for this bill, our local hospital will close, and you will be to blame."

752

job as a leader. And it was Kennedy's responsibility to set aside his ego, stubbornness, and White House ambition and show some modicum of loyalty to a Democratic president — and to avoid making the perfect the enemy of the good. This hurt not just Carter but also the cause to which Kennedy devoted so much of his career in the Senate.

As he neared the end of his life, Kennedy lamented not splitting the difference on a solid, moderate bill that President Nixon and his HEW secretary, Caspar Weinberger, had offered him in 1973–74. But his bitterness toward Carter was such that he could never accept blame for anything he did in 1979–80, no matter its impact in the years ahead on the health of millions of American families.

For his part, Carter regretted that in late 1978 he didn't appoint Archibald Cox to the federal bench when Kennedy came to the Oval Office and asked him to do so. Carter's reason — that Cox, at sixty-seven, was too old — was a poor excuse; he was still sore at Cox for criticizing him in Mo Udall's campaign ads in 1976 and didn't want to do Kennedy any favors. In retrospect, he said, he should have told the senator, "I'll accommodate you because you don't ask me for many things." Kennedy often cited this pettiness in explaining why he ran for president, but he likely would have done so anyway.

Ted Kennedy's views of the presidency had for years been caught in tragic crosscurrents of duty, doubt, and loss. The longest-running story in American politics had become a musty, repetitive guessing game full of clichés about "restoring

Camelot" and "passing the torch." Should Kennedy run? Would Kennedy run?

He never had before. In 1968 the Democratic National Convention was held only ten weeks after RFK was assassinated in Los Angeles. Had he set aside his grief and jumped in, the youngest Kennedy, a mere thirty-six years old, was seen as a good bet to be nominated in Chicago and beat Nixon in November. Everyone thought this — except for Ted Kennedy himself. Even in 1972 and 1976 he was plagued by feelings of inadequacy compared to his brothers. Both years, he let the cup pass, and not just because memories of Chappaquiddick were still fresh in voters' minds. Through much of this period, Kennedy was a good guy in a bad place: drinking too much, cheating on his wife, and wallowing in self-doubt even as he made respectable contributions in the Senate. He felt he could not possibly live up to the expectations now garlanded around his neck.

Even in 1979, "Teddy honestly doubted he could do the job," said his nephew Stephen Smith Jr., who sat in on most 1980 strategy sessions. "He hadn't fully resolved his fear and insecurity about being a good president."

Several of Kennedy's longtime aides thought he ran not because of health care or other liberal issues, or because he thought Carter was some kind of usurper, but out of an honest political assessment that Carter could not beat anyone the GOP put up. His Senate colleagues John Glenn and Pat Moynihan begged him to enter — then hid after he got in. Kennedy backers all felt at first that what one called Carter's "sanctimonious smallball" was a sure loser in 1980.

At first, the outlook for Kennedy seemed promising. The Congressional Black Caucus endorsed him, offering hope that he could peel off black voters from Carter. Mark Siegel, a former Carter adviser on Jewish affairs, defected to Kennedy, as did former Iowa senator Dick Clark, who was running refugee affairs for Carter, and former Wisconsin governor Patrick Lucey, Carter's ambassador to Mexico. On the Hill, Tip O'Neill and Scoop Jackson whispered to reporters about major losses in Congress if Carter was renominated. But loyal Joe Biden — who twenty-one months earlier had warned Carter that Kennedy was running for president — called the president in August to report that he had polled the fourteen Democrats up for reelection, and only one, New Hampshire senator John Durkin, wanted Kennedy to run.

The Kennedys believed the essence of politics is chemistry, and that Teddy's 30-point lead in the polls proved it. The Carters believed in engineering and mechanics. October 13, when neither candidate had formally announced yet, was the first test of their respective strength. As in 1976, the incipient Carter campaign was exceptionally well organized in Florida. A vote for county delegates went for Carter, 2 to 1. Jordan had dreaded Kennedy's entry but he felt this little victory validated his judgment that a Kennedy campaign would allow Carter to prosper as the "giant slayer."

Sunday, November 4, 1979, one year to the day before the 1980 election, was expected to include a happy moment for the Carter presidential campaign. Word had leaked to Hamilton Jordan that an interview with Ted Kennedy conducted by CBS News anchor Roger Mudd — airing that night in an hourlong prime-time special — had been a disaster, especially on the subject of Chappaquiddick.

Mudd, an old friend of the Kennedy family, had first interviewed the senator at Hyannis Port on September 29, then two weeks later in his Senate office. The first half hour was dominated by questions about his failing marriage — he and his wife, Joan, a recovering alcoholic, were separated — and a brutal reconstruction of Chappaquiddick, which included familiar but nonetheless shattering facts about the drowning of Mary Jo Kopechne and Kennedy's unconscionable decision not to report the accident until the next morning. The producer, Andrew Lack (later the president of NBC News), arranged for a camera to be affixed to Mudd's car as it rumbled along the same dirt road Kennedy's Plymouth Valiant traveled on that night a decade earlier when the senator seemed to be looking for a secluded spot for himself and Kopechne. The segment left little doubt Kennedy knew he was making a wrong turn toward the Dyke Bridge, where he drove his car into the water.

Mudd asked him how he would handle a heckler who yelled, "Kennedy, you know, you were drinking, you lied, and you covered up." Kennedy's lame answers were studded with "uh"s. The interview confirmed that Chappaquiddick — once thought to be disappearing as an issue — would be a major liability for him in the primaries and general election.

But the worst was yet to come. In the second half hour, Mudd asked Kennedy a simple question that would all but end his chances of winning: "Why do you want to be president?"

756

After a pause lasting a full four seconds, Kennedy replied: "Well, I'm, uh, were I to make the announcement to run, the reasons I would run is that I have a great belief in this country. We have more natural resources than any nation in the world . . . I would . . . basically . . . feel that . . . that it's imperative for this country to either move forward, that it can't stand still, or otherwise, it moves backward."

The interview competed with the movie *Jaws* — airing for the first time on TV on another network — but it lit up the political world. "Seventy-five percent of the country watched *Jaws,* twenty-five percent watched Roger Mudd, and half of them couldn't tell the difference," Senator Bob Dole quipped. Mudd himself was incredulous afterward: "It was like, 'I want to be president because the sea is so deep and the sky is so blue.' " Carl Wagner, the senator's chief strategist, remembered watching the interview in Kennedy's Senate office and almost fainting. "It was awful," he said. "A terrible moment."

Another terrible moment for the Kennedy campaign came that very night, though no one could know that yet. At four thirty in the morning, the president and his team heard from the White House Situation Room that the gates of the American embassy in Tehran had been breached and an undetermined number of hostages taken.

Hamilton Jordan remembered that he wasn't unduly alarmed. This had happened in February, he figured, and the hundred hostages were freed by the end of the day. His thoughts turned immediately to politics, and he told Phil Wise, Carter's longtime aide from Plains, "It'll be over in a few hours, but it could provide a nice contrast

757

between Carter and our friend from Massachusetts in how to handle a crisis."

# 33
## AMERICA HELD HOSTAGE

The admission of the shah of Iran to the United States for medical treatment in October 1979 was a seminal event in recent American history: it led to the takeover of the US embassy in Tehran, which, of all the events in Jimmy Carter's long life, is the one that sticks to him most. The fate of the fifty-two American hostages became Carter's own. Even though they all returned safely, their captivity stigmatized him forever as the personification of impotent American leadership and helped cause the end of his presidency.

Many times more people died in 1979 and 1980 in auto accidents, plane crashes, and fires. It was the anger, embarrassment, and shame enmeshed in the story that made Americans feel as if the country itself were a hostage. And the cliff-hanging drama was perfect for television. For 444 days, the crisis captivated the nation, with every morsel of news devoured by an anxious public. The shared sense of crisis tied a deeply divided country together with a yellow ribbon — the totem of the day, a symbol of hope for their safe return.★

★The 1973 number one hit "Tie a Yellow Ribbon 'Round the Ole Oak Tree," sung by Tony Orlando and Dawn, regained popularity in 1979 and 1980.

It's rare when a compelling human-interest story is also major foreign news. The hostage crisis thrust to the foreground difficult questions of national honor, presidential restraint, and military competence. For the first but hardly the last time, Americans were confronted with a bewildering force — radical Islam — that sought to turn back the clock on a modern world they had taken for granted.

In 1970 President Nixon had warned that if the United States did not expand the Vietnam War into Cambodia, it risked becoming "a helpless, pitiful giant." The overwrought line didn't work then except as an ironic jab at Nixon. When the war finally ended in 1975, it brought more relief than humiliation. But as blindfolded hostages, burning American flags, and chants of "Death to America!" appeared on television night after night in 1979 and 1980, the status of the United States as a great power was suddenly on the line.

For most of 1979, Carter and his national security team weren't feeling too bad about Iran. They knew they could have handled the February revolution better but felt the new government in Tehran, however chaotic, was far preferable to a pro-Soviet regime in Iran that could have changed the map of the Middle East. Less than three months after the shah's departure, his country was on the back burner in Washington — a subject to avoid if possible. On May 1 Zbigniew Brzezinski gave a long speech at the National Press Club roaming the horizon of American foreign policy and didn't even mention Iran.

Through the winter and spring, the administration strengthened its military ties to other nations in the region but also began communicating again with the Iranian government. This may have lulled the State Department into thinking of Tehran as just another hardship post. The presence at the US embassy was shrinking, but relations stabilized to the point that in August the United States resumed providing spare parts for the American-made weapons still in the arsenal of the Iranian military. Hopes rose of maintaining critical secret listening posts near the border with the Soviet Union.

To lessen the perception of having "lost" Iran, Carter needed to get the oil flowing again. That meant restoring relations with the revolutionary regime, whose prime minister, Mehdi Bazargan, was seen as a relative moderate. At the opening session of the UN General Assembly in late September, Cyrus Vance met with Ibrahim Yazdi, the graduate of the Baylor College of Medicine and naturalized US citizen who had appeased the Americans at the French inn and was now Iran's foreign minister. Yazdi told him that improving relations was not possible until the United States fully accepted the revolution, extradited all "criminals" (senior officials in the shah's government), and returned the frozen assets belonging to Iran — much of it held at the Chase Manhattan Bank. They resolved nothing, but diplomatic channels remained open.

In Tehran, the revolutionary forces were factionalized. The secular nationalists were split between moderates, led by Bazargan and Yazdi, and those with more Islamic ideals, such as Abol Hassan Bani-Sadr (who would later work both sides) and a collection of faceless hard-line mullahs. Khomeini dominated the clerics but had not yet

761

consolidated enough power to become "supreme leader." This he would do by exploiting anti-American fervor that was much more intense than Carter understood.

From the start, Carter's instincts told him it was wrong to bring the shah to the United States. After fleeing Iran, the demoralized monarch — who did not formally abdicate — had rested in Egypt, where he had never planned to stay long, before accepting an invitation from King Hassan II of Morocco to live there for a while. This suited Carter fine. "I believe the taint of the shah being in our country is not good for either us or him," he wrote in his diary on January 20, 1979.

But the shah's final journey was only beginning. By mid-February, King Hassan was worried that the shah's presence in Morocco would be awkward during the Arab summit scheduled for April in Rabat. On February 26 former Iranian ambassador Zahedi called Brzezinski to say the shah wanted to come to the United States immediately. When Brzezinski asked Carter to reconsider his decision barring him, Carter grew angry — he didn't want the shah to be his responsibility.

Even after he learned in mid-March that King Hassan was essentially expelling the shah, the president's position did not soften. He told Vance to scout other countries that might take him. Carter was eerily prescient: "What are you guys going to advise me to do if they overrun our embassy and take our people hostage?" No one had a good answer.

Vance tried to enlist Henry Kissinger and David Rockefeller to fly to Morocco to tell the shah that he should not expect to find new accommodations in the United States. They both indignantly refused, despite hearing intelligence reports from Iran that confirmed Carter's fears that admitting the shah could lead to the seizure of the American embassy. No country in Europe or the Middle East would step up, and the US ambassador to Morocco was finally instructed to tell the shah that his options had shrunk to South Africa and Paraguay.

On March 30 the shah and his party were hours away from departing for Johannesburg on King Hassan's plane when they were rerouted to the Bahamas, where Joseph Reed Jr., the Chase banker running Project Eagle, had found them temporary refuge. Just before his fatal heart attack in January, Nelson Rockefeller had arranged for his friend the shah to have the full-time services of his onetime gofer, a dapper young advance man named Robert Armao, who would meet him and his entourage (including two smelly dogs) at the Nassau airport. The twenty-nine-year-old Armao — Project Eagle's man on the ground — would become the shah's closest companion, bridge partner, and strongest advocate in the last sixteen months of his life. He would eventually run afoul of Carter, who came to believe the young man's deceptions helped wreck his presidency.

Project Eagle had all the trappings of a fevered conspiracy theory come to life: a cabal of scheming elites who actually were secretly controlling American foreign policy under the direction of the Rockefellers. The key players were David Rockefeller (whose Chase Manhattan Bank had syndicated $1.7 billion in Iranian loans and held $500 million of the country's deposits), Henry Kissinger (who had worked for the Rockefellers before Nixon and had subcontracted large chunks of American foreign policy to his friend the shah), and John J. McCloy (the so-called dean of the American foreign policy establishment, whose law firm represented the Pahlavi family) — with occasional help from former presidents Richard Nixon and Gerald Ford, Theodore Roosevelt's grandson Archie Roosevelt Jr. (whose cousin Kermit Jr. helped engineer the 1953 coup that put the shah in power), former CIA director and ambassador to Iran Richard Helms, and Jim Schlesinger, now out of government but never short of strong opinions.*

On April 9 David Rockefeller came by the Oval Office to tell Carter that after only nine days in the Bahamas, the shah already wanted to leave. He and his entourage felt they were being cheated by the lavish Paradise Island resort that hosted them, an argument that brought no sympathy from the president. That week, Kissinger called his old rival Brzezinski to lobby for the shah to come to the United States, and he followed up with a call to Carter himself, who respected Kissinger. After the calls, Carter asked his national security adviser, "What would you do if you were

*McCloy was a lawyer-diplomat best known for his World War II service as assistant secretary of war, a position in which he served ably but was also heavily involved in the internment of Japanese Americans and the decision not to bomb Nazi concentration camps. Thirty-five years later, McCloy besieged Carter, Vance, and others in the administration with letters about relocating the shah to the United States, but with no discernible impact on Carter's decisions.

president?" Brzezinski advised letting the shah in. He felt it was a matter of "national honor" built on the principle that the United States stands by its friends. Kissinger, meanwhile, went public and said that it was morally wrong for the United States to treat the shah "like a flying Dutchman seeking a port of call," a line used for months afterward by Carter's conservative critics.

In May the shah's Bahamas visa ran out, and the government declined to renew it. Rockefeller tried to arrange for Austria to welcome him, but no invitation materialized. The shah's first choice was Great Britain, and that looked promising for a time. During her 1979 campaign for prime minister, Margaret Thatcher pledged to admit him, but after she won, the foreign office advised that doing so would be dangerous for the British embassy in Tehran. Queen Elizabeth II, who had sounded welcoming, also got cold feet.

That left Mexico, where President López Portillo overruled the objections of the foreign ministry. Bob Armao found a Cuernavaca villa owned by a Palm Beach socialite, and on June 10, the shah, his queen, and their dwindling entourage decamped for what would be their fourth country in six months. In Mexico, the shah hosted Nixon, Kissinger, and other American friends who assured their royal friend that they were working to help him win entrance into the United States.

The president didn't like the pressure tactics of the establishment. Hamilton Jordan reported that the high-level lobbying campaign backfired and actually made Carter less sympathetic to the shah's plight. He reacted badly when Kissinger tried to link, in what Brzezinski facetiously called his "subtle fashion," his critically important support for SALT II to White House support for the shah. Senators Charles Percy, a Republican, and Claiborne Pell, a Democrat, ratcheted up the establishment pressure, implying that by denying the shah entrance the president was submitting to Iranian blackmail. Conservative critics argued that Carter was simultaneously weak for abandoning the shah and ungracious for not letting him in. "It is so sad that an administration that knows so much about morality has so little dignity," George Will wrote in his syndicated column.

At a July 27 national security breakfast in the Cabinet Room, Carter complained caustically that "Zbig bugged me on it [admitting the shah] every day." This was apparently only a slight exaggeration. Feelings in the meeting were still raw from the Cabinet purge ten days earlier, and the discussion about the shah grew testy. Vance produced staff studies showing that Iranians believed letting the shah into the United States would be a prelude to a 1953-style effort to undo the revolution and restore him to the throne. He reported that Bruce Laingen, the acting ambassador in Tehran, had cabled that admitting the shah could jeopardize the security of the embassy. All of this left Vance strongly opposed to welcoming him.

Kissinger, McCloy, and others associated with Project Eagle had been lobbying Walter Mondale for weeks, and it finally worked. The vice president now supported admitting the shah on the grounds of basic human decency. But the president remained adamant. Hundreds of Iranians — including the shah's longtime prime minister — had been executed since the revolution began, and memories of the February 14 assault on the US embassy remained fresh. More than once, Carter

766

asked his national security team about contingency planning. He reminded them that earlier in the year a pair of marines at a satellite observation post on the border with the Soviet Union had been briefly detained by militants. "What are we going to do if they take twenty of our marines and kill one of them every morning at sunrise?" Carter recalled saying. "Are we going to go to war with Iran?"

Brzezinski was undaunted, and he and Mondale pressed Carter. The president finally exploded: "Fuck the shah! I'm not going to let him in when he has other places to go where he'll be perfectly safe!" The room, by all accounts, went silent. "It was shocking to hear," Harold Brown remembered. "I'd never heard him use that word before." Carter went on to say that he didn't want the shah in the United States playing tennis while Americans in Tehran were kidnapped or even killed.

To prevent that, the United States was quietly extracting forty thousand Americans living in Iran — a complex and risky operation. Amid the revolution, no commercial flights went in or out of Tehran. That meant transporting the American expats by C-130 aircraft from heavily fortified military bases. The size of the US embassy, once the largest in the world, was being reduced from 1,100 to about 70 and the security upgraded — though in hindsight, not upgraded enough. It helped that Prime Minister Bazargan and Foreign Minister Yazdi had both made firm commitments to Laingen to protect the embassy. Laingen had been warning for months that the reaction in Tehran to admitting the shah would be terrible but would be "more defensible if we were seen to admit him under demonstrably humanitarian conditions."

Over the summer, the shah fell ill in Mexico, his skin a sickly yellow. His glamorous and quick-tempered twin sister, Princess Ashraf, wrote a plaintive letter to Carter vaguely describing "the quite noticeable impairment of his health in Mexico" and urging that he be granted asylum. Carter passed the letter along to the State Department, which offered a noncommittal response.

Now came a series of medical errors by squabbling, elbows-out doctors that show why prominent people so often receive poor care. On September 29 Project Eagle dispatched to Mexico a charming, domineering New York society doctor and friend of Joseph Reed named Benjamin Kean — an expert in pathology and tropical disease. Dr. Kean couldn't figure out the source of the shah's jaundice, in part because the shah's men gave him someone else's urine sample to keep the cancer a secret. Back in New York, Dr. Kean finally learned the truth from an alarmed Armao. On October 18 Dr. Kean returned to Cuernavaca, where Dr. Georges Flandrin, one of the French oncologists who had treated the shah for years, gave him the details of the chemotherapy regimen he was using. Upset that the hard-charging Dr. Kean — no cancer specialist — was now running the shah's cancer case, Dr. Flandrin abandoned his famous patient and returned to France.

What happened next became the subject of dispute. After consulting with Armao on the ground in Mexico, Joseph Reed of Project Eagle told old-boys-club friends at the State Department that the shah was receiving chemotherapy for "malignant lymphoma" compounded by a possible intestinal blockage that had caused the severe jaundice. The Project Eagle version was that Dr. Kean believed the shah had only days to live and needed a CAT scan and other diagnostic tests not available in Mexico. Reed, who later served as ambassador to Morocco and chief of protocol under Reagan and Bush, was described by Ambassador Nicholas Veliotes, a widely respected career diplomat, as a "compulsive liar." In this case, anyway, his lies had resounding consequences.

In truth, Mexican hospitals contained plenty of CAT scan machines and other state-of-the-art equipment, and many fine physicians from around the world came there for training. And oncologists could have easily been flown in from the United States. But the cursory report (lacking the opinion of an oncologist) prepared for Warren Christopher by the State Department's incompetent medical officer made no mention of this. It offered Reed's bogus claim that the shah must be treated in the United States.

Carter received Christopher's memo — stamped "Supersensitive" — on October 20 when he was in Boston speaking at the dedication of the new John F. Kennedy Presidential Library and Museum. This potentially awkward occasion, with Ted, Jackie, Caroline, and John Jr. in attendance, was eased by what everyone agreed was Carter's pitch-perfect speech (written by Rick Hertzberg). Carter's memory was that he learned in Boston that the shah was "at the point of death" and must be brought to the United States to save his life.

This was untrue. Dr. Kean insisted later that he never said the shah had only days to live and never claimed Mexico did not have CAT scans to diagnose him and radiation therapy departments to treat him — and that for Armao to say he felt the Mexicans lacked such facilities was "nonsense." Moreover, Dr. Flandrin, the French doctor who knew a lot more about the shah's cancer than Dr. Kean or anyone else, believed that while American hospitals might be superior, the shah could be properly diagnosed and treated in Mexico City. Although Armao would claim later that the only debate was over "optimal" care in the United States versus "acceptable" care in Mexico, this was not how he and Project Eagle framed it at the time. Had the possibility of "acceptable" care in Mexico been conveyed to the White House, the shah would never have been admitted to the United States — and events in late-twentieth-century America might have taken a dramatically different course.

Just as Carter had failed to read the full report on Bert Lance, he now failed to ask enough questions about Christopher's memo; his normal attention to detail flagged when he needed it most. On October 21 in Tehran, Laingen, the acting ambassador, and Henry Precht of the State Department — equipped with State's bogus medical report — briefed Prime Minister Bazargan and Foreign Minister Yazdi on the shah's condition and the urgent need for medical attention in the United States. The Iranian ministers were skeptical and warned, "You're opening a Pandora's box with this." But the two most senior Iranian officials said the embassy would be protected — as it had been in February — as long as the shah stayed in the United States only for

770

medical treatment and didn't engage in political activity.

Embassy security personnel in Tehran warned Washington that the compound was vulnerable, but because the warning didn't come from Laingen, it received no high-level attention and no decision was made to bolster security at the perimeter. "We were faced squarely with a decision in which common decency and humanity had to be weighed against possible harm to our embassy personnel in Tehran," Vance wrote later, explaining his change of heart. And there were political considerations. Hamilton Jordan warned Carter that Kissinger would have "a field day" if the shah was still rebuffed: "He'll say that first you caused the shah's downfall and now you've killed him."

Had Carter been tougher, he would have stuck to his original decision barring the shah. But his heart prevailed over his head and his gut. With no debate, the president made the most fateful decision of his presidency and agreed to admit the shah on humanitarian grounds, with the understanding that he would return to Mexico as soon as possible. "I was convinced that there would be no adverse consequences — that Bazargan and Yazdi would indeed protect our embassy," he explained later. He reasoned that no host government in the modern era had ever endorsed attacking an embassy or kidnapping a nation's diplomats. It was a bet he had not been willing to make over the previous nine months.

On the evening of October 22, a Gulfstream II jet carrying the shah landed at a private air terminal at LaGuardia Airport. Amid great secrecy, he was admitted to New York Hospital Center under the alias "David Newsom" (which was news to Undersecretary of State David Newsom). What followed was a new string of medical miscues. After word leaked of the shah's presence in New York, anti-shah demonstrators gathered every day to shout up toward his room.

At first it seemed as if the shah would receive excellent care. A well-respected New York oncologist, Dr. Morton Coleman, examined him and briefed the press with a prognosis that gave the celebrity patient a fifty-fifty chance of survival. But the case quickly turned peculiar. New York Hospital's radiation department was deemed inferior to that of nearby Sloan-Kettering, but the cancer center, concerned about possible terrorism, didn't want anyone to know it was treating the shah. So he was often transported there secretly at two in the morning in a wheelchair through an underground tunnel that connected the two hospitals. Sloan-Kettering doctors working a special night shift secretly administered radiation to his lymph nodes before he was wheeled back to New York Hospital.

Dr. Coleman was appalled to learn that a New York Hospital surgeon removed most of the shah's jaundiced gallstones without taking out his cancer-ridden spleen. This on-the-fly decision was seen later by several doctors as fatal to the shah. Then, once the shah's first round of chemo and radiation was completed, Dr. Kean, the tropical disease specialist, impulsively removed Dr. Coleman, the oncologist, from the case. This meant that until just before the end of his life, the shah's cancer would not be treated by a cancer doctor.

As news of the shah's entry to the United States

spread to Iran, a million protesters filled the streets of Tehran, very few of whom believed the shah had been admitted to the United States for medical reasons. A Tehran newspaper ran a picture of the shah looking healthy, with an accompanying article suggesting that he could not possibly have lymphoma because everyone knew that Iranians did not even get that kind of cancer.

On November 1 Brzezinski and one of his deputies, Robert Gates, a future secretary of defense, flew to Algiers to honor the twenty-fifth anniversary of Algerian independence. Prime Minister Bazargan and Foreign Minister Yazdi were there and asked for a meeting with Brzezinski, who rejected their urgent requests that the shah not be granted asylum. His message to the Iranians was blunt: "We will not betray him." Brzezinski was by then widely known inside Iran for having backed the shah's admission, and the photograph of him shaking hands with the prime minister and foreign minister played badly in Tehran. Within a week, both Iranian ministers would be gone, with fateful consequences.

If Carter had a better sense of the bitter anti-Americanism in Iran, he might have sensed trouble ahead. Instead, his only comment in his diary was that Brzezinski had wandered out of his lane on the trip (by meeting with Morocco's King Hassan) and that Vance had grown "emotional" about it: "Cy's so extremely jealous it's ridiculous — but I didn't interfere." Carter and his men were arguing on the edge of the abyss.

The following day, a twenty-four-year-old civil engineering student at the Tehran Polytechnic Institute strode into a makeshift meeting room.

Mohsen Mirdamadi moved with "the latent energy of a coiled spring," as a fellow student agitator who went by "Mary" wrote later. A dozen student representatives of radical Islamic groups from all four Tehran universities were gathered for this planning session, awaiting a decision on what should happen next.

"We've been under the thumb of the United States for more than fifty years," Mirdamadi told the group. "Now it's our chance to do something about it." The room was silent. Everyone felt certain that admitting the shah to the United States was the prelude to a coup d'etat, as in 1953, and that to protect the revolution, they needed to find the American documents detailing the plot. But how to prove its existence? At another meeting, a student named Ibrahim Asgharzadeh proposed a peaceful occupation of the US embassy, where the documents were kept. They would take Americans hostage — not as diplomatic personnel but as agents of the US government. Asgharzadeh, Mirdamadi, and a tiny group of other students (several of whom ended up decades later as prodemocracy reformers) were setting in motion events that would upend a six-hundred-year global tradition of diplomatic immunity.*

The next day, Khomeini validated their plans. Commemorating students killed in 1978 while protesting the shah, the ayatollah said, "It is incumbent upon students . . . to expand their attack on America and Israel." He would soon use

*Mohsen Mirdamadi was elected to parliament in 2000 but removed in 2006 and sentenced to prison in 2010 for protesting the rigged election of 2010.

their passion to consolidate his power. Mirdamadi persuaded the group, already called the Muslim Student Followers of the Imam's Line, to move up its timetable and stage the occupation immediately, before the United States tightened security.

It is one of the significant ironies of recent history that the student militants drew no distinction between Carter and his intensely pro-shah Republican predecessors. They were under the misimpression that Carter intended to restore the shah or another American puppet to power. Their motive for the embassy takeover was to prevent an outcome that Carter — trying to accommodate himself to the new regime — did not, in fact, seek. Of course, they had no reason to believe Carter's recent assurances of Iranian self-determination, if they heard them at all.

The students moved fast. Within a day, one found lookout points to sketch the embassy compound, while others produced 250 red armbands emblazoned with a small image of Khomeini and "Allahu Akbar" — insignia for the men and women authorized to be part of the operation. They would bring three days' worth of supplies. No one expected the occupation to last longer than that.

On Sunday morning, November 4, 1979, it was drizzling in Tehran. After attending a pro-Khomeini rally on campus, about four hundred students marched from Tehran University to the American embassy. Three days earlier, a mob had been repelled at the gates, but now they had a plan. Devout women hid bolt-cutting shears and a few guns under their chadors.

At ten in the morning, the students calmly

breached the front gate and told the fifteen or so Iranian police officers to step aside. Why they agreed to do so remains unclear. (Pre-9/11, the host country and its security apparatus handled perimeter security for all US embassies around the world.) The dozen US marines inside the compound saw what was happening on closed circuit TV, but they had long-standing orders not to use their weapons, lest a shooting at the embassy worsen whatever tense situation they faced. At first, only 150 or so student radicals entered, but soon thousands of exultant Iranians scaled the walls and swarmed the once-manicured twenty-seven-acre compound, a parklike symbol of privilege in the teeming city, now full of debris left over from the recent evacuations of foreign nationals.

Inside the embassy, American officials had a sense of déjà vu. They remembered the nerve-wracking Valentine's Day attack but also their rescue within hours by Yazdi and others from the Iranian government. Bazargan and Yazdi had lost power inside the regime, but no one knew it yet. Following protocols, the American diplomats alerted Washington — where it was three in the morning — and began destroying communications equipment and burning documents. The furnace wasn't working properly, though, so they had to switch to a shredder. Later, the captors, who called the embassy a "nest of spies," painstakingly reassembled the shredded documents in an effort to show the Americans were plotting to undermine the revolution. They were not, but the shredded files were incriminating enough to be useful as propaganda.

At first, the militants seemed underwhelming.

One soon-to-be hostage, John Graves, noticed that the first wave of students were polite, and many seemed to be women. He saw a sign in English: "Don't be afraid. We just want to set-in" — a translation problem suggesting that the action was akin to the sit-ins of the civil rights and antiwar movements in the United States.

By afternoon, the situation began unraveling. The American in charge, Bruce Laingen, was not in the US embassy at the time; he was over at the Iranian foreign ministry, where relations with the United States had been improving in the weeks before the shah was admitted. He called his colleagues barricaded inside the embassy and told them to surrender. "It looked hopeless for us to begin some Custer's Last Stand operation. I thought that would be very dangerous," he remembered. Any firefight would end badly for Americans, who would then be at the mercy of the mobs.

The US Marines briefly repelled women students led by "Mary" (Masoumeh Ebtekar, a future vice president of Iran) with tear gas and threats to use their guns. But after seeing that the women, who wore shirts with Khomeini's image, were prepared to die as martyrs, the embassy's chief of security ordered his men to stand down to avoid bloodshed. After he bravely went outside to negotiate with the lead captors, they put a gun to his head and forced him to scream to the others — barricaded behind inner heavy steel doors — that they would kill him if the Americans didn't open up. When the doors opened, the militants stormed in and rounded up dozens of Americans. The captors blindfolded them, tied their hands behind their backs, and hustled them to a nearby building — an image caught in photographs that would soon help define the era.

At first, no one grasped the full gravity of the situation. When Laingen sought out Yazdi — still unaware that he was about to be undercut by more radical forces inside the government — the foreign minister told him the whole thing would be resolved by morning. "What are you going to do with me?" he asked Yazdi, who advised him to go down to the diplomatic reception rooms of the foreign ministry and find a place to sleep there for the night. Along with two colleagues, Laingen would be held separately from the others for the duration — an odd combination of hostage and diplomat.

By some accounts, Khomeini was planning to order the hostages released a couple of days after documents were recovered. Then, on the first night, his son Ahmed Khomeini was hoisted over the wall and reported back that the takeover was the work of an impressive revolutionary force that should not be ignored. By the second day, it was clear that the ayatollah would not authorize even negotiations over the hostages, at which point both Bazargan and Yazdi — already weakened by the handshake with Brzezinski — resigned.

Inside Iran, the occupation of the embassy was expected to extend only through mid-November 1979, when the country would debate the adoption of a new constitution that would grant veto power to the mullahs and their canny supreme leader. If they weren't freed by then, some of the hostages were sure the cavalry would rescue them by Thanksgiving — Christmas at the latest. They settled in the dank basement of the embassy warehouse, which the hostages called "the Mushroom Inn" because it seemed perfect for growing them.

At first, the hostages numbered sixty-seven, but in mid-November the ayatollah ordered fifteen women and black hostages released. The United States thought that might mark a softening in Tehran's line, but it did not. For weeks, the hostages were not allowed to speak a single word, bathe, change clothes, or go outside. Some were beaten for minor infractions; awakened in the middle of the night, stripped to their underwear, and forced to face mock firing squads; and tormented with games of Russian roulette. The sole consolation was that the basement contained many good books that had been brought from the now-closed American international school in Tehran (including Aleksandr Solzhenitsyn's novel *The Gulag Archipelago,* about detention in Siberia). Throughout, the hostages had no idea if Laingen was dead or if the outside world was paying any attention to them.

Several of the captors had a love-hate relationship with the United States. They would beat the hostages — then say they hoped to get a visa for America when it was over. When the Reverend William Sloane Coffin (a longtime peace activist) and other clergymen were allowed to visit in late December for a Christmas party, a hostage whispered, "Don't believe what you are seeing; we're being treated like animals."

The day after the embassy takeover, November 5, was business as usual in Washington, a sign of how history can sneak up on policy makers. The CIA had no information about these "students" and their intentions. "We just plain fell asleep," CIA director Turner admitted later. In the afternoon, Warren Christopher sent the president a memo covering six pressing foreign policy matters. The first five were: relief snafus in Kampuchea (Cambodia); a coup in Bolivia; bank credits for Poland; a troubling speech by India's defense minister; and Colombia's chances of securing a seat on the Latin American Security Council. Number six was Iran, of which Christopher reported tersely, "We have made no progress today in securing the release of the hostages."

By the next day, it was clear that the immediate release of hostages that took place after the February takeover had not happened this time. At a meeting of the National Security Council, Carter listened to every possible option — "no matter how preposterous" — from delivering the shah back to the revolutionaries as they demanded (ensuring his death) to dropping an atomic bomb on Tehran. He didn't want the kidnappers called "students" anymore (they would be "militants" or "terrorists" moving forward) but urged everyone to avoid abusive language about Iranians that might provoke them into hurting the hostages.

"It's almost impossible to deal with a crazy man," Carter wrote in his diary that night. The only hope, he thought, was that as a religious figure, Khomeini would not want his reputation damaged by "committing murder in the name of religion" — a surprisingly clueless sentiment that placed faith over his usual empiricism. After all, extralegal executions had been under way in Iran for nine months.

With Bazargan and Yazdi gone, Carter asked Vance, "Who does that leave us to deal with?"

780

Vance peered over his reading glasses at Carter and said: "The Ayatollah Khomeini." This became the central problem of the next fourteen months — several Iranian officials claimed to speak for the country, but only one man did so, and he refused to authorize anyone to negotiate on his behalf much less meet with any foreigner himself. The Americans didn't know this yet. So Vance then suggested that they send former attorney general Ramsey Clark, a onetime opponent of the shah who knew Khomeini, to Tehran as an emissary, a mission that the PLO (hoping to improve its status) offered to help facilitate. Powell and Jordan looked at each other and rolled their eyes. For the previous decade, Clark had been involved in fringe Far Left causes. Carter had questions about that but was finally convinced it was worth a try.

Never one for superpower swagger, Carter wrote a polite private letter to the ayatollah asking him to receive Clark and to release the hostages "for humanitarian reasons." Instead of making demands, which he felt would be counterproductive, he closed with: "The people of the United States desire to have relations with Iran based on equality, mutual respect, and friendship." Khomeini never responded to Carter, and upon arrival in Tehran, Clark — like many others who would try in the months to come — was denied any meetings with anyone from the government unless the United States sent the shah back to Iran for trial and execution. Carter asked several Middle Eastern countries to intercede; it was hard to know how much they tried, but none was successful.

From the start, the presence of hostages severely

limited Carter's military options. So he took a series of other actions: ending oil purchases from Iran, banning pro-Khomeini demonstrations on federal property, deporting fifteen thousand pro-Khomeini students, and, eventually, freezing $12 billion in Iranian assets held in American banks, which turned out to be the smartest decision he made in the entire crisis.

On November 8, at Jordan's suggestion, Carter canceled a state visit to Canada to attend to the embassy seizure. This was the beginning of a new and self-defeating approach. In 1976 Carter had accused President Ford of adopting a "Rose Garden strategy" — using the power of incumbency to make news from the White House instead of mixing it up on the campaign trail. Now Carter chose to do the same thing, with the hostages as his explanation for not campaigning. "It was the first time we had placed Iran above everything else in Carter's presidency, and I felt largely responsible for the public trap we later found ourselves in," Jordan remembered.

In the first month of the crisis, Carter, Mondale, Vance, and others engineered a chorus of worldwide condemnation, though European allies refused to jeopardize their oil supplies and other economic ties with full-scale embargoes against Iran.

The political reaction at home was more supportive. In November Carter's approval rating jumped from 30 percent to 61 percent in the Gallup poll. After an impressive November 28 press conference devoted to the hostages, public approval for his handling of the crisis passed 75 percent in some polls. Clark Clifford came by to tell him that Kennedy's official entrance into the race (just three days after the Roger Mudd interview and the seizure of the embassy) would keep the Carter team on its toes and that beating him would give the campaign momentum going into the general election — as it turned out, spectacularly wrong advice.

Carter had planned to begin campaigning for reelection in early December, but he canceled his first road trip. On December 4 his campaign bought time on CBS for a speech in which he explained, "Abraham Lincoln said, 'I have but one task, and that is to save the Union.' Now I must devote my concerted efforts to resolving the Iranian crisis."

Jordan thought this was not smart politically; nobody was as good a campaigner as Carter, and he was confident his boss would thrash Kennedy on the trail. Rafshoon agreed and figured Carter was using the hostages as an excuse not to have to engage with a rival he considered a spoiled brat and unworthy of his time and attention.

It's easy to say in retrospect that Carter should have issued an ultimatum: release the hostages or the United States will start bombing. But doing so would have been unlikely to yield results. It's easy to forget that there was legitimate uncertainty in the early weeks of the crisis over whether Khomeini had fully consolidated power and exercised full control over the student militants who occupied the American embassy. Carter's first priority at the time — endorsed by almost every expert and commentator — was to avoid doing anything that might enrage the captors and lead to the death of the hostages.

Every official on the Special Coordination Committee (SCC) set up to handle the crisis operated under the assumption that any ultimatum must be backed up; otherwise it risked great harm to American credibility in the world. If Tehran called the bluff, and Washington launched a sustained bombing campaign or inserted ground forces, the United States would have to wage a long, grinding war in a country with many of the most advanced weapons systems in the world and a landmass more than five times the size of Vietnam. Every president knows (or should know) that getting out of a war is always much harder than getting in, and neither Ronald Reagan nor any of Carter's other hawkish successors seriously considered responding to hostage taking with major military action.

At Camp David on November 20, Carter heard the military options. Brzezinski favored seizing or blockading Kharg Island in the Persian Gulf, from which Iran exported most of its oil. Harold Brown preferred mining the entrances to Iranian harbors, which could be done with less danger to US warships. The group discussed bombing a major refinery at Abadan, in southwestern Iran. All could be executed immediately. A rescue attempt could not: the nearest US aircraft carrier was six hundred miles from Tehran, and the Army Rangers, Navy SEALs, and others who might be involved in such a mission would need months of special training.

Carter fretted over what he saw as his poor military options. He thought a naval blockade would set back chances of a negotiated settlement, while not inconveniencing Iran much, given its access to shipping goods from other countries and Khomeini's indifference to oil revenues. "If we seize Kharg Island, then what?" Jody Powell asked. "We have Kharg Island, and they have the hostages." Carter figured if the United States mined Iran's harbors, the Iranian government would almost certainly turn to the neighboring Soviet Union for minesweepers. (The atheism of the Soviet Union would have been no impediment for Khomeini and the mullahs. Within two years, they would be buying arms from Israel — "the Little Satan" — to fight Iraq.)

The Carter family was on the hawkish side. Miss Lillian didn't think her son was being tough enough on the ayatollah. "I'd get a couple of mafiosi and take him out," she told a friend.* Rosalynn described herself as "very impatient" and, as the days passed, began to say to him, "Do something! Do something!"† She fell silent when he asked her — as he had asked his aides the previous summer — how she would feel if the terrorists took a single hostage out, once a day, and executed him in front of the world. Cy Vance, Lloyd Cutler, Hamilton Jordan, and Jody Powell

*Miss Lillian's friend Maurice Sonnenberg, who later advised President Clinton on intelligence, said Carter should have told Khomeini that we were coming for the hostages, and if he didn't relinquish them unharmed, we would destroy the holy city of Qom. Sonnenberg's idea never reached the president.

†In 2001 the Carters took a fishing trip near Yellowstone National Park that included Supreme Court justice Sandra Day O'Connor. When the subject of Iran arose, Rosalynn grew tearful. If he had bombed Iran, "Jimmy would have been reelected," she said conclusively. "But all the hostages would have died."

agreed with the president's logic.

"The problem with all the military options," Carter said quietly in a November 9 meeting, "is that we could use them and feel good for a few hours — until we found out they had killed our people. And once we start killing people in Iran, where will it end?" A famously impatient president settled on patient diplomacy to secure their release. The American public and editorial pages agreed, at least for a while.

With no direct negotiations on the horizon, Carter tried any available connection to Iran. He had been embarrassed the previous August when his brother returned from Tripoli (his second trip) and bragged to reporters about all of the nice gifts he'd received from the Libyans. But now Rosalynn didn't hesitate to call Billy Carter and ask him to arrange a meeting with Libyan officials who might help free the hostages. On November 27 Brzezinski met secretly with Billy and representatives of the Libyan government. The meeting led to Mu'ammar Gadhafi sending the ayatollah a letter seeking the release of the hostages. It didn't work.

Years later, the president and his national security adviser would disagree on why the United States did not intervene militarily. Brzezinski thought Carter's reluctance to use force grew out of his faith; Carter felt he just had bad intelligence and few options. Either way, the president ignored the essential dynamic of the crisis: once he signaled that he would not even mount a token show of force, Khomeini had no reason to release the hostages.

In that sense, Carter's most fateful decision after letting the shah into the United States may have been traveling a few blocks to the State Department on November 10 and again on December 7 for private meetings with the families of the hostages. He was gracious and comforting, and many family members said afterward how grateful they were for his determination to bring home their loved ones. "I am not going to take any military action that would cause bloodshed or arouse the unstable captors of our hostages to attack them or punish them," the president told State Department personnel gathered in the lobby. "I'm going to be very moderate, very cautious." In essence, Carter tied his own hands with his compassion and noble intentions. The United States no longer had any leverage, and the standoff dragged on.

Even if one grants that military action would have been a mistake, Carter suffered from the failure of a quality he otherwise revered: boldness. In diplomacy, the element of surprise always helps. Carter never surprised the Iranians. They thought they had him figured out, and they were right. If, for instance, he had mined a harbor or two as a taste of what was to come if they didn't negotiate directly for the hostages' release, the Iranians might have thought twice about whether they truly wanted war with the United States. But Carter was, at bottom, a man who would take risks for peace but not for war. He would gamble with his own reputation but not with the lives of innocent Americans.

Carter knew that he was messing with male archetypes deeply embedded in the American psyche. "I could've been reelected if I'd taken military action against Iran, shown that I was strong and resolute and, um, manly," he said on his ninetieth birthday. "I could have wiped Iran off the map with the weapons that we had, but in the process a lot of innocent people would have been killed."

There were limits to his forbearance. After Carter moved naval forces into the Gulf, Khomeini responded on November 23 by saying that if the United States attacked or tried to rescue the hostages, he could not prevent the student captors from destroying the embassy and prisoners. In response, Carter used the Germans (because many of Iran's top civilian leaders had been educated in Germany) to deliver a message to Khomeini that if any hostage was hurt, the United States would cut off Iran from the outside world; if any hostage was killed, Washington would retaliate militarily. Carter felt that allowing the hostages to be put on trial would likely hasten their execution. He authorized Jody Powell to threaten "grave consequences" if they were brought into court. They never were, because Khomeini knew that doing so would bring war.

The following week, the president miscalculated. Angered by reports from the newly released black and women hostages that they had all been abused in captivity — bound, threatened with guns, and kept in unsanitary conditions for three weeks — Carter told a November 27 breakfast with Democratic congressional leaders that "the slate would not be wiped clean just by release of the hostages." Louisiana senator Bennett Johnston leaked these remarks to the press, which interpreted them to mean that Carter would retaliate against Iran *after* the hostages were freed. This obviously incentivized the Iranians to hold the hostages longer, lest they be attacked. It reinforced that the hostages were now the only cards the Iranians had to play. Releasing them would be seen at home as buckling to the country the protesters now called "the Great Satan." If Iranians looked like pawns of the West again, their revolution would be doomed.

Carter's advisers were growing concerned about appearances. On December 18 Brzezinski warned Carter that US policy looked "increasingly flabby" and that the potent effect of threatening military action "seems to have worn off." It was time, he said, to "make clear that sanctions are the last *peaceful* remedy but that other remedies are not excluded."

Carter nonetheless remained focused on the United Nations and other diplomatic efforts to convince allies to hold Iran in default and not take part in international tribunals directed at prosecuting the shah. A year-end visit to Tehran by UN Secretary General Kurt Waldheim was a complete failure. On his return, he recounted for Carter his terrifying experiences in Iran, where he felt his life was in danger on three occasions. There's no government in place, he told the president. Khomeini wouldn't see him, and the Revolutionary Council established after the shah fled was timid and ineffective.

A few Iranian officials were actually looking for plausible ways out. Abol Hassan Bani-Sadr, on his way up in Iranian politics, thought he had the answer. He would go to New York and present Iran's case against the shah to the UN Security Council. The United States, he figured, would strongly oppose this move but would have a hard time vetoing a resolution condemning the shah that was conditioned on the freeing of the hos-

789

tages. But Bani-Sadr recalled that when he was preparing to leave for New York on November 28, he heard on the radio that the ayatollah had ordered that no one could go to the United Nations on behalf of Iran. He said he traveled to the holy city of Qom to ask the ayatollah directly why he was preventing his trip. Khomeini "received us in a severe, distant manner" and offered irrelevant anti-UN arguments, Bani-Sadr wrote later. It was clear to Bani-Sadr that the ayatollah — whose hold on power was less firm than outsiders understood — did not want to end the crisis. Doing so would have given moderates too much legitimacy.

By year's end, Carter was willing to try virtually anything short of war. Through intermediaries, he asked Yāssir 'Arafāt to help, but the PLO leader, a Sunni Muslim, got nowhere with the Iranian Shiites. Next, with the president's tacit support, Muhammad Ali entered the ring. He offered Khomeini a "hostage swap" in which the recently retired boxer would agree to be held indefinitely in Tehran if the hostages were freed. Later, he promised to strap on the gloves again to fight the current heavyweight champion, Larry Holmes, in Tehran if he could return home with the hostages. While Ali managed, through an intermediary, to deliver a letter and gifts to the hostages at Christmas, which lifted their spirits, "the Greatest" never heard back from the Iranian government on any of his proposals.

Brzezinski wasn't a fan of desperate diplomacy. Without minimizing the importance of getting back the hostages, he worried about the "honor and dignity" of the United States and its foreign policy interests, and he felt Carter and Vance were

790

handcuffed by the administration's great diplomatic successes. Having prevailed on the Panama Canal and in peace talks between Israel and Egypt, they believed in the power of negotiation, even when the obstacles seemed overwhelming. It was hard for them to fathom that — after the bluster — a regime would not in the end be a rational actor pursuing its own national interests.

Carter believed he was rationally pursuing American national interests. Throughout the crisis, he was clear on his priorities: "To protect the interests and honor of my country and to bring all the hostages home to safety and freedom." The excruciating question for Carter and the country was whether he could do both at the same time.

After nearly six weeks in New York Hospital, the shah was scheduled for release, but he would not be going back to Cuernavaca. With the seizure of the US embassy in Tehran, Mexican President López Portillo issued a communique: "The shah is not welcome in Mexico." This angered Carter, who was now forced to supervise the shah's sleeping arrangements if he wanted the release of the hostages. He dispatched his new White House counsel, Lloyd Cutler, to visit the shah in the hospital and tell him he could not move into his sister Princess Ashraf's Beekman Place apartment on Manhattan's Upper East Side, as he had planned. "Goddamn it, Hamilton, you owe it to the shah!" Armao had protested to Jordan, who replied, in an echo of his boss: "The answer is, 'Fuck the shah.' "

The president wanted him out of New York and away from the media as soon as possible. On

December 2 Dr. Kean snipped the "David New-som" name tag off the shah's wrist, and, before dawn, the FBI escorted him to LaGuardia, where, under heavy armed guard, he boarded a US Air Force jet bound for Lackland Air Force Base, outside San Antonio. When the shah and his wife arrived, the spare military accommodations looked to the queen like a psychiatric ward. "Are we in jail?" she shouted to the shah. "Has Carter put us in jail?"

Carter was now under heavy pressure to get the shah out of the United States altogether. Kennedy led the charge. Why should "that individual" — he couldn't even mention his name — be allowed to "come here and stay here with his umpteen billions of dollars that he's stolen from Iran," the senator thundered, while Hispanics with green cards had to wait nine years to get their children in? The attack went over badly at the time; politicians on both sides of the aisle thought Kennedy was out of line with his rhetoric when the nation was in crisis. His campaign contributions immediately dried up. But everyone agreed on the basic point: it was time for the shah to go.

The State Department was having its familiar problem finding a country that would take him. Panamanian president Omar Torrijos, who adored Carter for giving back the Panama Canal, floated the idea of extending an invitation. Carter sent Hamilton Jordan on a secret mission to meet with Torrijos, whom he had bonded with during the canal debates. Torrijos, the dashing, sexually insatiable character immortalized in an admiring nonfiction book by Graham Greene, *Getting to Know the General,* would do what he could over the next few months to get the hostages released.

After their first late-night meeting, Jordan took Torrijos's letter of invitation back to the shah at Lackland. Jordan and Lloyd Cutler then cut a deal with the shah — called the Lackland Agreement — whereby he would go to Panama in exchange for a commitment (never honored) to let him back into the United States if he fell gravely ill. When Jordan asked the shah what had happened in Iran, he offered a long, incisive analysis that was full of regrets.

"If I had to do it over, I would have been firmer," he said, his voice thick with despair. "Iran is worth fighting for, and I should have led that fight!" But he and his family still blamed Carter for his punishing and wandering exile. Out of earshot of Jordan, he asked Armao bitterly: "Can you imagine Kennedy, FDR, Nixon — any of them — letting a bunch of thugs dictate who the United States invites?" On the way out, Jordan ran into Princess Ashraf in the hall. She wouldn't shake his hand.

On December 15, shortly before he left for Panama, the deposed monarch received an awkward courtesy call from Carter. It was their first contact in more than a year and the last time they would ever speak. Later that day, after less than two weeks in "Carter's jail," the ailing shah and his royal entourage left the United States for good.

In 1979 Roone Arledge, the legendary producer brought in from ABC Sports to jazz up lackluster ABC News, was eager to expand his empire. He wanted to grab the eleven-thirty-to-midnight half hour away from the affiliates, which were saving money by re-airing old episodes of *The Love Boat, Baretta,* and *Police Woman* instead of competing

793

directly with *Johnny Carson.*

Arledge got lucky with the timing of the embassy takeover. On the first day, only ABC News managed to get a crew into Iran, which had barred US reporters as the turmoil worsened. The crew shot the first footage of angry mobs shouting anti-American slogans and burning American flags outside the embassy.

At first, the news from Iran wasn't huge. The night the story broke, Ted Koppel, the ABC News diplomatic correspondent but out of favor with Arledge, didn't want to come into the Washington studio. Like the White House, he recalled the short-lived February takeover and figured the whole thing would be finished in a few hours or days. But Arledge noticed that cabdrivers, doormen, and others he met in New York were entranced by the story.

Starting eleven days after the takeover, Arledge grabbed the time slot every night for a special he called *The Iran Crisis: America Held Hostage,* which was soon anchored by Koppel. The ratings were so high that Arledge ordered specials even when there was no breaking news. With the price of satellite time plummeting, Koppel, an exceptionally skillful interviewer, could moderate a conversation across time zones, commonplace now but new and unusual in the 1970s.

In that pre-cable era, where the only network interview shows were on Sunday morning, *America Held Hostage* (renamed *Nightline* the following March and made permanent) changed the way Americans absorbed news. Along with Walter Cronkite's nightly tagline — "And that's the way it is, Tuesday, December 4, 1979, the thirtieth day of captivity for the American hostages in Iran" —

794

Koppel kept the story front and center almost every night and became a star. With endless questions about the origins of the takeover (Why hadn't the embassy been closed? Why was the shah so unpopular?) and plenty of local angles (the hometowns, friends, and families of hostages), the story never ran out of steam. When it looked as if it might, media-savvy Iranian officials would hint at progress or issue new demands or let the mother of a hostage come to Tehran and visit her son. Their willingness to square off via satellite with the family members of hostages was an early form of reality TV.

Koppel argued later that Carter played into the hands of the Iranians by saying that he thought about the hostages every day and would do nothing to jeopardize their safety: "It made holding the hostages look smart." Hodding Carter, the State Department spokesman, agreed. He said later, "The fundamental error was keeping this story on the front burner day in and day out. We talked about it every goddamn day."

It wasn't as if the White House had the option of tamping down such a big story. But Carter's decision to ditch the campaign trail so he could stay in the White House and work on freeing the hostages — while briefly helpful to him in the polls — proved a mistake, as he admitted later. "Carter was essentially making *himself* a hostage," Rick Hertzberg remembered. "Every single night it was, 'America is being humiliated because Carter is a wimp.' "

When Koppel ran into Carter years later, the former president told him, "You know, there were only two people who really benefited from all of that: you and the Ayatollah Khomeini."

■ ■ ■ ■

The Iranian revolution was only the first of several threats to American interests in the Muslim world. Shortly thereafter, the CIA learned that Pakistan — trying to keep pace with India's nascent nuclear weapons program — was secretly building a uranium-enrichment facility with the aim of developing "the Islamic Bomb." Pakistan's new dictator, General Muhammad Zia-ul-Haq, hanged Ali Bhutto, the democratically elected president he had pushed out of power in a 1977 coup. Zia canceled elections and began what became a long and bloody tradition of the Pakistani government supporting radical Islamists.

Those Islamists got a big boost on November 20, 1979, when Saudi extremists — angered by the House of Saud's Westernizing ways — seized the Great Mosque of Mecca, the holiest site in Islam, a huge pavilion constructed over the previous twenty-five years by the bin Laden family, one of Saudi Arabia's richest. The attack was a pivotal event in the Arab world, little understood in the United States at the time. After the Saudi royal family reclaimed and secured the Great Mosque with the help of France and Pakistan, the ruling sheiks shifted sharply right and began subsidizing Sunni religious schools that preached hate all over the world — a move that would ultimately lead to 9/11.

More immediately, Pakistani Islamists spread lies that the United States and Israel had conspired to launch the Mecca attack. The next day, November 21, Islamists burned down the US embassy in Islamabad, killing two Americans, and on December 2, they torched the US embassy in Tripoli, Libya.

The region seemed to be collapsing: Iran in revolutionary chaos and trampling diplomatic norms; Iraq — now under the boot of Saddam Hussein — itching for war with Iran; Pakistan losing its democracy to a military dictatorship; Saudi Arabia rocked by a major attack. And one of their poorer neighbors was about to become the focus of the greatest superpower tension in a generation.

# 34
# Reheating the Cold War

Unfortunately for Jimmy Carter, the big events in the Muslim world in 1979 were far removed from his life experience and that of almost anyone else in official Washington. Like every other president since FDR, he was a product of the Cold War, enmeshed in what John F. Kennedy called "a long twilight struggle" against Communism — a struggle that seemed to be heating up again.

As the seventies ended, most experts believed that the Soviet Union was stronger than at the beginning of the Cold War, when it was still reeling from having lost nearly seventeen million people in World War II. While OPEC squeezed the West, the Soviet Union was a net oil exporter. And with the Politburo's tight grip on power, the USSR could spend a much higher percentage of GDP on defense than the United States did. Between 1964 and 1979, the Soviets deployed thousands of new nuclear missiles (giving them numerical superiority, even if their technology was less advanced) and conscripted a million soldiers, which added an astonishing twenty-five divisions to the Red Army.

But underneath the buildup and the bravado, the Soviet Union was doomed — a decrepit system that didn't work for its people and was decaying from within. Strangely enough, almost no one knew it yet. Despite billions spent on espionage and satellite surveillance, the West was clueless about the future. Only Senator Daniel Patrick Moynihan and one or two outlier Soviet experts predicted the demise of Communism, and even they were shocked that the Berlin Wall and the Soviet empire collapsed within a decade and without violence.

Detente did not work well in the Carter years, a victim of Soviet adventurism in Angola and the Horn of Africa that Soviet ambassador Anatoly Dobrynin later admitted was unwise.* To Carter's chagrin, bad behavior by the Soviets had a good effect on the fortunes of Republicans. They had been deeply divided in 1976 between supporters of detente (the Nixon and Ford policy) and more hard-line conservatives (Reaganites). Once Carter was elected, they closed ranks and endlessly portrayed the Democratic president as "weak" on the Russians — an early example of the GOP's ability to drive a message.

"Our side didn't get that this wasn't a political disagreement — that they are trying to destroy us," Hodding Carter said later. "Kissinger was the worst, telling everyone that Carter was not only naive but dangerously wrong and that human rights was a disaster."

Carter's real sin in the eyes of many hard-liners

*Dobrynin wrote in his memoirs that interfering in those African countries made it seem as if the Soviet Union had designs on the whole continent, which it did not.

was that he tried to introduce some nuance into America's response to nationalism in the Third World. In February 1979 he told a conference of editors that he rejected "the temptation to see all changes as inevitably against the United States — as a kind of loss for us or a victory for 'them.' . . . We need to see what is happening not in terms of simplistic colors of black and white, but in more subtle shades." The Right ridiculed this fresh thinking as defeatism or the rationalization of radical Left regimes, but it was, in effect, just a more moral version of Kissingerian realpolitik, hardly worthy of the venom directed at it.

Hard-line neoconservatives, many of them former Democrats, relaunched an anti-Communist group from the 1950s called the Committee on the Present Danger. In 1977 the hard-liners used a hawkish former senior national security official, Paul Nitze, to publicly trash his erstwhile friend Paul Warnke, Carter's chief arms control negotiator, for being soft on the Soviets — a false charge that was designed to raise doubts about the president.

The neocons and much of the press punished Carter for killing two weapon systems. The first was the B-1 bomber, a hideously expensive plane ($250 million a copy, a huge sum in 1977) that the politically savvy Pentagon made sure had suppliers spread across almost every state and the congressional districts of powerful House members. Carter didn't let the daunting politics intimidate him out of deciding the issue on its merits. Jack Watson remembered walking into the president's study to find him comparing and contrasting something on a yellow legal pad. Carter said he was listing the pros of the B-1 bomber on one side and the cons on the other.*

Beyond cost, the biggest argument against the B-1 was that the Pentagon was at the time secretly developing a far-superior airplane — the B-2 stealth bomber, which would turn out to be one of the technological marvels of the age. Of course, Carter could not discuss the B-2 even in private because the development of that plane — which evades radar — was, he said, the most highly classified information of his entire administration. This meant that when he killed the B-1 the president had no choice but to take his lumps as a "unilateral disarmer," when he was, in fact, developing a weapon that would eventually do as much as any other to convince the Soviets that they couldn't catch up.

The second thorn in Carter's side was the neutron bomb: an enhanced radiation weapon. After reams of bad publicity about the bomb's creepy power to kill people without doing much damage to buildings, the president in 1978 awkwardly canceled deployment at the last minute. This bought him nothing with doves but angered Chancellor Schmidt, who told everyone

*The lobbying for the B-1 was so strong that the Pentagon was able to maintain R & D funding. Reagan revived the B-1 program at great expense, and a hundred planes were delivered by the late 1980s. Retrofitted versions eventually provided close air support for the air force, a mission for which the plane was not designed. Even Donald Rumsfeld, both President Ford's and President George W. Bush's defense secretary, felt the B-1 bomber had been a colossal waste of money.

he knew on both sides of the Atlantic that he had been misled and blindsided by Carter. In fact, the president simply changed his mind, although he admitted later he could have handled it better.

The cancellation of the two weapons clouded the real picture of a president who actually left a hawkish record on defense. He increased Pentagon spending by a healthy 5 percent, with new money for readiness and other improvements later credited to Reagan. He overcame opposition from the Left and in 1979 agreed (under pressure from Helmut Schmidt) to deploy scores of cruise missiles and new intermediate-range Pershing nuclear missiles on European soil, a critical display of firmness that helped future presidents negotiate with Moscow from strength. He moved forward, over loud and persuasive liberal objections, with the MX missile, a destabilizing land-based missile demanded by the Joint Chiefs of Staff in exchange for their support of SALT II — a reasonable if expensive bargain, Carter figured. And his support for Harold Brown's visionary R & D would ensure military primacy for the United States for decades to come.

Carter was also active in the battle of ideas. With sixteen new transmitters for Voice of America, Radio Free Europe, and Radio Liberty, the Carter administration pressed America's ideological advantage. Robert Gates said that the amplification of Carter's human rights policy made him the first president since Truman "to challenge directly the legitimacy of the Soviet government in the eyes of its own people."

As usual, Carter was willing to take political hits at home to advance long-term foreign policy interests. One example of this is the story of the

Crown of St. Stephen. When the Soviets occupied Hungary and the rest of Eastern Europe after the Second World War, Hungarian nationalists gave the thirteenth-century crown — the political and religious symbol of Hungarian nationhood — to American troops for safekeeping. For more than thirty years, the crown was held with the American gold supply at Fort Knox. Over the feverish objections of hundreds of thousands of anti-Communist Hungarian Americans in Ohio, Illinois, and other swing states, Carter, with the support of the Hungarian Church, made the tough decision to return the crown to Communist Hungary.

Besides thinking this was just the right thing to do, Carter and Vance figured that returning the sacred relic would make the United States more popular in Hungary and stir feelings of patriotic independence there that could eventually help draw that country out of the Soviet bloc. It worked. A policy that looked soft on Communism actually helped undermine it. Twelve years later, many Hungarians pointed to the return of the Crown of St. Stephen as a pivotal moment on their road away from Communism.

Even some of Carter's supporters felt he would have seemed stronger had he taken symbolically tough action early on, as President Reagan did in invading the tiny island of Grenada in 1983. But that wasn't how Carter rolled. He made concessions to the politics of national security but never felt the need to prove his toughness, especially if such gestures might cost American lives. To him, that wasn't tough but, rather, a sign of insecurity, and he viewed the killer instinct that he lacked as a bogus prerequisite for good leadership.

■ ■ ■ ■

Of all the issues that confronted him as president, Carter felt most deeply about arms control — the ultimate peace issue. As president-elect in late 1976, he shocked the Joint Chiefs of Staff by asking what it would take to reduce America's arsenal of land-based intercontinental ballistic missiles from 1,054 to 200 — still plenty to blow up the world. He backed off only when Harold Brown told him that such unilateral reductions of ICBMs would alarm NATO.

In his inaugural address, Carter mentioned only one specific issue: arms control. He pledged, "We will move this year a step toward [our] ultimate goal — the elimination of all nuclear weapons from this earth." Six days later, he sent Leonid Brezhnev a friendly letter urging cooperation on nuclear weapons, and the Soviet leader replied in kind, setting the stage for progress on negotiating SALT II.

As a former president, Carter wrote of his religious faith:

"The most important element of faith ever imposed on me, and on another person simultaneously [Brezhnev], involved the threat of a total elimination of all human life on earth by a nuclear war with the Soviet Union. . . . I learned soon after my election that [after a nuclear exchange] the resulting radiation and other collateral damage would kill most of the rest of the world's population."

And if it didn't? Carter the engineer planned for every contingency. He issued a series of secret presidential directives (PDs) culminating with

PD-59 in 1980, which clarified for the first time what the US government should do if nuclear hostilities commenced. When it leaked, PD-59, by making the survival of a nuclear war more "thinkable," upset thirty years of nuclear deterrence doctrine and rattled official Washington. The *New York Times* editorialized that it looked "callous" to plan to save the lives of generals as part of "strategic chess games" that left everyone else to die. "Dear Mr. President," Russell Baker wrote in his wry *Times* column, "I have just read about the plan to save certain people in caves and would very much like to be among them."

But declassification showed that PD-59 wasn't a full-scale war-fighting doctrine or a sign that Carter wanted a return to the pointless civil defense shelters of the past or wasn't serious about steep cuts in nuclear weapons. It was an elaborate and long-overdue acknowledgment that deterrence alone wasn't a viable policy once missiles were launched. The president simply wanted genuine continuity of government (COG) procedures and prudent emergency planning. He arranged for the congressional leadership to tour for the first time the underground bunker in Greenbrier County, West Virginia, where they would go in the event of full-scale war. And he broke precedent by personally visiting the presidential bunker at Raven Rock, near Camp David, and the much larger bunker for government officials at Mount Weather in the Virginia hills.*

*One night in November 1979 Brzezinski received back-to-back calls in the wee hours saying a full-scale nuclear attack against the United States was under way. The national security adviser was just seconds from

805

After several nuclear emergency drills were botched, Carter thought the government could do better disaster preparedness across the board. Eager to improve coordination after droughts, toxic waste spills, the 1980 volcanic eruption of Mount St. Helens, and other disasters, Carter issued an executive order consolidating government functions under a new Federal Emergency Management Agency.* When FEMA was led properly in later years, it would be one of the most effective federal agencies; when it was not, it would leave America at risk.

Carter had muffed his first effort at arms control. Just weeks after taking office, he sided with Cyrus Vance over Harold Brown and sent Moscow an ambitious plan to slash ICBMs. The proposal was badly tilted against the Soviets, who weren't ready for deep cuts of any kind. This was eight years before the arrival of Mikhail Gorbachev and reform; the Soviet old guard "thought these Americans are bonkers," Assistant Secretary of State Leslie Gelb remembered.

Or feckless. The most common foreign policy story of the Carter administration was that the president was caught between Vance the dove and Brzezinski the hawk. This was always an oversim-

---

waking Carter when a third call came telling him it was a false alarm. A training tape simulation had somehow slipped into the real-time network.

*On May 18, 1980, Mount St. Helens, a volcano in the Cascade Mountains in Washington State, expelled plumes of ash that killed fifty-seven people. It was the most destructive eruption in modern US history.

plification. While Brzezinski, a skilled bureaucratic knife fighter, eventually won his struggle with Vance, Carter was much too smart and independent minded to fall under his or anyone else's sway.

He did, however, sometimes try to split the difference. In June 1978 Carter gave a commencement address at Annapolis that felt like a blend of Vance's and Brzezinski's contrasting worldviews. Speechwriter Jim Fallows remembered literally stapling a Vance draft to a Brzezinski draft before trying for an awkward integration of them. Evans and Novak wrote a column charging that Carter's foreign policy was like a Chinese menu: one from column A, one from column B; the story fed the common perception that he was a waffler. In fact, the speech, largely in response to Soviet meddling in Africa, was tougher on the Soviet Union than anything that had come out of the Ford Administration, suggesting greater Brzezinski influence.

On the biggest issue, arms control, Carter, Vance, and Brzezinski were all on the same page. SALT II, negotiated by Paul Warnke and Ralph Earle and completed in early 1979, called for the first actual reductions in stockpiles since the dawn of the nuclear age. "I had a more difficult time convincing the Joint Chiefs of Staff than I did some of the Soviet leaders," Carter remembered. Under the complex deal, both sides limited MIRVs (missiles with multiple independent nuclear warheads) and began steps toward better verification, among other significant advances. The treaty's reductions were modest; each side would still be able to destroy the other thousands of times over. But at least the arms control process was moving in the right direction.

Scoop Jackson didn't think so. As Carter flew to Vienna in June of 1979 for the big summit, Jackson — the man Carter had nominated for president seven years earlier in Miami — compared the president's trip to Neville Chamberlain appeasing Adolf Hitler at Munich in 1938. Margaret Thatcher and Helmut Schmidt, still sore over Carter's reversal on the neutron bomb, didn't go that far, but they were upset that the US president hadn't done enough at the bargaining table to stop the Soviet SS-20 missiles and Backfire bombers that threatened Europe. They thought the American nuclear umbrella had a leak over their territory.

At the Hofburg Imperial Palace, Carter found the seventy-two-year-old Brezhnev — who looked fifteen years older and had a drinking problem — less addled than he had expected. He was surprised when Brezhnev, representing an atheist state, "said a very strange thing: 'If we do not succeed, God will not forgive us.'" It apparently didn't occur to Carter that an insincere Brezhnev might be trying to play him. He made progress, anyway. With his usual attention to detail, Carter personally negotiated a side agreement with Foreign Minister Andrey Gromyko that at least papered over the Backfire bomber question. At the banquet, Brezhnev offered frequent vodka toasts; on the first, Carter didn't turn his glass bottom up, and Brezhnev jovially mocked him for it. Carter had anticipated this and soon switched to a special, smaller glass brought along from the United States for just such a contingency.

At the signing ceremony, Carter shook Brezhnev's hand warmly and, to his surprise, Brezhnev leaned forward and put his cheek next to his for a

European-style kiss. Leslie Gelb, standing just behind the two leaders, knew instantly that the gesture was a disaster for Carter. "I thought, 'Uh-oh. It looks like he got taken in by the Russians.' " It was the only thing anyone remembered from the summit and a potent image for the Republicans in 1980.

Back home, debate erupted over the MX missile. It became Carter's bargaining chip not with the Soviets but with the Senate, especially Majority Leader Robert Byrd, without whose support the treaty would die. Byrd had come a long way since opposing FDR's wartime alliance with Stalin's "Communistic Russia" so fiercely that it helped motivate him as a young man to join the anti-Communist Ku Klux Klan in West Virginia. He approached the treaty with an open mind, consulting with NATO allies and experts on both sides of the debate. After Carter wrote him a letter pledging to proceed with the MX, Byrd gave a long speech on October 25 endorsing ratification and saying that, win or lose, it should go to the floor. But the Senate, being the Senate, got bogged down in other business. Before long, it was time for the Christmas recess, and SALT II had not yet come up for a vote. And it never would.

American hard-liners were about to receive a new cudgel to use against the president: Afghanistan. In 1978, Afghan Communists staged a revolution that overthrew a shaky regime that had enjoyed decent relations with the United States. Washington was alarmed, and, in the summer of 1979, Carter approved covert operations that aided anti-Communist mujahideen: impassioned Afghan rebels whom Brzezinski hoped would turn Afghanistan into "a Soviet Vietnam." As he admitted in 1998, "We didn't push the Russians to intervene, but we knowingly increased the probability that they would."*

Here the reigning dynamic of American foreign policy — the law of unintended consequences — began to take hold. The mujahideen of the 1980s became the Taliban and Al Qaeda of the turn of the century. In later years, Brzezinski was unapologetic, arguing that the disintegration of the Soviet empire (to the extent that Afghanistan was responsible) was more important to the history of the world than any downstream consequences.

Historians have long debated why the Soviets invaded Afghanistan — one of the great foreign policy blunders of the late twentieth century. Newly declassified documents from both the United States and the former Soviet Union offer important clues. They show that the Soviets feared "another Egypt," where seven years earlier Sadat had expelled them. They didn't want the leaders of Afghanistan doing the same. And there was fear of setting a precedent in the Soviet empire. As Averell Harriman, Franklin Roosevelt's ambassador to the Soviet Union, told Carter after the invasion, the Soviet Union had never let a Communist government loyal to Moscow fall, much less one that might defect to the West. The Soviets figured a stable Afghanistan firmly in their orbit was worth whatever criticism might come their way.

The Kremlin was also emboldened by previous presidential restraint. Brezhnev and other mem-

*Among the insurgents was a wealthy young Saudi named Osama bin Laden.

bers of the Politburo figured that President Eisenhower hadn't gone to war after they invaded Hungary in 1956, and President Johnson had not responded militarily after they invaded Czechoslovakia in 1968, so it was hard to imagine President Carter doing much.

The backstory of the invasion is one of murder and intrigue. By the summer of 1979, Afghanistan had descended into what would become a familiar national condition: civil war. The new Communist leader, President Noor Muhammad Taraki, warned Moscow that Islamic fundamentalism was a serious threat to his hold on power — a threat Brezhnev ignored. Taraki's more immediate challenge came from within his own government. In September Taraki tried to push out his prime minister, Hafizullah Amin, also ostensibly a Marxist-Leninist. But Amin was the slicker of the two, and he arrested Taraki, who was soon mysteriously smothered to death with pillows.

Shortly after taking power in October, Amin met with US ambassador Archer K. Blood and told him he wanted to improve relations with the United States. Blood was impressed by Amin, who had studied in America, but he replied that US aid could not resume until the Afghan government explained what happened in February when Blood's predecessor as ambassador, Adolph Dubs, had been abducted from the US embassy and killed.

When Yuri Andropov, head of the KGB, heard that Amin might be switching superpower allegiances, he advised Brezhnev to get rid of him. Failing to do so, Andropov concluded, could lead to a major geostrategic realignment in South

811

Central Asia. On December 12 the Politburo — with no debate — approved direct intervention in Afghanistan. Days later, incompetent KGB operatives tried to poison Amin's Coca-Cola (the carbonation diluted the toxic agent) and his food (Soviet doctors, unaware of the plot, saved him). Stronger measures would be required.

Christmas Day 1979 brought navigable skies in the Afghan capital. Suddenly huge Soviet military planes appeared on the Kabul horizon and began landing thousands of troops. By December 27, the world learned that the Soviet Union had engaged in its first major act of aggression outside Eastern Europe since World War II. That day, Amin was shot and killed at the palace and a Soviet puppet, Babrak Karmal, installed as the leader of Afghanistan.

Brezhnev, oblivious to what Taraki had reported to Moscow six months earlier about the strength of radical Islam, figured the war would be over in three weeks. It lasted nearly a decade, until a humiliating withdrawal signaled the approaching demise of the Soviet Union.

At Camp David, Jimmy and Rosalynn were shocked by the Christmas Day reports from Afghanistan. The next morning, Brzezinski wrote Carter that the invasion posed "an extremely grave challenge, both internationally and domestically." He argued that while Afghanistan could prove to be "a Soviet Vietnam," as he had hoped the previous summer, any comparison between the mujahideen and the Vietcong (who had outwitted the United States in South Vietnam for twenty years) was a stretch because the Afghan guerrillas were "badly organized and poorly led" and didn't have

812

an organized army or country (North Vietnam) behind them. American strategic challenges, he reported, had been transformed overnight.

The entire heavily armed region would be described in early 1980 as "an arc of crisis" — a description that would drive Carter's foreign policy for the rest of his tenure. Brzezinski argued that the invasion was meant to fulfill "the agelong dream of Moscow to have direct access to the Indian Ocean." This was a geographical reach: Afghanistan is landlocked, and the Soviets would have to move hundreds of miles through Iran to get to the Persian Gulf and the Indian Ocean. But maybe the Ayatollah Khomeini would let them.

On December 29 Carter used the hotline with Moscow to send a tough message of disapproval. Brezhnev responded that the president of Afghanistan had invited the Soviets in to protect the country from outside aggression.

In a much-discussed New Year's Eve interview with Frank Reynolds of ABC News, Carter explained that Brezhnev's account was a lie; the person the Soviets claimed had asked them in, President Amin, couldn't have done so because he had been "murdered or assassinated when the Soviets pulled their coup." Then Reynolds asked Carter if "you have changed your perceptions of the Russians" since becoming president. Carter answered, "My opinion of the Russians has changed [more] drastically in the last week than even the previous two and one-half years before that. It is only now dawning upon the world . . . the magnitude of the action that the Soviets undertook in invading Afghanistan."

As soon as the interview aired, Republicans leapt on Carter as naive. This became one of the most

813

explosive and enduring critiques of his presidency. In this case, anyway, it was a charge without merit. The comment to Reynolds would have been naive only had the Soviets' behavior not, in fact, represented a significant departure from the restrained way they had acted territorially in the previous decade.

And it wasn't as if Carter's record was one of naively turning a blind eye to the malevolence of the Soviet Union. He had confronted Moscow over its treatment of dissidents during the first week of his presidency — a more confrontational approach than that of Nixon and Ford. Carter had never been "soft" on the Soviets, unless one defined support for any arms control that way. His biggest mistake in the Reynolds interview may have been acting surprised, since he had signed off on covert aid to the mujahideen the summer before with the understanding that it might lure the Soviets into a quagmire in Afghanistan.

Later in the month, at Mondale's suggestion, Carter invited Norman Podhoretz, editor of *Commentary* magazine, and other neoconservatives (several of them nominally still Democrats) to the White House. They wanted the president to admit that the invasion had essentially caused the scales to fall from his eyes, and he now had fresh, hawkish views of the Soviet Union. But Carter denied the headline from the Reynolds interview, which disappointed the group. When retired Admiral Elmo Zumwalt told him — falsely, it turned out — that existing US navy forces were incapable of defending the Persian Gulf and Indian Ocean oil routes, the president responded with what was described by one attendee as "a stare that in a less democratic society would've meant he was destined for a firing squad."

At a critical meeting on January 2 in the Cabinet Room, Carter told his team that nothing could be done to get the Soviets to leave Afghanistan any time soon, but Russian actions over the next ten or twenty years "will be colored by our response to this crisis." That was the nub of it for him. The American response would shape Soviet behavior in the future.

In the meantime, his hand was being forced — by a Democratic union. Over the holidays, the fiercely anti-Communist International Longshoremen's Association told the White House that its members would no longer load ships with wheat and other products bound for the Soviet Union. This conditioned the discussion of how to retaliate. It meant that beyond yanking his ambassador, canceling cultural exchanges, and limiting technology transfers — all easy calls — the president's first big decision would be whether to impose a grain embargo.

Carter was a farmer and warehouseman with a son who owned a grain elevator. He followed commodity market fluctuations in his diary ("Corn was up 23 cents!") and how they affected ordinary Americans — on the farm and in the grocery store. But for him, this was about national security, not his personal interests or even the interests of a major sector of the economy. The minutes of the January 2 NSC meeting show that in two and a half hours, the president spent about thirty seconds describing what he thought an embargo might do to US grain export markets.

Mondale found it "outrageous" that longshoremen had taken foreign policy into their own hands over the holidays. The vice president pointed out that an embargo would require the US government to spend big money buying the grain contracted for but not yet delivered to the Soviet Union. Then grain prices would plummet, angering farmers and splitting them off from labor — a blow to the Democratic Party. He predicted the grain embargo would be ineffective abroad — other nations would supply the Soviet Union — and political poison at home.

Mondale explained to the president that politically, the whole thing was a simple math problem: all you had to do was take every farm state, multiply by two senators, and you had a majority of the Senate right there that would oppose the White House on the grain embargo. Carter didn't dispute the math, but he once again chose policy over politics. He sided with Cy Vance, who insisted that without an embargo, it would be nearly impossible to convince American allies to impose any economic restrictions on the Soviet Union. Harold Brown agreed, arguing that if we didn't do things that hurt us, we couldn't get others to make the necessary sacrifices. Rosalynn joined Mondale in thinking the whole thing was a political disaster in the upcoming Iowa caucuses and beyond.

After the embargo was imposed, Mondale turned out to be right. Brazil and Argentina immediately filled the wheat production gap, with Canada and Australia not far behind; the Soviet Union saw almost no interruption in its grain imports and used the experience to ramp up its own production enough to become a net wheat exporter. The embargo's inadvertent message was that the United States was no longer a reliable trading partner. Carter was in a state of semi-denial over it; when Agriculture Secretary Bob Bergland told the president that winter that he couldn't "sell" the embargo politically, Carter turned his icy blues on him and reiterated the grave national security threats involved.

Carter later convinced himself that American farmers supported the decision. They did so in the first polls, when the whole country rallied around the flag and the president. The patriotic feeling lasted long enough for Carter to beat Kennedy in the Iowa caucuses and other farm state primaries.

But by the middle of 1980, the grain embargo was killing Carter in the farm belt, where decades later, many older farmers still blamed him for their woes. In the 1970s, rural areas were not wedded to one party, with Democrats often winning in farm belt states that were later bright red. Dan Glickman, a Democrat congressman from Kansas who became Bill Clinton's agriculture secretary, believed the fallout from the 1980 grain embargo in the rural Midwest was akin to the role played by the Civil Rights Act of 1964 in turning the South solidly Republican. "It was that big," he said. In the name of protesting the invasion, Carter had ceded US dominance of the huge wheat export market. American farmers would never get it back — and they would never forget.

"There goes SALT II," Jimmy told Rosalynn after the Soviet invasion. On January 3 Carter wrote Majority Leader Byrd asking him to delay floor consideration of the treaty. While neither wanted it pulled from the Senate altogether, this meant

817

that SALT II — the focus of so much of Carter's attention over the previous three years — was effectively dead.*

The next evening, January 4, 1980, the president addressed the nation about the "extremely serious threat to peace" and said the United States would respond with suspension of grain shipments and technology transfers, possibly a boycott of the 1980 Summer Olympics in Moscow, and other measures that would "match the gravity of the Soviet action."

From the start, the most publicized option was the boycott of the Summer Olympics, scheduled to begin in Moscow on July 19. When debating the boycott in National Security Council meetings, Warren Christopher reported that West Germany's NATO representative worried the Moscow Games could be a repeat of the 1936 Berlin Games, which Adolf Hitler used to advance Nazi propaganda. Christopher ended up opposed to a boycott — he thought it would be "destructive of international community" — but most of Carter's other advisers favored it, arguing that this particular reprisal would be especially painful to the Soviets. Unlike the grain embargo, an Olympic boycott appealed to Mondale, who thought it could inspire Americans. Carter agreed, noting that the patriotic sacrifice that would be required "sends chills down my spine."

Carter said he "sweated the boycott" more than

*The failure to ratify the treaty was not a total loss. Both sides abided by all of its terms, which proved to be a solid basis for the Strategic Arms Reduction Treaty (START) talks that Ronald Reagan and Mikhail Gorbachev would launch in the 1980s.

any other issue in his presidency that wasn't life-or-death. But once Andrey Sakharov endorsed the idea in early January, he never agonized about the decision again.

On January 14 the White House announced that the United States would boycott the Summer Games if the Soviets did not withdraw from Afghanistan in one month, which no one expected. After Carter explained the reasons — to teach the Soviets a lesson and deter further aggression — support for the boycott in polls reached nearly 75 percent. NBC executives reported an unprecedented volume of calls to affiliates from viewers in favor — even more than after the malaise speech. But Carter knew it had to be seen as a genuine worldwide reaction, not just American, or "Howard Cosell [would tell] the sports fans that Jimmy Carter killed the Olympics." (In fact, Cosell, a popular and opinionated sportscaster, backed the boycott.)

Support built for a "counter Olympics." Montreal, which had held the 1976 Summer Games, was the most plausible alternative site, but the Canadians had torn down their Olympic Village, so the cost was prohibitive. Proposals to make Greece the permanent home of the Games went nowhere. The International Olympic Committee was adamantly opposed to any boycotts and insisted all along that the Games would take place in Moscow as planned. The US government eventually had to threaten to sue the IOC to disassociate itself from the Games.

Several gold medalists from earlier Summer Games supported the boycott, but the American sports community as a whole argued that the decision was about politics, not national security. The worried — and increasingly angry — 1980 athletes took hope from the fact that they technically answered to the United States Olympic Committee, not the US government. The USOC voted on January 7 to "resist political intrusion into the Games."

On January 23, 1980, Carter used what would be his final State of the Union address to rally the country around the flag and, not coincidentally, his reelection. He outlined what became known as the Carter Doctrine, which held that attempts by "any outside force [in other words, the Soviet Union] to gain control of the Persian Gulf region will be regarded as an assault on the vital interests of the United States of America [read oil supplies] and such an assault will be repelled by any means necessary, including military force." To conduct such military operations, the president established a new interservice Rapid Deployment Force for coordinated intervention in hot spots.*

The most controversial section of the 1980 State of the Union — especially among liberals and libertarians — was Carter's resumption of draft registration after a five-year hiatus. Before the speech, this prompted "practically a rebellion from

*In 1983 the RDF would become the US Central Command, which directed the 1991 Gulf War, the 2003 overthrow of Saddam Hussein, and the defeats of the Iraqi insurgency and the Islamic State (ISIS). All later interventions in the Middle East — almost all of which were opposed by Carter when he was out of office — were at least indirect Centcom applications of the Carter Doctrine.

Stu and Fritz," Carter wrote, "same timidity as on the 'malaise speech,' changing of the Cabinet . . . This is worse."[*] It was true that Carter's proposal that women should also register (unmentioned in the speech) was dead on arrival in Congress. And the president missed a golden opportunity to push for a broad national service program for all young Americans. But Eizenstat's and Mondale's concerns seemed overblown. The president was repeatedly interrupted by bipartisan applause, and his big lead over Kennedy in the polls solidified.

It wasn't clear then, but the Carter Doctrine — like US policy toward the shah — was based in part on faulty intelligence. For years, the CIA wrongly reported that the Soviet Union was running out of oil. Even after he left office, Carter still believed there was a genuine risk that the Soviets would use Afghanistan as a "launching pad" to seize control of the Persian Gulf through Iran, which was distracted and dysfunctional at the time, or even through Pakistan. "I reacted strongly because I wanted Brezhnev to know that if they did thrust toward the Persian Gulf, it would

[*]Over the summer, Congress approved draft registration for nineteen- and twenty-year-olds, though not Carter's proposal for women to be included. While the law required young men born starting January 1, 1960, to go to the post office to register, none was ever conscripted. Ted Kennedy and Ronald Reagan opposed the idea as unnecessary, and Reagan did nothing to enforce it as president. The law was never repealed, and in the twenty-first century, more than 95 percent of nineteen-year-olds of both sexes are automatically registered by the US government.

be the same as an attack on our country," he said in 1988, a view he did not amend in old age. Such was the fear of the Soviet Union and the dependence of the US economy on Middle Eastern oil in 1980.

The hawkish speech, praised across the political spectrum, brought Carter some much-needed validation. The day after the State of the Union, the House passed a resolution backing Carter's boycott of the Olympics, 386 to 12, and the Senate soon followed by a margin of 88 to 4. For now, at least, the country as a whole was strongly behind its president.

By March, it was clear that the Soviets had underestimated both the strength of the home-grown (though CIA-assisted) Afghan insurgency and the international outcry that greeted their invasion. But outrage within the Western alliance was spotty. Carter thought that Helmut Schmidt didn't understand the strategic stakes. Brzezinski disagreed. He figured the Europeans all knew perfectly well that any threat to Persian Gulf oil supplies would hurt them more than it would the United States; they were just acting irresponsibly by letting the Americans respond on their behalf. Harold Brown told Carter he needed to "rub their noses" in the strategic facts and shake them out of their appeasement. The Europeans sounded as if they wanted to continue detente with the Soviet Union even as the United States moved in a more hawkish direction. Brzezinski told Carter to his face that there was a good explanation for that: US foreign policy had not been "consistent."

At a March 18 National Security Council meeting in the Cabinet Room, Carter said the previous two weeks had been the worst of his presidency. The situations in both Iran and Afghanistan were "stagnant," and the same applied to Israeli-Egyptian post-treaty talks on moving forward as planned on the Palestinian question. He said he and Brezhnev didn't understand each other and that Americans were sick of the hostage crisis.

As dispirited as he felt, Carter was looking for some positive spin. He wanted the Joint Chiefs to move beyond complaining about the perceived inadequacies in the defense budget and explain where the United States was strong. The message coming through to the world was that "we are weak, we are second, and it's getting worse," he said. Carter felt that if Brown and military officials could not in good conscience testify that US military forces were superior, they should at least say that the United States and the Soviet Union were equal. He understood that even though he had been steadily modernizing American forces and increasing defense spending, the impression was hardening that the United States had fallen behind the Soviet Union — political dynamite as the 1980 campaign heated up.

Meanwhile, the USOC went into quiet opposition to the Olympics boycott, telling American athletes to keep training, planting stories that international support for the boycott was tepid, and suggesting that Carter might change his mind.* This was never a possibility, but the

*Emotions still ran high fifteen years later, when Carter carried the torch in Atlanta, home of the 1996 Olympics. The argument against him was that he had nearly wrecked the entire Olympic movement in 1980, and only the efforts of Peter Ueberroth — who ran the suc-

politics of the boycott were now in flux.

On March 21 Carter invited a hundred members of the 1980 team to the East Room of the White House. The athletes expected a forum on how to find a workable compromise, perhaps by competing in Olympic events but boycotting all ceremonies in Moscow. Instead, they got what several viewed as a condescending lecture on geopolitics from Brzezinski. When Carter entered, they did not stand and applaud, which the press reported as a snub. Carter quoted the minister of Bavaria saying that "if only the Olympics had not been held in Berlin in 1936, the course of history could have been different." When he told the athletes that the decision was final, his efforts to convey his angst ("It's not a pleasant time for me") did not go over well. In the weeks that followed, Carter pressed forward anyway, successfully pressuring NBC and advertisers to pull out (a huge revenue loss) and threatening to revoke the US passports of any Olympic athlete attempting to take part in the Games under a neutral banner.

When Carter announced on April 10 that the Justice Department would take legal action to enforce the boycott, the United States Olympic Committee — fearing for its future — caved. Meeting in Colorado Springs, the USOC's House of Delegates reversed the organization's previous opposition and endorsed the boycott, leaving most members of the US Olympic team heartbroken and bitter. Carter genuinely felt for the athletes, but he drew satisfaction from the reaction in

cessful 1984 Summer Games in Los Angeles — had rescued it.

824

Moscow. "There is nothing you could possibly have done to upset the Soviets more," a Polish diplomat told Ambassador Thomas Watson, the US envoy in Moscow, though Watson reported that the Soviets would host the Games even if only a handful of countries took part. They were especially intent on preventing Western European nations from joining the boycott.

Carter felt the new strategic balance allowed no retreat. China, still playing the American card, strongly supported the Olympic boycott and economic sanctions and later sent word to Washington through back channels that it would like to see the Soviets "bogged down" in Afghanistan. Muslim nations, including even revolutionary Iran, mostly committed to the boycott, though, of course, Afghanistan's small team planned to participate. African countries were the most reluctant to stay home, in part because their partial boycott of the 1976 Summer Games in Montreal over apartheid was not joined by other countries.

As with the hostages, Carter was willing to try anything — including once again enlisting Muhammad Ali, a 1960 Olympic champion. Reveling in the endorsement of the world's most famous man (Ali told the press he was instructing his tens of millions of American fans to vote for Carter-Mondale), the president in February dispatched him to five African countries to drum up support for the boycott. *Time* magazine called it "the most bizarre diplomatic mission in US history." Ali seemed to agree. "Maybe I'm being used to do something that ain't right," he admitted in Tanzania. "If I find out I'm wrong, I'm going back to America and cancel the whole trip." In Kenya, he said Carter sent him "around the world to take the whupping over American policies."

To make the boycott work, Carter needed Western Europe. For months, Germany's support had seemed lukewarm and conditional. By spring, Carter was so annoyed with Helmut Schmidt that he argued internally that right-wing Bavarian minister Franz Josef Strauss — Schmidt's nemesis — was "a breath of fresh air" despite his "scary rhetoric." At least Strauss wasn't telling him one thing privately and the press something else, as he felt Schmidt was doing. Strauss had advised Carter that Schmidt was "a fool" for not backing the Olympic boycott more sincerely. The Bavarian firebrand came back again and again to the argument that global participation in the 1936 Berlin Olympics — an event also in the news because of the death that spring of gold medalist sprinter Jesse Owens — emboldened Hitler.

Carter and Brzezinski had long found Schmidt exasperating. "I guess women are not the only ones that have periods," the president wrote in his diary after the chancellor seemed moody during an earlier meeting. Their mutual disregard boiled over at a June summit in Venice, when Schmidt — sitting knee-to-knee with Carter in a hotel suite — raged about a letter the president sent him opposing a freeze in the number of medium-range nuclear weapons in Europe, which Carter felt would have frozen Soviet advantages in place. Carter wrote that evening that Schmidt "acted like a paranoid child — ranting and raving."

The president was annoyed that his conservative critics were so sure that Schmidt was strong and sophisticated, while he was weak and naive. In fact, their respective positions on theater nuclear weapons suggested just the opposite. The German foreign minister, Hans-Dietrich Genscher, thanked Carter privately for not overreacting to Schmidt's often-bitter denunciations of the United States.

With key votes coming up in the West German and French Olympic committees, Carter called Schmidt and asked him to finally commit and to bring the French along. The chancellor came through in the end. He convinced French president Giscard d'Estaing to join him in announcing a boycott of the Games, though both France and Great Britain ended up having it both ways by sending some of their best athletes under other banners.

In Moscow that summer, sixty-five nations refused to participate, while eighty mostly smaller countries sent athletes. The Soviet Union and East Germany won more than half of the medals, in what Carter described as a "farce." By that time, the shock of the Soviet invasion had worn off, and most Americans felt sorry for the athletes — nearly half of whom would never get another chance to appear in the Olympic Games — and sorry for themselves that they had no Olympics to watch on TV in the summer of 1980. They blamed Jimmy Carter.

For a generation, Carter has been second-guessed from both the Left and the Right for his role in the resumption of serious tensions between the United States and the Soviet Union. The Left claimed he overreacted to the invasion of Afghanistan, that vital interests in the Persian Gulf were not truly at stake, and that he was just trying to look tough after the hostages were seized in Iran

— in short, that the Carter Doctrine was a jingoistic political move designed to aid his reelection. The Right insisted that Carter was naive about the Soviets, that he weakened American defenses, and that only Ronald Reagan showed the firmness necessary to win the Cold War.

Four decades later, neither of these interpretations holds up. Liberal critics ignore the geopolitical realities: the United States was, in fact, dangerously dependent on oil from the Gulf, and while the Soviets would not likely have moved to cut off supplies, the capacity to do so would have given them powerful new strategic leverage on the global chessboard.

It's true that Carter and his political advisers welcomed what critics routinely called "the distraction" that the invasion of Afghanistan provided from his failure to resolve the Iranian hostage crisis. And looking tough was certainly good for Carter politically. But if that had been his only motive — and if he had been a different kind of president — he might have sent troops somewhere (as six of his predecessors had) or bombed some country (as all of his successors have). That would have ultimately been more popular than canceling US participation in the Olympics and slamming the farm belt and nascent tech sector with embargoes. In the end, Carter managed to show resolve without imperiling American lives — just as he intended.

Conservative attacks on Carter's "softness" hold up even less well. His defense buildup — especially the development of stealth technology — and the Carter Doctrine did much to set the stage for the end of the Cold War a decade later. Detente had to die before the Cold War could end, and Carter was the one who killed it. Stigmatizing Moscow from the outside advanced the cause of reform on the inside in the 1980s. Had he minimized the invasion of Afghanistan and merely slapped the Soviets on the wrist, the war might have gone better for Moscow. And the pressures within Russian society that did more than anything else to unravel the Soviet regime might not have materialized, or at least not so soon.

In interviews after leaving the presidency, Carter consistently defended the Olympic boycott as an extremely tough decision that was necessary at the time. But he also began to rewrite history. "Both the Congress and the Olympic Committee voted overwhelmingly not to participate, and I reluctantly agreed with their decision," he wrote middle schoolers working on a history project in 2011. Later, Carter sat next to 1984 gold medalist wrestler Jeff Blatnick on an airplane. Blatnick, who had also been a member of the 1980 US Olympic team, remembered him saying, "That was a bad decision. I'm sorry."

It turned out that neither the boycott nor the grain embargo deterred Soviet behavior directly. But the arms for the mujahideen did. Over the next decade, the Afghan war went so badly that the Red Army lost its appetite and capacity for further incursions into foreign territory. That meant there was little chance of the Soviets invading one of their restless captive nations in Eastern Europe, as they had in 1956 and 1968. Moscow's flinch stimulated internal rebellion in those nations and signaled the end of the Soviet Empire.

While Mikhail Gorbachev's reformist vision and unwillingness to shed blood to save the Soviet Union remains the preeminent explanation for the end of the Cold War, the firmness and skill displayed by the three American presidents of this era were important factors. Carter confronted the Soviets on their reckless and dehumanizing behavior; Reagan turned the screws; George H. W. Bush refused to gloat when the collapse began. All of this helped bring a peaceful end to a brutal seventy-two-year-old Communist empire that by all historical odds should have gone down fighting.

# 35
## DISASTER AT DESERT ONE

Carter would later compare 1980 to 1954, when his warehouse business was doing so badly that he worried he would have to declare bankruptcy and go work for a defense contractor. "That's the way the hostage thing was for me for fourteen months," he said after leaving the White House. "No matter what else happened, it was always there — painful because I was failing to accomplish what seemed to be a simple task." At the time, he hid his insomnia and stress even from Rosalynn, but he admitted later that in 1980 he was less confident and prayed more than at any time he could remember. The idea of people being harmed or killed because of his decisions filled him with dread.

Ironically, Carter began 1980 on a high note. For much of 1979, he had trailed Ted Kennedy by 20 to 30 points in the polls. Now, benefitting from the rally-round-the-flag mood after the seizure of the hostages and the Soviet invasion of Afghanistan, he led Kennedy by 20 points — a 50-point swing between August 1979 and January 1980. Even in the less polarized political culture of the twentieth century, this was an unusual level of volatility.

It helped Carter that at first Kennedy was "a horrible candidate," as a Kennedy senior adviser, Peter Edelman, put it, with fumbling references to "fam farmilies" and the "United Notions," and rambling, inarticulate answers that made Carter look like Cicero. Watching his lackluster rallies, old friends in the press corps thought Teddy's heart wasn't in it. And his pro forma support for a president in crisis felt insincere and off-key. (In private, Kennedy thought Afghanistan was no more critical an ally than South Vietnam had been.)

On a December 24 conference call, Carter told his team that he would not take part in a January 7 debate with Kennedy and Jerry Brown, who would again enter a few primaries but was not seen as a serious contender. Carter believed this was the politically obvious move. When he had agreed to the debate, he was down 2-to-1 to Kennedy and didn't have foreign policy crises to worry about. "Now all those factors have changed, and Rosalynn thinks I'm right," he wrote in his journal, echoing his wife's view that he should stay "above the fray." Rafshoon, already in Iowa arranging debate logistics, wasn't alone in thinking this was a blunder. Carter was quicker and much more articulate than Kennedy and might have ended the senator's campaign on the spot by thrashing him.

In the meantime, domestic issues that could in any way be connected to national security started to go his way. For months, Carter had been struggling to win approval of $1.5 billion in loan guarantees for the Chrysler Corporation. Suddenly his argument that the rescue protected not just cars but also the Chrysler-built M-1 Abrams tank had more resonance. After a long struggle in Congress, he finally signed the package on January 7.

Chrysler CEO Lee Iacocca was so determined to maintain his bipartisan credentials that he didn't give Carter much credit for bailing out his company.* And the United Auto Workers stuck with Kennedy, which infuriated Carter, who considered the union ungrateful for the tens of thousands of jobs he saved at Chrysler and its suppliers and dealerships. At a December 1979 staff meeting, he simmered in fury at UAW president Doug Fraser, using his favorite expletive: "We ought not kiss his ass." Fraser was later remorseful. He said after the 1980 election that backing Kennedy was "the biggest political mistake I ever made." It never dawned on him, he said, that Reagan could possibly win.

It apparently never dawned on feminist leaders, either.† After being outorganized in the states by

---

*"This is the man that saved Chrysler!" Iacocca told employees, raising Carter's hand high — but only after the 1980 election. The Chrysler bailout was the precedent for Obama's 2009 bailout of General Motors and Chrysler. In both bailouts, bitterly opposed by free marketeers, the government got almost all of its money back.

†The leaders of the women's movement never came to terms with Kennedy's history with women. In the December 1979 issue of *Washington Monthly,* Suzannah Lessard wrote a bracing piece called "Kennedy's Women Problem/Women's Kennedy Problem," arguing that Kennedy's "pattern" of coming on to women constituted "a kind of narcissistic intemperance" even

conservative activist Phyllis Schlafly, the National Organization for Women (NOW), a large feminist organization then led by Eleanor Smeal, blamed Carter for the Equal Rights Amendment falling just three states shy of ratification. This was unfair to Carter, who started slow but, under prodding from Rosalynn, embraced the cause. He lobbied for — and in 1978 signed — a bill to extend the deadline for ratification until 1982, called dozens of state legislators (unheard of for a president), and made an unprecedented presidential address to the Illinois General Assembly, the first ever given by a president to a state government. (The ERA lost there anyway.) Rosalynn and her daughter-in-law Judy Langford Carter campaigned hard across the country for the ERA; Rosalynn said its failure was her "greatest disappointment" as first lady.

None of this was good enough for Smeal and other leading feminists. By December 1979, Kennedy was flailing, but the board of NOW nonetheless endorsed him over Carter on the grounds that Carter had neglected to use patronage to win ERA ratification — a strange argument considering that presidents no longer controlled state and local patronage the way they once did. NOW also announced that if Carter won the Democratic nomination, it would sit out the general election, an astonishing decision that it refused to revisit even after the GOP nominated Reagan. Decades later, Rosalynn still considered this unforgivable.

And yet at first, none of the intraparty strife affected Carter; he seemed to be unstoppable.

---

if the encounters were consensual.

Without campaigning for even a day, he beat Kennedy by 28 points in the January 21 Iowa caucuses. Afterward, Kennedy assembled his eight senior aides to vote on whether he should continue his campaign. Even Steve Smith, his brother-in-law and campaign manager, thought he should drop out. But the thrashing had energized the senator, who had never lost before and now relished the fight. "It's four to four, and the ayes have it," he told his team. "I'm staying in."

Bob Shrum thought Kennedy, like many losing candidates, felt liberated. "There is no malaise in the spirit of this country," he thundered. "It's just Mr. Carter."

At Georgetown University, Kennedy gave a combative policy speech (written by Shrum and Stephen Breyer) that blew apart the country's post-invasion unity. He attacked the president from both left and — amazingly — right, even mentioning the Brezhnev kiss. Carter, he sneered, was pursuing "foreign policy based on the pangs of unrequited love." On domestic policy, the senator swung sharply left, endorsing wage and price controls that had failed badly when tried in 1971 by President Nixon.

Carter won by 10 points in New Hampshire, but a newly amped Kennedy was competitive in Illinois. Chicago's Democratic mayor, Jane Byrne, had endorsed Carter the previous October before pretending she hadn't and switching to Kennedy. "This is a rare event in politics, when somebody deliberately lies," an irate Carter wrote in his journal. Naive as that sounds to twenty-first-century ears, it was an accurate depiction of the long-standing rules of engagement in American politics, where obvious lies usually boomeranged.

With the March 18 primary approaching, Kennedy found Byrne's endorsement a burden; she was a nasty and increasingly unpopular mayor. He even tried to ditch her at Chicago's Saint Patrick's Day parade so they would not be photographed together. The flap helped Carter, who won Illinois easily. What could stop him now?

While Carter was far ahead of Ronald Reagan, George H. W. Bush, and other potential opponents in head-to-head polling matchups, he worried that rampant inflation could threaten his reelection. The annual increase in the consumer price index had surged from 5 percent when he took office to 18 percent in March 1980. That this was caused largely by OPEC price hikes and Iranian supply disruptions was irrelevant politically; he would be blamed.

To align his fiscal policy with the Fed's tight monetary policy, Carter decided to rewrite his entire budget to make it more austere. At a March 14 press conference, he awkwardly invoked Benjamin Franklin: "It's as though we've come to believe a penny *borrowed* is a penny earned." He announced a freeze on all federal hiring and new initiatives, a balanced budget by October, and a pledge to veto any bill that exceeded the spending limits.* With inflation so high, freezing spending or even cutting the rate of spending growth amounted to a significant "cut." This was especially hard on seniors and others with fixed

*Carter felt the biggest threat to a balanced budget came from the business community, with its hundreds of tax favors and other hidden subsidies embedded in federal law.

incomes, whose grocery bills and rents rose faster than cost-of-living increases.

These budget cuts were small compared to what Republicans favored, but progressive rage was now directed at Carter, who — while far from a Wall Street Democrat — had appeased markets by appointing Paul Volcker and issuing a conservative budget. He was pushing his fourth anti-inflation plan in three years, and it managed to make him look desperate, stingy, and futile all at the same time.

At the *Boston Globe,* Kirk Scharfenberg wrote an editorial about Carter's opening remarks in his press conference; the piece was meant to have the headline "All Must Share the Burden," but as a playful placeholder he wrote, "Mush from the Wimp." That inside-joke headline accidentally ran in 161,000 copies of the paper and spread rapidly around the world.

For all the snickering and liberal blowback, the president proved surprisingly persuasive on the economy. His most significant short-term step was to impose a set of credit controls (lending limits administered by the Fed) to tamp down the spending boom that he felt was fueling inflation.*
Americans responded to the president's call to

---

*That month, Carter also signed the Depository Institutions Deregulation and Monetary Control Act of 1980, which was aimed at increasing the savings rate by freeing banks to charge whatever interest rates they wanted among other provisions designed to stabilize credit. It was the deregulation enacted in the Clinton and Bush II administrations — not this Carter-era bill — that led in part to the 2008 financial crisis.

borrow less with patriotic fervor, deluging the White House with cut-up credit cards. As consumers stopped going to the mall and paid off debt, the economy fell into what turned out to be a mild six-month recession, with unemployment peaking at 7.5 percent in May 1980. That downturn prompted the Fed to ease the credit controls and Carter and Congress enacted a small election-year stimulus and minor tax cuts. The vertiginous economy recovered quickly. This, in turn, triggered reductions in the Fed's money supply. Volcker admitted later that he was nonetheless surprised that interest rates shot up again in the fall, just in time for the election.

The economic funhouse mirror took a psychological toll on the country. Even though Social Security and many labor agreements included cost-of-living increases, the adjustments couldn't keep pace with inflation. The combination of unemployment and inflation — what economist Arthur Okun dubbed "the misery index" — hit 21.9 percent in June 1980, providing both Ted Kennedy and Ronald Reagan with killer sound bites. And the misery index didn't even include interest rates.

It took another three years before Volcker engineered a short, steep recession in 1982 that finally killed inflation for good. President Reagan got the credit for what Carter's man had done, leading directly to his famous "It's Morning in America" ad campaign and landslide reelection in 1984.

Carter soldiered through the early primaries by ditching the campaign trail and focusing mostly on the hostages. But as time wore on, the once-strong president was seen increasingly as being at the mercy of the Iranian militants — the "students" whom Mondale called "a bunch of twerps." It also made the president a tad rusty. He admitted later that he should have stumped more, so as not to lose touch with the American people.

Carter nonetheless seemed to be cruising toward a win in the March 25 New York primary, just a week after Illinois. A *New York Daily News* poll showed him up by 20 points; if the president won by any margin, Kennedy would have to withdraw.

But in early March, Carter's team made a mistake that would end up extending Kennedy's primary challenge throughout the spring. When the UN Security Council took up a resolution condemning Israel for illegal settlements on the West Bank, Carter made the same routine decision he and his predecessors had made in the past: the United States would abstain because the resolution included a paragraph questioning Israeli sovereignty over Jerusalem. This clause was also contrary to what had been agreed to at Camp David.

Vance then reported to the president that UN drafters had deleted all of the objectionable references to Jerusalem and adopted the amendments the Americans had requested. But they hadn't. Without checking the revisions with the White House, the State Department had instructed UN ambassador Donald McHenry to vote in favor of the resolution.

Many Jewish voters thought the United States had sold out Israel. Under pressure, Carter issued a statement saying the vote had been a "mistake" based on a "failure to communicate" between the White House and McHenry, a version of events that let Vance off the hook. Within hours, the United States rescinded its support for the resolution. Brzezinski, who strongly opposed the resolution, also strongly opposed the apology and retraction, which he thought "made the administration look silly and the president look weak."

Kennedy leapt on the UN screwup and, more ominously for Carter, so did New York mayor Ed Koch, who had decided the Carter administration was unreliable on Israel and said so loudly. With hundreds of thousands of Jewish voters in New York on the line, Koch called Vance, Brzezinski, Young, McHenry, and Assistant Secretary of State Harold Saunders the "Gang of Five" who were out to harm Israel, a comment Carter found "disgraceful."*

Beyond the UN snafu, Carter ran into trouble in New York on an issue that should have helped him: urban policy.

In 1977 and 1978 two of Carter's young hotshots — Roger Altman and Orin Kramer — had worked with Treasury Secretary Blumenthal to craft the final piece of Washington's historic rescue of New York City from bankruptcy, a series of loan guarantees in exchange for concessions by both unions and banks. Carter had lobbied the bill through Congress in 1978 — mostly by convincing twenty Republicans to abstain.

The New York City bailout was part of an innovative Carter urban policy that kicked off an era of public-private partnerships (most operating through HUD's new Urban Development Action

*This was a play on the Gang of Four, a faction of Chinese ultra-hard-liners, led by Mao Tsetung's widow, Jiang Qing, who abused power in the early 1970s.

Grant program). This culminated in the revitalization of downtown areas across the country — an important part of Carter's legacy. The little-noticed centerpiece was the landmark Community Reinvestment Act, signed by Carter in 1977, which used federal regulatory power to encourage banks to invest in low-income neighborhoods, effectively banning the practice of "redlining" by banks that for generations refused to make loans in black neighborhoods. The bill, pushed by Senator William Proxmire of Wisconsin and strengthened in later years, appealed to Carter's belief in racial justice. Over time the CRA, despite problems with predatory lenders, helped stimulate hundreds of billions of dollars of investment in minority communities.*

For all of its successes, Carter's urban policy was infected by grubby old-fashioned politics. While giving the president deniability, his political operatives weren't above using discretionary federal largesse to reward supportive mayors — including Koch, who in 1979 endorsed Carter for

---

*In 1976 candidate Carter toured the abandoned lots on Charlotte Street in the South Bronx, pledging to revive the neighborhood — a big overpromise, Jack Watson admitted. In 1980 Reagan made a point of visiting Charlotte Street, and it was still vacant. He turned this into a potent campaign taunt. In truth, something positive was starting to happen there. Reagan cut Carter's urban programs, but by the 1990s, the public-private partnerships made possible by the CRA and launched under Carter brought tidy, affordable new townhouses to once-desolate Charlotte Street.

reelection.*

But Carter's newly announced budget undermined all the political deal making done on his behalf. Its cuts hit New York especially hard. Just before the primary, Koch said that he not only opposed the budget cuts but also wanted yet more federal aid for New York City. He implied to millions of New Yorkers that despite his earlier endorsement, Carter didn't deserve their support.

Rosalynn was angry at Jimmy. She wondered why he couldn't have waited until the week after the New York primary to announce his budget cuts. "The psychology of inflation demands that something be done now," he told her. She wasn't convinced. When declining to make politically expedient decisions, Jimmy's explanation for his behavior was often, in Rosalynn's words, "seemingly pompous." He would say something like, "I'll never do anything to hurt my country." And she'd reply, "The thing you can do to hurt your country most is not get reelected."

On March 25 Kennedy won New York by 18 points, a staggering upset. (He carried Connecticut by 5 points the same day.) "It's a protest vote," Pat Caddell told the president, arguing that Jewish voters knew Carter had the nomination sewed up and wanted to send him a message.

The results all but guaranteed that Kennedy would stay in the race and helped encourage moderate Republican congressman John Anderson of Illinois, who had not won a single GOP

---

*Neil Goldschmidt, Carter's new transportation secretary, even admitted he might withhold discretionary transportation funds from mayors who endorsed Kennedy, which led to calls for his resignation.

842

primary, to swing left and weigh running in the fall as an independent. With the help of his depiction in Garry Trudeau's *Doonesbury* comic strip, Anderson had become a cult hero on college campuses and with young urban professionals who would soon be called "Yuppies." Now he threatened to complicate the general election.

In August the president was in New York for a speech and rode with Mayor Koch to the event. "I gave him hell for his daily stabbing me in the back," he wrote in his diary.* Hamilton Jordan joked that "if Ed Koch and Jane Byrne had a baby, it would have all the characteristics of a dog except loyalty."

One of Ted Koppel's frequent guests on *Nightline* was Iran's new foreign minister, Sadegh Ghotbzadeh, a dodgy diplomat in a silk suit who tried to perfume the ayatollah and the student militants while seeming to extend an olive branch to the United States. At the end of 1979, Ghotbzadeh saw a chance to secure his power base at home by extraditing the shah for a trial in Iran that would almost certainly lead to his execution.† He

---

*Carter didn't know the half of it. Roy Cohn revealed later that Koch met secretly with Republican county leaders in the fall and agreed to help Reagan's campaign by attacking Carter for hurting Israel and New York's Medicaid budget — in exchange for GOP support for Koch in future campaigns. Reagan carried New York State handily.

†It would be Ghotbzadeh himself who would be executed — by the Ayatollah Khomeini's regime — in 1982.

authorized two unlikely Paris-based intermediaries, a slick pro-revolutionary French lawyer, Christian Bourguet, and a rumpled Argentinian radical with shoulder-length hair, Hector Villalon, to negotiate with the Panamanians and Americans with an eye toward extraditing the shah from Panama.

Omar Torrijos's admiration for Carter meant that he would have gladly extradited the shah in exchange for release of the hostages — an outcome he presumed would result in the president's reelection. But Carter was adamantly opposed to extradition; he knew that if it seemed imminent, the shah would seek asylum in the United States to avoid sure death in Iran, and he would have no choice but to let him in again.

Bourguet and Villalon felt the State Department was dominated by Kissinger, Rockefeller, and other friends of the shah, leaving them loath to negotiate with anyone there. But they agreed to Torrijos's suggestion in January that they establish a back channel to his new buddy Hamilton Jordan. Carter signed off on the idea and agreed not to suspend all diplomatic relations with Iran, as he had been threatening to do, in order to give this back channel a chance.

On February 17 Jordan — traveling in partial disguise and under a false identity — met secretly in Paris with Ghotbzadeh, who told him that in order to get the hostages released, "all you have to do is kill the shah." An appalled Jordan said that would not happen, but the Iranian foreign minister continued to raise hopes in Washington. He instructed Bourguet in March to tell Jordan that the hostages would be freed — and the whole crisis ended — if the shah could be kept from leaving Panama (where extradition was possible) for Egypt (where his friend Sadat would protect him from extradition). Carter agreed that the shah should not go to Egypt, but for different reasons. "I will not do that to Anwar," he told Jordan. "He's got enough problems without having us dump the shah in his lap."

But keeping him in Panama so that Jordan could execute his deal was difficult. Torrijos was fed up with the shah's medical drama, which felt like déjà vu, with Armao and his American doctors (now including world-famous Houston heart surgeon Dr. Michael DeBakey) insulting local Panamanian physicians. His patience finally exhausted, Torrijos let the shah board a plane for Cairo on March 23.

Jordan was so anxious to keep the disappearing deal for the hostages' release alive that he called Secretary of Defense Harold Brown and asked him to have the Pentagon ground the shah's plane when it landed in the Azores islands for refueling. Brown complied, though the delay lasted only a couple of hours. Carter was "livid" when he found out and reproached Jordan for grossly overstepping his authority.

Two days later — the day of the New York primary — the president met with Jordan and Bourguet at the White House. Carter, slumped on the Oval Office couch, decried the "comic opera" under way. The Iranian government "didn't have the courage to take the hostages away from the terrorists," he told Bourguet. "Our patience is beginning to look like cowardice." When told that the Iranian people thought the hostages were being treated better than dissidents under the shah, Carter exploded. "I find that sickening! These fifty-three people have killed no one, while Khomeini has been responsible for the execution of six or eight hundred people." Carter felt that "to punish fifty-three innocent human beings violates all the teachings of Christianity and the Moslem faith that I know of." Carter, as usual, was choosing the religious ideal over the grim historical record; it was as if he had forgotten not just SAVAK's recent abuses but centuries of Christian and Muslim butchery toward infidels.

Bourguet claimed a deal to free the hostages was still possible and that Carter should write to Ghotbzadeh's rival, Abol Hassan Bani-Sadr, another *Nightline* favorite, who in January had become the nearly powerless president of Iran. Carter reluctantly wrote Bani-Sadr a conciliatory letter saying that in exchange for immediately releasing the hostages, the United States would normalize relations on Iran's schedule and offer the country a chance to air its grievances. He followed up on March 28 with a tougher message to both Bani-Sadr and Khomeini stating that there would be "serious consequences" if the hostages were not transferred by April 1.

But Bani-Sadr was stuck between the unruly parliament and Khomeini. Instead of responding to Carter's ultimatum, the ayatollah — trying to show he had humiliated the West — brandished a fake "letter of apology" from Carter that supposedly confessed America's sins. Many White House reporters, habituated to a cynical take on Carter, assumed the crude fake letter was real and Jody Powell's denial a lie.

On March 29 Jordan told Rosalynn there was "no way in God's world we [can] win Pennsylvania

846

[on April 22] unless something happened on the hostage situation." This made her feel sad, but her husband was unperturbed. "Jimmy said on Friday that if he could survive me and Hamilton — our feelings — that he would be all right," Rosalynn wrote in a journal she kept during this period.

The next day, Ghotbzadeh appeared on *Issues and Answers,* the ABC News Sunday show, and made it sound as if the release of the hostages was near. Vance told Carter the signs were positive. After Rosalynn woke from a nap, "Jimmy came into the room and said the Iranians are going to announce Monday at three o'clock in the morning our time that the hostages would be transferred from the students to the government and that the Revolutionary Council had already voted approval of this and Khomeini had already approved."

Jimmy and Rosalynn went to bed at 8:40 p.m., anticipating that they would arise at 3:00 a.m. on March 31 for an announcement from Tehran, though by this time they had been jerked around enough that they weren't confident that anything would happen. Rosalynn awoke at 11:00 p.m. and couldn't go back to sleep. The 3:00 a.m. announcement never came, nor did one scheduled for 10:30 a.m. Carter was then told that the Revolutionary Guard had been meeting for five hours to decide how to take the hostages from the students, where to put them, and other logistics. Now the announcement would come at 3:00 p.m. — twelve hours after it was originally scheduled. But again, nothing.

At dinnertime, Carter received a message through intermediaries that Khomeini had said the hostage release was off, with no explanation why. The Carters went to bed. Rosalynn went into the bathroom at eleven o'clock and cried for a while. She had invested so much emotional energy in worrying if the hostages were alive and well, and now she wouldn't know. She tried to find something positive in the mess. "Jimmy would have an excuse to get out and campaign, which I think he needs to do now," she confided in her journal. "He, in my opinion, is the hostage to this situation."

On April 1, primary day in Wisconsin, Carter assembled reporters in the Oval Office at seven thirty in the morning to tell them about the events of the past twenty-four hours, which — despite the ayatollah's last message — he described as the first "positive development" in Iran in the five months of the crisis. Jody Powell was later angry at himself for allowing this. A skeptical press corps thought the president was trying to influence the outcome in Wisconsin.

Carter won there by 26 points, but that morning's press conference made him look inept and manipulative at once. "He was left in an extremely awkward position," *New York Times* columnist James Reston wrote the next day, "accused at home of misleading the press and mocked abroad for trying to work out a secret compromise." Reston concluded that "none of his political opponents has a better answer," but that was cold comfort for the White House.

Polls now showed that for the first time, disapproval of Carter's handling of the hostage problem exceeded approval. Even so, Kennedy and later Reagan could criticize Carter only so much on the issue as long as the hostages were still being held.

Carter's family and friends saw his impatience as a defining trait, which made his months of forbearance during the hostage crisis all the more remarkable — a testament to his overarching preference for peace. That would now change. A week after the ayatollah's brush-off, Carter announced that he was breaking diplomatic relations with Iran, expelling all Iranian diplomats, and imposing a full embargo — all moves he had avoided over the winter to keep diplomacy on track. By now, rumors were swirling of some kind of US military action, though no one knew what form it would take.

When Jordan pointed out that Bourguet and Villalon hadn't given up, Carter cut him off: "Ham, the only people in the world who think we're going to get our people back soon are you and your French friends."

Planning for a possible rescue mission had been under way since the week after the hostages were seized in November. At last, with diplomacy failing and Carter's poll numbers dropping, it was time for a bold move.

The administration had already experienced some covert success. In January a CIA operative, Tony Mendez, gaincd entry into Iran under the guise of making a Hollywood science fiction movie. His mission was to spirit out of the country six American diplomats who on the day of the embassy seizure in November had taken refuge in the residence of the Canadian ambassador, Ken Taylor, and the home of another Canadian official. (Carter later thought *Argo,* the 2012 Oscar-winning movie based on the rescue, gave too much credit to the CIA and too little to the

Canadian government, especially Taylor, "the real hero.")

All winter, US military forces had been training for a raid on Tehran to free the hostages, and now they were ready. So was Carter, whose usual diffidence toward politics was quickly giving way to the same determination that helped him win in 1970 and 1976. He made no apologies for thinking politically in an election year. "The reason for the raid was that the Rose Garden strategy — the strategy of a president 'too good to go to war' — was no longer working, and the last possibility for a deal collapsed the day of the Wisconsin primary," Hodding Carter said. "The raid was necessary for the president to get reelected."

This is a little harsh; Carter's frustration, confidence in the military, and natural risk-taking also played important roles in his decision. And for all the political calculations, the administration's internal debates revolved around fundamental questions of American power. Vance, who favored sticking with diplomacy, had been deeply influenced by his experience as secretary of the army during the Vietnam War. He essentially believed, as Hodding Carter put it, that you could not take a platoon across a river at night without losing half your men. Brzezinski felt that Vance had been traumatized by Vietnam and favored a muscular military response. Harold Brown's view was in the middle: that "the rescue mission is the best of a lousy set of options."

For months, Vance had been weighing resignation. He was worn out from battling Brzezinski and suffering from gout. On the weekend of April 10, he took a much-needed break in Florida. In his absence, Brzezinski scheduled a National

Security Council meeting to decide on the mission. Deputy Secretary of State Warren Christopher represented Vance but stayed neutral because he had not been fully briefed. The others backed the rescue mission, and Carter approved it and scheduled a date: April 24. Vance remembered being "stunned and angry that so momentous a decision had been made in my absence."

Carter and Vance had been drifting apart for months, in part because the president was annoyed that his secretary of state wasn't more of a spokesman for American foreign policy. Vance was never comfortable going on Sunday shows or spinning important columnists, which Carter didn't want to do himself. ("I'd rather retire to Plains than spend an hour with Joe Kraft," he said after the pompous syndicated columnist lectured him on how to handle the shah.)

On his return, the president gave what he described as his "extremely despondent" secretary of state a chance to weigh in at another NSC meeting. Vance made a good argument that an attempt to extract hostages by force from a city of five million people carried unacceptable risks for the lives of the hostages and for the national interest. He noted that even if the hostages were rescued, thc Iranians could simply seize some of the thousands of Americans (mostly businessmen) who had elected to remain in Tehran. Carter said these individuals weren't government officials — and they had been advised by the State Department to leave months earlier. Even though his old friend David Rabhan was among them, they would not be his concern.

On the evening of April 16 General David Jones, chairman of the Joint Chiefs, and Major General

James Vaught, the commander of the rescue mission, came to the Situation Room for a final briefing for Carter and his senior team. They brought along Colonel Charles "Chargin' Charlie" Beckwith, the Vietnam War hero who in 1977 had created a small, specialized commando unit called Delta Force. Beckwith outlined the plan, codenamed Operation Eagle Claw.

Seven Sikorsky RH-53 Sea Stallion helicopters would fly more than 600 miles under cover of darkness from the aircraft carrier USS *Nimitz* in the Gulf of Oman to a remote rendezvous point at a dry lake bed in central Iran called Desert One. There the helicopters would meet six C-130 cargo planes — flown in from an island off Oman — loaded with 120 highly trained Delta Force commandos. After refueling at Desert One, the choppers would fly 270 miles northwest to a daytime hideout near Tehran, where Iranian agents working for the United States would put the men in trucks and drive them undetected to the US embassy, at which point the commandos would blow a hole in the outer wall of the compound before overpowering the heavily armed militants. The rescued hostages would then be spirited to a soccer stadium across the street from the embassy, where the helicopters would pick them up and fly them to an unused airfield fifty miles away; two hundred Rangers flown in from Egypt would protect the hostages as they boarded giant C-141 transport planes, which would then fly everyone out of the country, with the Iranian armed forces none the wiser.

What could possibly go wrong? Only everything. The mission may have been worth a try, but it was, by any standard, a highly risky jerry-rigged operation requiring the intricate cooperation of units from five different military branches that often engaged in poisonous rivalries. The plan was based in part on the famous 1976 Raid on Entebbe, where Israeli commandos freed hostages being held in Uganda. But skeptical Israeli intelligence officials — consulted on the planning — reminded their American counterparts that the Israeli hostages had been held at a remote airport, not in the center of a city.

Whatever the complications, Carter was grimly determined to proceed. He was impressed by the eight elaborate training exercises at various remote military bases but apparently never learned that not once did all of the services have a dress rehearsal to see how the many moving parts meshed.

What, the president asked, was the most difficult part of the mission? He was told there were two: going in undetected and "the helicopters." They weren't accustomed to flying long distances at low altitudes with heavy loads. The original military plan had included only six choppers, later bumped up to seven. Under prodding from Carter and Brzezinski, there would now be eight.

Carter wanted to know whether the commandos would distinguish between guards — peasant conscripts with no responsibility for seizing the hostages — and the militants inside. Beckwith said no. He explained that most or all of the Iranians in the embassy compound would be killed — shot twice each, right between the eyes. Beckwith told Jordan afterward that in the past he hadn't been a Carter fan, despite hailing from southwest Georgia. But he was impressed when the president pulled him aside and told him to tell his men that any failure was on him, not them. "The buck stops with me," Carter said. He was even more explicit with the military brass: "If we are successful, it will be your victory. If we are not successful, it will be my defeat."

Jordan traveled to Europe to meet again with Ghotbzadeh and reported to Carter on April 22 that his suspension of diplomatic relations had gone over badly with the Iranians, and there was now no chance for release of the hostages for "months and months." The same day, Bruce Laingen, still being held at the foreign ministry in Tehran, slipped out a message recommending strong action against Iran. While worried about security breaches, Carter made the final decision to proceed.

As rumors of some kind of military action swirled, Carter grew defensive about the reaction to his hardening line. The dovish General Conference of Methodists, meeting in Indianapolis, passed what Carter described as "an embarrassing resolution" accusing the United States of imperialism. When the church's top bishops sought to come see him, Carter asked Vance to meet with them instead. The secretary of state declined, which, Carter noted, was the first time anyone in his administration had refused to obey an official order.

Vance, now alone internally in his opposition to the rescue mission, which he believed was too complicated to succeed, submitted his resignation on April 21. This time Carter accepted it, effective after the mission was over.

Carter would consider April 24, 1980, one of the worst days of his life. For most of the afternoon,

Washington time, communications indicated that the mission was advancing according to plan. It wasn't. The C-130s arrived at Desert One at midnight, expecting sandy solitude. But the Americans encountered a busload of terrified Iranian pilgrims en route to a holy site. They were stopped and detained. Then Army Rangers spotted a truck speeding through the area, which turned out to be driven by a gasoline smuggler. A Ranger blew up the truck with an antitank missile; the driver miraculously survived and jumped out of the truck and into another car, which sped away. A night of confusion and disaster was just beginning.

Of the eight helicopters that had set out from the *Nimitz,* one turned back an hour into the mission because of what seemed like a cracked rotor blade, though it turned out later that after an emergency landing the *army* pilot hadn't known how to examine a *navy* blade, which was actually okay. The pilot of a second chopper — on radio silence to avoid detection — grew disoriented in a sandstorm, later likened to being inside a bottle of milk with clouds of fine powder penetrating the cockpit and caking your lips. The pilot turned around even though he was much closer to Desert One than to the *Nimitz.* Back on the carrier, his furious fellow marines soon nicknamed him "Turn Back."

The mission called for an absolute minimum of six helicopters. It looked as if they still had just enough to proceed. The helicopters refueled at Desert One and were preparing to lift off and head toward Tehran when one suddenly malfunctioned. Its backup hydraulic system was shot, likely from the dust.

Now what? The twenty-odd soldiers from that chopper couldn't squeeze into the remaining five helicopters without adding too much weight and leaving too little room for the rescued hostages. An officer asked Beckwith if they could proceed with twenty fewer shooters storming the embassy. "Fuck you," Beckwith said. "I ain't gonna do that. I don't know what I'm up against."

When word reached Washington that Beckwith wanted to abort, Brzezinski rushed to the Oval Office to convince Carter to press forward with only five helicopters. He found Carter on the phone with Harold Brown and heard him say, "Let's go with his [Beckwith's] recommendation." Then he put his head down on his desk and cradled it in his arms.

After the mission was scrapped, the choppers needed to clear the makeshift runway so the C-130s could take off for the return to the Oman base. But all the dust from five helicopters cut visibility, and one of them flew right into one of the C-130s, causing a huge explosion that killed three marines at the back of the helicopter and five airmen in the cockpit of the plane. The two aircraft were engulfed in flames; recovering the bodies proved impossible. Five wounded men and everyone else on-site were loaded onto the remaining C-130s and flown out. American soldiers and airmen had been at Desert One for three hours in the middle of the night. Now they were coming home in grief and failure.

By this time, Carter began to hear sketchy reports of further troubles on the ground. At 5:58 p.m., General Jones called. In the president's small study, Vance, Brown, Brzezinski, and Jordan watched as Carter — on the phone — closed his eyes; his jaw dropped and his face turned ashen. He hung up and in an even tone described early reports of the fiery collision. No one said a word, as the magnitude of what had happened sunk in. Vance's voice broke the stillness: "Mr. President, I'm very, very sorry." Jordan ducked into the president's private bathroom and "vomited my guts out."

Rosalynn was campaigning in Texas, and Jimmy didn't want to tell her what had happened over the phone. Back at the White House, she had trouble accepting the grim truth. "Like the night my father died, every time I woke up, I wanted to go back to sleep, hoping it would all go away," she wrote. The devastated president obtained a copy of John F. Kennedy's remarks after the 1961 Bay of Pigs fiasco (when a CIA-backed effort to liberate Cuba failed spectacularly), then slept a couple hours before getting up in the middle of the night to prepare his somber address to the nation at seven in the morning. He laid out the story of the "equipment failure" in detail and pledged to "pursue every possible avenue" to free the hostages. "It was my decision to attempt the rescue operation; it was my decision to cancel it," Carter said. "The responsibility is fully my own."

Three days later, Carter flew to the CIA base at Camp Peary, Virginia, where Beckwith was waiting for him. The tough colonel's chin quivered, and tears ran down his cheeks. "I opened my arms, and we embraced and wept together," Carter recalled. "Mr. President, I'm sorry we let you down!" Beckwith said, his voice breaking. For a few minutes, he couldn't talk, as Carter expressed his heartfelt appreciation for what he and his soldiers had done.

Vance quit as planned, the first time a secretary of state resigned on principle since William Jennings Bryan left Woodrow Wilson's cabinet in 1915 over his opposition to the United States drifting toward war. Carter was angry at him for leaving him when he was down but settled quickly on Maine senator Ed Muskie as Vance's replacement. As false news stories spread that Carter had terminated the mission over the objections of Delta Force, which wanted to go forward, Beckwith held a briefing for reporters on May 1 to set the record straight. Afterward, he told Jordan the president was "as tough as woodpecker lips," though he didn't describe him that way to reporters.

By now, air force general Richard Secord, just back from Iran, had already been assigned to try again. He put together an aggressive battle plan that this time would include overwhelming force (eighty-five helicopters) and the prospect of many Iranian casualties as American troops fought their way into Tehran. But after the abortive raid, the hostages had been scattered to unknown locations across the city. Once again, better intelligence might have made a difference. Stansfield Turner had slashed the clandestine service to find more money for space surveillance. But spy satellites, which did not yet have infrared technology to let them see at night, were of little use over Iran. And the HUMINT — human intelligence — on the ground was poor to nonexistent.

On the lawn of the captured US embassy, a radical mullah — a government official who had once strangled a cat in front of reporters to show what he wanted to do to the shah — assembled the Western press. With a flourish, he pulled back tarpaulins to show wooden crates full of shattered aircraft parts and the charred remains of the American airmen who had died on the mission. "This is the proof of Carter's crime," the mullah said.

The Pentagon's after-action reports were harsh. An obscure table in a weather report had warned of dust storms that night, but the helicopter pilots were never briefed on this. And the public learned that the refueling at Desert One was supposed to be the easy part of the operation. The chances of the rest of a complex forty-eight-hour mission succeeding without large-scale American and Iranian casualties seemed slim. The fiasco exposed the extent of interservice rivalry that Carter and several of his predecessors had allowed to fester. Within six years, the landmark Goldwater-Nichols bill would restructure the armed forces so that its different services could finally coordinate properly. Carter's humiliation (and similarly problematic rivalries during the 1983 invasion of Grenada, under Ronald Reagan) led to improved military performance.

Carter often said casually that he would have won a second term if the Pentagon had "sent one more helicopter" into the desert. "Had he pulled the chestnuts out of the fire, he would have been a fucking hero," Max Cleland, the VA administrator, said. "An Annapolis grad–commander in chief nailing these sons of bitches." But it's not clear that even a successful mission would have ensured his reelection.

As if inflation and the hostage rescue debacle weren't enough, Carter faced a big problem during the 1980 primary season with Cuban refugees.

Over the previous two years, he had tried to improve relations with Fidel Castro by lifting all travel restrictions and moving toward ending what the president considered a foolish trade embargo. This was long overdue — and more than thirty years ahead of President Obama's similar efforts — but it failed. Castro still thought the best way to stay in power was to bash the United States. He thumbed his nose at Carter by sending troops to Angola to fight on behalf of Marxist forces there, and US intelligence reports showed him backing Communist insurgencies in El Salvador, Nicaragua, and Grenada.

The previous fall, Senator Frank Church, worried about his right flank as he faced a tough 1980 reelection campaign in Idaho (which he would lose), had reported "evidence" of a new Soviet combat brigade of three thousand troops camped secretly near Havana's Jose Martí airport. Church's announcement, based on faulty intelligence, was a gift for neoconservatives who had been beating the drums over Carter's alleged naivete about Soviet intentions. Brzezinski, too, jumped on the report and confirmed it for the press, as did Vance.

The story was false, though it took the administration weeks to ascertain that. It turned out the "brigade" was the same collection of Soviet military personnel who had been in Cuba since the early 1960s. But the allegations had already done their intended work, helping prevent the SALT II treaty from coming to the Senate floor and nudging official Washington back into Cold War thinking. By the time of the Soviet invasion of Afghanistan at Christmas, Carter felt obliged to view Cuba through the same lens as every other president since Eisenhower.

Castro didn't help. In April 1980 he decided to wriggle out of a crisis at home by making it the problem of Carter and the United States. With ten thousand Cubans crowded in horrible conditions on the grounds of the Peruvian embassy in Havana, the Cuban dictator announced suddenly that dissatisfied citizens were free to leave the country. So began what became known as the Mariel boatlift, named for the Cuban port of departure. Carter was perturbed that Cubans were avoiding the established system for asylum seeking, but federal law required that he treat Cuban refugees more favorably than others. And his call for refugees to be welcomed with "open arms" was well received at home, where the US Coast Guard helped scores of fishing boats jammed with refugees land in Key West, Florida. Two decades after Castro had seized power, Americans still felt great sympathy for those fleeing his Communist rule.

That began to change when it became clear that in addition to large numbers of honest dissidents seeking a better life, many of the refugees were criminals and mental patients whom Castro had released from Cuban jails. As the number of refugees surged (including tens of thousands of Haitians whom Castro would not allow to stay in Cuba), Carter ordered the refugees detained for screening in resettlement camps hastily established on US military bases. All told, 125,000 refugees landed in 1980, which meant months of excruciating headlines for the administration. The overwhelmed resettlement process became its own story of bureaucratic ineptitude, laid at Carter's feet, of course.

The flashpoint came at the military detention center at Fort Chaffee, Arkansas, which had been used for Vietnamese refugees in the mid-1970s. The White House told the thirty-three-year-old governor of Arkansas, Bill Clinton, that the government would need Fort Chaffee again for Cubans. Clinton, unhappy to see Carter dump this problem on him, suggested that the United States first detain and screen the refugees on the US naval base in Guantanamo Bay, Cuba, then open the gate and have the worst of them walk back into Communist Cuba. When Carter rejected this intriguing idea out of hand, Clinton knew he had reason to be agitated.

By May 20, Fort Chaffee was bursting with more than eighteen thousand Cuban refugees. Clinton told Gene Eidenberg, the senior White House aide handling the issue, that Castro was making America look foolish and the president look powerless. On May 26 several dozen Cubans, angry at having been locked up for so long, slipped through an unguarded gate at dawn and caused a minor disturbance in the tiny neighboring town of Barling. Within hours, terrified residents had cleaned out the shelves of all gun shops in a fifty-mile radius.

By this time, allowing Cuban refugees into the United States had become enormously unpopular. On May 28 Clinton called the president, who promised to send more troops to help confine the Cubans to the base. This placated Clinton until the commanding officer of Fort Chaffee, General James "Bulldog" Drummond, told him that his superiors in the Pentagon had instructed him that under the hundred-year-old posse comitatus federal statute, he had no authority over civilian refugees, and thus they could send no more soldiers to Arkansas.

On June 1 a standoff turned into a riot. More than a thousand Cuban refugees stormed out of Fort Chaffee carrying sticks and bottles and chanting, "Libertad! Libertad!" US army troops lining Highway 20 did nothing. Anticipating trouble, Clinton had ordered a few dozen National Guardsmen and Arkansas state troopers to the scene. They now fired warning shots, and the Cubans returned to the base, where they rampaged through three buildings, destroying property. More than sixty people were injured in the melee, five from gunshots. It was a miracle no one was killed. When General Drummond argued that the US military wasn't to blame, Clinton snarled, "Well, shit, General, who left the wire cutters in the stockade if none of this was the military's fault?"

The first-term governor, running for reelection in the fall, was furious at Carter for not keeping his promise. He tried desperately to figure out who had "screwed" him in the three days between his phone call with the president and the riot. Was it Eidenberg? Harold Brown? Carter himself? He concluded it was none of the three but never learned the identity of the general or senior Pentagon official who ordered the federal troops to stand down. Exposed to renewed charges of incompetence, Carter apologized publicly to the state of Arkansas for causing so much anxiety. But he never called Clinton to do so privately.

The Mariel mess frosted the relationship between the two men for decades. Clinton narrowly lost that fall to a Republican and blamed Carter for his defeat. Two years later, he regained the governorship, and ten years after that, he was elected president. In 2004 Carter, speaking in Little Rock at the dedication of the Clinton Library, finally apologized to Clinton for "mistakes" at Fort Chaffee that "may have cost him his reelection." But even decades later, Clinton had trouble letting the grievance go. For his part, Carter concluded that over the course of knowing Clinton for more than forty years, certain constants remained. He was "always ambitious" and "concentrated on what was best for him."

For all the turmoil, Carter was still making some popular decisions that might help reelect him. In early April he signed a steep windfall profits tax on fossil fuel companies that gave him a little populist zing. And he soon hosted a celebration marking the establishment of the new Department of Education, which had been approved in 1979 after debate so fierce that it even split the two teachers' unions: the National Education Association (NEA) was in favor; the American Federation of Teachers (AFT), opposed.

During the 1976 campaign, Carter had argued that education was lost in the gargantuan Department of Health, Education, and Welfare (HEW); for decades, it seemed like education was mentioned only in reference to school desegregation and women's equity in sports. In exchange for support in the primaries, Carter promised the NEA that education would get its own department. But as president, he feared creating another bureaucracy and didn't like the watered-down version of the bill making its way through Congress. Mondale and Eizenstat reminded him that his promise had been explicit, and, for once, the political calculation won out. He green-lighted the new department but declined to lobby personally for it. It passed by a whisker.

Carter limped through late primaries. If Kennedy had lost New York, Pennsylvania, or California, he would almost certainly have dropped out of the 1980 race, his aides said later. But he won all three, thanks in part to going negative. Carroll O'Connor, the star of *All in the Family,* the top-rated TV show of the 1970s, cut a devastating ad for Kennedy saying that Carter "may be the most Republican president since Herbert Hoover, and he may give us a depression that makes Hoover's look like prosperity."

Carter told Rafshoon that the campaign should fight back hard. Man-on-the-street ads soon showed voters saying of Kennedy, "I don't trust him," "I don't believe him." Carter victories in four states and the District of Columbia on May 6 assured the president of a big delegate lead, but the ads ruptured the Carter-Kennedy relationship for good and ensured bad blood at the convention. "The Kennedy challenge hurt us very badly," Jordan wrote in a memo to Carter, "not only within the Democratic Party but with the electorate as a whole."

As summer began, Democratic delegates were divided between those furious at Kennedy for trying to take down a sitting president and those convinced that renominating Carter would mean certain defeat in November. On June 5 Kennedy came by the White House "completely obsessed," as Carter remembered, with getting the president to agree to debate him in advance of the convention. The meeting was apparently more acrimonious than either man admitted, but Carter soon decided that a debate with Kennedy would indeed be a good way to pivot to the fall campaign. Most of his campaign team and Cabinet agreed; they were confident Carter would crush any opponent.

On the other side of the argument, Mondale thought a debate might elevate Kennedy and give him momentum at the convention. Charlie Kirbo said that if Carter debated, he would quit as campaign chair. That led Carter to change his mind. When he heard the news, the president's twenty-five-year-old delegate-counting whiz, Tom Donilon, went into the bathroom and vomited — the second aide in six weeks to lose his lunch over the sinking fortunes of the president.

Decisions on debates were the least of Carter's problems. His family was cracking under the burdens of his presidency. Chip still showed the flag for his father in public appearances, but he was often too stoned or drunk to be of much help as a political operative. Family and staff worried that he would be arrested for drug use, blowing the reelection campaign sky-high.

Billy Carter had been cycling down for two years. Billy Beer sold well for a few months in 1977, but the Kentucky brewery that made it soon went bankrupt. After what he called his "redneck pose" wore thin, Billy fell into a depression and began consuming a half gallon of vodka a day. He developed a "love-hate relationship with fame," his wife, Sybil, said. They moved twenty-five miles north to the town of Buena Vista to get away from the tourists clogging the streets of Plains. His distaste for the attention directed at his brother was obvious. When Dale Russakoff of the *Atlanta Journal* chatted with Billy in front of a blaring TV, he made a point of turning away every time the president came on the screen and did nothing to defend him. After softball games in Plains, he would sometimes mock Jimmy to reporters.*

The embarrassments mounted. Billy urinated on an airport tarmac and ripped his home phone off the wall. He punched an old family friend, Hal Gulliver, and was nearly thrown off an airplane for donning an Indian headdress and chanting in the aisle. One day the man who had once stood up for the Koinonia interracial farm brought home a Ku Klux Klan leader. "Billy had suddenly turned into a racist," his son Buddy later wrote. "He was trying to prove a point that he would do whatever the hell he felt like doing, regardless of who his brother was." Even after Billy dried out for good at a naval hospital in Long Beach, California, Jimmy had to apply kid gloves to his kid brother. Everyone in the family knew that if you told him to do something, Billy would likely do the opposite.

Billy's most serious problem revolved around his work for Libya. In 1978 the Libyan government — seeking influence with the Carter administration — invited Billy to Tripoli, where he reviewed a military parade and got set up in business as a commission agent selling Libyan crude

*Billy was in a long line of brothers, half brothers, and children of presidents and vice presidents who ran into trouble for trading off the family name, including FDR's son Elliott Roosevelt and LBJ's brother, Sam Houston Johnson, as well as Donald Nixon, Neil Bush, Roger Clinton, Malik Obama, Ivanka Trump, and Hunter Biden.

oil. Representatives of Libya visited Billy in Plains, and he made a second trip to the country, with Sybil, in 1979. When the US government told Billy to register as a foreign agent, he refused. An independent counsel would eventually spend $30 million investigating whether Billy was also involved in arms trading and drug dealing, but it found nothing.

Jimmy felt conflicted. When the story of the first Libya trip broke, it fell to Greg Schneiders to brief the president. "What should I say?" Carter asked him. Schneiders suggested he announce that it had been a bad idea for Billy to go there. Carter's steely blues bored into him: "Thank you for advising me about my family relations," he snapped — though he complied.

A few months later, CBS's *Face the Nation* booked Billy, but Rafshoon convinced Carter that they had to keep his brother off the air. After Rafshoon gave Billy the bad news, he replied, "Fuck you." When Lesley Stahl of CBS News asked Rafshoon why Billy had been bumped from her broadcast, Rafshoon told her that having Billy as a guest was "beneath your show." Word got back to the president, who asked Rafshoon if he had, in fact, told Stahl that; he thought it smacked of northern condescension. Carter quickly forgave Rafshoon but not before telling him exactly what Billy had said when he'd heard the news: "That Jew bastard of yours pulled me off the show."

The Libya story exploded again on July 15, 1980 — the first day of the Republican Convention — with news that the Justice Department had filed a formal complaint against Billy for not registering as a lobbyist for the Libyans after accepting $220,000 from them. When the story broke, he agreed to register, but a series of other headlines spread across the front page: fugitive financier Robert Vesco claiming involvement in the payments to Billy; Jimmy admitting he shared State Department cables with Billy; Jimmy and Rosalynn enlisting Billy and the Libyans to help free the hostages.

Hamilton Jordan worried the story was "starting to smell like Watergate," and sure enough, it was quickly dubbed "Billygate." Unlike other presidents facing scandals, Carter opted for full transparency. He announced that he was "eager" to cooperate with a Senate probe (he was never called, though Billy was) and would not claim executive privilege. Inside the family, there was little turmoil. It made no sense, as Jordan put it, to get mad at the sober Billy for what the drinking Billy had said and done. When Rosalynn grew despondent about the headlines, Jimmy told her to read from John 14:1 ("Let not your heart be troubled"), and her spirits lifted before she embarked on a diplomatic mission to Peru. Republican senator Mark Hatfield of Oregon called Carter to say he was praying for him and referred him to Hebrews 11:1: "Faith is the substance of things hoped for, the evidence of things not seen."

"People think I'm a lot more burdened down and discouraged than I actually am," the president wrote in his diary on July 30. "I have a lot of problems on my shoulders, but strangely enough, I feel better as they pile up." He seemed to sense his relatively good spirits might be distorting his perspective: "My main concern is propping up people around me who tend to panic (and who might possibly have a better and clearer picture of the situation than I do)."

August 4, the day he would face the press to discuss Billy, was stressful. Admiral Rickover, now eighty years old and still on active duty, left a message that he was thinking of Carter and asked if there was anything he could do for him.* Amid the defection of important Democratic governors and senators who were calling for an "open convention" that freed delegates to "vote their consciences" (that is, for Kennedy), the president held an hourlong prime-time news conference devoted entirely to the Billygate scandal.

Carter refused to repudiate his brother. "We are personally close," he said. "I love him, and he loves me." But in a soft voice, he admitted, "I cannot control him." He announced an executive order prohibiting the president's relatives from lobbying or even communicating with US government officials. To put the story behind him, he released an exhaustive ninety-two-page report that was critical of Billy's poor judgment but convincingly refuted all allegations and rumors of wrongdoing. The report included diary excerpts showing Jimmy trying to dissuade his brother from traveling a second time to Libya and revealed that Carter knew Billy had created "an embarrassing

*Rickover would soon have his own problems. In 1981 he was forced out by Reagan's navy secretary, John Lehman, after revelations that he'd accepted thousands of dollars in trinkets from General Dynamics, a defense contractor he had bitterly attacked for shoddy workmanship. When Reagan offered to let him stay on as an energy adviser, he told the commander in chief, "This is bullshit," and walked out of the Oval Office.

incident" that would hurt Carter with Jewish voters.

The reaction to the press conference seemed favorable at first, with overwhelmingly positive calls to the White House and strong support from editorial writers. "It was the best of Carter, a profoundly caring man, loving his brother through stress, as honest as a political human knows how to be," wrote *Time*'s Hugh Sidey, usually a stout Carter critic, in a piece representative of the consensus in Washington. But the public was losing faith. An ABC News–Harris poll showed that only 23 percent of the public approved of Carter's job performance, down 12 points in a week. This was the worst rating for a president in the history of polling — even worse than Nixon's just before he resigned.

And yet in the more fluid, less polarized political climate of the day, Carter still had time to claw his way back — and he would.

# 36
## ARE YOU BETTER OFF?

Instead of coming together in advance of their August convention, Democrats split apart.

On July 28 Carter learned that Majority Leader Byrd had hosted a lunch at which he urged a few Democratic senators to accompany him to the White House to tell Carter that he should not seek renomination. None did, and Byrd himself chickened out. Three days later, Carter signed an international agreement for a coal liquefaction plant in West Virginia and, as he wrote in his diary that night, "introduced Bob Byrd graciously in spite of his trying to stab me in the back politically." Because Carter needed Byrd more than the other way around, he never confronted him about his disloyalty. But one Democratic senator, Daniel Inouye of Hawaii, a disabled war veteran and revered figure, never forgave Byrd for his betrayal of Carter, whom he admired greatly for his fortitude and sense of principle.

By summer, Carter was bombarded daily from his left, with John Anderson announcing that he would fold his independent campaign if his new pal Kennedy was the nominee. This was galling to Carter. In the 1960s, Anderson had been so conservative that three times he introduced constitutional amendments to "recognize the law and authority of Jesus Christ" over the United States. Through most of the 1970s, his House voting record was conservative. Now he was presenting himself as a liberal who backed the ERA and civil rights and opposed Carter's draft registration. To pick up Kennedy voters, Anderson chose a liberal running mate (Carter's former ambassador to Mexico, Pat Lucey, a progressive former governor of Wisconsin) and became the wild card of 1980. Laurence Tribe of Harvard Law School wrote in August that "the odds seem high" that Anderson's presence on the ballot would hold both Carter and Reagan below 270 electoral votes, throwing the election into the House of Representatives. This scenario faded when a Carter lawyer convinced banks that they risked penalties under campaign finance laws if they lent money to Anderson's campaign.*

The Republican National Convention, held in Detroit in mid-July, turned dramatic for a time when it seemed Reagan would pick former president Ford as his running mate. But after Ford signaled in interviews that he essentially expected a copresidency, Reagan rethought his decision and chose George H. W. Bush, who had finished a

*Tim Smith of the Carter campaign cleverly argued in public that if the Anderson campaign defaulted on its loans, the banks could be found guilty of making an illegal campaign contribution. The Federal Election Commission rejected that argument, but by that time it was too late. The banks didn't want the hassle of an FEC appeal, and Anderson didn't get the money he needed to make the race more competitive.

distant second in the GOP primaries.

The convention proved a sturdy launching pad for Reagan, who essentially ran as a hawkish Santa Claus promising to boost defense spending, slash income taxes, and balance the budget all at the same time. The idea behind this supply-side economics — which economist Arthur Laffer famously drew on a napkin for Donald Rumsfeld and Dick Cheney in 1974 — was that the new economic activity generated by cutting taxes would bring in huge, new tax receipts for the Treasury. This theory, denounced earlier in the year by Bush as "voodoo economics," set the stage for Reaganites to cast Carter as the Grinch. They and their cynical heirs in the GOP bet correctly that even if the so-called Laffer curve proved fallacious, which it did, President Reagan's record deficits wouldn't hurt the GOP.

Democrats convened again at Madison Square Garden, which this time would be filled with tension and ill will. The national news media was now openly hostile to the president. In a *Time* cover story that reflected the tone of the coverage, Hugh Sidey — who enjoyed a close friendship with George Bush — catalogued Carter's alleged foreign policy errors, arguing that "Carter's human rights campaign is now viewed as having often embarrassed US allies and hardened the opposition of adversaries." Viewed that way by whom? The powerful American foreign policy establishment, perhaps, but not by dissidents rotting in foreign jails. In Sidey's facile analysis, Carter hadn't grown at all in office and was "self-obsessed."

The night before the convention opened, *60 Minutes* — then the highest-rated show of any kind on American television (with thirty million viewers) — aired a Carter interview conducted by Dan Rather, the hottest star in news. It was a fiasco for the White House; the perfect illustration of how the Watergate-conditioned media devoured a politically clueless president who badly wanted to come across as a straight talker.

From the start, a prosecutorial Rather went after the president for Billygate and broken promises on reducing inflation, slashing the number of agencies, and overhauling the tax system. "Now, it strikes me that any reasonable person looking at that record would say that's a record of ineffective leadership," Rather said flatly, as if any "reasonable person" would know Carter's other accomplishments were not enough to merit his being reelected. "I hear it at truck stops, coffee shops, cafeterias," Rather said. "Jimmy Carter's a good and decent man . . . but the job's too big for him.' "

With that, Rather moved in for the kill. He noted that Carter had asked his White House staff to issue report cards grading their subordinates, A through F, and he asked Carter to grade himself. Rafshoon had warned Carter that this question might be coming, and he must dodge it — to say it was up to the voters to grade him. Anything but an answer. Carter tried to wiggle out like a normal politician, protesting that "this is a little bit embarrassing," but Rather bore down by reminding him, "You have prided yourself on your candor and straight talk."

"Maybe a B or C-plus on foreign policy," Carter said before adding, "but I'd like to equivocate some" because — given the peace in the world — "a disinterested observer would give me a little bit higher grade." Now, after abasing himself by answering the question, he was grade grubbing, too. And it got worse:

> RATHER: You give yourself a C-plus, but you think a B-minus might be justified?
> PRESIDENT CARTER: I think a B-minus. Let's say a B-minus.
> RATHER: Overall domestic policy.
> PRESIDENT CARTER: Under the circumstances, I think about a B. The — the actual results, maybe a C.

Carter made a game effort to recover by giving himself an A on energy and a B on overall leadership internationally, thanks to his focus on human rights. (It was too early to claim complete success for Camp David or normalization with China, and the Panama Canal Treaties were still unpopular.) "I don't want to be held to account on those scores," he said with a nervous laugh, clearly regretting his decision to take part in the exercise. "I'll see what the American people say in November."

Years later, Rather was stunned that the president answered the questions honestly. But Carter's stubborn pride in his candor would endure. When asked nearly forty years after the *60 Minutes* interview how he would revise those grades, he said, "They look okay to me."

Carter had won thirty-six out of forty-eight primaries and caucuses and led Kennedy by seven hundred delegates — plenty for the nomination — but Kennedy operatives came up with a way to throw the convention into chaos. They built support for a change in the rules to let delegates vote their consciences on the first ballot. It was a devastating sign of distaste for Carter that the Kennedy forces had a reasonable chance of convincing Carter delegates to betray their pledge to represent the voters who sent them to the convention.

The week before the convention, Carter's hardcount advantage on the so-called robot rule binding delegates slipped dangerously below a hundred delegates. The better-organized Carter forces worked feverishly to make sure the rules vote came before Kennedy's speech, which they feared would sway delegates. They prevailed, thereby securing Carter's renomination, but not until Hamilton Jordan and the Kennedy campaign's Paul Kirk hammered out a written agreement that Jordan felt was about as friendly as an estranged couple signing divorce papers. In exchange for Kennedy's withdrawal, Carter had to concede on two platform planks that challenged his economic policy from the Left by advocating a $12 billion stimulus package that the president considered inflationary and committing the party to prioritize combating unemployment over fighting inflation.

Kennedy delivered one of the best speeches of his life — passionate, eloquent (written largely by Shrum), and moving. With the winning smile of a happy warrior, he guided the delegates through Reagan's most outrageous statements ("Social Security should be voluntary," "80 percent of air pollution comes from plants and trees"), then asked them "to renew the commitment of the Democratic Party to economic justice." His peroration would join the ranks of the greatest in the history of American political conventions:

"For me, a few hours ago, this campaign came

to an end. For all those whose cares have been our concern, the work goes on, the cause endures, the hope still lives, and the dream shall never die."

It seemed to the Carter team as if the wild ovation and camera shots of weeping delegates would never end. "We may have won the nomination," Jordan conceded later. "But Ted Kennedy had won their hearts."

In 1980 the film devoted to the nominee was still critically important — a way to reintroduce him to tens of millions on NBC, CBS, ABC, and PBS, plus a few thousand on brand-new CNN. In Carter's film, Tip O' Neill made clear that, contrary to popular misconception, Congress had passed "about eighty percent of the programs the president sent up." Carter followed up on the point by saying, "We never thought it would take this long to reach the promised land, but we're moving in the right direction." To Rafshoon, that was the essential sound bite: "This was the preacher, and we needed to see more of him and less of the engineer."*

After finally winning the nomination, Carter went to bed at two in the morning and jogged in Central Park at six thirty, which meant that he gave his acceptance speech on Thursday night on little more than four hours' sleep. The teleprompter was malfunctioning, and, Carter recalled, "I had to make the entire speech either from memory or from glancing down at my written notes." Early on in a largely unmemorable

*After the film aired, Steve Smith called Rafshoon to complain that the Carter campaign hadn't obtained permission to use images of his brother-in-law JFK. Rafshoon practically hung up on him.

878

speech, he generated guffaws by calling the late Hubert Horatio Humphrey "Hubert Horatio Hornblower," the fictitious British admiral from the Napoleonic Wars he had read about as a boy.

Carter made the case for his reelection by saying that he had come to see his primary duty as president with "great clarity." The whole job, he said, boiled down to this: "Above all, I must look ahead, because the president of the United States is the steward of the nation's destiny. He must protect our children and the children they will have and the children of generations to follow. He must speak and act for them. That is his burden and his glory." At the time, this line was dismissed as a platitude if it was noticed at all, but it was a fair summary of what a good American president must do and an accurate reflection of Carter's legitimate pride in his farsightedness.

Afterward, Walter Cronkite — anchoring his last convention before retiring — stated the obvious by noting that Carter's reception from Democrats was "not as enthusiastic" as the one the night before for Kennedy. Over on NBC News, droll David Brinkley said of the comparatively tepid ovation, "Well, this is slightly awkward." From there, the coverage went downhill for the president. Dan Rather recounted how a Carter man had told him the speech was "very low wattage" and another complained, "Forget the hostages, we can't get the balloons down." It was true. The balloon drop from the rafters — an important visual for the final night of any convention — had malfunctioned.

Then came an even more sickening symbolic moment for Democrats. To show unity, Bob Strauss started summoning politicians to the stage. As the minutes ticked by, the party chairman was reduced to shouting out names of Democrats no one had ever heard of. Where was Kennedy? To the dismay of the Carter team, he had insisted on watching the speech from his suite at the Waldorf-Astoria Hotel, not the Garden. Bob Shrum denied that he and Kennedy took their own sweet time getting to the convention, but the twenty-block ride there seemed to take forever. By the time Kennedy arrived for the "money shot" with Carter — the time-honored image of former rivals raising their clasped hands in symbolic party unity — millions of viewers had already tuned out.

A subdued Kennedy finally mounted the crowded stage and shook hands a few times in a perfunctory way with the president, then hugged Tip O'Neill and began waving to the crowd. Contrary to some recollections, the president didn't chase the senator around the stage, but his eyes followed him, as if Kennedy, not he, were the leader. Mary McGrory wrote in the *Washington Star* that Carter looked like an airline pilot "whose passengers have defected to the hijacker."

Carter stuck out his hand once more for a unity clasp, which ended up only going about chest high — not good enough to work as an iconic front-page shot or newsmagazine cover — and was captured only from the rear by the podium camera, rendering it useless for much of the television audience.

Admitting later that he had "not expected to" raise the president's hand, Kennedy tried to shift blame: "I didn't elevate his hand; he made no effort to elevate mine! I thought it was proper enough." Asked in 2015 what he was thinking about Kennedy at that moment, Carter said simply: "That he was drunk."

After the convention, Carter fled New York for a bucolic "trout haven" in Huntingdon County, Pennsylvania, called Spruce Creek, where a new friend of his named Wayne Harpster had helped stir a passion for fly-fishing. Tying flies in the White House Residence was just about the only way he relaxed all year, and now he could use his best ones. It was the respite he had been looking forward to all week, but the president still scanned some of the coverage. Reading the Sunday *Washington Post,* "I couldn't believe the obvious hatred and vituperation leveled against me," he wrote in his diary. "It was as though I was a combination of Adolf Hitler and Goofy."

But the press coverage was misleading. Carter got a bounce out of the seemingly embarrassing convention and cut Reagan's lead in the polls from 25 points to the mid–single digits. Rosalynn said later that she had no sense of foreboding and fully expected the public to recognize her husband's fine qualities and reelect him.

The Carter camp wasn't so sanguine, in part because of money concerns. Steve Smith informed Jordan that Kennedy wouldn't have time to campaign for Carter if he had to raise money to erase his debt. "He's blackmailing us!" Carter fumed. He nonetheless held an awkward meeting with Kennedy in the White House family quarters, where he agreed to shift much-needed campaign funds to his former rival's account. In the fall, Kennedy traveled a fair amount speaking on behalf of Carter and the Democratic ticket, but to no avail. At the point in a speech to iron workers when he urged them to vote for Carter, no one applauded. David Broder of the *Washington Post* said that was when he knew the election was over.

Looking back on 1980, Walter Mondale called Kennedy's behavior "disgraceful." The former vice president believed the "death wish" of the party resulting from the Vietnam War and the economic woes of the 1970s "fueled a reckless divisiveness" that doomed the Democrats.

Carter had long sensed that Reagan might be a problem. When the president beat Kennedy in New Hampshire, Rafshoon told Carter he had a "bonus" for him: Reagan was handily winning the New Hampshire GOP primary and would be the GOP nominee. Carter said, "I'm not so sure that's good." After the primaries, Jerry Brown's father, Edmund G. "Pat" Brown — who lost his governorship to Reagan in 1966 — visited the White House and met with the political team. He had a warning for them: "You're going to say he's an actor, and it won't work. That he's not really that smart, and it won't work. That he's lazy, and it won't work."

One of Reagan's many strengths was his natural humor, which he deployed regularly with scripted one-liners: "Recession is when your neighbor loses his job. Depression is when you lose yours. And recovery is when Jimmy Carter loses his." It worked.

In focus groups, Carter's strengths were all personal — trust, courage, honesty — and his weaknesses were on the issues (especially the economy and Iran) and what Kennedy had solidified in the voters' minds: poor leadership. Curtis Wilkie of the *Boston Globe* asked him if he wasn't just "a good staff man" running against a man

882

who sought to be chairman of the board. That common appraisal was rooted in their TV skills. Reagan's background as a B-list movie actor (in 1951's *Bedtime for Bonzo,* he costarred with a chimp) and General Electric pitchman opened him to derision but also offered him critical experience as a television performer. Carter could never match the man who would soon be called the Great Communicator. Over time "the Gipper" (a nickname that came from his role as the dying college football player George Gipp in the 1940 film *Knute Rockne, All American*) fused optimism and patriotism with a sophisticated bit of passive-aggressive rhetoric. Reagan told voters to go ahead and reelect Carter "if he instills in you pride for your country and a sense of optimism about the future."

Reagan decided to launch his fall campaign at the Neshoba County Fair in Philadelphia, Mississippi, just a few miles from where civil rights activists Michael Schwerner, James Chaney, and Andrew Goodman had been murdered by white supremacists in 1964. His campaign claimed this was a coincidence, which seemed implausible, as the murders had received immense publicity. Reagan removed further doubt about the reasoning behind his appearance when he told the nearly all-white crowd, "I believe in states' rights" — unmistakable code for opposition to civil rights. Just before Election Day, Reagan campaigned with former Mississippi governor John Bell Williams, one of the most extreme segregationists of the early seventies.

Carter kicked off his general election drive on Labor Day in Tuscumbia, Alabama, part of his effort to hold on to his base in the South. But he wanted to send a very different message to the region than Reagan had in Mississippi. With musician Charlie Daniels on the stage beside him, he looked out over the enthusiastic crowd of twenty-five thousand and — noticing a small group of white-robed Klansmen who had come to protest against him — departed from his prepared text to call out "the cowards" in the audience:

"I say these people in white sheets do not understand our region and what it's been through. They do not understand what our country stands for. Our past is a rich source of inspiration. But the past is not a place to live."

A day later, Reagan wandered again onto racial terrain and blundered. He ignored what Carter had said and obtusely attacked him for launching his campaign in the birthplace of the KKK, which it was not (though parts of the Klan had recently moved their headquarters to Tuscumbia). Seven southern governors blasted Reagan for implying that the Klan represented the South, and his poll numbers dropped sharply, especially among women. But the back-and-forth on race eventually helped Reagan by pushing the president to say things out loud that were considered off-limits at the time — such as charging (even obliquely) that his opponent was fueling racism. At the Ebenezer Baptist Church in Atlanta, Carter said, "You've seen in this campaign the stirrings of hate and the rebirth of code words like 'states' rights' in a speech in Mississippi."

The press interpreted the Ebenezer speech as over the top. At a press conference on September 18, Sam Donaldson asked the president directly if he was "running a 'mean' campaign" — a version of the old "When are you going to stop beating your wife?" question, which the ABC News correspondent regretted after the election. The so-called meanness issue was driven not just by Carter's recent rhetoric but also by a general impression in the press corps that Carter could be harsher in private than his little-goody-two-shoes image suggested. No one provided any evidence of Carter being mean, but the word stuck to him anyway — just another example of Carter being a Velcro politician, while Reagan was usually coated with Teflon.

Jordan and Rafshoon thought the meanness charge, repeated ad nauseam, was hurting Carter, though, in retrospect, accusing Reagan of dividing the country — Carter's basic charge — was extremely tame by twenty-first-century standards. They told him not to hit Reagan so hard. "I'll hit him medium," Carter replied, but he kept flinging charges at Reagan, and it continued to boomerang on him, in part because the press corps as a whole — fatigued and annoyed by Carter — went easier on the challenger. While Reagan may have been too right-wing for reporters' personal tastes, he generated excitement and momentum that translated into relatively soft coverage. Through the fall, the former California governor didn't get a free ride, but he did go half fare.

In August and September the economy began rising fast, which helped pull up Carter's poll numbers. Almost any other Fed chair would have let the economy surge right through November. Not Paul Volcker. On September 25 the Fed raised the discount rate a point, sending the prime rate back up to 14 percent, which was lower than the 20 percent of April but higher than the 11 percent it had dipped to in July. Volcker thought holding off on raising interest rates until after the election risked runaway inflation. "I said, 'Shit, we'll show 'em,' " he recalled. "I wanted to send a message to the public that we're serious and to discipline ourselves to keep our feet to the fire."

Carter began complaining mildly on the campaign trail that higher interest rates were "unwarranted," but he never called out Volcker by name. He was trapped by his own appointee. The Fed's decision, wrote journalist William Greider, was "the last wound" to Carter. Small business owners across the country gave up on the president. Bob Kerrey, the future Democratic presidential candidate who was so moved in 1977 by Carter's brave amnesty for draft dodgers, was operating restaurants in Omaha and could barely keep them open under the pressure of crushing inflation and interest rates. He voted for Reagan.

So did evangelicals — a newly organized force in politics that had no problem castigating one of their own. They denounced Carter's refusal to restore the tax-exempt status of fundamentalist Bob Jones University (because it discriminated against blacks); his opposition to constitutional amendments that banned abortion and enshrined school prayer; his backing of the ERA; and his hosting of the June 1980 White House Conference on Families, which evangelicals opposed because it counted single mothers as families and allowed discussion of contraception and divorce. (The fact that Reagan was divorced and didn't go to church often was apparently a nonissue for them.)

Reverend Jerry Falwell Sr. of the Moral Majority, a Christian Right political organization

886

founded only a year earlier, claimed that during an Oval Office meeting, Carter had bragged to him about having homosexuals on his staff. But there was never any meeting with Falwell or anyone from his group; Falwell had made it up — "a total lie," Carter wrote with disgust in his diary. Bailey Smith, president of the immense Southern Baptist Convention, did come by and accuse Carter of being a "secular humanist," the latest evangelical slur on liberals. Carter told him he had never even heard the expression before.

With the help of excessive media coverage, the Moral Majority grew to about four hundred thousand members — less than 1 percent of the electorate, and thus hardly a "majority." But Falwell skillfully created a new political identity for conservative evangelicals that would help power the presidential and congressional candidates they supported in 1980 and beyond. The fact that Carter himself was an evangelical Christian made their takedown of him all the more significant.

Even as he was hammered by right-wing Christians as a libertine, the president seemed to many other Americans like a pious, sober killjoy. Tom Wolfe, who four years earlier had viewed Carter's spiritualism as an appealing part of the ascendant Me Decade, wrote after the 1980 election that Carter was essentially arguing, "Despite all the fun they [Americans] seemed to be having, deep in their hearts they were sinners."

With interest groups, the Carter team often felt no good deed went unpunished. On veterans' affairs, Carter and Max Cleland had overcome Republican opposition and sharply upgraded VA hospitals. They also expanded the GI Bill, which financed the education of hundreds of thousands of veterans. But their attention to Vietnam veterans and those with service-connected disabilities made millions of men who served in World War II and the Korean War (often in noncombat roles) feel neglected. The Veterans of Foreign Wars (VFW) broke precedent and formed a PAC for Reagan. "The animosity toward us was so thick you could cut it," Cleland remembered. Carter was a hunter, but the National Rifle Association, until then neutral in presidential elections, endorsed Reagan, apparently because Carter had appointed Abner Mikva, a leading advocate of gun control, to the federal bench and prevented hunting in certain Alaskan wildlife refuges.

All year, there was growing thunder on the Right. Even so, if the economy had been good — and the hostages free — the new noise from conservatives would not likely have been loud enough to jeopardize Carter's reelection.

In late spring Drs. Kean, Coleman, and Flandrin had reassembled in Cairo, where Dr. Michael De-Bakey finally operated on the shah of Iran's spleen. It was no use. At the end, the physicians squabbled over who was responsible for the shah's shoddy care. He died on July 27, 1980, and beyond the expected treatment in Iranian state media ("bloodsucker of the century"), his demise was anticlimactic. Anwar Sadat gave him a grand send-off — attended by Henry Kissinger and some of the Project Eagle crowd — and a fancy Muslim tomb. The Carter administration issued an anodyne statement.

The shah's death did nothing to hasten the release of the hostages. In August a frustrated Carter asked his new secretary of state, Ed Muskie, to propose a series of new diplomatic initiatives. Carter scribbled "Expedite," "Move on it," "Pursue aggressively," and "Why wait?" across sections of Muskie's long memo, the only part of which would bear fruit was a plan to use the Algerian government as an intermediary.

The main reason the Ayatollah Khomeini finally agreed to indirect negotiations was the outbreak of the Iran-Iraq War, which by the time it ended in 1988 was the bloodiest global conflict since World War II. When Saddam Hussein's Iraq invaded Iran on September 22, Tehran suddenly needed the assets frozen in American banks to pay for weapons and spare parts. The ayatollah — noticing that the United States was staying conspicuously neutral — signed off on conditions for hostage negotiations that were still full of "Great Satan" rhetoric but nonetheless suggested he was looking for an exit strategy.

By fall, the Reagan campaign began coordinating with the Rockefeller team to spread unfounded rumors that the Carter administration was paying off Iranians to free the hostages in time for the election. With the shah dead, Joseph Reed changed the original objective of Project Eagle from getting the shah into the United States to preventing the release of the hostages. After the election, Reed wrote to his family that "I had given my all" to thwarting Carter's efforts "to pull off the long-suspected 'October surprise.'" Here was a banker and pillar of the establishment — a future ambassador and chief of protocol in Republican administrations — who got up every day in the fall of 1980 trying to prolong the captivity of other Americans.

Reed worked closely with Reagan's campaign manager, William Casey, who had run the European intelligence branch of the Office of Strategic Services (OSS) — the precursor to the CIA — during World War II. Casey, slated to become Reagan's CIA director the following January, enlisted 120 "foreign policy consultants" — many still working for the US government — to monitor diplomatic channels and US military bases for early word on release of the hostages. The sooner Reagan campaign operatives learned the hostages had been freed, the sooner they could spin it.

That would be the job of Robert Gray, a Republican PR guru who would go on to manage the Reagan inaugural. In an internal memo, Gray explained how the campaign's network would obtain advance word of which military bases or other venues the Carter administration would use to celebrate the freeing of the hostages: "If we leak to news sources our knowledge of the Carter planned events, we can get the press [to] say Carter is politicizing the issue." This was a clever jiujitsu: to make a politically inept president look excessively political if he succeeded in executing an "October Surprise" that freed the hostages just in time for the election.

Did Reed's Project Eagle and Casey's and Gray's network of consultants go beyond defending against a Carter October Surprise to planning one of their own? There would soon be reason to suspect they did.

About two weeks before the election, Carter staffers had a bad feeling. Polls showed the South moving heavily toward Reagan. That meant the president would need to win California, which had gone for Ford in 1976. But Reagan was from California, and his support showed no signs of softening. So even though several national polls had the two candidates neck and neck, the outlook in the electoral college was troubling. "You could feel it slipping away," Mondale remembered. Returning from the trail, Carter confided to his vice president, "They aren't listening to me anymore." Mondale thought Carter was losing confidence in himself.*

The time-honored white-tie Al Smith Dinner in New York on October 16 was an omen. Carter, who had been campaigning his heart out, looked tired, and his jokes were shopworn, while Reagan looked rested, and his jokes were spot-on. His easy way reminded some in the audience of JFK, even if Reagan was twenty-five years older than Kennedy in 1960. The old comparisons of Carter to the hero of his young adulthood had long since been forgotten.

But Reagan's handlers still worried he would lose if the hostages were freed, and they fretted

*Even a twenty-five-year-old loner named John Hinckley thought Carter was no longer the favorite. Hinckley became obsessed with the actress Jodie Foster after seeing her in the 1976 movie *Taxi Driver*. He decided he would kill President Carter to impress her, just as Robert De Niro's character, Travis Bickle, targets a presidential candidate in the film. In September he followed Carter to Dallas and to Dayton, Ohio, where he managed to shake his hand. On October 9 he made plans to kill Carter in Nashville but decided Reagan was more likely to win so he would shoot him instead, which he did the following March.

that women voters remained afraid of their hawk-ish candidate. For weeks, they had dodged a one-on-one debate with Carter, insisting that any debate with him include Anderson, who had debated Reagan one-on-one earlier in the fall. Now their calculation changed. Stuart Spencer, Reagan's chief strategist, said the Al Smith Din-ner was when the Reagan team decided to agree to what would become the only 1980 general elec-tion debate involving the two major candidates. It would take place in Cleveland on October 28, one week before the election.

Unlike Carter, Reagan had debated during the primaries. But at sixty-nine, he had lost a step, and his aides worried about how he would perform against a sharp and exceptionally well-informed incumbent. Fortunately for them, they had a cheat sheet — thanks to a roguish Kennedy family retainer named Paul Corbin, who despised Car-ter. At the urging of Bill Casey, Corbin, who dwelled in the underbelly of politics, somehow obtained copies of the briefing books the Carter campaign used to prepare the president for the debate. They showed where Carter was likely to attack and with what evidence of Reagan's short-comings.

All told, thirteen Reagan staffers and advisers saw the material, including Jim Baker, David Ger-gen, and George Will, the syndicated columnist, who was secretly helping Reagan.* A 1983 House

*Will landed in hot water for his role in Reagan's debate prep. On ABC News after the debate, Will had praised Reagan's "thoroughbred performance." Carter learned of this breach after the election and attacked Will for it, though in 1996 he publicly forgave him.

investigation led by Democratic representative Donald Albosta of Michigan was unable to identify the mole inside the Carter campaign, and more recent speculation about his or her identity has proven unfounded. It's unlikely that what came to be known as "Debategate" changed the outcome of the debate, much less the election. But it did suggest the Reaganites would break the rules to win.

Carter's own debate prep offered a preview of trouble ahead. In rehearsing his answers, the president tried to conjure the threat to peace that electing Reagan would pose for future generations, as LBJ did against Barry Goldwater in 1964 in his famous "Daisy" ad. Carter mentioned that he had recently talked with thirteen-year-old Amy about preventing nuclear war, which she thought was the most important issue in the world. To his advisers, it sounded peculiar to be consulting a child. Caddell remembered, "We all said, 'Uh, Mr. President, you can't do that!' " He said, "Okay, I won't do it."

Onstage in Cleveland, he did: "I had a discussion with my daughter, Amy, the other day, before I came here, to ask her what the most important issue was. She said she thought nuclear weaponry — and the control of nuclear arms." Even admiring Democrats winced. If Reagan had told a homey story about his family, he would have framed it in a cheerful, winning way. Carter was ham-handed by comparison. Republicans predictably used the Amy reference to suggest Carter was letting his daughter run the country.

But it was hardly the only reason an otherwise calm and thoughtful president lost the debate. While Carter won easily on points, Reagan won the expectations game just by showing up and not sounding like a trigger-happy right-winger unfit for office. By softly puncturing Carter's claims that he was reckless, the two-term governor eased concerns about his suitability, especially among women voters. When Carter brought up Reagan's past opposition to Medicare — a fair jab — Reagan, who likely saw it coming, said with a winning smile, "There you go again." It worked so well stylistically that no one remembered that Reagan's answer on Medicare was deceptive.

Toward the end of the debate, Reagan said, "I never made the statement that nuclear proliferation is none of our business." This was untrue. But in those pre-Internet days, the press could do little or no real-time fact-checking of politicians, and it took the Carter campaign forty-eight hours to dig up the videotape from ABC's Jacksonville affiliate to prove Reagan had indeed said what Carter alleged. By that time, the postdebate coverage was over, and "Amy" — not Reagan's lies and distortions — was the story.

Reagan arguably sewed up the election with his brilliantly simple closing statement. "Are you better off than you were four years ago?" he asked Americans. "Is it easier for you to go and buy things in the stores than it was four years ago? Is there more or less unemployment in the country than there was four years ago? Is America as respected throughout the world as it was?"* This

*Before the 1938 midterm elections, FDR, then in his second term, asked the country, "Are you better off than you were last year?" It's unclear whether Reagan, who voted for Roosevelt four times, picked it up from him.

894

would become the permanent new standard for incumbent presidents.

In the two days after the debate, Carter lost 6 points in Caddell's internal polls, and Anderson began cratering, with a larger share of his voters and undecideds heading to Reagan. This raised the intriguing question of whether Carter had it wrong about Anderson all along, and that his presence in the race had been helping him. Whatever the flux meant, Carter seemed to be reviving on Friday, four days before the election, when several polls showed the candidates within the margin of error.

Then over the weekend, Caddell saw serious erosion among late-deciding blue-collar voters. Carter's team knew all along they would lose if the 1980 campaign became a referendum on his presidency instead of a choice between him and Reagan. Choice was giving way to referendum. Voters were still echoing Rafshoon's TV ads, telling pollsters that Reagan was too old and shot from the hip. But as one woman said, "If this little bastard can't handle the ayatollah, I'll take my chances with the cowboy."

In the final week, Republican worries about a last-minute release of the hostages seemed justified. On October 30, with the Carter camp still reeling from the debate, Warren Christopher received word through Swiss intermediaries that the Iranian parliament — known as the Majlis — had scheduled a meeting Sunday morning, November 2, and the Iranians were expected to produce a specific proposal to end the crisis. At 3:45 a.m. on Sunday morning, Carter was awakened in his Chicago hotel room with the first reports of the

Majlis's new conditions, which had not yet been fully translated. Hamilton Jordan advised the president to cut the campaign trip short and return to Washington to consult his advisers and formulate a response. Ted Kennedy quickly agreed to fill in for Carter in Detroit and Philadelphia. Aboard Air Force One, Carter mused over the strangeness of a homestretch "that will be decided not in Michigan or Pennsylvania or New York — but in Iran."

In the Cabinet Room, Carter scanned the translation, pulled off his reading glasses, and noted calmly that the Majlis had merely repackaged the same untenable conditions that Khomeini had approved in September. No one on his foreign policy team said anything, but the whole room knew the hostages would not be freed before voters went to the polls in two days.

Caddell's numbers showed Carter down by 5 points and falling. Monday's early tracking was worse. It was cold comfort that Gallup's final poll showed Carter slightly ahead. Caddell's explanation for the erosion was that Election Day, November 4, was the first anniversary of the seizure of the hostages, which occasioned newsmagazine cover stories and long retrospectives on all three network evening news programs — still the main source of national news in the United States — reminding voters of their anger over America's humiliation.

The Carter campaign believed that year-old images of blindfolded hostages — the last message Americans received before going to the polls — led to a final gut check on the economy and huge movement toward Reagan in northern states. Without the anniversary and this last-minute shift,

Reagan would likely have won anyway, but the margin would have been much smaller.

Carter ended his final campaign with a thirty-six-hour mad dash across the country, ending with a raucous rally before thirty thousand supporters crammed into a Seattle airport hangar. He was on fire in ways that had eluded him in the past. Afterward, Rick Hertzberg joked, "You finally got that stump speech down, Mr. President!" At 2:45 a.m. eastern standard time, with the rally still under way, Jordan, Rafshoon, and Caddell called Powell from the White House. "We're gonna win this fucker!" Powell exulted as he picked up. The Carter entourage was deluded by the same large, enthusiastic crowds that greeted Barry Goldwater and George McGovern and would later scream for Michael Dukakis and Mitt Romney at the end of their losing general election campaigns. Sure enough, Jordan told Powell their final poll showed Reagan ahead by 10 points: "It's over, Jody."

Back aboard Air Force One, Carter was in such good spirits that he grabbed the flight attendant's speakerphone as music blared and shouted with uncharacteristic playfulness to reporters, "Hey slackers, are you having a party?" Then, before Powell could break the news, the president met for forty-five minutes with the press pool and told them how good he felt — how the momentum was moving his way. When Jordan, Caddell, and Rafshoon called back, Carter passed Powell in the aisle and asked who was on the line. He grabbed the phone with a smile and a cheery greeting.

After a brief silence, Rafshoon, losing his courage, stammered: "You tell him, Pat." Caddell went through the numbers quickly, took a deep breath, and said, "Mr. President, I'm afraid that it's gone." He explained how the hostage crisis had triggered pent-up frustrations among voters about the administration: "A lot of working-class Democrats are going to wake up tomorrow and for the first time in their lives vote Republican."

His entourage saw Carter turn pale and sit down as he absorbed the news. Then he instructed them: "Don't tell Rosalynn." He wanted to let her know in person when he got home to Plains that day to vote. After the call, Susan Clough remembered the president sitting alone, pensively holding a tribal scepter he had received from an African visitor.

Election Day was strangely anticlimactic. Just as in 1976, Carter addressed the hometown crowd from the old Plains railroad depot, only this time he did so knowing he had already lost the election. He skipped anything sentimental in favor of one final argument for a national TV audience about how he had kept the peace and made tough, unpopular decisions. Even then, there was something almost quaint about the adultness of this appeal. He thanked his neighbors for traveling around the country on his behalf. "I've tried to honor my commitment" — here his voice broke — "to you."

Then he flew to Washington, where he met with his inner circle in the Oval Office. Carter's analysis before the polls opened of why he was going to lose that night was that most of his major decisions in office cost him votes and that "the Kennedy attacks for eight months hurt a lot." He admitted he had to spend too much of his time in the fall "trying to recruit back the Democratic constituency that should have been naturally supportive: Jews, Hispanics, blacks, the poor, labor, and so forth." He consoled his glum team, "Don't second-guess yourself. You did a good job." Rafshoon, realizing it was the first time Carter had ever told him that, began crying. Jordan was so overcome he couldn't speak.

It was only five thirty California time when the White House placed a call to the Reagan home in Pacific Palisades. Nancy answered the phone in the bath and handed the receiver to her husband as he emerged from the shower. As he toweled off, Carter congratulated him on his election.

The networks called the election by eight o'clock on the East Coast, and Carter didn't want to wait until eleven — when the last polls closed on the West Coast — to concede. He told Powell that he was afraid people would think he was sulking bitterly in the White House. Jordan advised him to hold off, but Carter insisted on getting it over with, even at the risk of hurting down-ballot Democrats — "vintage Carter at his dead worst," said Representative Tom Foley, a future House speaker. At around nine thirty, surrounded on the stage at the Washington Sheraton Hotel by family and staff, he forced a smile, glanced at note cards, and said: "I promised you four years ago that I would never lie to you, so I can't stand here tonight and say it doesn't hurt."

Reagan won the popular vote by nearly 10 points — 50.7 percent to 41.0 for Carter and 6.6 for Anderson. He trounced Carter 489 to 49 in the electoral college and carried forty-four states. (Carter prevailed only in Georgia, Hawaii, Maryland, Minnesota, Rhode Island, and West Virginia.) The GOP took twenty Senate seats, giving it control of the upper chamber for the first time in twenty-six years. Columnist Mary McGrory wrote: "That was no election. That was Mount St. Helens, pouring hot ash over the whole political landscape, burying a president and much of his party."

On Wednesday Carter held an early-morning press conference with a dozen reporters in the Oval Office. The in-box with "The Buck Stops Here" sign on it was empty, but he had some suggestions for the public. He advocated a single six-year term for presidents so that they could operate without the constant pressure of politics. When asked how he felt, he went off the record momentarily to remark, "I guess I felt bad when I heard Falwell say, 'I'm glad we'll now have a real Christian in the White House.'" Sam Donaldson remembered wanting to go behind the desk and comfort him.

Carter mused later that had there been one more helicopter at Desert One, he would have been reelected. Maybe. More likely, the president still would have faced the Kennedy mutiny, the Cuban refugee crisis, Billygate, a talented GOP nominee with far superior candidate skills, and — most of all — a dismal economy. Bert Lance figured that if interest rates had ticked down in October, Carter would probably still have lost, but by a narrow margin.

At Wayne Harpster's fishing camp in the mid-1980s, Paul Volcker approached Carter and asked him if he thought the Fed's monetary policy had cost him the election. Carter smiled one of his genuine smiles and replied, "I think there were a few other factors as well." Volcker wrote later, "I have become a strong admirer of the man."

900

September 1978:
Thinking time amid
thirteen grueling days
trying to secure the
Camp David Accords.

Israeli Prime Minister
Menachem Begin
(left) plays chess with
National Security
Adviser Zbigniew
Brzezinski.

During emotional day trip to Gettysburg, flanked by Egyptian president Anwar Sadat and
Begin, with Moshe Dayan (with eye patch) on right. Carter's much-maligned attention to
detail saved the historic deal after each side repeatedly threatened to walk out.

4

5

Gas lines in 1979 sent Carter's
popularity plummeting.

Paul Volcker, Carter's choice as chairman
of the Federal Reserve, jacked up interest
rates to end double-digit inflation.

6

7

As Carter sunk lower in the
polls, a peculiar incident
with a swamp rabbit
approaching his fishing boat
made him seem hapless.

Heavily favored Ted Kennedy—
at odds with the president over health
care—blew a famous interview the
same day as the US embassy
takeover in Iran.

The shah of Iran, tear-gassed at the White House, was deposed in a major revolution. Carter got duped into letting him into the United States for medical attention, which precipitated the embassy seizure.

Mural of the Ayatollah Khomeini on outer wall of the former US embassy in Tehran. Khomeini essentially held Carter hostage— and America, too.

Remains of a burned-out US helicopter at Desert One. The abortive Delta Force raid to free the fifty-two hostages was a disaster from the start.

With (from near right) Vice President Walter Mondale, Secretary of State Cyrus Vance, and Secretary of Defense Harold Brown. Besieged by the hostage crisis and the Soviet invasion of Afghanistan, Carter looked swamped.

Soviet Premier Leonid Brezhnev kissing Carter after they signed the doomed SALT II treaty. "Uh-oh. It looks like he got taken in by the Russians," a US official fretted, though he hadn't been.

Carter led a successful if ultimately unpopular boycott of the 1980 Summer Olympic Games in Moscow.

On the podium of the 1980 Democratic Convention at Madison Square Garden with House Speaker Tip O'Neill, party chairman Bob Strauss and a chilly Kennedy. At right, Amy and Rosalynn. Carter said later that he thought Kennedy was drunk.

Signing the 1980 Alaska Lands Bill, which made Carter the greatest environmental president since Theodore Roosevelt. (Inset map of Alaska.) Carter signed more major legislation than any postwar president except President Lyndon Johnson.

18

Long underestimated, Ronald Reagan won the only 1980 debate, in part by asking voters "Are you better off than you were four years ago?" The answer was no.

19

White House all-nighter: Catching a little rest during the final hours of his presidency after successfully negotiating an end to the 444-day hostage crisis.

20

Iran tried to humiliate Carter by freeing the hostages moments after Reagan was sworn in. But he was elated they came home safely.

Rosalynn (left) and Jimmy empathize
as a worm emerges from the foot of a
Ghanaian child. The Carter Center saved
millions from Guinea worm disease,
among other global health successes.

Ship ahoy with Kim Il-sung,
North Korea's brutal founder, 1994.
Carter made no apologies
for his peace talks
with dictators.

Handing the keys to a new homeowner. Each year, the Carters spend a week building
houses for Habitat for Humanity.

January 2009: Outgoing President George W. Bush hosts President-Elect Barack Obama and ex-presidents. Carter's barbed comments about his successors ensured that he would remain outside their club.

Renaissance man: A master woodworker with one of his cabinets, Plains home office, 2015.

The longest-living and longest-married American president.

# 37
## Inaugural Drama

The year 1980 may have been a political disaster for Carter, but it was a legislative triumph. He signed bills that dramatically expanded food stamp eligibility, virtually ending extreme hunger in many places; established special courts under the Foreign Intelligence Surveillance Act (FISA) to oversee the intelligence community for the first time; and provided generous new aid to higher education that within a few years would help power the information economy.

In October he signed the first and most important piece of mental health legislation ever enacted by Congress, a product of Rosalynn's four years of tireless and politically skillful work. At the bill signing, Carter joked, "When Senator Kennedy and I were communicating, um, through the media" — at which point the Kennedy and Carter Democrats in attendance all guffawed — "quite often I would come in and find Rosalynn and him communicating very intimately about the Mental Health Systems Act."

Rosalynn's comprehensive bill mandated that mental illness be put on par with other diseases in the eyes of the government; it fully funded transitional housing and community mental health centers, a huge shift from large mental institutions that were already emptying patients into the streets — where they often became homeless. One of the first things the Reagan administration did was to gut the bill, stripping it of appropriations, which left Rosalynn feeling betrayed. But the ideas she championed were now permanently embedded within the new Department of Health and Human Services and at the state and local levels — and they changed prevention, research, and services for the mentally ill. While funding still lagged, almost all of her bill's provisions were resurrected nearly thirty years later in the Affordable Care Act.

Mental health was just one of the thorny issues Carter tackled at the end. The president signed a landmark bill establishing the Superfund, which compels chemical polluters to pay for the cleanup of hazardous waste dumps. He was prompted by the environmental disaster at Love Canal, an upstate New York community located near a chemical plant that had dumped thousands of tons of chemicals over several decades, contaminating the ground. The residents nearby were found to suffer abnormally high incidences of miscarriages, birth defects, and cancer. The federal government relocated some eight hundred families, reimbursing them for their lost homes, many of which had to be demolished. The Superfund doesn't always work as well as it should, and estimating how many lives it has saved is impossible. But this Carter-era idea, which has led to the clean-up of hundreds of contaminated sites since Love Canal, has unquestionably prevented thousands or even millions of serious health problems.

As in Georgia, Carter proved to be a fine steward of public lands. Over four years, he was responsible for thirty-nine new National Park Service designations, with a special emphasis on urban parks that could be accessed by millions. He finished work he had begun as governor by federally protecting Atlanta's Chattahoochee River, and he designated the Santa Monica Mountains in Los Angeles as a national recreational area, preventing development in what is now one of the largest urban national parks in the world.

Carter's least-known major accomplishment may be saving California's redwood forest. Theodore Roosevelt had protected Muir Woods near San Francisco, and Redwood National Park was established under LBJ in 1968. But clear-cutting on the park borders created terrible erosion that dammed up rivers and imperiled the two-thousand-year-old redwoods and giant sequoias. Carter and his inspired interior secretary, Cecil Andrus, studied the matter closely and won congressional approval for the most expensive land condemnation in US history. The result was expansion of Redwood National Park and protection of an area often compared to the Grand Canyon.

Carter's greatest natural legacy — unmatched by any president before or since — was secured only seven weeks before he left office. On December 2, 1980, the final day of the lame duck session, he signed what came to be known as the Alaska Lands bill, which protected 104 million acres (25 percent of the state) — a landmass the size of California. With one stroke of the pen, he doubled the size of the national park system, tripled wilderness areas, and preserved twenty-five free-flowing rivers, thus ensuring his place in the first rank of conservationist presidents. The debate that led to the new law was fierce; the difference once again was Carter's grit and passion for the environment, and his often-maligned attention to detail.

In 1978, when the votes weren't there yet for legislation, the president settled on a clever strategy. He moved unilaterally to protect fifty-eight million acres as national monuments by executive order under the 1906 Antiquities Act. Executive orders creating national monuments can be undone by future presidents; Carter and Andrus bet that the threat of possible reversals would generate important backing from local environmentalists. The executive order created a firestorm in Alaska, where Carter was burned in effigy. But even Alaska Republicans suddenly realized that they had better come up with something legislative so they could have some voice in the process. This hardly meant they reconciled themselves to Carter's bill. As the measure moved forward, more people lined up at the Alaska State Fair to pummel a Carter dummy than one of the Ayatollah Khomeini.

While Democrats Mo Udall and John Dingell pushed the bill in Congress for years, Jim Schlesinger argued hard internally to allow drilling inside an oil-rich 1.5-million-acre subset of the Arctic National Wildlife Refuge, a relatively small portion (less than 2 percent) of the protected Alaska wilderness. Andrus worried about the effects on endangered caribou in the region. When the division in the Cabinet came to a head in a climactic meeting, it was no contest. Carter sided

904

with Andrus, and the final bill contained language saying it would take an act of Congress to allow drilling in ANWR.*

In July 1980, when the bill was finally debated in the Senate, hundreds of Native Americans came to Washington to lobby for it. Carter held an event at the White House where the Tlingit tribe made him an honorary member and wrapped him in a ceremonial blanket. At the suggestion of Kathy Fletcher, his aide on the issue, Carter said thank you in their language — Tlingit — and told them that the bill was the most important environmental legislation of his lifetime. The event left Fletcher in tears because, she said, Carter's "concern about the environment was so real — so inside his soul and without political calculation."

That commitment even extended to defying his strongest supporters. When Native Americans sought exemptions from International Whaling Commission rules, Carter was unmoved: "I will not approve the killing of whales," he wrote on one of Fletcher's memos. He reluctantly signed off on the reasonable whaling compromise that Mondale negotiated, but not until after tribal hunting was regulated in more environmentally sound ways.

The Alaska Lands bill took four years because Carter and the Democrats were determined that it not be undermined by the Alaska delegation. When the outcome hung in the balance, Republi-

*For nearly four decades, ANWR has been a partisan issue, with Democrats opposing drilling and Republicans supporting it. Democrats prevailed until 2017, when the Trump tax bill gave the interior secretary authority to allow drilling on a million acres.

can senator Ted Stevens — until then, a fierce opponent — asked for an appointment with Carter.
He brought maps with him and told Carter he
could make sure the bill became law if the
president accepted his minor modifications, none
of which, he claimed, would hurt the environment. But it turned out Carter knew the maps in
such detail that he could not be buffaloed by
Stevens, who was just trying to help developers.
He understood exactly which sections lay at critical headwaters or spawning grounds and refused
to make concessions. On the way back to the Hill,
Stevens — soon to vote no — told an aide, "That
son of a bitch knew as much about my state as I
did."

To avoid leaving the fate of the Alaska wilderness to Reagan Republicans, the Democratic Senate stopped squabbling and finally approved the
bill. All the while, Carter remained deeply unpopular in Alaska. He received only 26 percent of
the vote there in the 1980 presidential election. In
September 1981 he landed in Anchorage to refuel
en route to Tokyo. With Alaskans still predicting
economic ruin, the Secret Service advised him
not to leave the air base for his own safety. But by
2000, a billion-dollar tourism industry had blos-
somed in Alaska, and polls showed residents
favored Carter's landmark achievement. When he
visited that year, he was greeted by six hundred
cheering supporters — a big crowd anywhere for
a former president — and they interrupted his
speech five times for standing ovations.

Jimmy Carter was the first leader anywhere in the
world to recognize the problem of climate change.
In 1977, scratching his itch as a planner and

steward of the earth, he commissioned the *Global 2000 Report to the President,* an ambitious effort to explore environmental challenges and the prospects of sustainable development over the next twenty years. As part of that process, the White House Council on Environmental Quality (CEQ) issued three reports contending with global warming, the last of which — issued the week before Carter left office — was devoted entirely to the long-term threat of what a handful of scientists then called "carbon dioxide pollution."

The report, written by Gus Speth, Carter's top aide on the environment, urged "immediate action" and included calculations on $CO_2$ emissions in the next decades that proved surprisingly accurate. The large-scale burning of oil, coal, and other fossil fuels could lead to "widespread and pervasive changes in global climatic, economic, social, and agricultural patterns," the CEQ report concluded with great prescience. One recommendation — covered in the last paragraph of the *New York Times* story on page A13 — urged industrialized nations to reach agreement on the safe maximum level of carbon dioxide released into the atmosphere. The CEQ report suggested trying to limit global average temperature to two degrees centigrade above preindustrial levels — precisely the standard agreed to by the nations of the world thirty-five years later in the Paris Climate Agreement.

With these facts in hand, the results of the 1980 election take on a tragic dimension: Carter had acted on every CEQ report issued in the previous four years with aggressive legislation and executive orders. He almost certainly would have done

907

so on this one, too, had he been reelected. Gains made under Carter's presidential leadership in the early 1980s might have bought the planet precious time. Instead, for the next twelve years, under Reagan and Bush I, the US government would view global warming as largely unworthy of study, much less action. Then came twenty-five years of stop-and-start efforts under administrations of both parties, followed by a return to denial under President Trump.

The Carter-Reagan transition was one of the strangest and most dramatic in American history. The president-elect made it clear he wanted nothing to do with Carter, which Carter said left him "in despair." At a November 20 meeting in the White House, the president presented Reagan with a list of twenty-eight challenges he would face, from the hostages, to a squabble between Anwar Sadat and Mu'ammar Gadhafi, to the new Superfund, with which Reagan seemed unfamiliar. "Reagan had zero interest in any of it," Carter remembered. His only happy moment was thinking that Helmut Schmidt, Menachem Begin, and Sam Donaldson were now Reagan's problems. Carter deadpanned to friends that one of the best parts of leaving office was that he would never again have to listen to Bob Byrd play the fiddle.

Word reached Rosalynn that Nancy Reagan felt the Carters were leaving the White House in poor condition, especially the doors. Rosalynn had them checked and could find nothing wrong with them. UPI then reported that Nancy felt it would be appropriate for the Carters to move across the street into Blair House (where foreign dignitaries stay) so that she could redecorate the White House before she and Ronnie moved in. Nancy denied the story, but Reagan's aides reminded the boss to spare the insults — that while the American people overwhelmingly rejected *President* Carter, "they continue to like Jimmy Carter personally."

Predictably, Carter used the platform of the presidency to the very end. He championed Lech Wałesa's Solidarity movement in Gdańsk, where Polish shipyard workers staged historic strikes that created a chain reaction of resistance to Communist authorities across Eastern Europe. In assessing how Communism fell, Wałesa said later that Carter's tough statement of December 3, 1980, which sharply warned the Soviets against a military buildup on Poland's border, was a key moment in the struggle. It sent a signal to Moscow that the United States would intervene if the Soviets rolled their tanks into Warsaw. Deterring the Soviet military — which Reagan continued — helped give the fledgling Solidarity movement the breathing room it needed to grow.

The quality of Carter's farewell address, written with the help of Rick Hertzberg, was exceeded only by those delivered by George Washington and Dwight Eisenhower. It resonates more powerfully in our own time than his other speeches, in part for its evocation of values at risk.

Carter began by stressing "the inner strength of our country — the unchanging value of our principles and ideals, the stability of our political system, the ingenuity and the decency of our people." After a section describing the threat posed by special interests and the specter of nuclear war, Carter focused on what makes the United States exceptional. "Our American values are not luxuries but necessities — not the salt in our bread but the bread itself," he said:

America did not invent human rights. In a very real sense, it is the other way around. Human rights invented America. Ours was the first nation in the history of the world to be founded explicitly on such an idea. It is both our history and our destiny.

It was legacy time. Max Cleland came by with a plaque that Carter would always treasure. It contained this quote from Thomas Jefferson:

I Have the Consolation to Reflect
That During the Period of My
Administration Not a Drop
Of the Blood of a Single Citizen
Was Shed by the Sword of War

Carter was the first president since Jefferson who could claim that distinction. Even if the hostage rescue mission had reached Tehran and led to casualties, Carter never dropped a bomb or launched a missile while in office, and he was proud of it.

True to form, his final message to his Cabinet included a soft-spoken admonition: "I hope you will go out and pay it back." At a farewell dinner just before the inaugural, an emotional Mondale turned to Carter and said, "Never once did you put me down. Never once did you fail to treat me with dignity." Then he toasted what they had all accomplished:

"We told the truth. We obeyed the law. We kept the peace."

Carter added later, "And we championed human rights."

At the time, these might have seemed modest accomplishments — the minimum requirements for the job. But considering what came before (Vietnam and Watergate) and after (the Iran-Contra scandal, endless wars in Iraq and Afghanistan, two impeachments), Mondale's summary was meaningful. In later years, Carter made it the unofficial epitaph of his presidency.

After the election, the hostages slipped from view in both countries. In the United States, all eyes were on Reagan. In Iran, they were on Iraq. Reeling from Saddam Hussein's blows to key oil refineries, the Tehran regime cracked down on all dissent, uniting the people behind the war effort. Firmly in control, the mullahs had no need to show their toughness by holding American hostages. More urgent was the need for money for the war effort. Their estimates of the shah's hidden overseas wealth — $20 billion to $60 billion — were off by a thousandfold (the real figure was $20 million to $60 million), but at a minimum, they had to get their hands on the several billion in frozen state assets held by US banks.

In the end, the release of the hostages was likely the result of a good cop (Carter) doing the hard, painstaking negotiations for which he was perfectly suited, while the bad cop (Reagan) hovered offstage. Reagan's role was to be the trigger-happy menace in Iran's future. The regime no doubt heard Reagan say after Christmas, "I don't think you pay ransom for people who have been kidnapped by barbarians." Some Iranians might have even heard the joke "What's flat, red, and glows in the dark? Answer: Tehran, after Reagan becomes president." There's no documentary proof, but the Iranians likely figured that — desperate for cash — they would do better with Carter than starting all over again with a new administration whose president was making threatening noises.

In bashing diplomacy, Republican hawks of later years argued that it was just the threat of Reagan coming to office that led the Iranians to capitulate. In their telling, Carter's negotiations for the release of the hostages was "weak." This is a myth. Without both the carrot and the stick, the crisis might not have been resolved peacefully.

The final deal was negotiated through Algeria, whose diplomats had good contacts with both the Iranians and the Americans, represented by Deputy Secretary of State Warren Christopher and White House Counsel Lloyd Cutler. The negotiations were slow and conducted mostly in French, with the involvement of banks in several countries adding to the already cumbersome process.

Carter quickly rejected Iranian proposals for an American apology and reparations before agreeing that in return for Iran freeing the hostages, the United States would stop interfering in Iranian domestic affairs; unfreeze Iranian assets (determined, after endless haggling, to be $7.9 billion); end crippling trade sanctions; and make sure the dead shah's smaller-than-expected fortune was returned.

A month before the inaugural, the Iranians made a final demand: indemnify the Iranian government against lawsuits launched by the hostages seeking compensation for their days of suffering. This was a bitter pill for the Americans, but they finally agreed to the creation of the Iran–United

States Claims Tribunal, which removed cases against Iran from US courts.

Before signing off on the last, painful concession, Carter consulted with the hostage families. They told him to go ahead because they wanted their loved ones back. This would prove a source of contention for decades. "I would rather have stayed longer," Barry Rosen, one of the better-known hostages, said later. "Don't do me a favor by getting me out and telling me that I don't have a right to sue." Brzezinski conceded that it was "not a very good bargain," and he didn't blame the hostages for being angry.

The banking transactions involved in finalizing the Algiers Accords were mind-numbingly complex and — because of language barriers — prone to misunderstanding. Two of the twelve overseas branches of the American banks holding Iranian assets brought in lawyers to argue they should keep the interest accrued since the embassy takeover. Carter and Cutler overruled them. Even after pressure from the Algerian foreign minister, Iran's Bank Markazi did not agree to the basic terms the bank had already signed. The Iranians were clearly stalling, determined to avoid letting Carter get credit for ending the crisis. The president knew this but stayed focused. He worried that if the Algerian channel collapsed, the hostages might never come home.

Carter didn't go to bed in the forty-eight hours before Reagan's inauguration, which was shaping up to be one of the most emotionally fraught passages of power in American history. The outgoing president monitored the situation around the world from the Oval Office, where stewards brought blankets so that he could nap on the couch. The deal called for the Federal Reserve Bank to transfer a portion of the frozen assets to a London bank, from which it would go through the Bank of England and into an Algerian escrow account.

In the wee hours of January 20, one of the Federal Reserve attorneys who had traveled to Algiers refused to sign papers, claiming the Fed's independence from the Treasury. Carter barked into the phone, "Let's move!" When a Fed lawyer seemed to have fainted from fatigue, Carter told a New York Fed official to rouse him and order him to sign, then held a conference call at four thirty in the morning assuring Algerian officials that all the details were straight. By seven o'clock, the transfers were complete.

"We're not cutting it close enough," Jordan said sarcastically. "We still have five hours before the inauguration."

Rosalynn came by with a barber, and Jimmy went back to his small study for a haircut and a shave. Carter had tried phoning Reagan earlier with news of the impending release, only to be told by one of his top lieutenants, Edwin Meese, that the president-elect was not to be disturbed. This time he reached him, then got off one of those dry lines the public never saw. "I briefed him on what was happening with the hostages," Carter said with a straight face. "When I finished, he said, 'What hostages?' " The Oval Office, stripped bare but now full of officials, exploded in laughter.

Around nine o'clock, with three hours to go in his presidency, Carter received word on his red secure phone that two Algerian planes were taxiing on the runway in Tehran. Cutler reported to the group, "Chris [Warren Christopher] has been told that they will take off, quote, 'Within your administration.' " It was not to be. The best bet is that the Iranians decided to deliver one final insult to Carter, but even decades later, no one has identified an Iranian official who gave an order to delay takeoff from Tehran Airport until noon Washington time, when Reagan was sworn in. While several of the former captors said they did not want to give Carter the satisfaction of having the hostages freed on his watch, none identified points of contact with the pilots or air traffic control.

The transfer of the hostages out of Iran was handled by the Swiss. Flavio Meroni, the meticulous deputy Swiss ambassador to Iran, attributed the last-minute delay to "the procedure I insisted on completing to take delivery of the hostages." Meroni went up and down the aisle exchanging a few words with each hostage and obtaining fifty-two signatures ascertaining that each was in "acceptable" health. He recounted that Iranian officials at the airport showed no concern that the transfer of power in Washington was less than an hour away — and no indication they had been told to delay takeoff — only fear that an Iraqi fighter jet might intercept the plane on its way to Turkey.

On the ride down Pennsylvania Avenue, while Carter's mind was on the hostages, Reagan — "an affable and decent man" — told "a series of anecdotes that were remarkably pointless," Carter remembered. One long story involved Jack Warner, the late studio boss. When they emerged from the limo, a preoccupied Carter asked an aide: "Who is Jack Warner?"

Reagan took the oath at noon, and just after an inaugural address that Carter described as "hackneyed," a Secret Service agent whispered that the plane bearing the hostages was headed toward the Turkish border. The now-former president described this as "one of the happiest moments of my life," though he was disappointed not to be able to announce it to the American people.

At the congressional luncheon inside the Capitol Rotunda, the new president — hoisting a glass of champagne — told the world "the plane bearing our prisoners has left Iranian airspace." That night, Reagan lent Carter Air Force One to fly to Wiesbaden, West Germany, to meet the hostages, who were undergoing a battery of physical and psychological examinations. The flight over and back was like a bittersweet party for senior staff — relief and regret mixing freely. Carter told Jordan, "Nineteen eighty was pure hell: the Kennedy challenge, Afghanistan, having to put the SALT treaty on the shelf, Ronald Reagan, the hostages — always the hostages! It was one crisis after another." Many years later, George Packer wrote, "Carter finished his term like a man staring under the hood of his car in the middle of a mudslide."

In Wiesbaden, the fifty-two hostages were safe and in fair condition, considering their 444-day ordeal. All but a half dozen agreed to see Carter and Mondale, who both grew emotional as they hugged the freed Americans and shared their tears. During a closed-door meeting, one former hostage asked the president why the shah had been admitted. Carter said he had been given assurances by the Iranian government that the embassy would be protected. Another stood up and said, "Mr. President, with all due respect, I

916

and others wrote [Washington] that those assurances were not worth the paper they were written on."

Others were more complimentary. Colonel Thomas Schaefer, who as the defense attaché received especially harsh treatment in captivity, told the press that Jimmy Carter "displayed the patience, the maturity, and, most of all, the dignity of the office of the president."

The world will likely never know for sure whether the Reagan campaign went beyond improperly monitoring Carter's negotiations to actually conspiring with Iran to delay the release of the hostages until after the election — the new definition of the October Surprise.

By the mid-1980s, a cottage industry of October Surprise theories arose, bolstered by the details of the Iran-Contra scandal, in which the Reagan administration secretly provided arms (through Israel) to Iran in exchange for the release of seven hostages in Lebanon and secret funding for the anti-Communist contras in Nicaragua.

The core of Iran-Contra — using Israeli middlemen to trade arms for hostages — closely paralleled what was alleged in the October Surprise. In fact, they may have been part of the same scandal.* The first secret arms shipments to Iran began in 1981, just weeks after Reagan took office

---

*October Surprise theories gained credibility in part because the motives for it extended beyond the Reagan campaign. After Carter and Stansfield Turner cleaned house at the CIA, the world was awash in former intelligence operatives bent on revenge against Carter. Several figured in both October Surprise theories and

and three years *before* American hostages were seized in Lebanon. Ambassador Nicholas Veliotes, a career diplomat, testified that in 1981, when he was assistant secretary of state for the Middle East, "Indeed, we had agreed that the Israelis could transship to Iran some American-made military equipment." Veliotes later reiterated that he was certain such approval was granted by Secretary of State Alexander Haig and that he also learned of the crash of an Argentine airliner loaded with weapons being shipped to Iran by Israeli arms dealers in violation of US law. This raised questions that have never been answered definitively: Were those weapons a payoff for delaying release of the hostages? Why would the Reagan administration be secretly sending arms to an enemy nation so soon after it had held American hostages?*

---

the established facts of the Iran-Contra scandal. Shortly before his death in 2016, Duane "Dewey" Clarridge, a legendary CIA operative, said the events depicted in George Cave's 2013 novel, *October 1980,* were real — that a deal was struck and that infamous Iran-Contra middleman Manucher Ghorbanifar won huge Las Vegas bets by accurately predicting the exact date of the hostage release: January 20, 1981. Cave, also a former CIA operations officer, said his novel was fictitious and denied knowing that the Reagan campaign struck a deal.

*Veliotes believed the Reagan administration was hostile to the Iranian mullahs — with Casey even discussing a coup to put the shah's son on the throne — and he speculated that the arms shipments were "an

The most sensational allegation was that vice presidential candidate George Bush met secretly with Iranians in Paris in October 1980. The story was almost certainly false: Bush had an airtight alibi, and the idea of him secretly leaving the United States seventeen days before the election was implausible. When this and other conspiracy theories were debunked, it undermined legitimate October Surprise reporting.

Gary Sick, Carter's well-regarded NSC expert on Iran, came closest to cracking the case. In 1991 Sick, by then a professor at Columbia University, made a circumstantial argument: in July 1980 William Casey, while serving as Reagan's campaign manager, slipped out of a World War II history conference in London, flew to Madrid, and met in a hotel with intelligence operatives and one of Khomeini's closest associates. According to Sick and sources interviewed by PBS's investigative news program *Frontline* and other news outlets, a follow-up meeting several weeks later finalized a deal whereby the Iranians would coordinate with the Reagan campaign on the timing of the release of the hostages in exchange for a promise that, after he was elected, the new president would unfreeze their assets and — through the Israelis — provide spare parts for Iranian weapons.

After many allegations and denials — tantalizing clues and disputed theories — the validity of the October Surprise story came down to whether Casey went to Madrid. In January 1993 a special

---

Israeli initiative." Others, including several sources whose credibility has been challenged, alleged that it was all part of an elaborate deal.

bipartisan House panel, cochaired by Democrat Lee Hamilton of Indiana, issued a 960-page report that found plenty of smoke but no smoking gun — "no credible evidence" that Casey was in Madrid or that the Reagan campaign colluded with Iranians.

Much later, Hamilton was dismayed to learn that his probe had been denied a key piece of evidence. In preparing to cooperate with that investigation in 1992, the State Department's legal counselor found a cable from the Madrid embassy from July 1980 "indicating that Bill Casey was in town, for purposes unknown." Paul Beach, a deputy White House counsel under President George H. W. Bush, memorialized this incriminating cable but his superiors failed to turn it over to the Hamilton Committee, apparently fearing that revelations of an October Surprise would hurt Bush's reelection chances in 1992. By the time investigative reporter Robert Parry, now deceased, found the critical document at the Bush Presidential Library in 2013, Washington had long since lost any interest in reopening the investigation.

Gary Sick remained convinced that hotel and other records that might have further confirmed the Madrid meeting were destroyed by "professionals" before Hamilton's committee investigators could find them, but he acknowledged he had no definitive proof.

For the Carters, who strongly suspected that Casey had cut a deal to delay the release of the hostages, vindication would remain just out of reach.

*Jimmy and Rosalynn honored with a gift of traditional attire, Ghana, 2007.*

■ ■ ■ ■ ■

# PART SEVEN:
# GLOBAL CITIZEN

■ ■ ■ ■

# 38
## EXILE

Jimmy Carter had what the poet William Butler Yeats called "a pilgrim soul." His winding trek after leaving office was something unique among former presidents — a sustained effort to improve both himself and the wider world. Over a forty-year period, Carter combined intense self-discovery with inspiring selflessness: he learned to be a writer, poet, and painter (among other new skills), while patiently pursuing peace and global health in long-forsaken countries.

At first, there was a reputation to repair. It was hard for the Carters to live with the idea that the hostage crisis and the devastating 1980 election would be the last word on them. But this better explains Rosalynn's motivation than Jimmy's. After writing his memoirs, Carter spent relatively little time justifying his performance in office. Instead, driven by his Christian faith, he searched for new ways to leverage his status to do good.

That leverage was much reduced after he left Washington. James Laney, the president of Emory University, liked to say that Carter was "the only president who ever used the White House as a stepping-stone." But to what? For all the accomplishments of the Carter Center, there is no higher and more powerful platform than the one Jimmy Carter relinquished. Contrary to myth, nothing Carter achieved after leaving the presidency exceeded what he did in office.

But the effort itself defined him. The hallmark of Carter's later years, Hamilton Jordan wrote in an unpublished account, was "his total commitment to making a difference — his willingness to try and fail, to invest his time and emotions, and to risk his reputation" helping people. He also relished his chance to satisfy his boundless curiosity; to "learn something new every day," as he often said. By the turn of the century, Carter would routinely describe the decades after his "involuntary retirement" as "the best years of my life."

Over time, his dizzying activity — almost always with Rosalynn at his side — made him a world-class humanitarian and set a new standard for former presidents. His successors know their contributions after leaving the White House will be judged against his. To their annoyance, Carter sometimes let his self-righteousness get in the way, acting as if he were due more deference than he owed those who were running the country. The man who canceled "Hail to the Chief" sometimes acted as if he were still the president of the United States — or at least secretary of state.

But that was just another part of his paradoxical nature: patient and impatient, humble and proud. The one constant was ceaseless effort. Carter's cross-country coach at Annapolis in the mid-1940s had taken note of the teenager's stamina and competitive drive. Nearly eight decades later, he was still using those traits to squeeze everything he possibly could out of being Jimmy Carter — to

926

satisfy his ego, yes, but also to better the lives of strangers living thousands of miles away.

The Trailways bus wound its way up the interstate, a twenty-seven-hour journey from Americus, Georgia, to New York City. Aboard all night were the former leader of the free world and thirty-nine other bleary-eyed volunteers, many of whom called their old friend nothing more formal than "Jimmy."

In the nearly four years since leaving Washington, Jimmy and Rosalynn had come to believe they needed to do more for the poor than merely bring a turkey to the food pantry on Thanksgiving and Christmas. They had helped build a few houses in Sumter County but were ready for a bigger project that might spread the word about a charity they admired.

The group planned to renovate a six-story abandoned building at 742 East Sixth Street in what was then a run-down area of Manhattan's Lower East Side. Accommodations for the week were at the Metro Baptist Church, right by the grimy entrance to the Lincoln Tunnel. When the Carters learned that a husband and wife from Americus were on their honeymoon, they gave the couple their bedroom in the vestry and slept on bunk beds with the other volunteers.

The next day, they set to work. Jimmy, a skilled carpenter, replaced rotted beams and laid new floors with the help of some of the future owners, each of whom was granted an interest-free loan to buy one of the renovated apartments. Carter told the *New York Times* that while he was honorary chairman of many charities, Habitat for Humanity was the only one to which he devoted his time and labor.*

Habitat was founded and operated by Millard Fuller, a millionaire businessman who experienced a spiritual crisis in the mid-1960s and ended up at Koinonia Farm, where he came to revere Clarence Jordan. In 1969 Jordan suffered a fatal heart attack. When the white supremacist authorities who despised Jordan's interracial community would not send the coroner, Fuller packed the corpse in his station wagon and drove it to the morgue.

As Koinonia's housing ministry evolved into Habitat, the Carters changed from skittish neighbors into enthusiastic volunteers. Starting with the New York project, they spearheaded thirty-seven Habitat for Humanity "builds" in fourteen countries, each of which tapped into a spirit of modesty and civic engagement that offered a refreshing counterpoint to the materialism of the age.

After the 1984 New York project, Jimmy and Rosalynn set aside time every year to spend a week building a house — one year overseas, the next year in the United States. Even in his nineties, Carter could drive a three-and-a-half-inch nail into a stud wall with eight hard hammer strokes or fewer. He was a demanding foreman, barking out orders like the submarine captain he never got to be. In Thailand, when he saw a government minister walking around the site, he snapped, "Why aren't you working?"

Contrary to popular belief, Carter never ran Habitat for Humanity. But he was an active board

*The front-page story by Esther B. Fein helped put Habitat on the map.

928

chairman and the public face of a Christian organization that has constructed a million houses and become the largest not-for-profit home builder in the world.

The first year out of office felt like exile. When he left the White House, Carter's approval rating stood at 34 percent, the same as George W. Bush's at the end of his eight-year presidency; only Truman and Nixon were less popular. At first, Rosalynn was in denial. She remembered the presidential helicopter, Marine One, lifting off from the South Lawn for the last time and thinking, "He'll win [in 1984], and we'll come back." She soon sank into what her friend Rita Thompson described as a "clinical depression," though she wouldn't admit it, and developed psychosomatic muscle ailments that Amy remembered left her in bed for much of the day. For her part, Amy despised Plains and the Sumter County consolidated high school where "boys made fun of my clothes, and everyone hated Dad." She soon fled to a boarding school in Atlanta, further demoralizing her parents.

Jimmy, by contrast, didn't miss Washington or harbor dreams of a return; he saw Plains as "a place to heal our wounds when we're disappointed." And yet he admitted later that he was "despondent" and in "despair" for months: "I felt I had a vacuum in my life if I don't have something that occupies my time and effort." Chip, who returned to Plains to help his parents settle into their new life, remembered his father "in a pissy mood for a long time. Thank God for the wood shop." As a farewell gift, the White House staff gave him the tools and tables he had wanted ever since the navy, which he set up in the garage. This brought some solace, but Betty Pope described the Carters as still "grieving" over the what-ifs. What if they hadn't taken in the shah of Iran? What if they'd had another helicopter? Billy's alcoholism and public disintegration had "broken Jimmy's heart." To visitors, Jimmy said he wasn't bitter — and Rosalynn said she was bitter enough for the both of them.

One satisfying moment came in October 1981, when Carter forced the long-hostile *Washington Post* to grovel. The Ear, a *Post* gossip column, had printed an outlandish item alleging that the Carters had bugged Blair House when the Reagans stayed there before the inauguration. The story was completely false, and Carter — both sensing a chance for payback and legitimately worried that foreign heads of state would never agree to be guests at Blair House again — instructed his personal lawyer, Terry Adamson, to sue for libel. For nearly two weeks, the *Post* tried to weasel out of accountability. "How do you make a public apology?" *Post* editor Ben Bradlee asked. "Run up and down Pennsylvania Avenue bare bottomed, shouting, 'I'm sorry'?" Adamson deadpanned to CNN that he would present that proposal to his client. The *Post* finally printed an embarrassing front-page retraction and apology. This hardly made up for what Carter considered four years of snobby treatment — but it was something.

During this time, Jim Laney reached out to Carter, whom he described as "at the nadir of his life and not well received anywhere," to offer the former president an association with Emory. Carter became a University Distinguished Professor

930

and found that he loved teaching. He eventually lectured — he was proud to say — in every major college and school in the university.

One day Laney introduced Carter to Karl Deutsch, a renowned political scientist visiting from Harvard. Deutsch told Carter that a thousand years from now, only a handful of American presidencies would be remembered, but that his would be among them because of his focus on human rights. Carter's eyes welled with tears. He teared up again during one of his annual appearances before Emory freshmen when a student asked him, "Would your father be proud of you?"

Carter regained his composure and said, "Yes, I think he would be."

Before Jimmy could raise money for his library, he had to make money for his family. Just after the 1980 election, Charlie Kirbo, the trustee of the Carters' blind trust, came for a drink on the Lincoln Balcony. He told Jimmy and Rosalynn he had good news and bad news. The good news was that, back home in Plains, the trees were in bloom. "The bad news is you're a million in debt." From 1977 to 1981, Sumter County had experienced one of its worst-ever droughts, and all across the country, the farm economy had been battered during the Carter years.

For a time, it seemed as if the Carters would have to sell their land — most of it worth only $1,500 an acre — to pay off debts. Their house in Plains was worth a mere $100,000 and they owned few stocks, which had flatlined along with the broader market in the 1970s. Fortunately for the family, Archer Daniels Midland — whose savvy CEO, Dwayne Andreas, was a big contributor to both parties — decided to go into the peanut business. The agricultural conglomerate paid $1.2 million for Carter's Warehouse, enough to cover its liabilities. But the Carters remained cash poor.

As a former president, Carter had an easy option. Philip Alston, his ambassador to Australia and just about the only member of the Atlanta establishment who had stuck by him all the way through the presidency, recommended he go on corporate boards and start playing golf again, which would get him more business contacts. Alston said if Carter's game improved, he might be able to get him into the exclusive Augusta National Golf Club, home of the Masters Tournament.

Hamilton Jordan, present during this conversation, had trouble imagining Carter in lime-green golf slacks with little whales on them, teeing off with Republican CEOs before retiring to the clubhouse to relive each hole over mint juleps. But even he wasn't prepared for Carter's answer. Jimmy told Alston he had "zero interest" in being on the boards of already successful companies and that he "hated golf" because it took too long to play eighteen holes and wasn't even good exercise.

Carter had already told the press on the day after the election that he would emulate Harry Truman and refuse to "enrich myself" from the presidency. Unlike Gerald Ford, the first ex-president to use his stature to cash in big, he would turn down not just corporate boards but also speaking fees, except a few he gave to charity — a "naive but sincere commitment that I have honored," he said later. His successors all did the opposite, with the Clintons and Obamas each amassing $100 million in net worth within a few years of leaving office.* Carter was built differently. He had spent his life as a relentless striver, much of it in business. But the rewards were not about money: "It just never had been my ambition to be rich."

To support his family, he became an author, which — unlike giving the same paid corporate speech over and over — required real work. In the early 1980s, both Carters wrote their memoirs. Rosalynn's were more vivid and became a number one best seller, which his — to his chagrin — did not. Jimmy's account of his White House years, entitled *Keeping Faith: Memoirs of a President,* was more cathartic. He banged out a chapter settling scores with the press but decided not to publish it because it was "childish." But he was glad to get his feelings "out of my system."

By 2020, Carter had written thirty-two books — about one every fifteen months — on everything from fishing, to faith, to the Mideast. He even wrote a children's book about a boy and a sea monster, *The Little Baby Snoogle Fleejer,* based

*Ronald Reagan pocketed $2 million for speaking in Japan. George H. W. Bush, already well-to-do, made less than Reagan per speech but accepted discreet paying gigs. Bill Clinton, who said he left the presidency "dead broke," made $104.9 million giving 542 speeches — most of them abroad — in the first twelve years after he left office. George W. Bush spoke about two hundred times in his first five years out of office, for $150,000 or so a pop. The Obamas signed a $65 million book deal and a lucrative Netflix deal, and made hundreds of thousands of dollars per speech.

on a bedtime story he used to tell Amy, who did the illustrations. The best, *An Hour Before Daylight: Memories of a Rural Boyhood,* was a finalist for the 2002 Pulitzer Prize.

Carter brought his usual competitive streak to his new career. On tour, he kept score of exactly how fast he was signing copies and greeted those who waited in line coldly if they brought along one of his earlier books for signature but hadn't purchased his new one. But he knew how to sell. When a woman came up and said, "If you still lust in your heart, Mr. President, I'm available," he told the story on late-night talk shows. He was affable in public but with a purpose. Flying commercial, he made a habit of working his way up and down the aisles shaking hands with all the passengers shortly after boarding. The move was classic Carter: it made a great impression while also allowing him to get the well-wishing out of the way so he could work undisturbed for the duration of the flight.

Ironically, the biggest rift in the Carters' relationship since Jimmy left the navy was over a 1986 book that he and Rosalynn wrote together on how to find happiness in late middle age. Jimmy said coauthoring *Everything to Gain: Making the Most of the Rest of Your Lives* almost ruined their marriage. It got so bad that Rosalynn put a Do Not Disturb Me sign on her door. They began communicating only through notes and ate in silence or at different times. Jimmy thought Rosalynn treated his chapters "like rough, rough drafts," while viewing her own as "sent down from Mount Sinai." Rosalynn called her daughter-in-law Judy in tears, complaining that Jimmy changed her prose, when hers was better. Jimmy was misremembering, she insisted, or not getting to the heart of things. They decided to return the $60,000 advance. Their editor at Random House, Peter Osnos, traveled to Plains and worked out a truce: each would write different sections, with a "JC" or "RC" at the bottom of the page. The book was published, did reasonably well, and their marriage healed.

Jimmy and Rosalynn still fought, but Jimmy could not handle even relatively short separations. Once, when Rosalynn had been gone for a few days, he told Faye Perdue, a friend and aide, that he "actually ached from missing Rosalynn." After an especially hurtful spat, Jimmy retired to his woodshop and cut out a thin sheet of walnut about the size of a check and carved on it: "Each evening, forever, this is good for an apology — or forgiveness — as you desire, Jimmy."

For the first four decades of their marriage, Jimmy's obsessive punctuality led to many arguments. Desperate for a last-minute birthday gift in 1984, he wrote a note to her: "Rosalynn, I promise you that for the rest of our marriage, I will never again make an unfavorable remark about tardiness." She said it was the best present she ever received. But with the rest of his family, Carter acted as he had with tardy reporters. On annual family vacations with his children and grandchildren, he printed a White House–style schedule and ordered the bus to leave for sightseeing exactly on time — whether or not relatives were left behind.

The exacting engineer continued to have little influence over his children. Amy, shy and cerebral, abandoned her studies at Brown University and became an activist engaged in civil disobedience. She was handcuffed in 1985 at an antiapartheid demonstration in front of the South African embassy, where she told reporters, "I'm proud to be my father's daughter." Jimmy and Rosalynn were proud of her, too. In 1987 Amy and former Chicago Seven defendant Abbie Hoffman were among those tried and acquitted for protesting CIA recruitment at the University of Massachusetts Amherst. As a former president, Jimmy might have been expected to back the CIA but he was again fully supportive, and not just because Amy was his daughter.

Carter was moving left from the hawkishness of his defense budget and the Carter Doctrine, though he wouldn't admit it, claiming that he hadn't changed his politics but was simply free in his postpresidency to speak his mind and meet with whomever he pleased. There was some truth in this: his views on peace had not changed much since he finally abandoned support for the Vietnam War in 1974. But his children all agreed that both Jimmy and Rosalynn, while still difficult to pigeonhole, were no longer conservative on much beyond federally funded abortions and premarital sex.

Amy sometimes got angry with her father for his refusal to get angry. She felt his rationality and eerie calm could be off-putting — "like an obnoxious moral high ground." But their bond remained strong. In 1994 twenty-six-year-old Amy was preparing to get married in Memphis, where she had earned a degree at art school in preparation for her career as an elementary school art teacher in Atlanta. Carter had booked the Peabody Hotel and paid for everything, when, the night before the wedding, Amy backed out. Rosalynn was upset, but this time Amy admired how calmly her father reacted. He just wanted to talk about a few things. She remembered being touched and amused that he worried that no other man might love her if she wasn't still a virgin, not comprehending that she hadn't been a virgin for several years. Amy remained quietly independent. When she married someone else in 1996, she refused to be given away by her father because she "belonged to no one," which he accepted with equanimity.

While Jimmy remained close with Amy, and he got on well with Chip and Jeff, his relationship with Jack continued to be difficult. Jack faced several business reversals, starting with the failure of a grain elevator he bought in Calhoun. He moved with his family to Chicago in the 1980s to work at the Board of Trade and invest in other businesses, some of which also had trouble. Carter and his firstborn son seldom spoke on the phone — replicating the distance between Jimmy and Mr. Earl when Jimmy was in the navy. Judy Langford felt one of the reasons that she and Jack divorced in 1988 was that she was still close to Rosalynn, and Jack blamed her for siding with his parents.

After he remarried, Jack was disappointed that his parents traveled all over the world but never once visited him in the decade that he lived in Bermuda; he found them self-absorbed and uninterested in his new life and career. According to family members, Jimmy in the 1980s and 1990s viewed Jack as he did Chip, saying things like, "He should grow up. He's an adult now."

In 2006 Jack won the Democratic primary for a US Senate seat from Nevada but faced a daunting campaign against incumbent John Ensign. In September Jack ate some tainted spinach and contracted an *E. coli* infection that spread rapidly through his body. His doctor called Jimmy and Rosalynn and said he wasn't sure Jack would live through the weekend. They rushed to his bedside, and Jimmy and Chip campaigned on his behalf in the weeks that he spent recovering in the hospital. He ultimately lost the election.

When Chip's drug and alcohol problems worsened, Jimmy visited him in rehab and expressed appropriate regret about not having been more understanding toward him. By the 2000s, substance abuse was afflicting a third generation of Carters; Jimmy and Rosalynn helped pay for therapy for Chip and two grandsons, Jeremy and James.

The Carter children were all open about their setbacks, and Rosalynn, with her expertise in mental health and caregiving, confronted family problems head-on.* But in his books, Jimmy never even alluded to these problems and how they might have touched or changed him. He wasn't comfortable enough to explore anything truly personal, which he considered out-of-bounds for a former president.

Like many parents of troubled baby boomers, the Carters focused more on their grandchildren. When Jack and Judy's son, Jason, was about to graduate from Duke in 1997, Jimmy told Edna Langford, "I don't much care what my kids think

*The Rosalynn Carter Institute for Caregiving at Georgia Southwestern State University does important work in providing caregivers long-overdue recognition and support.

938

of me, but I really care what my grandchildren think." He and Rosalynn visited Jason when he was in the Peace Corps in South Africa; Jason would much later become his designated successor at the Carter Center.

Out of office, Rosalynn worried that "Jimmy's miserable if he's not doing anything." So she was happy when he renewed his yen for self-improvement. He thought of cultivating the fine arts almost as an engineering project.

When he decided to learn how to paint, he met with artists for tips on brushes, easels, and canvases. Over the years, he completed more than a hundred colorful paintings, mostly of local people and scenes.

His poetry came more slowly. From the time he fell in love with Dylan Thomas's verse, Carter dreamed of writing his own. He had written poems for Rosalynn while in the navy but lost them. When he finally had time to write again after leaving office, he asked for instruction from accomplished Arkansas poets Miller Williams and Jim Whitehead. After they told him his first poems rhymed awkwardly, he stopped rhyming.

He invited both men to Plains along with other poets, two of whom brought their guitars. "I rushed to write in fumbling lines why we should care about a distant starving child," he wrote in a poem about their visit. He tried writing about outer space and why "we reject peace as weakness." These were big themes that preoccupied Carter, but they didn't make for good poems. The words rarely flowed, and when they came, he found the results underwhelming. Family members felt he could never account for the gap between his passion to help the "distant starving child" — an abstraction — and his curious indifference to the details of his own children's lives. But he did find resonance in "closer, simpler themes" from his childhood, such as passing through a pasture gate (one of his best poems) and a possum hunt. He learned from poetry that "art is best derived from artless things." Over time he concluded, "I express my feelings more honestly in my poetry than in prose."

Carter worked on his poems for seven years before sending them to his editor at Random House. After Peter Osnos rejected the collection, Jimmy wrote him and attached what he considered a bad poem by Jean Valentine, who went on to win the National Book Award for poetry. To try to make his point, he wrote some doggerel ("Poems editors seem to buy / they don't amuse or edify") meant to say: If people will publish this junk, what's wrong with *my* stuff? Osnos eventually arranged for publication and Carter received what he remembered as a "tiny advance." *Always a Reckoning and Other Poems,* a collection of what *Booklist* magazine called "44 humble but competent enough poems," sold much better than expected. The poems were evocative, nostalgic, and provided insights into his inner life.

Carter also tried his hand at fiction, the first American president to do so. He sought advice from the Emory creative writing department on how to write a novel and, after six years, produced *The Hornet's Nest,* a fact-filled historical novel about the Revolutionary War in the South, with cover art he painted himself. The plot contained a cringe-worthy sex scene ("He was overwhelmed with a feeling of tenderness and also aroused sexu-

940

ally, which his tight trousers made obvious to both of them") that a seventy-nine-year-old Carter read aloud in 2003 to a bemused Jay Leno on the *Tonight* show.

Among other DIY skills, Carter learned to make his own wine and cook bear meat. "The only time people back away is when he sings," Chip said. When Jimmy was sixty-two and Rosalynn fifty-nine, they learned to downhill ski at Crested Butte, the Colorado resort owned by Bo Callaway, his old rival and new friend. Two years later, they came within seven hundred feet of the summit of Mount Kilimanjaro, and six years after that, climbed Mount Fuji; at ninety, Jimmy learned to snorkel. The Carters undertook many separate activities — a secret of their long marriage, they said — but especially enjoyed fly-fishing and bird-watching together. On long international trips, they used the layover time to jog around the airport.

Of all his activities, the one closest to his heart was woodworking. Over four decades, he built beautiful wooden tables, chairs, armoires, four-poster beds, cabinets, closets, cradles for each grandchild, and chess sets with finely crafted inlaid boards and pieces. He made almost all of the furniture in the house in Plains and in a cabin the Carters owned with John and Betty Pope in the mountains of northern Georgia. With the help of inmates he requested from a Georgia penitentiary, he built carved wooden railings for a restored Depression-era elevator at the Plains Historic Inn, a charming, small hotel where Rosalynn decorated each of the seven rooms with authentic furnishings from seven decades of the twentieth century.

Woodworking drew Carter back to when he plowed the land with Emma the mule. The work could be boring, but it brought the comfort and satisfaction of knowing that "I had done all that was humanly possible, even as a young boy, and had left behind me the visible proof of my work."

In 1983 Lillian Carter, surrounded by her family, died of breast cancer at eighty-eight. Her closet at home still contained a complete uniform of her beloved Los Angeles Dodgers, including cleats. Just a month earlier, Ruth Carter Stapleton, only fifty-four, died of pancreatic cancer after a short illness. The cause of death hit the Carters especially hard because Earl had died of the same thing thirty years earlier. Like substance abuse, pancreatic cancer was now clearly something that ran in the family. Jimmy, of course, studied the disease, underwent a series of tests, and concluded that being a nonsmoker lessened though hardly eliminated his chances of suffering from this especially fatal form of cancer.

In 1988 Billy, only fifty-one, was told he had it, too. He hadn't smoked for years but bought two cartons of Pall Malls after the diagnosis. At his funeral later that year, Sybil chose his friend Tom T. Hall, the popular country singer and songwriter, to deliver the eulogy, a sign that not all of the old grievances against Jimmy had died with her husband.

Gloria was sixty-three when she fell sick in 1990, the fourth Carter with the same cancer. Years earlier, she and Walter had constructed a four-hole outhouse in their backyard that accommodated several dozen bikers passing through. Many of them now returned to Plains to pay

942

tribute to the patron saint of the biker community. Two bikers stood guard at all times outside her hospital room. Her funeral cortège was led by a long line of Harley-Davidson motorcycles, and her tombstone reads: "She rides in Harley heaven."

With the passing of his three siblings, all from the same disease, Jimmy would live the rest of his life with even more urgency, as if under a death sentence. He was determined to make the most of it.

# 39
# THE CARTER CENTER

One night in 1982 Carter woke with a start. He was only fifty-eight years old, and the path for the rest of his life suddenly struck him with astonishing clarity. Rosalynn arose and asked if he was sick. Jimmy said no, but he had figured out how to turn his presidential library into something more than a repository for his papers. He would make it a "small Camp David" — a place to solve problems and resolve disputes.

A year earlier, the Carters had toured a thirty-three-acre piece of land on the hill where Union general William Tecumseh Sherman watched Atlanta burn in the final months of the Civil War. The state of Georgia had acquired the property as part of a long-standing plan to build an east-west highway nearby. If Carter could accept the highway, he would get the property for free.

This was an ideal site for the Jimmy Carter Presidential Library and Museum, and for what would eventually become the Carter Center. But there was a problem. Many Atlantans didn't want a four-lane elevated high-speed expressway scarring their neighborhoods and beautiful parks designed by Frederick Law Olmsted.

The battle over "the parkway" split Atlanta.

944

Mayor Andrew Young and his successor, Maynard Jackson, supported it, while Atlanta City Council member John Lewis, the civil rights icon and veteran of the Carter administration — where he ran VISTA and other national service programs — opposed what he saw as the despoiling of a historic black community. Lewis would come to revere Carter as an "Energizer Bunny" for peace and for the world's dispossessed, but he wished he had applied those values more in his own neighborhood. Carter claimed to donors that "I have divorced myself from the parkway issue, leaving it completely in the hands of state and local authorities." While this was technically true, he was, as usual, immersed in the details and discussed them with the commissioner of the Georgia Department of Transportation. But he kept mum in public. "I could never understand how Mr. Carter could champion world peace yet not seek peace with his neighbors," recalled Cathy Bradshaw, a community activist.

In the end, a judge forced the DOT and community groups together and a series of compromises (putting the road at street level, eliminating the plan for ugly elevated off-ramps) resolved the matter. The new tree-lined road, called Freedom Parkway, was built so tastefully that everyone was satisfied. When the campus that included the library, museum, and center was completed in 1986, it drew people to the neighborhood and helped revive the surrounding area.

The Carter Center, which eventually employed more than three thousand people (mostly abroad), bent quickly to its founder's will. The Atlanta buildings were designed to be energy efficient, and the former president himself could sometimes

945

be found putting up Post-it Notes reading: "Do Not Touch This Thermostat." Instead of using a portion of their apartment in the presidential library as a bedroom, as other ex-presidents did, the Carters made it an office for Rosalynn. During the one week per month they spent in Atlanta, Jimmy and Rosalynn slept on a Murphy bed in the den.

Looking back, Carter said he wouldn't trade the Carter Center for a second term. If he had served eight years in the presidency, he reflected, he might not have had the same motivation to start something as ambitious after leaving office — or as expensive. Carter needed to raise millions not just for his library but also for the ongoing expenses of his ambitious new projects. He set his mind to doing so. The only thing Carter liked less than fund-raising was the prospect of being forgotten.

Carter affiliated his new nonpartisan center with Emory University, which put up most of the early money, but he still spent months on the road with a tin cup. While wealthy Atlantans like CNN founder Ted Turner and Home Depot co-founder Arthur Blank kicked in, he didn't do as well in New York, where real estate developer Donald Trump was impressed that he had "the nerve and the guts" to ask him for $5 million but gave him nothing. The same happened with several other potential donors, who saw him as a failed figure from the past.

And so Carter turned to a collection of unsavory but generous characters from overseas. His first big foreign partner was Ryoichi Sasakawa, an elderly Japanese philanthropist who had been imprisoned by the United States as a war criminal after World War II and went on to make his fortune in gambling interests (mostly speedboat racing) with ties to the Japanese underworld. Another early benefactor was Agha Abedi, the Pakistani founder of the Bank of Credit and Commerce International (BCCI), which was soon enveloped in scandal. In later years, King Fahd of Saudi Arabia and the Sultan of Oman — big contributors to several American universities — were among the Carter Center's multimillion-dollar donors. But, contrary to some reports, the center was never dependent on Arab benefactors.

By the mid-1980s, the indefatigable Carters were throwing themselves into trouble spots around the world — traveling an astonishing 150 days a year for peacemaking, election monitoring, and other projects. But even with highly publicized conferences that lured major leaders from around the world to Atlanta and splashy new initiatives, they knew their center lacked focus. Jim Laney of Emory wanted it to be more academic; Carter, more practical. Of course, Carter won. Studying issues and producing fat reports bored him. He was determined to solve problems, even if that meant diving headfirst into complex social issues that no one fully understood.

An early and frustrating failure was an overly ambitious effort called the Atlanta Project, which enlisted corporations and nonprofit organizations to address a wide variety of social ills afflicting four million people in the city. The project, which included door-to-door organizing and effective outreach to churches, drew strong involvement from Atlanta's African American community. But it was beset by turf fights and poor implementa-

947

tion, as Carter learned the hard way that he had more influence over narrow conditions overseas than broad ones at home. The hubris was matched by a lack of sophistication about the dense tangle of social factors connected to poverty. An internal report in 1994 found that "the record with regard to schools is particularly dismal."

The lesson Carter drew was that NGOs must specialize in a few discrete areas to succeed. From then on, the Carter Center focused almost all its efforts on conflict resolution, global health, and promoting democracy and human rights. It dedicated itself to empowering people in the developing world with new "skills, knowledge, and access to resources" and adopted the motto "Waging Peace. Fighting Disease. Building Hope."

Carter was the first American president to visit sub-Saharan Africa, and he returned to the continent, at least briefly, more than two dozen times in the years after leaving office. This made him a hero there. Even the most anti-American leaders received him graciously; children were named for him. He knew he could do more there — with less — than anywhere else in the world.

Africa spoke to the Carters. "In many villages, I felt at home," Jimmy said. On landing, he thought often of his own life in the Jim Crow South; of his feelings for Jack and Rachel Clark and the other African Americans he had known. Carter never said explicitly that his humanitarian commitments at home and abroad were at least in part an attempt to atone for having ducked the civil rights movement — but he came close. In his nineties, he acknowledged that what he called "my late full awareness" of the persecution of African Americans "obviously made me much more avid in treating them as equals and trying when possible to compensate."

In Africa, Carter teamed up with Norman Borlaug, the heroic agronomist who had won the Nobel Peace Prize for saving millions of lives in Latin America, India, and Pakistan in the 1960s with his development of high-yield strains of wheat. Hoping to revive "the Green Revolution," Ryoichi Sasakawa funded an initiative called Global 2000 to apply Borlaug's astonishingly effective agricultural techniques to the famine and disease spreading across Africa in the 1980s.

In partnership with the Carter Center, Global 2000 began in Ghana, where local farmers were offered expert advice and special seeds and fertilizer at harvest time. The so-called Borlaug-Carter method proved successful, in part because of Carter's diplomatic work. He befriended Jerry Rawlings, the thirty-four-year-old revolutionary who had seized power and now backed their efforts enthusiastically. By the late 1980s, more than a hundred thousand farmers had adopted the new techniques, and Ghana no longer needed to import food.

The turn of the century brought a stunning turnaround in Ethiopia and a dozen smaller African countries no longer experiencing famine, thanks partly to the Sasakawa Africa Association, and to a lesser degree, the Carter Center.

But it was Carter's prescient focus on global health that would become his most impressive postpresidential achievement. In 1987 Jimmy and Rosalynn traveled to two villages in Ghana, where, in just a few minutes, they saw more than a

949

hundred people with worms two to three feet in length that Carter described as "coming out of their ankles, knees, groins, legs, arms, and other parts of their bodies." At one point, they thought they were looking at the black hair of a baby being cradled, but it was actually the mother's breast, hideously discolored by worms.

The Carters' old friend Peter Bourne had introduced them to the problem of Guinea worm disease in 1985; "We almost got nauseated at lunch," Jimmy remembered. (Carter himself later shocked a luncheon by discussing the pustules caused by Guinea worm just as the main course was served.) He was intrigued that the affliction was referred to in the Bible as the "fiery serpent" and that it had apparently inspired the ancient depiction of staff and serpent that has become the oft-used symbol of medicine. The Carters were shocked to learn that nearly ten million people a year, mostly in Africa, were stricken with this easily preventable disease, spread by contaminated water.

Guinea worm was a perplexing affliction: not fatal, but incurable and devastating to rural areas. Its crippling aftereffects, which resembled polio, ensured dire poverty by sidelining farmers, preventing children from going to school, and keeping mothers from caring for their infants. The solution was neither a vaccine (preventative) nor an antibiotic (treatment). Instead, eradication required mass behavioral changes in drinking, bathing, and washing, which many global health experts considered impractical.

When in office, Jimmy Carter was the first American president to show interest in global health. Now, with his late mother's values alive in him, he called on Dr. Bill Foege to help him make the Carter Center a leader in this vital area. In the 1960s, the heroic six-foot-seven epidemiologist developed the vaccination strategy that reduced smallpox from two million cases worldwide to none by 1975. As Carter's director of the Centers for Disease Control, Foege expanded the agency into global health and made great progress on measles inoculation.* In 1986 Carter tapped him to become the executive director of the Carter Center, where he and another talented CDC veteran, Donald Hopkins, figured out creative ways to use the former president's star power to propel progress against Guinea worm.

They attacked the problem on several fronts at once. Using his diplomatic skills, Carter got his big donor, Agha Abedi of Pakistan, to spend $10 million on clean water wells and convinced Jerry Rawlings of Ghana and Zia-ul-Haq of Pakistan to embrace the cause. He cleverly figured that Ghana's progress would incentivize nearby Nigeria to catch up, while Pakistan's gain would get India's attention.

Under prodding from Carter, corporate America pitched in. With Camp David–style skills, he convinced American Cyanamid, the only manufacturer of Abate (the larvicide that kills the water flea hosts), to provide its product to Africa for free. And in 1989 Carter persuaded DuPont to donate one million square yards of cloth filters that were normally used to make parachutes and bulletproof vests. One square yard could yield as

*The Carter administration also continued a mass vaccination campaign against swine flu begun under Gerald Ford.

many as nine filters, and, unlike cash, the cloth couldn't be converted to other uses. The DuPont gift gave the Carter Center leverage with other foreign leaders, who, once offered free filters, were unable to resist fighting the disease.

Critically, the Carter Center paid locals a $100 bounty for reporting the presence of Guinea worms (an idea borrowed from Foege's smallpox initiative) and trained thousands of workers to use the filters to test for parasites and to urge villagers to stay away from infected ponds.

In his first meeting with Bill Gates, in 1986, Carter — at Foege's urging — didn't ask for money. Instead, he began an ongoing conversation about how to get results in global health, a subject that Gates was just beginning to embrace. Jimmy invited Bill Gates Sr., who helped run his son's foundation, to tour Africa with him. Melinda Gates remembered Carter telling her in Seattle, " 'Melinda, anything you do has to be owned by the local people. And when it's owned by them, and their voices are heard, and they truly believe in it, then they will take it up. And when you leave, the program will still exist.' And he was absolutely right."

When his talks with the Bill & Melinda Gates Foundation got serious, Carter insisted that Gates skip the usual capacity-building phase, standard spadework for a foundation, and move directly to eradicating the disease. He wanted immediate results. This caused some tension, but over time the foundation came to trust the Carter Center and eventually put tens of millions into Guinea worm programs across the continent.

Starting in 1988, Carter went on a Guinea worm trip abroad almost every year — monitor-

952

ing progress and keeping the heat on local leaders. "When he locked on to something, he became very tenacious," Hopkins recalled. In 2007 the former president grew furious at Ghanaian authorities for neglecting to maintain the clean water supply. As he told a press conference, "If Ghana keeps dragging its feet, we will rename it *Ghana worm disease*." Shortly thereafter, the number of cases in Ghana plummeted.

By the early 2000s, the Carter Center was making jaw-dropping progress, especially for a relatively small nonprofit. When Carter first focused on Guinea worm in 1986, the disease afflicted 3.5 million people. By 2014, it was down to 130 cases worldwide.

Jimmy and Rosalynn soon grew interested in other parasites, especially the one that caused river blindness (onchocerciasis), which presented as intensely itchy rashes and over time robbed victims of their sight. Fortunately, doctors at Merck had developed a drug sold under the brand name Mectizan that — administered once or twice a year — knocked out the disease. The pharmaceutical company's public-spirited CEO, Dr. Roy Vagelos, set out to take Merck's treatment global. In the mid-1980s, Vagelos — a rare combination of scientist and hugely successful manager — convinced his board to manufacture as many Mectizan tablets as necessary and give them away for free. He would eventually build a large factory just for this philanthropic purpose. But Vagelos still needed a way to distribute the medicine, which many Africans wrongly thought a greedy pharmaceutical giant was simply dumping on the developing world. That's where Carter and Foege came in.

After a trip to Chad with Carter in 1994, Vagelos realized that Carter, in his down-to-earth way, "had become our best salesman." Carter was often asked on his travels why a former president of the United States would do this kind of humanitarian work. He always explained that he was a farmer, which sometimes turned out to be the most persuasive entry on his resume.

The Carter Center's original goal was to get six million people treated for river blindness in six countries in six years. With the help of thousands of locals, it accomplished that goal ahead of schedule, cutting the infection rate in central Nigeria, for instance, from 55 percent in 1991 to 0.4 percent in 2009. By 2015, Merck had provided one billion free treatments, and river blindness, while not eradicable, was greatly reduced across Africa and Latin America.

Carter also worked to remove the stigma attached to AIDS.* In 2002 he held babies suffering from the disease with Nelson Mandela in Soweto and toured clinics treating HIV-positive prostitutes with Bill Gates Sr. Then he flew to Cape Town, where South African president Thabo Mbeki, who claimed antiretroviral medicine was toxic, told Carter, "South Africans have different blood than the rest of the world." An outraged Carter accused him publicly of "turning your

---

*The Carter Center lacked the resources to be a major player on AIDS. It was the Clinton Foundation that did important work on AIDS in Africa, especially to lower the cost of antiretroviral drugs to fight the disease.

954

back" on dying people. He would later say, "That's the closest I've come to getting into a fist-fight with a head of state."

By then, nearly two-thirds of the Carter Center's budget was devoted to global health, with workers in more than eighty countries fighting not just Guinea worm and river blindness but also trachoma, schistosomiasis, lymphatic filariasis, and malaria. When the Ebola virus struck Africa in 2013–14, the Carter Center had been on the ground in Liberia (a locus of the epidemic) since 2010. To combat the virus, the center coordinated the training of four thousand village elders and provided what was often the first information about the disease that villagers received. The Carter Center's Mental Health Program, launched by Rosalynn, helped the Liberian government train its first mental health workers and reduce the stigma of mental illness, a cause to which Rosalynn devoted herself worldwide.

Carter believed passionately in democratic accountability — that freedom must be bolstered and defended by fair and peaceful elections with uniform standards. Since the mid-1980s, the Carter Center has monitored more than a hundred elections — roughly three a year — mostly in Latin America at first, and then in Africa and Asia. Carter has been present for about half of them. Into their nineties, he and Rosalynn would immerse themselves in the complexities of an election in a distant country, jump on a plane, and visit as many as forty polling stations a day. They and dozens of other two-person teams would fan out across rural areas and then gather in the capital to announce any irregularities.

In Nigeria in 1999, for instance, the Carter Center found that more votes had been cast than there were registered voters, which brought back memories of stuffed ballot boxes in his 1962 state senate race in Quitman County, Georgia. Carter issued a statement criticizing the outcome, even though another group of observers, headed by retired general Colin Powell, praised the election — happy that anyone had voted at all. The fact that two groups were watching that day was a testament to Carter's pioneering efforts at election monitoring.

The duty could be dangerous. In Guyana in 1992, rioting broke out. Carter and his party were detained at the airport when they tried to leave the country, then were trapped in a building surrounded by an angry mob that had stolen their computers. Carter threatened to contact Washington and arrange for military evacuation before the regime — embarrassed by having lost the election — finally relented and set the group free. Mozambique's 1999 election took place when the roads were still lined with thousands of land mines. This meant that the monitors often had no choice but to relieve themselves in the middle of the road.

The Carter Center won't monitor an election in any country that lacks a formalized national postelection process for dealing with voting irregularities. The United States, where elections are handled by states and counties, has no such national process and is thus ineligible for the Center's seal of approval.

Carter has nonetheless worked to repair American democracy. After the disputed outcome of the extremely close 2000 presidential election, he and former president Ford cochaired a commission whose recommendations were largely adopted in the 2002 Help America Vote Act, which provided federal support to help states upgrade their voting systems and required them to provide provisional ballots and voter registration information that are important bulwarks against voter suppression. In 2004, Carter and former secretary of state James A. Baker cochaired a second commission that recommended eighty-seven more common-sense reforms, including ideas to expand participation. The commission found that while mail-in ballots "remain the largest source of potential voter fraud," such ballots were a good idea, and Oregon, which pioneered vote-by-mail in 1998, was a national model for how to do it right. In 2020, amid the coronavirus pandemic, Carter urged "immediate steps to expand vote-by-mail and other measures that can help protect the core of American democracy: the right of our citizens to vote."

Surprisingly, the Carter Center for many years was not a major player on human rights. Carter preferred to act quietly in private with heads of state; he was more of what foreign policy types call "an engagement guy," meaning that he was less interested in speaking truth to power than in getting to know foreign leaders so that he could influence their behavior.

Carter did host human rights conferences, cosponsored a prestigious human rights award with the philanthropist Dominique de Menil, strongly supported the 1998 establishment of the International Criminal Court (despite US opposition) and sent dozens of letters over the years that led to the release of hundreds of political prisoners. But he rarely used his meetings with thuggish leaders to pressure them on human rights.

There were exceptions. In 2002 Carter went to Cuba and called out President Fidel Castro on live TV over his human rights violations, the first time since the 1959 Cuban Revolution that Cubans had heard any criticism at home of their government. But he usually gave preference to peacekeeping. During the conflict in Bosnia, for instance, he reasoned that if you could stop the war, you would stop the "rape camps" established by Serbs in the 1990s. He was only partially right about this: after Carter engineered a brief cease-fire, some abuses ended, but many others did not.

Out of office, Carter had much less leverage to bring about change — no foreign aid to withhold or sanctions to impose. His approach was to convince authoritarian leaders to step down with the promise that they would receive amnesty. This worked in Haiti and a few other places, but more often, the dictator continued his atrocities while enjoying the stature that came from having met with a former American president. This lessened the impact of Carter's work, but it didn't keep him from trying the same thing with the next tyrant.

If Carter's belief in human rights grew out of his experience in the Jim Crow South, so did his layered attitude toward human rights abusers. He knew firsthand that even the worst southern racist had some good qualities. Now he set about looking for something to work with in the collection of louts, crooks, and killers who too often became militia leaders or heads of state. When Carter was president, he met with them because of their positions; after leaving office, he met with them because, for better or worse, they held the keys to peace, public health, and at least the chance for better treatment of their people.

As a Christian, Carter believed even the worst human beings are redeemable. "He always looked for — and believed in — the inherent good in each person," recalled Jennifer McCoy, a Carter Center official who accompanied Jimmy and Rosalynn on several trips. He figured that somewhere, buried deep, these men contained a tiny reservoir of humanity that could be harnessed to their naked self-interest. In order to make any progress as a mediator, he needed warring thugs and dictators to trust him. But just because he wanted them to trust him didn't mean that he ever trusted them. For all the charges of softness, there was always a hard, pragmatic imperative at work. "We fill vacuums," he said. "We reach out to bad guys if it can stop a war." The advantage of dealing with dictators over democrats — as Carter first learned with Anwar Sadat and Menachem Begin — is that dictators more often have the power to make good on their commitments.

All of this was hard for the human rights community to accept. Any time Carter met with murderous dictators like Mobutu Sese Seko of Zaire or Mengistu Haile Mariam of Ethiopia, Karin Ryan, the director of the Carter Center's human rights program, would field angry calls. "My human rights friends would yell at me, 'How can he shake hands with these monsters?' I'd say, 'He's wearing a flak jacket.' "

Sometimes that was literally true. In Liberia in 1989, the Carters were circling the airport above the capital city of Monrovia but couldn't land

959

because of gunfire on the runway. They had donned flak jackets and prepared to enter a war zone when a Carter aide got Charles Taylor, an American-educated warlord, on the phone and persuaded him to order an immediate cease-fire. Two years later, the Carters, accompanied by son Jeff, arrived back in Monrovia amid random gunfire and decapitations in the street. Carter arranged to see Taylor at the rubber plantation he used as his rebel headquarters and convinced him to release hundreds of hostages, which he did after seizing their shoes and forcing them to walk barefoot back to the capital.

A Baptist and lover of classical music, Taylor charmed many Americans, including televangelist Pat Robertson (who got into the diamond business with him). While Jimmy and Rosalynn saw that he was "corrupt and a despot," they thought he had what Carter called "a good side" — something he had said about some of his white supremacist neighbors in Sumter County.

After helping to mediate the end to a long civil war, Carter convinced Taylor to submit to elections in 1997, which he won with the slogan "He killed my ma, he killed my pa, but I will vote for him." After his victory, Taylor at first refused to cooperate with Carter Center health workers. "I can bring enough vaccinations here for every child in the country, but I can't gather people to come out and be inoculated," Rosalynn told him sharply. "That's your job."

Taylor would continue to plunder Liberia's wealth and that of neighboring Sierra Leone. His army, which included twelve-year-old soldiers armed with AK-47s, was responsible for violence that left 250,000 dead before he was finally removed from power in 2003. Once again, the Carters were there to help pick up the pieces, monitoring elections and working to establish a justice system for the country.

Even in the face of depravity, Carter felt that pounding the table was pointless. Karin Ryan noticed that her boss had a quality of looking people in the eye and making them think he was their friend. "He can tell you to go to hell, and you think you'll enjoy the trip," Andrew Young recalled. "He has the ability to reach for the best in that person — an almost magical power to inspire someone by telling them, 'You can make history.'"

After a disappointing trip to Tunisia, Ryan asked him, "When are you going to get mad?" The answer was never. Ryan saw Carter as an "informed optimist." He went into meetings with one thing on his mind: preventing bullets from flying. Everything else was secondary, and he grew impatient when other people couldn't see it that way. Carter's belief in avoiding war was so strong that he once wrote an essay on how the American Civil War (with casualties of around 750,000) was not, as most historians conclude, an "irrepressible conflict," and might have been prevented with a negotiated settlement that left slavery to die more slowly.

In 1994 Carter faced a rebellion within the human rights community. Michael Posner of the Lawyers Committee for Human Rights and Kenneth Roth of Human Rights Watch — arguably the top two human rights experts in the United States — came to Atlanta for a tense meeting. They were concerned that Carter had helped cut a deal granting amnesty to Haitian strongman

Raoul Cédras. Worse, Carter had met with Radovan Karadzic and other Bosnian Serbs then making headlines for engaging in "ethnic cleansing" — genocide — against Bosnian Muslims. He even kept a picture of himself with Karadzic in his office.

Richard Holbrooke, a former assistant secretary of state under Carter now working in the Balkans as a top diplomat for Clinton, thought Carter figured he might be able to save the souls of war criminals. The truth was more prosaic: Carter felt that human rights are impossible to secure in a society wracked by violence. He wasn't prioritizing peace over human rights so much as saying the former was a prerequisite for the latter. He believed "war is the greatest violation of human rights" and vowed to continue talking to war criminals because they were the ones with the power to stop people from killing each other.

Posner and Roth felt that Carter had it backward: if the international community ostracized human rights abusers, there would be fewer wars. They remember Carter's response as being along the lines of "That's nice in theory, but I'm sitting there with people who have weapons, and you're not." Rosalynn grew emotional during the meeting and said passionately that she and Jimmy would do whatever it took to stop the fighting.

Sudan soon became a flashpoint in the continuing argument. President Omar al-Bashir, who had sheltered every terrorist from Osama bin Laden to Carlos the Jackal, was a notorious war criminal. Carter developed a special fondness for Sudan and visited repeatedly to negotiate cease-fires between al-Bashir's regime and the separatists of the south. He was photographed smiling and

962

shaking hands with the tyrant, which rankled human rights activists; al-Bashir felt free to persecute people without worry of being rebuked even by one of the world's great champions of human rights. Carter, they charged, was "enabling impunity."

After George W. Bush took office in 2001, the new president made the ritual call to Carter and asked if there was anything he could do for him. Carter said, yes: focus more on Sudan. Bush complied. A 2005 agreement negotiated by the State Department resolved the civil war and led to an independent South Sudan, but the talks hardly ended the violence. Genocide continued in the Darfur region of Sudan, where hundreds of thousands of people were killed and millions displaced, mostly by al-Bashir's Janjaweed militias.

When al-Bashir was indicted by the International Criminal Court in 2008 for genocide and war crimes, Ryan instructed the Carter Center staff not to take any more pictures of Carter shaking his hand. The conflict resolution team didn't like the indictment, but Carter on this occasion sided more with the Center's human rights staffers. He scrawled on the memo detailing al-Bashir's indictment: "This will put more pressure on him."

In 2019 al-Bashir was finally deposed in a coup after a thirty-year reign. During all that time, Jimmy and Rosalynn never flagged in their quest for peace in Sudan. The Carter Center's observation missions and election monitoring and the former president's deep personal commitment helped build a fragile civil society in one of the most desperate regions of the world.

For Carter, peace would always be preeminent.

963

He was not a pacifist, but Hamilton Jordan thought he was close to one. He believed, as an article of faith, in exhausting all diplomatic options before war.

To the chagrin of his successors, he would pursue world peace whether they liked it or not.

# 40
## FREELANCE SECRETARY OF STATE

Carter traveled to more than 140 countries after leaving office — returning to several of them more than a dozen times — and he said he always kept the State Department apprised of his trips. But the notifications were often pro forma, as if he merely had to check a box before going off on his own.

It was no secret that Carter was not a member in good standing of the ex-presidents' club, in part because he never accepted their code. The unwritten rules aren't complicated: former presidents are expected to build their libraries and at least try to hold their tongues about the incumbent, not complain — as Carter often did — that the policy is wrong or they are underused by the president. No one sitting in the Oval Office likes the idea of a freelance secretary of state. At the same time, five of the six presidents who succeeded Carter (all except Reagan) recognized the usefulness of his vast knowledge and high-level contacts. The challenge for them was managing their high-maintenance predecessor.

When Carter was president, he took care to cultivate relationships with his living predecessors — Richard Nixon and Gerald Ford — and he welcomed their support on China, the Panama Canal, and other issues. After leaving office, he got along exceptionally well with Ford, who joined him on several postpresidential projects. Ford and Carter promised that each would deliver the eulogy if the other died first. Ford did, and Carter remembered him warmly at his funeral in 2006. George H. W. Bush believed the Ford-Carter bond "set a wonderful example of cooperation and friendship" between old rivals.

Carter's successors were a different matter. He said he had "okay relations" with the Bushes — especially George H. W. Bush — and Donald Trump in his first two years. It was the Democratic presidents, Clinton and Obama, whom he found "cooler and more aloof." No one who watched their interactions over the years would be left to wonder why.

If he had been reelected in 1980, Carter's top priority was to complete what he'd started at Camp David and bring peace and a Palestinian homeland to the Middle East. As president, he might have had the clout to get it done. Out of office, he soldiered on, working the periphery as if it were the center of the action. After the Syrians were implicated in a 1984 attempt to blow up an Israeli airliner, the Reagan administration banned high-level contacts with Damascus. Carter, who believed drawing Syrian president Hafiz al-Assad into the peace process was critical to its success, blithely ignored the restrictions and spent nine hours in talks with Assad, just one of many fruitless visits.

This unfinished business of his presidency now preoccupied him. In the summer of 1987 alone,

Carter met with Mikhail Gorbachev, Deng Xiao-ping, and Margaret Thatcher on Middle East peace. But with the Reagan administration uninterested in the process he had launched, his efforts went nowhere.

This irked Carter, who blamed Reagan not just for the stalemate in the Middle East but for dangerous militarism and the growing gap between rich and poor at home. "He stopped upward mobility," he said later. But he also knew he had been bested by a political master. At the dedication of the Carter Library in 1986, Reagan gave a gracious speech, praising Carter's "passionate intellect and commitment." Carter replied with more than mock sincerity, "As I listened to you talk, I understood more clearly than I ever did in my life why you won in 1980 and I lost."

Rosalynn adopted the habit of avoiding any mention of Reagan's name, preferring "the next administration" or "Jimmy's successor." She felt Reagan "made us [Americans] comfortable with our prejudices" and that much of the progress in Plains on race relations was reversed once Reagan became president. She believed the climate Reagan fostered helped explain why the Lion's Club swimming pool near their house in Plains that Jimmy had helped build in the 1950s and helped integrate in the late 1960s had — in the 1980s — been turned into an all-white private club. And the personal snubs continued to hurt. "Even when we left the White House, we were 'country come to town' as far as they [the Reagans] were concerned," Rosalynn remembered. The Carters weren't even invited to the White House for the unveiling of their official portraits.

■ ■ ■ ■

After George H. W. Bush was elected in 1988, Secretary of State James Baker consulted Carter often. Carter helped Bush out in Panama in 1989 by confronting Manuel Noriega after he rigged an election. He told the dictator and his henchmen, "You are thieves." But his most conspicuous early diplomatic success was in Nicaragua, which he visited eight times in a five-year period. In February 1990, for the first time since the Russian Revolution, a Communist regime (the Sandinistas) lost a democratic election. If the shocking results held, Violeta Chamorro, a newspaper publisher, would replace President Daniel Ortega and become the first female head of state in the Americas.

But five decades had passed since the last peaceful transfer of power in Nicaragua, and this one was by no means assured. Ortega had been confident of reelection — all the polls showed him well ahead — and he was not inclined to relinquish power. The Carter Center monitored the election, and, after finding it fair, Carter met with Ortega late into the night. He told Ortega, who had followed the familiar trajectory of dashing revolutionary to repressive thug, that he knew what it felt like to lose and that he could perhaps make a comeback someday. (He did.) Carter's personal experience in 1980 impressed Ortega, and he left office peacefully. President Bush was thrilled with Carter's role. "This sent a powerful message throughout the region and to Moscow," he recalled. Later, Carter resolved devilishly complex disputes between the Sandinistas and those whose

968

property they had seized during their revolution.

In the run-up to the 1991 Gulf War, Carter's relationship with President Bush turned sour. Carter felt passionately that Saddam Hussein's invasion of Kuwait wasn't worth going to war over, even though Bush cited the Carter Doctrine in justifying it. The former president said so publicly, then took matters a fateful step further, writing each member of the UN Security Council and urging them to vote against the United States on the resolution authorizing coalition forces to intervene. Canadian prime minister Brian Mulroney received Carter's letter and alerted the Bush White House.

Carter argued that there was no difference between expressing one's views publicly and privately. Bush, who recalled "working night and day" to bring the allies aboard, vehemently disagreed. "We only have one president at a time," he said in 2016. He was appalled that a former president would "foment opposition to the policy objective of his own country." Even many Democrats felt Bush had the better argument.

Carter didn't care about procedural niceties or whether Bush would stop liking him. When he was trying to keep the bullets from flying, his Plains friend Jill Stuckey explained, he never "gave a rat's ass what people thought of him." Rick Hertzberg noted that Americans admire ruthlessness in the waging of war but not peace. Carter was "a Patton of peace," Hertzberg said, referring to General George S. Patton, whose single-minded devotion to achieving his objectives during World War II was remembered longer than the harsh criticism he received from many contemporaries for improper behavior.

Bush's apoplectic team briefly considered charging Carter with violation of the Logan Act, the 1799 federal law that criminalizes unauthorized negotiation with a foreign power. Bush himself was more merciful. After he won UN approval and liberated Kuwait, he dropped the matter. In 2006 Carter infuriated Bush again when he used his eulogy at Coretta Scott King's funeral to implicitly criticize President George W. Bush's response to Hurricane Katrina the year before. Bush Sr. thought Carter's comments about his son were "out of line and untrue," but at the end of his life, he made a point of saying, "I respect this good man."

Carter's most infamous connection after leaving the presidency was with Yāssir 'Arafāt, the PLO chairman whose fingerprints were on several terrorist acts against Israel. On his own authority, he undertook a decadelong effort to buff 'Arafāt's global reputation. Carter's goal was legitimate: to make the PLO a plausible negotiating partner for Israel. To that end, he helped nudge 'Arafāt down the road toward recognizing Israel's right to exist, a prerequisite for peace. Where he erred was in moving from engagement to something closer to friendship, though Carter later claimed the two men never fully trusted each other. It helped that 'Arafāt told Carter after his presidency that rejecting Camp David was one of the worst mistakes he ever made.* Later, Carter made a point of hosting 'Arafāt in Plains, where the PLO leader was

*Israeli Prime Minister Benjamin Netanyahu, by contrast, told Carter at a funeral that Camp David, including peace with Egypt, was a mistake.

970

incredulous that the Carters lived in such a modest house.

Carter worked sincerely to convince the Palestinians to emphasize nonviolent resistance, which he thought was both more moral and — as the American civil rights movement proved — more effective than terrorism.

But for all of his private diplomacy, the peace process proceeded largely independent of his efforts. It was the 1991 Madrid Conference, organized by George H. W. Bush and Jim Baker, that led to the establishment of the Palestinian Authority and the first direct negotiations between Israel and the Palestinians. In the next few years, Carter sometimes darted out ahead of the process. After 'Arafāt returned from exile in 1994 and held two elections, Carter rashly called him "the president of Palestine." This assumed statehood was a fait accompli after elections instead of the product of negotiations, as Carter himself envisioned at Camp David.

Throughout this period, Carter's views on the substance of the peace process were fairly conventional. He consistently favored a two-state solution along borders established by the United Nations in 1967 and spoke out against violence on all sides. But after so many years of American politicians ardently backing Israel or at least appearing evenhanded, his obvious sympathy with the Palestinians disturbed many American Jews. They felt, with some justification, that his condemnations of Israeli behavior were stronger than any criticism he leveled at Arabs. Carter bristled at the idea that he was guilty of a double standard; for all of the Arab abuses, Carter felt Israel was the guiltier party because it was the primary

971

country in the region acting in violation of international law.

Carter's sympathy for the Palestinians grew partly out of guilt for failing to resolve their fate at Camp David. But there were deeper motivations at work. The Palestinians reminded him of blacks in South Africa or the Jim Crow South: a beaten-down people, stripped of their land and persecuted by much wealthier and more powerful neighbors. In 2006, he went on Israel Radio to say that the country's West Bank policy "perpetuates even worse instances of apartness, or apartheid, than we witnessed even in South Africa."

Progressives around the world — especially Europeans — thought Carter was brave for making this argument. But many Jews and conservatives agreed with Natan Sharansky that Carter's "blind sympathy for the suffering" caused him to lose "moral clarity" on the stakes in the region. "We saw Carter as incredibly self-centered, stubborn, and dangerously naive" on the Mideast, recalled Brent Scowcroft, Bush's national security adviser.

This was unduly harsh. Most of the time he was just doing what all good diplomats — official and nonofficial — should do: namely, talk and talk and talk some more. The problem came when he undermined those efforts with his prickly pride.

During the 1992 presidential campaign, the tensions between Carter and Bill Clinton of a dozen years earlier resurfaced. "People are looking for somebody who is honest and tells the truth," Carter said in a remark that took on added meaning because it came amid the first national stories of Governor Clinton lying about sex. Clinton, for his part, worried that Carter's failures as president would rub off on another southern governor and hurt his chances.

After the election, Clinton wouldn't take Carter's calls. He finally handed him off to Warren Christopher, his transition director and choice for secretary of state. "Chris" quickly grew tired of Carter, too, and fobbed him off on his undersecretary, Peter Tarnoff. Carter felt snubbed. Clinton's basic problem with Carter was that he too often crossed the line from expressing his views on a subject to saying the president "should" do something. Carter admitted later that while he didn't intend to be personally critical, "I may not always have succeeded."

Case in point: a week before Clinton's inauguration, Carter told the New York Times that he was "disappointed" that thirteen-year-old Chelsea Clinton would not be attending public school in Washington, DC, as Amy had. Carter's comments to the Times were widely viewed as self-righteous, but few knew that they were also hypocritical: he and Rosalynn had sent Jeff to the private Woodward Academy in Atlanta when he was governor, and Amy attended the same boarding school when she transferred from the Sumter County system in the early 1980s.

The Clintons retaliated in a petty fashion. It was no coincidence that the Carters were seated far back at the inaugural gala. Onstage, Clinton thanked Barbra Streisand, Michael Jackson, and other celebrities for attending but not the most recent Democratic president. Terry Adamson, the Carters' longtime attorney, said he had never seen Rosalynn so upset. Over the next eight years, Hillary Clinton made several trips to Atlanta and never stopped by to say hello to her.

By contrast, Bill Clinton would have to deal with Jimmy Carter and his unique role on the world stage whether he liked it or not. This was particularly so in the case of the Middle East peace process. Carter's contacts with 'Arafāt helped set the table for the Oslo Accords, facilitated by the Norwegians and signed in 1993 at the White House, where Clinton convinced 'Arafāt and a reluctant-looking Israeli prime minister Yitzhak Rabin to shake hands. What had seemed far-fetched — negotiating with 'Arafāt — was now considered more acceptable, thanks in part to Carter.

As Carter moved around the world, the Clinton White House had no confidence that he would limit himself to his assigned mission without making concessions that the president never approved. The White House knew that Carter understood that recalling a former chief executive like some errant ambassador was difficult if not impossible, which meant that he could hog glory and operate outside the president's control. This happened twice in 1994, a year that was simultaneously the peak of Carter's success as a peacemaker and the nadir of his forty-year relationship with Clinton.

The first flashpoint was over Korea. Kim Il-sung, the founder of North Korea, had written President-Elect Carter in 1976 proposing direct ties between Pyongyang and Washington. Even after Carter failed to fulfill his campaign promise to withdraw US forces from South Korea, "the Great Leader," as Kim was known inside his totalitarian country, kept writing the president through intermediaries. Out of office, Carter wanted to meet with Kim, but in 1989, Secretary of State Baker nixed the trip.

Then US–North Korean relations took a nose-dive. In 1992 International Atomic Energy Agency inspectors concluded that North Korea was diverting enough plutonium from its Yongbyon nuclear power plant for one or two Hiroshima-style nuclear bombs. By early 1994, an air of crisis had enveloped Washington, with even some liberal pundits in support of bombing the reactor. Kim again invited Carter to visit, and this time it was President Clinton who vetoed the trip. Instead, he sent evangelist Billy Graham, who informed him upon returning home that the person Kim really wanted to see was Carter. Jim Laney, who had left the presidency of Emory to become Clinton's ambassador to South Korea, flew back from Seoul in February to warn Clinton in person that he could have "fifty thousand body bags coming home" if Clinton didn't tamp down the war fever.

When Kim invited Carter a third time, Vice President Al Gore — Carter's biggest backer in the administration — advised Clinton to let him go to Pyongyang. Clinton did so reluctantly, with the proviso that Carter make it clear he was acting as a private citizen, not an official envoy. While Washington worried about appeasement, Seoul feared a cataclysmic war. On June 15, the day the Carters crossed the Demilitarized Zone into North Korea, Brent Scowcroft cowrote an op-ed piece in the *Washington Post* advocating the destruction of the Yongbyon facility in a US air strike: "The time for temporizing is over." Scowcroft's views were largely shared by Clinton's defense secretary, William Perry.

His first full day in Pyongyang, Carter awoke at

three in the morning and wrote a letter to be delivered to Clinton if his mission did not bear fruit. He felt failure meant war unless the president announced immediate talks. Upon arriving at the presidential palace, Carter found the eighty-two-year-old Kim much warmer and more alert than expected. Kim fumed over Clinton's taunts but offered the broad outlines of a deal: North Korea would stop developing its nuclear program if the United States helped supply light-water reactors for peaceful use. When Carter raised the issue of the two IAEA inspectors threatened with expulsion from the Yongbyon reactor, Kim, a crafty despot, feigned ignorance.

That was the opening Carter needed. The next day, he reported back to Washington that Kim had agreed to a nuclear freeze and would let the inspectors stay. He told Robert Gallucci, the official US negotiator, that he was about to announce the deal on CNN International, which had a camera crew and uplink capacity with him in North Korea. Gallucci didn't understand at first how this would box in Clinton, whose threat of sanctions — opposed at the United Nations by China and Russia — was now fatally weakened. On the air, Carter made Kim seem reasonable and said that "very positive steps" had been taken to end the crisis.

Clinton was having one of his purple fits, raging to aides. He had dispatched Carter on a kind of reconnaissance mission, and now he seemed to be selling out the US position and negotiating on cable TV. One Cabinet member called Carter a "treasonous prick," and the president did not disagree. Gore, by contrast, saw a chance "to make lemonade out of this lemon." He contacted the South Koreans, and they jointly developed an ad hoc plan to move forward. Carter was instructed to send Kim Il-sung a letter with specific American conditions. Kim not only agreed to all of the conditions, but also invited the Carters aboard his yacht for a cruise down the Taedong River. At first, Carter pressed Kim forcefully on recovering the hidden remains of American soldiers killed in the Korean War. But then, with the CNN cameras rolling, he got far out ahead of US policy by saying the Clinton administration had "stopped the sanctions activity at the United Nations." Within an hour, the State Department issued a statement that the former president was mistaken.

This freelancing on sanctions, which badly undercut the president, grew out of Carter's deepest convictions. After having imposed harsh sanctions against the Soviet Union as president, he was now philosophically opposed to them unless they were narrowly focused on restricting the travel and finances of leaders; otherwise he felt broad economic sanctions just let regimes blame all of their problems on the United States, which simultaneously exalted the dictators and hurt their people. This was certainly true in the case of the trade embargo with Cuba. But Carter ignored the fact that sanctions can provide crucial leverage — for example, in the case of helping Barack Obama achieve a nuclear deal with Iran in 2015 — and that lifting them simply rewarded bad actors.

In this case, Carter's unorthodox approach proved sound. Just when his mission seemed doomed, it came up aces. Carter convinced Kim Il-sung and South Korean president Kim Young-sam to schedule the first-ever summit between the two Koreas, to be followed by real arms reduction talks. Don Oberdorfer, for decades the top American correspondent in Korea, marveled that the prospect of a meeting meant "the immense tension and great danger in the Korean peninsula" had given way "to the greatest hope in years."

When he arrived back in Washington, Carter learned that Clinton, still irate and ungrateful, had no interest in seeing him. White House aides were chilly, and TV talking heads compared Carter to Neville Chamberlain. But by giving Kim Il-sung the status of hosting an American president, Carter helped him to back down without losing face, always a critical factor in power relations. In doing so, Carter helped avert a devastating war that many expected.*

Three weeks later, Kim Il-sung dropped dead of a heart attack. Carter heard the news in Japan, just after he'd climbed more than twelve thousand feet to the summit of Mount Fuji. Kim's son Kim Jong-il wasn't nearly strong enough to bring off the historic summit with South Korea, which never happened. But Carter's mission bore fruit nonetheless. On October 21, 1994, the United States and North Korea — meeting in Geneva — signed the Agreed Framework, which froze the North Korean nuclear program and, at least in theory, allowed its spent fuel to be monitored by inspectors.

In the years that followed, Washington dragged its feet on providing the light-water reactors and strengthening relations. Pyongyang, which at first

*President Trump tried something similar in 2018. The difference was that Trump had no plan for moving forward with negotiations.

abided by the terms of the agreement, announced that if the United States was reneging, it would, too. After George W. Bush's election in 2000, his point man, UN Ambassador John Bolton, scuttled the whole deal without even bothering to protest North Korea's violations. Some hard-liners have argued that if Clinton had bombed the Yongbyon reactor in 1994 instead of letting Carter cut a deal, North Korea would be nuclear free today. This is at odds with everything we know about how that country reacts to outside pressure. Carter was out of line, but he cooled tensions on the Korean peninsula and set up the first bilateral talks.

In 1993 as many as two hundred thousand Haitians were poised to board makeshift boats and set out for the Florida coast, fleeing Haitian strongman General Raoul Cédras, who had taken power in a coup. It looked like another Mariel boatlift. With Haiti experiencing a return to the bad old days of dictators "Papa Doc" and "Baby Doc" Duvalier, Clinton refocused policy on returning the democratically elected former president, Jean-Bertrand Aristide, to power. As the drums began sounding for a "humanitarian" military intervention, Carter — who had already made eight trips to Haiti to lessen tensions — pointed out that nearly eighty years had passed since the US Marines last landed in Port-au-Prince, and when they did, they stayed for nearly two decades.

When Haitian protests forced a US ship, the USS *Harlan County,* to turn back from the Haitian coast, Clinton was embarrassed. In 1994 he issued an ultimatum to Cédras and obtained a UN

Security Council resolution authorizing an invasion. The Pentagon drew up plans for deploying twenty-five thousand troops from the US Army's Eighty-Second Airborne and Tenth Mountain Divisions.

As war loomed, Cédras invited Carter to talk, which the Clinton White House figured was just a ploy to stay in power. But once again, as in the North Korean crisis three months earlier, Al Gore thought it was a good idea to send the former president to a hot spot. Clinton and Warren Christopher felt they had seen this movie before. As George Stephanopoulos, then a top Clinton aide, wrote later, Carter's "pacifist leanings could undercut Clinton's ultimatum. He was also a bit of a Lone Ranger." So Senator Sam Nunn and Colin Powell, former chairman of the Joint Chiefs of Staff and eager to get his feet wet as a diplomat, were recruited to join the team.

Clinton rashly set a timetable: if General Cédras didn't resign by September 19, the United States would invade. "Your time is up," Clinton told the dictator publicly. Carter, Nunn, and Powell arrived with only thirty-six hours to negotiate an agreement that would avoid a war in the Caribbean. Powell told the Haitian junta: "Let me make sure you understand what you're facing," then ticked off the specifics of the overwhelmingly military force sitting just offshore. Bill Bush, a longtime Secret Service agent for Carter, was on the verge of extracting him from Haiti for his own safety, leaving behind Powell and Nunn, who were not the Secret Service's responsibility.

As the talks wore on, Carter asked to see the general's wife, Yannick, and their family. This was a clever move that softened up Cédras for a few concessions, but he still refused to relinquish power. General Hugh Shelton, commander of the US invasion force, was worried that Carter, Nunn, and Powell would be taken hostage. He phoned the White House and shouted, "Goddamn it! Get them out of there!" But Carter and his team still refused to give up. When one of Cédras's generals burst into the room waving a submachine gun, Carter's face turned beet red. "You must accept this agreement now, or your children will be killed," he said. "Your country will be burned." Powell was impressed by Carter's toughness, but Cédras remained unmoved.

Nunn said later that the breakthrough came when Carter — over the objections of the State Department — had the inspired idea of circumventing Cédras and negotiating instead with the eighty-one-year-old provisional president, Emil Jonassaint, whom everyone had assumed was completely under Cédras's control. Jonassaint was indeed powerless — a ceremonial interim president — but he rose to the occasion and suddenly assumed moral authority over the junta: "Can you defend our country from an attack by the United States? Can you?" he scolded Cédras. The general finally agreed to a deal in which the junta stepped back from power and allowed US forces to enter Haiti on friendly terms. The crisis was over.

But once again, Carter's ego got in the way of his triumph. Back in Washington, he got up early and sinned again on CNN, praising Cédras and downplaying his human rights abuses. Decades later, Carter had no regrets: "It was the only way to report the facts to the public." He still didn't see what was wrong with appearing on TV before briefing the sitting president. "Carter has no clear idea of the shrine he seeks except that it is built for him," wrote columnist Murray Kempton.

The meeting that morning at the White House was perhaps the most contentious ever between a president and a former president. Clinton, failing to appreciate that Carter and company had spared him a bloody and open-ended intervention, was indignant over Carter's unauthorized victory lap; Carter gave Clinton an earful for issuing ultimatums while his emissaries were still on the ground in Haiti. Nunn made peace between them in time for the East Room news conference, but Carter blew himself up all over again by telling Maureen Dowd of the *New York Times* that he was "ashamed" of Clinton's sanctions on Haiti, which hurt the poor. He then came across as flaky when he showed reporters a peace-loving poem from his upcoming poetry collection; the next week's cover stories in *Time* and *Newsweek* would be less than flattering. Senator Daniel Patrick Moynihan — understanding that peace was more important than the bruised feelings of an incumbent president — dissented from the disdain. He thought Carter deserved "five Nobel Prizes" for Haiti alone, but — no surprise, given the controversy — he didn't get one.

Late 1994 brought a final peacemaking challenge for Carter in Bosnia. After much wrangling, he negotiated a brief cease-fire at Christmas. This was his third diplomatic win of the year, but it fell apart within a month.* Clinton was through with

*In 1995, when Richard Holbrooke, Clinton's envoy for the former Yugoslavia, was negotiating with Radovan Karadzic, the Serbian war criminal, Karadzic told him, "If we can't get anything done here, I will call

982

him. The Carters were never invited to a state dinner, and Jimmy felt unwelcome at the 1996 Democratic Convention in Chicago, so he went fishing instead. Late in his second term, Clinton named a *Seawolf*-class nuclear submarine for Carter and awarded him the Presidential Medal of Freedom, and Carter spoke graciously at the dedication of the Clinton Library in 2004. But the wounds never healed. The entire Carter family favored Barack Obama over Hillary Clinton in 2008 and Bernie Sanders over her in 2016.

Carter didn't know it yet, but the year 1994 was a marker in his life. At age seventy, his days as a presidential emissary were largely over. For the next twenty-five years, he would continue to meet often with foreign leaders in war-torn countries, and to use his resourcefulness and experience to settle disputes, free prisoners, and work tirelessly as a warrior for peace. But well into his nineties, he waited in vain by the phone for his successors to tap him for major diplomatic assignments. While this dismissive treatment of a difficult predecessor was understandable from their perspective, they often failed to realize that the interests and prerogatives of the president — while hardly irrelevant — were not always the same as the larger interests of the nation and the international community, which continued to be advanced by the Carters' constant efforts to confront many of the major challenges of their times.

---

President Carter. I am in regular contact with him." Holbrooke had to remind him that while he respected his old boss, Carter was merely a private citizen: "We take orders only from President Clinton."

# 41

## SUNDAY SCHOOL TEACHER

When he left office, Carter was ranked in the bottom third of presidents, but by 2002, a Gallup survey showed him in the top third, a sign, apparently, that his inspiring postpresidency had helped resurrect the reputation of his administration. Of course, the venom from conservatives continued, and even liberals settled into the cliché that he would be remembered as a great *former* president. This would annoy Jimmy and Rosalynn for the rest of their days.

Ever since he missed out in 1979 for Camp David, Carter yearned for a Nobel Peace Prize. But he was embarrassed to be nominated — then passed over — year after year. After he lost in 2000, Rosalynn reported to Hamilton Jordan that "Jimmy is livid" and had drafted a letter to the Nobel Committee stating that he would not accept the prize if offered it. When Carter came on the phone, he told Jordan, "They can take their damn prize and shove it!" Jordan advised him the letter would look like sour grapes, and Carter never sent it.

In 2002 he finally won, but, as was often the case with Carter, his triumph was not unalloyed. Gunnar Berge, chairman of the Nobel Peace Prize

Committee, used the prize as a cudgel against George W. Bush: he said the award to Carter "must also be seen as criticism of the line the current US administration has taken on Iraq." Carter was proud of his early and loud opposition to the Iraq War in speeches and op-ed pieces, and so this unorthodox announcement did nothing to dampen his satisfaction. He brought a planeload of family and friends (including Willie Nelson) to Oslo for the ceremony, where he explained in his short speech that without Martin Luther King Jr., the 1964 winner, a white southerner like him could never have been president. He decried "the growing chasm between the richest and poorest people on earth" and argued that "war may sometimes be a necessary evil. But no matter how necessary, it is always an evil, never a good."

The Nobel hardly turned Carter into a universally admired humanitarian. The first decade of the twenty-first century would show that his days as a juicy target were not yet behind him.

In late 2000, as President Clinton prepared to leave office, his peace initiative fell just short. Yāssir 'Arafāt proved to be a poor leader — tolerant of corruption and full of false promises — and that year he rejected a generous offer of a Palestinian state from the Israeli prime minister, Ehud Barak. Carter was of no help to Clinton in trying to get 'Arafāt to change his mind. Carter's view — common in the region — was that 'Arafāt would be assassinated by Arab extremists if he accepted the deal.

In January 2006 Hamas, one of the most lethal terrorist organizations in the world, won a stunning victory in the first elections in the West Bank and Gaza. Three months later, Carter met in Syria with Khaled Meshaal, head of Hamas. Carter insisted that he had cleared the meeting with President George W. Bush's State Department and was doing nothing to legitimize terrorists. He had agreed to meet with Meshaal only after Hamas won the election, a point he would later reinforce in a speech to the Israeli Knesset. His goal throughout was to end Hamas's schism with the less radical (if more corrupt) party Fatah so that Israel would have a single Palestinian negotiating partner and could move toward peace.

In private, Carter chastised both Hamas and Fatah for arresting each other's leaders, making it harder to unify. But in public, he praised Hamas and said "there's a good chance" it would change its charter to renounce violence and its long-standing commitment to destroy Israel. Even after Hamas, unchastened by the responsibilities of governing Gaza, stepped up its brutality, Carter continued to hold out hope that it might change. Had he engaged in wishful thinking? "I engaged in wishful thinking on all sides," he concluded later. That hope, he felt, was the only way to move forward, even if it looked naive.

The Israeli critique of Carter was that as a liberal Christian who felt guilty about Jim Crow segregation, he would always side with the dispossessed out of a sense of social justice, even if the weaker party was a bunch of terrorists. Ami Ayalon, former chief of Israeli internal security and a liberal supporter of a Palestinian state, gave Carter full credit for his towering achievement at Camp David, which he thought other Israelis devalued unfairly. But, he said, "We believe he hates us. He cannot understand Israeli fear [of suicide bombers and rocket launchers]. He could care less about that." Ironically, some of the fiercest criticism of him came from Russian Jews who were allowed to immigrate to Israel in the late 1970s thanks in large part to the efforts of the Carter administration.

In November 2006 Carter published a book, *Palestine: Peace Not Apartheid,* that caused a huge backlash. The problem was not the book itself, which offered fairly traditional ideas on the peace process and the need for a two-state solution; it was the title, which seemed to compare Israelis to racist Afrikaners. Before publication, Carter's literary agent, Lynn Nesbit, and his editor at Simon & Schuster, Alice Mayhew, strongly advised him to change the title, but he refused. He thought a provocative title would stir much-needed debate on the Israeli occupation. Instead, the debate was about Carter's inflammatory rhetoric.* He later regretted his decision, because

*The book caused another flap when former US negotiator Dennis Ross said Carter had misconstrued Ross's proposed maps for the region. And Carter misstated some history. He understated anti-Jewish violence in Jerusalem in the early twentieth century and wrote, not for the first time, that Israel attacked Jordan in the 1967 Six Day War. In fact, Israel had preemptively attacked Egypt and Syria to cripple their militaries before they could destroy Israel's. King Hussein of Jordan then decided his army needed to join the fight. By most neutral accounts, Israel did not seize the West Bank from Jordan in an act of aggression; it occupied that territory after beating back Jordan's attack.

987

the book, which sold poorly, "harmed my relationship with the Jewish community," though the largest Jewish donors to the Carter Center remained loyal.

Carter noted correctly that the word "apartheid" was already used by former prime minister Ehud Barak and other liberals in parliamentary debates inside Israel; he joined other analysts in explaining how much was at risk for Israel's future if it didn't move to break the stalemate and embrace a two-state solution. But many Jews didn't like hearing the South African analogy from a non-Jewish former president famous for sympathizing with the Palestinians. Carter's use of the word let the enemies of Israel weaponize the charge, even as it proved prescient. Within a decade, even many American Jews were using "apartheid" when describing the future of the West Bank under Israeli rule.

In 2007, Kenneth Stein, who had run the Carter Center for a short time in the mid-1980s and accompanied Carter on three trips to the Middle East, wrote a scathing takedown of his old boss. Unlike some Jews drawing unwarranted conclusions from afar, Stein never found him anti-Semitic.* But he felt Carter had begun operating out of emotion rather than logic: "He has shifted

*When he was president, Carter taught a Sunday School lesson in Washington in which he seemed to suggest that "Jewish leaders" killed Christ. He issued a statement repudiating the ancient canard that the Jewish people as a whole were "Christ killers," describing it as "that unjust accusation which has been exploited as a basis and rationalization for anti-Semitism."

from annoyance to exasperation [with Israel], from frustration to anger, and from partial blame upon the Palestinians to their exculpation." Stein's most serious charge was that Carter had moved from the standard "Land for Peace" to something closer to "Land for Talks" — a formulation that would require Israel to hand over the occupied territories to the Palestinians in exchange for nothing more than further negotiations.

In his mideighties, Carter was still determined to go the last mile for peace. In 2008 he made the tense overland journey into Gaza. En route through the Erez Crossing, he learned that Al Qaeda–affiliated groups had planted improvised explosive devices on the road, mostly to embarrass Hamas. Between meetings, Carter was informed that both Israel and the United States wanted him to leave Gaza for his own safety. He waved off the warnings. In Gaza, he met human rights activists who had been imprisoned by both the Israelis and Hamas. Carter worked hard on the case of the kidnapped Israeli soldier Gilad Shalit, pushing Hamas to hand him over. He failed but won points in Israel for the effort.

That summer, Carter's meetings with Hamas became a campaign issue in the race between Barack Obama, then a senator from Illinois, and Arizona Senator John McCain, who charged that Obama's election would mean "a second term" for Carter. Obama's response was to reduce Carter's remarks at the 2008 Democratic National Convention in Denver to a ninety-second introduction of a short film, a move that the Carters found belittling.

Back in the Middle East in 2009, Carter's visit with former Israeli prime minister Shimon Peres proved painful. Carter and Peres had always gotten along well, but now, inside Peres's home, their exchange grew uncharacteristically emotional. "You're treating Palestinians like animals," Carter snapped. Peres tried to soothe him: "Jimmy, Jimmy, no." Peres agreed to Carter's pleas to consider an "interim border" in the West Bank (the first outlines of statehood), which, like so many peace initiatives in the region, went nowhere.

During Obama's first term, neither the president nor Secretary of State Hillary Clinton had any interest in Carter's advice. He described his relationship with them as "nonexistent," which, in the case of Obama, whom he had admired greatly in 2008, was personally hurtful.* The fact that he and Obama had only ceremonial contacts embittered Carter and — in his mind — freed him to knock the president, as he had Clinton. Carter had known embattled Syrian president Bashar al-Assad since he was an ophthalmology student, and he publicly criticized Obama for issuing futile demands for Assad's removal. Obama's second-term secretary of state, John Kerry, was more solicitous of Carter and checked in regularly to see what he had learned about Syria peace plans in his meetings with Vladimir Putin and other

*He was, however, pleased when Obama wrote his grandson James Earl Carter IV, a talented opposition researcher in the Democratic Party, thanking him for his role in bringing to public attention a bartender's videotape of Mitt Romney criticizing "47 percent" of American voters as entitled and seeking government handouts, which helped Obama win the 2012 election.

leaders. Kerry found that even at ninety, Carter still had fresh information and penetrating insights into geopolitics.

Carter's greatest contribution to the Obama administration came through an innovative Carter Center program — adopted by the State Department — that used sophisticated mapping of social media posts to show where the Syrian and Russian militaries were targeting moderate forces and civilians inside Syria instead of ISIS. Other than that, he was viewed by the Obama White House as yesterday's news.*

If Carter's political influence was waning, his moral stature among moderate and progressive American Baptists was surging.

Many cheered when he took on the Southern Baptist Convention, the largest Protestant denomination in the United States. With nearly fifty thousand mostly white Baptist churches coming under its umbrella, the SBC had always allowed local autonomy for its churches. That began to change in the 1980s, when ultraconservative leaders turned the SBC into a political organization.

In 1998 the SBC decreed that women must submit to their husbands and could no longer be pastors. It elevated the literal Bible above the message of Jesus, a move Carter rejected, and kicked independent-minded churches out of the convention — a clear violation, Carter believed, of the principle of local control. Two years later, he quit the SBC in protest. Carter decried what he called

*Rosalynn felt that she was old news, too. She was hurt that Michelle Obama did not invite her to a luncheon on mental health, her signature issue.

991

an "inexorable merger" of the Southern Baptists with the "conservative wing of the Republican Party." His 2005 book *Our Endangered Values: America's Moral Crisis* included a sharp attack on right-wing evangelicals, and he lectured often on "narrow, self-serving . . . authoritarian males" who are so convinced of their own morality "that they cast the opposition not just as wrong, but as evil."

Carter was giving more voice to long-held liberal views. He spoke out strongly against the death penalty (which Rosalynn had converted him on) and against the "war on drugs" and mass incarceration in the United States. In 2012, he began publicly supporting gay marriage. He noted that homosexuality was well known in the ancient world, and "Jesus never said a word about it" and would have felt it was "very fine for gay people to be married in civil ceremonies." Carter drew the line at requiring churches to perform gay weddings. And while he viewed abortion rights as fully constitutional, he continued to believe Jesus would have opposed abortion except in cases of rape or incest or if the mother's life was in danger.

Carter soon became a major voice in encouraging Baptists to form new partnerships. In 2008 he spearheaded the New Baptist Covenant, which brought together black and white churches around racial justice. He also helped more moderate (Carter called them traditional) Baptists form the Cooperative Baptist Fellowship, which grew to about 1,900 affiliated churches. In an effort to find common ground with conservatives, Carter accepted an invitation to speak at Liberty University, founded by Jerry Falwell Sr., and was warmly received. "He represents the best of what it means

992

to be a Baptist in the twenty-first century," said Amy Butler, who served as the pastor of New York's Riverside Church.

In his ninetieth year, 2014, Carter wrote one of his best books, *A Call to Action: Women, Religion, Violence, and Power,* a searing depiction of what he called "the worst human rights abuse on earth": the mistreatment of women. Carter detailed how 160 million girls were eliminated through selective abortion or infanticide, mostly in China and India, and that genital mutilation remained a problem in many of the countries he'd visited. Carter was especially distressed to learn that Atlanta's huge international airport, which he had helped finish when he was governor, had become a hub for human trafficking, with girls bought there for $1,000 and sold into sex slavery. Before the #MeToo movement emerged, he blasted military leaders and college presidents for covering up sexual assaults.

When Carter first heard in the mid-1970s that his eccentric old friend David Rabhan had moved to Iran and started a fish meal protein business, he didn't think much of it. Rabhan — who had done so much to make him governor and president — was always dreaming up moneymaking schemes. But Rabhan stayed in Iran too long and made the wrong enemies. In 1980, amid the revolution, Iranian authorities seized his $7 million in assets and threw him into prison, where he was beaten and spent thirteen months in solitary confinement.

Rabhan's Iranian captors came across details of his friendship with Carter, including Rabhan's joking line in the American press that they had occasionally slept in the same bed in Atlanta in the 1970 campaign. During one of his four trials in Iran, in 1984, a prosecutor charged: "Jimmy Carter was a queer." Rabhan replied, "If you can prove that, you can make a fortune."

When he was president, Carter had other hostages to worry about, and Reagan showed no interest in Rabhan's fate. But Carter was a loyal friend, and he looked for ways to free him. In 1988 he wrote the Ayatollah Khomeini seeking the release of the American hostages in Lebanon. He added a postscript regarding "a matter of personal interest": a request for help in "the release of a US citizen by the name of David Rabhan." He received no reply.

Carter wrote Rabhan long, chatty letters in prison expressing his friendship and support, signed, "Your 1834H copilot, Jimmy." Rabhan replied with one of his little jokes that Carter loved: "I also shudder to think that I may go *free* thanks to you — then you'll be telling me for the rest of my life how you sprung me from jail. But I'll tell you this, and you can count on it — when you go to jail, I will do the same for you — so don't worry!" Carter finally got through to Rabhan by phone and urged good behavior to hasten his release: "For once in your life, go back to your cell and try to be nice."

With the help of Yāssir 'Arafāt, Rabhan was finally released in 1989. When his plane landed in Atlanta, Jimmy and Jeff were waiting for him. Ten brutal years in an Iranian prison had apparently not cured Rabhan of his taste for questionable business deals. Not long after returning home, he pled guilty in cases involving a Georgia catfish processing plant and a candy factory in Swaziland.

In an unusual though not improper move akin to testifying as a character witness, Carter called Judge Berry Avant Edenfield, whom he had appointed to the federal bench in 1978, to say that Rabhan had suffered greatly in an Iranian prison for a decade and deserved to have his sentence reduced. Judge Edenfield declined to do so, and Rabhan served five more years in prison, this time in the United States.

Carter was adept at handling sensitive matters that never surfaced in the press. After Millard Fuller was caught a second time making unwanted advances to women staffers at Habitat for Humanity, Carter negotiated his friend's painful departure from the organization he had founded.

In 2016, the squabbling children of Martin Luther King Jr. needed Carter to mediate. They were at one another's throats over their family's possessions, including an old pool table. Brothers Marty and Dexter teamed up to sue sister Bernice, who had possession of their father's Bible (used by Barack Obama to take the oath of office) and his Nobel Peace Prize. Carter's approach was the same as at Camp David: both sides would agree at the end of the process to one document. This time, the document went through six or seven drafts, with the parties finally agreeing that Carter's decisions on what would be sold or kept were to be final. One night Carter would be hard on Bernice; the next, on Dexter or Marty. Carter finally determined — and a judge soon ratified — that Marty, as chairman of the estate, had control of the Bible and the Nobel, but they would be displayed at the King Center in Atlanta, not sold.

One day a visitor to Plains came upon an old man

in a cap mowing the grass behind a church. "Isn't that the place where Jimmy Carter teaches Sunday school?" the visitor asked. "Yes, it is," Jimmy Carter replied with a smile before resuming his chores. Inside the 350-seat sanctuary, Rosalynn was vacuuming. Jimmy and Rosalynn could often be found in Plains eating off paper plates at church suppers, chatting with visitors as if they were just another elderly couple in town.

Jimmy was more than just a deacon at Maranatha Baptist Church. He made the wooden cross and wooden collection plates on a lathe. And once or twice a month from 1981 until late 2019, he donned a bolero tie with a turquoise stone and stood to teach a warm and engaging Sunday school lesson to a small group of his neighbors and a much larger assemblage of visitors from all over the world. Carter still sometimes found it easier to connect to strangers than old friends, who could find his fanatical self-discipline and unrelenting pace of good deeds intimidating. "As much as I love Jimmy Carter," said Andrew Young, "he makes you feel guilty around him."

After Carter was diagnosed with cancer in 2015, he saw himself transported in the public mind to a place beyond politics. Thousands made the pilgrimage to Maranatha, camping out in front of the church all night for the chance to see him teach and to cross something off their bucket lists. Most settled for a video feed in the overflow room. He and Rosalynn would slip in about ten in the morning, after the visitors had been instructed not to applaud or ask him how he was feeling when they had their pictures taken with them.

The gentle lessons, usually drawn from the New Testament, were charming and inspiring even for nonbelievers. He taught often on forgiveness and "agape love," which he described as "self-sacrificial love, love for people who are not lovable, loving without expecting to be loved back." He might work in what he had learned from Eloy Cruz on his Baptist mission a half century earlier: "We must love God and love the person in front of us at any time."

The message was inclusive and focused on deeds on earth. "A good person is someone who follows the example of Jesus Christ," he said in church in 2017. He made no claim that believing in Christ's divinity was critical to being good; he simply made the case that one treat others well, as Christ did.

Carter would often try to connect his diplomatic experience to daily life. "Wars between two countries, civil wars inside a country, disagreements between a husband and wife that lead to divorce, are all caused by the same thing," he said. "That is, an honest and sincere difference of opinion and an unwillingness to communicate."

Amid the warm public smiles and self-effacing remarks came occasional glimpses of the demanding Carter. He sometimes referred to Jesus' brother, James, who taught, in Carter's words, that "if your life is not filled with peace, joy, and thanksgiving, it's your fault." James's instruction was direct: "With our freedom, every one of us can make a basic decision: 'What kind of person do I, myself, choose to be?' " Every person, he said, "can be a complete success in the eyes of God." He would often conclude by asking everyone in church to try to do something nice for someone at least once a month.

As president, Carter was often respected without

997

being liked; afterward, he was admired without being loved. In their nineties, he and Rosalynn were finally beloved for all they had done for humanity and for the grace with which they did it. And to keep the good deeds flowing, Jimmy's hobbies were still convertible into cash. The live and silent auctions held at the annual Carter Center Weekend — a festive event for donors — always brought impressive sums: a wooden dresser that Jimmy built in his nineties went for more than $1 million, and his old tennis shoes fetched $11,500.

In 2015 Jimmy and Rosalynn turned over the board chairmanship of the Carter Center to Jack's son, Jason Carter, a veteran of the Peace Corps who had served in the Georgia State Senate and run a strong but unsuccessful race for governor in 2014. Jason would carry the Carter Center into what he called its "adolescence," certain that his grandparents' mission "to alleviate suffering and advance human rights globally has never been more urgent." The transition wasn't entirely seamless. Jason shifted most of the major decision-making from the board, where Jimmy still served, to an executive committee. "This feels like we're being pushed to the side," Jimmy told his grandson, who replied that the restructuring was inevitable and was best done while "Papaw," as his grandchildren called him, was still alive.

There were other disappointments. Guinea worm seemed on course to be the only human disease other than smallpox to be eradicated — and Carter had every reason to believe he would live to see it. But in 2017 the disease was found in dogs in Chad, and soon a few new cases in humans were reported in Angola. In late 2019 the

World Health Organization (WHO) quietly announced that it had moved back the target date for eradication from 2020 to 2030, when if Jimmy Carter was still alive, he would be 106 years old.

Jason believed that Carter's two big goals at the end of his life were peace in the Mideast and fixing the Baptist Church, neither of which was likely. Privately, Jimmy was contemptuous of Israel's intransigence but even tougher on the narrow, far-right Baptists of the Southern Baptist Convention, whom he called Philistines.

As Carter grew older, his critique of America grew harsher. He felt the 2010 Supreme Court decision in the *Citizens United* case (opening the floodgates of money into campaigns) and rampant gerrymandering had turned the United States into what he described as "an oligarchy." One day Carter looked up something he had been wondering about on Wikipedia. He found that in the 242 years since the Declaration of Independence, the United States had enjoyed only 16 years of full peace. Four of the years without any hostilities came when he was president. That meant, he concluded, that "our country has been the foremost warlike nation on earth." Worse, many of the wars were motivated by domestic politics. "Most presidents look at war as a way of going from beleaguered civilian administrator to being commander in chief," he said.

To work for peace and human rights, Carter had joined the Elders, a group of a half dozen former heads of state assembled in 2007 by Nelson Mandela. The group included Mary Robinson, the first woman president of Ireland; Ban Ki-moon, former secretary-general of the United Nations; and others who, unlike former

American presidents, readily accepted Carter into their club. He liked the camaraderie of the august group but also found himself drawn to figures of peace who lacked stature.

In 2001 Carter struck up an unusual friendship with Mattie J. T. Stepanek, a brilliant and wry eleven-year-old Maryland boy afflicted with a fatal neuromuscular disease. Mattie had made a request from his hospital bed to meet his hero, Jimmy Carter. Over the next three years, Mattie wrote *Heartsongs,* a best-selling book of poetry, among other volumes, and became a widely recognized peace activist and favorite guest of Oprah Winfrey on her television show. From that first meeting, Mattie and Jimmy exchanged several letters exploring how, in Mattie's words, "to make peace an attitude and a habit and a reality." Carter was especially struck by the boy's concept of "just peace." To the eternal question of "What can we do?" Carter answered: "What we can do individually is adopt Mattie's apparently naive commitment to a coalescence of the finest human traits: including peace, justice, equity, humility, service, compassion, and love."

When Mattie died in 2004, Carter delivered the eulogy. "There's no doubt that Mattie was an angel of God, a messenger of God," Carter told the mourners, and he meant it.

Just after the 2008 election, outgoing president George W. Bush invited all of the living former presidents to the White House for a private lunch with President-Elect Obama. A memorable Oval Office photograph shows the Bushes, Bill Clinton, and Obama chatting like old friends on the left, with Carter standing alone on the right. One of

1000

the presidents confided later that the photo perfectly captured the chemistry of their meeting and lunch that day. The other presidents gave Obama convivial advice on the peculiarities of the office, while Carter wanted to press his serious policy agenda. Carter later told Brian Williams of NBC News that the body language was deliberate because "I feel that my role as a former president is probably superior to that of other presidents." Judging by the amount of golf the others played over the years while Carter was doing good in Africa, this was an accurate but — as he recognized — ill-advised statement. The next day he tried to walk back the boast by saying he meant to refer to the "good deeds" of the Carter Center.

And it got worse in the ex-presidents club. In October 2017 the five living former presidents, including new member Barack Obama, gathered at Texas A&M University to raise money for hurricane relief. In the holding area, aides saw on their phones a column by Maureen Dowd in the *New York Times* entitled "Jimmy Carter Lusts for a Trump Posting." In it, Carter admitted that at Zbigniew Brzezinski's funeral, he had lobbied Trump's (second of several) national security adviser, H. R. McMaster, to be dispatched to North Korea, and — not coincidentally — he refused to say anything negative about Trump. At the same time, he didn't hold back on the two other living Democratic ex-presidents. Carter said that Obama "reneged" on his early promise to work on Mideast peace and that he went overboard on authorizing drone strikes, especially in Yemen, a country that the always-adventurous Carter, late in life, called the most fascinating he had ever visited. (He even tried khat, a shrub used in the Horn of Africa as a stimulant.)

The Clinton Foundation had always been a sore spot. "Rosie and I put money in the Carter Center; we never take any out," he told Dowd, an apparent shot not just at the Clintons' ethics but also at a foundation struggling after Trump's election. Before going onstage, Carter tried to joke that Dowd often misquoted all of them. Clinton and Obama weren't buying it.

For the first two years of the Trump administration, Carter was critical of Trump's habit of lying, but he didn't yet think he was the worst president in American history, a distinction he reserved for George W. Bush because of all the blood he felt had been needlessly spilled on his watch. Bush's idea of preemptive war struck Carter as a "radical departure" from other presidents.

In April 2019 Carter wrote Trump what Trump described as a "beautiful" letter on dealing with China, and the president called him to discuss it. Carter's big point (which he made in many venues) was that China hadn't fought a war since 1949 and had thus — unlike the United States — been able to spend trillions of dollars on education, health care, and infrastructure instead of armaments. Afterward, Trump said, "I've always liked Jimmy Carter." But by summer, it was clear that Trump wasn't about to dispatch Carter to China, North Korea, or anywhere else. Rebuffed at ninety-four in his final bid to return to the action, Carter felt free to resume his practice of speaking his mind about the incumbent. He fastened on Trump's threats to democracy and called his Mexican border policy a "disgrace." At the 2019 Carter Center Weekend, he said flatly that Russia's successful interference in the 2016 election had rendered Trump an illegitimate president. Carter felt it likely that "Trump didn't actually win the office — he was put into office through Russian efforts." Trump predictably responded by calling Carter a failure as president.

This prompted several prospective 2020 Democratic presidential candidates, including Cory Booker, Amy Klobuchar, and Pete Buttigieg (all of whom had made pilgrimages to Plains), to leap to the defense of their party's newly revered senior statesman. Carter preferred such younger candidates. He made news by calling for an age limit on the presidency, arguing that he didn't think he could have handled the job after age eighty. But when seventy-eight-year-old Joe Biden — his first supporter in the Senate in 1976 — clinched the Democratic nomination in 2020, Carter was all in.

In 2015 doctors found a mass on Carter's liver: metastatic melanoma, which had spread to his brain. He was told he could be dead within weeks. After surgery and radiation, he received a miraculous new immunotherapy drug called Keytruda, which, along with prayer, he credited with saving his life. When he arrived back in Plains from Emory University Hospital, the town was festooned with signs reading "Jimmy Carter for Cancer Survivor." The cancer left no lasting effects, and he quickly resumed his old routines.

After the diagnosis, Jack took steps to ease their long estrangement. He traveled alone to Plains for the first time since he was first married in 1971 and took a long walk with his father. They had a good conversation, and Jimmy expressed some regret about their relationship, but Jack still felt his father had never come to terms with his shortcomings as a parent. Chip and Jeff were more forgiving.

As Christmas neared, Jeff and Annette's son Jeremy, a sweet young man who loved hunting with his grandfather, was living at his parents' new home in Peachtree City, Georgia, and getting set to enroll again in college. Jeremy, who had struggled for years with substance abuse, had felt poorly for days and was sitting in the kitchen with his mother when he suffered an apparent heart attack. Annette tried to resuscitate him, but he died at the hospital on December 20, 2015, at age twenty-eight. No autopsy was ever conducted. At a small family dinner five months after his death, Jimmy thanked the Lord for taking care of his family, then presented Jeff and Annette with a portrait he had painted of Jeremy. Jeff wasn't ready for it and fled in tears, upset that his father had not asked him beforehand whether he would want such a gift.

By 2019, Carter was the longest-living president, with the longest postpresidency and the longest marriage. Rick Hertzberg compared him to Mahatma Gandhi, a peacemaker who exasperated many followers with his showy righteousness. But as George Orwell, who counted himself as among those irritated by Gandhi, put it about the Indian leader more than seventy years ago: "How clean a smell he has managed to leave behind!" Carter's family agreed. At Jimmy and Rosalynn's seventieth wedding anniversary in 2016, Jeff toasted his parents for "saving more lives than possibly any couple in the history of the world." Amy thought her parents' lives raised an intriguing question for everyone: "How much more would you do if every minute could make a profound change in the world?" The answer the Carters offered was that if Jimmy and Rosalynn could do so much, everyone else could at least do a little more.

In their nineties, the Carters were still building houses for Habitat. At night, the people on the "builds" loved hearing Jimmy discourse intelligently on many subjects: epidemiology, physics, theology, the history of Native Americans. Wearing his trademark blue work shirt and red bandana, he could still handle the band saw well and teach the uninitiated his swift and unusual two-handed hammer stroke. Rosalynn, too, hammered better than most of the volunteers on the site, many of whom were a third her age.

Closer to home, the Carters arranged in 2018 for the first health clinic in Plains since the closing of the Wise Sanitarium, where Jimmy was born. Up close, the level of their commitment to their little town inspired anyone who made the long trek to visit. For decades, they had worked to improve Plains with all the energy they devoted to projects half a world away. No one wanted to contemplate what would happen to Plains after they were gone.

The Carters' energy levels were exhausting for people half their age. Thanks to double knee replacement, Jimmy walked briskly until his early nineties and could stand for hours in a stream. In 2012 they caught Pacific salmon on Russia's pristine Kamchatka peninsula; in 2014, the year Jimmy turned ninety and Rosalynn eighty-seven, they went to the Kola peninsula — on the other side of the Russian landmass, where they rose at three in the morning and caught thirty-eight

Atlantic salmon.

As late as 2018, Carter still sat for as many as six long meetings a day, where he held forth without any loss of mental acuity. He went on talk shows at ninety-three and cracked up hosts with his drollery. When he broke a wrist riding a scooter at ninety-four, his staff fretted that he was too old to know his limits, not realizing that this was who he had always been, going back to when he was seventeen and broke his wrist trying to impress a girl with his tumbling skills.

Carter felt he had mellowed a bit. "I think I am less intense now than I was back then," he reflected. "I've tried to get rid of those animosities I used to cherish." When he memorized the poem "Invictus" at Annapolis in 1943, he had not believed that he was "master of my fate, captain of my soul." Nor during his years in politics. But looking back at his postpresidency, he felt he had become that master. "Captain of my soul"? He didn't hesitate: "Oh, I am."

In early 2019 Carter awoke before dawn and dressed in hunting clothes. He hadn't bagged his quota of turkeys and wanted to shoot more. He fell in the dark on the way out of the house, and the Secret Service rushed him to the hospital, where hip replacement surgery went surprisingly well. By now, Carter concluded that his globe-trotting days were finally over. Even if he had the strength — and he always assumed he did — Rosalynn was frail. After she was hospitalized in 2018 for intestinal surgery, he grew scared she would die and vowed not to leave her side.

The Carters' thirty-sixth Habitat "build" was in 2019 in Nashville, where, the week after Jimmy turned ninety-five, they joined country music stars Garth Brooks and Trisha Yearwood, just two of the many ardent admirers who had helped them build houses over the years. Jimmy had recently fallen again and received fourteen stitches around his left eye, but he happily hammered away, oblivious to the bruises on his face. Only later did doctors learn that the fall had caused a subdural hematoma, which required fluid to be drained from his brain. It took Carter weeks after being released from the hospital to recover his speech and to move around again, now with a walker. With his eyesight impaired, he needed someone to read to him — just as his near-blind teacher, Miss Julia Coleman, did in the 1930s. This didn't stop her then, and it wouldn't stop her prize student now.

Just 150 yards from the Carters' modest house on Woodland Drive lies a ten-acre field that has been in the family for generations. In 2019 Carter arranged for the installation of 3,500 solar panels, which would soon provide more than half the power for the people of Plains. Carter was proud of the example he was setting but also a little wistful. In 1979, when he placed the solar panels on the roof of the White House, he committed the nation to using renewable resources for 20 percent of its energy by the year 2000. Had he been reelected, he said, the United States would have been well on its way to achieving that goal.

Now, in 2020, green energy still lagged behind fossil fuels, but a new generation of idealistic young Americans gave Carter great hope that the problems he had devoted himself to addressing were being tackled anew.

He believed that among those challenges would be global health. In March 2020 the Carters and their grandson Jason asked all donors to forgo their next gift to the Carter Center and direct it to groups working to reduce the suffering caused by the Covid-19 pandemic. With its experience combating the ravages of the Ebola virus and other infectious diseases, the Center would soon be called on to help confront the coronavirus in developing countries where it had some infrastructure in place. In the meantime, Jimmy and Rosalynn were photographed wearing masks.

Amid the national upheaval after Minneapolis police murdered George Floyd in May 2020, Carter touched on his own experience with race "as a white male of the South [who knows] all too well the impact of segregation and injustice to African Americans."

With "great sorrow and disappointment," he noted that it was necessary, nearly five decades later, to repeat the message of his 1971 inaugural address: "The time for racial discrimination is over." He said that he and Rosalynn had seen in their travels abroad for human rights that "silence can be as deadly as violence." Between the lines of his June 3 statement lay regrets about the seventeen years in the 1950s and 1960s when he stayed mostly silent about civil rights at home. He reminded those who had not yet made their own redemptive journeys that "people of power, privilege, and moral conscience must stand up and say 'No more' to a racially discriminatory police and justice system, immoral economic disparities between whites and blacks, and government actions that undermine our unified democracy."

He concluded with a variation on the line that had made him president: "We need a government as good as its people, and we are better than this."

Jimmy and Rosalynn sheltered at home and didn't much like the Zoom version of church. They were thrilled to step outside and hear a small concert that included music from guitars made from an empress tree on their land. When they left their house to walk a little, they could glimpse the section of their property set aside for their graves.

Not long before the pandemic, Jimmy explained in Sunday school that he was "completely at ease with death." His Christian faith, he told congregants and visitors, made him absolutely confident that "I'm going to live again after I die."

For nearly a century, he had already lived again and again and again — constantly reimagining himself and what was possible for a barefoot boy from southwest Georgia with a moral imagination and a driving ambition to live his faith. That passionate commitment — sustained long after others of his generation had left the field — would take him to the farthest corners of the earth, but he always came full circle to Plains, where his inner and outer selves could find repose.

By the time he was in his midninetics, the shortcomings and contradictions of Jimmy Carter's long life seemed even to his critics to have given way to an appreciation of his core decency. Beyond his heavenly reward lay his earthly example: a life of ceaseless effort, not just for himself but for the world he helped shape.

# ACKNOWLEDGMENTS

This book combines traditional scholarly research and extensive interviewing and I am enormously grateful to the scores of people who helped me with both. I spent many happy weeks in Atlanta at the Jimmy Carter Presidential Library and Museum, where Meredith Evans is the director and Keith Schuler, Christopher Geissler, Aisha Johnson-Jones, and especially David Stanhope provided invaluable help. They were of assistance remotely, too. I'm also grateful to Ru Story-Huffman, director of the James Earl Carter Library at Georgia Southwestern State University in Americus; Christian Lopez and Jason Hasty at the Richard Russell Library at the University of Georgia in Athens; Steven Engerrand at the Georgia State Archive; Courtney Chartier at the Emory University Library; Thomas van der Voort at the Miller Center, University of Virginia; and my old friend Tom Blanton at the National Security Archive, among others who helped me navigate through the millions of documents amassed about any American president.

I was a beneficiary of the 2017 posting of twelve million additional pages of recently declassified documents on the CIA Records Search Tool

(CREST) system, which I was able to access while at the Carter Library. And the Freedom of Information Act Electronic Reading Room offered me access to many documents not previously available to historians. The declassified minutes of key National Security Council meetings were especially helpful in fashioning a fresh perspective on Carter's misunderstood foreign policy.

At the Carter Center, located on the same campus, I was aided by Kathy Cade, Deanna Congileo, Beth Davis, Lauren Gay, and Patricia Rafshoon Simon, not to mention all of the experts there whom I interviewed. Special thanks to Jay Beck, Rita Thompson, and Steve Hochman, a thoughtful, meticulous historian who did much to improve my understanding of Jimmy Carter. In Plains, I was greatly dependent on Jill Stuckey, my wonderful friend and host.

This book would not have been possible without the extensive cooperation of Jimmy Carter and eighteen members of his family, all of whom were exceptionally generous with their time. Beyond the former president, I am especially indebted to Rosalynn Carter for sharing with me her husband's love letters from the navy, which have never been even reviewed by scholars before, much less published. She also provided me with the periodic unpublished journal entries she kept during the Camp David peace talks in 1978, which offered a new angle of vision on that historic event; in the Middle East in 1979; and when it looked for a time as if the hostages in Iran might be released during her husband's time in office. Extensive and highly useful entries of President Carter's diaries from his years in the White House were published in 2010, but he allowed me to request unpublished

1012

entries as well, and I found no evidence that he withheld anything of significance. His diary from his plebe year at Annapolis was also revealing.

I am hugely grateful to each of the more than 250 people who granted me interviews of varying lengths, often on several occasions. Carter's White House inner circle has thinned out in recent years. (Hamilton Jordan and Jody Powell both died before I started my research in 2015.) But I tapped relevant documents and oral histories and was able to interview all of those still alive who saw him every day in the White House. Of former White House aides, special thanks to Phil Wise, Susan Clough, and Jerry Rafshoon. Jerry's many amusing and insightful stories kept me entertained throughout a grueling process, and they all checked out. Of personal friends, David Rabhan — without whom Carter would likely have been neither governor nor president — was kind enough to share his recollections and privately published memoir. Among other unpublished work, the diaries of Jerry Doolittle and Landon Butler were especially helpful.

I'm often asked why Jimmy Carter has never before been the subject of a major independent biography. I have no answer, except to note that the misimpression of him ran so deep that it discouraged such efforts. I nonetheless owe a debt of gratitude to my predecessors who have tackled the subject. Two fine, ambitious works came out in the 1990s, one by Douglas Brinkley on Carter's impactful postpresidency through 1997, and the other by Peter Bourne, a friend and health policy adviser to Carter from 1970 to 1978. Another former senior aide, Stuart Eizenstat, who worked at Carter's side from 1970 to 1981, wrote a comprehensive and important 2018 account of the White House years. A 1980 book by Betty Glad was instructive, as was Stanly Godbold's account of Carter's time in Georgia. Randall Ballmer's *Redeemer* offers a revealing look at his spiritual life, and Julian Zelizer's 150-page overview contains penetrating insights. Finally, I mined most of Jimmy Carter's own books, which contained well-scrubbed but important stories from his life.

My deepest thanks to those who read chapters or the whole book before publication: Charlotte Alter, Ethan Bronner, Landon Butler, Mark Chiusano, David Farber, Jim Free, Julian Gewirtz, Gordon Goldstein, Steve Hochman, Brooks Jackson, Andrew Koenig, Evan Kutzler, Zachary J. Lechner, Jamie Alter Lynton, Martin Marty, David McKean, Melissa Montgomery, Jerry Rafshoon, Cliff Sloan, Michael Waldman, Mark Whitaker, and Phil Wise. Special thanks to the brilliant Bill Drayton and to several members of Biographers International Organization.

I received good research, fact-checking, and transcription help from Jonathan Aronoff, Ariel Doctoroff, Jeremy Fassler, Evan Kutzler (my scholar in Plains), and the indefatigable Andrew Koenig, who along with Crary Pullen, Bob Shapiro, and Keith Ulrich were lifesavers at the end of the process.

At Simon & Schuster, I'm most indebted to the late, great Alice Mayhew, a legendary editor (for good reason) who edited my three previous books with great skill and enthusiasm. This biography was essentially Alice's idea, and when she died in early 2020, I felt adrift. But Priscilla Painton and Megan Hogan stepped smartly into the breach and got me over the finish line. Thanks also to Stuart Roberts, Julia Prosser, Caitlyn Reuss, Hana Park, Lisa Healy, Jonathan Evans, Phil Bashe, and Jackie Seow. Jon Karp and the late Carolyn Reidy provided strong support from the top.

My greatest debt, as usual, is to my family. My siblings, Jennifer Warden, Jamie Lynton, and Harrison Alter, and my children Tommy Alter and Molly Alter offered great moral support through the long years of writing. Our older daughter, Charlotte Alter, and son-in-law, Mark Chiusano, are strong, demanding editors and greatly enhanced the book. And my lovely, patient, and tough-minded wife, Emily Lazar, saved me from myself, as she usually does.

# NOTES

## Abbreviations
**CC** Carter Center
**CREST** CIA Records Search Tool
**C/S-FOHP** Carter/Smith Family Oral History Project
**FP** Family Papers, JCPLM
**GSA** Georgia State Archive
**GSWSU** Georgia Southwestern State University
**int.** Author interview
**JCPLM** Jimmy Carter Presidential Library and Museum
**NSA** National Security Archive, George Washington University
**OH** Oral history
**PPPJC** Public Papers of the President, Administration of Jimmy Carter
**ROGP** Reflections on Georgia Politics OH
**SCOHP** Sumter County Oral History Project
**SSF** Staff Secretary Files, JCPLM
**UVA-MC** University of Virginia, Miller Center

## Author Interviews
Joshua Abram, Morton Abramowitz, Elliott Abrams, Terry Adamson, William Alford, Roger Altman, Robert Armao, Bernard Aronson, Ami

1017

Ayalon, Martha Baker, Gerald Barney, Shahnaz Batmanghelidj, Richard Beattie, Mary Beazley, Jay Beck, Bob Beckel, Joe Biden, Jimmy Bishop, Jim Blanchard, Barbara Blum, Michael Blumenthal, Bill Boggs, Peter Bourne, Cathy Bradshaw, Jimmy Breslin, Tom Brokaw, Chris Brown, Harold Brown, Sam Brown, Diane Bryant, Zbigniew Brzezinski, Tim Buchanan, Janet Bunde, Bill Bush, George H. W. Bush, Amy Butler, Landon Butler, Pat Caddell, Kathy Cade, Joseph Califano, Tim Carden, David Carroll, Amy Carter, Annette Carter, Becky Carter, Buddy Carter, Chip Carter, Don Carter, Hodding Carter, Jack Carter, James Carter, Jason Carter, Jeff Carter, Jeremy Carter, Joshua Carter, Jimmy Carter, Kate Carter, Margaret Carter, Rosalynn Carter, Sally Carter, Sarah Carter, Sybil Carter, Jim Cheevers, Max Cleland, Eleanor Clift, Susan Clough, Adam Clymer, Richard Cohen, Roberta Cohen, Mort Coleman, Jim Copeland, Joseph Crespino, Tom Crick, John Dalton, Andy DeRoche, Chris Dickey, John Dinges, Evan Dobelle, Sam Donaldson, Tom Donilon, Jerome Doolittle, Ralph Earle, Peter Edelman, Joe Eldridge, Peter Emerson, Edward Elson, James Fallows, Kane Farabaugh, Kambiz Fattahi, Kathy Fletcher, Bill Foege, Warren Fortson, Les Francis, Linda Francke, A. D. Fraser, Jim Free, David Freeman, Robert Frosch, Paul Gaddis, Felice Gaer, Peter Galbraith, Richard Gardner, Leslie Gelb, Michael Giles, Dan Glickman, Boze Godwin, Peter Goldman, Barry Golson, Gordon Goldstein, Douglas Grant, Rex Granum, Gene Griessman, Thom Gunn, Bernard Gwirtzman, Jay Hakes, Pete Hamill, Lee Hamilton, Steve Hammond, Richard Harden, John Hardman, Bruce Harlan, Wayne Harpster, Herky

Harris, Tex Harris, Jim Hershberg, Rick Hertzberg, Carlton Hicks, Steve Hochman, Donald Hopkins, Ben Huberman, Rick Hutcheson, Tim Hutchinson, Daniel Inouye, Brooks Jackson, Larry Jacobs, Barry Jagoda, Leroy Johnson, Clovis Jones, Imara Jones, Hamilton Jordan Jr., Kathleen Jordan, Vernon Jordan, Seth Kaller, John Kaminsky, Robert Kapp, Juratc Kazickas, Bob Kerrey, Mary King, Paul Kirk, Henry Kissinger, Curtis Kohlhass, Ted Koppel, Ed Kosner, Tim Kraft, Orin Kramer, Moon Landrieu, Jim Laney, Jim Langford, Judy Langford, Dan Lee, John Lewis, Robert Lifset, Jennie Lincoln, Robert MacNeil, John Maltese, Martin Marty, Ray Marshall, Keith Mason, Bob McBarton, Jennifer McCoy, David McCullough, Jim McIntyre, Joel McLeary, Hannah McMahan, John McMillan, G Juan Mendez, Flavio Meroni, Abner Mikva, George Miller, Newt Minow, Walter Mondale, Richard Moe, Frank Moore, Liz Moynihan, Reg Murphy, Lynn Nesbit, Barry Nickelsberg, Sam Nunn, Tom Oliphant, Steve Oney, Peter Osnos, Richard Ossoff, Richard Ottinger, Dot Padgett, Alex Parker, Will Pattiz, Faye Perdue, Giancarlo Peressuti, William Perry, Charles Peters, Mary Ann Peters, Betty Pope, Nan Powell, Nelson Price, David Rabhan, Jerry Rafshoon, Eleanor Randolph, Dan Rather, Johnny Raven, Jonathan Reckford, Mike Reiss, John Rendon, Leo Ribuffo, Gene Roberts, Bill Roper, Gerald Rosenthal, Bobby Rowan, Robert Rubin, David Rubinstein, Al Rusher, Dale Russakoff, Jan Ryan, Karin Ryan, Peter Sahlins, Rita Jackson Samuels, Lon Saavedra, Robert Scheer, Mark Schneider, Greg Schneiders, Robert Schule, Richard Secord, Clarence Seeliger, Bill Shipp, Adam Shrum, Gary Sick, Mark Silk, Steve Simon, Jan

Simpson, Sam Singer, Alicia Smith, Stephen Smith Jr., Tim Smith, Maurice Sonnenberg, Gillian Sorensen, Lauren Speeth, Gus Speth, Joe Sports, Kenneth Stein, Jeni Smith Stepanek, Patty Stonesifer, Jonathan Stonestreet, Ru Story-Huffman, Jill Stuckey, Joe Tanner, Dan Tate, Michael Terry, Rita Thompson, Richard Tofel, Roy Vagelos, Gordon Van Ness, Cyrus Vance Jr., William vanden Heuvel, Nicholas Veliotes, Paul Volcker, Carl Wagner, Jane Wales, Jack Watson, Drew Weston, Curtis Wilkie, Phil Wise, Bob Woodward, Andrew Young.

## Preface

" 'The worst thing' ": Gunnar Berge, Nobel Peace Prize Award Ceremony Speech, December 10, 2002, https://www.nobelprize.org/prizes/peace/2002/ceremony-speech.

"the meanest man": Taylor Branch, *Parting the Waters: America in the King Years, 1954–63* (New York: Simon & Schuster, 1988), 561.

"That I was weak": Jimmy Carter int., November 19, 2015.

"a bastard": Hunter S. Thompson, "Jimmy Carter and the Great Leap of Faith," *Rolling Stone*, June 3, 1976.

"human heart": Henry James, *The Notebooks of Henry James*, ed. Francis Otto Matthiessen and Kenneth Ballard Murdock (New York: Oxford University Press, 1961), 74.

## Prologue

"Gas . . . died": John Updike, *Rabbit Is Rich* (New York: Alfred A. Knopf, 1981), 17. See also Meg Jacobs, *Panic at the Pump: The Energy Crisis and the Transformation of American Politics in the 1970s* (New York: Hill and Wang, 2016).

*surveys in June 1979:* Gallup, "Presidential Approval Ratings — Gallup Historical Statistics and Trends, Low Individual Measurements," https://news.gallup.com/poll/116677/presidential-approval-ratings-gallup-historical-statistics-trends.aspx.

*"Energy is our Vietnam":* "Special Report: The Energy Crisis: A Program for the 80s," *Newsweek,* July 16, 1979.

*handwrote a reference:* Jerry Doolittle, unpublished diary, May 22, 1978.

*"solar power":* Jimmy Carter, "Solar Energy: Remarks Announcing Administration Proposals, June 20, 1979," *PPPJC,* 1979, vol. 1 (Washington, DC: US Government Printing Office, 1980), 1095–99.

*"this solar heater":* Martin Tolchin, "Carter Welcomes Solar Power," *New York Times,* June 21, 1979.

*"federal judiciary":* SCOTUSblog, October 31, 2017.

*Averell Harriman . . . "most extraordinary":* *Washington Post,* September 29, 1978.

*"three smiles":* Zbigniew Brzezinski int., March 1, 2016.

**Part 1: Sources of Strength**
*Chapter 1: Daddy and Hot*

*pellets the size of grits:* Jimmy Carter, *An Hour Before Daylight: Memories of a Rural Boyhood* (New York: Simon & Schuster, 2001), 15, 78.

*"an immersion in the natural world":* Jimmy Carter, preface, in Fred Brown and Sherri M. L. Smith, *The Flint River: A Recreational Guidebook to the Flint River and Environs* (Atlanta: CI Publishing, 2001).

*an aroma so sublime:* Jimmy Carter, *Hour Before Daylight,* 178.

*"fly rod":* Jimmy Carter, *Living Faith* (New York: Times Books, 1996), 49.

*"We despised it":* James T. Wooten, *Dasher: The Roots and the Rising of Jimmy Carter* (New York: Summit Books, 1978), 133.

*missing picnic:* Dorothy Padgett, *Jimmy Carter: Elected President with Pocket Change and Peanuts* (Macon, GA: Mercer University Press, 2016), 6–7.

*"so little and forlorn":* Peter Goldman, "Sizing Up Carter: The Question of Character," *Newsweek,* September 13, 1976.

*his tenacity:* Jimmy Carter int., September 15, 2017.

*"equaled any other ambition":* Jimmy Carter, *Hour Before Daylight,* 165.

*"do it better":* ibid., 166.

*fresh brains:* ibid., 170–71.

*"blinked or smiled":* Jimmy Carter, "Prosperity Doesn't Suit Everyone," in *Always a Reckoning and Other Poems* (New York: Times Books, 1995), 97.

*"back with us, Hot":* Jimmy Carter, *Living Faith,* 14; Jimmy Carter, *Hour Before Daylight,* 81–82.

*"the last money I ever stole":* Jimmy Carter, *Hour Before Daylight,* 226.

*turkey at a nearby farm . . . young widow:* ibid., 206.

*"showed much emotion or love":* Jimmy Carter, lecture, Emory University, Atlanta, February 15, 2017.

*"This is a pain":* Jimmy Carter, "I Wanted to Share

My Father's World," in *Always a Reckoning,* 99.

Chapter 2: The Carters and the Gordys

*Carter's genes:* Jeff Carter, *Ancestors of Jimmy and Rosalynn Carter* (Jefferson, NC: McFarland, 2012), 38.

*"To have it taken away . . . terrible":* Jimmy Carter: *Man from Plains,* directed and written by Jonathan Demme (Los Angeles: Participant Media/ Sony Pictures Classics, 2007); Jimmy Carter, *A Full Life: Reflections at Ninety* (New York: Simon & Schuster, 2015), 231–32.

*There was violence:* Jeff Carter, *Ancestors,* 59–60.

*"I haven't been very belligerent":* AARP Bulletin online, June 2015, https://www.aarp.org/ politics-society/history/info-2015/ jimmy-carter-reflections-at-90.html.

*"Damn! Damn! Damn!":* Ruth Carter Stapleton, *Brother Billy* (New York: Harper & Row, 1978), 17–18.

*"Some think I'm queer":* Duane Hutchinson, *Jimmy Carter's Hometown: People of Plains* (Lincoln, NE: Foundation Books, 2003), 23.

*pollster without polls:* Jimmy Carter, *Turning Point: A Candidate, a State, and a Nation Come of Age* (New York: Times Books, 1992), 3–4.

*revering Watson anyway:* Hutchinson, *Jimmy Carter's Hometown,* 11–12.

*twenty-five chin-ups:* Jimmy Carter int., June 13, 2015.

*"We hire rednecks for that":* Jerry Rafshoon int., May 18, 2015.

*"his looks":* Lillian Carter, C/S-FOHP, September 26, 1978.

*"He was the kind":* Jimmy Carter, *Hour Before*

*Daylight,* 119–22.

*"I knew I wasn't a virgin":* Wooten, *Dasher,* 87.

*"the leader":* Martin Schram, *Running for President, 1976: The Carter Campaign* (New York: Stein and Day, 1977), 39.

*"most brilliant":* Paul H. Elovitz, "Three Days in Plains," *Journal of Psychohistory* 5, no. 2 (Fall 1977): 177.

*"not altogether healthy":* Ruth Carter Stapleton, *The Gift of Inner Healing* (Waco, TX: Word Books, 1976), 16.

*"a mistake":* Lillian Carter, C/S-FOHP, September 26, 1978.

*"I'm just as busy":* Jimmy Carter, *A Remarkable Mother* (New York: Simon & Schuster, 2008), 23, 45.

*"He never plowed":* Lillian Carter, C/S-FOHP, September 26, 1978.

*"It told accurately":* Nicholas Dawidoff, "The Riddle of Jimmy Carter," *Rolling Stone,* February 2, 2011.

*"A buck a day":* Jimmy Carter, "The Day No One Came to the Peanut Picker," in *Always a Reckoning,* 48.

*"hateful man":* Goldman, "Sizing Up Carter."

*"poorest of the poor":* Richard R. Wright Jr. and John R. Hawkins, *Centennial Encyclopaedia of the African Methodist Episcopal Church,* vol. 1 (Philadelphia: Book Concern of the AME Church, 1916), 137.

*"epitome of success":* Jimmy Carter, *Hour Before Daylight,* 23.

*"Cadillac after Cadillac":* ibid., 24.

*"I knew Rachel Clark":* Demme, *Man from Plains;* Jimmy Carter, *Hour Before Daylight,* 41.

*"Swim, son, swim":* Betty Glad, *Jimmy Carter: In*

*Search of the Great White House* (New York: W. W. Norton, 1980), 37.

*"acute attention"*: Jimmy Carter, *Hour Before Daylight,* 76.

*"She'd tell how"*: Jimmy Carter, "Rachel," in *Always a Reckoning,* 4.

*"You're the cause"*: Hutchinson, *Jimmy Carter's Hometown,* 90–93.

*"a more affectionate father"*: Lillian Carter, C/S-FOHP, September 26, 1978.

*"breach of southern etiquette"*: Jimmy Carter, *Why Not the Best?* (Nashville: Broadman Press, 1975), 32; Jimmy Carter, *Hour Before Daylight,* 24; Jimmy Carter, *Turning Point,* 17.

*I have never had a black person:* Lillian Carter, C/S-FOHP, September 26, 1978; Elovitz, "Three Days in Plains," 185.

*"People just didn't"*: ibid.

*Miscegenation is wrong:* Wooten, *Dasher,* 79.

*"We called them niggers then"*: Willard Slappey, C/S-FOHP, 1979.

*"I ain't going nowhere"*: Elovitz, "Three Days in Plains," 195.

*As late as the 1970s . . . let the word slip:* Eleanor Randolph, "The Carter Complex," *Esquire,* November 1977.

*she gave him a whipping:* William "Buddy" Carter, *Billy Carter: A Journey Through the Shadows* (Lanham, MD: Taylor Trade, 1999), 53.

*"She loved to laugh"*: Jimmy Carter, "Miss Lillian," in *Always a Reckoning,* 19.

*"only as histrionics"*: Jimmy Carter int., May 5, 2016.

*"not polite"*: Jimmy and Rosalynn Carter, *First Family from Plains,* interview by Judy Woodruff, PBS, October 1, 2014, https://www.pbs.org/

show/first-family-plains.

*" 'I'm just reading' "*: Gloria Carter Spann, C/S-FOHP, 1988; Elovitz, "Three Days in Plains," 185.

*"This was my first picture"*: Jimmy Carter, *Hour Before Daylight,* 56.

*"The working man in Georgia"*: George B. Tindall, *The Emergence of the New South: 1913–1945* (Baton Rouge: Louisiana State University Press, 1967), 616.

*"my first picture"*: Jimmy Carter, *Hour Before Daylight,* 65–67.

*"Children who cling"*: Jimmy Carter, *Remarkable Mother,* 64.

*"She would nurse"*: Jimmy Carter, "Miss Lillian," in *Always a Reckoning,* 19.

Chapter 3: Miss Julia

*"we were country"*: Hutchinson, *Jimmy Carter's Hometown,* 323.

*"that 'metropolitan' community' "*: Jimmy Carter, *Why Not the Best?,* 15.

*"like breathing"*: Jimmy Carter, *Hour Before Daylight,* 96.

*"nobody in there colored but me"*: Goldman, "Sizing Up Carter."

*"I was two different people"*: Jimmy Carter, *Hour Before Daylight,* 207–8.

*"a nagging degree of skepticism"*: Jimmy Carter, *Living Faith,* 17–18.

*Davis was arrested:* Elovitz, "Three Days in Plains," 192; Hutchinson, *Jimmy Carter's Hometown,* 93; Jimmy Carter int., September 2, 2017.

*"race and race"*: Jimmy Carter, "The Pasture

Gate," in *Always a Reckoning,* 34.

*Plains High School:* Betty Jennings Carter, C/S-FOHP.

*"the most resonating":* Jimmy Carter and Martin Marty, "What Happens to Children in Peril?," forum, Emory University, Atlanta, 2003.

*"He wasn't shy":* Kandy Stroud, *How Jimmy Won: The Victory Campaign from Plains to the White House* (New York: Morrow, 1977), 128.

*Miss Julia routinely shouted "Projection!":* Hugh Carter, and Frances Spatz Leighton, *Cousin Beedie and Cousin Hot: My Life with the Carter Family of Plains, Georgia* (Englewood Cliffs, NJ: Prentice-Hall, 1978), 54.

*"common, ordinary people":* Jimmy Carter, *Why Not the Best?,* 31.

*"her eyes":* Kathryn Bacon Maudlin to Jimmy Carter, June 16, 1970. FP. Box 17.

*"Expecting to accomplish":* William Patrick O'Brien, Jimmy Carter National Historic Site; Elovitz, "Three Days in Plains," 186.

*Eloise "Teenie" Ratliff:* Elovitz, "Three Days in Plains," 195.

*the importance of nonconformity:* Jimmy Carter, commencement address, Leslie High School, May 29, 1963, FP, JCPLM.

*"I love you":* Jimmy Carter int., September 15, 2015; Jimmy Carter, *Hour Before Daylight,* 228; Peter G. Bourne, *Jimmy Carter: A Comprehensive Biography from Plains to Post-Presidency* (New York: Scribner, 1997), 42.

*"no white man":* Wooten, *Dasher,* 104.

*lynched in Americus:* Richard Kluger, *Simple Justice: The History of Brown v. Board of Education and Black America's Struggle for Equality*

(New York: Alfred A. Knopf, 1976), 518.

*"We could hear them screaming"*: Lillian Carter, C/S-FOHP, September 26, 1978.

*"had been honored"*: Jimmy Carter, *Hour Before Daylight,* 33.

*"Almost ignored"*: Jimmy Carter, "Peanuts," in *Always a Reckoning,* 43.

*unselfconscious then:* Jimmy Carter, *Hour Before Daylight,* 152–53.

*stubborn righteousness:* ibid., 70–71.

*"go to Annapolis"*: Jimmy Carter, *Sharing Good Times* (New York: Simon & Schuster, 2004), 13.

*"college education"*: Jimmy Carter int., June 14, 2015.

*"Like a parrot"*: Jack Sheehan, *Class of '47: Annapolis — America's Best* (Las Vegas: Stephens Press, 2007), 11.

*"that last clinging drop"*: Jimmy Carter, *Why Not the Best?,* 43.

*Roxy Jo Logan:* Bourne, *Jimmy Carter,* 46–47.

*he peed on an electric fence:* Jimmy Carter int., August 3, 2018.

*put on more pounds:* Goldman, "Sizing Up Carter."

*alternative career:* Glad, *Jimmy Carter: In Search,* 48.

*insisted he never:* Jimmy Carter int., September 2, 2017.

*went fishing:* Randolph, "Carter Complex."

*"Dear Folks"*: Jimmy Carter to parents, n.d., JCPLM.

*Chapter 4: Annapolis*

*"I was a landlubber"*: Sheehan, *Class of '47,* 20.

*"telling a lie":* Jimmy Carter int., May 5, 2016.

*hazing of 1943–44:* Sheehan, *Class of '47,* 12.

*"assaulted from all sides":* Bruce Mazlish and Edwin Diamond, *Jimmy Carter: An Interpretive Biography* (New York: Simon & Schuster, 1979), 98.

*"It hurt like heck":* Jimmy Carter int., May 20, 2016.

*Carter was fried:* Jimmy Carter, unpublished journal, July 7, 1943–July 24, 1943.

*"Over five months til Xmas":* ibid., August 14, 1943–August 22, 1943.

*"Never kick":* Goldman, "Sizing Up Carter."

*"get his d—d nose":* Jimmy Carter, unpublished journal, October 6, 1943.

*"Brace up!":* *Lucky Bag,* US Naval Academy yearbook, 176.

*"I'm practically bilging Bull":* Jimmy Carter, unpublished journal, May 24, 1944.

*A Jewish midshipman, Howie Weiss:* Robert J. Schneller Jr., *Breaking the Color Barrier: The U.S. Naval Academy's First Black Midshipmen and the Struggle for Racial Equality* (New York: New York University Press, 2005), 233.

*"as if he was traitor":* ibid., 218.

*Brown's backside:* Jimmy Carter, *Full Life,* 34; Paul Vitello, "Wesley Brown, Pioneer as Black Naval Graduate, Dies at 85," *New York Times,* May 24, 2012; Padgett, *Pocket Change and Peanuts,* 3.

*"hang in there":* Padgett, *Pocket Change and Peanuts,* 3.

*"Liebestod":* Dan Thanh Dang, "Carter Tells Ex-Classmates to Boost 'Academy's Image' — 370 from Class of 1947 Recall Life as Midshipmen," *Baltimore Sun* online, June 5, 1996, https://www.baltimoresun.com/news/bs-xpm-

1996-06-05-1996157011-story.html.

*compassion and sensitivity:* Al Rusher int., July 10, 2015.

*officially graduating 60th: Annual Register of the U.S. Naval Academy, Class of 1946–47,* 33.

*"did not really excel":* Jimmy Carter, *Full Life,* 36.

*"Long-distance runners":* Glad, *In Search,* 51.

*"a loner":* Mazlish and Diamond, *Jimmy Carter: Interpretive Biography,* 100.

*details of captivity:* Tom Gordy File, "Diary, 1942," "Prisoner of War Manuscript, 1941–1945," box 1, Emily Dolvin Collection, FP.

*"city ways were considered strange":* Jimmy Carter, "The Ballad of Tom Gordy," in *Always a Reckoning,* 29.

*Dorothy married a fireman:* Jimmy Carter, *Hour Before Daylight,* 253; Jimmy Carter, *Full Life,* 51; Jimmy Carter, *Remarkable Mother,* 35; Jimmy Carter, "Ballad of Tom Gordy," in *Always a Reckoning,* 30.

Chapter 5: Rosalynn

*"guilty conscience for years":* Rosalynn Carter, *First Lady from Plains* (Boston: Houghton Mifflin, 1984), 14.

*"depending on you to be strong":* ibid., 17.

*Edgar's bed:* Allie Smith, C/S-FOHP, 1978.

*"I'd pay to sit behind her":* Jimmy Carter, "Rosalynn," in *Always a Reckoning,* 87.

*"She was remarkably beautiful":* Jimmy Carter, *Full Life,* 38.

*"She's Ruth's friend":* Wooten, *Dasher,* 179.

*"the wrong side of the tracks":* Carter and Leighton, *Cousin Beedie and Cousin Hot,* 65–66.

*"He had all these expectations":* Rosalynn Carter

1030

int., November 18, 2015.

*so solicitous:* Jimmy Carter int., November 18, 2015.

*"Everybody here . . . in Times Square etc.":* Jimmy Carter to Jacquelyn Reid, August 10, 1945, Early American History Auctions, https://www .liveauctioneers.com/item/27817031_1945- jimmy-carter-als-as-us-navy-midshipman.

*"I'm really looking forward . . . darling":* ibid., September 17, 1945.

*engraved with "ILYTG":* Rosalynn Carter int., May 13, 2016; Bourne, *Jimmy Carter,* 53.

*"I couldn't wait":* Rosalynn Carter, *First Lady,* 26.

*"You, darling":* JCPLM exhibit.

*"the perfect extension of myself":* Jimmy Carter, remarks, CC Weekend, 2016.

*insisted they weren't late:* Hutchinson, *Jimmy Carter's Hometown,* 48; Jimmy Carter int., June 15, 2016.

*"felt cheated":* Stapleton, *Brother Billy,* 49, 94.

*"very jealous":* Rosalynn Carter, *First Lady,* 26.

*"He berated me":* Jimmy Carter int., February 17, 2017.

*weighed leaving the navy:* Jimmy Carter, *Turning Point,* 55.

*"fed up with navy life":* Jimmy Carter, *Full Life,* 40.

*"at the pleasure of the president":* Jimmy Carter int., February 17, 2017.

*"constant separations . . . ecstatic reunions":* Jimmy Carter, *Why Not the Best?,* 68–69.

*"an independence . . . of my life":* JCPLM exhibit.

*"I could do anything":* Rosalynn Carter int., June 13, 2015.

*"her tears":* Rosalynn Carter, *First Lady,* 28; Jimmy Carter; *Living Faith,* 40.

*"real peculiar-looking guy"*: Mazlish and Diamond, *Jimmy Carter: Interpretive Biography,* 102.

*Elizabethan scholar . . . nervous breakdown:* Bourne, *Jimmy Carter,* 64.

*killed himself:* Jimmy Carter, *Full Life,* 42.

*confirmed to be safe:* Glad, *In Search,* 60; Jimmy Carter, *Full Life,* 48.

*"fragile was my existence"*: Jimmy Carter, *Full Life,* 53.

*"remarkably high native intelligence"*: *Report on the Fitness of Officers,* United States Navy, May 31, 1949, FP.

*"pleasant personality"*: ibid., June 30, 1949.

*"finest of submarine officers"*: ibid., July 10, 1950.

*"the boss"*: Goldman, "Sizing Up Carter."

*"seaman . . . being seasick"*: ibid.

*"the whole cruise"*: Jimmy Carter to Rosalynn Carter, October 14, 1949.

*"Jimmy was not one of the guys"*: T. R. Reid, "Carter Is Remembered as Diligent but Distant Sailor," *Washington Post,* December 1, 1976.

*In Honolulu . . . spirit of adventure:* Jimmy Carter, *Sharing Good Times,* 25.

*"single-minded commitment"*: ibid., 18.

*"Rosalynn, it's probably my imagination"*: Jimmy Carter to Rosalynn Carter, August 18, 1949.

*"quite a few nightclubs"*: ibid.

*"The Aloha party"*: ibid., August 21, 1949.

*"all business, no fooling"*: Mazlish and Diamond, *Jimmy Carter: Interpretive Biography,* 115.

*"but it was not . . . a close friendship"*: Goldman, "Sizing Up Carter."

*"a workshop with my own tools"*: Jimmy Carter to parents, n.d., FP.

*"The governor-general was absolutely right"*: Jimmy Carter, *Full Life,* 61.

*"too soon for . . . a dance together":* Jimmy Carter, *Turning Point,* 46.

*Chapter 6: The Rickover Way*

*"no social skills":* John Dalton int., June 15, 2016.

*"fight against stupidity":* Norman Polmar and Thomas B. Allen, *Rickover* (New York: Simon & Schuster, 1982), 462.

*"a 'nucleus of martyrs' ":* ibid., 640.

*"Start talking":* ibid.

*"Did you always do your best?"* Jimmy Carter int., February 15, 2017.

*"Why not?":* Jimmy Carter, *Why Not the Best?,* 63–64.

*"a PhD isn't worth anything":* William J. Crowe Jr. with David Chanoff, *The Line of Fire: From Washington to the Gulf, the Politics and Battles of the New Military* (New York: Simon & Schuster, 1993), 51.

*"cold and humorless":* Jimmy Carter int., June 14, 2015.

*"the smartest man":* Dave Schechter, "A Bible Study Led by 92-Year-Old Jimmy Carter Isa Sightto Behold," Religion News Service, July 31, 2017, https://religionnews.com/?s=%22 the+smartest+man%22.

*"Rickover has set an example":* Jimmy Carter, Address to the Alabama American Legion Convention, July 14, 1973, GSA.

*"The absence of . . . compliment":* Jimmy Carter int., May 20, 2016.

*Rickover was still up and scribbling:* Jimmy Carter int., May 13, 2016.

*superhuman work ethic:* Jimmy Carter, *Why Not the Best?,* 61.

*"he valued me":* Jimmy Carter int., June 14, 2015.

*he rated him "outstanding":* H. G. Rickover, *Report on the Fitness of Officers,* April 24, 1953, VF, Carter, J., Navy Records, JCPLM.

*"I . . . do the best I can":* Goldman, "Sizing Up Carter."

*Chalk River:* Gordon Edwards, "Reactor Accidents at Chalk River: The Human Fallout," Canadian Coalition for Nuclear Responsibility, http://www.ccnr.org/paulson_legacy.html. See also W. B. Lewis, *The Accident to the NRX Reactor on December 12, 1952* (report DR-32) (Chalk River, Ont.: Atomic Energy of Canada, July 13, 1953), available at US Department of Energy, Office of Scientific and Technical Information online, https://www.osti.gov/servlets/purl/4379334); D. G. Hurst, *The Accident to the NRX Reactor on December 12, 1952, Pt. 2* (report GPI-14) (Atomic Energy of Canada, October 1953).

*"how diverse . . . a man's life could be":* Jimmy Carter, *Full Life,* 65.

*"besieged by an unwelcome comparison":* Jimmy Carter, *Hour Before Daylight,* 259.

*"Nobody would care":* Goldman, "Sizing Up Carter"; Jimmy Carter, *Hour Before Daylight,* 259; Jimmy Carter, *Full Life,* 65–66.

*"It was agony":* ibid.

*"still not completely clear to me":* Jimmy Carter, *Sharing Good Times,* 26.

*"God did not . . . kill people":* Bourne, *Jimmy Carter,* 81.

*"the past resentment of the boy":* Jimmy Carter, "Wanted to Share My Father's World," in *Always a Reckoning,* 100.

*"Something's . . . driving you":* Frank Bruni, "Losing Fathers, Then Making History," *New York*

*Times,* June 17, 2018.

*"astounded and furious":* Rosalynn Carter, *First Lady,* 36.

*"She almost quit on me":* Stuart E. Eizenstat, *President Carter: The White House Years* (New York: Thomas Dunne Books, 2018), 22.

*"His mind was made up":* Rosalynn Carter int., June 14, 2015.

*"thought that . . . we weren't worth having":* Jimmy Carter int., June 14, 2015.

*special dispensation:* E. L. Forrester to Vice Admiral James L. Holloway Jr., August 28, 1953, JCPLM.

*"relations between us remained quite cool":* Jimmy Carter, *Full Life,* 67.

*"Jack . . . stop at a restroom":* ibid.; Jimmy Carter int., June 16, 2015.

*"I had . . . varied public service":* Jimmy Carter, *Why Not the Best?,* 65.

**Part 2: Georgia on His Mind**

*Chapter 7: The Joiner*

*"There's no house big enough":* King, Rainone, and Bourne, "Lillian Carter on Her Own: Talking About Racism, the Kennedys, and 'Jimmy's Reign,' " *Ms.,* October 1976; Rosalynn Carter int., May 13, 2016.

*nuclear reactor . . . simple by comparison:* Jimmy Carter, *Full Life,* 70.

*"gnawing away":* Jimmy Carter, OH, UVA-MC, 1988.

*"we might as well be really successful":* Kati Marton, *Hidden Power: Presidential Marriages That Shaped History* (New York: Pantheon Books, 2001), 222.

*"Can't we relax?":* Rosalynn Carter, *First Lady,* 42.

*"to get people to buy peanuts":* Jimmy Carter int., September 5, 2015.

*"Get up! . . . excel!":* Jeff Carter int., June 26, 2015.

*"eventually I won":* Jack Carter int., August 27, 2015.

*One of the only fights:* Jeff Carter int., June 16, 2015; Jack Carter int., August 27, 2015; Chip Carter int., May 17, 2016; Jack Carter, OH, JCPLM, June 25, 2003.

*"extremely strict . . . perhaps excessively":* Jimmy Carter int., May 13, 2016.

*"real pistol":* Grant Hayter-Menzies, *Lillian Carter: A Compassionate Life* (Jefferson, NC: McFarland, 2014), 84–85.

*Animal Farm:* Chip Carter, remarks, CC Weekend, June 29, 2019.

*on fertilizer sacks:* Harvey Shapiro, "A Conversation with Jimmy Carter," *New York Times Book Review,* June 19, 1977, 1.

*"the insensitivity . . . in power":* ibid.

*Poets' Corner:* see John Malcolm Brinnin, Comment, *New Yorker,* March 29, 1982; Jimmy Carter, *White House Diary* (New York: Farrar, Straus and Giroux, 2010), 49.

*"on the toilet . . . of the warehouse":* Jimmy Carter int., February 17, 2017.

*"hired hand":* William "Buddy" Carter, *Billy Carter,* 22, 26, and 53.

*ready to work:* Jimmy Carter int., May 13, 2016.

*Chapter 8: "There's Nothing I Can Do"*

*"I never claimed":* Jimmy Carter int., September 15, 2015.

*"a mean and starved back corner":* Garry Wills, *Lead Time: A Journalist's Education* (Boston: Houghton Mifflin, 1984), 250.

*"the secret shame":* Charles Mohr: "Carter Credibility Issue: Calley and Vietnam War," *New York Times,* May 21, 1976, 1.

*Rosalynn remembered . . . racial integration:* Rosalynn Carter, *First Lady,* 42.

*"do away with the public school system":* Roy Harris, "Strictly Personal," *Augusta (GA) Courier,* October 2, 1950.

*"obviously a mistake on my part":* Robert Scheer, "Jimmy, We Hardly Know Y'All," *Playboy,* November 1976.

*board acted as though nothing had changed:* Board of Education Meeting Minutes, January 18, 1956, 299, Sumter County Board of Education Ledger, September 1931–January 1956, Sumter County Board of Education, Americus.

*"minimize simultaneous traffic":* ibid.

*"Lexie, there's nothing I can do":* Goldman, "Sizing Up Carter."

*"Koinonia was Communist . . . everybody said":* Rosalynn Carter int., May 13, 2016.

*"That's scared":* Alan Anderson, SCOHP, June 2, 2003; Jim Auchmutey, *The Class of '65: A Student, a Divided Town, and the Long Road to Forgiveness* (New York: PublicAffairs, 2015), 47.

*"ship the nuts out":* William Bailey Williford, *Americus Through the Years: The Story of a Georgia Town and Its People, 1832–1975* (Atlanta: Cherokee, 1975), 337.

*Jack Singletary:* Bourne, *Jimmy Carter,* 98; Robert Scheer int., September 16, 2017; Scheer, "Jimmy, We Hardly Know Y'All," in Robert Scheer, *Playing President: My Close Encounters with Nixon, Carter, Bush I, Reagan, and Clinton — and How They Did Not Prepare Me for*

*George W. Bush* (New York: Akashic Books, 2006), 117.

*Carter's Warehouse and Koinonia did transact some business:* Auchmutey, *Class of '65,* 41; Robert Scheer int., September 16, 2017; Steve Hammond int., November 17, 2017.

*"It's a shame":* Goldman, "Sizing Up Carter"; Auchmutey, *Class of '65,* 41.

*"infect" other children:* Auchmutey, *Class of '65,* 60.

*chairman Carter . . . "disagreed strongly":* Board of Education Minutes, November 6, 1960, 88.

*"If you wanted to queer something":* Bourne, *Jimmy Carter,* 115; Warren Fortson, int., March 29, 2017.

*"stinging disappointment":* Jimmy Carter, *Why Not the Best?,* 88.

*"I sat there . . . crying inside":* Rosalynn Carter, *First Lady,* 46.

*"COONS AND CARTERS GO TOGETHER":* Deanna L. Michael, *Jimmy Carter as Educational Policymaker: Equal Opportunity and Efficiency* (Albany: State University of New York Press, 2008), 28–29.

*"You fellas don't mind":* Goldman, "Sizing Up Carter."

*"somewhat shaky voice":* Jimmy Carter, *Living Faith,* 65.

*" 'down the toilet' ":* Jimmy Carter, *Turning Point,* 22–23.

*suspiciously colorful coda:* Jimmy Carter, *Full Life,* 78.

*"the meanest man in the world":* Branch, *Parting the Waters,* 561.

*Chappell was . . . a caricature:* John Perdew and Randy Battle, "A Kitchen Table Conversation:

Events in Dawson and Americus, Georgia," Civil Rights Movement Archive, October 2005, https://www.crmvet.org/nars/perdew1.htm.

*"very solid people":* Andrew Young, *An Easy Burden: The Civil Rights Movement and the Transformation of America* (New York: HarperCollins, 1996), 168–69.

*"seventy-five thousand members?":* Jimmy Carter, *Turning Point,* 63; Jimmy Carter, *Keeping Faith: Memoirs of a President* (New York: Bantam Books, 1982), 9; Bourne, *Jimmy Carter,* 113.

*Chapter 9: Senator Carter*

*"isolated and withdrawn sometimes":* Stroud, *How Jimmy Won,* 11.

*"it's Jimmy":* Goldman, "Sizing Up Carter."

*"stuff the ballot box":* Sam Singer int., February 7, 2016; Jimmy Carter, *Turning Point,* 84.

*("square-danced . . . elected"):* Jimmy Carter int., February 15, 2017.

*"so naive":* Jimmy Carter, *Full Life,* 85.

*"he wouldn't pretend . . . like most of us":* Charles Kirbo, OH, UVA-MC, January 5, 1983.

*"I nearly fainted":* ibid.

*" 'We have just won this thing' ":* Warren Fortson int., March 29, 2017.

*take the oath:* Sam Singer int., February 7, 2016; Jimmy Carter, *Turning Point,* 182.

*"thirty questions":* Jimmy Carter, *Living Faith,* 121.

*"fearful of the news": Addresses of Jimmy Carter (James Earl Carter), Governor of Georgia, 1971–1975* (Atlanta: B. W. Fortson, Secretary of State, 1975), 260–61.

*rights of atheists:* Jimmy Carter, *Why Not the Best?,* 101.

*"This sometimes made him unpopular":* Bobby

Rowan int., June 26, 2016.

*speed-reading:* Marcia Biederman, *Scan Artist: How Evelyn Wood Convinced the World That Speed-Reading Worked* (Chicago: Chicago Review Press, 2019), 181.

*"Go through . . . what you don't like":* Jimmy Carter, *Why Not the Best?,* 99.

*"grab ass":* Bobby Rowan int., June 2, 2016.

*"straight arrow":* ibid.

*"were seldom spoken with affection or even warmth":* Hamilton Jordan, unpublished book proposal, June 16, 2003.

*" 'Good morning, Senator' ":* Leroy Johnson int., May 17, 2016.

*pronunciation of the word* Negro: Jimmy Carter int., May 17, 2016; Leroy Johnson int., May 17, 2016; Leroy Johnson, ROGP-016, February 27, 2007.

*" 'Run, nigger, run' ":* Kathy Fletcher, SCOHP, March 6, 2004.

*"without parallel in" . . . a desegregation campaign:* Claude Sitton, "Strict Law Enforcement Stifles Negroes' Drive in Americus, GA," *New York Times,* September 29, 1963.

*"plotting his own future":* Morris B. Abram, interviewed by Lorraine Nelson Spritzer, January 4, 1978 (P1978-02, Series G, The Belle of Ashby Street), Georgia Government Documentation Project (GGDP), Special Collections and Archives, Georgia State University Library; Morris B. Abram, *The Day Is Short: An Autobiography* (New York: Harcourt Brace Jovanovich, 1982), 139.

*Chip picked up a chair:* Chip Carter int., August 12, 2017.

*declined to punish him:* Rosalynn Carter, *First Lady,* 49.

*pelted with rocks and bricks:* Bobby Fuse Jr., SCOHP, July 30, 2003.

*"learn to box":* Wooten, *Dasher,* 255.

*drive-by shooting:* Gene Roberts, "White Youth Is Shot Near Georgia Rally," *New York Times,* July 29, 1965, 1.

*Klan rally:* Gene Roberts, "Americus Names Negroes to Jobs as Polling Clerks," *New York Times,* August 7, 1965, 1.

*"We'll kill . . . tonight!":* Auchmutey, *Class of '65,* 147–48.

*"We have no other choice":* Tom Brokaw int., May 30, 2016.

*Rosalynn pleaded:* Rosalynn Carter int., November 17, 2015.

*"This is . . . not your house":* Goldman, "Sizing Up Carter."

*voter registration march: Americus (GA) Times-Recorder,* August 9, 1965.

*"caught a lot of unshirted hell":* Gene Roberts, "Americus Whites Ask Peace Talks," *New York Times,* August 4, 1965, 18; Warren Fortson int., May 7, 2017.

*"Bircher" lies about the Carters:* Jimmy Carter, *Living Faith,* 68–69; Jimmy Carter int., February 17, 2017.

*"nothing to say":* Gene Roberts int., December 16, 2015.

*"Plains . . . a wonderful place to live":* Jimmy Carter, *Always a Reckoning,* vii; Jimmy Carter, *Living Faith,* 70.


Chapter 10: The Greasy Pole

*"I'm a Dick Russell Democrat": Atlanta Constitution,*

April 12, 1966.

*"You'd better get a chair":* Rosalynn Carter int., November 17, 2015.

*"You'd never . . . switched":* Bobby Rowan int., June 2, 2016.

*"I hadn't the strength":* Schram, *Running for President,* 42.

*"I have never been so happy":* Hayter-Menzies, *Lillian Carter,* 119.

*"unnatural and even forced":* Hamilton Jordan, unpublished book proposal, June 16, 2003.

*"no other human being":* Hamilton Jordan, *A Boy from Georgia: Coming of Age in the Segregated South,* ed. Kathleen Jordan (Athens: University of Georgia Press, 2015), 221–26.

*"I have never met Bobby Kennedy":* "Carter Denies Association with Kennedys," *Augusta (GA) Chronicle-Herald,* August 21, 1966.

*"I'll show you a loser":* Hamilton Jordan, *Boy from Georgia,* 222.

*Chapter 11: Born Again*

*"profoundly depressed":* Bourne, *Jimmy Carter,* 165.

*wandering aimlessly:* Carter and Leighton, *Cousin Beedie and Cousin Hot,* 117.

*"Everything . . . was not gratifying":* Jimmy Carter int., February 17, 2017.

*"I was disillusioned":* Jimmy Carter, *Living Faith,* 96.

*"torturous time of searching":* ibid., 24.

*"The turning point":* ibid., 95.

*"doubt . . . one element of faith":* Leo P. Ribuffo, *The Limits of Moderation: Jimmy Carter and the Ironies of American Liberalism,* draft manuscript,

1042

225, 227.

*"personal courage . . . my Christian life"*: Jimmy Carter, *Living Faith*, 2.

*"faith . . . to God"*: ibid., 8.

*"inner healing"*: Goldman, "Sizing Up Carter."

*"communicating love to . . . a human being"*: Wolfgang Saxon, "Ruth Carter Stapleton Dies: Evangelist and Faith Healer," *New York Times*, September 27, 1983.

*"a bunch of crap"*: Jimmy Carter, *Living Faith*, 201–2; Nancy Gibbs and Michael Duffy, *The Preacher and the Presidents: Billy Graham in the White House* (New York: Center Street, 2007), 243.

*"I had to forget"*: *Washington Post*, March 12, 1976.

*Jimmy remembered*: Goldman, "Sizing Up Carter"; Jules Witcover, *Marathon: The Pursuit of the Presidency, 1972–1976* (New York: Viking Press, 1977), 270.

*"I rejected her advice"*: Jimmy Carter, *Hour Before Daylight*, 264.

*"a Timothy"*: Nelson Price int., September 22, 2017.

*"Being born again . . . to Christ"*: Jimmy Carter, *Living Faith*, 22.

*"It was a sobering thought"*: ibid., 208.

*"they weren't planning on having me"*: Amy Carter int., November 18, 2015.

*"She had four fathers"*: Rosalynn Carter int., November 17, 2015.

*"Yours in Christ"*: Jimmy Carter to Milo Pennington, August 1, 1968, JCPLM.

*"I have no idea"*: Hutchinson, *Jimmy Carter's Hometown*, 327.

*"Jimmy got down on his knees"*: James C. Hefley and Marti Hefley, *The Church That Produced a*

*President* (New York: Wyden Books, 1977), 66.

*"most moving religious experiences":* Goldman, "Sizing Up Carter."

*"a great man":* Jimmy Carter, *Living Faith,* 218.

*"tough as nails inside":* Goldman, "Sizing Up Carter."

*"A man needs only two loves":* Jimmy Carter, sermon, Church of the Exceptional, Macon, GA, March 18, 1974, JCPLM.

*"don't please everyone":* Lillian Carter and Gloria Carter Spann, *Away from Home: Letters to My Family* (New York: Simon & Schuster, 1977), 153.

*"Becoming the leader . . . in a segregated state":* Nancy Gibbs and Michael Duffy, *The Presidents Club: Inside the World's Most Exclusive Fraternity* (New York: Simon & Schuster, 2012), 244; Bobby Fuse Jr., SCOHP, July 30, 2003.

*"I am at best a mediocre Christian":* Jimmy Carter, address to Detroit Christian Business Men's Committee, May 11, 1974, JCPLM.

*"sin of pride":* Jimmy Carter, *Living Faith,* 219; Ribuffo, *Limits of Moderation,* 224.

*Chapter 12: The Code Word Campaign*

*"Are we done talking about this yet?":* Jimmy Carter int., November 19, 2015.

*free beer:* Rosalynn Carter, *First Lady,* 61.

*"Jimmy and I . . . sleep in the same bed":* William Safire, "Mr. Carter's Cover-Up," *New York Times,* December 6, 1976, 33; Jimmy Carter int., November 19, 2015.

*Rabhan recalled pitching:* David Rabhan int., September 8, 2017.

*"poison apple"*: David Rabhan int., September 5, 2017.

*"he had a better way"*: Padgett, *Pocket Change and Peanuts,* 407.

*"better than anyone except my wife"*: ibid.

*"icy stare"*: Jack Carter int., August 27, 2015; Jack Carter, OH, JCPLM, June 25, 2003.

*Jimmy was simply repeating:* Judy Langford int., December 4, 2015.

*his parents' intervention . . . saved his life:* Chip Carter, remarks, CC Weekend, June 28, 2019.

*mental health:* E. Stanly Godbold Jr., *Jimmy and Rosalynn Carter: The Georgia Years, 1924–1974* (New York: Oxford University Press, 2010), 151.

*"law and order"*: Jimmy Carter, draft announcement, April 3, 1970, JCPLM.

" 'consider *voting for me*' ": Bobby Rowan int., June 2, 2016.

*"I don't think it is right . . . stifling communications with another state"*: Bourne, *Jimmy Carter,* 192.

*"our kind"*: Dan T. Carter, *From George Wallace to Newt Gingrich: Race in the Conservative Counterrevolution, 1963–1994* (Baton Rouge: Louisiana State University Press, 1996), 46–48.

*"peanuts, pennies, and people"*: Randy Sanders, *Mighty Peculiar Elections: The New South Gubernatorial Campaigns of 1970 and the Changing Politics of Race* (Gainesville: University Press of Florida, 2002), 160.

*"Cufflinks Carl"*: *Columbus (GA) Ledger,* August 28, 1970.

*"ignorant, racist, backward . . . peanut farmer"*: Robert A. Strong, "Jimmy Carter: Life Before the Presidency," UVA-MC online, https://millercenter.org/president/carter/life-before-

the-presidency.

*"rich liberal interests"*: Bill Shipp int., August 23, 2016.

*"champagne shampoo"*: Atlanta Journal, March 21, 1970.

*"a dangerous smear . . . campaign"*: Atlanta Constitution, June 11, 1970.

*"nigger campaign"*: Sanders, *Mighty Peculiar Elections*, 164.

*"Carter's attitude"*: Jerry Rafshoon int., August 7, 2017.

*"I was shocked"*: Reg Murphy int., August 23, 2016.

*"right of center, but not far right"*: Atlanta Journal, July 28, 1970.

*"so that they . . . register everybody"*: Kings Bay (GA) Periscope, February 1970, JCPLM.

*"We're too busy working"*: video collection, JCPLM.

*Carter mentioned . . . double the buy*: Jerry Rafshoon int., September 3, 2015.

*"Carter is . . . undermined by political ambition"*: "Carter's Bitterness Taints His Credibility," *Macon (GA) News*, August 31, 1970.

*"Jimmy . . . works hard"*: Columbus (GA) Enquirer, editorial, September 14, 1970.

*Carter was "atheistic"*: ibid.

*"race mixers"*: Atlanta Constitution, August 8, 1970.

*"The tiniest drop"*: Wooten, *Dasher*, 267.

*"playing the race card"*: Carl Sanders, interviewed by Bob Short, October 1, 2006, ROGP (video, ROGP-005), Richard B. Russell Library for Political Research and Studies, University of Georgia Libraries, Athens, GA.

*"rednecks, whitenecks, and blacknecks"*: Harry Murphy, "Carter Wooing Rednecks, Whitenecks, and Blacknecks," *Atlanta Constitution*,

October 17, 1970.

*Story of Carter's pledge to Rabhan on Cessna:* ibid.; David Rabhan int., September 5, 2017, March 26, 2019; Jimmy Carter int., September 5, 2017; Douglas Brinkley, "What It Takes," *New Yorker,* October 21, 1996.

*"I need your continuing prayers":* Eloy Cruz to Jimmy Carter, November 13, 1970.

*Chapter 13: "He Said Whaaat?"*

*"the neurosis, the despair":* Michael Paterniti, "Jimmy Carter for Higher Office," *GQ* online, June 25, 2018, https://www.gq.com/story/jimmy-carter-for-higher-office.

*"kidney stone of a decade":* Garry Trudeau, *Doonesbury,* December 7, 1979.

*"the ghettos":* Charles Kirbo to Jimmy Carter, December 28, 1970.

*"I say . . . simple justice":* inauguration address draft, January 12, 1971.

*"You could just feel the shock":* Jimmy and Rosalynn Carter, *First Family from Plains,* https://www.pbs.org/show/first-family-plains.

*"It looked like a stake":* Bill Shipp int., August 23, 2016.

*"Wallace's old pal":* *Atlanta Constitution,* January 13, 1971.

*"enigma and a contradiction":* Jon Nordheimer, "New Georgia Governor Urges End of Racial Bias," *New York Times,* January 13, 1971; Jon Nordheimer, "Yes, That Was Georgia Governor Speaking," *New York Times,* January 17, 1971.

*"His liberalism was there all the time":* Jerry Rafshoon int., August 7, 2017.

*"his stance overnight":* Godbold Jr., *Jimmy and Rosalynn Carter,* 174.

*"That nigger-loving bastard"*: Bobby Rowan int., June 2, 2016.

*"Pay no attention"*: Vernon Jordan int., May 9, 2016.

*"He said* whaaat*?"*: Rita Jackson Samuels int., May 17, 2016.

*"I have just got one purpose"*: Lester Maddox, interviewed by John Allen, November 22, 1988, and July 26, 1989 (P1988-22, series A), Georgia Governors, Georgia Government Documentation Project (GGDP), Special Collections and Archives, Georgia State University Library.

*"I wasn't abusive"*: Jimmy Carter int., February 17, 2017.

*"those are his exact words"*: Maddox, GGDP, July 26, 1989.

*"a bald-faced liar"*: Gary M. Fink, *Prelude to the Presidency: The Political Character and Legislative Leadership Style of Governor Jimmy Carter* (Westport, CT: Greenwood Press, 1980), 30–33.

*"Georgia's Hitler"*: Godbold Jr., *Jimmy and Rosalynn Carter,* 178; Hamilton Jordan, unpublished book proposal, June 16, 2003.

*"We are not limousine people"*: Emily Dolvin, FP.

*she still sometimes spelled Rosalynn "Rosalyn"*: Lillian Carter to Jimmy Carter, c. 1972.

*"Please . . . I'm too humble"*: Lillian Carter to Jimmy Carter, n.d.

*"a dictator"*: Jimmy Carter int., February 17, 2017.

*"you are just 'Great' "*: Bert Lance to Jimmy Carter, April 26, 1971.

*"One of the bright spots"*: Jimmy Carter to Bert Lance, May 17, 1971.

*"Beware!"*: ibid., May 28, 1971.

*"personal visits . . . smoke signals"*: Bert Lance with Bill Gilbert, *The Truth of the Matter: My Life In and Out of Politics* (New York: Summit Books, 1991), 38.

*"Repeat after me"*: Jerry Rafshoon int., May 20, 2020.

*"You are the greatest"*: Bert Lance to Jimmy Carter, December 3, 1971.

*"Your accomplishments . . . for Georgia"*: ibid., March 9, 1972.

*"crack heads"*: *Atlanta Constitution,* January 15, 1973.


*Chapter 14: Jungle Jimmy*

*"Harmless enough . . . precision"*: Michiko Kakutani, *The Death of Truth: Notes on Falsehood in the Age of Trump* (New York: Tim Duggan Books, 2018), 100.

*"shuffling boxes"*: ibid.

*"The list is disgusting"*: Jimmy Carter to Frank Moore, August 25, 1971, JCPLM.

*"I've never been so surprised and disappointed"*: Jimmy Carter to Sam Nunn, May 16, 1972.

*Nunn . . . pulled the ads:* Sam Nunn int., June 7, 2017.

*"You sold the farm"*: Goldman, "Sizing Up Carter."

*"kick my ass if . . . I was doing something wrong"*: Jimmy Carter to Arthur Bolton, July 16, 1972.

*"I'm not going to . . . be gutted"*: Fink, *Prelude to the Presidency,* 93–96.

*"Jimmy sailed high"*: Warren Fortson int., March 29, 2017.

*"He doesn't go around . . . until the log gives way"*: ibid.

*"do as fine a job as that boy"*: Charles Kirbo, OH,

UVA-MC, January 5, 1983.

*"selfish, petty bastards":* Hamilton Jordan to Jimmy Carter, n.d.

*contingency fund:* Bourne, *Jimmy Carter,* 219.

*"son of a bitch":* "Carter's Testimony, on Videotape, Is Given in Georgia Gambling Trial," *New York Times,* April 20, 1978, A20.

*"it is . . . a miracle":* Hamilton Jordan to Jimmy Carter, n.d.

*Only decades later:* Jimmy Carter int., June 14, 2015.

*threatened to arrest them for trespassing:* Joe Tanner int., June 8, 2016; Jimmy Bishop int., February 21, 2018.

*Blum confessed she never got the hang of it:* Barbara Blum int., October 24, 2016.

*Maddox whispered, "Commie":* ibid.

*"a congressman's highest goals":* Carter, preface, in Brown and Smith, *Flint River;* Jimmy Carter int., November 18, 2015.

*"a wild river":* Claude Terry interviewed, Georgia Canoe Association newsletter, June 30, 2010; *The Wild President,* directed by Will Staufer-Norris (Moscow, ID: NRS Films/Vimeo, 2017).

*"The Georgia children . . . improvements":* Jimmy Carter to George L. Smith, May 3, 1973.

*sent absenteeism past 50 percent: Americus (GA) Times-Recorder,* April 6, 1972.

*"degenerating rapidly":* ibid., June 7, 1971.

*"I just can't stand to see my own county":* Jimmy Carter to Tommy Hooks III, April 24, 1972.

*"Christian witness":* Jimmy Carter to Allen Ault, November 26, 1974.

*free eyeglasses:* Jimmy Carter to Harold Clayton, March 19, 1963.

" 'Paved roads all around' ": Lance with Gilbert, *Truth of the Matter,* 40.

*"You know, JC only stands for 'Jimmy Carter' ":* Jerry Rafshoon int., April 28, 2015.

*"a cancer":* Goldman, "Sizing Up Carter."

*"You mean . . . in private?":* Felicity Barringer, "Celestine Sibley Is Dead at 85; Columnist Embodied the South," *New York Times,* August 17, 1999, C21.

*"It was a bit schoolmarmish":* Reg Murphy int., August 23, 2016.

*"I've been here all day!":* Greg Schneiders int., September 1, 2015.

*"I don't like watermelon that much":* Carlton Hicks int., May 4, 2015.

*"Pardon Williams":* Chip Carter and Jerry Rafshoon int., June 15, 2015.

*"When they spoke . . . like people in South Georgia":* Godbold, *Jimmy and Rosalynn Carter,* 1–2.

*"We discovered part of ourselves": New York Times,* May 15, 2008.

## Part 3: Dark Horse
*Chapter 15: Jimmy Who?*

*"becoming again":* Wooten, *Dasher,* 187.

*"Dixie Whistles a Different Tune":* "A New Day Coming in the South," *Time,* May 31, 1971.

*Norman Mailer . . . admired Carter's "arrogance":* Norman Mailer, "The Search for Carter," *New York Times Magazine,* September 26, 1976.

*"vile language":* Bourne, *Jimmy Carter,* 228.

*"No . . . I ran for governor":* Witcover, *Marathon,* 106.

*"We think you should run for . . . p-p-p-president":* Jerry Rafshoon int., June 15, 2015; Bourne, *Jimmy Carter,* 233.

*"I've got other plans":* Dan Tate int., July 20, 2015.

*"President of what?":* Al Rusher int., July 10, 2015.

*Jordan wrote with uncanny foresight:* Hamilton Jordan to Jimmy Carter, November 4, 1972.

*"believed very deeply that the Jews . . . deserved their own nation":* Jimmy Carter, *Keeping Faith,* 274.

*he would be Orthodox:* Jerry Rafshoon int., June 15, 2015.

*"reports have reached our office":* Hayden C. Hewes to Jimmy Carter, September 14, 1973, GSA.

*"about same size as [the] moon maybe":* Jimmy Carter to Hayden C. Hewes, September 18, 1973, GSA.

a *barium cloud was launched:* Jere Justus to Steven H. Hochman, February 27, 2020; *US Space Science Program Report to COSPAR* (QB504.U54), vol. 8 (Washington, DC: National Academy of Sciences–National Research Council, 1970), appendix 1, 154.

*"six hundred thousand for me":* Jimmy Carter, Sunday school class, Maranatha Baptist Church, Plains, GA, September 16, 2015.

*"what God has in mind for you":* Nelson Price int., September 22, 2017.

*three reasons:* Vernon E. Jordan Jr. with Annette Gordon-Reed, *Vernon Can Read!: A Memoir* (New York: PublicAffairs, 2001), 271; Vernon Jordan int., May 9, 2016.

*"save face":* Jimmy Carter, interview A-0066, SOHPC (#4007), 1974.

*"The picture will be placed in the capitol":* Rita Jackson Samuels int., May 17, 2016.

*"weathered . . . the race issue":* Jimmy Carter, ap-

pearance on NBC's *Meet the Press,* June 2, 1974.

*"I was . . . berserk":* Thompson, "Jimmy Carter and the Great Leap of Faith."

*"puzzlingly changeable":* Edward Kennedy, *True Compass: A Memoir* (New York: Twelve, 2009), 353; Paul Kirk int., August 11, 2017; Peter Bourne int., September 25, 2019.

*"I was looking . . . parochial point of view":* Ed Pilkington, "Jimmy Carter Calls for Fresh Moratorium on Death Penalty," *Guardian* (US edition), November 11, 2013.

*"I listened . . . poor and weak":* Jimmy Carter, *Living Faith,* 113.

*"Dad really isn't an orator":* Jack Carter, OH, JCPLM, June 25, 2003.

*"one of the strangest":* Thompson, "Jimmy Carter and the Great Leap of Faith."

*"Carter-Fuller brushes":* ibid.

*"painfully timid":* Jeff Cochran, "When Jimmy Carter Met Bob Dylan," Atlanta Loop, October 1, 2016.

*"First thing he did": Jimmy Carter: Rock and Roll President,* directed by Mary Wharton, written by Bill Flanagan (Not Just Peanuts/CNN, 2020).

*Carter thought he was "stoned":* Jerry Rafshoon int., June 15, 2015.

*"Jimmy will be the next president":* ibid., May 11, 2017.

*"Jimmy Carter Is Running for* What*?":* Atlanta Constitution, editorial, July 10, 1974.

*"bottom of the list":* Ellis Arnall, interviewed by James F. Cook, March 25 and April 17, 1986 (P1986-03, Series A), Georgia Governors, Georgia Government Documentation Project

(GGDP), Special Collections and Archives, Georgia State University Library online, Atlanta.

*"Where the devil is William Clinton?":* C-SPAN, Dedication of Clinton Library, Little Rock, AR, November 18, 2004; Frank Moore int., February 20, 2018.

*"Watergate Babies":* Abner Mikva int., July 20, 2015.

*"Holiday Inns":* Witcover, *Marathon,* 127.

*Bentsen:* Edward Elson int., October 10, 2019.

*"Being president is not . . . the world to me":* Wayne King, "Georgia's Gov. Carter Enters Democratic Race for President," *New York Times,* December 13, 1974, 1.

*"I was put off by the title":* Jack Carter int., August 23, 2016.

*"Well, Jack . . . your best":* Wooten, *Dasher,* 29.

*"Nobody will work harder":* *Newsweek,* December 23, 1974.

*he took his dark-blue overcoat:* Jerry Rafshoon int., December 6, 2015.

*Chapter 16: The Long March*

*"One, that I'll do my best":* Fletcher Knebel, *Dark Horse* (Garden City, NY: Doubleday, 1972), 57.

*called Carter "bionic":* Eleanor Clift int., May 8, 2019.

*"just the opposite":* Witcover, *Marathon,* 211.

*"personal rosary":* ibid., 197–98.

*"enveloping them with . . . love":* ibid., 233.

*he first heard Carter's "mawkish":* Thompson, "Jimmy Carter and the Great Leap of Faith."

*The meeting was canceled:* Robert Rubin int., October 30, 2018.

*"would put Muhammad Ali to shame"*: Bill Boggs int., August 24, 2017.

*"your Judeo-Christian vows?"*: Jerry Rafshoon int., May 12, 2017.

*"we carried Iowa"*: Jimmy Carter, eulogy for Jody Powell, September 17, 2009.

*"Anyone with . . . ecstasy"*: ibid.

*they would scribble "WH"*: Witcover, *Marathon,* 199.

*Carter avoided the salutation:* Jerry Rafshoon int., June 15, 2015.

*"extremely wasteful"*: Jimmy Carter to Rosalynn Carter, Hamilton Jordan, and Jody Powell, FP, July 19, 1975.

*"Anyone who can snag you"*: Phil Wise int., May 18, 2016.

*"everything I do"*: Rosalynn Carter int., September 1, 2015.

*national strategies:* Hamilton Jordan, memo to Jimmy Carter, 1976 campaign files, n.d.

*"I had already won"*: Jimmy and Rosalynn Carter, *First Family from Plains,* https://www.pbs.org/show/first-family-plains.

*Only three freshmen showed up:* Peter Sahlins and Richard Tofel int., November 7, 2019.

*"healing process"*: Julia M. Klein, "Jimmy Carter Tells Law School Forum He'll Restore Faith," *Harvard Crimson,* September 27, 1975.

*In the ads, Carter says, "I'll never tell a lie"*: tape collection, JCPLM.

*"If it hadn't been for Gregg Allman"*: Jimmy Carter, Sunday school class, Maranatha Baptist Church, Plains, GA, June 5, 2017.

*"the great Allman Brothers!"*: Jimmy Carter, Allman Brothers Band concert (audio), Providence, RI, November 25, 1975, available on YouTube, https://www.youtube.com/watch?v=

ZPR9bf19ums.

*"Jimmy passed the test"*: Andrew Young int., June 10, 2015.

*the soundman . . . threatening to throw a table:* Thom Gund int., June 17, 2017.

*entire Congressional Black Caucus:* Andrew Young int., June 10, 2015.

*"solid lead"*: R. W. Apple Jr., "Carter Appears to Hold a Solid Lead in Iowa as the Campaign's First Test Approaches," *New York Times,* October 27, 1975, 17; Tim Kraft, unpublished account, 2015.

*"We're going to lose the liar vote"*: Jerry Rafshoon, OH, UVA-MC, April 8, 1983; Jerry Rafshoon int., July 10, 2019.

*"I open every letter"*: Steven Brill, "Jimmy Carter's Pathetic Lies," *Harper's,* March 1976.

*"That's what made our campaign"*: Pat Caddell int., April 8, 2016.

## Chapter 17: Front-runner

*"I guess . . . Alaska now"*: Carter-Mondale letter, spring 2015.

*a different kind of southerner:* ibid.

*"Jimmy Carter? How can that be?"*: Richard J. Ellis, *The Development of the American Presidency* (New York: Routledge, 2012), 52.

*If he won blacks in the North:* Pat Caddell int., April 8, 2016.

*single biggest handicap:* Schram, *Running for President,* 33.

*"He was very direct"*: Greg Schneiders int., September 1, 2015.

*"I got better coverage than I deserved"*: Jimmy Carter int., February 15, 2017.

*"I never . . . would approve abortion"*: ibid., June

1056

14, 2015.

*"with an accent?"*: Witcover, *Marathon,* 265.

*"like grits at a seder"*: Schram, *Running for President,* 80; Richard Gardner int., January 9, 2016.

*"because of the times"*: Schram, *Running for President,* 39.

*lighter fluid:* Jerry Rafshoon int., October 19, 2017; Hunter S. Thompson with David Streitfeld, *Hunter S. Thompson: The Last Interview and Other Conversations* (Brooklyn, NY: Melville House, 2018), 68.

*"meanest men I ever met"*: Anita Thompson, ed., *Ancient Gonzo Wisdom: Interviews with Hunter S. Thompson* (Cambridge: Da Capo Press, 2009), 74.

*"Wee Jimmy"*: James Reston, "What's in a Name?," *New York Times,* March 7, 1976.

*"It is said . . . in ten years"*: *New York Times,* February 20, 1977.

*"That's bigotry"*: Murray Illson, "Washington Chief of A.C.L.U. Resigns," *New York Times,* April 10, 1976.

*"two faces"*: Scheer, *Playing President,* 126.

*"Symbolic communication"*: Richard Reeves, "Carter's Secret," *New York,* March 22, 1976.

*"cried like a baby"*: Myra MacPherson, *Washington Post,* March 12, 1976.

*"prays three times a day"*: Richard Gardner int., March 17, 2016.

*Truman was a Baptist:* Schram, *Running for President,* 94–95.

*"He talks about spending all that time on his kneeeeeees"*: Elizabeth Drew, *American Journal: The Events of 1976* (New York: Random

House, 1977); Schram, *Running for President,* 100.

*"this man who I love and believe in":* Witcover, *Marathon,* 302–7; Schram, *Running for President,* 123; *Atlanta Constitution,* April 14, 1976.

*"I am not sure . . . other than yourself":* Robert Shrum, "No Private Smiles," *New Times,* June 11, 1976; Schram, *Running for President,* 136.

*"he may be a one-term president":* John Dickerson, "What Happened When President Carter Fired Five Cabinet Officials," *Slate,* August 2, 2017.

*mob lawyer Sidney Korshak:* Joel McLeary int., December 16, 2015.

*"as the underdog . . . we did all right":* Schram, *Running for President,* 5.

Chapter 18: Grits and Fritz

*"That's why I won":* Jerry Rafshoon int., November 18, 2015.

*"that was costly":* Jimmy Carter, OH, UVA-MC, 1988; Jimmy Carter int., June 15, 2015.

*"hypocrites" at church:* Dawidoff, "Riddle of Jimmy Carter."

*("Lillian, you should have stayed a virgin"):* ibid.

*her jealous streak:* Stroud, *How Jimmy Won,* 80.

*"mostly niggers":* Randolph, "Carter Complex."

*"A good ol' boy is":* Stroud, *How Jimmy Won,* 42.

*"I'm not the Carter who never lies":* Stapleton, *Brother Billy,* 109–10.

*"he's around people that kiss his ass":* ibid., 104.

*"He can be a real prick":* Adam Clymer int., November 15, 2016.

*"I don't like women reporters":* Stroud, *How Jimmy Won,* 78.

*"Remember how . . . pretty you were?":* *Los Angeles Times,* February 13, 1999.

*"Don't cry"*: Stroud, *How Jimmy Won,* 221.

*literal Bible:* Richard Cohen int., April 12, 2015.

*"He is a very tough fellow"*: Judy Woodruff with Kathleen Maxa, *"This Is Judy Woodruff at the White House"* (Reading, MA: Addison-Wesley, 1982), 127.

*"quintessential American cleanliness"*: Mailer, "Search for Carter."

*"our backgrounds were similar"*: Walter Mondale, remarks, CC Weekend, June 28, 2019.

*"someone who is handsome"*: Jimmy Carter and Walter Mondale, remarks, CC Weekend, 2016.

*Dewey . . . "for a change"*: Jimmy Carter, *"I'll Never Lie to You": Jimmy Carter in His Own Words,* compiled by Robert L. Turner (New York: Ballantine Books, 1976), 11.

*"My friends call me Jerden"*: Richard Reeves, "Shhh, Don't Wake the Democrats," *New York,* July 26, 1976, 26.

*"I'll denounce your dictators"*: Sam Brown int., January 21, 2019.

*"quiet, brooding emotion"*: Stapleton, *Brother Billy,* 79.

*"my brother, Billy"*: ibid.

*("My main advantage")*: *New York Times,* February 20, 1977.

*"My name is Jimmy Carter"*: "Transcript of Carter Address Accepting Democratic Nomination for Presidency," *New York Times,* July 16, 1976.

*"astonishingly nice smile"*: Mailer, "Search for Carter."

*"so that . . . in twenty years"*: R. W. Apple Jr., "Carter Gives Insight on Decision-Making," *New York Times,* July 15, 1976.

*"a snowball's chance at first?"*: Sam Donaldson, ABCnewsvideosource.com.

*high point of his political career:* Richard Reeves, "The Night Carter Took Over the Party," *New York Times Magazine,* February 20, 1977, 32.

*"the servant-leader" model:* "Bill Moyers Interview with Jimmy Carter," PBS, May 6, 1976; Schram, *Running for President,* 97.

*"Dole was a disaster":* Jimmy Carter, *White House Diary,* February 2, 1979, 287.

*"Nobody really knows Ford":* Zachary J. Lechner, "Fuzzy as a Georgia Peach: The Ford Campaign and the Challenge of Jimmy Carter's Southerness," *Southern Cultures* 23, no. 4 (Winter 2017): 62–81.

*Boston busing crisis:* ibid.

*" 'I know what's good for America' ":* Jerry Rafshoon, OH, UVA-MC, April 8, 1983.

*"bosses" and "leaders":* Tim Kraft int., July 15, 2015.

*Caddell grew worried:* Pat Caddell int., April 8, 2016.

*Chapter 19: "Lust in My Heart"*

*"reasonably sure":* Theodore White, *In Search of History: A Personal Adventure* (New York: HarperCollins, 1978), 529.

*"as hard-drinking":* Scheer, *Playing President,* 103–4.

*"relative degree of sinfulness":* Scheer, "Jimmy, We Hardly Know Y'All."

*"Smile If You're Horny":* Bob Scheer int., September 16, 2017; Barry Golson int., December 15, 2018.

*"People should watch out":* Gibbs and Duffy, *Preacher and the Presidents,* 251.

*"You tell Oral":* Kenneth L. Woodward, "Sister Ruth," *Newsweek,* July 17, 1978.

*"I did worry":* Rosalynn Carter int., November 17, 2015.

*"close to the edge":* Dominic Sandbrook, *Mad as Hell: The Crisis of the 1970s and the Rise of the Populist Right* (New York: Alfred A. Knopf, 2011), 204.

*"moral issue":* Jimmy Carter, *White House Diary,* 367.

*the exposure he needed: New York Times,* November 7, 1976.

*"nit-shitting": New York Times,* September 25, 1976.

*"extravagantly negative comments":* Bourne, *Jimmy Carter,* 350–51.

*"surreptitiously restarted the tape recorder": New York Times,* December 17, 1996.

*"unsung hero in his brother's election":* Lance with Gilbert, *Truth of the Matter,* 74.

*Dickey . . . showed up drunk:* John Meroney, " 'There's an Awakening in Our Country': A Q&A with Jimmy Carter," *Atlantic,* July 13, 2015.

*"catch rhetorical fire":* Jimmy Carter to James Dickey, October 7, 1976.

*"He is a sitting duck":* James Dickey to Jimmy Carter, September 29, 1976, box 236, folders 21 and 22, James Dickey Papers Circa 1914–1997, Stuart A. Rose Manuscript, Archives, and Rare Book Library, Emory University, Atlanta.

*"the KGB recruited":* Office of the Director of National Intelligence, National Intelligence Council, Intelligence Community Assessment, *Assessing Russian Activities and Intentions in Recent US Elections* (ICA 2017-01D), January 6, 2017, R, https://www.dni.gov/files/docu ments/ICA_2017_01.pdf.

*Mondale replied that Dole was a "hatchet man":* Time, November 15, 1976.

*"N-E-G-R-O-E-S!":* Glad, In Search, 396.

*"emotionally and mentally disturbed":* New York Times, November 1, 1976.

*"Somebody should have shot":* Wooten, Dasher, 86.

*television . . . appearance:* Jerry Rafshoon int., November 18, 2015.

*"lonely candidate":* ibid., June 15, 2015.

*"It's all right to . . . vote for Jimmy Carter":* Jim Free int., February 5, 2016.

*"Marxist, right?":* Wooten, Dasher, 371.

*"Y'all ain't trash no more":* Carter-Mondale letter, fall 2016.

*"He won!":* Rock and Roll President, 2020.

*"political redemption":* Jimmy Carter, Keeping Faith, 22.

*"The son of a bitch":* Jerry Rafshoon int., November 18, 2015; Curtis Wilkie int., November 15, 2015; Greg Schneiders int., May 1, 2016.

*the American Dream come true:* Bourne, Jimmy Carter, 356.

*"phone book to be president":* Hendrik Hertzberg, Politics: Observations & Arguments, 1966–2004 (New York: Penguin Press, 2004), 60.

*"deeds not declarations":* New York Times, November 5, 1976.

*privately more comfortable:* Abner Mikva int., July 20, 2015.

*"the emerging Republican majority":* Kevin P. Phillips, The Emerging Republican Majority, (New Rochelle, NY: Arlington House, 1969).

**Part 4: Outsider President**
*Chapter 20: "Let's Go!"*
*"the worst mistake I made":* Jimmy Carter int.,

February 17, 2017.

*"going to cocktail parties"*: Hamilton Jordan memo to Jimmy Carter, November 1976, JCPLM.

*"assistant president"*: Jimmy Carter, lecture, 92nd Street Y, New York, December 6, 2018.

*"Boy . . . did that change the attitude of the DOD"*: Walter Mondale to Jimmy Carter, memo, "The Role of the Vice President in the Carter Administration," December 9, 1976, available at Minnesota Historical Society online, https://www.mnhs.org/collections/upclose/Mondale-CarterMemo-Scanned.pdf; Mondale, remarks, CC Weekend, 2016.

*weekly lunch:* Walter F. Mondale, and David Hage, *The Good Fight: A Life in Liberal Politics* (New York: Scribner, 2010), 171–83.

*radical shift:* Walter Mondale int., June 9, 2015; Jimmy Carter int., June 15, 2015; Richard Moe int., August 9, 2019.

*"has a cast-iron rear end"*: Lance with Gilbert, *Truth of the Matter,* 83.

*Bush . . . offered his resignation:* George H. W. Bush int., October 11, 2016.

*her husband should have fought harder:* Rosalynn Carter int., June 15, 2015.

*"Above all . . . gain or profit"*: Jimmy Carter, presidential transition press release, December 31, 1976, JCPLM.

*"sober optimism"*: Haynes Johnson, "Carter Is Sworn In as President, Asks 'Fresh Faith in Old Dream,' " *Washington Post,* January 21, 1977.

*"So together, in a spirit of individual sacrifice"*: Jimmy Carter, *Keeping Faith,* 19.

*"rather silly"*: ibid., 16–17.

*"a reduction in the imperial status"*: Jimmy Carter,

*White House Diary,* 10.

*"Let's go!":* Atlanta Journal-Constitution, January 17, 2017.

*"tears of joy ran down my cold cheeks":* Jimmy Carter, *Keeping Faith,* 17–18.

*"was game changing":* Lesley Stahl, CBS News, January 20, 1977.

*"dramatized in deed":* ibid.

*"most disgraceful":* Michael J. Gerhardt, *The Forgotten Presidents: Their Untold Constitutional Legacy* (New York: Oxford University Press, 2013), 227.

*"sense of Christian forgiveness":* Max Cleland int., December 23, 2015.

*"Most presidents get a honeymoon":* Tim Kraft int., July 15, 2015.

*"obsessed, maybe to excess":* Jimmy Carter, OH, UVA-MC, November 29, 1982.

*Chapter 21: The Moral Equivalent of War*

*"our country and our people are in trouble":* Tip O'Neill to Jimmy Carter, January 27, 1977, JCPLM.

*"It's a bitch!":* Rosalynn Carter, *First Lady,* 367.

*"Our energy policy":* Eizenstat, *Carter: White House Years,* 165.

*the cardigan . . . fresh and comforting:* Jerry Rafshoon int., June 12, 2016; Rosalynn Carter int., June 14, 2015; Barry Jagoda int., September 16, 2018.

*"He was folks, and folks is in":* "The Administration: Warm Words from Jimmy Cardigan," *Time,* February 14, 1977.

New York Times *editorial . . . "masterful":* "The Chat by the Fire," editorial, *New York Times,* February 4, 1977.

*"calculating and remote":* Woodruff with Maxa, *"This Is Judy,"* 127.

*"Okay, you did some orange sunshine":* Kali Holloway, "11 of 'Saturday Night Live' 's Most Hilarious Election-Year Sketches," Salon, October 6, 2015, https://www.salon.com/2015/10/05/11_best_snl_sketches_partner.

*75 percent, his all-time high:* Gallup, "Presidential Approval Ratings — Gallup Historical Statistics and Trends, High Individual Measurements."

*"You don't have to prove":* Lance with Gilbert, *Truth of the Matter,* 113.

*eleventh-grade reading level:* Martin Longman, "Maybe Dumbing It Down Is Good Politics," *Washington Monthly,* October 8, 2018.

*Carter agreed and said, "I'm him":* David Freeman int., June 27, 2015.

*popular book:* E. F. Schumacher, *Small Is Beautiful: Economics As If People Matter* (New York: Harper and Row, 1975).

*"Jimmy's problem in the White House": Newsweek,* November 13, 1976.

*"it looked more like a smorgasbord than an agenda":* Lance with Gilbert, *Truth of the Matter,* 128.

*"front-loaded pain and back-loaded pleasure":* Walter Mondale int., June 9, 2015.

*"war with his own best soldiers":* Lance with Gilbert, *Truth of the Matter,* 118.

*"I'm gonna kick his ass":* Jerry Rafshoon int., June 26, 2019.

*"There was no groundswell":* Jimmy Carter, OH, UVA-MC, 1988.

*"To fight moral equivalent of war":* Jerry Doolittle, unpublished diary, October 24, 1977.

*energy efficiency on easy-to-read labels:* Carl M.

Cannon, "Trump Is Looking for a Way Out," Real Clear Politics, June 12, 2016.

Chapter 22: The Steel Magnolia

*"Note the order"*: Hugh Sidey, "Second Most Powerful Person," The Presidency, *Time,* May 7, 1979.

*"very equal partnership"*: Judy Woodruff, *First Family from Plains,* 2016.

*"He said, 'I'll get Rosalynn' "*: B. Drummond Ayres Jr., "The Importance of Being Rosalynn," *New York Times,* June 3, 1979.

*"Well, Rosie . . . what's on your agenda this week?"*: ibid.

*his wife should attend Cabinet meetings:* Rosalynn Carter int., June 14, 2015.

*"Ambassador Rosalynn Carter"*: David Vidal, "Ambassador Rosalynn Carter," *New York Times,* June 14, 1977.

*"my number one diplomat"*: Jimmy Carter, remarks, CC Weekend, 2019.

*"one tough lady"*: Ayres Jr., "Importance of Being Rosalynn."

*Colombia . . . cocaine cartel:* Jimmy Carter, *White House Diary.*

*"Give me a smile"*: George Packer, "The Republican Class War," The Political Scene, *New Yorker,* November 2, 2015.

*"I've approved Beattie (white male), but this can't go on"*: Jimmy Carter to Joseph Califano, May 10, 1979, Richard Beattie Papers.

*"mankind" or "the common man"*: *Washington Post,* July 6, 1977.

*"How many law review articles?"*: Terry Adamson int., February 28, 2019.

*He replaced tokenism with . . . affirmative action:*

Mary L. Clark, "Carter's Ground-breaking Appointment of Women to the Federal Bench: His Other 'Human Rights' Record," *American University Journal of Gender, Social Policy & the Law* 11, no. 3 (2003): 1131–63.

*" 'Well, did you always want to be a judge?' "*: Irin Carmon and Shana Knizhnik, *Notorious RBG: The Life and Times of Ruth Bader Ginsburg* (New York: Dey Street Books, 2015), 77.

*"She's gotten younger, healthier, prettier"*: Jimmy Carter, *White House Diary*, 273.

*" 'us against the world' "*: Jeff Carter int., June 26, 2016.

*Like . . . Ronald and Nancy Reagan*: Chip Carter int., May 17, 2016.

*a different woman in all fifty states*: ibid.

*Mary Prince . . . took care of Amy*: Jimmy Carter, *Our Endangered Values: America's Moral Crisis* (New York: Simon & Schuster, 2005), 84.

*"I have never met an ugly Italian!"*: Jimmy Carter, *White House Diary*, 205.

*"a damn foreigner"*: ibid., 260.

*Billy Beer*: Chip Carter, ROGP, June 25, 2008.

*"never been good at personal counseling"*: Kenneth L. Woodward, "Sister Ruth."

*"Do your best"*: Jimmy Carter, *Always a Reckoning*, 6; Rachel Clark, C/S-FOHP, September 9, 1978.

*"If you do your best"*: Hutchinson, *Jimmy Carter's Hometown*, 90–93.


*Chapter 23: His Inner Engineer*

*"He didn't seem to have the political adrenalin"*: David McCullough int., July 14, 2016.

*"thinking time"*: Charles Kirbo, OH, UVA-MC, January 5, 1983.

*"three key questions"*: Jimmy Carter, *Living Faith,* 104–5.

*"permissive abortion"*: Jimmy Carter, *White House Diary,* 361.

*through his poetry*: Jimmy Carter int., June 14, 2015.

*"I never could understand why"*: Mel Ayton, *Hunting the President: Threats, Plots, and Assassination Attempts — from FDR to Obama* (Washington, DC: Regnery History, 2014), 128.

*"rocks in his head"*: Jerry Smith, C/S-FOHP.

*"with our butts in the air"*: Jimmy Carter, *White House Diary,* 174.

*"painted us as country farm people"*: Susan Swain, *First Ladies: Presidential Historians on the Lives of 45 Iconic American Women* (New York: PublicAffairs, 2015), 379.

*"How the fuck did I get here?"*: Willie Nelson and David Ritz, *It's a Long Story: My Life* (New York: Little, Brown, 2015), 250–51; *Washingtonian,* June 2019.

*"We de-pomped the White House"*: Jerry Rafshoon, OH, UVA-MC, April 8, 1983.

*"Goddamn it, Frank, you're stupid"*: Frank Moore int., January 27, 2017.

*"tight as bark on a tree"*: Dawidoff, "The Riddle of Jimmy Carter."

*bury the expense as "props"*: Jerry Rafshoon int., October 13, 2018.

*"Politics is about credit taking"*: Ray Marshall int., September 6, 2016.

*"willingness to be difficult"*: Landon Butler int., June 22, 2016.

*"I have a good ability to rationalize"*: Jimmy Carter and Rosalynn Carter int., June 14, 2015.

*"I can read faster than people can talk"*: Kevin Matt-son, *"What the Heck Are You Up To, Mr. President?": Jimmy Carter, America's "Malaise," and the Speech That Should Have Changed the Country* (New York: Bloomsbury, 2009), 25.

*"In his own scary-smart way"*: Tim Smith int., May 12, 2016.

*"not the bad things you were avoiding"*: Abner Mikva int., July 20, 2015.

*"Nixon had his enemies list"*: Jules Witcover, *Joe Biden: A Life of Trial and Redemption* (New York: William Morrow/HarperCollins, 2010), 138; Joe Biden int., October 9, 2016.

*"Pennsylvania Avenue is a two-way street"*: Evan Dobelle, "A Study of the Creation of a Federal Cabinet-Level Department of Education 1857–1979: with an Analysis of Executive Branch Public Policy 1977–1979" (PhD diss., University of Massachusetts-Amherst, 1987), 241.

*"You said to play tennis"*: Frank Moore int., January 27, 2017.

*"a bunch of disorganized juvenile delinquents"*: Jimmy Carter, *White House Diary,* 192.

*"People . . . pissed on"*: Christopher Matthews, *Hardball: How Politics Is Played, Told by One Who Knows the Game* (New York: Simon & Schuster, 1999), 33–34.

*"a genuine affection between us"*: Tip O'Neill and William Novak, *Man of the House: The Life and Political Memoirs of Speaker Tip O'Neill* (New York: Random House, 1987), 296.

*"would feel less like a man"*: Jerry Rafshoon int., October 13, 2018.

*"If that's the best you can do"*: Barry Jagoda int., September 16, 2018.

*"eyes shone like diamonds"*: Bob Beckel and John

David Mann, *I Should Be Dead: My Life Surviving Politics, TV, and Addiction* (New York: Hachette Books, 2015), 117.

*"emphatic but not mean spirited"*: Jay Beck int., February 17, 2017.

*"Fuck you, Jimmy!"*: Jerry Rafshoon int., June 22, 2016.

*With the cameras rolling . . . a tall stack of paper off his desk*: Hertzberg, *Politics,* 55.

*"afflicted with Montezuma's revenge"*: Jimmy Carter, "Mexico City, Mexico: Toasts at the Luncheon Honoring President Carter, February 14, 1979," *PPPJC,* 1979, vol. 1, 276.

*"It's genital"*: DOJ memo, May 13, 1977, Terry Adamson Personal Papers.

*"Strauss was working very hard on the shoe import"*: Randolph, "Carter Complex."

*"living in sin"*: Jimmy Carter, *White House Diary,* 18.

*"You will obey [the law], or . . . . seek employment elsewhere"*: Jimmy Carter to senior staff, July 24, 1978, box 34, Office of the Chief of Staff, JCPLM.

*"Do you intend to marry her?"*: Sam Brown int., January 21, 2019.

*"I get it: Jordan's president, and Carter's chief of staff"*: Peggy Noonan, *What I Saw at the Revolution: A Political Life in the Reagan Era* (New York: Random House, 1990), 170.

*quickly grasped Frosch's technical explanations*: Robert Frosch int., October 12, 2019.

*"likely to survive a billion years"*: Jimmy Carter, "Voyager Spacecraft: Statement by the President, July 29, 1977," *PPPJC,* 1977, vol. 2 (Washington, DC: US Government Printing Office, 1978), 1379.

*"It's . . . just a contrivance to keep NASA alive":* Jimmy Carter, *White House Diary,* 63.

*"the group around him slumbers":* James Fallows, "The Passionless Presidency," *Atlantic,* May 1979.

*Carter personally supervised . . . White House tennis court:* Jimmy Carter int., September 4, 2019; Frank Moore int., July 16, 2015; James Fallows int., April 11, 2020; Tim Smith int., May 16, 2016; Susan Clough int., December 26, 2015.

*Chapter 24: "Bert, I'm Proud of You"*

*Jody Powell passed along a message . . . Fuck you:* Bob Woodward int., May 21, 2019.

*"a sickening sense of foreboding":* Bob Woodward, *Shadow: Five Presidents and the Legacy of Watergate* (New York: Simon & Schuster, 1999), 198.

*press coverage . . . as bad as Nixon's:* Tom Wicker, *One of Us: Richard Nixon and the American Dream* (New York: Random House, 1991), 444.

*"I underestimated that":* Jimmy Carter, OH, UVA-MC, 1988.

*"They don't want a president; they want Bob Hope":* Jerry Doolittle, unpublished diary, April 30, 1977.

*"his politically maladroit . . . defeat":* Eizenstat, *Carter: White House Years,* 295.

*"Should produce a real winner":* Jerry Doolittle, unpublished diary, September 19, 1978.

*"If it ain't broke, don't fix it":* Gary Martin, The Phrase Finder, https://www.phrases.org.uk/meanings/if-it-aint-broke-dont-fix-it.html.

*"That's foolishness":* Lance with Gilbert, *Truth of the Matter,* 133.

*"seemed so inordinately pure"*: Walter Mondale int., June 9, 2015.

*"sweetheart loan"*: William Safire, "Carter's Broken Lance," *New York Times,* July 21, 1977, 23.

*"Lance was a corner cutter, not a criminal"*: Michael Blumenthal int., December 15, 2015.

*"hired the only dumb Jewish lawyer in Atlanta"*: Jerry Rafshoon int., April 26, 2019.

*"a loud-mouthed, pushy little broad"*: William Grimes, "Midge Costanza, a Top Assistant to Carter, Dies at 77," *New York Times,* March 24, 2010.

*"half-truths and misrepresentations, innuendos, and the like?"*: Lance with Gilbert, *Truth of the Matter,* 139–42.

*"I could see that LaBelle was creating a very serious problem"*: Jimmy Carter, *White House Diary,* 102–3.

*"you can go with the rest of the jackals"*: Lance with Gilbert, *Truth of the Matter,* 130–31.

*the president . . . said quietly: "Vultures"*: James Schlesinger, OH, UVA-MC, July 19, 1984.

*"spared any allegations of impropriety"*: "Excerpts from Text of Pres. Carter's Press Conference," *Washington Post,* September 22, 1977, A16.

*"He'd lost his self-confidence"*: James Schlesinger, OH, UVA-MC, July 19, 1984.

*"Lancegate is no Watergate"*: William Safire, "Lancegate: Why Carter Stuck It Out," *New York Times,* October 16, 1977, 221.

*remembered how Burns:* Lance with Gilbert, *Truth of the Matter,* 155–56.

*They feared that Lance, as Fed chair:* ibid.

*"I've always wanted to see the pyramids"*: Sam Donaldson int., March 16, 2017; Sally Quinn, "Where Did All the Good Times Go?," *Wash-*

*ington Post,* December 18, 1977.

*"Hamilton had come to be viewed":* Jody Powell, *The Other Side of the Story* (New York: Morrow, 1984), 109.

*Carter called the memo "superb":* Landon Butler, unpublished diary, December 16, 1977.

*"But the big four didn't pass":* Frank Moore, OH Exit Interview Project, JCPLM, December 17, 1980.

*"My advice hadn't been sought. My input's not in it":* Eizenstat, *Carter: White House Years,* 317.

*"much more conservative":* Jimmy Carter, *White House Diary,* 75.

*"a complete waste of time . . . entertaining":* ibid., 164–65.

*Nader and Peterson were enraged:* Mark J. Green, *Bright, Infinite Future: A Generational Memoir on the Progressive Rise* (New York: St. Martin's Press, 2016), 74–76; Eizenstat, *Carter: White House Years,* 388–89.

*"tremendous legislative achievement":* Charles S. Clark, "After 40 Years: A Look Back at the Unlikely Passage of Civil Service Reform," Government Executive, July 3, 2018.

**Part 5: Peacemaker**

*Chapter 25: Human Rights*

*"was the one who broke the ice":* Jimmy Carter, remarks, CC Weekend, June 28, 2019.

*"frozen indifference":* Murray Kempton, *Rebellions, Perversities, and Main Events* (New York: Times Books, 1994), 418.

*"isolated and little-known":* Robert Gates, *From the Shadows: The Ultimate Insider's Story of Five Presidents and How They Won the Cold War* (New York: Simon & Schuster, 1996).

*"interference in our internal affairs":* Leonid Brezhnev to Jimmy Carter, February 25, 1977, in Mary E. King, *The New York Times on Emerging Democracies in Eastern Europe* (Washington, DC: CQ Press, 2010), 27; Zbigniew Brzezinski, *Power and Principle: Memoirs of the National Security Adviser, 1977–1981* (New York: Farrar, Straus and Giroux, 1983), 154–55.

*"microscopic dot of no importance to anyone":* Jimmy Carter, *White House Diary,* 105.

*"It's never too late":* Jimmy Carter, *White House Diary,* 155.

Carter *"was almost never willing to back his rhetoric":* Natan Sharansky with Ron Dermer, *The Case for Democracy: The Power of Freedom to Overcome Tyranny and Terror* (New York: PublicAffairs, 2004), 131.

*"We've fought fire with fire":* Jimmy Carter, "University of Notre Dame, Address at Commencement Exercises at the University, May 22, 1977," *PPPJC,* 1977, vol 1. (Washington, DC: US Government Printing Office, 1977), 954.

*Freedom would be that potent dousing force:* Juan Mendez int., June 16, 2016; John Dinges int., October 13, 2015.

*"No member of the UN can claim . . . its own business":* "Jimmy Carter on Human Rights," History.com, March 17, 1977, https://www.history.com/topics/us-presidents/jimmy-carter-on-human-rights-video.

*"I never thought I'd concede this":* Association of Diplomatic Studies and Training, Foreign Affairs OH Project, August 13, 1988.

*"add her own feelings":* Jimmy Carter, remarks, CC Weekend, 2019.

*"ambiguous, ambivalent, and ambidextrous"*: Hodding Carter int., April 15, 2017.

*"planting the seeds for a change of thinking"*: Roberta Cohen int., March 20, 2017.

*Carter met with . . . Deutsch family:* CC video archive, 2014.

*Operation Condor:* National Security Archive Report, May 6, 2015.

*Carter proposed . . . that the dictator step down and agree to elections:* Jimmy Carter, *White House Diary,* 248, 257.

*White House secretly tried to convince Pope John Paul II:* Betty Glad, *An Outsider in the White House: Jimmy Carter, His Advisors, and the Making of American Foreign Policy* (Ithaca, NY: Cornell University Press, 2009), 250–60.

*"But she didn't march with King, and you did":* Andrew Young int., June 10, 2015.

*Uganda's dictator, Idi Amin, was an exception:* Jerry Doolittle, unpublished diary, December 6, 1978; Jimmy Carter, *White House Diary,* 29.

*"too timid":* Jimmy Carter, *White House Diary,* 39.

*Carter publicly blasted apartheid:* ibid.; Andrew Young int., June 10, 2015.

*"weak-kneed approach":* Jimmy Carter, *White House Diary,* 37.

*Carter relieved him of his command:* ibid., 455.

*wanted to normalize with Hanoi:* ibid., 215.

*"I should have denounced them more forcefully":* Jimmy Carter int., August 3, 2018.

*"I encouraged the Chinese to support Pol Pot":* Elizabeth Becker, "Pol Pot's End Won't Stop U.S. Pursuit of His Circle," *New York Times,* April 17, 1998, 15.

*Carter's explanation . . . was practical but unpersuasive:* Jimmy Carter, *White House Diary,* 463.

*deleted references to "disappearances": Human Rights and U.S. Foreign Policy, The First Decade, 1973–1983* (New York: American Association for the International Commission of Jurists, 1984), 25.

*"the results of our commitment were often disappointing":* ibid.

*their power in Italy receded:* Richard Gardner int., March 17, 2016; Elliott Abrams int., August 3, 2018.

*"taught the young there was another life":* Jonathan Alter, *Between the Lines: A View Inside American Politics, People, and Culture* (Ann Arbor: State Street Books, 2008), 239.

*"played significant role":* Anatoly Dobrynin, *In Confidence: Moscow's Ambassador to America's Six Cold War Presidents (1962–1986)* (New York: Times Books, 1995), 352.

*Carter's policy . . . undermined "the self-confidence" of the Soviet bloc:* Douglas Brinkley, *The Unfinished Presidency: Jimmy Carter's Journey Beyond the White House* (New York: Viking, 1998), 22.

*Chapter 26: Panama Canal Squeaker*

*"Suppose there is no second term?":* Eizenstat, *Carter: White House Years,* 558.

*"utter disaster":* Adam Clymer int., November 15, 2016.

*dealt at length with three of Carter's lifelong interests:* David McCullough int., July 14, 2016.

*"a diplomatic cancer":* Jimmy Carter, *Keeping Faith,* 155.

*"litmus test throughout the world":* Jimmy Carter, *Living Faith,* 156.

*"use your best judgment":* Eizenstat, *Carter: White*

*House Years,* 560.

*"enjoyed his role as the political emancipator":* Brzezinski, *Power and Principle,* 137.

*Torrijos broke down in tears:* Jimmy Carter, *Keeping Faith,* 161; Jimmy Carter, *White House Diary,* September 7, 1977.

*"subhuman" and Torrijos a "drunken dictator":* Jimmy Carter, *White House Diary,* 81.

*The Carters hosted him and his wife, Erma:* ibid., 85.

*"more responsible than he is ambitious":* Landon Butler int., September 1, 2015.

*the senator snapped, "So be it":* Adam Clymer, *Drawing the Line at the Big Ditch: The Panama Canal Treaties and the Rise of the Right* (Lawrence: University Press of Kansas, 2008), 78.

*"the right thing":* Jerry Rafshoon int., March 11, 2019.

*"A leaden, heavy, shapeless, and disorganized piece of work":* Jerry Doolittle, unpublished diary, November 26, 1978.

*"expectations so low that nobody particularly noticed [it] sucked":* ibid., January 31, 1978, February 3, 1978.

*"shaky feeling":* Clymer, *Drawing the Line,* 93.

*"all the people who write me hysterical letters":* John Wayne to Jimmy Carter, October 12, 1977.

*"point by God damn point":* Clymer, *Drawing the Line,* 94–95.

*the doubts . . . were the greatest of his presidency:* Jimmy Carter int., November 19, 2015.

*"the skunk at the garden party":* Clymer, *Drawing the Line,* 101.

*"the bully boys of the radical Right":* ibid., 110.

*a bizarre tale surfaced of a secret diplomatic cable:*

Beckel and Mann, *I Should Be Dead,* 120–21.

*"He wished he could share his lunch":* Jimmy Carter, *White House Diary,* 318.

*he received $50,000 in cash . . . to conduct opposition research:* ibid., 106.

*"His heart wasn't in it":* Frank Moore int., January 27, 1917.

*Cannon finally had the cover he needed:* Jimmy Carter, *Keeping Faith,* 176–77.

*"one of the worst days of my political life":* Jimmy Carter, *White House Diary,* 177.

*"worked over a problem like a piece of broken machinery":* Mailer, "Search for Carter."

*Arizona's Dennis DeConcini almost did:* Beckel and Mann, *I Should Be Dead,* 109–10.

*"first display of emotion I've seen":* Jerry Doolittle, unpublished diary, March 16, 1978.

*plan to play on the senator's vanity:* Walter Mondale int., June 9, 2015.

*"do you need to meet with Sam Hayakawa?":* J. Lee Annis, *Howard Baker: Conciliator in an Age of Crisis* (Knoxville: Howard H. Baker Jr. Center for Public Policy, University of Tennessee, 1995), 130–35.

*Carter . . . read the dense academic tome:* Jimmy Carter, *White House Diary,* 189.

*"Sam, I couldn't possibly limit our visits":* Walter Mondale int., June 9, 2015.

*barricaded himself in a telephone booth:* Dan Tate int., July 20, 2015.

*He found Abourezk "flighty":* Jimmy Carter, *White House Diary,* April 18, 1978, 189.

*"trying to blackmail me":* ibid., 183.

*Carter got word . . . Abourezk would vote yes:* Jimmy Carter, *Keeping Faith,* 177.

*"We were planning for massive violence":* Jimmy

Carter, *White House Diary,* 189.

*"Your badges of courage":* "Senate Leaders and the Panama Canal Treaties, April 18, 1978," United States Senate online, senate.gov.

*wanted to celebrate . . . by visiting Panama:* Jerry Doolittle, unpublished diary, June 13, 1978.

*"groups of thirty or forty ad nauseam":* Jimmy Carter, OH, UVA-MC, 1988.

*"Has been a bitch ever since":* Jimmy Carter, *White House Diary,* 358.

*eight Democratic senators . . . defeated:* Adam Clymer, "Robert B. Morgan, Senator Undone by His Panama Canal Votes, Dies at 90," *New York Times,* July 18, 2016.

*Reagan won by losing on Panama:* William F. Buckley, *Overdrive: A Personal Documentary* (New York: Doubleday, 1983), 119.

*"success story":* UPI, October 1, 1982.

*"They said . . . gone as far as they could":* Jimmy Carter, OH, UVA-MC, July 19, 1984.

*"protect the integrity of the Panama Canal Treaties":* Carl T. Bogus, "The Invasion of Panama and the Rule of Law," *International Lawyer* 26, no. 3 (Fall 1992): 781–87.

Chapter 27: Camp David

*"very stubborn and somewhat ill at ease":* Jimmy Carter, *White House Diary,* 31.

*The Syrian leader soon found several ways to . . . "sabotage":* Jimmy Carter, *Keeping Faith,* 286.

*"quite congenial, dedicated, sincere, deeply religious":* ibid., 290.

*"We had quite an argument at breakfast":* Jimmy Carter, *White House Diary,* 168.

*"a small man with limited vision":* ibid., 193.

*"Are you willing to be the scapegoat?":* Rosalynn

Carter, *First Lady,* 238.

*"They get over here, and this blows up":* Walter Mondale int., June 9, 2015.

*"I slowly became hardened":* Jimmy Carter, *Keeping Faith,* 317.

*"Sadat seemed to trust me too much":* ibid., 322.

*"Barbara Walters syndrome":* Lawrence Wright, *Thirteen Days in September: Carter, Begin, and Sadat at Camp David* (New York: Alfred A. Knopf, 2014), 9.

*"the courage of my father":* ibid., 35.

*Sadat . . . ate the cracker right out of her hand:* Amy Carter int., November 18, 2015.

*"Jimmy, is Anwar Sadat married?"* Jerry Rafshoon int., February 16, 2017.

*"We can do it, Mr. President!":* Rosalynn Carter, unpublished diary.

*"stop assing around":* ibid.

*"What chutzpah!":* Ezer Weizman, *The Battle for Peace* (New York: Bantam Books, 1981), 353–54.

*"Security, yes! Land, no!":* Jimmy Carter, unpublished diary; Jimmy Carter, *Keeping Faith,* 351.

*the two leaders had been "mean":* Rosalynn Carter, unpublished diary.

*"This is still my prayer!":* Jimmy Carter, *Keeping Faith,* 358.

*Sadat said angrily that a "stalemate" had been reached:* ibid., 359.

*"strong proposal":* Jimmy Carter, unpublished diary.

*found her hiding . . . in the ladies' room:* Jerry Rafshoon int., February 16, 2017.

*" 'that man' acts as though I have done nothing":* Rosalynn Carter, unpublished diary.

*"My good friend Jimmy":* Jimmy Carter, *White*

House Diary, 227.

*Sadat was being so "tough and mean":* Rosalynn Carter, unpublished diary.

*"locked into positions by his past":* ibid.

*they drank at lunch:* ibid.

*"Jimmy and I come across as exotic to Jewish people":* Rosalynn Carter, remarks, CC Weekend, 2015.

*"a concentration camp deluxe":* Wright, *Thirteen Days,* 201.

*The two men had met . . . when Brzezinski traveled:* Zbigniew Brzezinski int., March 1, 2016.

*"Carter at the periscope":* Weizman, *Battle for Peace,* 359.

*"Do you reject United Nations Resolution 242?":* Jimmy Carter, *Keeping Faith,* 373–74.

*"It looks like subterfuge":* Jimmy Carter, unpublished diary.

*"You will have to accept it!":* Weizman, *Battle for Peace,* 365.

*Carter . . . doubted Begin's "rationality":* Jimmy Carter, unpublished diary.

*Begin was a "psycho":* Brzezinski, *Power and Principle,* 262.

*"Mr. Weizman!":* Weizman, *Battle for Peace,* 261.

*"Their hatred and distrust":* Wright, *Thirteen Days,* 187.

*"troubled and was somewhat evasive":* Jimmy Carter, *Keeping Faith,* 384–85.

*"It's all right":* ibid., 385.

*"unpleasant and repetitive":* ibid., 386–87.

*He was angry and discouraged:* Rosalynn Carter, unpublished diary.

*Carter turned icy:* ibid.; Jimmy Carter, *White House Diary,* 236.

*"I'm worried about his safety":* Rosalynn Carter,

unpublished diary.

*"lived under an occupying power"*: Jimmy Carter, *White House Diary*, 245.

*"I think it's all coming together now"*: Rosalynn Carter, unpublished diary.

*"All bad. We've failed"*: ibid.

*"I went to my bedroom, knelt down, and prayed"*: Jimmy Carter, *White House Diary*, 237.

*"I will stick with you to the end"*: Jimmy Carter, *Keeping Faith*, 392–93; Rosalynn Carter, unpublished diary.

*"among the most unpleasant he had ever experienced"*: Rosalynn Carter, unpublished diary.

*"felt Sadat had been planning . . . to embarrass Begin"*: ibid.

*"You've restored my faith in lawyers!"*: David Landau, *Arik: The Life of Ariel Sharon* (New York: Alfred A. Knopf, 2013), 160.

*"political suicide"*: Jimmy Carter, unpublished diary.

*disputed meaning of "during the negotiations"*: Jimmy Carter, *Keeping Faith*, 397; Cyrus Vance, *Hard Choices: Critical Years in American Foreign Policy* (New York: Simon & Schuster, 1983), 228.

*"All of you are plumbers!"*: Wright, *Thirteen Days*, 255.

*"Love and Best Wishes"*: Susan Clough int., May 6, 2015, September 24, 2016; Jimmy Carter, remarks, CC Weekend, 2015; Jimmy Carter, unpublished diary.

*"love feast"*: Jimmy Carter, unpublished diary; Jimmy Carter, *Keeping Faith*, 400.

*"a surprising flexibility"*: Jimmy Carter, unpublished diary.

*"Begin showed courage in giving up the Sinai"*:

Jimmy Carter, *White House Diary,* 508.

*"The process . . . becomes virtually irreversible":* Jimmy Carter, unpublished diary.

*"We're coming home!":* Rosalynn Carter, *First Lady,* 267.

*"Mama, we'll go down in history books!":* Rosalynn Carter, unpublished diary.

*smartest, shrewdest, and ablest:* Landon Butler, unpublished diary, September 17, 1978.

*"full autonomy" for the Palestinians:* Jimmy Carter, *Keeping Faith,* 376–77.

*"The Camp David conference should be renamed":* Menachem Begin, Camp David Accords press conference, Associated Press, September 17, 1978.

*"we all shared faith in the same God":* Sam Cahnman, "My Visit with the Carters in Plains," *Illinois Times* (Springfield), March 9, 2017; Jimmy Carter, lecture, 92nd Street Y, New York, December 6, 2018.

*had never seen such an outpouring of emotion:* Rosalynn Carter, unpublished diary.

*"I was certain Sadat would be killed":* Steven M. Gillon, *The Democrats' Dilemma: Walter F. Mondale and the Liberal Legacy* (New York: Columbia University Press, 1992), 237.

*Chapter 28: Recognizing China*

*normalizing relations longest-lasting achievement:* Jimmy Carter, lecture, 92nd Street Y, New York, December 6, 2018.

*a governing philosophy:* Brzezinski, *Power and Principle,* 201.

*"First one to the top gets to fight the Russians!":* *New Republic,* editorial, October 4, 1980.

*The educational exchanges would exceed the wild-*

*est:* Jimmy Carter, speech to US-China Relations Forum, CC, November 10, 2013.

*"I don't give a shit what the Soviets think":* Ben Huberman int., May 20, 2015; Vance, *Hard Choices,* 110–11.

*The president later expressed pleasant surprise:* Jimmy Carter, *Keeping Faith,* 211.

*"Carter Is a Bastard": Newsweek,* January 8, 1979.

*"Three decades of acrimony":* Ji Chaozhu, *The Man on Mao's Right: From Harvard Yard to Tiananmen Square, My Life Inside China's Foreign Ministry* (New York: Random House, 2008), 298.

*Deng "small, tough, intelligent, frank":* Jimmy Carter, *White House Diary,* 283.

*"They insulted us":* Jimmy Carter int., June 14, 2015.

*"Do me a favor":* ibid.

*"They will drown in many people's wars":* Zbigniew Brzezinski int., March 1, 2016.

*"will generate major international turmoil":* Zbigniew Brzezinski to Jimmy Carter, February 6, 1979, CREST, JCPLM.

*"defensive counterattack":* Oriana Fallaci, *Interviews with History and Conversations with Power* (New York: Rizzoli, 2011), 371.

*"a genuine sense of emotion":* Jimmy Carter, *White House Diary,* 285.

*"In one simple gesture . . . imbibing American life and culture":* Orville Schell, *"Watch Out for the Foreign Guests!": China Encounters the West* (New York: Pantheon Books, 1980), 125.

*"let people worship freely, to own Bibles":* Jimmy Carter, *White House Diary,* 284; Jimmy Carter int., June 14, 2015.

*Schlesinger advised Chinese on coal:* James Schlesinger, OH, UVA-MC, July 20, 1984.

**Part 6: Swamped**

*Chapter 29: The Fall of the Shah*

*"I didn't see [it] as the major burning issue":* Jimmy Carter int., August 18, 2015.

*"I owe my throne to God":* William Shawcross, *The Shah's Last Ride: The Fate of an Ally* (New York: Simon & Schuster, 1988), 264.

*"It was* really *rough":* Jimmy Carter, *White House Diary,* 135.

*"draw a crowd":* "Toasts of the President and the Shah at a Dinner Honoring the Shah," The American Presidency Project, www.presidency.ucsb.edu.

*"no fingernails":* Doolittle, unpublished diary, November 16, 1977.

*Visitors to the palace . . . "shattered":* Gary Sick, *All Fall Down: America's Tragic Encounter with Iran* (New York: Random House, 1985), 60–61; Michael Blumenthal int., December 15, 2015.

*"the calmest, stillest man":* Kambiz Fattahi, "Two Weeks in January: America's Secret Engagement with Khomeini," BBC Persian Service, June 3, 2016; Robert MacNeil int., September 16, 2019.

*"Our destiny is to work with the shah":* Brzezinski, *Power and Principle,* 359–62.

*"confusing and contradictory":* Sick, *All Fall Down,* 87; see also Mohammad Reza Pahlavi, *Answer to History* (New York: Stein and Day, 1980).

*undermining his "self-confidence":* Robert Armao int., August 12, 2016.

*"relied on the US as a safety net":* Henry Kissinger int., April 21, 2016.

*"I will not pass on the throne to my son on a foundation of blood":* Robert Armao int., August 12, 2016.

*a "Gandhi-like" role:* Sick, *All Fall Down,* 194.

*"is not in a revolutionary . . . situation":* Jimmy Carter, *Keeping Faith,* 438.

*"let Carter down badly":* Stansfield Turner, *Burn Before Reading: Presidents, CIA Directors, and Secret Intelligence* (New York: Hachette, 2005), 180–81.

*explaining . . . what an "ayatollah" was:* Gary Sick int., June 6, 2019.

*"very, very negative in his attitude":* Jimmy Carter, *White House Diary,* 262.

*"acting in a completely irresponsible way":* Jimmy Carter, *Keeping Faith,* 405.

*"He's trying to welsh on the deal":* Jimmy Carter, *White House Diary,* 249.

*had not given up on option C:* Brzezinski, *Power and Principle,* 397.

*"a wobbler":* James Schlesinger, OH, UVA-MC, July 19, 1984.

*"We personally prefer that the shah maintain a major role":* Jim Hoagland, "Carter Hints Shah Could Fall," *Washington Post,* December 8, 1978.

*"bouts of conscience and apologize":* James Schlesinger OH, UVA-MC, July 19, 1984.

*"choose without delay":* Vance, *Hard Choices,* 333.

*"determined, even quixotic man":* ibid., 338.

*"neutralize the army":* Leonard Downie Jr., "Shah Says U.S. Worked Actively for His Ouster," *Washington Post,* December 8, 1979.

*The top generals, he said, were "gutless":* David D. Kirkpatrick, "How a Chase Bank Chairman Helped the Deposed Shah of Iran Enter the U.S.," *New York Times,* December 29, 2019.

*a source of stability:* Brzezinski, *Power and Principle,* 377.

*"Jim [Callaghan] complained":* ibid.

"one of the most enjoyable times I've ever had": Jimmy Carter, *White House Diary,* 276.

"not a kindergarten": Brzezinski, *Power and Principle,* 380.

"gross and perhaps irretrievable mistake": William H. Sullivan cable, JCPLM; Jimmy Carter, *Keeping Faith,* 446.

"bordered on insolence": Jimmy Carter, *Keeping Faith,* 446.

"nothing could be worse than a half-assed coup": Landon Butler, unpublished diary, January 23, 1979.

"Your Majesty . . . we are talking about you": Robert Huyser, *Mission to Tehran* (Southwold, UK: Bookthrift, 1990), 290.

going "on vacation": Jimmy Carter, *Keeping Faith,* 447.

"Oh, boy, another week to excel!": Max Cleland, personal notes on Cabinet meeting, January 15, 1979, Max Cleland Papers, Stetson University Archive.

a voice that could "boil the fat off a taxi driver's neck": Jonathan Mahler, *Ladies and Gentlemen, the Bronx Is Burning* (New York: Farrar, Straus and Giroux, 2005), 70.

"the Friday Afternoon Massacre": Jerry Rafshoon int., March 2, 2019.

"We are pushing hard": Jimmy Carter, *White House Diary,* 278.

"close the airports": Jimmy Carter, *Keeping Faith,* 280.

More likely, news of Bakhtiar's consorting . . . accelerated the revolution: Brzezinski, *Power and Principle,* 387; see also Glad, *In Search,* 173.

"a humanitarian one": Fattahi, "Two Weeks in January."

*"drowned in mullahs"*: ibid.

*"a misperception on my part"*: Zbigniew Brzezinski int., March 1, 2016.

*Secord warned him against it*: Richard Secord int., May 2, 2016.

*Brzezinski heard separate reports*: Gary Sick int. June 6, 2019.

*In his nineties, Henry Kissinger still insisted*: Henry Kissinger int., April 21, 2016.

*"the player who smashes his fist"*: Sick, *All Fall Down*, 45.

*"convinced the peace effort was at an end"*: Jimmy Carter, *Keeping Faith*, 415.

*"It got kinda ugly"*: Jimmy Carter, OH, UVA-MC, 1988.

*he would likely face a public relations disaster*: Jimmy Carter, *Keeping Faith*, 416; Jimmy Carter int., September 1, 2017.

*"keep Carter honest"*: Jerry Rafshoon int., March 11, 2019.

*"so completely disgusted"*: Rosalynn Carter, unpublished diary.

*decided to go over Begin's head*: Jimmy Carter, *White House Diary*, 301.

*"All negative," he said*: Rosalynn Carter, unpublished diary.

*Carter's Knesset speech was so persuasive*: Stephen Rosenfeld to Rick Hertzberg, April 30, 1979, Hendrik Hertzberg Papers.

*"You see, I'm only one member!"*: Jimmy Carter, *Keeping Faith*, 422–23.

*"Being charitable to Begin"*: Rosalynn Carter, unpublished diary.

*"Everyone was so pessimistic and 'down'"*: ibid.

*"You boys like the King David?"*: Jerry Rafshoon int., March 2, 2019.

*"I made one final effort"*: Jimmy Carter, *White House Diary,* 303.

*"breech birth"*: Eizenstat, *Carter: White House Years,* 547.

*"It's a miracle!"*: Jimmy Carter, *White House Diary,* 303.

*Sadat's wife, Jehan, told Rosalynn tearfully . . . faith in God:* Rosalynn Carter, unpublished diary.

*intriguing revisionist history:* see Seth Anziska, *Preventing Palestine: A Political History from Camp David to Oslo* (Princeton, NJ: Princeton University Press, 2018).

*"too often seems to absolve the Palestinians"*: Dennis Ross, "Did Camp David Doom the Palestinians?," *Foreign Policy,* October 19, 2018.

*"Tell Brzezinski to fuck off"*: William H. Sullivan, *Mission to Iran: The Last Ambassador* (New York: W. W. Norton, 1989), 252–53.

*"I'm firing all of you"*: Leslie Gelb int., December 15, 2015; Jimmy Carter, *Keeping Faith,* 450; Walter Mondale int., June 9, 2015.

*"we thought would be friendly"*: Jimmy Carter int., November 18, 2015.


Chapter 30: The "Malaise" Speech

*"est, gestalt therapy, bioenergetics"*: Jerry Rubin, *Growing (Up) at Thirty-Seven* (New York: M. Evans, 1976), 20.

*one historian called "the Great Funk"*: see Thomas Hine, *The Great Funk: Falling Apart and Coming Together (On a Shag Rug) in the Seventies* (New York: Farrar, Straus and Giroux, 2007).

*Carter's experience as a planner:* Gene Eidenberg, OH, WH Exit Interview Project, JCPLM, June 10, 1981.

*"New Foundation":* Robert Schlesinger, *White House Ghosts* (New York: Simon & Schuster, 2008), 296; Rick Hertzberg int., June 7, 2015.

*"to* look *like you're providing leadership":* Jerry Rafshoon, quoted in Schlesinger, *White House Ghosts,* 298.

*"Glory comes only in great danger":* Pat Caddell int., April 8, 2016.

*popular sociological analysis:* see Christopher Lasch, *The Culture of Narcissism: American Life in an Age of Diminishing Expectations* (New York: W. W. Norton, 1978).

*"on the order of a Lincoln":* Pat Caddell, "Of Crisis and Opportunity," April 23, 1979, JCPLM.

*"a continuing political campaign":* see Sidney Blumenthal, *The Permanent Campaign* (New York: Simon & Schuster, 1982); Joe Klein, *Politics Lost: How American Democracy Was Trivialized by People Who Think You're Stupid* (New York: Doubleday, 2006), 39.

*"transformational leadership . . . seeks":* see James MacGregor Burns, *Leadership* (New York: HarperCollins, 1978).

*"getting him out of chickenshit":* Charles Peters int., March 21, 2015.

*thought it was "crap":* Walter Mondale int., June 9, 2015.

*"I became really depressed":* ibid.

*"I'll be better if you quit":* Joan Mondale, quoted in Gillon, *Democrats' Dilemma,* 259.

*meeting with Emperor Hirohito:* Jimmy Carter, *White House Diary,* 334.

*"Back home, everything is going down the drain":* Hendrik Hertzberg Papers.

*"a clear enemy":* Martin Schram, "Carter Urged to Blame OPEC, Save Himself," *Washington*

*Post,* July 7, 1979.

*"one of the most brilliant analyses":* Jimmy Carter, *White House Diary,* 340.

*"almost a Rasputin":* Eizenstat, *Carter: White House Years,* 673.

*"bullshit the American people":* Hendrik Hertzberg Papers.

*"President Cancels Address on Energy":* Hendrick Smith, "President Cancels Address on Energy; No Reason Offered," *New York Times,* July 5, 1979.

*"President Carter has reached the low point":* Tom Wicker, "Carter on the Precipice," *New York Times,* July 10, 1979.

*"almost felt I was at a seance":* Eizenstat, *Carter: White House Years,* 679.

*"You've become part of the Washington system":* Elizabeth Drew, "Phase: In Search of a Definition," *New Yorker,* August 27, 1979.

*"We got elected . . . a government as good as its people":* Walter Mondale int., June 9, 2015.

*"I think we're goners":* Eizenstat, *Carter: White House Years,* 679.

*"You have a style problem":* ibid.

*"shaking like a leaf":* Pat Caddell int., April 8, 2016.

*"preeminently a place of moral leadership":* New York Times Magazine, September 11, 1932.

*"quite distraught":* Jimmy Carter, *White House Diary,* 341.

*"Their criticisms of me were much more severe":* ibid., 342.

*"the worst of the week":* ibid.

*"Don't just preach sacrifice":* Eizenstat, *Carter: White House Years,* 686.

*"the God Squad":* Mattson, "What the Heck Are You

*Up To, Mr. President?,"* 142.

*would be "self-righteous":* ibid., 143.

*"a teaching president":* ibid.

*"counterproductive, even a disaster":* Hendrik Hertzberg Papers.

*Stewart . . . "I'm bored":* Schlesinger, *White House Ghosts,* 303.

*"In a nation that was proud of hard work":* ibid.

*"How else were voters to feel?":* Richard Wirthlin, *The Greatest Communicator: What Ronald Reagan Taught Me About Politics, Leadership, and Life* (Hoboken, NJ: John Wiley & Sons, 2004), 35–36.

*Caddell used "malaise":* Jerry Rafshoon int., June 7, 2015.

*"No president since Abraham Lincoln":* Theodore H. White, *America in Search of Itself: The Making of the President, 1956–1980* (New York: Harper & Row, 1982), 268.

*"The president's comments on the mood":* Office of the White House Press Secretary, news release, July 19, 1979, JCPLM.

*"by far the best formal address":* "Out in Front," *New York Daily News,* July 17, 1979.

*"Suddenly last night, the nation saw an old friend":* " 'Crisis of Confidence,' " editorial, *Baltimore Sun,* July 16, 1979.

*"truthful and prescient diagnosis":* Hertzberg, *Politics,* 63.

*"You should fire people":* Eizenstat, *Carter: White House Years,* 694.

*"shocking" and "brutal" tone:* ibid., 697.

*"acting like Moses":* Harold Brown int., August 20, 2016.

*"awful advice":* Jerry Rafshoon int., March 11, 2019.

*Georgians thought . . . Blumenthal was a leaker:* Michael Blumenthal int., December 15, 2015.

*"If I had to do it all again":* Jimmy Carter int., June 14, 2015.

*"one of the best and strongest":* Jimmy Carter, *White House Diary,* 262.

*"On smoking, you were right, and I was wrong":* Joseph Califano int., May 19, 2015; Jimmy Carter int., June 14, 2015.

*"He's like a football player":* Mary Russell, "On the Hill: One Step Forward for Carter — and One Back," *Washington Post,* July 20, 1979.

*"I handled the Cabinet changes very poorly":* Jimmy Carter, *Keeping Faith,* 121.

*"Are we falling apart?":* Walter Mondale int., June 9, 2015.

*"a ship that seemed rudderless":* ibid.

*Mondale claimed later that he was merely blowing off steam:* Eizenstat, *Carter: White House Years,* 704–7.

*"That day, he was a gone duck":* James Schlesinger, OH, UVA-MC, July 20, 1984.

*"Jimmy Carter must be the sexiest man in the country":* Jerry Rafshoon int., March 13, 2019.

*Chapter 31: Touching Bottom*

*scores of bottles began exploding:* Jimmy Carter, *Hour Before Daylight,* 201.

*"Congress and Labor were our natural enemies":* quoted in Judith Stein, *Pivotal Decade: How the United States Traded Factories for Finance in the Seventies* (New Haven, CT: Yale University Press, 2010), 181.

*That was pathetic:* Jimmy Carter int., November 19, 2015.

*"snobbish, arrogant, distrustful":* Leonard Silk and

1093

Mark Silk, *The American Establishment* (New York: Avon Books, 1981), ix.

*"You have to understand":* Paul Volcker obituary, *New York Times,* December 10, 2019.

*Volcker felt he had talked too much:* Paul Volcker int., May 5, 2015; Paul Volcker with Christine Harper, *Keeping at It: The Quest for Sound Money and Good Government* (New York: PublicAffairs, 2018), 103.

*Peggy Clausen changed American history:* Richard Moe int., August 9, 2019.

*"You gotta tell Jimmy":* Jerry Rafshoon int., March 13, 2019.

*how excited she and Jimmy:* John Dalton int., March 26, 2019.

*"It will be very austere":* Jacobs, *Panic at the Pump,* 197.

*"practically nothing in savings":* Paul Volcker int., May 5, 2015.

*Charlie Schultze . . . called Volcker with a final plea:* William Greider, *Secrets of the Temple: How the Federal Reserve Runs the Country* (New York: Simon & Schuster, 1989), 123.

*"indifferent" to his political fate:* ibid., 214.

*thought the probe was a "travesty":* Jimmy Carter, *White House Diary,* 354.

*"ridiculous reason":* ibid., 374.

*"Bunny Goes Bugs":* Brooks Jackson, "Bunny Goes Bugs: Rabbit Attacks President," *Washington Post,* August 30, 1979; Brooks Jackson int., June 3, 2020; Susan Clough int., December 26, 2015.

*"enormous swimming rabbit":* Dave Barry, *Dave Barry Slept Here: A Sort of History of the United States* (New York: Random House, 1989), 219.

*the president . . . seemed incapable of laughing at*

*himself:* Patrick Anderson, *Electing Jimmy Carter: The Campaign of 1976* (Baton Rouge: Louisiana State University Press, 1994), 168.

*"beginning to think Richard Nixon got a raw deal":* Eleanor Clift, remarks, CC Weekend, June 28, 2019.

*"perhaps thousands of political prisoners":* Associated Press, "Political Prisoners in U.S., Young Says," *New York Times,* July 13, 1978, A3.

*accepted Young's resignation:* Andrew Young int., June 10, 2015.

*he would have kept Young and cut Vance loose:* Jimmy Carter int., November 19, 2015; see also Garry Wills, *Certain Trumpets: The Call of Leaders* (New York: Simon & Schuster, 1994), 77.

*"the long knives at the State Department":* John Herbers, "Aftermath of Andrew Young Affair: Blacks, Jews, and Carter All Could Suffer Greatly," *New York Times,* September 6, 1979.

*"too much pain, too much suffering":* ibid.

*"I'm going to find somewhere else to take my vote":* ibid.

*"You want me to change":* Evan Dobelle int., February 8, 2020.

"They had to drag me off.": Sarah Pileggi, "Jimmy Carter Runs into the Wall," *Sports Illustrated,* September 24, 1979.

*Chapter 32: Ready for Teddy?*

*malaise speech:* Kennedy, *True Compass,* 366–67.

*"divide the country":* William vanden Heuvel int., May 10, 2015.

*"If Kennedy runs, I'll whip his ass":* Newsweek, June 25, 1979.

*Carter thought his feisty answer was the best:*

Jimmy Carter, *White House Diary,* 332.

*John White . . . felt obliged to say he was neutral:* Adam Clymer, "Move Grows in Capitol to Urge Carter to Shun Race," *New York Times,* September 13, 1979.

*"Southerners took over; now Yankees unhappy":* Pat Caddell int., April 8, 2016.

*"Why is he perceived as a weak leader?":* Wendell Rawls Jr., "Carter's Poll-Taker Seems to Voice 1980 Catchwords," *New York Times,* August 14, 1979.

*"I'm the King's man":* Pat Caddell int., April 8, 2016.

*the* "appearance *of listening":* Kennedy, *True Compass,* 360–61.

*"he reserved a special place in his animus toward me":* ibid., 352.

*"a reader in the White House":* Eizenstat, *Carter: White House Years,* 363.

*"a miracle achievement":* Jimmy Carter, *White House Diary,* 444.

*"just-in-time":* Cynthia Engel, "Competition Drives the Trucking Industry," *Monthly Labor Review* 121, no. 4 (April 1998): 34–41; Thomas Gale Moore, "Unfinished Business in Motor Carrier Deregulation," *Regulation* 14, no. 7 (Summer 1991): 33–41.

*He suggested coverage be expanded in phases:* Jimmy Carter, *White House Diary,* 203.

*"squandering a real opportunity":* Kennedy, *True Compass,* 359–60.

*single-payer system . . . . "politically impossible":* ibid., 359.

*"blasting us":* Jimmy Carter, *White House Diary,* 208–209.

*"would be excessively expensive":* ibid., 295.

*"This is* the *vote to fight inflation":* Jimmy Carter to Tip O'Neill, November 9, 1979.

*"all pain and no gain":* Eizenstat, *Carter: White House Years,* 817–18; see also Joseph A. Califano Jr., *Governing America: An Insider's Report from the White House and Cabinet* (New York: Simon & Schuster, 1981), 152.

*"Why, at this point . . . elect Reagan?":* Walter Mondale int., June 9, 2015.

*"What would the downside have been?"* Carl Wagner int., December 31, 2015.

*"Kennedy, continuing . . . abusive attitude":* Jimmy Carter, *White House Diary,* 325.

*"putting an elephant through a keyhole":* Eizenstat, *Carter: White House Years,* 832.

*"worst example of a powerful special interest":* Jimmy Carter, *White House Diary,* 370.

*"would have been a huge victory":* Kennedy, *True Compass,* 360.

*"if you vote for this bill":* Frank Moore int., February 20, 2018.

*wished he had handled the Kennedy challenge better:* Jimmy Carter int., August 3, 2018.

*"I'll accommodate you":* Jimmy Carter int., June 14, 2015.

*"Teddy honestly doubted he could do job":* Stephen Smith Jr., int., July 24, 2015.

*At first, the outlook for Kennedy seemed promising:* Jimmy Carter, *White House Diary,* 362.

*"Seventy-five percent of the country watched* Jaws": John Dickerson, *Whistlestop: My Favorite Stories from Presidential Campaign History* (New York: Twelve, 2016), 350.

*"It was like . . . 'the sky is so blue' ":* quoted in Jack W. Germond and Jules Witcover, *Blue Smoke and Mirrors: How Reagan Won and Why*

*Carter Lost the Election of 1980* (New York: Viking, 1982), 70.

*"It'll be over in a few hours"*: Hamilton Jordan, *Crisis,* 19.

## Chapter 33: America Held Hostage

*"the taint of the shah"*: ibid., January 20, 1979; Jimmy Carter, *Keeping Faith,* 448.

*"What . . . if they overrun our embassy and take our people hostage?"*: Jimmy Carter, OH, UVA-MC, 1988; also see Mark Bowden, *Guests of the Ayatollah: The First Battle in America's War with Militant Islam* (New York: Atlantic Monthly Press, 2006), 19.

*Vance tried to enlist Henry Kissinger:* Terence Smith, "Why Carter Admitted the Shah," *New York Times,* May 17, 1981.

*Armao . . . would eventually run afoul of Carter:* Robert Armao int., August 12, 2016.

*"national honor"*: Brzezinski, *Power and Principle,* 474.

*"like a flying Dutchman seeking a port of call"*: Henry Kissinger, "Kissinger On the Controversy Over the Shah," *Washington Post,* November 29, 1979.

*In May the shah's Bahamas visa ran out:* Shawcross, *Shah's Last Ride,* 228–29.

*"subtle fashion"*: Brzezinski, *Power and Principle,* 474.

*"It is so sad"*: quoted in Kai Bird, *The Chairman: John J. McCloy and the Making of the American Establishment* (New York: Simon & Schuster, 1992), 648–49.

*"Zbig bugged me on it"*: Brzezinski, *Power and Principle,* 474.

*"Are we going to go to war with Iran?"*: Jimmy Car-

ter, OH, UVA-MC, November 29, 1982.

*"Fuck the shah!":* Brzezinski, *Power and Principle,* 474.

*"It was shocking to hear":* Harold Brown int., August 20, 2016.

*Carter . . . didn't want the shah in the United States:* Shawcross, *Shah's Last Ride,* 241; David R. Farber, *Taken Hostage: The Iran Hostage Crisis and America's First Encounter with Radical Islam* (Princeton, NJ: Princeton University Press, 2005), 125.

*"more defensible":* quoted in Bowden, *Guests of the Ayatollah,* 33; Jimmy Carter, OH, UVA-MC, 1988.

*"compulsive liar":* Nicholas Veliotes int., May 20, 2020.

*"at point of death":* Jimmy Carter int., June 14, 2015.

*Dr. Kean insisted . . . was "nonsense":* Lawrence K. Altman, "The Shah's Health: A Political Gamble," *New York Times,* May 17, 1981.

*"optimal" . . . "acceptable":* Robert Armao int., August 12, 2016, September 17, 2019; for more on the shah's entrance to the United States, see Shawcross, *Shah's Last Ride,* 250–51; Eizenstat, *Carter: White House Years,* 761–63.

*"You're opening a Pandora's box":* Smith, "Why Carter Admitted the Shah."

*"a field day":* Hamilton Jordan, *Crisis: The Last Year of the Carter Presidency* (New York: G. P. Putnam's Sons, 1982), 31.

*"I was convinced":* Jimmy Carter, OH, UVA-MC, 1988.

*picture of the shah looking healthy:* Farber, *Taken Hostage,* 127.

*"Cy's so extremely jealous it's ridiculous":* Jimmy Carter, *White House Diary,* 364.

*The students moved fast:* Massoumeh Ebtekar, *Takeover in Tehran: The Inside Story of the 1979 Embassy Capture* (Burnaby, BC: Talonbooks, 2000), 49–55.

*"Don't be afraid":* Tim Wells, *444 Days: The Hostages Remember* (San Diego: Harcourt Brace Jovanovich, 1985), 39.

*"It looked hopeless":* Nate Penn, "444 Days in the Dark: An Oral History of the Iran Hostage Crisis," *GQ,* November 3, 2009.

*"What are you going to do with me?":* Neil Genzlinger, "L. Bruce Laingen, Senior Hostage During Iran Crisis, Dies at 96," *New York Times,* July 19, 2019, A24.

*the hostages were not allowed to speak:* Harrison Smith, "Bruce Laingen, Top-Ranking U.S. Diplomat Held in Iran Hostage Crisis, Dies at 96," *Washington Post,* July 17, 2019.

*"Don't believe what you are seeing":* see Bowden, *Guests of the Ayatollah;* Farber, *Taken Hostage,* 134–35.

*"We just plain fell asleep":* Chris Whipple, *The Gatekeepers: How White House Chiefs of Staff Define Every Presidency* (New York: Crown, 2017), 105.

*"We have made no progress":* Warren Christopher to Jimmy Carter, November 5, 1979, NLC, 128141337 CREST, JCPLM.

*"no matter how preposterous":* Jimmy Carter, *Keeping Faith,* 459.

*"It's almost impossible to deal with a crazy man":* Jimmy Carter, *White House Diary,* 368.

*"for humanitarian reasons":* Jimmy Carter to Ayatollah Khomeini, November 6, 1979,

JCPLM.

*"It was the first time":* Hamilton Jordan, *Crisis,* 44.

*"Lincoln said, 'I have but one task' ":* Jimmy Carter, "1980, Remarks Concerning Candidacy and Campaign Plans, December 4, 1979," *PPPJC,* 1979, vol. 2, 2194.

*Brzezinski favored seizing or blockading Kharg Island:* Zbigniew Brzezinski int., March 1, 2016.

*Harold Brown preferred mining the entrances:* Harold Brown int., August 20, 2016.

*"I'd get a couple of mafioso":* Maurice Sonnenberg int., September 21, 2017.

*"Do something! Do something!":* Rosalynn Carter, *First Lady,* 312.

*"The problem with all the military options":* Hamilton, Jordan, *Crisis,* 52.

*"Jimmy would have been reelected":* Carol Butler, unpublished diary, August 21, 2002.

*Brzezinski met secretly with Billy:* "Text of Statement by Brzezinski," *New York Times,* October 3, 1980.

*"I am not going to take any military action": Desert One,* directed by Barbara Kopple (Cabin Creek Films, 2020).

*"resolute and, um, manly":* CNBC Meets, October 1, 2014.

*In response, Carter used the Germans:* Jimmy Carter int., June 14, 2015.

*"grave consequences":* Bernard Gwertzman, "Carter Warns Iran on Hostages," *New York Times,* November 24, 1979.

*"slate would not be wiped clean":* Jimmy Carter, unpublished diary, November 27, 1979.

*"increasingly flabby":* Special Coordination Committee minutes, December 18, 1979, CREST, JCPLM.

*he recounted for Carter his terrifying experiences in Iran:* Jimmy Carter, *White House Diary,* 389.

*"received us in a severe, distant manner":* Abol Hassan Bani-Sadr, *My Turn to Speak: Iran, the Revolution, and Secret Deals with the U.S.* (Potomac Books, 1991), 24.

*"To protect . . . and to bring all the hostages home":* Jimmy Carter, OH, UVA-MC, 1988.

*"Goddamn it, Hamilton, you owe it to the shah!":* Robert Armao int., August 12, 2016.

*"Are we in jail?":* Shawcross, *Shah's Last Ride,* 292.

*Why should "that individual":* ibid., 297.

*"If I had to do it over":* Robert Armao int., August 12, 2016.

*Princess Ashraf . . . wouldn't shake his hand:* Hamilton Jordan, *Crisis,* 94.

*he thought about the hostages every day:* Ted Koppel int., August 30, 2019.

*"The fundamental error":* Penn, "444 Days in the Dark."

*"Carter was essentially making himself a hostage":* ibid.

*"there were only two people who really benefited":* Ted Koppel int., August 30, 2019.

*Chapter 34: Reheating the Cold War*

*Soviets deployed thousands of new nuclear missiles:* Cyrus Vance, telegram, February 17, 1980, NSA.

*Detente did not work well:* Dobrynin, *In Confidence,* 402–3.

*"Kissinger was the worst":* Hodding Carter int., April 15, 2017.

*"We need to see . . . in more subtle shades":* Terence Smith, "President Cautions Foreign

Policy Foes," *New York Times,* February 23, 1979.

*"to challenge directly the legitimacy":* Robert M. Gates, *From the Shadows: The Ultimate Insider's Story of Five Presidents and How They Won the Cold War* (New York: Simon & Schuster, 1996), 95.

*The most important element of faith:* Jimmy Carter, *Faith: A Journey for All* (New York: Simon & Schuster, 2018), 8.

*"Dear Mr. President":* Russell Baker, *New York Times,* August 13, 1980, quoted in Garrett M. Graff, *Raven Rock: The Story of the U.S. Government's Secret Plan to Save Itself — While the Rest of Us Die* (New York: Simon & Schuster, 2017), 274.

*PD-59 wasn't a full-scale war-fighting doctrine:* Briefing Book #390, the Nuclear Vault, NSA, September 14, 2012.

*And he broke precedent by personally visiting the presidential bunker:* Graff, *Raven Rock,* 274.

*"thought these Americans are bonkers":* Leslie Gelb int., December 15, 2015.

*caught between Vance and Brzezinski:* see Robert A. Strong, *Working in the World: Jimmy Carter and the Making of American Foreign Policy* (Baton Rouge: Louisiana State University Press, 2012), 108–21.

*"more difficult time convincing the Joint Chiefs":* Jimmy Carter, OH, UVA-MC, 1988.

*" 'God will not forgive us' ":* see Jimmy Carter, *White House Diary,* 328–30.

*Brezhnev offered frequent vodka toasts:* New York Times, Washington Post, June 15–18.

*"I thought, 'Uh-oh.' ":* Jimmy Carter, *White House*

*Diary,* 331; Leslie Gelb int., December 21, 2015.

*helped motivate him as a young man:* see Robert C. Byrd, *Child of the Appalachian Coalfields* (Morgantown: University of West Virginia Press, 2005), 406.

*"a Soviet Vietnam":* Zbigniew Brzezinski, quoted in "Les Révélations d'un Ancien Conseiller de Carter: 'Oui, la CIA est Entrée en Afghanistan avant les Russes . . .' " *Le Nouvel Observateur,* January 15, 1998.

*"We didn't push the Russians to intervene":* ibid., January 21, 1998.

*Brzezinski was unapologetic:* Zbigniew Brzezinski int., March 1, 2016.

*Newly declassified documents . . . offer important clues:* Briefing Book #657, NSA, January 29, 2019.

*"extremely grave challenge":* Zbigniew Brzezinski to Carter, December 29, 1979, National Security Archive, www. nsarchive2.gwu.edu doc 5696260.

*"My opinion of the Russians": Foreign Relations of the United States, 1977–1980,* vol. 1, *Foundation of Foreign Policy.* US Department of State, Office of the Historian.

*"destined for a firing squad":* Steven Hayward, "Ben Wattenberg, RIP," Power Line, June 29, 2015, https://www.powerlineblog.com/archives/2015/06/ben-wattenberg-rip.php.

*"Corn was up 23 cents!":* Jimmy Carter, *White House Diary,* 391.

*Mondale found it "outrageous":* Walter Mondale int., June 9, 2015.

*couldn't "sell" the embargo: Brainerd Dispatch,* September 16, 2019, JCPLM.

*"It was that big"*: Dan Glickman int., July 24, 2018.

*"There goes SALT II"*: Rosalynn Carter, *First Lady,* 314.

*Carter wrote . . . to delay floor consideration of the treaty:* Jimmy Carter to Robert Byrd, January 3, 1980, JCPLM.

*"extremely serious threat to peace"*: "Transcript of President's Speech on Soviet Military Intervention in Afghanistan," *New York Times,* January 5, 1980.

*"sweated the boycott"*: NSC6090, declassified minutes of NSC meeting, January 2, 1980, JCPLM.

*"Howard Cosell . . . killed the Olympics"*: Hamilton Jordan, *Crisis,* 113.

*"counter Olympics"*: Barry Lorge, "White House Clout Could Make Boycott Stick," *Washington Post,* April 4, 1980.

*threaten to sue the IOC:* ABC News–Harris Survey, March 27, 1980.

*The USOC voted . . . to "resist"*: Terence Smith, "The President Said 'Nyet'," *New York Times,* January 20, 1980.

*"practically a rebellion from Stu and Fritz"*: Jimmy Carter, *White House Diary,* 394.

*"I reacted strongly"*: Jimmy Carter, OH, UVA-MC, 1988.

*Harold Brown told Carter he needed to "rub their noses"*: NSC027, declassified minutes of NSC meeting, March 18, 1980, JCPLM.

*"we are weak, we are second, and it's getting worse"*: ibid.

*("It's not a pleasant time for me"):* Jimmy Carter, "White House Briefing on the 1980 Summer Olympics, Remarks to Representatives of U.S.

Teams, March 21, 1980," *PPPJC,* 1980, vol. 1, 519.

*"There is nothing . . . to upset the Soviets more":* Zbigniew Brzezinski to Jimmy Carter, Daily Report, January 24, 1980, JCPLM.

*"bogged down":* Special Coordination Committee Summary of Conclusions, January 22, 1980, Defense Policy Coordination to Brzezinski, January 30, 1980, CREST, JCPLM.

*"around the world to take the whupping":* Michael Ezra, "Muhammad Ali's Strange, Failed Diplomatic Career," *Politico,* June 5, 2016.

*"I guess women are not the only ones that have periods":* Jimmy Carter, *White House Diary,* 172.

*"acted like a paranoid child — ranting and raving":* ibid., 439–40.

*Carter called Schmidt and asked him to finally commit:* Lloyd Cutler to Jimmy Carter, May 10, 1980, JCPLM.

*in what Carter described as a "farce":* Jimmy Carter, *White House Diary,* 449.

*"I reluctantly agreed with their decision":* Henry Bushnell, "Ghost Olympians: The Lives Forever Changed by the 1980 Boycott," Yahoo! Sports, May 19, 2020.

*"That was a bad decision. I'm sorry":* Associated Press, April 12, 2020.


*Chapter 35: Disaster at Desert One*

*prayed more than at any time he could remember:* Jimmy Carter int., June 14, 2015.

*"above the fray":* Jimmy Carter, *White House Diary,* 381.

*"We ought not kiss his ass":* Eizenstat, *Carter: White House Years,* 839.

*"the biggest political mistake I ever made":* Jimmy

Carter, *White House Diary*, 497.

*"This is the man that saved Chrysler!":* ibid.

*"greatest disappointment":* Rosalynn Carter, *First Lady,* 286.

*NOW also announced:* Adam Clymer, "Board of NOW to Oppose Carter, Charging Lag on Women's Issues," *New York Times,* December 11, 1979.

*Rosalynn still considered this unforgivable:* Rosalynn Carter int., November 17, 2015.

*"a kind of narcissistic intemperance":* Suzannah Lessard, "Kennedy's Woman Problem. Women's Kennedy Problem," *Washington Monthly,* December 1979; see also Jon Ward, *Camelot's End: Carter vs. Kennedy and the Fight That Broke the Democratic Party* (New York: Twelve, 2019), 158–77; *Ted Kennedy — Part Five* (*Boston Globe* film).

*"foreign policy based on . . . unrequited love":* Christian Science Monitor, January 30, 1980.

*"This is a rare event in politics":* Jimmy Carter, *White House Diary,* 365.

*"made the administration look silly":* Brzezinski, *Power and Principle,* 442.

*a comment Carter found "disgraceful":* Jimmy Carter, *White House Diary,* 409; *New York Times,* February 5, 1984; Jimmy Carter, *Keeping Faith,* 492–94.

*"seemingly pompous":* Rosalynn Carter, *First Lady,* 165.

*Carter toured . . . South Bronx:* Jack Watson int., November 19, 2015.

*"I gave him hell":* Jimmy Carter, *Keeping Faith,* 550.

*"if Ed Koch and Jane Byrne had a baby":* Jerry Rafshoon int., January 25, 2019.

*Koch met secretly with Republican county leaders:*

"Carter Contends Koch Harmed '80 Campaign, *New York Times,* May 12, 1986, B5.

*"all you have to do is kill the shah":* Hamilton Jordan, *Crisis,* 165; Shawcross, *Shah's Last Ride,* 352.

*"I will not do that to Anwar":* Hamilton Jordan, *Crisis,* 216.

*Carter was "livid":* ibid., 227.

*"I find that sickening!":* ibid., 233.

*"he could survive me and Hamilton":* Rosalynn Carter, unpublished diary, March 31, 1980.

*"Jimmy came into the room":* ibid.

*"He, in my opinion, is the hostage":* ibid.

*"He was left in an extremely awkward position":* James Reston, "The Diplomatic War," *New York Times,* March 2, 1980.

*"Ham, the only people . . . are you and your French friends":* Hamilton Jordan, *Crisis,* 246.

*(Taylor, "the real hero"):* Associated Press, February 12, 2013.

*"The raid was necessary . . . to get reelected":* Hodding Carter int., April 15, 2017.

*you could not take a platoon across a river:* ibid.

*"the rescue mission is the best":* Hamilton Jordan, *Crisis,* 249.

*"stunned and angry":* Vance, *Hard Choices,* 409.

*"extremely despondent":* Jimmy Carter, *Keeping Faith,* 510.

*"the helicopters":* Hugh Sidey, "Assessing a Presidency," Nation, *Time,* August 18, 1980.

*"The buck stops with me":* Hamilton Jordan, *Crisis,* 263; see David C. Martin and John Walcott, *Best-Laid Plans: The Inside Story of America's War Against Terrorism* (New York: Harper & Row, 1988), 4.

*"months and months"*: Hamilton Jordan, *Crisis*, 266.

*"Fuck you," Beckwith said:* Penn, "444 Days in the Dark."

*"Let's go with [Beckwith's] recommendation"*: Martin and Walcott, *Best-Laid Plans*, 23.

*"Mr. President, I'm very, very sorry"*: Hamilton Jordan, *Crisis*, 272–73.

*"It was my decision"*: "Transcript of President Carter's Statement on the Hostage Situation," *New York Times*, April 26, 1980.

*"when my father died"*: Rosalynn Carter, *First Lady*, 327.

*"I opened my arms, and we embraced"*: Jimmy Carter, *Keeping Faith*, 519.

*"as tough as woodpecker lips"*: Jimmy Carter, *White House Diary*, 424.

*He put together an aggressive battle plan:* Richard Secord int., May 2, 2016.

*"Had he pulled the chestnuts out of fire"*: Max Cleland int., December 23, 2015.

*beating the drums over Carter's alleged naivete:* Hedley Donovan to Jimmy Carter, February 2, 1980, JCPLM.

*"Well, shit, General"*: David Maraniss, *First in His Class: A Biography of Bill Clinton* (New York: Simon & Schuster, 1995), 378.

*He tried desperately to figure out who had "screwed" him:* Bill Clinton, *My Life* (New York: Alfred A. Knopf, 2004), 274–78.

*"mistakes . . . may have cost him his reelection"*: C-SPAN, November 18, 2004; Jimmy Carter, *White House Diary*, 433.

*"always ambitious" and "concentrated on what was best"*: Jimmy Carter int., November 19, 2015.

*If Kennedy had lost:* Stephen Smith Jr. int., July

26, 2015.

*Kennedy and Carter TV ads:* video collection, JCPLM.

*"Kennedy challenge hurt us very badly":* Hamilton Jordan, *Crisis,* 306.

*"completely obsessed":* Jimmy Carter, *White House Diary,* 435.

*"redneck pose":* " 'Mobituaries': Remembering First Brother Billy Carter," CBS News, November 1, 2019.

*"love-hate relationship with fame":* Sybil Carter int., September 28, 2015.

*he made a point of turning away:* Dale Russakoff int., July 4, 2019.

*"had suddenly turned into racist":* Buddy Carter, *Billy Carter,* 174.

*"Thank you for advising me":* Greg Schneiders int., September 1, 2015.

*"That Jew bastard of yours":* Jerry Rafshoon int., January 25, 2019.

*it was quickly dubbed "Billygate":* Hamilton Jordan, *Crisis,* 312.

*"People think I'm a lot more burdened down":* Jimmy Carter, *White House Diary,* 452.

*"This is bullshit":* Jimmy Carter, *White House Diary,* 492–93.

*"an embarrassing incident":* "Text of Report by President's Counsel to Panel Conducting Billy Carter Inquiry," *New York Times,* August 5, 1980.

*"It was the best of Carter":* Sidey, "Assessing a Presidency," *Time,* August 18, 1980.

*Chapter 36: Are You Better Off?*

*"introduced Bob Byrd graciously":* Jimmy Carter, *White House Diary,* 451, 453, 486.

*But one Democratic senator . . . never forgave Byrd:* Daniel Inouye int., August 27, 2008.

*"the odds seem high":* Laurence Tribe and Thomas M. Rollins, "Deadlock," *Atlantic,* October 1980.

*"Carter's human rights campaign":* Sidey, "Assessing a Presidency."

*Tim Smith and FEC:* see Dennis L. Dresang, *Patrick J. Lucey: A Lasting Legacy* (Madison: Wisconsin Historical Society Press, 2020).

*"Maybe a B or C-plus on foreign policy": 60 Minutes,* August 10, 1980.

*Rather was stunned:* Dan Rather int., July 19, 2016.

*"They look okay to me":* Jimmy Carter int., August 3, 2018.

*robot rule:* Tom Oliphant int., July 28, 2017.

*as friendly as an estranged couple:* Hamilton Jordan, *Crisis,* 320.

*"We may have won the nomination":* ibid., 330.

*"I had to make the entire speech":* Jimmy Carter, *White House Diary,* 457.

*"Forget the hostages":* Dan Rather int., July 19, 2016.

*"money shot":* Robert Shrum int., August 30, 2016.

*"whose passengers have defected":* Mary McGrory, *Washington Star,* August 19, 1980, JCPLM.

*stuck out his hand:* NBC News and CBS News video, JCPLM.

*"I didn't elevate his hand":* Edward Kennedy, OH, UVA-MC, 2005.

*"That he was drunk":* Jimmy Carter int., June 14, 2015.

*"Adolf Hitler and Goofy":* Jimmy Carter, *White*

*House Diary,* 458.

*"fueled a reckless divisiveness":* Walter Mondale int., June 27, 2019.

*Rafshoon told Carter he had a "bonus":* Jerry Rafshoon int., January 25, 2019.

*"You're going to say he's an actor, and it won't work":* Chris Matthews, *Tip and the Gipper: When Politics Worked* (New York: Simon & Schuster, 2013), 3.

*"a good staff man": Boston Globe,* August 22, 1980.

*"if he instills in you pride":* Mark Lilla, *The Once and Future Liberal: After Identity Politics* (New York: Harper, 2017), 39.

*"I say these people in white sheets do not understand":* Edward Walsh, "Carter: Appealing to the South to Support One of Its Own," *Washington Post,* September 2, 1980.

*"running a 'mean' campaign":* Sam Donaldson int., March 16, 2017; "Transcript of the President's News Conference on Foreign and Domestic Matters," *New York Times,* September 19, 1980.

*the former California governor . . . did go half fare:* Jonathan Alter, "Rooting for Reagan," *Washington Monthly,* January 1981.

*"I said, 'Shit, we'll show 'em' ":* Greider, *Secrets of Temple,* 216.

*"the last wound":* ibid.

*He voted for Reagan:* Bob Kerrey int., May 11, 2018.

*"secular humanist":* Jimmy Carter, *White House Diary,* 455.

*"Despite all the fun . . . they were sinners":* Tom Wolfe, "Summing Up the Seventies," *Esquire,* June 1983.

*"The animosity toward us was so thick"*: Max Cleland int., December 23, 2015.

*"Why wait?"*: Edmund Muskie to Jimmy Carter, August 1, 1980, NLC 13281447 CREST, JCPLM.

*"to pull off the long-suspected 'October surprise' "*: Kirkpatrick, "How a Chase Bank Chairman Helped the Deposed Shah."

*"I had given my all"*: ibid.

*"If we leak"*: Debategate Report, archive.org, appx. 4, 1,489.

*"You could feel it slipping away"*: Walter Mondale int., June 9, 2015.

*Even . . . John Hinckley thought Carter was no longer the favorite*: Jared Cohen, *Accidental Presidents: Eight Men Who Changed America* (New York: Simon & Schuster, 2019), 365; Aynton, *Hunting the President,* 139–40.

*known as "Debategate"*: Craig Shirley, *Rendezvous with Destiny: Ronald Reagan and the Campaign That Changed America* (Wilmington, DE: Intercollegiate Studies Institute, 2009), 440.

*"thoroughbred performance"*: Eric Alterman, *Sound and Fury: The Making of the Punditocracy* (New York: HarperCollins, 1992), 101.

*"We all said, 'Uh, Mr. President, you can't do that!' "*: Pat Caddell int., April 8, 2016; Jerry Rafshoon int., January 25, 2019.

*"If this little bastard . . . I'll take my chances with the cowboy"*: Jerry Rafshoon int., January 25, 2019.

*"that will be decided not in Michigan . . . but in Iran"*: Hamilton Jordan, *Crisis,* 362.

*Caddell's explanation for erosion*: Pat Caddell int., April 8, 2016.

*"Don't tell Rosalynn"*: Caddell, Clough, Hertzberg, Rafshoon ints.; Germond and Witcover, *Blue*

*Smoke and Mirrors,* 302–6; Hamilton Jordan, *Crisis,* 368.

*"I've tried to honor my commitment":* Germond and Witcover, *Blue Smoke and Mirrors,* 306.

*"the Kennedy attacks for eight months hurt":* Jimmy Carter, *White House Diary,* 480.

*"Don't second-guess yourself":* Jerry Rafshoon int., December 7, 2015.

*"vintage Carter at his dead worst":* Eizenstat, *Carter: White House Years,* 891.

*"I promised you":* Edward Walsh, "A Concession with Grace and Class," *Washington Post,* November 5, 1980.

*"That was no election":* John Norris, *Mary McGrory: The First Queen of Journalism* (New York: Viking, 2016), 209.

*"I guess I felt bad":* Sam Donaldson int., March 17, 2017.

*Bert Lance figured . . . but by a narrow margin:* Greider, *Secrets of the Temple,* 218.

*"I think there were a few other factors":* Paul Volcker int., May 5, 2015; Volcker and Harper, *Keeping at It,* 111, Jimmy Carter int., June 14, 2015.

*Chapter 37: Inaugural Drama*
*"When Senator Kennedy and I were communicating, um":* Patrick Kennedy and Stephen Fried, *A Common Struggle: A Personal Journey Through the Past and Future of Mental Illness and Addiction* (New York: Blue Rider Press, 2015), 63.

*saving California's redwood forest:* see Nathaniel Pryor Reed, *The Battle over the Tall Tree Corridor at Redwood National Park* (published privately).

*Carter's "concern about the environment was so real":* Kathy Fletcher int., April 5, 2018.

*"That son of a bitch knew as much"*: Jim Free int., February 25, 2016, June 22, 2016.

*"carbon dioxide pollution"*: see Gus Speth, "Global Energy Futures and the Carbon Dioxide Problem," *Boston College Environmental Affairs Law Review* 9, no. 1 (1980).

*CEQ report on safe maximum level of carbon dioxide:* Philip Shabecoff, "U.S. Study Warns of Extensive Problems from Carbon Dioxide Pollution," *New York Times,* January 14, 1981; Gus Speth int., November 17, 2017.

*Nancy Reagan felt the Carters were leaving the White House in poor condition:* Rosalynn Carter int., November 17, 2015.

*"they continue to like Jimmy Carter personally"*: Peter Baker, review of *President Carter: The White House Years,* by Stuart E. Eizenstat, *New York Times,* June 10, 2018.

*It contained this quote from Thomas Jefferson:* Jimmy Carter, *Keeping Faith,* 596.

*"I hope you will go out and pay it back"*: Ray Marshall int., September 6, 2016.

*"We told the truth"*: Walter Mondale int., June 9, 2015.

*"What's flat, red, and glows in the dark?"*: Penn, "444 Days in the Dark."

*"I would rather have stayed longer"*: ibid.

*Several of the former captors:* Mark Bowden, *Guests of the Ayatollah,* 629.

*Last hours of Carter administration:* Hamilton Jordan, *Crisis,* 399–402; Jimmy Carter, *White House Diary,* 513; Gary Sick int., June 6, 2019.

*"the procedure I insisted on completing to take delivery of the hostages"*: Flavio Meroni int., June 22, 2018; Jimmy Carter int., June 15, 2015.

*"an affable and decent man"*: Jimmy Carter, *White House Diary,* 513.

*"one of the happiest moments of my life"*: ibid.

*events depicted in George Cave's 2013 novel:* Nicholas Schou, "The 'October Surprise' Was Real, Legendary Spymaster Hints in Final Interview," *Newsweek,* April 24, 2016.

*"an Israeli initiative"*: Nicholas Veliotes int., May 18, 2020.

*"no credible evidence": oint Report of the Task Force to Investigate Certain Allegations Concerning the Holding of American Hostages by Iran in 1980* (Washington, DC: US Government Printing Office, January 3, 1993).

*Casey in Madrid:* Paul Beach, "Memorandum for the Record: Meeting with Ed Williamson — October Surprise," November 4, 1991, George H. W. Bush Presidential Library and Museum; see also Robert Parry, *America's Stolen Narrative: From Washington and Madison to Nixon, Reagan and the Bushes to Obama* (Arlington, VA: Media Consortium, 2012).

*Hamilton was dismayed:* Lee Hamilton int., June 1, 2020.

*destroyed by "professionals"*: Gary Sick int., June 6, 2019.

**Part 7: Global Citizen**

*Chapter 38: Exile*

*"a pilgrim soul"*: W. B. Yeats, "When You Are Old."

*"used the White House as a stepping-stone"*: Jim Laney, Emory Report, May 1, 2006.

*"his total commitment"*: Hamilton Jordan, unpublished book proposal, June 16, 2003.

*only one to which he devoted time and labor:* Esther B. Fein, "Carpenter Named Carter Comes to New York," *New York Times,* September 3, 1984.

*"Why aren't you working?":* Jonathan Reckford int., November 2, 2015.

*"He'll win" [in 1984]:* Rosalynn Carter int., November 17, 2015.

*"boys made fun":* Amy Carter int., November 18, 2015.

*"despondent" and in "despair":* Diane Rehm Show, NPR, October 9, 2007.

*"I had a vacuum in my life":* Jimmy Carter int., May 20, 2016.

*still "grieving" over the what-ifs:* Betty Pope int., September 15, 2015.

*Carter forced the long-hostile* Washington Post *to grovel:* Phil Gailey, "Carter Intent on Suing *Washington Post* over Rumor," *New York Times,* October 15, 1981; *Washington Post,* editorial, October 22, 1981.

*"hated golf":* Hamilton Jordan, unpublished book proposal, June 16, 2003, 56.

*"naive but sincere commitment":* Sara Rimer, "Enjoying the Ex-Presidency? Never Been Better," *New York Times,* February 16, 2000.

*"childish"* . . . *"out of my system":* Jimmy Carter, OH, UVA-MC, 1988.

*coauthoring . . . almost ruined their marriage:* Diane Rehm Show, NPR, July 9, 2015; Judy Langford int., December 4, 2015; Jimmy Carter, lecture, Emory University, Atlanta, February 15, 2017.

*Peter Osnos . . . worked out truce:* Peter Osnos int., December 14, 2017.

*"actually ached from missing Rosalynn":* Faye Perdue int., September 24, 2015.

*"Each evening, forever, this is good for an apology":*

Jimmy Carter, *Living Faith,* 88.

*"Rosalynn, I promise you"*: ibid., 76.

*"I'm proud to be my father's daughter"*: "Amy Carter Arrested," *New York Times,* April 9, 1985.

*"like an obnoxious moral high ground"*: Amy Carter int., November 18, 2015.

*Jack blamed her for siding with his parents:* Judy Langford int., December 4, 2015.

*never once visited him:* Jack Carter int., August 23, 2016.

*"I don't much care what my kids think of me"*: Judy Langford int., December 4, 2015.

*"art is best derived from artless things"*: Jimmy Carter, "Itinerant Songsters Visit Our Village," in *Always a Reckoning,* 51–52.

*"I express my feelings"*: Jimmy Carter int., February 15, 2017.

*Osnos rejected the collection:* Peter Osnos int., July 17, 2015.

*"The only time people back away is when he sings"*: Chip Carter int., June 12, 2015.

*"I had done all that was humanly possible"*: Jimmy Carter, *The Craftsmanship of Jimmy Carter* (Macon, GA: Mercer University Press, 2017).

*Chapter 39: The Carter Center*

*"small Camp David"*: Jimmy Carter, remarks, CC Weekend, June 28, 2019.

*"Energizer Bunny"*: John Lewis int., March 4, 2015.

*"I have divorced myself"*: Jimmy Carter to donors, May 12, 1983.

*"how Mr. Carter could champion world peace"*: Cathy Bradshaw int., September 13, 2016.

*"the nerve and the guts" to ask him for $5 million:* Maureen Dowd, "Jimmy Carter Lusts for a

1118

Trump Posting," *New York Times,* October 21, 2017.

*"The record with regard to schools is particularly dismal":* Michael Giles, CC report, 1994.

*"In many African villages, I felt at home":* Jimmy Carter int., August 4, 2018.

*"coming out of their ankles":* Jimmy Carter, "The Modern Horror of an Ancient Scourge," *Washington Post,* April 24, 1990.

*the mother's breast, hideously discolored:* Donald Hopkins int., August 10, 2015.

"we almost got nauseated": Jimmy Carter, lecture, 92nd Street Y, New York, December 6, 2018.

*Dr. Bill Foege in Carter administration:* Jimmy Carter, "Chief Delegate, Delegates, and Alternate Delegates from the United States to the Thirtieth World Health Assembly, May 3, 1977," *PPPJC,* 1977, vol. 1, 806.

" *'Melinda, anything you do' ":* John Legend, "Melinda Gates Is Proud Women Are Becoming More Empowered — But It's Not Happening Quickly Enough," *Town and Country,* Summer 2019.

*He wanted immediate results:* Patty Stonesifer int., February 3, 2016.

*"When he locked on to something":* Donald Hopkins int., July 16, 2015.

*"If Ghana keeps dragging its feet":* ibid.

*"had become our best salesman":* Roy Vagelos int., January 11, 2016.

*Merck had provided one billion:* ibid.

*"South Africans have different blood":* Jimmy Carter, "Africa Trip Report, March 2002," Carter Center, March 1, 2002.

*"That's the closest . . . fistfight":* Erica Ritz, "Former President Jimmy Carter Reveals the Only Time

He Almost Got in a 'Fist Fight' with Another Head of State," *The Hill,* November 4, 2013.

*"remain the largest source of potential voter fraud":* Jessica Huseman, "Voting by Mail Would Reduce Coronavirus Tramsission, but It Has Other Risks," ProPublica, March 24, 2020.

*"immediate steps to expand vote-by-mail":* "Carter Center Statement on Voting by Mail for 2020 U.S. Elections," Carter Center, May 6, 2020.

*"He always looked for . . . the inherent good":* Jennifer McCoy int., July 16, 2015.

*"We fill vacuums":* Jimmy Carter int., July 16, 2019.

*"I can bring enough vaccinations":* Annette Carter int., July 16, 2019.

*"irrepressible conflict":* Harold Holzer, Joshua Wolf Shenk, and James H. Billington, *In Lincoln's Hand: His Original Manuscripts* (New York: Bantam Dell, 2009), 102.

*"war is the greatest violation of human rights":* Hamilton Jordan, *Crisis,* 344.

*"This will put more pressure":* Karin Ryan int., March 9, 2017.

*Chapter 40: Freelance Secretary of State*

*"set a wonderful example":* George H. W. Bush int., October 11, 2016.

*"cooler and more aloof":* Jimmy Carter int., March 22, 2019.

*"He stopped upward mobility":* ibid., November 17, 2015.

*"passionate intellect and commitment":* David Treadwell, " 'You Gave of Yourself: Reagan Praises Carter at Library Dedication," *Los Angeles Times,* October 2, 1986.

*" 'country come to town' ":* Rosalynn Carter int., November 17, 2015.

*"This sent a powerful message":* George H. W. Bush int., October 11, 2016.

*resolved devilishly complex disputes:* Jennifer McCoy int., July 16, 2015.

*"working night and day":* George H. W. Bush int., October 11, 2016.

*"a Patton of peace":* Hertzberg, *Politics,* 50.

*"out of line and untrue":* ibid.

*'Arāfat told Carter . . . rejecting Camp David was one of the worst mistakes:* Jimmy Carter int., April 12, 2019.

*"blind sympathy for the suffering":* Sharansky with Dermer, *The Case for Democracy,* xxi.

*"We saw Carter as incredibly self-centered":* Brinkley, *Unfinished Presidency,* 345.

*"I may not always have succeeded":* Jimmy Carter int., November 19, 2015.

*he was "disappointed":* Alessandra Stanley, "On Tour with Jimmy Carter: Words of Advice, Bittersweet," *New York Times,* January 14, 1993.

*"The time for temporizing is over":* Brent Scowcroft and Arnold Kanter, "Korea: Time for Action," *Washington Post,* June 15, 1994.

*feigned ignorance:* Jimmy Carter, "Report of Our Trip to Korea," Carter Center, June 1994.

*"treasonous prick":* Brinkley, *Unfinished Presidency,* 405.

*"to make lemonade out of this lemon":* ibid.

*"stopped the sanctions":* David E. Sanger, "Carter Visit to North Korea: Whose Trip Was It Really?," *New York Times,* June 18, 1994.

*Carter ignored the fact that sanctions can provide crucial leverage:* Jimmy Carter int., August 3, 2018.

*"the immense tension":* Don Oberdorfer, *The Two*

*Koreas: A Contemporary History* (Boston: Little, Brown, 1998), 334.

*"pacifist leanings could undercut"*: George Stephanopoulos, *All Too Human: A Political Education* (Boston: Little, Brown, 1999), 313.

*"Goddamn it! Get them out of there!"*: Brinkley, *Unfinished Presidency,* 427.

*"You must accept this agreement"*: ibid.

*"Can you defend our country?"*: Sam Nunn int., June 9, 2017.

*"It was the only way"*: Jimmy Carter int., August 3, 2018.

*"the shrine he seeks"*: Murray Kempton, "St. Jimmy's Halo Askew," *Newsday,* September 22, 1994.

*"ashamed" of Clinton's harsh sanctions:* Maureen Dowd, "Despite Role as Negotiator, Carter Feels Unappreciated," *New York Times,* September 21, 1994.

*"We take orders"*: Richard Holbrooke, *To End a War* (New York: Random House, 1998), 150.

*Chapter 41: Sunday School Teacher*

*"They can take their damn prize!"*: Hamilton Jordan, unpublished book proposal, June 16, 2003.

*"must also be seen as criticism"*: Alan Riding, "Nobel Committee Wins Praise and Criticism for Prize to Carter," *New York Times,* October 12, 2002.

*"I engaged in wishful thinking"*: Jimmy Carter int., September 1, 2017.

*"We believe he hates us"*: Ami Ayalon int., November 2, 2017.

*"harmed my relationship"*: Jimmy Carter int., June 13, 2015.

*"He has shifted from annoyance"*: Kenneth W. Stein, "My Problem with Jimmy Carter's Book," *Middle East Quarterly* 14, no. 2 (Spring 2007): 3–15.

*still determined to go the last mile for peace*: Karin Ryan int., March 9, 2017.

*"a second term"*: NBC Nightly News, June 9, 2008.

*"that unjust accusation"*: *New York Times,* May 15, 1977.

*"Jimmy, Jimmy"*: Karin Ryan int., March 9, 2017.

*"nonexistent"*: Jimmy Carter int., June 14, 2015.

*"Jimmy Carter was a queer"*: David Rabhan int., September 4, 2017.

*"a matter of personal interest"*: Jimmy Carter to Ayatollah Khomeini, October 28, 1988.

*"Your 1834H copilot, Jimmy"*: Jimmy Carter to David Rabhan, December 7, 1989, Rabhan private papers.

*"I also shudder to think . . . I may go free"*: David Rabhan to Jimmy Carter, November 21, 1988, Rabhan private papers.

*"For once . . . go back to your cell"*: David Rabhan int., September 5, 2017.

*Carter called Judge Berry Avant Edenfield:* Jimmy Carter int., September 8, 2017.

*"A good person"*: Cahnman, "My Visit with the Carters in Plains."

*"if your life is not filled with peace"*: Travis Loller, "Despite Fall, Former President Carter Helps Build Home," Associated Press, October 7, 2019.

*"to alleviate suffering"*: Ernie Suggs, "Carter Center Appoints Paige Alexander as New CEO," *Atlanta Journal-Constitution,* February 14, 2020.

*the World Health Organization (WHO) . . . moved back the target date:* Tim McDonnell, "The

End of Guinea Worm Was Just Around the Corner. Not Anymore," NPR, October 4, 2019.

*"our country . . . the foremost warlike nation":* Jimmy Carter, remarks, CC Weekend, June 28, 2019.

*"to make peace an attitude":* Mattie J. T. Stepanek with Jimmy Carter, *Just Peace: A Message of Hope* (Kansas City, MO: Andrews McMeel, 2006), 158.

*"There's no doubt that Mattie was an angel":* ibid., 189; Jeni Smith Stepanek int., November 5, 2015.

*"I feel that my role . . . is probably superior to that of other presidents":* Dowd, "Carter Lusts for Trump Posting."

*"radical departure": Diane Rehm Show,* NPR, October 9, 2007.

*"I've always liked Jimmy Carter":* NBC News, October 7, 2019.

*calling for an age limit:* ibid., September 18, 2019.

*"How clean a smell":* Hertzberg, *Politics,* 69.

*"saving more lives than possibly any couple":* Jeff Carter, remarks, CC Weekend, June 22, 2016.

*"I think I am less intense now":* Jimmy Carter int., September 5, 2015.

*"Oh, I am":* Jimmy Carter int., February 17, 2017.

*"Great sorrow and disappointment":* Jimmy Carter, Carter Center, June 3, 2020.

*"completely at ease with death":* Alan Judd, "In Good Humor, Carter Returns to Sunday School After Fall," *Atlanta Journal-Constitution,* October 21, 2019.

# SELECT BIBLIOGRAPHY

Abram, Morris B. *The Day Is Short: An Autobiography.* New York: Harcourt Brace Jovanovich, 1982.

Alter, Jonathan. *Between the Lines: A View Inside American Politics, People, and Culture.* Ann Arbor: State Street Books, 2008.

Alterman, Eric. *Sound and Fury: The Making of the Punditocracy.* New York: HarperCollins, 1992.

Anderson, Patrick. *Electing Jimmy Carter: The Campaign of 1976.* Baton Rouge: Louisiana State University Press, 1994.

Annis, J. Lee. *Howard Baker: Conciliator in an Age of Crisis.* Knoxville: Howard H. Baker Jr. Center for Public Policy, University of Tennessee, 1995.

Anziska, Seth. *Preventing Palestine: A Political History from Camp David to Oslo.* Princeton, NJ: Princeton University Press, 2018.

Auchmutey, Jim. *The Class of '65: A Student, a Divided Town, and the Long Road to Forgiveness.* New York: PublicAffairs, 2015.

Ayton, Mel. *Hunting the President: Threats, Plots, and Assassination Attempts — from FDR to Obama.* Washington, DC: Regnery History, 2014.

Ballmer, Randall. *Redeemer: The Life of Jimmy Carter.* New York: Basic Books, 2014.

Bani-Sadr, Abol Hassan. *My Turn to Speak: Iran, the Revolution, and Secret Deals with the U.S.* Potomac Books, 1991.

Barone, Michael. *Our Country: The Shaping of America From Roosevelt to Reagan.* New York: Free Press, 1990.

Barry, Dave. *Dave Barry Slept Here: A Sort of History of the United States.* New York: Random House, 1989.

Beckel, Bob, and John David Mann. *I Should Be Dead: My Life Surviving Politics, TV, and Addiction.* New York: Hachette Books, 2015.

Biederman, Marcia. *Scan Artist: How Evelyn Wood Convinced the World That Speed-Reading Worked.* Chicago: Chicago Review Press, 2019.

Bill, James A. *The Eagle and the Lion: The Tragedy of American-Iranian Relations.* New Haven: Yale University Press, 1988.

Bird, Kai. *The Chairman: John J. McCloy and the Making of the American Establishment,* New York: Simon & Schuster, 1992.

Biven, W. Carl. *Jimmy Carter's Economy: Policy in an Age of Limits.* Chapel Hill: The University of North Carolina Press, 2002.

Blount, Roy, Jr. *Crackers.* New York: Simon & Schuster, 1977.

Blumenthal, W. Michael. *From Exile to Washington: A Memoir of Leadership in the Twentieth Century.* New York: Harry N. Abrams, 2013.

Bourne, Peter G. *Jimmy Carter: A Comprehensive Biography from Plains to Post-Presidency.* New York: Scribner, 1997.

Bowden, Mark. *Guests of the Ayatollah: The Iran*

*Hostage Crisis: The First Battle in America's War with Militant Islam.* New York: Atlantic Monthly Press, 2006.

Branch, Taylor. *Parting the Waters: America in the King Years, 1954–63.* New York: Simon & Schuster, 1988.

Brinkley, Douglas. *The Unfinished Presidency: Jimmy Carter's Journey Beyond the White House.* New York: Viking, 1998.

Brower, Kate Anderson. *The Residence: Inside the Private World of the White House.* New York: HarperCollins, 2015.

Brown, Fred, and Sherri M. L. Smith. *The Flint River: A Recreational Guidebook.* Atlanta: CIPublishing, 2001.

Brzezinski, Zbigniew K. *Power and Principle: Memoirs of the National Security Adviser, 1977–1981.* New York: Farrar, Straus and Giroux, 1983.

Buckley, William F. *Overdrive: A Personal Documentary.* New York: Doubleday, 1983.

Burns, James MacGregor. *Leadership.* New York: HarperCollins, 1978.

Byrd, Robert C. *Child of the Appalachian Coalfields.* Morgantown: University of West Virginia Press, 2005.

Califano, Joseph A., Jr. *Governing America: An Insider's Report from the White House and the Cabinet.* New York: Simon & Schuster, 1981.

Cannon, Lou. *President Reagan: The Role of a Lifetime.* New York: Simon & Schuster, 2001.

Carmon, Irin, and Shana Knizhnik. *Notorious RBG: The Life and Times of Ruth Bader Ginsburg.* New York: Dey Street Books, 2015.

Carter, Dan T. *From George Wallace to Newt Gin-*

grich: *Race in the Conservative Counter-revolution, 1963–1994.* Baton Rouge: Louisiana State University Press, 1996.

Carter, Hugh A., and Frances Spatz Leighton. *Cousin Beedie and Cousin Hot: My Life with the Carter Family of Plains, Georgia.* Englewood Cliffs, NJ: Prentice-Hall, 1978.

Carter, Jeff. *Ancestors of Jimmy and Rosalynn Carter.* Jefferson, NC: McFarland, 2012.

Carter, Jimmy. *Addresses of Governor Jimmy Carter, 1971–75.* Atlanta: Georgia Department of Archives and History, 1975.

——. *Always a Reckoning and Other Poems.* New York: Times Books, 1995.

——. *The Blood of Abraham: Insights into the Middle East.* Boston: Houghton Mifflin, 1985.

——. *A Call to Action: Women, Religion, Violence, and Power.* New York: Simon & Schuster, 2014.

——. *Christmas in Plains.* New York: Simon & Schuster, 2001.

——. *The Craftsmanship of Jimmy Carter.* Macon, GA: Mercer University Press, 2017.

——. *Faith: A Journey for All.* New York: Simon & Schuster, 2018.

——. *A Full Life: Reflections at Ninety.* New York: Simon & Schuster, 2015.

——. *The Hornet's Nest: A Novel of the Revolutionary War.* New York: Simon & Schuster, 2003.

——. *An Hour Before Daylight: Memories of a Rural Boyhood.* New York: Simon & Schuster, 2001.

——. *Keeping Faith: Memoirs of a President.* New York: Bantam Books, 1982.

——. *The Little Baby Snoogle-Fleejer.* Illustrated

1128

by Amy Carter. Fayetteville: University of Arkansas Press, 2014.

———. *Living Faith.* New York: Times Books, 1996.

———. *Our Endangered Values: America's Moral Crisis.* New York: Simon & Schuster, 2005.

———. *The Paintings of Jimmy Carter.* Macon, GA: Mercer University Press, 2017.

———. *Palestine: Peace Not Apartheid.* New York: Simon & Schuster., 2006.

———. *A Remarkable Mother.* New York: Simon & Schuster, 2008.

———. *Sharing Good Times.* New York: Simon & Schuster, 2004.

———. *Turning Point: A Candidate, a State, and a Nation Come of Age.* New York: Times Books, 1992.

———. *White House Diary.* New York: Farrar, Straus and Giroux, 2010.

———. *Why Not the Best?* Nashville: Broadman Press, 1975.

Carter, Jimmy, and Rosalynn Carter. *Everything to Gain: Making the Most of the Rest of Your Life.* New York: Random House, 1987.

Carter, Jimmy, with Steve Halliday. *Through the Year with Jimmy Carter: 366 Daily Meditations from the 39th President.* Grand Rapids, MI: Zondervan, 2011.

Carter, Jimmy, and Wesley G. Pippert. *The Spiritual Journey of Jimmy Carter, in His Own Words.* New York: Macmillan, 1978.

Carter, Lillian, and Gloria Carter Spann. *Away from Home: Letters to My Family.* New York: Simon & Schuster, 1977.

Carter, Rosalynn. *First Lady from Plains.* Boston:

Houghton Mifflin, 1984.

Carter, William "Buddy." *Billy Carter: A Journey Through the Shadows.* Lanham, MD: Taylor Trade, 1999.

Christison, Kathleen, *Perceptions of Palestine: Their Influence on U.S. Middle East Policy.* Berkeley: University of California Press, 1999.

Clymer, Adam. *Drawing the Line at the Big Ditch: The Panama Canal Treaties and the Rise of the Right.* Lawrence: University Press of Kansas, 2008.

Cohen, Jared. *Accidental Presidents: Eight Men Who Changed America.* New York: Simon & Schuster, 2019.

Cooper, Andrew Scott. *The Fall of Heaven: The Pahlavis and the Final Days of Imperial Iran.* New York: Henry Holt, 2016.

Crowe, William J., and David Chanoff. *The Line of Fire: From Washington to the Gulf, the Politics and Battles of the New Military.* New York: Simon & Schuster, 1993.

Delbanco, Andrew. *The War Before the War: Fugitive Slaves and the Struggle for America's Soul from the Revolution to the Civil War.* New York: Penguin Press, 2018.

Dickerson, John. *Whistlestop: My Favorite Stories from Presidential Campaign History.* New York: Twelve, 2016.

Dobrynin, Anatoliy Fedorovich. *In Confidence: Moscow's Ambassador to America's Six Cold War Presidents (1962–1986).* New York: Times Books, 1995.

Drew, Elizabeth. *American Journal: The Events of 1976.* New York: Random House, 1977.

Dumbrell, John. *The Carter Presidency: A Re-*

*Evaluation.* New York: Manchester University Press, 1993.

Ebtekar, Massoumeh. *Takeover in Tehran: The Inside Story of the 1979 U.S. Embassy Capture.* Burnaby, BC: Talonbooks, 2000.

Eizenstat, Stuart. *President Carter: The White House Years.* New York: Thomas Dunne Books, 2018.

Ellis, Richard J. *The Development of the American Presidency.* New York: Routledge, 2012.

Fallaci, Oriana. *Interviews with History and Conversations with Power.* New York: Rizzoli, 2011.

Farber, David. *Taken Hostage: The Iran Hostage Crisis and America's First Encounter with Radical Islam.* Princeton, NJ: Princeton University Press, 2005.

Farrell, John A. *Tip O'Neill and the Democratic Century: A Biography.* Boston: Little, Brown, 2001.

Fink, Gary M. *Prelude to the Presidency: The Political Character and Legislative Leadership Style of Governor Jimmy Carter.* Westport, CT: Greenwood Press, 1980.

Fink, Gary M. and Hugh Davis Graham, eds. *The Carter Presidency: Policy Choices in the Post–New Deal Era.* Lawrence: University Press of Kansas, 1999.

FitzGerald, Frances. *The Evangelicals: The Struggle to Shape America.* New York: Simon & Schuster, 2017.

Frisch, Scott A. and Sean Q. Kelly, *Jimmy Carter and the Water Wars: Presidential Influence and the Politics of Pork.* Amherst, NY: Cambria Press, 2008.

Frum, David. *How We Got Here: The '70s.* New

York: Random House, 2000.

Gates, Robert M. *From the Shadows: The Ultimate Insider's Story of Five Presidents and How They Won the Cold War.* New York: Simon & Schuster, 1996.

Gerhardt, Michael J. *The Forgotten Presidents: Their Untold Constitutional Legacy.* New York: Oxford University Press, 2013.

Germond, Jack W., and Jules Witcover. *Blue Smoke and Mirrors: How Reagan Won and Why Carter Lost the Election of 1980.* New York: Viking, 1982.

Gibbs, Nancy, and Michael Duffy. *The Preacher and the Presidents: Billy Graham in the White House.* New York: Center Street, 2007.

———. *The Presidents Club: Inside the World's Most Exclusive Fraternity.* New York: Simon & Schuster, 2012.

Gillon, Steven M. *The Democrats' Dilemma: Walter F. Mondale and the Liberal Legacy.* New York: Columbia University Press, 1992.

Glad, Betty. *Jimmy Carter: In Search of the Great White House.* New York: W. W. Norton, 1980.

———. *An Outsider in the White House: Jimmy Carter, His Advisors, and the Making of American Foreign Policy.* Ithaca, NY: Cornell University Press, 2009.

Godbold, E. Stanly, Jr. *Jimmy and Rosalynn Carter: The Georgia Years, 1924–1974.* New York: Oxford University Press, 2010.

Graff, Garrett M. *Raven Rock: The Story of the U.S. Government's Secret Plan to Save Itself — While the Rest of Us Die.* New York: Simon & Schuster, 2017.

Green, Mark J. *Bright, Infinite Future: A Generational*

*Memoir on the Progressive Rise.* New York: St. Martin's Press, 2016.

Greider, William. *Secrets of the Temple: How the Federal Reserve Runs the Country.* New York: Simon & Schuster, 1989.

Hargrove, Erwin C. *Jimmy Carter as President: Leadership and the Politics of the Public Good.* Baton Rouge: Louisiana State University Press, 1988.

Hayter-Menzies, Grant. *Lillian Carter: A Compassionate Life.* Jefferson, NC: McFarland Publishers, 2014.

Hayward, Steven F. *The Real Jimmy Carter: How Our Worst Ex-President Undermines American Foreign Policy, Coddles Dictators, and Created the Party of Clinton and Kerry.* Washington, DC: Regnery, 2004.

Hefley, James C., and Marti Hefley. *The Church That Produced a President.* New York: Wyden Books, 1977.

Hertzberg, Hendrik. *Politics: Observations & Arguments, 1966–2004.* New York: Penguin Books, 2004.

Hine, Thomas. *The Great Funk: Falling Apart and Coming Together (on a Shag Rug) in the Seventies.* New York: Farrar, Straus and Giroux, 2007.

Hutchinson, Duane. *Jimmy Carter's Hometown: People of Plains.* Lincoln, NE: Foundation Books, 2003.

Huyser, Robert. *Mission to Tehran.* Southwold, UK: Bookthrift, 1990.

Jacobs, Meg. *Panic at the Pump: The Energy Crisis and the Transformation of American Politics in the 1970s.* New York: Hill and Wang, 2016.

James, Henry. *The Notebooks of Henry James.* Edited by Francis Otto Matthiessen and Kenneth Ballard Murdock. New York: Oxford University Press, 1961.

Ji, Chaozhu. *The Man on Mao's Right: From Harvard Yard to Tiananmen Square, My Life Inside China's Foreign Ministry.* New York: Random House, 2008.

Jones, Charles O. *The Trusteeship Presidency: Jimmy Carter and the United States Congress.* Baton Rouge: Louisiana State University Press, 1988.

Jordan, Hamilton. *Crisis: The Last Year of the Carter Presidency.* New York: G. P. Putnam's Sons, 1982.

Jordan, Hamilton, and Kathleen Jordan, ed. *A Boy from Georgia: Coming of Age in the Segregated South.* Athens: University of Georgia Press, 2015.

Jordan, Vernon E., and Annette Gordon-Reed. *Vernon Can Read!: A Memoir.* New York: PubliAffairs, 2001.

Kakutani, Michiko. *The Death of Truth: Notes on Falsehood in the Age of Trump.* New York: Tim Duggan Books, 2018.

Kaplan, Fred. *The Bomb: Presidents, Generals and the Secret History of Nuclear War.* New York: Simon & Schuster, 2020.

Kaufman, Burton I. and Scott I. Kaufman. *The Presidency of James Earl Carter Jr.* Lawrence: The University Press of Kansas, 2006.

Kempton, Murray. *Rebellions, Perversities, and Main Events.* New York: Times Books, 1994.

Kennedy, Edward M. *True Compass: A Memoir.* New York: Twelve, 2009.

Kennedy, Patrick, and Stephen Fried. *A Common Struggle: A Personal Journey Through the Past and Future of Mental Illness and Addiction.* New York: Blue Rider Press, 2015.

King, Mary E. *The New York Times on Emerging Democracies in Eastern Europe.* Washington, DC: CQ Press, 2010.

Kluger, Richard. *Simple Justice: The History of Brown v. Board of Education and Black America's Struggle for Equality.* New York: Alfred A. Knopf, 1975.

Knebel, Fletcher. *Dark Horse.* Garden City, NY: Doubleday, 1972.

Lance, Bert, with Bill Gilbert. *The Truth of the Matter: My Life In and Out of Politics.* New York: Summit Books, 1991.

Landau, David. *Arik: The Life of Ariel Sharon.* New York: Alfred A. Knopf, 2013.

Langford, Edna, and Linda Maddox. *Rosalynn: Friend and First Lady.* Old Tappen, NJ: Ravelle, 1980.

Lasch, Christopher. *The Culture of Narcissism: American Life in an Age of Diminishing Expectations.* New York: W. W. Norton, 1978.

Mahler, Jonathan. *Ladies and Gentlemen, the Bronx Is Burning.* New York: Farrar, Straus and Giroux, 2005.

Martin, David C., and John Walcott. *Best-Laid Plans: The Inside Story of America's War Against Terrorism.* New York: Harper & Row, 1988.

Marton, Kati. *Hidden Power: Presidential Marriages That Shaped Our History.* New York: Pantheon Books, 2001.

Matthews, Christopher. *Hardball: How Politics Is Played, Told by One Who Knows the Game.* New

York: Simon & Schuster, 1999.

Mattingly, Doreen J. *A Feminist in the White House: Midge Costanza, the Carter Years and America's Culture Wars.* Oxford: Oxford University Press, 2016.

Mattson, Kevin. *"What the Heck Are You up to, Mr. President?": Jimmy Carter, America's "Malaise," and the Speech That Should Have Changed the Country.* New York: Bloomsbury, 2009.

Mazlish, Bruce, and Edwin Diamond. *Jimmy Carter: An Interpretive Biography.* New York: Simon & Schuster, 1979.

McCullough, David G. *The Path Between the Seas: The Creation of the Panama Canal, 1870–1914.* New York: Simon & Schuster, 1977.

McGarr, Kathryn, J. *The Whole Damn Deal: Robert Strauss and the Art of Politics.* New York: Public Affairs, 2011.

McFadden, Robert, Joseph B. Treaster, and Maurice Carroll. *No Hiding Place: The New York Times Inside Report on the Hostage Crisis.* New York: Times Books, 1981.

Michael, Deanna L. *Jimmy Carter as Educational Policymaker: Equal Opportunity and Efficiency.* Albany: State University of New York Press, 2008.

Mitchell, Nancy. *Jimmy Carter in Africa: Race and the Cold War.* Stanford, CA: Stanford University Press, 2016.

Mondale, Walter F., and Dave Hage. *The Good Fight: A Life in Liberal Politics.* New York: Scribner, 2010.

Morris, Kenneth. *Jimmy Carter, American Moralist.* Athens: University of Georgia Press, 1996.

Nelson, Willie, and David Ritz. *It's a Long Story:*

*My Life.* New York: Little, Brown, 2015.

Noonan, Peggy. *What I Saw at the Revolution: A Political Life in the Reagan Era.* New York: Random House, 1990.

Norris, John. *Mary McGrory: The First Queen of Journalism.* New York: Viking, 2016.

Oberdorfer, Don. *The Two Koreas: A Contemporary History.* Boston: Little, Brown, 1998.

O'Neill, Tip, and William Novak. *Man of the House: The Life and Political Memoirs of Speaker Tip O'Neill.* New York: Random House, 1987.

Packer, George. *Our Man: Richard Holbrooke and the End of the American Century.* New York: Alfred A. Knopf, 2019.

Padgett, Dorothy. *Jimmy Carter: Elected President with Pocket Change and Peanuts.* Macon, GA: Mercer University Press, 2016.

Pahlavi, Mohammad Reza. *Answer to History.* New York: Stein and Day, 1980.

Phillips, Kevin. *The Emerging Republican Majority.* New Rochelle, NY: Arlington House, 1969.

Polmar, Norman, and Thomas B. Allen. *Rickover.* New York: Simon & Schuster, 1982.

Powell, Colin. *My American Journey.* New York: Random House, 1995.

Powell, Jody. *The Other Side of the Story.* New York: Morrow, 1984.

Power, Samantha. *A Problem From Hell: America in the Age of Genocide.* New York: Basic Books, 2002.

Quandt, William B. *Camp David: Peacemaking and Politics.* Washington, DC: Brookings. 1986.

Rabhan, David. *Conscious Coma: Ten Years in an Iranian Prison.* Xlibris, 2018.

Reeves, Richard. *Convention.* New York: Harcourt

Brace Jovanovich, 1977.

Ribuffo, Leo P. *Right, Center, Left.* New Brunswick, NJ: Rutgers University Press, 1992.

Richardson, Don, ed. *Conversations with Carter.* Boulder, CO: Lynne Rienner Publishers, 1998.

Rockwell, Theodore. *The Rickover Effect: How One Man Made a Difference.* Annapolis, MD: Naval Institute Press, 1992.

Rubin, Jerry. *Growing (Up) at Thirty-Seven.* New York: M. Evans, 1976.

Sandbrook, Dominic. *Mad as Hell: The Crisis of the 1970s and the Rise of the Populist Right.* New York: Alfred A. Knopf, 2011.

Sanders, Randy. *Mighty Peculiar Elections: The New South Gubernatorial Campaigns of 1970 and the Changing Politics of Race.* Gainesville: University Press of Florida, 2002.

Scheer, Robert. *Playing President: My Close Encounters with Nixon, Carter, Bush I, Reagan, and Clinton — and How They Did Not Prepare Me for George W. Bush.* New York: Akashic Books, 2006.

Schell, Orville. *"Watch Out for the Foreign Guests!": China Encounters the West.* New York: Pantheon Books, 1980.

Schlesinger, Robert. *White House Ghosts.* New York: Simon & Schuster, 2008.

Schneller, Robert John. *Breaking the Color Barrier: The U.S. Naval Academy's First Black Midshipmen and the Struggle for Racial Equality.* New York: New York University Press, 2005.

Schram, Martin. *Running for President, 1976: A Journal of the Carter Campaign.* New York: Pocket Books, 1976.

Shawcross, William. *The Shah's Last Ride: The*

*Fate of an Ally.* New York: Simon & Schuster, 1988.

Sheehan, Jack. *Class of '47: Annapolis — America's Best.* Las Vegas: Stephens Press, 2007.

Shirley, Craig. *Rendezvous with Destiny: Ronald Reagan and the Campaign That Changed America.* Wilmington, DE: Intercollegiate Studies Institute, 2009.

Shrum, Robert. *No Excuses: Confessions of a Serial Campaigner.* New York: Simon & Schuster, 2007.

Sick, Gary. *All Fall Down: America's Tragic Encounter with Iran.* New York: Random House, 1985.

———. *October Surprise: America's Hostages in Iran and the Election of Ronald Reagan.* New York: Crown, 1991.

Silk, Leonard, and Mark Silk. *The American Establishment.* New York: Avon Books, 1981.

Stapleton, Ruth Carter. *Brother Billy.* New York: Harper & Row, 1978.

———. *The Gift of Inner Healing.* Waco, TX: Word Books, 1976.

Stein, Judith. *Pivotal Decade: How the United States Traded Factories for Finance in the Seventies.* New Haven: Yale University Press, 2010.

Stein, Kenneth W. *Heroic Diplomacy: Sadat, Kissinger, Carter, Begin and the Quest for Arab-Israeli Peace.* Philadelphia: Routledge, 1999.

Stepanek, Jeni. *Messenger: The Legacy of Mattie J. T. Stepanek and Heartsongs.* New York: Dutton, 2009.

Stepanek, Mattie J. T., with Jimmy Carter. *Just Peace: A Message of Hope.* Kansas City: Andrews McMeel Universal, 2006.

Stephanopoulos, George. *All Too Human: A Politi-*

*cal Education.* Boston: Little, Brown, 1999.

Strong, Robert A. *Working in the World: Jimmy Carter and the Making of American Foreign Policy.* Baton Rouge: Louisiana State University Press, 2012.

Stroud, Kandy. *How Jimmy Won: The Victory Campaign from Plains to the White House.* New York: Morrow, 1977.

Sullivan, William H. *Mission to Iran: The Last U.S. Ambassador.* New York: W. W. Norton, 1989.

Swain, Susan. *First Ladies: Presidential Historians on the Lives of 45 Iconic American Women.* New York: PublicAffairs, 2015.

Thompson, Hunter S. *The Great Shark Hunt.* New York: Simon & Schuster, 1979.

Troester, Rod. *Jimmy Carter as Peacemaker: A Post-Presidential Biography.* Westport, CT: Praeger Publishers, 1996.

Turner, Stansfield. *Burn Before Reading: Presidents, CIA Directors, and Secret Intelligence.* New York: Hachette, 2005.

Updegrove, Mark K. *Second Acts: Presidential Lives and Legacies After the White House.* Guilford, CT: The Lyons Press, 2006.

Updike, John. *Rabbit Is Rich.* New York: Alfred A. Knopf, 1981.

Vance, Cyrus. *Hard Choices: Critical Years in America's Foreign Policy.* New York: Simon & Schuster, 1983.

Volcker, Paul, with Christine Harper. *Keeping at It: The Quest for Sound Money and Good Government.* New York: PublicAffairs, 2018.

Ward, Jon. *Camelot's End: Kennedy vs. Carter and the Fight That Broke the Democratic Party.* New York: Twelve, 2019.

Weizman, Ezer. *The Battle for Peace.* New York: Bantam Books, 1981.

Whipple, Chris. *The Gatekeepers: How the White House Chiefs of Staff Define Every Presidency.* New York: Crown, 2017.

White, Theodore. *In Search of History: A Personal Adventure.* New York: HarperCollins, 1978.

Wicker, Tom. *One of Us: Richard Nixon and the American Dream.* New York: Random House, 1991.

Williford, William Bailey. *Americus Through the Years: The Story of a Georgia Town and Its People, 1832–1975.* Atlanta: Cherokee, 1975.

Wills, Garry. *Certain Trumpets: The Call of Leaders.* New York: Simon & Schuster, 1994.

———. *Lead Time: A Journalist's Education.* Boston: Houghton Mifflin, 1984.

Wirthlin, Richard. *The Greatest Communicator: What Ronald Reagan Taught Me About Politics, Leadership, and Life.* Hoboken, NJ: John Wiley & Sons, 2004.

Witcover, Jules. *Joe Biden: A Life of Trial and Redemption.* New York: William Morrow/Harper Collins, 2010.

———. *Marathon: The Pursuit of the Presidency, 1972–1976.* New York: Viking Press, 1977.

Woodruff, Judy, with Kathleen Maxa. *"This Is Judy Woodruff at the White House."* Reading, MA: Addison-Wesley, 1982.

Woodward, Bob. *Shadow: Five Presidents and the Legacy of Watergate.* New York: Simon & Schuster, 1999.

Wooten, James T. *Dasher: The Roots and the Rising of Jimmy Carter.* New York: Summit Books, 1978.

Wright, Lawrence. *Thirteen Days in September: Carter, Begin, and Sadat at Camp David.* New York: Alfred A. Knopf, 2014.

Wright, Richard R. *Centennial Encyclopaedia of the African Methodist Episcopal Church, 1816–1916.* Forgotten Books, 2018.

Young, Andrew. *An Easy Burden: The Civil Rights Movement and the Transformation of America.* New York: HarperCollins, 1996.

Zelizer, Julian E. American Presidents Series: *Jimmy Carter.* New York: Times Books, 2010.

# PHOTO CREDITS

**Photo Insert 1**

1. The Jimmy Carter Presidential Library and Museum
2. The Jimmy Carter Presidential Library and Museum
3. The Jimmy Carter Presidential Library and Museum
4. The Jimmy Carter Presidential Library and Museum
5. The Jimmy Carter Presidential Library and Museum
6. Courtesy of Sally Carter
7. Naval History and Heritage Command
8. PJF Military Collection/Alamy
9. The Jimmy Carter Presidential Library and Museum
10. The Jimmy Carter Presidential Library and Museum
11. Bettmann/Getty Images
12. Charles Pugh/Atlanta Journal-Constitution Photographs/George State University
13. AP/Shutterstock
14. Doug Woodward
15. AP/Shutterstock
16. Alamy

17. The Jimmy Carter Presidential Library and Museum
18. The Jimmy Carter Presidential Library and Museum
19. Ken Hawkins/Alamy
20. Thomas O'Halloran/U.S. News & World Report Magazine Photograph Collection/Library of Congress
21. The Print Collector/Alamy Stock Photo
22. Harvey Georges/AP/Shutterstock
23. The Jimmy Carter Presidential Library and Museum
24. The Jimmy Carter Presidential Library and Museum
25. The Jimmy Carter Presidential Library and Museum
26. Ken Hawkins/Alamy
27. Everett/Shutterstock
28. The Jimmy Carter Presidential Library and Museum
29. Ken Hawkins/Alamy

**Photo Insert 2**
1. The Jimmy Carter Presidential Library and Museum
2. The Jimmy Carter Presidential Library and Museum
3. The Jimmy Carter Presidential Library and Museum
4. Warren K. Leffler/U.S. News & World Report/LOC
5. Mccool/Alamy
6. © 1979 William T. Coulter, for The Washington Post
7. Wally McNamee/Corbis/Getty ImagesFrancois Lonchon/Gamma-Rapho via Getty Images

8. Jon Arnold Images Ltd/Alamy
9. AP/Shutterstock
10. Universal History Archive/Universal Images Group via Getty Images
11. World History Archive/Alamy
12. Tony Duffy/Getty Images
13. Douglas Kirkland/Corbis/Getty Images
14. AP/Shutterstock
15. Bettmann Getty Images
16. National Park Service
17. The Jimmy Carter Presidential Library and Museum
18. The Jimmy Carter Presidential Library and Museum
19. AP/Shutterstock
20. The Carter Center
21. Korean Central News Agency via The New York Times/Redux
22. Habitat for Humanity International
23. Mark Wilson/Getty Images
24. Jonathan Alter
25. John Bazemore/AP/Shutterstock

**Photos Throughout**

Page 34: The Jimmy Carter Presidential Library and Museum
Page 154: The Jimmy Carter Presidential Library and Museum
Page 300: The Jimmy Carter Presidential Library and Museum
Page 432: The Jimmy Carter Presidential Library and Museum
Page 536: The Jimmy Carter Presidential Library and Museum
Page 650: US Army
Page 922: The Carter Center

# ABOUT THE AUTHOR

**Jonathan Alter** is an award-winning author, columnist, and documentary filmmaker. An MSNBC political analyst and former senior editor at *Newsweek,* he is the author of three *New York Times* bestsellers: *The Center Holds: Obama and His Enemies* (2013), *The Promise: President Obama, Year One* (2010), and *The Defining Moment: FDR's Hundred Days and the Triumph of Hope* (2006).

The employees of Thorndike Press hope you have enjoyed this Large Print book. All our Thorndike, Wheeler, and Kennebec Large Print titles are designed for easy reading, and all our books are made to last. Other Thorndike Press Large Print books are available at your library, through selected bookstores, or directly from us.

For information about titles, please call:
(800) 223-1244

or visit our website at:
gale.com/thorndike

To share your comments, please write:
Publisher
Thorndike Press
10 Water St., Suite 310
Waterville, ME 04901